JAVA™

A Desktop Quick Reference

THE JAVA™ SERIES

Learning Java™

Java™ Threads

Java™ Network Programming

Database Programming with JDBC™ and Java™

Java™ Distributed Computing

Developing Java Beans™

Java™ Security

Java™ Cryptography

Java™ Swing

Java™ Servlet Programming

Java™ I/O

Java™ 2D Graphics

Enterprise JavaBeans™

Creating Effective JavaHelp™

Java™ and XML

Java™ Performance Tuning

Java™ Internationalization

JavaServer™ Pages

Java™ Native Methods

Java™ Message Service

Also from O'Reilly

Java™ in a Nutshell

Java™ Enterprise in a Nutshell

Java™ Foundation Classes in a Nutshell

Java™ Examples in a Nutshell

Jini™ in a Nutshell

Enterprise Java™ CD Bookshelf

JAVA™

A Desktop Quick Reference

Third Edition

David Flanagan

O'REILLY®

Beijing • Cambridge • Farnham • Köln • Paris • Sebastopol • Taipei • Tokyo

Java™ in a Nutshell, Third Edition

by David Flanagan

Copyright © 1999, 1997, 1996 O'Reilly & Associates, Inc. All rights reserved.
Printed in the United States of America

Published by O'Reilly & Associates, Inc., 101 Morris Street, Sebastopol, CA 95472.

Editor: Paula Ferguson

Production Editor: Mary Anne Weeks Mayo

Printing History:

February 1996:	First Edition.
May 1997:	Second Edition.
November 1999:	Third Edition.
December 2000:	Java Library Set Casebound Edition.

ISBN: 1-56592-487-8 (softcover)
ISBN: 0-596-00111-8 (hardcover)
[C]

Table of Contents

Preface

This book is a desktop quick reference for Java™ programmers, designed to sit faithfully by your keyboard while you program. Part I of the book is a fast-paced, "no-fluff" introduction to the Java programming language and the core APIs of the Java platform. Part II is a quick-reference section that succinctly details every class and interface of those core APIs. The book covers Versions 1.0, 1.1, 1.2, and 1.3 of Java.

Changes Since the Second Edition

Readers who are familiar with the second edition of this book will notice a number of changes in this edition. Most notably, the AWT and applet APIs are no longer documented in this book. The Java platform tripled in size between Java 1.1 and Java 1.2. Accordingly, and unavoidably, *Java in a Nutshell* has been split into three volumes. The volume you are now reading documents only the essential APIs of the platform, including the basic language and utility classes, as well as classes for input/output, networking, and security. See the Table of Contents for a complete list of the packages documented here.

If you are a client-side programmer who is working with graphics or graphical user interfaces, you will probably want to supplement this book with *Java Foundation Classes in a Nutshell*, which documents all the graphics- and GUI-related classes, including the AWT, Swing, Java 2D, and applet APIs. And, if you are a server-side or enterprise programmer, you will likely be interested in *Java Enterprise in a Nutshell*.

Another big change is that Part I of this book has been almost entirely rewritten. The first and second editions of this book assumed knowledge of and experience with C or C++. Now that Java has come thoroughly into its own, that assumption no longer seems appropriate, so I have rewritten and expanded Chapters 2 and 3 to explain Java without any reference to C, C++, or any other programming language. Programmers with a modest amount of experience should now be able to learn Java programming from this book. These introductory chapters are written in a tight, concise style, so programmers who already know Java should find them useful as a language reference.

Another new feature of Part I is Chapter 4, *The Java Platform*. This chapter is an introduction to the APIs documented in the reference section of the book. It includes more than 60 detailed API usage examples that show how to accomplish common tasks with the predefined classes of the Java platform.

Finally, the quick-reference section in Part II of the book has a new look that dramatically improves the readability of the reference material and packs even more API information into a small space. Even if you are already familiar with the second edition, you should take the time to read the *How To Use This Quick Reference* section at the beginning of Part II; it explains the new quick-reference format and shows you how to get the most out of it.

Contents of This Book

The first eight chapters of this book document the Java language, the Java platform, and the Java development tools that are supplied with Sun's Java SDK (software development kit):

Chapter 1: Introduction
> This chapter is an overview of the Java language and the Java platform that explains the important features and benefits of Java. It concludes with an example Java program and walks the new Java programmer through it line by line.

Chapter 2: Java Syntax From the Ground Up
> This chapter explains the details of the Java programming language. It is a long and detailed chapter. Experienced Java programmers can use it as a language reference. Programmers with substantial experience with languages such as C and C++ should be able to pick up Java syntax by reading this chapter. The chapter does not assume years of programming experience, or even familiarity, with C or C++, however. Even beginning programmers, with only modest experience, should be able to learn Java programming by studying this chapter carefully.

Chapter 3: Object-Oriented Programming in Java
> This chapter describes how the basic Java syntax documented in Chapter 2 is used to write object-oriented programs in Java. The chapter assumes no prior experience with OO programming. It can be used as a tutorial by new programmers or as a reference by experienced Java programmers.

Chapter 4: The Java Platform
> This chapter is an overview of the essential Java APIs covered in this book. It contains numerous short examples that demonstrate how to perform common tasks with the classes and interfaces that comprise the Java platform. Programmers who are new to Java, and especially those who learn best by example, should find this a valuable chapter.

Chapter 5: Java Security

This chapter explains the Java security architecture that allows untrusted code to run in a secure environment from which it cannot do any malicious damage to the host system. It is important for all Java programmers to have at least a passing familiarity with Java security mechanisms.

Chapter 6: JavaBeans

This chapter documents the JavaBeans™ component framework and explains what programmers need to know to create and use the reusable, embeddable Java classes known as beans.

Chapter 7: Java Programming and Documentation Conventions

This chapter documents important and widely adopted Java programming conventions and also explains how you can make your Java code self-documenting by including specially formatted documentation comments.

Chapter 8: Java Development Tools

The Java SDK shipped by Sun includes a number of useful Java development tools, most notably the Java interpreter and the Java compiler. This chapter documents those tools.

These first eight chapters teach you the Java language and get you up and running with the Java APIs. The bulk of the book, however, is the API quick reference, Chapters 9 through 29, which is a succinct but detailed API reference formatted for optimum ease of use. Please be sure to read the *How To Use This Quick Reference* section, which appears at the beginning of the reference section; it explains how to get the most out of this section.

Related Books

O'Reilly & Associates, Inc. publishes an entire series of books on Java programming. These books include *Java Foundation Classes in a Nutshell* and *Java Enterprise in a Nutshell*, which, as mentioned earlier, are companions to this book.

A related reference work is the *Java Power Reference*. It is an electronic Java quick reference on CD-ROM that uses the *Java in a Nutshell* style. But since it is designed for viewing in a web browser, it is fully hyperlinked and includes a powerful search engine. It is wider in scope but narrower in depth than the *Java in a Nutshell* books. The *Java Power Reference* covers all the APIs of the Java 2 platform, plus the APIs of many standard extensions. But it does not include tutorial chapters on the various APIs, nor does it include descriptions of the individual classes.

You can find a complete list of Java books from O'Reilly & Associates at *http://java.oreilly.com/*. Books that focus on the core Java APIs, as this one does, include:

Exploring Java, by Pat Niemeyer and Joshua Peck

A comprehensive tutorial introduction to Java, with an emphasis on client-side Java programming.

Java Threads, by Scott Oaks and Henry Wong
> Java makes multithreaded programming easy, but doing it right can still be tricky. This book explains everything you need to know.

Java I/O, by Elliotte Rusty Harold
> Java's stream-based input/output architecture is a thing of beauty. This book covers it in the detail it deserves.

Java Network Programming, by Elliotte Rusty Harold
> This book documents the Java networking APIs in detail.

Java Security, by Scott Oaks
> This book explains the Java access-control mechanisms in detail and also documents the authentication mechanisms of digital signatures and message digests.

Java Cryptography, by Jonathan Knudsen
> Thorough coverage of the Java Cryptography Extension, the `javax.crypto.*` packages, and everything you need to know about cryptography in Java.

Developing Java Beans, by Robert Englander
> A complete guide to writing components that work with the JavaBeans API.

Java Programming Resources Online

This book is a quick reference designed for speedy access to frequently needed information. It does not, and cannot, tell you everything you need to know about Java. In addition to the books listed earlier, there are several valuable (and free) electronic sources of information about Java programming.

Sun's main web site for all things related to Java is *http://java.sun.com/*. The web site specifically for Java developers is *http://developer.java.sun.com/*. Much of the content on this developer site is password-protected, and access to it requires (free) registration.

Sun distributes electronic documentation for all Java classes and methods in its *javadoc* HTML format. Although this documentation is somewhat difficult to navigate and is rough or outdated in places, it is still an excellent starting point when you need to know more about a particular Java package, class, method, or field. If you do not already have the *javadoc* files with your Java distribution, see *http://java.sun.com/docs/* for a link to the latest available version. Sun also distributes its excellent *Java Tutorial* online. You can browse and download it from *http://java.sun.com/docs/books/tutorial/*.

For Usenet discussion (in English) about Java, try the *comp.lang.java.programmer* and related *comp.lang.java.** newsgroups. You can find the very comprehensive *comp.lang.java.programmer* FAQ by Peter van der Linden at *http://www.afu.com/javafaq.htm*.

Finally, don't forget O'Reilly's Java web site. *http://java.oreilly.com/* contains Java news and commentary and a monthly tips-and-tricks column by O'Reilly Java author Jonathan Knudsen.

Examples Online

The examples in this book are available online and can be downloaded from the home page for the book at *http://www.oreilly.com/catalog/javanut3*. You also may want to visit this site to see if any important notes or errata about the book have been published there.

Conventions Used in This Book

We use the following formatting conventions in this book:

Italic
> Used for emphasis and to signify the first use of a term. Italic is also used for commands, email addresses, web sites, FTP sites, file and directory names, and newsgroups.

Bold
> Occasionally used to refer to particular keys on a computer keyboard or to portions of a user interface, such as the **Back** button or the **Options** menu.

`Letter Gothic`
> Used in all Java code and generally for anything that you would type literally when programming, including keywords, data types, constants, method names, variables, class names, and interface names.

`Letter Gothic Oblique`
> Used for the names of function arguments and generally as a placeholder to indicate an item that should be replaced with an actual value in your program.

Franklin Gothic Book Condensed
> Used for the Java class synopses in the quick-reference section. This very narrow font allows us to fit a lot of information on the page without a lot of distracting line breaks. This font is also used for code entities in the descriptions in the quick-reference section.

Franklin Gothic Demi Condensed
> Used for highlighting class, method, field, property, and constructor names in the quick-reference section, which makes it easier to scan the class synopses.

Franklin Gothic Book Compressed Italic
> Used for method parameter names and comments in the quick-reference section.

Request for Comments

Please help us improve future editions of this book by reporting any errors, inaccuracies, bugs, misleading or confusing statements, and even plain old typos that you find. Please also let us know what we can do to make this book more useful to you. We take your comments seriously and will try to incorporate reasonable suggestions into future editions. You can contact us by writing:

O'Reilly & Associates, Inc.
101 Morris Street
Sebastopol, CA 95472
1-800-998-9938 (in the United States or Canada)
1-707-829-0515 (international/local)
1-707-829-0104 (fax)

You can also send us messages electronically. To be put on the mailing list or request a catalog, send email to:

info@oreilly.com

To ask technical questions or comment on the book, send email to:

bookquestions@oreilly.com

We have a web site for the book, where we'll list examples, errata, and any plans for future editions. You can access this page at:

http://www.oreilly.com/catalog/javanut3/

For more information about this book and others, see the O'Reilly web site:

http://www.oreilly.com

How the Quick Reference Is Generated

For the nerdy or merely inquisitive reader, this section explains a bit about how the quick-reference material in *Java in a Nutshell* and related books is created.

As Java has evolved, so has my system for generating Java quick-reference material. The current system is part of a larger commercial documentation browser system I'm developing (visit *http://www.davidflanagan.com/Jude/* for more information about it). The program works in two passes: the first pass collects and organizes the API information, and the second pass outputs that information in the form of quick-reference chapters.

The first pass begins by reading the class files for all of the classes and interfaces to be documented. Almost all of the API information in the quick reference is available in these class files. The notable exception is the names of method arguments, which are not stored in class files. These argument names are obtained by parsing the Java source file for each class and interface. Where source files are not available, I obtain method argument names by parsing the API documentation generated by *javadoc*. The parsers I use to extract API information from the source files and *javadoc* files are created using the Antlr parser generator developed by Terrence Parr of the Magelang Institute. (See *http://www.antlr.org/* for details on this very powerful programming tool.)

Once the API information has been obtained by reading class files, source files, and *javadoc* files, the program spends some time sorting and cross-referencing everything. Then it stores all the API information into a single large data file.

The second pass reads API information from that data file and outputs quick-reference chapters using a custom SGML format. The SGML markup is fairly complex, but the code that generates it is quite mundane. Once I've generated the SGML output, I hand it off to the production team at O'Reilly & Associates. They process it and convert it to troff source code. The troff source is processed with the GNU *groff* program (*ftp://ftp.gnu.org/gnu/groff/*) and a custom set of troff macros to produce PostScript output that is shipped directly to the printer.

Acknowledgments

Many people helped in the creation of this book, and I am grateful to them all. I am indebted to the many, many readers of the first two editions who wrote in with comments, suggestions, bug reports, and praise. Their many small contributions are scattered throughout the book. Also, my apologies to those who made the many good suggestions that could not be incorporated into this edition.

Paula Ferguson, a friend and colleague, has been the editor of all three editions of this book. Her careful reading and always-practical suggestions have made the book stronger, clearer, and more useful. She guided the evolution of *Java in a Nutshell* from a single book into a three-volume series and, at times, juggled editing tasks for all three books at once. Finally, Paula went above and beyond the call of editorial duty by designing the hierarchy diagrams found at the start of each reference chapter.

Mike Loukides provided high-level direction and guidance for the first edition of the book. Eric Raymond and Troy Downing reviewed that first edition—they helped spot my errors and omissions and offered good advice on making the book more useful to Java programmers.

For the second edition, John Zukowski reviewed my Java 1.1 AWT quick-reference material, and George Reese reviewed most of the remaining new material. The second edition was also blessed with a "dream team" of technical reviewers from Sun. John Rose, the author of the Java inner class specification, reviewed the chapter on inner classes. Mark Reinhold, author of the new character stream classes in java.io, reviewed my documentation of these classes. Nakul Saraiya, the designer of the new Java Reflection API, reviewed my documentation of the java.lang.reflect package. I am very grateful to these engineers and architects; their efforts made this a stronger, more accurate book.

The third edition also benefited greatly from the contributions of reviewers who are intimately familiar with the Java platform. Joshua Bloch, one of the primary authors of the Java collections framework, reviewed my descriptions of the collections classes and interfaces. Joshua was also helpful in discussing the Timer and TimerTask classes of Java 1.3 with me. Mark Reinhold, creator of the java.lang.ref package, explained the package to me and reviewed my documentation of it. Scott Oaks reviewed my descriptions of the Java security and cryptography classes and interfaces. Joshua, Mark, and Scott are all engineers with Sun Microsystems, and I'm very grateful for their time. The documentation of the javax.crypto package and its subpackages was also reviewed by Jon Eaves. Jon worked on a clean-room implementation of the Java Cryptography Extension (which is available from *http://www.aba.net.au/*), and his comments were quite helpful. Jon now works for Fluent Technologies (*http://www.fluent.com.au/*) consulting in Java and electronic commerce. Finally, Chapter 1 was improved by the comments of reviewers who were *not* already familiar with the Java platform:

Christina Byrne reviewed it from the standpoint of a novice programmer, and Judita Byrne of Virginia Power offered her comments as a professional COBOL programmer.

The O'Reilly & Associates production team has done its usual fine work of creating a book out of the electronic files I submit. My thanks to them all. And a special thanks to Lenny Muellner and Chris Maden, who worked overtime to implement the new and improved format of the quick-reference section.

As always, my thanks and love to Christie.

David Flanagan
http://www.davidflanagan.com/
September 1999

PART I

Introducing Java

Part I is an introduction to the Java language and the Java platform. These chapters provide enough information for you to get started using Java right away.

CHAPTER 1

Introduction

Welcome to Java. Since its introduction in late 1995, the Java language and platform have taken the programming world by storm. This chapter begins by explaining what Java is and why it has become so popular. Then, as a tutorial introduction to the language, it walks you through a simple Java program you can type in, compile, and run.

What Is Java?

In discussing Java, it is important to distinguish between the Java programming language, the Java Virtual Machine, and the Java platform. The Java programming language is the language in which Java applications (including applets, servlets, and JavaBeans components) are written. When a Java program is compiled, it is converted to byte codes that are the portable machine language of a CPU architecture known as the Java Virtual Machine (also called the Java VM or JVM). The JVM can be implemented directly in hardware, but it is usually implemented in the form of a software program that interprets and executes byte codes.

The Java platform is distinct from both the Java language and Java VM. The Java platform is the predefined set of Java classes that exist on every Java installation; these classes are available for use by all Java programs. The Java platform is also sometimes referred to as the Java runtime environment or the core Java APIs (application programming interfaces). The Java platform can be extended with optional standard extensions. These extension APIs exist in some Java installations, but are not guaranteed to exist in all installations.

The Java Programming Language

The Java programming language is a state-of-the-art, object-oriented language that has a syntax similar to that of C. The language designers strove to make the Java language powerful, but, at the same time, they tried to avoid the overly complex features that have bogged down other object-oriented languages, such as C++. By keeping the language simple, the designers also made it easier for programmers to write robust, bug-free code. As a result of its elegant design and next-generation features, the Java language has proved wildly popular with programmers, who typically find it a pleasure to work with Java after struggling with more difficult, less powerful languages.

The Java Virtual Machine

The Java Virtual Machine, or Java interpreter, is the crucial piece of every Java installation. By design, Java programs are portable, but they are only portable to platforms to which a Java interpreter has been ported. Sun ships VM implementations for its own Solaris operating system and for Microsoft Windows (95/98/NT) platforms. Many other vendors, including Apple and various Unix vendors, provide Java interpreters for their platforms. There is a freely available port of Sun's VM for Linux platforms, and there are also other third-party VM implementations available. The Java VM is not only for desktop systems, however. It has been ported to set-top boxes, and versions are even available for hand-held devices that run Windows CE and PalmOS.

Although interpreters are not typically considered high-performance systems, Java VM performance is remarkably good and has been improving steadily. Of particular note is a VM technology called just-in-time (JIT) compilation, whereby Java byte codes are converted on-the-fly into native-platform machine language, boosting execution speed for code that is run repeatedly. Sun's new Hotspot technology is a particularly good implementation of JIT compilation.

The Java Platform

The Java platform is just as important as the Java programming language and the Java Virtual Machine. All programs written in the Java language rely on the set of predefined classes* that comprise the Java platform. Java classes are organized into related groups known as *packages*. The Java platform defines packages for functionality such as input/output, networking, graphics, user-interface creation, security, and much more.

The Java 1.2 release was a major milestone for the Java platform. This release almost tripled the number of classes in the platform and introduced significant new functionality. In recognition of this, Sun named the new version the Java 2 Platform. This is a trademarked name created for marketing purposes; it serves to emphasize how much Java has grown since its first release. However, most programmers refer to the Java platform by its official version number, which, at the time of this writing, is 1.3.

It is important to understand what is meant by the term platform. To a computer programmer, a platform is defined by the APIs he or she can rely on when writing programs. These APIs are usually defined by the operating system of the target computer. Thus, a programmer writing a program to run under Microsoft Windows must use a different set of APIs than a programmer writing the same program for

---

* A *class* is a module of Java code that defines a data structure and a set of methods (also called procedures, functions, or subroutines) that operate on that data.

the Macintosh or for a Unix-based system. In this respect, Windows, Macintosh, and Unix are three distinct platforms.

Java is not an operating system.* Nevertheless, the Java platform—particularly the Java 2 Platform—provides APIs with a comparable breadth and depth to those defined by an operating system. With the Java 2 Platform, you can write applications in Java without sacrificing the advanced features available to programmers writing native applications targeted at a particular underlying operating system. An application written on the Java platform runs on any operating system that supports the Java platform. This means you do not have to create distinct Windows, Macintosh, and Unix versions of your programs, for example. A single Java program runs on all these operating systems, which explains why "Write once, run anywhere" is Sun's motto for Java.

It also explains why companies like Microsoft might feel threatened by Java. The Java platform is not an operating system, but for programmers, it is an alternative development target and a very popular one at that. The Java platform reduces programmers' reliance on the underlying operating system, and, by allowing programs to run on top of any operating system, it increases end users' freedom to choose an operating system.

Versions of Java

As of this writing, there have been four major versions of Java. They are:

Java 1.0
> This was the first public version of Java. It contained 212 classes organized in 8 packages. There is a large installed base of web browsers that run this version of Java, so this version is still in use for writing simple applets—Java programs that are included in web pages. (See *Java Foundation Classes in a Nutshell* (O'Reilly) for a discussion of applets.)

Java 1.1
> This release of Java doubled the size of the Java platform to 504 classes in 23 packages. It introduced inner classes, an important change to the Java language itself, and included significant performance improvements in the Java VM. This version of Java is out of date, but is still in use on systems that do not yet have a stable port of Java 1.2.

Java 1.2
> This was a very significant release of Java; it tripled the size of the Java platform to 1520 classes in 59 packages. Because of the many new features included in this release, the platform was renamed and is now called the Java 2 Platform.

Java 1.3
> This release migrates JNDI and Java Sound (which were previously extensions) to the core Java platform. It adds support for RMI over the IIOP protocol, and ships with the new high-performance "HotSpot" virtual machine.

---

* There is a Java-based operating system, however; it is known as JavaOS.

Mostly, however, this update consists of minor corrections and updates. The most interesting new classes are probably `java.util.Timer` and `java.lang.reflect.Proxy`.

In addition, Sun has instituted a process for proposing and developing standard extensions to the Java platform. In the future, most new functionality is expected to take the form of a standard extension, rather than be a required part of every Java installation.

In order to work with Java 1.0 or Java 1.1, you have to obtain the Java Development Kit (JDK) for that release. As of Java 1.2, the JDK has been renamed and is now called a Software Development Kit (SDK), so we have the Java 2 SDK or, more precisely, the Java 2 SDK, Standard Edition, Version 1.3. Despite the new name, many programmers still refer to the development kit as the JDK.

Don't confuse the JDK (or SDK) with the Java Runtime Environment (JRE). The JRE contains everything you need to run Java programs, but does not contain the tools you need to develop Java programs (i.e., the compiler). You should also be aware of the Java Plug-in, a version of the JRE that is designed to be integrated into the Netscape Navigator and Microsoft Internet Explorer web browsers.

In addition to evolving the Java platform over time, Sun is also trying to produce different versions of the platform for different uses. The Standard Edition is the only version currently available, but Sun is also working on the Java 2 Platform, Enterprise Edition (J2EE), for enterprise developers and the Java 2 Platform, Micro Edition, for consumer electronic systems, like handheld PDAs and cellular telephones.

Key Benefits of Java

Why use Java at all? Is it worth learning a new language and a new platform? This section explores some of the key benefits of Java.

Write Once, Run Anywhere

Sun identifies "Write once, run anywhere" as the core value proposition of the Java platform. Translated from business jargon, this means that the most important promise of Java technology is that you only have to write your application once— for the Java platform—and then you'll be able to run it *anywhere*.

Anywhere, that is, that supports the Java platform. Fortunately, Java support is becoming ubiquitous. It is integrated, or being integrated, into practically all major operating systems. It is built into the popular web browsers, which places it on virtually every Internet-connected PC in the world. It is even being built into consumer electronic devices, such as television set-top boxes, PDAs, and cell phones.

Security

Another key benefit of Java is its security features. Both the language and the platform were designed from the ground up with security in mind. The Java platform allows users to download untrusted code over a network and run it in a secure environment in which it cannot do any harm: untrusted code cannot infect the host system with a virus, cannot read or write files from the hard drive, and so forth. This capability alone makes the Java platform unique.

The Java 2 Platform takes the security model a step further. It makes security levels and restrictions highly configurable and extends them beyond applets. As of Java 1.2, any Java code, whether it is an applet, a servlet, a JavaBeans component, or a complete Java application, can be run with restricted permissions that prevent it from doing harm to the host system.

The security features of the Java language and platform have been subjected to intense scrutiny by security experts around the world. Security-related bugs, some of them potentially serious, have been found and promptly fixed. Because of the security promises Java makes, it is big news when a new security bug is found. Remember, however, that no other mainstream platform can make security guarantees nearly as strong as those Java makes. If Java's security is not yet perfect, it has been proven strong enough for practical day-to-day use and is certainly better than any of the alternatives.

Network-centric Programming

Sun's corporate motto has always been "The network is the computer." The designers of the Java platform believed in the importance of networking and designed the Java platform to be network-centric. From a programmer's point of view, Java makes it unbelievably easy to work with resources across a network and to create network-based applications using client/server or multitier architectures. This means that Java programmers have a serious head start in the emerging network economy.

Dynamic, Extensible Programs

Java is both dynamic and extensible. Java code is organized in modular object-oriented units called *classes*. Classes are stored in separate files and are loaded into the Java interpreter only when needed. This means that an application can decide as it is running what classes it needs and can load them when it needs them. It also means that a program can dynamically extend itself by loading the classes it needs to expand its functionality.

The network-centric design of the Java platform means that a Java application can dynamically extend itself by loading new classes over a network. An application that takes advantage of these features ceases to be a monolithic block of code. Instead, it becomes an interacting collection of independent software components. Thus, Java enables a powerful new metaphor of application design and development.

Internationalization

The Java language and the Java platform were designed from the start with the rest of the world in mind. Java is the only commonly used programming language that has internationalization features at its very core, rather than tacked on as an afterthought. While most programming languages use 8-bit characters that represent only the alphabets of English and Western European languages, Java uses 16-bit Unicode characters that represent the phonetic alphabets and ideographic character sets of the entire world. Java's internationalization features are not restricted to just low-level character representation, however. The features permeate the Java platform, making it easier to write internationalized programs with Java than it is with any other environment.

Performance

As I described earlier, Java programs are compiled to a portable intermediate form known as byte codes, rather than to native machine-language instructions. The Java Virtual Machine runs a Java program by interpreting these portable byte-code instructions. This architecture means that Java programs are faster than programs or scripts written in purely interpreted languages, but they are typically slower than C and C++ programs compiled to native machine language. Keep in mind, however, that although Java programs are compiled to byte code, not all of the Java platform is implemented with interpreted byte codes. For efficiency, computationally intensive portions of the Java platform—such as the string-manipulation methods—are implemented using native machine code.

Although early releases of Java suffered from performance problems, the speed of the Java VM has improved dramatically with each new release. The VM has been highly tuned and optimized in many significant ways. Furthermore, many implementations include a just-in-time compiler, which converts Java byte codes to native machine instructions on the fly. Using sophisticated JIT compilers, Java programs can execute at speeds comparable to the speeds of native C and C++ applications.

Java is a portable, interpreted language; Java programs run almost as fast as native, non-portable C and C++ programs. Performance used to be an issue that made some programmers avoid using Java. Now, with the improvements made in Java 1.2 and 1.3, performance issues should no longer keep anyone away. In fact, the winning combination of performance plus portability is a unique feature no other language can offer.

Programmer Efficiency and Time-to-Market

The final, and perhaps most important, reason to use Java is that programmers like it. Java is an elegant language combined with a powerful and well-designed set of APIs. Programmers enjoy programming in Java and are usually amazed at how quickly they can get results with it. Studies have consistently shown that switching to Java increases programmer efficiency. Because Java is a simple and elegant language with a well-designed, intuitive set of APIs, programmers write better code with fewer bugs than for other platforms, again reducing development time.

An Example Program

Example 1-1 shows a Java program to compute factorials.* The numbers at the beginning of each line are not part of the program; they are there for ease of reference when we dissect the program line-by-line.

Example 1-1: Factorial.java: A Program to Compute Factorials

```
 1 /**
 2  * This program computes the factorial of a number
 3  */
 4 public class Factorial {              // Define a class
 5   public static void main(String[] args) { // The program starts here
 6     int input = Integer.parseInt(args[0]); // Get the user's input
 7     double result = factorial(input);   // Compute the factorial
 8     System.out.println(result);         // Print out the result
 9   }                                     // The main() method ends here
10
11   public static double factorial(int x) { // This method computes x!
12     if (x < 0)                          // Check for bad input
13       return 0.0;                       //   if bad, return 0
14     double fact = 1.0;                  // Begin with an initial value
15     while(x > 1) {                      // Loop until x equals 1
16       fact = fact * x;                  //   multiply by x each time
17       x = x - 1;                        //   and then decrement x
18     }                                   // Jump back to start of loop
19     return fact;                        // Return the result
20   }                                     // factorial() ends here
21 }                                       // The class ends here
```

Compiling and Running the Program

Before we look at how the program works, we must first discuss how to run it. In order to compile and run the program, you need a Java software development kit (SDK) of some sort. Sun Microsystems created the Java language and ships a free Java SDK for its Solaris operating system and also for Linux and Microsoft Windows platforms. At the time of this writing, the current version of Sun's SDK is entitled Java 2 SDK, Standard Edition, Version 1.3.0 and is available for download from *http://java.sun.com/*. Be sure to get the SDK and not the Java Runtime Environment. The JRE enables you to run existing Java programs, but not to write your own.

Sun supports its SDK only on Solaris, Linux, and Windows platforms. Many other companies have licensed and ported the SDK to their platforms, however. Contact your operating-system vendor to find if a version of the Java SDK is available for your system.

The Sun SDK is not the only Java programming environment you can use. Companies such as Borland, Inprise, Metrowerks, Oracle, Sybase, and Symantec offer commercial products that enable you to write Java programs. This book assumes

---

* The factorial of an integer is the product of the number and all positive integers less than the number. So, for example, the factorial of 4, which is also written 4!, is 4 times 3 times 2 times 1, or 24. By definition, 0! is 1.

that you are using Sun's SDK. If you are using a product from some other vendor, be sure to read that vendor's documentation to learn how to compile and run a simple program, like that shown in Example 1-1.

Once you have a Java programming environment installed, the first step towards running our program is to type it in. Using your favorite text editor, enter the program as it is shown in Example 1-1. Omit the line numbers, as they are just there for reference. Note that Java is a case-sensitive language, so you must type lowercase letters in lowercase and uppercase letters in uppercase. You'll notice that many of the lines of this program end with semicolons. It is a common mistake to forget these characters, but the program won't work without them, so be careful! If you are not a fast typist, you can omit everything from // to the end of a line. Those are *comments*; they are there for your benefit and are ignored by Java.*

When writing Java programs, you should use a text editor that saves files in plain-text format, not a word processor that supports fonts and formatting and saves files in a proprietary format. My favorite text editor on Unix systems is *emacs*. If you use a Windows system, you might use *Notepad* or *WordPad*, if you don't have a more specialized programmer's editor. If you are using a commercial Java programming environment, it probably includes an appropriate text editor; read the documentation that came with the product. When you are done entering the program, save it in a file named *Factorial.java*. This is important; the program will not work if you save it by any other name.

After writing a program like this one, the next step is to compile it. With Sun's SDK, the Java compiler is known as *javac*. *javac* is a command-line tool, so you can only use it from a terminal window, such as an MS-DOS window on a Windows system or an *xterm* window on a Unix system. Compile the program by typing the following command line:†

```
C:\> javac Factorial.java
```

If this command prints any error messages, you probably got something wrong when you typed in the program. If it does not print any error messages, however, the compilation has succeeded, and *javac* creates a file called *Factorial.class*. This is the compiled version of the program.

Once you have compiled a Java program, you must still run it. Unlike some other languages, Java programs are not compiled into native machine language, so they cannot be executed directly by the system. Instead, they are run by another program known as the Java interpreter. In Sun's SDK, the interpreter is a command-line program named, appropriately enough, *java*. To run the factorial program, type:

```
C:\> java Factorial 4
```

java is the command to run the Java interpreter, *Factorial* is the name of the Java program we want the interpreter to run, and *4* is the input data—the number we

---

* I recommend that you type this example in by hand, to get a feel for the language. If you *really* don't want to, however, you can download this, and all examples in the book, from *http://www.oreilly.com/catalog/javanut3/*.

† The "C:\>" characters represent the command-line prompt; *don't* type these characters yourself.

---

want the interpreter to compute the factorial of. The program prints a single line of output, telling us that the factorial of 4 is 24:

```
C:\> java Factorial 4
24.0
```

Congratulations! You've just written, compiled, and run your first Java program. Try running it again to compute the factorials of some other numbers.

Analyzing the Program

Now that you have run the factorial program, let's analyze it line by line, to see what makes a Java program tick.

Comments

The first three lines of the program are a comment. Java ignores them, but they tell a human programmer what the program does. A comment begins with the characters /* and ends with the characters */. Any amount of text, including multiple lines of text, may appear between these characters. Java also supports another type of comment, which you can see in lines 4 through 21. If the characters // appear in a Java program, Java ignores those characters and any other text that appears between those characters and the end of the line.

Defining a class

Line 4 is the beginning of the program. It says that we are defining a class named Factorial. This explains why the program had to be stored in a file named *Factorial.java*. That filename indicates that the file contains Java source code for a class named Factorial. The word public is a *modifier*; it says that the class is publicly available and that anyone may use it. The open curly-brace character ({) marks the beginning of the body of the class, which extends all the way to line 21, where we find the matching close curly-brace character (}). The program contains a number of pairs of curly braces; the lines are indented to show the nesting within these braces.

A class is the fundamental unit of program structure in Java, so it is not surprising that the first line of our program declares a class. All Java programs are classes, although some programs use many classes instead of just one. Java is an object-oriented programming language, and classes are a fundamental part of the object-oriented paradigm. Each class defines a unique kind of object. Example 1-1 is not really an object-oriented program, however, so I'm not going to go into detail about classes and objects here. That is the topic of Chapter 3, *Object-Oriented Programming in Java*. For now, all you need to understand is that a class defines a set of interacting *members*. Those members may be fields, methods, or other classes. The Factorial class contains two members, both of which are methods. They are described in upcoming sections.

Defining a method

Line 5 begins the definition of a *method* of our Factorial class. A method is a named chunk of Java code. A Java program can call, or *invoke*, a method to execute the code in it. If you have programmed in other languages, you have probably seen methods before, but they may have been called functions, procedures, or subroutines. The interesting thing about methods is that they have *parameters* and *return values*. When you call a method, you pass it some data you want it to operate on, and it returns a result to you. A method is like an algebraic function:

    y = f(x)

Here, the mathematical function f performs some computation on the value represented by x and returns a value, which we represent by y.

To return to line 5, the public and static keywords are modifiers. public means the method is publicly accessible; anyone can use it. The meaning of the static modifier is not important here; it is explained in Chapter 3. The void keyword specifies the return value of the method. In this case, it specifies that this method does not have a return value.

The word main is the name of the method. main is a special name. When you run the Java interpreter, it reads in the class you specify, then looks for a method named main().* When the interpreter finds this method, it starts running the program at that method. When the main() method finishes, the program is done, and the Java interpreter exits. In other words, the main() method is the main entry point into a Java program. It is not actually sufficient for a method to be named main(), however. The method must be declared public static void exactly as shown in line 5. In fact, the only part of line 5 you can change is the word args, which you can replace with any word you want. You'll be using this line in all of your Java programs, so go ahead and commit it to memory now!†

Following the name of the main() method is a list of method parameters, contained in parentheses. This main() method has only a single parameter. String[] specifies the type of the parameter, which is an array of strings (i.e., a numbered list of strings of text). args specifies the name of the parameter. In the algebraic equation f(x), x is simply a way of referring to an unknown value. args serves the same purpose for the main() method. As we'll see, the name args is used in the body of the method to refer to the unknown value that is passed to the method.

As I've just explained, the main() method is a special one that is called by the Java interpreter when it starts running a Java class (program). When you invoke the Java interpreter like this:

---

* By convention, when this book refers to a method, it follows the name of the method by a pair of parentheses. As you'll see, parentheses are an important part of method syntax, and they serve here to keep method names distinct from the names of classes, fields, variables, and so on.

† All Java programs that are run directly by the Java interpreter must have a main() method. Programs of this sort are often called *applications*. It is possible to write programs that are not run directly by the interpreter, but are dynamically loaded into some other already running Java program. Examples are *applets*, which are programs run by a web browser, and *servlets*, which are programs run by a web server. Applets are discussed in *Java Foundation Classes in a Nutshell* (O'Reilly), while servlets are discussed in *Java Enterprise in a Nutshell* (O'Reilly). In this book, we consider only applications.

```
C:\> java Factorial 4
```

the string "4" is passed to the main() method as the value of the parameter named args. More precisely, an array of strings containing only one entry, "4", is passed to main(). If we invoke the program like this:

```
C:\> java Factorial 4 3 2 1
```

then an array of four strings, "4", "3", "2", and "1", are passed to the main() method as the value of the parameter named args. Our program looks only at the first string in the array, so the other strings are ignored.

Finally, the last thing on line 5 is an open curly brace. This marks the beginning of the body of the main() method, which continues until the matching close curly brace on line 9. Methods are composed of *statements*, which the Java interpreter executes in sequential order. In this case, lines 6, 7, and 8 are three statements that compose the body of the main() method. Each statement ends with a semicolon to separate it from the next. This is an important part of Java syntax; beginning programmers often forget the semicolons.

Declaring a variable and parsing input

The first statement of the main() method, line 6, declares a variable and assigns a value to it. In any programming language, a *variable* is simply a symbolic name for a value. Think back to algebra class again:

$$c^2 = a^2 + b^2$$

The letters a, b, and c are names we use to refer to unknown values. They make this formula (the Pythagorean theorem) a general one that applies to arbitrary values of a, b, and c, not just a specific set like:

$$5^2 = 4^2 + 3^2$$

A variable in a Java program is exactly the same thing: it is a name we use to refer to a value. More precisely, a variable is a name that refers to a storage space for a value. We often say that a variable holds a value.

Line 6 begins with the words int input. This declares a variable named input and specifies that the variable has the type int; that is, it is an integer. Java can work with several different types of values, including integers, real or floating-point numbers, characters (e.g., letters, digits), and strings. Java is a *strongly typed* language, which means that all variables must have a type specified and can only refer to values of that type. Our input variable always refers to an integer; it cannot refer to a floating point number or a string. Method parameters are also typed. Recall that the args parameter had a type of String[].

Continuing with line 6, the variable declaration int input is followed by the = character. This is the assignment operator in Java; it sets the value of a variable. When reading Java code, don't read = as "equals," but instead read it as "is assigned the value." As we'll see in Chapter 2, *Java Syntax from the Ground Up*, there is a different operator for "equals."

The value being assigned to our input variable is Integer.parseInt(args[0]). This is a method invocation. This first statement of the main() method invokes another method whose name is Integer.parseInt(). As you might guess, this method "parses" an integer; that is, it converts a string representation of an integer, such as "4", to the integer itself. The Integer.parseInt() method is not part of the Java language, but it is a core part of the Java API or Application Programming Interface. Every Java program can use the powerful set of classes and methods defined by this core API. The second half of this book is a quick-reference that documents that core API.

When you call a method, you pass values (called *arguments*) that are assigned to the corresponding parameters defined by the method, and the method returns a value. The argument passed to Integer.parseInt() is args[0]. Recall that args is the name of the parameter for main(); it specifies an array (or list) of strings. The elements of an array are numbered sequentially, and the first one is always numbered 0. We only care about the first string in the args array, so we use the expression args[0] to refer to that string. Thus, when we invoke the program as shown earlier, line 6 takes the first string specified after the name of the class, "4", and passes it to the method named Integer.parseInt(). This method converts the string to the corresponding integer and returns the integer as its return value. Finally, this returned integer is assigned to the variable named input.

Computing the result

The statement on line 7 is a lot like the statement on line 6. It declares a variable and assigns a value to it. The value assigned to the variable is computed by invoking a method. The variable is named result, and it has a type of double. double means a double-precision floating-point number. The variable is assigned a value that is computed by the factorial() method. The factorial() method, however, is not part of the standard Java API. Instead, it is defined as part of our program, by lines 11 through 19. The argument passed to factorial() is the value referred to by the input variable, which was computed on line 6. We'll consider the body of the factorial() method shortly, but you can surmise from its name that this method takes an input value, computes the factorial of that value, and returns the result.

Displaying output

Line 8 simply calls a method named System.out.println(). This commonly used method is part of the core Java API; it causes the Java interpreter to print out a value. In this case, the value that it prints is the value referred to by the variable named result. This is the result of our factorial computation. If the input variable holds the value 4, the result variable holds the value 24, and this line prints out that value.

The System.out.println() method does not have a return value, so there is no variable declaration or = assignment operator in this statement, since there is no value to assign to anything. Another way to say this is that, like the main() method of line 5, System.out.println() is declared void.

The end of a method

Line 9 contains only a single character, }. This marks the end of the method. When the Java interpreter gets here, it is done executing the main() method, so it stops running. The end of the main() method is also the end of the *variable scope* for the input and result variables declared within main() and for the args parameter of main(). These variable and parameter names have meaning only within the main() method and cannot be used elsewhere in the program, unless other parts of the program declare different variables or parameters that happen to have the same name.

Blank lines

Line 10 is a blank line. You can insert blank lines, spaces, and tabs anywhere in a program, and you should use them liberally to make the program readable. A blank line appears here to separate the main() method from the factorial() method that begins on line 11. You'll notice that the program also uses spaces and tabs to indent the various lines of code. This kind of indentation is optional; it emphasizes the structure of the program and greatly enhances the readability of the code.

Another method

Line 11 begins the definition of the factorial() method that was used by the main() method. Compare this line to line 5 to note its similarities and differences. The factorial() method has the same public and static modifiers. It takes a single integer parameter, which we call x. Unlike the main() method, which had no return value (void), factorial() returns a value of type double. The open curly brace marks the beginning of the method body, which continues past the nested braces on lines 15 and 18 to line 20, where the matching close curly brace is found. The body of the factorial() method, like the body of the main() method, is composed of statements, which are found on lines 12 through 19.

Checking for valid input

In the main() method, we saw variable declarations, assignments, and method invocations. The statement on line 12 is different. It is an if statement, which executes another statement conditionally. We saw earlier that the Java interpreter executes the three statements of the main() method one after another. It always executes them in exactly that way, in exactly that order. An if statement is a flow-control statement; it can affect the way the interpreter runs a program.

The if keyword is followed by a parenthesized expression and a statement. The Java interpreter first evaluates the expression. If it is true, the interpreter executes the statement. If the expression is false, however, the interpreter skips the statement and goes to the next one. The condition for the if statement on line 12 is x < 0. It checks whether the value passed to the factorial() method is less than zero. If it is, this expression is true, and the statement on line 13 is executed. Line 12 does not end with a semicolon because the statement on line 13 is part of the if statement. Semicolons are required only at the end of a statement.

Line 13 is a `return` statement. It says that the return value of the `factorial()` method is 0.0. `return` is also a flow-control statement. When the Java interpreter sees a `return`, it stops executing the current method and returns the specified value immediately. A `return` statement can stand alone, but in this case, the `return` statement is part of the `if` statement on line 12. The indentation of line 13 helps emphasize this fact. (Java ignores this indentation, but it is very helpful for humans who read Java code!) Line 13 is executed only if the expression on line 12 is `true`.

Before we move on, we should pull back a bit and talk about why lines 12 and 13 are necessary in the first place. It is an error to try to compute a factorial for a negative number, so these lines make sure that the input value x is valid. If it is not valid, they cause `factorial()` to return a consistent invalid result, 0.0.

An important variable

Line 14 is another variable declaration; it declares a variable named `fact` of type `double` and assigns it an initial value of 1.0. This variable holds the value of the factorial as we compute it in the statements that follow. In Java, variables can be declared anywhere; they are not restricted to the beginning of a method or block of code.

Looping and computing the factorial

Line 15 introduces another type of statement: the `while` loop. Like an `if` statement, a `while` statement consists of a parenthesized expression and a statement. When the Java interpreter sees a `while` statement, it evaluates the associated expression. If that expression is `true`, the interpreter executes the statement. The interpreter repeats this process, evaluating the expression and executing the statement if the expression is `true`, until the expression evaluates to `false`. The expression on line 15 is x > 1, so the `while` statement loops *while* the parameter x holds a value that is greater than 1. Another way to say this is that the loop continues *until* x holds a value less than or equal to 1. We can assume from this expression that if the loop is ever going to terminate, the value of x must somehow be modified by the statement that the loop executes.

The major difference between the `if` statement on lines 12–13 and the `while` loop on lines 15–18 is that the statement associated with the `while` loop is a *compound statement*. A compound statement is zero or more statements grouped between curly braces. The `while` keyword on line 15 is followed by an expression in parentheses and then by an open curly brace. This means that the body of the loop consists of all statements between that opening brace and the closing brace on line 18. Earlier in the chapter, I said that all Java statements end with semicolons. This rule does not apply to compound statements, however, as you can see by the lack of a semicolon at the end of line 18. The statements inside the compound statement (lines 16 and 17) do end with semicolons, of course.

The body of the `while` loop consists of the statements on line 16 and 17. Line 16 multiplies the value of `fact` by the value of x and stores the result back into `fact`. Line 17 is similar. It subtracts 1 from the value of x and stores the result back into x. The * character on line 16 is important: it is the multiplication *operator*. And, as you can probably guess, the - on line 17 is the subtraction operator. An operator is a key part of Java syntax: it performs a computation on one or two *operands* to produce a new value. Operands and operators combine to form *expressions*, such as fact * x or x - 1. We've seen other operators in the program. Line 15, for example, uses the greater-than operator (>) in the expression x > 1, which compares the value of the variable x to 1. The value of this expression is a boolean truth value—either true or false, depending on the result of the comparison.

To understand this while loop, it is helpful to think like the Java interpreter. Suppose we are trying to compute the factorial of 4. Before the loop starts, fact is 1.0, and x is 4. After the body of the loop has been executed once—after the first *iteration*—fact is 4.0, and x is 3. After the second iteration, fact is 12.0, and x is 2. After the third iteration, fact is 24.0, and x is 1. When the interpreter tests the loop condition after the third iteration, it finds that x > 1 is no longer true, so it stops running the loop, and the program resumes at line 19.

Returning the result

Line 19 is another return statement, like the one we saw on line 13. This one does not return a constant value like 0.0, but instead returns the value of the fact variable. If the value of x passed into the factorial() function is 4, then, as we saw earlier, the value of fact is 24.0, so this is the value returned. Recall that the factorial() method was invoked on line 7 of the program. When this return statement is executed, control returns to line 7, where the return value is assigned to the variable named result.

Exceptions

If you've made it all the way through the line-by-line analysis of Example 1-1, you are well on your way to understanding the basics of the Java language.* It is a simple but nontrivial program that illustrates many of the features of Java. There is one more important feature of Java programming I want to introduce, but it is one that does not appear in the program listing itself. Recall that the program computes the factorial of the number you specify on the command line. What happens if you run the program without specifying a number?

```
C:\> java Factorial
java.lang.ArrayIndexOutOfBoundsException: 0
        at Factorial.main(Factorial.java:6)
C:\>
```

And what happens if you specify a value that is not a number?

```
C:\> java Factorial ten
java.lang.NumberFormatException: ten
```

---

* If you didn't understand all the details of this factorial program, don't worry. We'll cover the details of the Java language a lot more thoroughly in Chapter 2 and Chapter 3. However, if you feel like you didn't understand any of the line-by-line analysis, you may also find that the upcoming chapters are over your head. In that case, you should probably go elsewhere to learn the basics of the Java language and return to this book to solidify your understanding, and, of course, to use as a reference. One resource you may find useful in learning the language is Sun's online Java tutorial, available at *http://java.sun.com/docs/books/tutorial/*.

```
    at java.lang.Integer.parseInt(Integer.java)
    at java.lang.Integer.parseInt(Integer.java)
    at Factorial.main(Factorial.java:6)
C:\>
```

In both cases, an error occurs or, in Java terminology, an *exception* is thrown.
When an exception is thrown, the Java interpreter prints out a message that
explains what type of exception it was and where it occurred (both exceptions
above occurred on line 6). In the first case, the exception is thrown because there
are no strings in the args list, meaning we asked for a nonexistent string with
args[0]. In the second case, the exception is thrown because Integer.parseInt()
cannot convert the string "ten" to a number. We'll see more about exceptions in
Chapter 2 and learn how to handle them gracefully as they occur.

CHAPTER 2

Java Syntax
from the Ground Up

This chapter is a terse but comprehensive introduction to Java syntax. It is written primarily for readers who are new to the language, but have at least some previous programming experience. Determined novices with no prior programming experience may also find it useful. If you already know Java, you should find it a useful language reference. In previous editions of this book, this chapter was written explicitly for C and C++ programmers making the transition to Java. It has been rewritten for this edition to make it more generally useful, but it still contains comparisons to C and C++ for the benefit of programmers coming from those languages.*

This chapter documents the syntax of Java programs by starting at the very lowest level of Java syntax and building from there, covering increasingly higher orders of structure. It covers:

- The characters used to write Java programs and the encoding of those characters.

- Data types, literal values, identifiers, and other tokens that comprise a Java program.

- The operators used in Java to group individual tokens into larger expressions.

- Statements, which group expressions and other statements to form logical chunks of Java code.

- Methods (also called functions, procedures, or subroutines), which are named collections of Java statements that can be invoked by other Java code.

---

* Readers who want even more thorough coverage of the Java language should consider *The Java Programming Language, Second Edition,* by Ken Arnold and James Gosling (the creator of Java) (Addison Wesley Longman). And hard-core readers may want to go straight to the primary source: *The Java Language Specification,* by James Gosling, Bill Joy, and Guy Steele (Addison Wesley Longman). This specification is available in printed book form, but is also freely available for download from Sun's web site at *http://java.sun.com/docs/books/jls/.* I found both documents quite helpful while writing this chapter.

- Classes, which are collections of methods and fields. Classes are the central program element in Java and form the basis for object-oriented programming. Chapter 3, *Object-Oriented Programming in Java*, is devoted entirely to a discussion of classes and objects.

- Packages, which are collections of related classes.

- Java programs, which consist of one or more interacting classes that may be drawn from one or more packages.

The syntax of most programming languages is complex, and Java is no exception. In general, it is not possible to document all elements of a language without referring to other elements that have not yet been discussed. For example, it is not really possible to explain in a meaningful way the operators and statements supported by Java without referring to objects. But it is also not possible to document objects thoroughly without referring to the operators and statements of the language. The process of learning Java, or any language, is therefore an iterative one. If you are new to Java (or a Java-style programming language), you may find that you benefit greatly from working through this chapter and the next *twice*, so that you can grasp the interrelated concepts.

The Unicode Character Set

Java programs are written using the Unicode character set. Unlike the 7-bit ASCII encoding, which is useful only for English, and the 8-bit ISO Latin-1 encoding, which is useful only for major Western European languages, the 16-bit Unicode encoding can represent virtually every written language in common use on the planet. Very few text editors support Unicode, however, and in practice, most Java programs are written in plain ASCII. 16-bit Unicode characters are typically written to files using an encoding known as UTF-8, which converts the 16-bit characters into a stream of bytes. The format is designed so that plain ASCII and Latin-1 text are valid UTF-8 byte streams. Thus, you can simply write plain ASCII programs, and they will work as valid Unicode.

If you want to embed a Unicode character within a Java program that is written in plain ASCII, use the special Unicode escape sequence \u*xxxx*. That is, a backslash and a lowercase u, followed by four hexadecimal characters. For example, \u0020 is the space character, and \u03c0 is the character π. You can use Unicode characters anywhere in a Java program, including comments and variable names.

Comments

Java supports three types of comments. The first type is a single-line comment, which begins with the characters // and continues until the end of the current line. For example:

```
int i = 0;   // initialize the loop variable
```

The second kind of comment is a multiline comment. It begins with the characters /* and continues, over any number of lines, until the characters */. Any text between the /* and the */ is ignored by the Java compiler. Although this style of comment is typically used for multiline comments, it can also be used for single-line comments. This type of comment cannot be nested (i.e., one /* */ comment cannot appear within another one). When writing multiline comments, programmers often use extra * characters to make the comments stand out. Here is a typical multiline comment:

```
/*
 * Step 4: Print static methods, both public and protected,
 *         but don't list deprecated ones.
 */
```

The third type of comment is a special case of the second. If a comment begins with /**, it is regarded as a special *doc comment*. Like regular multiline comments, doc comments end with */ and cannot be nested. When you write a Java class you expect other programmers to use, use doc comments to embed documentation about the class and each of its methods directly into the source code. A program named *javadoc* extracts these comments and processes them to create online documentation for your class. A doc comment can contain HTML tags and can use additional syntax understood by *javadoc*. For example:

```
/**
 * Display a list of classes, many to a line.
 *
 * @param classes The classes to display
 * @return <tt>true</tt> on success,
 * <tt>false</tt> on failure.
 * @author David Flanagan
 */
```

See Chapter 7, *Java Programming and Documentation Conventions*, for more information on the doc-comment syntax and Chapter 8, *Java Development Tools*, for more information on the *javadoc* program.

Identifiers and Reserved Words

An *identifier* is any symbolic name that refers to something in a Java program. Class, method, parameter, and variable names are all identifiers. An identifier must begin with a letter, an underscore (_), or a Unicode currency symbol (e.g., $, £, ¥). This initial letter can be followed by any number of letters, digits, underscores, or currency symbols. Remember that Java uses the Unicode character set, which contains quite a few letters and digits other than those in the ASCII character set. The following are legal identifiers:

```
i
engine3
theCurrentTime
the_current_time
θ
```

Identifiers can include numbers, but cannot begin with a number. In addition, they cannot contain any punctuation characters other than underscores and currency characters. By convention, dollar signs and other currency characters are reserved for identifiers automatically generated by a compiler or some kind of code preprocessor. It is best to avoid these characters in your own identifiers.

Another important restriction on identifiers is that you cannot use any of the keywords and literals that are part of the Java language itself. These reserved words are listed in Table 2-1.

Table 2-1: Java Reserved Words

abstract	do	if	package	synchronized
boolean	double	implements	private	this
break	else	import	protected	throw
byte	extends	instanceof	public	throws
case	false	int	return	transient
catch	final	interface	short	true
char	finally	long	static	try
class	float	native	strictfp	void
const	for	new	super	volatile
continue	goto	null	switch	while
default				

Note that const and goto are reserved words, but aren't part of the Java language.

Primitive Data Types

Java supports eight basic data types known as *primitive types*. In addition, it supports classes and arrays as composite data types, or reference types. Classes and arrays are documented later in this chapter. The primitive types are: a boolean type, a character type, four integer types, and two floating-point types. The four integer types and the two floating-point types differ in the number of bits that represent them, and therefore in the range of numbers they can represent. Table 2-2 summarizes these primitive data types.

Table 2-2: Java Primitive Data Types

Type	Contains	Default	Size	Range
boolean	true or false	false	1 bit	NA
char	Unicode character	\u0000	16 bits	\u0000 to \uFFFF
byte	Signed integer	0	8 bits	−128 to 127
short	Signed integer	0	16 bits	−32768 to 32767
int	Signed integer	0	32 bits	−2147483648 to 2147483647
long	Signed integer	0	64 bits	−9223372036854775808 to 9223372036854775807
float	IEEE 754 floating point	0.0	32 bits	±1.4E-45 to ±3.4028235E+38
double	IEEE 754 floating point	0.0	64 bits	±4.9E-324 to ±1.7976931348623157E+308

The boolean Type

The boolean type represents a truth value. There are only two possible values of this type, representing the two boolean states: on or off, yes or no, true or false. Java reserves the words true and false to represent these two boolean values.

C and C++ programmers should note that Java is quite strict about its boolean type: boolean values can never be converted to or from other data types. In particular, a boolean is not an integral type, and integer values cannot be used in place of a boolean. In other words, you cannot take shortcuts such as the following in Java:

```
if (o) {
  while(i) {
  }
}
```

Instead, Java forces you to write cleaner code by explicitly stating the comparisons you want:

```
if (o != null) {
  while(i != 0) {
  }
}
```

The char Type

The char type represents Unicode characters. It surprises many experienced programmers to learn that Java char values are 16 bits long, but in practice this fact is totally transparent. To include a character literal in a Java program, simply place it between single quotes (apostrophes):

```
char c = 'A';
```

You can, of course, use any Unicode character as a character literal, and you can use the \u Unicode escape sequence. In addition, Java supports a number of other escape sequences that make it easy both to represent commonly used nonprinting ASCII characters such as newline and to escape certain punctuation characters that have special meaning in Java. For example:

```
char tab = '\t', apostrophe = '\'', nul = '', aleph='\u05D0';
```

Table 2-3 lists the escape characters that can be used in char literals. These characters can also be used in string literals, which are covered later in this chapter.

Table 2-3: Java Escape Characters

Escape Sequence	Character Value
\b	Backspace
\t	Horizontal tab
\n	Newline
\f	Form feed

Table 2–3: Java Escape Characters (continued)

Escape Sequence	Character Value
\r	Carriage return
\"	Double quote
\'	Single quote
\\	Backslash
\xxx	The Latin-1 character with the encoding *xxx*, where *xxx* is an octal (base 8) number between 000 and 377. The forms \x and \xx are also legal, as in '\0', but are not recommended because they can cause difficulties in string constants where the escape sequence is followed by a regular digit.
\uxxxx	The Unicode character with encoding *xxxx*, where *xxxx* is four hexadecimal digits. Unicode escapes can appear anywhere in a Java program, not only in character and string literals.

char values can be converted to and from the various integral types. Unlike byte, short, int, and long, however, char is an unsigned type. The Character class defines a number of useful static methods for working with characters, including isDigit(), isJavaLetter(), isLowerCase(), and toUpperCase().

Integer Types

The integer types in Java are byte, short, int, and long. As shown in Table 2-2, these four types differ only in the number of bits and, therefore, in the range of numbers each type can represent. All integral types represent signed numbers; there is no unsigned keyword as there is in C and C++.

Literals for each of these types are written exactly as you would expect: as a string of decimal digits. Although it is not technically part of the literal syntax, any integer literal can be preceded by the unary minus operator to indicate a negative number. Here are some legal integer literals:

```
0
1
123
-42000
```

Integer literals can also be expressed in hexadecimal or octal notation. A literal that begins with 0x or 0X is taken as a hexadecimal number, using the letters A to F (or a to f) as the additional digits required for base-16 numbers. Integer literals beginning with a leading 0 are taken to be octal (base-8) numbers and cannot include the digits 8 or 9. Java does not allow integer literals to be expressed in binary (base-2) notation. Legal hexadecimal and octal literals include:

```
0xff           // Decimal 255, expressed in hexadecimal
0377           // The same number, expressed in octal (base 8)
0xCAFEBABE     // A magic number used to identify Java class files
```

Integer literals are 32-bit int values unless they end with the character L or l, in which case they are 64-bit long values:

```
1234        // An int value
1234L       // A long value
0xffL       // Another long value
```

Integer arithmetic in Java is modular, which means that it never produces an overflow or an underflow when you exceed the range of a given integer type. Instead, numbers just wrap around. For example:

```
byte b1 = 127, b2 = 1;         // Largest byte is 127
byte sum = (byte)(b1 + b2);    // Sum wraps to -128, which is the smallest byte
```

Neither the Java compiler nor the Java interpreter warns you in any way when this occurs. When doing integer arithmetic, you simply must ensure that the type you are using has a sufficient range for the purposes you intend. Integer division by zero and modulo by zero are illegal and cause an ArithmeticException to be thrown.

Each integer type has a corresponding wrapper class: Byte, Short, Integer, and Long. Each of these classes defines MIN_VALUE and MAX_VALUE constants that describe the range of the type. The classes also define useful static methods, such as Byte.parseByte() and Integer.parseInt(), for converting strings to integer values.

Floating-Point Types

Real numbers in Java are represented with the float and double data types. As shown in Table 2-2, float is a 32-bit, single-precision floating-point value, and double is a 64-bit, double-precision floating-point value. Both types adhere to the IEEE 754-1985 standard, which specifies both the format of the numbers and the behavior of arithmetic for the numbers.

Floating-point values can be included literally in a Java program as an optional string of digits, followed by a decimal point and another string of digits. Here are some examples:

```
123.45
0.0
.01
```

Floating-point literals can also use exponential, or scientific, notation, in which a number is followed by the letter e or E (for exponent) and another number. This second number represents the power of ten by which the first number is multiplied. For example:

```
1.2345E02    // 1.2345 × 10², or 123.45
1e-6         // 1 × 10⁻⁶, or 0.000001
6.02e23      // Avagadro's Number: 6.02 × 10²³
```

Floating-point literals are double values by default. To include a float value literally in a program, follow the number by the character f or F:

```
double d = 6.02E23;
float f = 6.02e23f;
```

Floating-point literals cannot be expressed in hexadecimal or octal notation.

Most real numbers, by their very nature, cannot be represented exactly in any finite number of bits. Thus, it is important to remember that float and double values are only approximations of the numbers they are meant to represent. A float is a 32-bit approximation, which results in at least 6 significant decimal digits, and a double is a 64-bit approximation, which results in at least 15 significant digits. In practice, these data types are suitable for most real-number computations.

In addition to representing ordinary numbers, the float and double types can also represent four special values: positive and negative infinity, zero, and NaN. The infinity values result when a floating-point computation produces a value that overflows the representable range of a float or double. When a floating-point computation underflows the representable range of a float or a double, a zero value results. The Java floating-point types make a distinction between positive zero and negative zero, depending on the direction from which the underflow occurred. In practice, positive and negative zero behave pretty much the same. Finally, the last special floating-point value is NaN, which stands for not-a-number. The NaN value results when an illegal floating-point operation, such as 0.0/0.0, is performed. Here are examples of statements that result in these special values:

```
double inf = 1.0/0.0;        // Infinity
double neginf = -1.0/0.0;    // -Infinity
double negzero = -1.0/inf;   // Negative zero
double NaN = 0.0/0.0;        // Not-a-Number
```

Because the Java floating-point types can handle overflow to infinity and underflow to zero and have a special NaN value, floating-point arithmetic never throws exceptions, even when performing illegal operations, like dividing zero by zero or taking the square root of a negative number.

The float and double primitive types have corresponding classes, named Float and Double. Each of these classes defines the following useful constants: MIN_VALUE, MAX_VALUE, NEGATIVE_INFINITY, POSITIVE_INFINITY, and NaN.

The infinite floating-point values behave as you would expect. Adding or subtracting anything to or from infinity, for example, yields infinity. Negative zero behaves almost identically to positive zero, and, in fact, the == equality operator reports that negative zero is equal to positive zero. One way to distinguish negative zero from positive, or regular, zero is to divide by it. 1.0/0.0 yields positive infinity, but 1.0 divided by negative zero yields negative infinity. Finally, since NaN is not-a-number, the == operator says that it is not equal to any other number, including itself! To check whether a float or double value is NaN, you must use the Float.isNaN() and Double.isNaN() methods.

Strings

In addition to the boolean, character, integer, and floating-point data types, Java also has a data type for working with strings of text (usually simply called *strings*). The String type is a class, however, and is not one of the primitive types of the language. Because strings are so commonly used, though, Java does have a syntax for including string values literally in a program. A String literal consists of arbitrary text within double quotes. For example:

```
"Hello, world"
"'This' is a string!"
```

String literals can contain any of the escape sequences that can appear as char literals (see Table 2-3). Use the \" sequence to include a double-quote within a String literal. Strings and string literals are discussed in more detail later in this chapter. Chapter 4, *The Java Platform*, demonstrates some of the ways you can work with String objects in Java.

Type Conversions

Java allows conversions between integer values and floating-point values. In addition, because every character corresponds to a number in the Unicode encoding, char types can be converted to and from the integer and floating-point types. In fact, boolean is the only primitive type that cannot be converted to or from another primitive type in Java.

There are two basic types of conversions. A *widening conversion* occurs when a value of one type is converted to a wider type—one that has a larger range of legal values. Java performs widening conversions automatically when, for example, you assign an int literal to a double variable or a char literal to an int variable.

Narrowing conversions are another matter, however. A *narrowing conversion* occurs when a value is converted to a type that is not wider than it. Narrowing conversions are not always safe: it is reasonable to convert the integer value 13 to a byte, for example, but it is not reasonable to convert 13000 to a byte, since byte can only hold numbers between −128 and 127. Because you can lose data in a narrowing conversion, the Java compiler complains when you attempt any narrowing conversion, even if the value being converted would in fact fit in the narrower range of the specified type:

```
int i = 13;
byte b = i;      // The compiler does not allow this
```

The one exception to this rule is that you can assign an integer literal (an int value) to a byte or short variable, if the literal falls within the range of the variable.

If you need to perform a narrowing conversion and are confident you can do so without losing data or precision, you can force Java to perform the conversion using a language construct known as a *cast*. Perform a cast by placing the name of the desired type in parentheses before the value to be converted. For example:

```
int i = 13;
byte b = (byte) i;    // Force the int to be converted to a byte
i = (int) 13.456;     // Force this double literal to the int 13
```

Casts of primitive types are most often used to convert floating-point values to integers. When you do this, the fractional part of the floating-point value is simply truncated (i.e., the floating-point value is rounded towards zero, not towards the nearest integer). The methods Math.round(), Math.floor(), and Math.ceil() perform other types of rounding.

The char type acts like an integer type in most ways, so a char value can be used anywhere an int or long value is required. Recall, however, that the char type is *unsigned*, so it behaves differently than the short type, even though both of them are 16 bits wide:

```
short s = (short) 0xffff;  // These bits represent the number -1
char c = '\uffff';         // The same bits, representing a Unicode character
int i1 = s;                // Converting the short to an int yields -1
int i2 = c;                // Converting the char to an int yields 65535
```

Table 2-4 is a grid that shows which primitive types can be converted to which other types and how the conversion is performed. The letter N in the table means that the conversion cannot be performed. The letter Y means that the conversion is a widening conversion and is therefore performed automatically and implicitly by Java. The letter C means that the conversion is a narrowing conversion and requires an explicit cast. Finally, the notation Y* means that the conversion is an automatic widening conversion, but that some of the least significant digits of the value may be lost by the conversion. This can happen when converting an int or long to a float or double. The floating-point types have a larger range than the integer types, so any int or long can be represented by a float or double. However, the floating-point types are approximations of numbers and cannot always hold as many significant digits as the integer types.

Table 2-4: Java Primitive Type Conversions

Convert From:	Convert To:							
	boolean	byte	short	char	int	long	float	double
boolean	–	N	N	N	N	N	N	N
byte	N	–	Y	C	Y	Y	Y	Y
short	N	C	–	C	Y	Y	Y	Y
char	N	C	C	–	Y	Y	Y	Y
int	N	C	C	C	–	Y	Y*	Y
long	N	C	C	C	C	–	Y*	Y*
float	N	C	C	C	C	C	–	Y
double	N	C	C	C	C	C	C	–

Reference Types

In addition to its eight primitive types, Java defines two additional categories of data types: classes and arrays. Java programs consist of class definitions; each class defines a new data type that can be manipulated by Java programs. For example, a program might define a class named Point and use it to store and manipulate X,Y points in a Cartesian coordinate system. This makes Point a new data type in that program. An array type represents a list of values of some other type. char is a data type, and an array of char values is another data type, written char[]. An array of `Point` objects is a data type, written `Point[]`. And an array of `Point` arrays is yet another type, written `Point[][]`.

As you can see, there are an infinite number of possible class and array data types. Collectively, these data types are known as *reference types*. The reason for this name will become clear later in this chapter. For now, however, what is important to understand is that class and array types differ significantly from primitive types, in that they are compound, or composite, types. A primitive data type holds exactly one value. Classes and arrays are aggregate types that contain multiple values. The `Point` type, for example, holds two `double` values representing the X and Y coordinates of the point. And `char[]` is obviously a compound type because it represents a list of characters. By their very nature, class and array types are more complicated than the primitive data types. We'll discuss classes and arrays in detail later in this chapter and examine classes in even more detail in Chapter 3.

Expressions and Operators

So far in this chapter, we've learned about the primitive types that Java programs can manipulate and seen how to include primitive values as *literals* in a Java program. We've also used *variables* as symbolic names that represent, or hold, values. These literals and variables are the tokens out of which Java programs are built.

An *expression* is the next higher level of structure in a Java program. The Java interpreter *evaluates* an expression to compute its value. The very simplest expressions are called *primary expressions* and consist of literals and variables. So, for example, the following are all expressions:

```
1.7       // A floating-point literal
true      // A boolean literal
sum       // A variable
```

When the Java interpreter evaluates a literal expression, the resulting value is the literal itself. When the interpreter evaluates a variable expression, the resulting value is the value stored in the variable.

Primary expressions are not very interesting. More complex expressions are made by using *operators* to combine primary expressions. For example, the following expression uses the assignment operator to combine two primary expressions—a variable and a floating-point literal—into an assignment expression:

```
sum = 1.7
```

But operators are used not only with primary expressions; they can also be used with expressions at any level of complexity. Thus, the following are all legal expressions:

```
sum = 1 + 2 + 3*1.2 + (4 + 8)/3.0
sum/Math.sqrt(3.0 * 1.234)
(int)(sum + 33)
```

Operator Summary

The kinds of expressions you can write in a programming language depend entirely on the set of operators available to you. Table 2-5 summarizes the operators available in Java. The P and A columns of the table specify the precedence and associativity of each group of related operators, respectively.

Table 2–5: Java Operators

P	A	Operator	Operand Type(s)	Operation Performed
15	L	.	object, member	object member access
		[]	array, int	array element access
		(args)	method, arglist	method invocation
		++, --	variable	post-increment, decrement
14	R	++, --	variable	pre-increment, decrement
		+, -	number	unary plus, unary minus
		~	integer	bitwise complement
		!	boolean	boolean NOT
13	R	new	class, arglist	object creation
		(type)	type, any	cast (type conversion)
12	L	*, /, %	number, number	multiplication, division, remainder
11	L	+, -	number, number	addition, subtraction
		+	string, any	string concatenation
10	L	<<	integer, integer	left shift
		>>	integer, integer	right shift with sign extension
		>>>	integer, integer	right shift with zero extension
9	L	<, <=	number, number	less than, less than or equal
		>, >=	number, number	greater than, greater than or equal
		instanceof	reference, type	type comparison
8	L	==	primitive, primitive	equal (have identical values)
		!=	primitive, primitive	not equal (have different values)
		==	reference, reference	equal (refer to same object)
		!=	reference, reference	not equal (refer to different objects)
7	L	&	integer, integer	bitwise AND
		&	boolean, boolean	boolean AND
6	L	^	integer, integer	bitwise XOR
		^	boolean, boolean	boolean XOR
5	L	|	integer, integer	bitwise OR

Table 2–5: Java Operators (continued)

P	A	Operator	Operand Type(s)	Operation Performed
		|	boolean, boolean	boolean OR
4	L	&&	boolean, boolean	conditional AND
3	L	||	boolean, boolean	conditional OR
2	R	?:	boolean, any, any	conditional (ternary) operator
1	R	=	variable, any	assignment
		*=, /=, %=,	variable, any	assignment with operation
		+=, -=, <<=,		
		>>=, >>>=,		
		&=, ^=, |=		

Precedence

The P column of Table 2-5 specifies the *precedence* of each operator. Precedence specifies the order in which operations are performed. Consider this expression:

```
a + b * c
```

The multiplication operator has higher precedence than the addition operator, so a is added to the product of b and c. Operator precedence can be thought of as a measure of how tightly operators bind to their operands. The higher the number, the more tightly they bind.

Default operator precedence can be overridden through the use of parentheses, to explicitly specify the order of operations. The previous expression can be rewritten as follows to specify that the addition should be performed before the multiplication:

```
(a + b) * c
```

The default operator precedence in Java was chosen for compatibility with C; the designers of C chose this precedence so that most expressions can be written naturally without parentheses. There are only a few common Java idioms for which parentheses are required. Examples include:

```
// Class cast combined with member access
((Integer) o).intValue();

// Assignment combined with comparison
while((line = in.readLine()) != null) { ... }

// Bitwise operators combined with comparison
if ((flags & (PUBLIC | PROTECTED)) != 0) { ... }
```

Associativity

When an expression involves several operators that have the same precedence, the operator associativity governs the order in which the operations are performed. Most operators are left-to-right associative, which means that the operations are performed from left to right. The assignment and unary operators, however, have right-to-left associativity. The A column of Table 2-5 specifies the associativity of each operator or group of operators. The value L means left to right, and R means right to left.

The additive operators are all left-to-right associative, so the expression a+b-c is evaluated from left to right: (a+b)-c. Unary operators and assignment operators are evaluated from right to left. Consider this complex expression:

```
a = b += c = -~d
```

This is evaluated as follows:

```
a = (b += (c = -(~d)))
```

As with operator precedence, operator associativity establishes a default order of evaluation for an expression. This default order can be overridden through the use of parentheses. However, the default operator associativity in Java has been chosen to yield a natural expression syntax, and you rarely need to alter it.

Operand number and type

The fourth column of Table 2-5 specifies the number and type of the operands expected by each operator. Some operators operate on only one operand; these are called unary operators. For example, the unary minus operator changes the sign of a single number:

```
-n              // The unary minus operator
```

Most operators, however, are binary operators that operate on two operand values. The - operator actually comes in both forms:

```
a - b           // The subtraction operator is a binary operator
```

Java also defines one ternary operator, often called the conditional operator. It is like an if statement inside an expression. Its three operands are separated by a question mark and a colon; the second and third operands must be convertible to the same type:

```
x > y ? x : y  // Ternary expression; evaluates to the larger of x and y
```

In addition to expecting a certain number of operands, each operator also expects particular types of operands. Column four of the table lists the operand types. Some of the codes used in that column require further explanation:

number
    An integer, floating-point value, or character (i.e., any primitive type except boolean)

integer
    A byte, short, int, long, or char value (long values are not allowed for the array access operator [])

reference
> An object or array

variable
> A variable or anything else, such as an array element, to which a value can be
> assigned

Return type

Just as every operator expects its operands to be of specific types, each operator
produces a value of a specific type. The arithmetic, increment and decrement, bitwise, and shift operators return a `double` if at least one of the operands is a `dou-
ble`. Otherwise, they return a `float` if at least one of the operands is a `float`.
Otherwise, they return a `long` if at least one of the operands is a `long`. Otherwise,
they return an `int`, even if both operands are `byte`, `short`, or `char` types that are
narrower than `int`.

The comparison, equality, and boolean operators always return `boolean` values.
Each assignment operator returns whatever value it assigned, which is of a type
compatible with the variable on the left side of the expression. The conditional
operator returns the value of its second or third argument (which must both be of
the same type).

Side effects

Every operator computes a value based on one or more operand values. Some
operators, however, have *side effects* in addition to their basic evaluation. If an
expression contains side effects, evaluating it changes the state of a Java program
in such a way that evaluating the expression again may yield a different result. For
example, the ++ increment operator has the side effect of incrementing a variable.
The expression ++a increments the variable a and returns the newly incremented
value. If this expression is evaluated again, the value will be different. The various
assignment operators also have side effects. For example, the expression a*=2 can
also be written as a=a*2. The value of the expression is the value of a multiplied
by 2, but the expression also has the side effect of storing that value back into a.
The method invocation operator ( ) has side effects if the invoked method has side
effects. Some methods, such as `Math.sqrt()`, simply compute and return a value
without side effects of any kind. Typically, however, methods do have side effects.
Finally, the `new` operator has the profound side effect of creating a new object.

Order of evaluation

When the Java interpreter evaluates an expression, it performs the various operations in an order specified by the parentheses in the expression, the precedence of
the operators, and the associativity of the operators. Before any operation is performed, however, the interpreter first evaluates the operands of the operator. (The
exceptions are the &&, | |, and ?: operators, which do not always evaluate all their
operands.) The interpreter always evaluates operands in order from left to right.
This matters if any of the operands are expressions that contain side effects. Consider this code, for example:

```
int a = 2;
int v = ++a + ++a * ++a;
```

Although the multiplication is performed before the addition, the operands of the + operator are evaluated first. Thus, the expression evaluates to 3+4*5, or 23.

Arithmetic Operators

Since most programs operate primarily on numbers, the most commonly used operators are often those that perform arithmetic operations. The arithmetic operators can be used with integers, floating-point numbers, and even characters (i.e., they can be used with any primitive type other than boolean). If either of the operands is a floating-point number, floating-point arithmetic is used; otherwise, integer arithmetic is used. This matters because integer arithmetic and floating-point arithmetic differ in the way division is performed and in the way underflows and overflows are handled, for example. The arithmetic operators are:

Addition (+)

The + operator adds two numbers. As we'll see shortly, the + operator can also be used to concatenate strings. If either operand of + is a string, the other one is converted to a string as well. Be sure to use parentheses when you want to combine addition with concatenation. For example:

```
System.out.println("Total: " + 3 + 4);    // Prints "Total: 34", not 7!
```

Subtraction (−)

When − is used as a binary operator, it subtracts its second operand from its first. For example, 7−3 evaluates to 4. The − operator can perform unary negation.

Multiplication (*)

The * operator multiplies its two operands. For example, 7*3 evaluates to 21.

Division (/)

The / operator divides its first operand by its second. If both operands are integers, the result is an integer, and any remainder is lost. If either operand is a floating-point value, however, the result is a floating-point value. When dividing two integers, division by zero throws an ArithmeticException. For floating-point calculations, however, division by zero simply yields an infinite result or NaN:

```
7/3        // Evaluates to 2
7/3.0f     // Evaluates to 2.333333f
7/0        // Throws an ArithmeticException
7/0.0      // Evaluates to positive infinity
0.0/0.0    // Evaluates to NaN
```

Modulo (%)

The % operator computes the first operand modulo the second operand (i.e., it returns the remainder when the first operand is divided by the second operand an integral number of times). For example, 7%3 is 1. The sign of the result is the same as the sign of the first operand. While the modulo operator is typically used with integer operands, it also works for floating-point values. For example, 4.3%2.1 evaluates to 0.1. When operating with integers, trying to compute a value modulo zero causes an `ArithmeticException`. When working with floating-point values, anything modulo 0.0 evaluates to `NaN`, as does infinity modulo anything.

Unary Minus (–)

When – is used as a unary operator, before a single operand, it performs unary negation. In other words, it converts a positive value to an equivalently negative value, and vice versa.

String Concatenation Operator

In addition to adding numbers, the + operator (and the related += operator) also concatenates, or joins, strings. If either of the operands to + is a string, the operator converts the other operand to a string. For example:

```
System.out.println("Quotient: " + 7/3.0f);  // Prints "Quotient: 2.3333333"
```

As a result, you must be careful to put any addition expressions in parentheses when combining them with string concatenation. If you do not, the addition operator is interpreted as a concatenation operator.

The Java interpreter has built-in string conversions for all primitive types. An object is converted to a string by invoking its `toString()` method. Some classes define custom `toString()` methods, so that objects of that class can easily be converted to strings in this way. An array is converted to a string by invoking the built-in `toString()` method, which, unfortunately, does not return a useful string representation of the array contents.

Increment and Decrement Operators

The ++ operator increments its single operand, which must be a variable, an element of an array, or a field of an object, by one. The behavior of this operator depends on its position relative to the operand. When used before the operand, where it is known as the *pre-increment* operator, it increments the operand and evaluates to the incremented value of that operand. When used after the operand, where it is known as the *post-increment* operator, it increments its operand, but evaluates to the value of that operand before it was incremented.

For example, the following code sets both i and j to 2:

```
i = 1;
j = ++i;
```

But these lines set i to 2 and j to 1:

```
i = 1;
j = i++;
```

Similarly, the –– operator decrements its single numeric operand, which must be a variable, an element of an array, or a field of an object, by one. Like the ++ operator, the behavior of –– depends on its position relative to the operand. When used before the operand, it decrements the operand and returns the decremented value.

When used after the operand, it decrements the operand, but returns the *un-decremented* value.

The expressions x++ and x-- are equivalent to x=x+1 and x=x-1, respectively, except that when using the increment and decrement operators, x is only evaluated once. If x is itself an expression with side effects, this makes a big difference. For example, these two expressions are not equivalent:

```
a[i++]++;            // Increments an element of an array
a[i++] = a[i++] + 1;  // Adds one to an array element and stores it in another
```

These operators, in both prefix and postfix forms, are most commonly used to increment or decrement the counter that controls a loop.

Comparison Operators

The comparison operators consist of the equality operators that test values for equality or inequality and the relational operators used with ordered types (numbers and characters) to test for greater than and less than relationships. Both types of operators yield a boolean result, so they are typically used with if statements and while and for loops to make branching and looping decisions. For example:

```
if (o != null) ...;       // The not equals operator
while(i < a.length) ...;   // The less than operator
```

Java provides the following equality operators:

Equals (==)
> The == operator evaluates to true if its two operands are equal and false otherwise. With primitive operands, it tests whether the operand values themselves are identical. For operands of reference types, however, it tests whether the operands refer to the same object or array. In other words, it does not test the equality of two distinct objects or arrays. In particular, note that you cannot test two distinct strings for equality with this operator.
>
> If == is used to compare two numeric or character operands that are not of the same type, the narrower operand is converted to the type of the wider operand before the comparison is done. For example, when comparing a short to a float, the short is first converted to a float before the comparison is performed. For floating-point numbers, the special negative zero value tests equal to the regular, positive zero value. Also, the special NaN (not-a-number) value is not equal to any other number, including itself. To test whether a floating-point value is NaN, use the Float.isNan() or Double.isNan() method.

Not Equals (!=)
> The != operator is exactly the opposite of the == operator. It evaluates to true if its two primitive operands have different values or if its two reference operands refer to different objects or arrays. Otherwise, it evaluates to false.

The relational operators can be used with numbers and characters, but not with boolean values, objects, or arrays because those types are not ordered. Java provides the following relational operators:

Less Than (<)
> Evaluates to true if the first operand is less than the second.

Less Than or Equal (<=)
> Evaluates to true if the first operand is less than or equal to the second.

Greater Than (>)
> Evaluates to true if the first operand is greater than the second.

Greater Than or Equal (>=)
> Evaluates to true if the first operand is greater than or equal to the second.

Boolean Operators

As we've just seen, the comparison operators compare their operands and yield a boolean result, which is often used in branching and looping statements. In order to make branching and looping decisions based on conditions more interesting than a single comparison, you can use the Boolean (or logical) operators to combine multiple comparison expressions into a single, more complex, expression. The Boolean operators require their operands to be boolean values and they evaluate to boolean values. The operators are:

Conditional AND (&&)
> This operator performs a Boolean AND operation on its operands. It evaluates to true if and only if both its operands are true. If either or both operands are false, it evaluates to false. For example:
>
> ```
> if (x < 10 && y > 3) ... // If both comparisons are true
> ```
>
> This operator (and all the Boolean operators except the unary ! operator) have a lower precedence than the comparison operators. Thus, it is perfectly legal to write a line of code like the one above. However, some programmers prefer to use parentheses to make the order of evaluation explicit:
>
> ```
> if ((x < 10) && (y > 3)) ...
> ```
>
> You should use whichever style you find easier to read.
>
> This operator is called a conditional AND because it conditionally evaluates its second operand. If the first operand evaluates to false, the value of the expression is false, regardless of the value of the second operand. Therefore, to increase efficiency, the Java interpreter takes a shortcut and skips the second operand. Since the second operand is not guaranteed to be evaluated, you must use caution when using this operator with expressions that have side effects. On the other hand, the conditional nature of this operator allows us to write Java expressions such as the following:
>
> ```
> if (data != null && i < data.length && data[i] != -1) ...
> ```
>
> The second and third comparisons in this expression would cause errors if the first or second comparisons evaluated to false. Fortunately, we don't have to worry about this because of the conditional behavior of the && operator.

Conditional OR (||)

This operator performs a Boolean OR operation on its two `boolean` operands. It evaluates to `true` if either or both of its operands are `true`. If both operands are `false`, it evaluates to `false`. Like the && operator, || does not always evaluate its second operand. If the first operand evaluates to `true`, the value of the expression is `true`, regardless of the value of the second operand. Thus, the operator simply skips that second operand in that case.

Boolean NOT (!)

This unary operator changes the `boolean` value of its operand. If applied to a `true` value, it evaluates to `false`, and if applied to a `false` value, it evaluates to `true`. It is useful in expressions like these:

```
if (!found) ...           // found is a boolean variable declared somewhere
while (!c.isEmpty()) ... // The isEmpty() method returns a boolean value
```

Because ! is a unary operator, it has a high precedence and often must be used with parentheses:

```
if (!(x > y && y > z))
```

Boolean AND (&)

When used with `boolean` operands, the & operator behaves like the && operator, except that it always evaluates both operands, regardless of the value of the first operand. This operator is almost always used as a bitwise operator with integer operands, however, and many Java programmers would not even recognize its use with `boolean` operands as legal Java code.

Boolean OR (|)

This operator performs a Boolean OR operation on its two `boolean` operands. It is like the || operator, except that it always evaluates both operands, even if the first one is `true`. The | operator is almost always used as a bitwise operator on integer operands; its use with `boolean` operands is very rare.

Boolean XOR (^)

When used with `boolean` operands, this operator computes the Exclusive OR (XOR) of its operands. It evaluates to `true` if exactly one of the two operands is `true`. In other words, it evaluates to `false` if both operands are `false` or if both operands are `true`. Unlike the && and || operators, this one must always evaluate both operands. The ^ operator is much more commonly used as a bitwise operator on integer operands. With `boolean` operands, this operator is equivalent to the != operator.

Bitwise and Shift Operators

The bitwise and shift operators are low-level operators that manipulate the individual bits that make up an integer value. The bitwise operators are most commonly used for testing and setting individual flag bits in a value. In order to understand their behavior, you must understand binary (base-2) numbers and the twos-complement format used to represent negative integers. You cannot use these operators with floating-point, `boolean`, array, or object operands. When used with `boolean` operands, the &, |, and ^ operators perform a different operation, as described in the previous section.

If either of the arguments to a bitwise operator is a `long`, the result is a `long`. Otherwise, the result is an `int`. If the left operand of a shift operator is a `long`, the result is a `long`; otherwise, the result is an `int`. The operators are:

Bitwise Complement (˜)

The unary ˜ operator is known as the bitwise complement, or bitwise NOT, operator. It inverts each bit of its single operand, converting ones to zeros and zeros to ones. For example:

```
byte b = ˜12;            // ˜00001100 ==> 11110011 or -13 decimal
flags = flags & ˜f;      // Clear flag f in a set of flags
```

Bitwise AND (&)

This operator combines its two integer operands by performing a Boolean AND operation on their individual bits. The result has a bit set only if the corresponding bit is set in both operands. For example:

```
10 & 7                   // 00001010 & 00000111 ==> 00000010 or 2
if ((flags & f) != 0)    // Test whether flag f is set
```

When used with `boolean` operands, & is the infrequently used Boolean AND operator described earlier.

Bitwise OR (|)

This operator combines its two integer operands by performing a Boolean OR operation on their individual bits. The result has a bit set if the corresponding bit is set in either or both of the operands. It has a zero bit only where both corresponding operand bits are zero. For example:

```
10 | 7                   //·00001010 | 00000111 ==> 00001111 or 15
flags = flags | f;       // Set flag f
```

When used with `boolean` operands, | is the infrequently used Boolean OR operator described earlier.

Bitwise XOR (ˆ)

This operator combines its two integer operands by performing a Boolean XOR (Exclusive OR) operation on their individual bits. The result has a bit set if the corresponding bits in the two operands are different. If the corresponding operand bits are both ones or both zeros, the result bit is a zero. For example:

```
10 ˆ 7                   // 00001010 ˆ 00000111 ==> 00001101 or 13
```

When used with `boolean` operands, ˆ is the infrequently used Boolean XOR operator.

Left Shift (<<)

The << operator shifts the bits of the left operand left by the number of places specified by the right operand. High-order bits of the left operand are lost, and zero bits are shifted in from the right. Shifting an integer left by n places is equivalent to multiplying that number by 2^n. For example:

```
10 << 1    // 00001010 << 1 = 00010100 = 20 = 10*2
7 << 3     // 00000111 << 3 = 00111000 = 56 = 7*8
-1 << 2    // 0xFFFFFFFF << 2 = 0xFFFFFFFC = -4 = -1*4
```

If the left operand is a `long`, the right operand should be between 0 and 63. Otherwise, the left operand is taken to be an `int`, and the right operand should be between 0 and 31.

Signed Right Shift (>>)

The >> operator shifts the bits of the left operand to the right by the number of places specified by the right operand. The low-order bits of the left operand are shifted away and are lost. The high-order bits shifted in are the same as the original high-order bit of the left operand. In other words, if the left operand is positive, zeros are shifted into the high-order bits. If the left operand is negative, ones are shifted in instead. This technique is known as *sign extension*; it is used to preserve the sign of the left operand. For example:

```
10 >> 1     // 00001010 >> 1 = 00000101 = 5 = 10/2
27 >> 3     // 00011011 >> 3 = 00000011 = 3 = 27/8
-50 >> 2    // 11001110 >> 2 = 11110011 = -13 != -50/4
```

If the left operand is positive and the right operand is n, the >> operator is the same as integer division by 2^n.

Unsigned Right Shift (>>>)

This operator is like the >> operator, except that it always shifts zeros into the high-order bits of the result, regardless of the sign of the left-hand operand. This technique is called *zero extension*; it is appropriate when the left operand is being treated as an unsigned value (despite the fact that Java integer types are all signed). Examples:

```
-50 >>> 2    // 11001110 >>> 2 = 00110011 = 51
0xff >>> 4   // 11111111 >>> 4 = 00001111 = 15  = 255/16
```

Assignment Operators

The assignment operators store, or assign, a value into some kind of variable. The left operand must evaluate to an appropriate local variable, array element, or object field. The right side can be any value of a type compatible with the variable. An assignment expression evaluates to the value that is assigned to the variable. More importantly, however, the expression has the side effect of actually performing the assignment. Unlike all other binary operators, the assignment operators are right-associative, which means that the assignments in a=b=c are performed right-to-left, as follows: a=(b=c).

The basic assignment operator is =. Do not confuse it with the equality operator, ==. In order to keep these two operators distinct, I recommend that you read = as "is assigned the value."

In addition to this simple assignment operator, Java also defines 11 other operators that combine assignment with the 5 arithmetic operators and the 6 bitwise and shift operators. For example, the += operator reads the value of the left variable, adds the value of the right operand to it, stores the sum back into the left variable as a side effect, and returns the sum as the value of the expression. Thus, the expression x+=2 is almost the same as x=x+2. The difference between these two expressions is that when you use the += operator, the left operand is evaluated only once. This makes a difference when that operand has a side effect. Consider the following two expressions, which are not equivalent:

```
a[i++] += 2;
a[i++] = a[i++] + 2;
```

The general form of these combination assignment operators is:

```
var op= value
```

This is equivalent (unless there are side effects in var) to:

```
var = var op value
```

The available operators are:

```
+=    -=    *=    /=    %=     // Arithmetic operators plus assignment
&=    |=    ^=                 // Bitwise operators plus assignment
<<=   >>=   >>>=              // Shift operators plus assignment
```

The most commonly used operators are += and -=, although &= and |= can also be useful when working with boolean flags. For example:

```
i += 2;          // Increment a loop counter by 2
c -= 5;          // Decrement a counter by 5
flags |= f;      // Set a flag f in an integer set of flags
flags &= ~f;     // Clear a flag f in an integer set of flags
```

The Conditional Operator

The conditional operator ?: is a somewhat obscure ternary (three-operand) operator inherited from C. It allows you to embed a conditional within an expression. You can think of it as the operator version of the if/else statement. The first and second operands of the conditional operator are separated by a question mark (?), while the second and third operands are separated by a colon (:). The first operand must evaluate to a boolean value. The second and third operands can be of any type, but they must be convertible to the same type.

The conditional operator starts by evaluating its first operand. If it is true, the operator evaluates its second operand and uses that as the value of the expression. On the other hand, if the first operand is false, the conditional operator evaluates and returns its third operand. The conditional operator never evaluates both its second and third operand, so be careful when using expressions with side effects with this operator. Examples of this operator are:

```
int max = (x > y) ? x : y;
String name = (name != null) ? name : "unknown";
```

Note that the ?: operator has lower precedence than all other operators except the assignment operators, so parentheses are not usually necessary around the operands of this operator. Many programmers find conditional expressions easier to read if the first operand is placed within parentheses, however. This is especially true because the conditional if statement always has its conditional expression written within parentheses.

The instanceof Operator

The `instanceof` operator requires an object or array value as its left operand and the name of a reference type as its right operand. It evaluates to `true` if the object or array is an *instance* of the specified type; it returns `false` otherwise. If the left operand is `null`, `instanceof` always evaluates to `false`. If an `instanceof` expression evaluates to `true`, it means that you can safely cast and assign the left operand to a variable of the type of the right operand.

The `instanceof` operator can be used only with array and object types and values, not primitive types and values. Object and array types are discussed in detail later in this chapter. Examples of `instanceof` are:

```
"string" instanceof String       // True: all strings are instances of String
"" instanceof Object              // True: strings are also instances of Object
new int[] {1} instanceof int[]    // True: the array value is an int array
new int[] {1} instanceof byte[]   // False: the array value is not a byte array
new int[] {1} instanceof Object   // True: all arrays are instances of Object
null instanceof String            // False: null is never instanceof anything

// Use instanceof to make sure that it is safe to cast an object
if (object instanceof Point) {
  Point p = (Point) object;
}
```

Special Operators

There are five language constructs in Java that are sometimes considered operators and sometimes considered simply part of the basic language syntax. These "operators" are listed in Table 2-5 in order to show their precedence relative to the other true operators. The use of these language constructs is detailed elsewhere in this chapter, but is described briefly here, so that you can recognize these constructs when you encounter them in code examples:

Object member access (`.`)

An *object* is a collection of data and methods that operate on that data; the data fields and methods of an object are called its members. The dot (`.`) operator accesses these members. If `o` is an expression that evaluates to an object reference, and `f` is the name of a field of the object, `o.f` evaluates to the value contained in that field. If `m` is the name of a method, `o.m` refers to that method and allows it to be invoked using the `()` operator shown later.

Array element access (`[]`)

An *array* is a numbered list of values. Each element of an array can be referred to by its number, or *index*. The `[]` operator allows you to refer to the individual elements of an array. If `a` is an array, and `i` is an expression that evaluates to an `int`, `a[i]` refers to one of the elements of `a`. Unlike other operators that work with integer values, this operator restricts array index values to be of type `int` or narrower.

Method invocation (( ))

A *method* is a named collection of Java code that can be run, or *invoked*, by following the name of the method with zero or more comma-separated expressions contained within parentheses. The values of these expressions are the *arguments* to the method. The method processes the arguments and optionally returns a value that becomes the value of the method invocation expression. If o.m is a method that expects no arguments, the method can be invoked with o.m( ). If the method expects three arguments, for example, it can be invoked with an expression such as o.m(x,y,z). Before the Java interpreter invokes a method, it evaluates each of the arguments to be passed to the method. These expressions are guaranteed to be evaluated in order from left to right (which matters if any of the arguments have side effects).

Object creation (new)

In Java, objects (and arrays) are created with the new operator, which is followed by the type of the object to be created and a parenthesized list of arguments to be passed to the object *constructor.* A constructor is a special method that initializes a newly created object, so the object creation syntax is similar to the Java method invocation syntax. For example:

```
new ArrayList();
new Point(1,2)
```

Type conversion or casting (( ))

As we've already seen, parentheses can also be used as an operator to perform narrowing type conversions, or casts. The first operand of this operator is the type to be converted to; it is placed between the parentheses. The second operand is the value to be converted; it follows the parentheses. For example:

```
(byte) 28           // An integer literal cast to a byte type
(int) (x + 3.14f)   // A floating-point sum value cast to an integer value
(String)h.get(k)    // A generic object cast to a more specific string type
```

Statements

A *statement* is a single "command" that is executed by the Java interpreter. By default, the Java interpreter runs one statement after another, in the order they are written. Many of the statements defined by Java, however, are flow-control statements, such as conditionals and loops, that alter this default order of execution in well-defined ways. Table 2-6 summarizes the statements defined by Java.

Table 2-6: Java Statements

Statement	Purpose	Syntax
expression	side effects	*var = expr*;
		expr++;
		method( );
		new *Type*( );
compound	group statements	{ *statements* }

Table 2-6: Java Statements (continued)

Statement	Purpose	Syntax
empty	do nothing	;
labeled	name a statement	label : statement
variable	declare a variable	[final] type name [= value] [, name [= value]] ... ;
if	conditional	if (expr) statement [else statement]

switch	conditional	switch (expr) {
		[case expr : statements] ...
		[default: statements]
		}

while	loop	while (expr) statement
do	loop	do statement while (expr);
for	simplified loop	for (init ; test ; increment) statement
break	exit block	break [label] ;
continue	restart loop	continue [label] ;
return	end method	return [expr] ;
synchronized	critical section	synchronized (expr) { statements }
throw	throw exception	throw expr ;
try	handle exception	try { statements } [catch (type name) { statements }] ... [finally { statements }]

Expression Statements

As we saw earlier in the chapter, certain types of Java expressions have side effects. In other words, they do not simply evaluate to some value, but also change the program state in some way. Any expression with side effects can be used as a statement simply by following it with a semicolon. The legal types of expression statements are assignments, increments and decrements, method calls, and object creation. For example:

```
a = 1;                              // Assignment
x *= 2;                             // Assignment with operation
i++;                               // Post-increment
--c;                               // Pre-decrement
System.out.println("statement");    // Method invocation
```

Compound Statements

A *compound statement* is any number and kind of statements grouped together within curly braces. You can use a compound statement anywhere a statement is required by Java syntax:

```
for(int i = 0; i < 10; i++) {
   a[i]++;                // Body of this loop is a compound statement.
```

```
    b[i]--;                         // It consists of two expression statements
  }                                 // within curly braces.
```

The Empty Statement

An *empty statement* in Java is written as a single semicolon. The empty statement doesn't do anything, but the syntax is occasionally useful. For example, you can use it to indicate an empty loop body of a for loop:

```
for(int i = 0; i < 10; a[i++]++)    // Increment array elements
    /* empty */;                    // Loop body is empty statement
```

Labeled Statements

A *labeled statement* is simply a statement that has been given a name by prepending an identifier and a colon to it. Labels are used by the break and continue statements. For example:

```
rowLoop: for(int r = 0; r < rows.length; r++) {      // A labeled loop
    colLoop: for(int c = 0; c < columns.length; c++) {  // Another one
        break rowLoop;                               // Use a label
    }
}
```

Local Variable Declaration Statements

A *local variable*, often simply called a variable, is a symbolic name for a location where a value can be stored that is defined within a method or compound statement. All variables must be declared before they can be used; this is done with a variable declaration statement. Because Java is a strongly typed language, a variable declaration specifies the type of the variable, and only values of that type can be stored in the variable.

In its simplest form, a variable declaration specifies a variable's type and name:

```
int counter;
String s;
```

A variable declaration can also include an *initializer*: an expression that specifies an initial value for the variable. For example:

```
int i = 0;
String s = readLine();
int[] data = {x+1, x+2, x+3};  // Array initializers are documented later
```

The Java compiler does not allow you to use a local variable that has not been initialized, so it is usually convenient to combine variable declaration and initialization into a single statement. The initializer expression need not be a literal value or a constant expression that can be evaluated by the compiler; it can be an arbitrarily complex expression whose value is computed when the program is run.

A single variable declaration statement can declare and initialize more than one variable, but all variables must be of the same type. Variable names and optional initializers are separated from each other with commas:

```
int i, j, k;
float x = 1.0, y = 1.0;
String question = "Really Quit?", response;
```

In Java 1.1 and later, variable declaration statements can begin with the `final` keyword. This modifier specifies that once an initial value is specified for the variable, that value is never allowed to change:

```
final String greeting = getLocalLanguageGreeting();
```

C programmers should note that Java variable declaration statements can appear anywhere in Java code; they are not restricted to the beginning of a method or block of code. Local variable declarations can also be integrated with the *initialize* portion of a `for` loop, as we'll discuss shortly.

Local variables can be used only within the method or block of code in which they are defined. This is called their *scope* or *lexical scope*:

```
void method() {          // A generic method
  int i = 0;             // Declare variable i
  while (i < 10) {       // i is in scope here
    int j = 0;           // Declare j; the scope of j begins here
    i++;                 // i is in scope here; increment it
  }                      // j is no longer in scope; can't use it anymore
  System.out.println(i); // i is still in scope here
}                        // The scope of i ends here
```

The if/else Statement

The `if` statement is the fundamental control statement that allows Java to make decisions or, more precisely, to execute statements conditionally. The `if` statement has an associated expression and statement. If the expression evaluates to `true`, the interpreter executes the statement. If the expression evaluates to `false`, however, the interpreter skips the statement. For example:

```
if (username == null)    // If username is null,
  username = "John Doe"; // define it.
```

Although they look extraneous, the parentheses around the expression are a required part of the syntax for the `if` statement.

As I already mentioned, a block of statements enclosed in curly braces is itself a statement, so we can also write `if` statements that look as follows:

```
if ((address == null) || (address.equals(""))) {
  address = "[undefined]";
  System.out.println("WARNING: no address specified.");
}
```

An `if` statement can include an optional `else` keyword that is followed by a second statement. In this form of the statement, the expression is evaluated, and, if it is `true`, the first statement is executed. Otherwise, the second statement is executed. For example:

```
if (username != null)
  System.out.println("Hello " + username);
else {
```

```
    username = askQuestion("What is your name?");
    System.out.println("Hello " + username + ". Welcome!");
}
```

When you use nested if/else statements, some caution is required to ensure that the else clause goes with the appropriate if statement. Consider the following lines:

```
if (i == j)
  if (j == k)
    System.out.println("i equals k");
else
  System.out.println("i doesn't equal j");    // WRONG!!
```

In this example, the inner if statement forms the single statement allowed by the syntax of the outer if statement. Unfortunately, it is not clear (except from the hint given by the indentation) which if the else goes with. And in this example, the indentation hint is wrong. The rule is that an else clause like this is associated with the nearest if statement. Properly indented, this code looks like this:

```
if (i == j)
  if (j == k)
    System.out.println("i equals k");
  else
    System.out.println("i doesn't equal j");    // WRONG!!
```

This is legal code, but it is clearly not what the programmer had in mind. When working with nested if statements, you should use curly braces to make your code easier to read. Here is a better way to write the code:

```
if (i == j) {
  if (j == k)
    System.out.println("i equals k");
}
else {
  System.out.println("i doesn't equal j");
}
```

The else if clause

The if/else statement is useful for testing a condition and choosing between two statements or blocks of code to execute. But what about when you need to choose between several blocks of code? This is typically done with an else if clause, which is not really new syntax, but a common idiomatic usage of the standard if/else statement. It looks like this:

```
if (n == 1) {
  // Execute code block #1
}
else if (n == 2) {
  // Execute code block #2
}
else if (n == 3) {
  // Execute code block #3
}
else {
  // If all else fails, execute block #4
}
```

There is nothing special about this code. It is just a series of if statements, where each if is part of the else clause of the previous statement. Using the else if idiom is preferable to, and more legible than, writing these statements out in their fully nested form:

```java
if (n == 1) {
  // Execute code block #1
}
else {
  if (n == 2) {
    // Execute code block #2
  }
  else {
    if (n == 3) {
      // Execute code block #3
    }
    else {
      // If all else fails, execute block #4
    }
  }
}
```

The switch Statement

An if statement causes a branch in the flow of a program's execution. You can use multiple if statements, as shown in the previous section, to perform a multi-way branch. This is not always the best solution, however, especially when all of the branches depend on the value of a single variable. In this case, it is inefficient to repeatedly check the value of the same variable in multiple if statements.

A better solution is to use a switch statement, which is inherited from the C programming language. Although the syntax of this statement is not nearly as elegant as other parts of Java, the brute practicality of the construct makes it worthwhile. If you are not familiar with the switch statement itself, you may at least be familiar with the basic concept, under the name computed goto or jump table. A switch statement has an integer expression and a body that contains various numbered entry points. The expression is evaluated, and control jumps to the entry point specified by that value. For example, the following switch statement is equivalent to the repeated if and else/if statements shown in the previous section:

```java
switch(n) {
  case 1:                      // Start here if n == 1
    // Execute code block #1
    break;                     // Stop here
  case 2:                      // Start here if n == 2
    // Execute code block #2
    break;                     // Stop here
  case 3:                      // Start here if n == 3
    // Execute code block #3
    break;                     // Stop here
  default:                     // If all else fails...
                               // Execute code block #4

    break;                     // Stop here
}
```

As you can see from the example, the various entry points into a switch statement are labeled either with the keyword case, followed by an integer value and a colon, or with the special default keyword, followed by a colon. When a switch statement executes, the interpreter computes the value of the expression in parentheses and then looks for a case label that matches that value. If it finds one, the interpreter starts executing the block of code at the first statement following the case label. If it does not find a case label with a matching value, the interpreter starts execution at the first statement following a special-case default: label. Or, if there is no default: label, the interpreter skips the body of the switch statement altogether.

Note the use of the break keyword at the end of each case in the previous code. The break statement is described later in this chapter, but, in this case, it causes the interpreter to exit the body of the switch statement. The case clauses in a switch statement specify only the *starting point* of the desired code. The individual cases are not independent blocks of code, and they do not have any implicit ending point. Therefore, you must explicitly specify the end of each case with a break or related statement. In the absence of break statements, a switch statement begins executing code at the first statement after the matching case label and continues executing statements until it reaches the end of the block. On rare occasions, it is useful to write code like this that falls through from one case label to the next, but 99% of the time you should be careful to end every case and default section with a statement that causes the switch statement to stop executing. Normally you use a break statement, but return and throw also work.

A switch statement can have more than one case clause labeling the same statement. Consider the switch statement in the following method:

```java
boolean parseYesOrNoResponse(char response) {
  switch(response) {
    case 'y':
    case 'Y': return true;
    case 'n':
    case 'N': return false;
    default: throw new IllegalArgumentException("Response must be Y or N");
  }
}
```

There are some important restrictions on the switch statement and its case labels. First, the expression associated with a switch statement must have a byte, char, short, or int value. The floating-point and boolean types are not supported, and neither is long, even though long is an integer type. Second, the value associated with each case label must be a constant value or a constant expression the compiler can evaluate. A case label cannot contain a runtime expressions involving variables or method calls, for example. Third, the case label values must be within the range of the data type used for the switch expression. And finally, it is obviously not legal to have two or more case labels with the same value or more than one default label.

The while Statement

Just as the if statement is the basic control statement that allows Java to make decisions, the while statement is the basic statement that allows Java to perform repetitive actions. It has the following syntax:

```
while (expression)
  statement
```

The while statement works by first evaluating the *expression*. If it is false, the interpreter skips the *statement* associated with the loop and moves to the next statement in the program. If it is true, however, the *statement* that forms the body of the loop is executed, and the *expression* is reevaluated. Again, if the value of *expression* is false, the interpreter moves on to the next statement in the program; otherwise it executes the *statement* again. This cycle continues while the *expression* remains true (i.e., until it evaluates to false), at which point the while statement ends, and the interpreter moves on to the next statement. You can create an infinite loop with the syntax while(true).

Here is an example while loop that prints the numbers 0 to 9:

```
int count = 0;
while (count < 10) {
  System.out.println(count);
  count++;
}
```

As you can see, the variable count starts off at 0 in this example and is incremented each time the body of the loop runs. Once the loop has executed 10 times, the expression becomes false (i.e., count is no longer less than 10), the while statement finishes, and the Java interpreter can move to the next statement in the program. Most loops have a counter variable like count. The variable names i, j, and k are commonly used as a loop counters, although you should use more descriptive names if it makes your code easier to understand.

The do Statement

A do loop is much like a while loop, except that the loop expression is tested at the bottom of the loop, rather than at the top. This means that the body of the loop is always executed at least once. The syntax is:

```
do
  statement
while ( expression ) ;
```

There are a couple of differences to notice between the do loop and the more ordinary while loop. First, the do loop requires both the do keyword to mark the beginning of the loop and the while keyword to mark the end and introduce the loop condition. Also, unlike the while loop, the do loop is terminated with a semicolon. This is because the do loop ends with the loop condition, rather than simply ending with a curly brace that marks the end of the loop body. The following do loop prints the same output as the while loop shown above:

```
int count = 0;
do {
  System.out.println(count);
  count++;
} while(count < 10);
```

Note that the do loop is much less commonly used than its while cousin. This is because, in practice, it is unusual to encounter a situation where you are sure you always want a loop to execute at least once.

The for Statement

The for statement provides a looping construct that is often more convenient than the while and do loops. The for statement takes advantage of a common looping pattern. Most loops have a counter, or state variable of some kind, that is initialized before the loop starts, tested to determine whether to execute the loop body, and then incremented, or updated somehow, at the end of the loop body before the test expression is evaluated again. The initialization, test, and update steps are the three crucial manipulations of a loop variable, and the for statement makes these three steps an explicit part of the loop syntax:

```
for(initialize ; test ; increment)
    statement
```

This for loop is basically equivalent to the following while loop:*

```
initialize;
while(test) {
  statement;
  increment;
}
```

Placing the *initialize, test,* and *increment* expressions at the top of a for loop makes it especially easy to understand what the loop is doing, and it prevents mistakes such as forgetting to initialize or increment the loop variable. The interpreter discards the values of the *initialize* and *increment* expressions, so in order to be useful, these expressions must have side effects. *initialize* is typically an assignment expression, while *increment* is usually an increment, decrement, or some other assignment.

The following for loop prints the numbers 0 to 9, just as the previous while and do loops have done:

```
int count;
for(count = 0 ; count < 10 ; count++)
  System.out.println(count);
```

Notice how this syntax places all the important information about the loop variable on a single line, making it very clear how the loop executes. Placing the increment expression in the for statement itself also simplifies the body of the

---

* As you'll see when we consider the continue statement, this while loop is not exactly equivalent to the for loop.

loop to a single statement; we don't even need to use curly braces to produce a statement block.

The `for` loop supports some additional syntax that makes it even more convenient to use. Because many loops use their loop variables only within the loop, the `for` loop allows the *initialize* expression to be a full variable declaration, so that the variable is scoped to the body of the loop and is not visible outside of it. For example:

```
for(int count = 0 ; count < 10 ; count++)
    System.out.println(count);
```

Furthermore, the `for` loop syntax does not restrict you to writing loops that use only a single variable. Both the *initialize* and *increment* expressions of a `for` loop can use a comma to separate multiple initializations and increment expressions. For example:

```
for(int i = 0, j = 10 ; i < 10 ; i++, j--)
    sum += i * j;
```

Even though all the examples so far have counted numbers, `for` loops are not restricted to loops that count numbers. For example, you might use a `for` loop to iterate through the elements of a linked list:

```
for(Node n = listHead; n != null; n = n.nextNode())
    process(n);
```

The *initialize, test,* and *increment* expressions of a `for` loop are all optional; only the semicolons that separate the expressions are required. If the *test* expression is omitted, it is assumed to be `true`. Thus, you can write an infinite loop as `for(;;)`.

The break Statement

A `break` statement causes the Java interpreter to skip immediately to the end of a containing statement. We have already seen the `break` statement used with the `switch` statement. The `break` statement is most often written as simply the keyword `break` followed by a semicolon:

```
break;
```

When used in this form, it causes the Java interpreter to immediately exit the innermost containing `while`, `do`, `for`, or `switch` statement. For example:

```
for(int i = 0; i < data.length; i++) {  // Loop through the data array.
    if (data[i] == target) {            // When we find what we're looking for,
        index = i;                      // remember where we found it
        break;                          // and stop looking!
    }
}   // The Java interpreter goes here after executing break
```

The `break` statement can also be followed by the name of a containing labeled statement. When used in this form, `break` causes the Java interpreter to immediately exit from the named block, which can be any kind of statement, not just a loop or `switch`. For example:

```
testfornull: if (data != null) {          // If the array is defined,
    for(int row = 0; row < numrows; row++) {  // loop through one dimension,
        for(int col = 0; col < numcols; col++) { // then loop through the other.
            if (data[row][col] == null)       // If the array is missing data,
                break testfornull;            // treat the array as undefined.
        }
    }
} // Java interpreter goes here after executing break testfornull
```

The continue Statement

While a break statement exits a loop, a continue statement quits the current iteration of a loop and starts the next one. continue, in both its unlabeled and labeled forms, can be used only within a while, do, or for loop. When used without a label, continue causes the innermost loop to start a new iteration. When used with a label that is the name of a containing loop, it causes the named loop to start a new iteration. For example:

```
for(int i = 0; i < data.length; i++) {  // Loop through data.
    if (data[i] == -1)                  // If a data value is missing,
        continue;                       // skip to the next iteration.
    process(data[i]);                   // Process the data value.
}
```

while, do, and for loops differ slightly in the way that continue starts a new iteration:

* With a while loop, the Java interpreter simply returns to the top of the loop, tests the loop condition again, and, if it evaluates to true, executes the body of the loop again.

* With a do loop, the interpreter jumps to the bottom of the loop, where it tests the loop condition to decide whether to perform another iteration of the loop.

* With a for loop, the interpreter jumps to the top of the loop, where it first evaluates the *increment* expression and then evaluates the *test* expression to decide whether to loop again. As you can see, the behavior of a for loop with a continue statement is different from the behavior of the "basically equivalent" while loop I presented earlier; *increment* gets evaluated in the for loop, but not in the equivalent while loop.

The return Statement

A return statement tells the Java interpreter to stop executing the current method. If the method is declared to return a value, the return statement is followed by an expression. The value of the expression becomes the return value of the method. For example, the following method computes and returns the square of a number:

```
double square(double x) {      // A method to compute x squared
    return x * x;              // Compute and return a value
}
```

Some methods are declared void to indicate they do not return any value. The Java interpreter runs methods like this by executing its statements one by one until it reaches the end of the method. After executing the last statement, the interpreter returns implicitly. Sometimes, however, a void method has to return explicitly before reaching the last statement. In this case, it can use the return statement by itself, without any expression. For example, the following method prints, but does not return, the square root of its argument. If the argument is a negative number, it returns without printing anything:

```
void printSquareRoot(double x) {      // A method to print square root of x
  if (x < 0) return;                  // If x is negative, return explicitly
  System.out.println(Math.sqrt(x));   // Print the square root of x
}                                     // End of method: return implicitly
```

The synchronized Statement

Since Java is a multithreaded system, you must often take care to prevent multiple threads from modifying an object simultaneously in a way that might corrupt the object's state. Sections of code that must not be executed simultaneously are known as *critical sections*. Java provides the synchronized statement to protect these critical sections. The syntax is:

```
synchronized ( expression ) {
  statements
}
```

expression is an expression that must evaluate to an object or an array. The statements constitute the code of the critical section and must be enclosed in curly braces. Before executing the critical section, the Java interpreter first obtains an exclusive lock on the object or array specified by expression. It holds the lock until it is finished running the critical section, then releases it. While a thread holds the lock on an object, no other thread can obtain that lock. Therefore, no other thread can execute this or any other critical sections that require a lock on the same object. If a thread cannot immediately obtain the lock required to execute a critical section, it simply waits until the lock becomes available.

Note that you do not have to use the synchronized statement unless your program creates multiple threads that share data. If only one thread ever accesses a data structure, there is no need to protect it with synchronized. When you do have to use synchronized, it might be in code like the following:

```
public static void SortIntArray(int[] a) {
  // Sort the array a. This is synchronized so that some other thread
  // cannot change elements of the array while we're sorting it (at
  // least not other threads that protect their changes to the array
  // with synchronized).
  synchronized (a) {
    // Do the array sort here...
  }
}
```

The synchronized keyword is also available as a modifier in Java and is more commonly used in this form than as a statement. When applied to a method, the synchronized keyword indicates that the entire method is a critical section. For a synchronized class method (a static method), Java obtains an exclusive lock on the class before executing the method. For a synchronized instance method, Java obtains an exclusive lock on the class instance. (Class and instance methods are discussed in Chapter 3.)

The throw Statement

An *exception* is a signal that indicates some sort of exceptional condition or error has occurred. To *throw* an exception is to signal an exceptional condition. To *catch* an exception is to handle it—to take whatever actions are necessary to recover from it.

In Java, the throw statement is used to throw an exception:

throw *expression* ;

The *expression* must evaluate to an exception object that describes the exception or error that has occurred. We'll talk more about types of exceptions shortly; for now, all you need to know is that an exception is represented by an object. Here is some example code that throws an exception:

```
public static double factorial(int x) {
  if (x < 0)
    throw new IllegalArgumentException("x must be >= 0");
  double fact;
  for(fact=1.0; x > 1; fact *= x, x--)
    /* empty */ ;            // Note use of the empty statement
  return fact;
}
```

When the Java interpreter executes a throw statement, it immediately stops normal program execution and starts looking for an exception handler that can catch, or handle, the exception. Exception handlers are written with the try/catch/finally statement, which is described in the next section. The Java interpreter first looks at the enclosing block of code to see if it has an associated exception handler. If so, it exits that block of code and starts running the exception-handling code associated with the block. After running the exception handler, the interpreter continues execution at the statement immediately following the handler code.

If the enclosing block of code does not have an appropriate exception handler, the interpreter checks the next higher enclosing block of code in the method. This continues until a handler is found. If the method does not contain an exception handler that can handle the exception thrown by the throw statement, the interpreter stops running the current method and returns to the caller. Now the interpreter starts looking for an exception handler in the blocks of code of the calling method. In this way, exceptions propagate up through the lexical structure of Java methods, up the call stack of the Java interpreter. If the exception is never caught, it propagates all the way up to the main() method of the program. If it is not handled in that method, the Java interpreter prints an error message, prints a stack trace to indicate where the exception occurred, and then exits.

Exception types

An exception in Java is an object. The type of this object is java.lang.Throwable, or more commonly, some subclass of Throwable that more specifically describes the type of exception that occurred.* `Throwable` has two standard subclasses: `java.lang.Error` and `java.lang.Exception`. Exceptions that are subclasses of `Error` generally indicate unrecoverable problems: the virtual machine has run out of memory, or a class file is corrupted and cannot be read, for example. Exceptions of this sort can be caught and handled, but it is rare to do so. Exceptions that are subclasses of `Exception`, on the other hand, indicate less severe conditions. These are exceptions that can be reasonably caught and handled. They include such exceptions as `java.io.EOFException`, which signals the end of a file, and `java.lang.ArrayIndexOutOfBoundsException`, which indicates that a program has tried to read past the end of an array. In this book, I use the term "exception" to refer to any exception object, regardless of whether the type of that exception is `Exception` or `Error`.

Since an exception is an object, it can contain data, and its class can define methods that operate on that data. The `Throwable` class and all its subclasses include a `String` field that stores a human-readable error message that describes the exceptional condition. It's set when the exception object is created and can be read from the exception with the `getMessage()` method. Most exceptions contain only this single message, but a few add other data. The `java.io.InterruptedIOException`, for example, adds a field named `bytesTransferred` that specifies how much input or output was completed before the exceptional condition interrupted it.

Declaring exceptions

In addition to making a distinction between `Error` and `Exception` classes, the Java exception-handling scheme also makes a distinction between checked and unchecked exceptions. Any exception object that is an `Error` is unchecked. Any exception object that is an `Exception` is checked, unless it is a subclass of `java.lang.RuntimeException`, in which case it is unchecked. (`RuntimeException` is a subclass of `Exception`.) The reason for this distinction is that virtually any method can throw an unchecked exception, at essentially any time. There is no way to predict an `OutOfMemoryError`, for example, and any method that uses objects or arrays can throw a `NullPointerException` if it is passed an invalid `null` argument. Checked exceptions, on the other hand, arise only in specific, well-defined circumstances. If you try to read data from a file, for example, you must at least consider the possibility that a `FileNotFoundException` will be thrown if the specified file cannot be found.

Java has different rules for working with checked and unchecked exceptions. If you write a method that throws a checked exception, you must use a `throws` clause to declare the exception in the method signature. The reason these types of exceptions are called checked exceptions is that the Java compiler checks to make sure you have declared them in method signatures and produces a compilation error if you have not. The `factorial()` method shown earlier throws an exception of type `java.lang.IllegalArgumentException`. This is a subclass of `RuntimeException`, so it is an unchecked exception, and we do not have to declare it with a `throws` clause (although we can if we want to be explicit).

---

* We haven't talked about subclasses yet; they are covered in detail in Chapter 3.

Even if you never throw an exception yourself, there are times when you must use a throws clause to declare an exception. If your method calls a method that can throw a checked exception, you must either include exception-handling code to handle that exception or use throws to declare that your method can also throw that exception.

How do you know if the method you are calling can throw a checked exception? You can look at its method signature to find out. Or, failing that, the Java compiler will tell you (by reporting a compilation error) if you've called a method whose exceptions you must handle or declare. The following method reads the first line of text from a named file. It uses methods that can throw various types of java.io.IOException objects, so it declares this fact with a throws clause:

```
public static String readFirstLine(String filename) throws IOException {
    BufferedReader in = new BufferedReader(new FileReader(filename));
    return in.readLine();
}
```

We'll talk more about method declarations and method signatures later in this chapter.

The try/catch/finally Statement

The try/catch/finally statement is Java's exception-handling mechanism. The try clause of this statement establishes a block of code for exception handling. This try block is followed by zero or more catch clauses, each of which is a block of statements designed to handle a specific type of exception. The catch clauses are followed by an optional finally block that contains cleanup code guaranteed to be executed regardless of what happens in the try block. Both the catch and finally clauses are optional, but every try block must be accompanied by at least one or the other. The try, catch, and finally blocks all begin and end with curly braces. These are a required part of the syntax and cannot be omitted, even if the clause contains only a single statement.

The following code illustrates the syntax and purpose of the try/catch/finally statement:

```
try {
    // Normally this code runs from the top of the block to the bottom
    // without problems. But it can sometimes throw an exception,
    // either directly with a throw statement or indirectly by calling
    // a method that throws an exception.
}
catch (SomeException e1) {
    // This block contains statements that handle an exception object
    // of type SomeException or a subclass of that type. Statements in
    // this block can refer to that exception object by the name e1.
}
catch (AnotherException e2) {
    // This block contains statements that handle an exception object
    // of type AnotherException or a subclass of that type. Statements
    // in this block can refer to that exception object by the name e2.
}
```

```
finally {
    // This block contains statements that are always executed
    // after we leave the try clause, regardless of whether we leave it:
    //    1) normally, after reaching the bottom of the block;
    //    2) because of a break, continue, or return statement;
    //    3) with an exception that is handled by a catch clause above; or
    //    4) with an uncaught exception that has not been handled.
    // If the try clause calls System.exit(), however, the interpreter
    // exits before the finally clause can be run.
}
```

try

The try clause simply establishes a block of code that either has its exceptions handled or needs special cleanup code to be run when it terminates for any reason. The try clause by itself doesn't do anything interesting; it is the catch and finally clauses that do the exception-handling and cleanup operations.

catch

A try block can be followed by zero or more catch clauses that specify code to handle various types of exceptions. Each catch clause is declared with a single argument that specifies the type of exceptions the clause can handle and also provides a name the clause can use to refer to the exception object it is currently handling. The type and name of an exception handled by a catch clause are exactly like the type and name of an argument passed to a method, except that for a catch clause, the argument type must be Throwable or one of its subclasses.

When an exception is thrown, the Java interpreter looks for a catch clause with an argument of the same type as the exception object or a superclass of that type. The interpreter invokes the first such catch clause it finds. The code within a catch block should take whatever action is necessary to cope with the exceptional condition. If the exception is a java.io.FileNotFoundException exception, for example, you might handle it by asking the user to check his spelling and try again. It is not required to have a catch clause for every possible exception; in some cases the correct response is to allow the exception to propagate up and be caught by the invoking method. In other cases, such as a programming error signaled by NullPointerException, the correct response is probably not to catch the exception at all, but allow it to propagate and have the Java interpreter exit with a stack trace and an error message.

finally

The finally clause is generally used to clean up after the code in the try clause (e.g., close files, shut down network connections). What is useful about the finally clause is that it is guaranteed to be executed if any portion of the try block is executed, regardless of how the code in the try block completes. In fact, the only way a try clause can exit without allowing the finally clause to be executed is by invoking the System.exit() method, which causes the Java interpreter to stop running.

In the normal case, control reaches the end of the try block and then proceeds to the finally block, which performs any necessary cleanup. If control leaves the try block because of a return, continue, or break statement, the finally block is executed before control transfers to its new destination.

If an exception occurs in the try block, and there is an associated catch block to handle the exception, control transfers first to the catch block and then to the finally block. If there is no local catch block to handle the exception, control transfers first to the finally block, and then propagates up to the nearest containing catch clause that can handle the exception.

If a finally block itself transfers control with a return, continue, break, or throw statement or by calling a method that throws an exception, the pending control transfer is abandoned, and this new transfer is processed. For example, if a finally clause throws an exception, that exception replaces any exception that was in the process of being thrown. If a finally clause issues a return statement, the method returns normally, even if an exception has been thrown and has not been handled yet.

try and finally can be used together without exceptions or any catch clauses. In this case, the finally block is simply cleanup code that is guaranteed to be executed, regardless of any break, continue, or return statements within the try clause.

In previous discussions of the for and continue statements, we've seen that a for loop cannot be naively translated into a while loop because the continue statement behaves slightly differently when used in a for loop than it does when used in a while loop. The finally clause gives us a way to write a while loop that handles the continue statement in the same way that a for loop does. Consider the following generalized for loop:

```
for( initialize ; test ; increment )
    statement
```

The following while loop behaves the same, even if the statement block contains a continue statement:

```
initialize ;
while ( test ) {
    try { statement }
    finally { increment ; }
}
```

Note, however, that placing the increment statement within a finally block causes this while loop to respond to break statements differently than the for loop does.

Methods

A *method* is a named sequence of Java statements that can be invoked by other Java code. When a method is invoked, it is passed zero or more values known as arguments. The method performs some computations and, optionally, returns a value. A method invocation is an expression that is evaluated by the Java interpreter. Because method invocations can have side effects, however, they can also be used as expression statements.

You already know how to define the body of a method; it is simply an arbitrary sequence of statements enclosed within curly braces. What is more interesting about a method is its *signature*. The signature specifies:

- The name of the method

- The type and name of each of the parameters used by the method

- The type of the value returned by the method

- The checked exceptions that the method can throw (the signature may also list unchecked exceptions, but these are not required)

- Various method modifiers that provide additional information about the method

A method signature defines everything you need to know about a method before calling it. It is the method *specification* and defines the API for the method. The reference section of this book is essentially a list of method signatures for all publicly accessible methods of all publicly accessible classes of the Java platform. In order to use the reference section of this book, you need to know how to read a method signature. And, in order to write Java programs, you need to know how to define your own methods, each of which begins with a method signature.

A method signature looks like this:

```
modifiers type name ( paramlist ) [ throws exceptions ]
```

The signature (the method specification) is followed by the method body (the method implementation), which is simply a sequence of Java statements enclosed in curly braces. In certain cases (described in Chapter 3), the implementation is omitted, and the method body is replaced with a single semicolon.

Here are some example method definitions. The method bodies have been omitted, so we can focus on the signatures:

```
public static void main(String[] args) { ... }
public final synchronized int indexOf(Object element, int startIndex) { ... }
double distanceFromOrigin() { ... }
static double squareRoot(double x) throws IllegalArgumentException { ... }
protected abstract String readText(File f, String encoding)
        throws FileNotFoundException, UnsupportedEncodingException;
```

modifiers is zero or more special modifier keywords, separated from each other by spaces. A method might be declared with the `public` and `static` modifiers, for example. Other valid method modifiers are `abstract`, `final`, `native`, `private`, `protected`, and `synchronized`. The meanings of these modifiers are not important here; they are discussed in Chapter 3.

The *type* in a method signature specifies the return type of the method. If the method returns a value, this is the name of a primitive type, an array type, or a class. If the method does not return a value, *type* must be `void`. A *constructor* is a special type of method used to initialize newly created objects. As we'll see in Chapter 3, constructors are defined just like methods, except that their signatures do not include this *type* specification.

The *name* of a method follows the specification of its modifiers and type. Method names, like variable names, are Java identifiers and, like all Java identifiers, can use any characters of the Unicode character set. It is legal (and sometimes useful) to define more than one method with the same name, as long as each version of the method has a different parameter list. Defining multiple methods with the same name is called *method overloading*. The System.out.println() method we've seen so much of is an overloaded method. There is one method by this name that prints a string and other methods by the same name that print the values of the various primitive types. The Java compiler decides which method to call based on the type of the argument passed to the method.

When you are defining a method, the name of the method is always followed by the method's parameter list, which must be enclosed in parentheses. The parameter list defines zero or more arguments that are passed to the method. The parameter specifications, if there are any, each consist of a type and a name and are separated from each other by commas (if there are multiple parameters). When a method is invoked, the argument values it is passed must match the number, type, and order of the parameters specified in this method signature line. The values passed need not have exactly the same type as specified in the signature, but they must be convertible to those types without casting. C and C++ programmers should note that when a Java method expects no arguments, its parameter list is simply (), not (void).

The final part of a method signature is the throws clause, which I first described when we discussed the throw statement. If a method uses the throw statement to throw a checked exception, or if it calls some other method that throws a checked exception and does not catch or handle that exception, the method must declare that it can throw that exception. If a method can throw one or more checked exceptions, it specifies this by placing the throws keyword after the argument list and following it by the name of the exception class or classes it can throw. If a method does not throw any exceptions, it does not use the throws keyword. If a method throws more than one type of exception, separate the names of the exception classes from each other with commas.

Classes and Objects

Now that we have introduced operators, expressions, statements, and methods, we can finally talk about classes. A *class* is a named collection of fields that hold data values and methods that operate on those values. Some classes also contain nested inner classes. Classes are the most fundamental structural element of all Java programs. You cannot write Java code without defining a class. All Java statements appear within methods, and all methods are defined within classes.

Classes are more than just another structural level of Java syntax. Just as a cell is the smallest unit of life that can survive and reproduce on its own, a class is the smallest unit of Java code that can stand alone. The Java compiler and interpreter do not recognize fragments of Java code that are smaller than a class. A class is the basic unit of execution for Java, which makes classes very important. Java actually defines another construct, called an *interface*, that is quite similar to a class. The distinction between classes and interfaces will become clear in Chapter 3, but for now I'll use the term "class" to mean either a class or an interface.

Classes are important for another reason: every class defines a new data type. For example, you can define a class named `Point` to represent a data point in the two-dimensional Cartesian coordinate system. This class can define fields (each of type `double`) to hold the X and Y coordinates of a point and methods to manipulate and operate on the point. The `Point` class is a new data type.

When discussing data types, it is important to distinguish between the data type itself and the values the data type represents. `char` is a data type: it represents Unicode characters. But a `char` value represents a single specific character. A class is a data type; the value of a class type is called an *object*. We use the name class because each class defines a type (or kind, or species, or class) of objects. The `Point` class is a data type that represents X,Y points, while a `Point` object represents a single specific X,Y point. As you might imagine, classes and their objects are closely linked. In the sections that follow, we will be discussing both.

Defining a Class

Here is a possible definition of the `Point` class we have been discussing:

```
/** Represents a Cartesian (x,y) point */
public class Point {
  public double x, y;               // The coordinates of the point.
  public Point(double x, double y) {  // A constructor that
    this.x = x; this.y = y;          // initializes the fields.
  }

  public double distanceFromOrigin() {  // A method that operates on
    return Math.sqrt(x*x + y*y);        // the x and y fields.
  }
}
```

This class definition is stored in a file named *Point.java* and compiled to a file named *Point.class*, at which point it is available for use by Java programs and other classes. This class definition is provided here for completeness and to provide context, but don't expect to understand all the details just yet; most of Chapter 3 is devoted to the topic of defining classes. Do pay extra attention to the first (non-comment) line of the class definition, however. Just as the first line of a method definition—the method signature—defines the API for the method, this line defines the basic API for a class (as described in the next chapter).

Keep in mind that you don't have to define every class you want to use in a Java program. The Java platform consists of over 1500 predefined classes that are guaranteed to be available on every computer that runs Java.

Creating an Object

Now that we have defined the `Point` class as a new data type, we can use the following line to declare a variable that holds a `Point` object:

```
Point p;
```

Declaring a variable to hold a `Point` object does not create the object itself, however. To actually create an object, you must use the `new` operator. This keyword is followed by the object's class (i.e., its type) and an optional argument list in parentheses. These arguments are passed to the constructor method for the class, which initializes internal fields in the new object:

```
// Create a Point object representing (2,-3.5) and store it in variable p
Point p = new Point(2.0, -3.5);

// Create some other objects as well
Date d = new Date();        // A Date object that represents the current time
Vector list = new Vector();  // A Vector object to hold a list of objects
```

The new keyword is by far the most common way to create objects in Java. There are a few other ways that are worth mentioning, however. First, there are a couple of classes so important that Java defines special literal syntax for creating objects of those types (as we'll discuss in the next section). Second, Java supports a dynamic loading mechanism that allows programs to load classes and create instances of those classes dynamically. This dynamic instantiation is done with the newInstance() methods of java.lang.Class and java.lang.reflect.Constructor. Finally, in Java 1.1 and later, objects can also be created by deserializing them. In other words, an object that has had its state saved, or serialized, usually to a file, can be recreated using the java.io.ObjectInputStream class.

Object Literals

As I just said, Java defines special syntax for creating instances of two very important classes. The first class is String, which represents text as a string of characters. Since programs usually communicate with their users through the written word, the ability to manipulate strings of text is quite important in any programming language. In some languages, strings are a primitive type, on a par with integers and characters. In Java, however, strings are objects; the data type used to represent text is the String class.

Because strings are such a fundamental data type, Java allows you to include text literally in programs by placing it between double-quote (") characters. For example:

```
String name = "David";
System.out.println("Hello, " + name);
```

Don't confuse the double-quote characters that surround string literals with the single-quote (or apostrophe) characters that surround char literals. String literals can contain any of the escape sequences char literals can (see Table 2-3). Escape sequences are particularly useful for embedding double-quote characters within double-quoted string literals. For example:

```
String story = "\t\"How can you stand it?\" he asked sarcastically.\n";
```

String literals cannot contain comments, and may consist of only a single line. Java does not support any kind of continuation-character syntax that allows two separate lines to be treated as a single line. If you need to represent a long string of text that does not fit on a single line, break it into independent string literals and use the + operator to concatenate the literals. For example:

```
String s = "This is a test of the       // This is illegal; string literals
            emergency broadcast system";  // cannot be broken across lines.
```

```
String s = "This is a test of the " +        // Do this instead.
           "emergency broadcast system";
```

This concatenation of literals is done when your program is compiled, not when it is run, so you do not need to worry about any kind of performance penalty.

The second class that supports its own special object literal syntax is the class named Class. Class is a (self-referential) data type that represents all Java data types, including primitive types and array types, not just class types. To include a Class object literally in a Java program, follow the name of any data type with .class. For example:

```
Class typeInt = int.class;
Class typeIntArray = int[].class;
Class typePoint = Point.class;
```

This feature is supported by Java 1.1 and later.

The Java reserved word null is a special literal that can be used with any class. Instead of representing a literal object, it represents the absence of an object. For example:

```
String s = null;
Point p = null;
```

Finally, objects can also be included literally in a Java program through the use of a construct known as an anonymous inner class. Anonymous classes are discussed in Chapter 3.

Using an Object

Now that we've seen how to define classes and instantiate them by creating objects, we need to look at the Java syntax that allows us to use those objects. Recall that a class defines a collection of fields and methods. Each object has its own copies of those fields and has access to those methods. We use the dot character (.) to access the named fields and methods of an object. For example:

```
Point p = new Point(2, 3);         // Create an object
double x = p.x;                    // Read a field of the object
p.y = p.x * p.x;                   // Set the value of a field
double d = p.distanceFromOrigin(); // Access a method of the object
```

This syntax is central to object-oriented programming in Java, so you'll see it a lot. Note, in particular, the expression p.distanceFromOrigin(). This tells the Java compiler to look up a method named distanceFromOrigin() defined by the class Point and use that method to perform a computation on the fields of the object p. We'll cover the details of this operation in Chapter 3.

Array Types

Array types are the second kind of reference types in Java. An array is an ordered collection, or numbered list, of values. The values can be primitive values, objects, or even other arrays, but all of the values in an array must be of the same type.

The type of the array is the type of the values it holds, followed by the characters []. For example:

```
byte b;                         // byte is a primitive type
byte[] arrayOfBytes;            // byte[] is an array type: array of byte
byte[][] arrayOfArrayOfBytes;   // byte[][] is another type: array of byte[]
Point[] points;                 // Point[] is an array of Point objects
```

For compatibility with C and C++, Java also supports another syntax for declaring variables of array type. In this syntax, one or more pairs of square brackets follow the name of the variable, rather than the name of the type:

```
byte arrayOfBytes[];            // Same as byte[] arrayOfBytes
byte arrayOfArrayOfBytes[][];   // Same as byte[][] arrayOfArrayOfBytes
byte[] arrayOfArrayOfBytes[];   // Ugh! Same as byte[][] arrayOfArrayOfBytes
```

This is almost always a confusing syntax, however, and it is not recommended.

With classes and objects, we have separate terms for the type and the values of that type. With arrays, the single word array does double duty as the name of both the type and the value. Thus, we can speak of the array type int[] (a type) and an array of int (a particular array value). In practice, it is usually clear from context whether a type or a value is being discussed.

Creating Arrays

To create an array value in Java, you use the new keyword, just as you do to create an object. Arrays don't need to be initialized like objects do, however, so you don't pass a list of arguments between parentheses. What you must specify, though, is how big you want the array to be. If you are creating a byte[], for example, you must specify how many byte values you want it to hold. Array values have a fixed size in Java. Once an array is created, it can never grow or shrink. Specify the desired size of your array as a non-negative integer between square brackets:

```
byte[] buffer = new byte[1024];
String[] lines = new String[50];
```

When you create an array with this syntax, each of the values held in the array is automatically initialized to its default value. This is false for boolean values, '\u0000' for char values, 0 for integer values, 0.0 for floating-point values, and null for objects or array values.

Using Arrays

Once you've created an array with the new operator and the square-bracket syntax, you also use square brackets to access the individual values contained in the array. Remember that an array is an ordered collection of values. The elements of an array are numbered sequentially, starting with 0. The number of an array element refers to the element. This number is often called the *index*, and the process of looking up a numbered value in an array is sometimes called *indexing* the array.

To refer to a particular element of an array, simply place the index of the desired element in square brackets after the name of the array. For example:

```
String[] responses = new String[2];    // Create an array of two strings
responses[0] = "Yes";                   // Set the first element of the array
responses[1] = "No";                    // Set the second element of the array

// Now read these array elements
System.out.println(question + " (" + responses[0] + "/" +
                   responses[1] + " ): ");
```

In some programming languages, such as C and C++, it is a common bug to write code that tries to read or write array elements that are past the end of the array. Java does not allow this. Every time you access an array element, the Java interpreter automatically checks that the index you have specified is valid. If you specify a negative index or an index that is greater than the last index of the array, the interpreter throws an exception of type ArrayIndexOutOfBoundsException. This prevents you from reading or writing nonexistent array elements.

Array index values are integers; you cannot index an array with a floating-point value, a boolean, an object, or another array. char values can be converted to int values, so you *can* use characters as array indexes. Although long is an integer data type, long values cannot be used as array indexes. This may seem surprising at first, but consider that an int index supports arrays with over two billion elements. An int[] with this many elements would require eight gigabytes of memory. When you think of it this way, it is not surprising that long values are not allowed as array indexes.

Besides setting and reading the value of array elements, there is one other thing you can do with an array value. Recall that whenever we create an array, we must specify the number of elements the array holds. This value is referred to as the length of the array; it is an intrinsic property of the array. If you need to know the length of the array, append .length to the array name:

```
if (errorCode < errorMessages.length)
  System.out.println(errorMessages[errorCode]);
```

Every array has a length field that specifies the number of elements it contains. Note that this field is read-only: you can use it to read the length of the array, but you cannot assign any value to it or use it to set or change the length of an array.

In the previous example, the array index within square brackets is a variable, not an integer literal. In fact, arrays are most often used with loops, particularly for loops, where they are indexed using a variable that is incremented or decremented each time through the loop:

```
int[] values;                    // Assume array is created and initialized elsewhere
int total = 0;                   // Store sum of elements here
for(int i = 0; i < values.length; i++) // Loop through array elements
  total += values[i];            // Add them up
```

In Java, the first element of an array is always element number 0. If you are accustomed to a programming language that numbers array elements beginning with 1, this will take some getting used to. For an array a, the first element is a[0], the second element is a[1], and the last element is:

```
a[a.length - 1]        // The last element of any array named a
```

Array Literals

The null literal used to represent the absence of an object can also be used to represent the absence of an array. For example:

```
char[] password = null;
```

In addition to the null literal, Java also defines special syntax that allows you to specify array values literally in your programs. There are actually two different syntaxes for array literals. The first, and more commonly used, syntax can be used only when declaring a variable of array type. It combines the creation of the array object with the initialization of the array elements:

```
int[] powersOfTwo = {1, 2, 4, 8, 16, 32, 64, 128};
```

This creates an array that contains the eight int elements listed within the curly braces. Note that we don't use the new keyword or specify the type of the array in this array literal syntax. The type is implicit in the variable declaration of which the initializer is a part. Also, the array length is not specified explicitly with this syntax; it is determined implicitly by counting the number of elements listed between the curly braces. There is a semicolon following the close curly brace in this array literal. This is one of the fine points of Java syntax. When curly braces delimit classes, methods, and compound statements, they are not followed by semicolons. However, for this array literal syntax, the semicolon is required to terminate the variable declaration statement.

The problem with this array literal syntax is that it works only when you are declaring a variable of array type. Sometimes you need to do something with an array value (such as pass it to a method) but are going to use the array only once, so you don't want to bother assigning it to a variable. In Java 1.1 and later, there is an array literal syntax that supports this kind of anonymous arrays (so called because they are not assigned to variables, so they don't have names). This kind of array literal looks as follows:

```
// Call a method, passing an anonymous array literal that contains two strings
String response = askQuestion("Do you want to quit?",
                              new String[] {"Yes", "No"});

// Call another method with an anonymous array (of anonymous objects)
double d = computeAreaOfTriangle(new Point[] { new Point(1,2),
                                               new Point(3,4),
                                               new Point(3,2) });
```

With this syntax, you use the new keyword and specify the type of the array, but the length of the array is not explicitly specified.

It is important to understand that the Java Virtual Machine architecture does not support any kind of efficient array initialization. In other words, array literals are created and initialized when the program is run, not when the program is compiled. Consider the following array literal:

```
int[] perfectNumbers = {6, 28};
```

This is compiled into Java byte codes that are equivalent to:

```java
int[] perfectNumbers = new int[2];
perfectNumbers[0] = 6;
perfectNumbers[1] = 28;
```

Thus, if you want to include a large amount of data in a Java program, it may not be a good idea to include that data literally in an array, since the Java compiler has to create lots of Java byte codes to initialize the array, and then the Java interpreter has to laboriously execute all that initialization code. In cases like this, it is better to store your data in an external file and read it into the program at runtime.

The fact that Java does all array initialization explicitly at runtime has an important corollary, however. It means that the elements of an array literal can be arbitrary expressions that are computed at runtime, rather than constant expressions that are resolved by the compiler. For example:

```java
Point[] points = { circle1.getCenterPoint(), circle2.getCenterPoint() };
```

Multidimensional Arrays

As we've seen, an array type is simply the element type followed by a pair of square brackets. An array of char is char[], and an array of arrays of char is char[][]. When the elements of an array are themselves arrays, we say that the array is *multidimensional*. In order to work with multidimensional arrays, there are a few additional details you must understand.

Imagine that you want to use a multidimensional array to represent a multiplication table:

```java
int[][] products;     // A multiplication table
```

Each of the pairs of square brackets represents one dimension, so this is a two-dimensional array. To access a single int element of this two-dimensional array, you must specify two index values, one for each dimension. Assuming that this array was actually initialized as a multiplication table, the int value stored at any given element would be the product of the two indexes. That is, products[2][4] would be 8, and products[3][7] would be 21.

To create a new multidimensional array, use the new keyword and specify the size of both dimensions of the array. For example:

```java
int[][] products = new int[10][10];
```

In some languages, an array like this would be created as a single block of 100 int values. Java does not work this way. This line of code does three things:

- Declares a variable named products to hold an array of arrays of int.

- Creates a 10-element array to hold 10 arrays of int.

- Creates 10 more arrays, each of which is a 10-element array of int. It assigns each of these 10 new arrays to the elements of the initial array. The default value of every int element of each of these 10 new arrays is 0.

To put this another way, the previous single line of code is equivalent to the following code:

```
int[][] products = new int[10][];    // An array to hold ten int[] values.
for(int i = 0; i < 10; i++)          // Loop ten times...
    products[i] = new int[10];       // ...and create ten arrays.
```

The new keyword performs this additional initialization automatically for you. It works with arrays with more than two dimensions as well:

```
float[][][] globalTemperatureData = new float[360][180][100];
```

When using new with multidimensional arrays, you do not have to specify a size for all dimensions of the array, only the leftmost dimension or dimensions. For example, the following two lines are legal:

```
float[][][] globalTemperatureData = new float[360][][];
float[][][] globalTemperatureData = new float[360][180][];
```

The first line creates a single-dimensional array, where each element of the array can hold a float[][]. The second line creates a two-dimensional array, where each element of the array is a float[]. If you specify a size for only some of the dimensions of an array, however, those dimensions must be the leftmost ones. The following lines are not legal:

```
float[][][] globalTemperatureData = new float[360][][100];  // Error!
float[][][] globalTemperatureData = new float[][180][100];  // Error!
```

Like a one-dimensional array, a multidimensional array can be initialized using an array literal. Simply use nested sets of curly braces to nest arrays within arrays. For example, we can declare, create, and initialize a 5×5 multiplication table like this:

```
int[][] products = { {0, 0, 0, 0, 0},
                     {0, 1, 2, 3, 4},
                     {0, 2, 4, 6, 8},
                     {0, 3, 6, 9, 12},
                     {0, 4, 8, 12, 16} };
```

Or, if you want to use a multidimensional array without declaring a variable, you can use the anonymous initializer syntax:

```
boolean response = bilingualQuestion(question, new String[][] {
                                     { "Yes", "No" },
                                     { "Oui", "Non" }});
```

When you create a multidimensional array using the new keyword, you always get a *rectangular* array: one in which all the array values for a given dimension have the same size. This is perfect for rectangular data structures, such as matrixes. However, because multidimensional arrays are implemented as arrays of arrays in Java, instead of as a single rectangular block of elements, you are in no way constrained to use rectangular arrays. For example, since our multiplication table is symmetrical about the diagonal from top left to bottom right, we can represent the same information in a nonrectangular array with fewer elements:

```
int[][] products = { {0},
                     {0, 1},
                     {0, 2, 4},
```

```
                    {0, 3, 6, 9},
                    {0, 4, 8, 12, 16} };
```

When working with multidimensional arrays, you'll often find yourself using nested loops to create or initialize them. For example, you can create and initialize a large triangular multiplication table as follows:

```
int[][] products = new int[12][];          // An array of 12 arrays of int.
for(int row = 0; row < 12; row++) {         // For each element of that array,
  products[row] = new int[row+1];           // allocate an array of int.
  for(int col = 0; col < row+1; col++)      // For each element of the int[],
    products[row][col] = row * col;         // initialize it to the product.
}
```

Reference Types

Now that we have discussed the syntax for working with objects and arrays, we can return to the issue of why classes and array types are known as reference types. As we saw in Table 2-2, all the Java primitive types have well-defined standard sizes, so all primitive values can be stored in a fixed amount of memory (between one and eight bytes, depending on the type). But classes and array types are composite types; objects and arrays contain other values, so they do not have a standard size, and they often require quite a bit more memory than eight bytes. For this reason, Java does not manipulate objects and arrays directly. Instead, it manipulates *references* to objects and arrays. Because Java handles objects and arrays by reference, classes and array types are known as reference types. In contrast, Java handles values of the primitive types directly, or by value.

A reference to an object or an array is simply some fixed-size value that refers to the object or array in some way.* When you assign an object or array to a variable, you are actually setting the variable to hold a reference to that object or array. Similarly, when you pass an object or array to a method, what really happens is that the method is given a reference to the object or array through which it can manipulate the object or array.

C and C++ programmers should note that Java does not support the & address-of operator or the * and -> dereference operators. In Java, primitive types are always handled exclusively by value, and objects and arrays are always handled exclusively by reference. Furthermore, unlike pointers in C and C++, references in Java are entirely opaque: they cannot be converted to or from integers, and they cannot be incremented or decremented.

Although references are an important part of how Java works, Java programs cannot manipulate references in any way. Despite this, there are significant differences between the behavior of primitive types and reference types in two important areas: the way values are copied and the way they are compared for equality.

---

* Typically, a reference is the memory address at which the object or array is stored. However, since Java references are opaque and cannot be manipulated in any way, this is an implementation detail.

Copying Objects and Arrays

Consider the following code that manipulate a primitive int value:

```
int x = 42;
int y = x;
```

After these lines execute, the variable y contains a copy of the value held in the variable x. Inside the Java VM, there are two independent copies of the 32-bit integer 42.

Now think about what happens if we run the same basic code but use a reference type instead of a primitive type:

```
Point p = new Point(1.0, 2.0);
Point q = p;
```

After this code runs, the variable q holds a copy of the reference held in the variable p. There is still only one copy of the Point object in the VM, but there are now two copies of the reference to that object. This has some important implications. Suppose the two previous lines of code are followed by this code:

```
System.out.println(p.x);   // Print out the X coordinate of p: 1.0
q.x = 13.0;                // Now change the X coordinate of q
System.out.println(p.x);   // Print out p.x again; this time it is 13.0
```

Since the variables p and q hold references to the same object, either variable can be used to make changes to the object, and those changes are visible through the other variable as well.

This behavior is not specific to objects; the same thing happens with arrays, as illustrated by the following code:

```
char[] greet = { 'h','e','l','l','o' };  // greet holds an array reference
char[] cuss = greet;                     // cuss holds the same reference
cuss[4] = '!';                           // Use reference to change an element
System.out.println(greet);               // Prints "hell!"
```

A similar difference in behavior between primitive types and reference types occurs when arguments are passed to methods. Consider the following method:

```
void changePrimitive(int x) {
  while(x > 0)
    System.out.println(x--);
}
```

When this method is invoked, the method is given a copy of the argument used to invoke the method in the parameter x. The code in the method uses x as a loop counter and decrements it to zero. Since x is a primitive type, the method has its own private copy of this value, so this is a perfectly reasonable thing to do.

On the other hand, consider what happens if we modify the method so that the parameter is a reference type:

```
void changeReference(Point p) {
  while(p.x > 0)
    System.out.println(p.x--);
}
```

When this method is invoked, it is passed a private copy of a reference to a Point object and can use this reference to change the Point object. Consider the following:

```
Point q = new Point(3.0, 4.5);   // A point with an X coordinate of 3
changeReference(q);              // Prints 3,2,1 and modifies the Point
System.out.println(q.x);         // The X coordinate of q is now 0!
```

When the changeReference() method is invoked, it is passed a copy of the reference held in variable q. Now both the variable q and the method parameter p hold references to the same object. The method can use its reference to change the contents of the object. Note, however, that it cannot change the contents of the variable q. In other words, the method can change the Point object beyond recognition, but it cannot change the fact that the variable q refers to that object.

The title of this section is "Copying Objects and Arrays," but, so far, we've only seen copies of references to objects and arrays, not copies of the objects and arrays themselves. To make an actual copy of an object or an array, you must use the special clone() method (inherited by all objects from java.lang.Object):

```
Point p = new Point(1,2);       // p refers to one object
Point q = (Point) p.clone();    // q refers to a copy of that object
q.y = 42;                       // Modify the copied object, but not the original

int[] data = {1,2,3,4,5};       // An array
int[] copy = (int[]) data.clone();  // A copy of the array
```

Note that a cast is necessary to coerce the return value of the clone() method to the correct type. The reason for this will become clear later in this chapter. There are a couple of points you should be aware of when using clone(). First, not all objects can be cloned. Java only allows an object to be cloned if the object's class has explicitly declared itself to be cloneable by implementing the Cloneable interface. (We haven't discussed interfaces or how they are implemented yet; that is covered in Chapter 3.) The definition of Point that we showed earlier does not actually implement this interface, so our Point type, as implemented, is not cloneable. Note, however, that arrays are always cloneable. If you call the clone() method for a non-cloneable object, it throws a CloneNotSupportedException, so when you use the clone() method, you may want to use it within a try block to catch this exception.

The second thing you need to understand about clone() is that, by default, it is implemented to create a shallow copy of an object or array. The copied object or array contains copies of all the primitive values and references in the original object or array. In other words, any references in the object or array are copied, not cloned; clone() does not recursively make copies of the objects or arrays referred to by those references. A class may need to override this shallow copy behavior by defining its own version of the clone() method that explicitly performs a deeper copy where needed. To understand the shallow copy behavior of clone(), consider cloning a two-dimensional array of arrays:

```
int[][] data = {{1,2,3}, {4,5}};       // An array of 2 references
int[][] copy = (int[][]) data.clone();  // Copy the 2 refs to a new array
copy[0][0] = 99;                         // This changes data[0][0] too!
copy[1] = new int[] {7,8,9};             // This does not change data[1]
```

If you want to make a deep copy of this multidimensional array, you have to copy each dimension explicitly:

```
int[][] data = {{1,2,3}, {4,5}};      // An array of 2 references
int[][] copy = new int[data.length][]; // A new array to hold copied arrays
for(int i = 0; i < data.length; i++)
  copy[i] = (int[]) data[i].clone();
```

Comparing Objects and Arrays

We've seen that primitive types and reference types differ significantly in the way they are assigned to variables, passed to methods, and copied. The types also differ in the way they are compared for equality. When used with primitive values, the equality operator (==) simply tests whether two values are identical (i.e., whether they have exactly the same bits). With reference types, however, == compares references, not actual objects or arrays. In other words, == tests whether two references refer to the same object or array; it does not test whether two objects or arrays have the same content. For example:

```
String letter = "o";
String s = "hello";                   // These two String objects
String t = "hell" + letter;           // contain exactly the same text.
if (s == t) System.out.println("equal"); // But they are not equal!

byte[] a = { 1, 2, 3 };               // An array.
byte[] b = (byte[]) a.clone();        // A copy with identical content.
if (a == b) System.out.println("equal"); // But they are not equal!
```

When working with reference types, there are two kinds of equality: equality of reference and equality of object. It is important to distinguish between these two kinds of equality. One way to do this is to use the word "equals" when talking about equality of references and the word "equivalent" when talking about two distinct object or arrays that have the same contents. Unfortunately, the designers of Java didn't use this nomenclature, as the method for testing whether one object is equivalent to another is named equals(). To test two objects for equivalence, pass one of them to the equals() method of the other:

```
String letter = "o";
String s = "hello";                   // These two String objects
String t = "hell" + letter;           // contain exactly the same text.
if (s.equals(t))                      // And the equals() method
   System.out.println("equivalent");  // tells us so.
```

All objects inherit an equals() method (from Object), but the default implementation simply uses == to test for equality of references, not equivalence of content. A class that wants to allow objects to be compared for equivalence can define its own version of the equals() method. Our Point class does not do this, but the String class does, as indicated by the code above. You can call the equals() method on an array, but it is the same as using the == operator, because arrays always inherit the default equals() method that compares references rather than array content. Starting in Java 1.2, you can compare arrays for equivalence with the convenience method java.util.Arrays.equals(). Prior to Java 1.2, however, you must loop through the elements of the arrays and compare them yourself.

The null Reference

We've seen the null keyword in our discussions of objects and arrays. Now that we have described references, it is worth revisiting null to point out that it is a special value that is a reference to nothing, or an absence of a reference. The default value for all reference types is null. The null value is unique in that it can be assigned to a variable of any reference type whatsoever.

Terminology: Pass by Value

I've said that Java handles arrays and objects "by reference." Don't confuse this with the phrase "pass by reference."* "Pass by reference" is a term used to describe the method-calling conventions of some programming languages. In a pass-by-reference language, values—even primitive values—are not passed directly to methods. Instead, methods are always passed references to values. Thus, if the method modifies its parameters, those modifications are visible when the method returns, even for primitive types.

Java does *not* do this; it is a "pass by value" language. However, when a reference type is involved, the value that is passed is a reference. But this is not the same as pass-by-reference. If Java were a pass-by-reference language, when a reference type was passed to a method, it would be passed as a reference to the reference.

Memory Allocation and Garbage Collection

As we've already noted, objects and arrays are composite values that can contain a number of other values and may require a substantial amount of memory. When you use the new keyword to create a new object or array or use an object or array literal in your program, Java automatically creates the object for you, allocating whatever amount of memory is necessary. You don't need to do anything to make this happen.

In addition, Java also automatically reclaims that memory for reuse when it is no longer needed. It does this through a process called *garbage collection*. An object is considered garbage when there are no longer any references to it stored in any variables, the fields of any objects, or the elements of any arrays. For example:

```
Point p = new Point(1,2);              // Create an object
double d = p.distanceFromOrigin();     // Use it for something
p = new Point(2,3);                    // Create a new object
```

After the Java interpreter executes the third line, a reference to the new Point object has replaced the reference to the first one. There are now no remaining references to the first object, so it is garbage. At some point, the garbage collector will discover this and reclaim the memory used by the object.

C programmers, who are used to using malloc() and free() to manage memory, and C++ programmers, who are used to explicitly deleting their objects with delete, may find it a little hard to relinquish control and trust the garbage

---

* Unfortunately, previous editions of this book may have contributed to the confusion!

collector. Even though it seems like magic, it really works! There is a slight performance penalty due to the use of garbage collection, and Java programs may sometimes slow down noticeably while the garbage collector is actively reclaiming memory. However, having garbage collection built into the language dramatically reduces the occurrence of memory leaks and related bugs and almost always improves programmer productivity.

Reference Type Conversions

When we discussed primitive types earlier in this chapter, we saw that values of certain types can be converted to values of other types. Widening conversions are performed automatically by the Java interpreter, as necessary. Narrowing conversions, however, can result in lost data, so the interpreter does not perform them unless explicitly directed to do so with a cast.

Java does not allow any kind of conversion from primitive types to reference types or vice versa. Java does allow widening and narrowing conversions among certain reference types, however. As we've seen, there are an infinite number of potential reference types. In order to understand the conversions that can be performed among these types, you need to understand that the types form a hierarchy, usually called the *class hierarchy*.

Every Java class *extends* some other class, known as its *superclass*. A class inherits the fields and methods of its superclass and then defines its own additional fields and methods. There is a special class named Object that serves as the root of the class hierarchy in Java. It does not extend any class, but all other Java classes extend Object or some other class that has Object as one of its ancestors. The Object class defines a number of special methods that are inherited (or overridden) by all classes. These include the toString(), clone(), and equals() methods described earlier.

The predefined String class and the Point class we defined earlier in this chapter both extend Object. Thus, we can say that all String objects are also Object objects. We can also say that all Point objects are Object objects. The opposite is not true, however. We cannot say that every Object is a String because, as we've just seen, some Object objects are Point objects.

With this simple understanding of the class hierarchy, we can return to the rules of reference type conversion:

- An object cannot be converted to an unrelated type. The Java compiler does not allow you to convert a String to a Point, for example, even if you use a cast operator.

- An object can be converted to the type of a superclass. This is a widening conversion, so no cast is required. For example, a String value can be assigned to a variable of type Object or passed to a method where an Object parameter is expected. Note that no conversion is actually performed; the object is simply treated as if it were an instance of the superclass.

- An object can be converted to the type of a subclass, but this is a narrowing conversion and requires a cast. The Java compiler provisionally allows this kind of conversion, but the Java interpreter checks at runtime to make sure it is valid. Only cast an object to the type of a subclass if you are sure, based on the logic of your program, that the object is actually an instance of the subclass. If it is not, the interpreter throws a ClassCastException. For example, if we assign a String object to a variable of type Object, we can later cast the value of that variable back to type String:

```
Object o = "string";    // Widening conversion from String to Object
// Later in the program...
String s = (String) o;  // Narrowing conversion from Object to String
```

- All array types are distinct, so an array of one type cannot be converted to an array of another type, even if the individual elements could be converted. For example, although a byte can be widened to an int, a byte[] cannot be converted to an int[], even with an explicit cast.

- Arrays do not have a type hierarchy, but all arrays are considered instances of Object, so any array can be converted to an Object value through a widening conversion. A narrowing conversion with a cast can convert such an object value back to an array. For example:

```
Object o = new int[] {1,2,3};  // Widening conversion from array to Object
// Later in the program...
int[] a = (int[]) o;            // Narrowing conversion back to array type
```

Packages and the Java Namespace

A *package* is a named collection of classes (and possibly subpackages). Packages serve to group related classes and define a namespace for the classes they contain.

The Java platform includes packages with names that begin with java, javax, and org.omg. (Sun also defines standard extensions to the Java platform in packages whose names begin with javax.) The most fundamental classes of the language are in the package java.lang. Various utility classes are in java.util. Classes for input and output are in java.io, and classes for networking are in java.net. Some of these packages contain subpackages. For example, java.lang contains two more specialized packages, named java.lang.reflect and java.lang.ref, and java.util contains a subpackage, java.util.zip, that contains classes for working with compressed ZIP archives.

Every class has both a simple name, which is the name given to it in its definition, and a fully qualified name, which includes the name of the package of which it is a part. The String class, for example, is part of the java.lang package, so its fully qualified name is java.lang.String.

Defining a Package

To specify the package a class is to be part of, you use a package directive. The package keyword, if it appears, must be the first token of Java code (i.e., the first thing other than comments and space) in the Java file. The keyword should be followed by the name of the desired package and a semicolon. Consider a file of Java code that begins with this directive:

```
package com.davidflanagan.jude;
```

All classes defined by this file are part of the package named com.davidflanagan.jude.

If no package directive appears in a file of Java code, all classes defined in that file are part of a default unnamed package. As we'll see in Chapter 3, classes in the same package have special access to each other. Thus, except when you are writing simple example programs, you should always use the package directive to prevent access to your classes from totally unrelated classes that also just happen to be stored in the unnamed package.

Importing Classes and Packages

A class in a package p can refer to any other class in p by its simple name. And, since the classes in the java.lang package are so fundamental to the Java language, any Java code can refer to any class in this package by its simple name. Thus, you can always type String, instead of java.lang.String. By default, however, you must use the fully qualified name of all other classes. So, if you want to use the File class of the java.io package, you must type java.io.File.

Specifying package names explicitly all the time quickly gets tiring, so Java includes an import directive you can use to save some typing. import is used to specify classes and packages of classes that can be referred to by their simple names instead of by their fully qualified names. The import keyword can be used any number of times in a Java file, but all uses must be at the top of the file, immediately after the package directive, if there is one. There can be comments between the package directive and the import directives, of course, but there cannot be any other Java code.

The import directive is available in two forms. To specify a single class that can be referred to by its simple name, follow the import keyword with the name of the class and a semicolon:

```
import java.io.File;    // Now we can type File instead of java.io.File
```

To import an entire package of classes, follow import with the name of the package, the characters .*, and a semicolon. Thus, if you want to use several other classes from the java.io package in addition to the File class, you can simply import the entire package:

```
import java.io.*;   // Now we can use simple names for all classes in java.io
```

This package import syntax does not apply to subpackages. If I import the java.util package, I must still refer to the java.util.zip.ZipInputStream class by its fully qualified name. If two classes with the same name are both imported from different packages, neither one can be referred to by its simple name; to resolve this naming conflict unambiguously, you must use the fully qualified name of both classes.

Globally Unique Package Names

One of the important functions of packages is to partition the Java namespace and prevent name collisions between classes. It is only their package names that keep the java.util.List and java.awt.List classes distinct, for example. In order for this to work, however, package names must themselves be distinct. As the developer of Java, Sun controls all package names that begin with java, javax, and sun.

For the rest of us, Sun proposes a package-naming scheme, which, if followed correctly, guarantees globally unique package names. The scheme is to use your Internet domain name, with its elements reversed, as the prefix for all your package names. My web site is *davidflanagan.com*, so all my Java packages begin with com.davidflanagan. It is up to me to decide how to partition the namespace below com.davidflanagan, but since I own that domain name, no other person or organization who is playing by the rules can define a package with the same name as any of mine.

Java File Structure

This chapter has taken us from the smallest to the largest elements of Java syntax, from individual characters and tokens to operators, expressions, statements, and methods, and on up to classes and packages. From a practical standpoint, the unit of Java program structure you will be dealing with most often is the Java file. A Java file is the smallest unit of Java code that can be compiled by the Java compiler. A Java file consists of:

- An optional package directive

- Zero or more import directives

- One or more class definitions

These elements can be interspersed with comments, of course, but they must appear in this order. This is all there is to a Java file. All Java statements (except the package and import directives, which are not true statements) must appear within methods, and all methods must appear within a class definition.

There are a couple of other important restrictions on Java files. First, each file can contain at most one class that is declared public. A public class is one that is designed for use by other classes in other packages. We'll talk more about public and related modifiers in Chapter 3. This restriction on public classes only applies to top-level classes; a class can contain any number of nested or inner classes that are declared public, as we'll see in Chapter 3.

The second restriction concerns the filename of a Java file. If a Java file contains a public class, the name of the file must be the same as the name of the class, with the extension *.java* appended. Thus, if Point is defined as a public class, its source code must appear in a file named *Point.java*. Regardless of whether your classes are public or not, it is good programming practice to define only one per file and to give the file the same name as the class.

When a Java file is compiled, each of the classes it defines is compiled into a separate *class file* that contains Java byte codes to be interpreted by the Java Virtual Machine. A class file has the same name as the class it defines, with the extension *.class* appended. Thus, if the file *Point.java* defines a class named Point, a Java compiler compiles it to a file named *Point.class*. On most systems, class files are stored in directories that correspond to their package names. Thus, the class com.davidflanagan.jude.DataFile is defined by the class file *com/davidflanagan/jude/DataFile.class*.

The Java interpreter knows where the class files for the standard system classes are located and can load them as needed. When the interpreter runs a program that wants to use a class named com.davidflanagan.jude.DataFile, it knows that the code for that class is located in a directory named *com/davidflanagan/jude* and, by default, it "looks" in the current directory for a subdirectory of that name. In order to tell the interpreter to look in locations other than the current directory, you must use the -classpath option when invoking the interpreter or set the CLASSPATH environment variable. For details, see the documentation for the Java interpreter, *java*, in Chapter 8.

Defining and Running Java Programs

A Java program consists of a set of interacting class definitions. But not every Java class or Java file defines a program. To create a program, you must define a class that has a special method with the following signature:

```
public static void main(String[] args)
```

This main() method is the main entry point for your program. It is where the Java interpreter starts running. This method is passed an array of strings and returns no value. When main() returns, the Java interpreter exits (unless main() has created separate threads, in which case the interpreter waits for all those threads to exit).

To run a Java program, you run the Java interpreter, *java*, specifying the fully qualified name of the class that contains the main() method. Note that you specify the name of the class, *not* the name of the class file that contains the class. Any additional arguments you specify on the command line are passed to the main() method as its String[] parameter. You may also need to specify the -classpath option to tell the interpreter to look for the classes needed by the program. Consider the following command:

```
% java -classpath /usr/local/Jude com.davidflanagan.jude.Jude datafile.jude
```

java is the command to run the Java interpreter. *-classpath /usr/local/Jude* tells the interpreter where to look for *.class* files. com.davidflanagan.jude.Jude is the name of the program to run (i.e., the name of the class that defines the main() method). Finally, *datafile.jude* is a string that is passed to that main() method as the single element of an array of String objects.

In Java 1.2, there is an easier way to run programs. If a program and all its auxiliary classes (except those that are part of the Java platform) have been properly bundled in a Java archive (JAR) file, you can run the program simply by specifying the name of the JAR file:

```
% java -jar /usr/local/Jude/jude.jar datafile.jude
```

Some operating systems make JAR files automatically executable. On those systems, you can simply say:

```
% /usr/local/Jude/jude.jar datafile.jude
```

See Chapter 8 for details.

Differences Between C and Java

If you are a C or C++ programmer, you should have found much of the syntax of Java—particularly at the level of operators and statements—to be familiar. Because Java and C are so similar in some ways, it is important for C and C++ programmers to understand where the similarities end. There are a number of important differences between C and Java, which are summarized in the following list:

No preprocessor
Java does not include a preprocessor and does not define any analogs of the #define, #include, and #ifdef directives. Constant definitions are replaced with static final fields in Java. (See the java.lang.Math.PI field for an example.) Macro definitions are not available in Java, but advanced compiler technology and inlining has made them less useful. Java does not require an #include directive because Java has no header files. Java class files contain both the class API and the class implementation, and the compiler reads API information from class files as necessary. Java lacks any form of conditional compilation, but its cross-platform portability means that this feature is very rarely needed.

No global variables
Java defines a very clean namespace. Packages contain classes, classes contain fields and methods, and methods contain local variables. But there are no global variables in Java, and, thus, there is no possibility of namespace collisions among those variables.

Well-defined primitive type sizes
All the primitive types in Java have well-defined sizes. In C, the size of short, int, and long types is platform-dependent, which hampers portability.

No pointers
Java classes and arrays are reference types, and references to objects and arrays are akin to pointers in C. Unlike C pointers, however, references in Java are entirely opaque. There is no way to convert a reference to a primitive type, and a reference cannot be incremented or decremented. There is no address-of operator like &, dereference operator like * or ->, or sizeof operator. Pointers are a notorious source of bugs. Eliminating them simplifies the language and makes Java programs more robust and secure.

Garbage collection
The Java Virtual Machine performs garbage collection so that Java programmers do not have to explicitly manage the memory used by all objects and arrays. This feature eliminates another entire category of common bugs and all but eliminates memory leaks from Java programs.

No goto statement

Java doesn't support a goto statement. Use of goto except in certain well-defined circumstances is regarded as poor programming practice. Java adds exception handling and labeled break and continue statements to the flow-control statements offered by C. These are a good substitute for goto.

Variable declarations anywhere

C requires local variable declarations to be made at the beginning of a method or block, while Java allows them anywhere in a method or block. Many programmers prefer to keep all their variable declarations grouped together at the top of a method, however.

Forward references

The Java compiler is smarter than the C compiler, in that it allows methods to be invoked before they are defined. This eliminates the need to declare functions in a header file before defining them in a program file, as is done in C.

Method overloading

Java programs can define multiple methods with the same name, as long as the methods have different parameter lists.

No struct and union types

Java doesn't support C struct and union types. A Java class can be thought of as an enhanced struct, however.

No enumerated types

Java doesn't support the enum keyword used in C to define types that consist of fixed sets of named values. This is surprising for a strongly typed language like Java, but there are ways to simulate this feature with object constants.

No bitfields

Java doesn't support the (infrequently used) ability of C to specify the number of individual bits occupied by fields of a struct.

No typedef

Java doesn't support the typedef keyword used in C to define aliases for type names. Java's lack of pointers makes its type-naming scheme simpler and more consistent than C's, however, so many of the common uses of typedef are not really necessary in Java.

No method pointers

C allows you to store the address of a function in a variable and pass this function pointer to other functions. You cannot do this with Java methods, but you can often achieve similar results by passing an object that implements a particular interface. Also, a Java method can be represented and invoked through a java.lang.reflect.Method object.

No variable-length argument lists

Java doesn't allow you to define methods such as C's printf() that take a variable number of arguments. Method overloading allows you to simulate C varargs functions for simple cases, and arguments can also be passed as an Object[], but there's no general replacement for this feature.

CHAPTER 3

Object-Oriented Programming in Java

Java is an object-oriented programming language. As we discussed in Chapter 2, *Java Syntax from the Ground Up*, all Java programs use objects, and every Java program is defined as a class. The previous chapter explained the basic syntax of the Java programming language, including data types, operators, and expressions, and even showed how to define simple classes and work with objects. This chapter continues where that one left off, explaining the details of object-oriented programming in Java.

If you do not have any object-oriented (OO) programming background, don't worry; this chapter does not assume any prior experience. If you do have experience with OO programming, however, be careful. The term "object-oriented" has different meanings in different languages. Don't assume that Java works the same way as your favorite OO language. This is particularly true for C++ programmers. We saw in the last chapter that close analogies can be drawn between Java and C. The same is not true for Java and C++, however. Java uses object-oriented programming concepts that are familiar to C++ programmers and even borrows C++ syntax in a number of places, but the similarities between Java and C++ are not nearly as strong as those between Java and C. Don't let your experience with C++ lull you into a false familiarity with Java.

The Members of a Class

As we discussed in Chapter 2, a class is a collection of data, stored in named fields, and code, organized into named methods, that operates on that data. The fields and methods are called *members* of a class. In Java 1.1 and later, classes can also contain other classes. These member classes, or inner classes, are an advanced feature that is discussed later in the chapter. For now, we are going to discuss only fields and methods. The members of a class come in two distinct types: class, or static, members are associated with the class itself, while instance members are associated with individual instances of the class (i.e., with objects). Ignoring member classes for now, this gives us four types of members:

- Class fields

- Class methods

- Instance fields

- Instance methods

The simple class definition for the class Circle, shown in Example 3-1, contains all four types of members.

Example 3-1: A Simple Class and its Members

```
public class Circle {
  // A class field
  public static final double PI= 3.14159;     // A useful constant

  // A class method: just compute a value based on the arguments
  public static double radiansToDegrees(double rads) {
    return rads * 180 / PI;
  }

  // An instance field
  public double r;                  // The radius of the circle

  // Two instance methods: they operate on the instance fields of an object
  public double area() {            // Compute the area of the circle
    return PI * r * r;
  }
  public double circumference() {   // Compute the circumference of the circle
    return 2 * PI * r;
  }
}
```

Class Fields

A *class field* is associated with the class in which it is defined, rather than with an instance of the class. The following line declares a class field:

```
public static final double PI = 3.14159;
```

This line declares a field of type double named PI and assigns it a value of 3.14159. As you can see, a field declaration looks quite a bit like the local variable declarations we discussed in Chapter 2. The difference, of course, is that variables are defined within methods, while fields are members of classes.

The static modifier says that the field is a class field. Class fields are sometimes called static fields because of this static modifier. The final modifier says that the value of the field does not change. Since the field PI represents a constant, we declare it final so that it cannot be changed. It is a convention in Java (and many other languages) that constants are named with capital letters, which is why our field is named PI, not pi. Defining constants like this is a common use for class fields, meaning that the static and final modifiers are often used together. Not all class fields are constants, however. In other words, a field can be declared static without declaring it final. Finally, the public modifier says that anyone can use the field. This is a visibility modifier, and we'll discuss it and related modifiers in more detail later in this chapter.

The key point to understand about a static field is that there is only a single copy of it. This field is associated with the class itself, not with instances of the class. If you look at the various methods of the `Circle` class, you'll see that they use this field. From inside the `Circle` class, the field can be referred to simply as `PI`. Outside the class, however, both class and field names are required to uniquely specify the field. Methods that are not part of `Circle` access this field as `Circle.PI`.

A class field is essentially a global variable. The names of class fields are qualified by the unique names of the classes that contain them, however. Thus, Java does not suffer from the name collisions that can affect other languages when different modules of code define global variables with the same name.

Class Methods

As with class fields, *class methods* are declared with the `static` modifier:

```
public static double radiansToDegrees(double rads) { return rads * 180 / PI; }
```

This line declares a class method named `radiansToDegrees()`. It has a single parameter of type `double` and returns a `double` value. The body of the method is quite short; it performs a simple computation and returns the result.

Like class fields, class methods are associated with a class, rather than with an object. When invoking a class method from code that exists outside the class, you must specify both the name of the class and the method. For example:

```
// How many degrees is 2.0 radians?
double d = Circle.radiansToDegrees(2.0);
```

If you want to invoke a class method from inside the class in which it is defined, you don't have to specify the class name. However, it is often good style to specify the class name anyway, to make it clear that a class method is being invoked.

Note that the body of our `Circle.radiansToDegrees()` method uses the class field `PI`. A class method can use any class fields and class methods of its own class (or of any other class). But it cannot use any instance fields or instance methods because class methods are not associated with an instance of the class. In other words, although the `radiansToDegrees()` method is defined in the `Circle` class, it does not use any `Circle` objects. The instance fields and instance methods of the class are associated with `Circle` objects, not with the class itself. Since a class method is not associated with an instance of its class, it cannot use any instance methods or fields.

As we discussed earlier, a class field is essentially a global variable. In a similar way, a class method is a global method, or global function. Although `radiansToDegrees()` does not operate on `Circle` objects, it is defined within the `Circle` class because it is a utility method that is sometimes useful when working with circles. In many non-object-oriented programming languages, all methods, or functions, are global. You can write complex Java programs using only class methods. This is not object-oriented programming, however, and does not take advantage of the power of the Java language. To do true object-oriented programming, we need to add instance fields and instance methods to our repertoire.

Instance Fields

Any field declared without the `static` modifier is an *instance field*:

```
public double r;    // The radius of the circle
```

Instance fields are associated with instances of the class, rather than with the class itself. Thus, every `Circle` object we create has its own copy of the `double` field `r`. In our example, `r` represents the radius of a circle. Thus, each `Circle` object can have a radius independent of all other `Circle` objects.

Inside a class definition, instance fields are referred to by name alone. You can see an example of this if you look at the method body of the `circumference()` instance method. In code outside the class, the name of an instance method must be prepended by a reference to the object that contains it. For example, if we have a `Circle` object named `c`, we can refer to its instance field `r` as `c.r`:

```
Circle c = new Circle(); // Create a new Circle object; store it in variable c
c.r = 2.0;               // Assign a value to its instance field r
Circle d = new Circle(); // Create a different Circle object
d.r = c.r * 2;           // Make this one twice as big
```

Instance fields are key to object-oriented programming. Instance fields define an object; the values of those fields make one object distinct from another.

Instance Methods

Any method not declared with the `static` keyword is an instance method. An *instance method* operates on an instance of a class (an object) instead of operating on the class itself. It is with instance methods that object-oriented programming starts to get interesting. The `Circle` class defined in Example 3-1 contains two instance methods, `area()` and `circumference()`, that compute and return the area and circumference of the circle represented by a given `Circle` object.

To use an instance method from outside the class in which it is defined, we must prepend a reference to the instance that is to be operated on. For example:

```
Circle c = new Circle();  // Create a Circle object; store in variable c
c.r = 2.0;                // Set an instance field of the object
double a = c.area();      // Invoke an instance method of the object
```

If you're new to object-oriented programming, that last line of code may look a little strange. I did not write:

```
a = area(c);
```

Instead, I wrote:

```
a = c.area();
```

This is why it is called object-oriented programming; the object is the focus here, not the function call. This small syntactic difference is perhaps the single most important feature of the object-oriented paradigm.

The point here is that we don't have to pass an argument to `c.area()`. The object we are operating on, `c`, is implicit in the syntax. Take a look at Example 3-1 again.

You'll notice the same thing in the signature of the area() method: it doesn't have a parameter. Now look at the body of the area() method: it uses the instance field r. Because the area() method is part of the same class that defines this instance field, the method can use the unqualified name r. It is understood that this refers to the radius of whatever Circle instance invokes the method.

Another important thing to notice about the bodies of the area() and circumference() methods is that they both use the class field PI. We saw earlier that class methods can use only class fields and class methods, not instance fields or methods. Instance methods are not restricted in this way: they can use any member of a class, whether it is declared static or not.

How instance methods work

Consider this line of code again:

```
a = c.area();
```

What's going on here? How can a method that has no parameters know what data to operate on? In fact, the area() method does have a parameter. All instance methods are implemented with an implicit parameter not shown in the method signature. The implicit argument is named this; it holds a reference to the object through which the method is invoked. In our example, that object is a Circle.

The implicit this parameter is not shown in method signatures because it is usually not needed; whenever a Java method accesses the fields in its class, it is implied that it is accessing fields in the object referred to by the this parameter. The same is true when an instance method invokes another instance method in the same class. I said earlier that to invoke an instance method you must prepend a reference to the object to be operated on. When an instance method is invoked within another instance method in the same class, however, you don't need to specify an object. In this case, it is implicit that the method is being invoked on the this object.

You can use the this keyword explicitly when you want to make it clear that a method is accessing its own fields and/or methods. For example, we can rewrite the area() method to use this explicitly to refer to instance fields:

```
public double area() {
  return Circle.PI * this.r * this.r;
}
```

This code also uses the class name explicitly to refer to class field PI. In a method this simple, it is not necessary to be explicit. In more complicated cases, however, you may find that it increases the clarity of your code to use an explicit this where it is not strictly required.

There are some cases in which the this keyword *is* required, however. For example, when a method parameter or local variable in a method has the same name as one of the fields of the class, you must use this to refer to the field, since the field name used alone refers to the method parameter or local variable. For example, we can add the following method to the Circle class:

```
public void setRadius(double r) {
  this.r = r;        // Assign the argument (r) to the field (this.r)
                     // Note that we cannot just say r = r
}
```

Finally, note that while instance methods can use the this keyword, class methods cannot. This is because class methods are not associated with objects.

Instance methods or class methods?

Instance methods are one of the key features of object-oriented programming. That doesn't mean, however, that you should shun class methods. There are many cases in which is is perfectly reasonable to define class methods. When working with the Circle class, for example, you might find there are many times you want to compute the area of a circle with a given radius, but don't want to bother creating a Circle object to represent that circle. In this case, a class method is more convenient:

```
public static double area(double r) { return PI * r * r; }
```

It is perfectly legal for a class to define more than one method with the same name, as long as the methods have different parameters. Since this version of the area() method is a class method, it does not have an implicit this parameter and must have a parameter that specifies the radius of the circle. This parameter keeps it distinct from the instance method of the same name.

As another example of the choice between instance methods and class methods, consider defining a method named bigger() that examines two Circle objects and returns whichever has the larger radius. We can write bigger() as an instance method as follows:

```
// Compare the implicit "this" circle to the "that" circle passed
// explicitly as an argument and return the bigger one.
public Circle bigger(Circle that) {
  if (this.r > that.r) return this;
  else return that;
}
```

We can also implement bigger() as a class method as follows:

```
// Compare circle a to circle b and return the one with the larger radius
public static Circle bigger(Circle a, Circle b) {
  if (a.r > b.r) return a;
  else return b;
}
```

Given two Circle objects, x and y, we can use either the instance method or the class method to determine which is bigger. The invocation syntax differs significantly for the two methods, however:

```
Circle biggest = x.bigger(y);        // Instance method: also y.bigger(x)
Circle biggest = Circle.bigger(x, y); // Static method
```

Neither option is the correct choice. The instance method is more formally object-oriented, but its invocation syntax suffers from a kind of asymmetry. In a case like this, the choice between an instance method and a class method is simply a design decision. Depending on the circumstances, one or the other will likely be the more natural choice.

A Mystery Solved

As we saw in Chapters 1 and 2, the way to display textual output to the terminal in Java is with a method named System.out.println(). Those chapters never explained why this method has such an long, awkward name or what those two periods are doing in it. Now that you understand class and instance fields and class and instance methods, it is easier to understand what is going on. Here's the story: System is a class. It has a class field named out. The field System.out refers to an object. The object System.out has an instance method named println(). Mystery solved! If you want to explore this in more detail, you can look up the java.lang.System class in Chapter 12, *The java.lang Package*. The class synopsis there tells you that the field out is of type java.io.PrintStream, which you can look up in Chapter 11, *The java.io Package*.

Creating and Initializing Objects

Take another look at how we've been creating Circle objects:

```
Circle c = new Circle();
```

What are those parentheses doing there? They make it look like we're calling a method. In fact, that is exactly what we're doing. Every class in Java has at least one *constructor*, which is a method that has the same name as the class and whose purpose is to perform any necessary initialization for a new object. Since we didn't explicitly define a constructor for our Circle class in Example 3-1, Java gave us a default constructor that takes no arguments and performs no special initialization.

Here's how a constructor works. The new operator creates a new, but uninitialized, instance of the class. The constructor method is then called, with the new object passed implicitly (a this reference, as we saw earlier), and whatever arguments that are specified between parentheses passed explicitly. The constructor can use these arguments to do whatever initialization is necessary.

Defining a Constructor

There is some obvious initialization we could do for our circle objects, so let's define a constructor. Example 3-2 shows a new definition for Circle that contains a constructor that lets us specify the radius of a new Circle object. The constructor also uses the this reference to distinguish between a method parameter and an instance field that have the same name.

Example 3-2: A Constructor for the Circle Class

```
public class Circle {
    public static final double PI = 3.14159;  // A constant
    public double r;    // An instance field that holds the radius of the circle
```

Example 3-2: A Constructor for the Circle Class (continued)

```
// The constructor method: initialize the radius field
public Circle(double r) { this.r = r; }

// The instance methods: compute values based on the radius
public double circumference() { return 2 * PI * r; }
public double area() { return PI * r*r; }
}
```

When we relied on the default constructor supplied by the compiler, we had to write code like this to initialize the radius explicitly:

```
Circle c = new Circle();
c.r = 0.25;
```

With this new constructor, the initialization becomes part of the object creation step:

```
Circle c = new Circle(0.25);
```

Here are some important notes about naming, declaring, and writing constructors:

- The constructor name is always the same as the class name.

- Unlike all other methods, a constructor is declared without a return type, not even void.

- The body of a constructor should initialize the this object.

- A constructor should not return this or any other value.

Defining Multiple Constructors

Sometimes you want to initialize an object in a number of different ways, depending on what is most convenient in a particular circumstance. For example, we might want to initialize the radius of a circle to a specified value or a reasonable default value. Since our Circle class has only a single instance field, there aren't too many ways we can initialize it, of course. But in more complex classes, it is often convenient to define a variety of constructors. Here's how we can define two constructors for Circle:

```
public Circle() { r = 1.0; }
public Circle(double r) { this.r = r; }
```

It is perfectly legal to define multiple constructors for a class, as long as each constructor has a different parameter list. The compiler determines which constructor you wish to use based on the number and type of arguments you supply. This is simply an example of method overloading, which we discussed in Chapter 2.

Invoking One Constructor from Another

There is a specialized use of the this keyword that arises when a class has multiple constructors; it can be used from a constructor to invoke one of the other constructors of the same class. In other words, we can rewrite the two previous Circle constructors as follows:

```
// This is the basic constructor: initialize the radius
public Circle(double r) { this.r = r; }
// This constructor uses this() to invoke the constructor above
public Circle() { this(1.0); }
```

The this() syntax is a method invocation that calls one of the other constructors of the class. The particular constructor that is invoked is determined by the number and type of arguments, of course. This is a useful technique when a number of constructors share a significant amount of initialization code, as it avoids repetition of that code. This would be a more impressive example, of course, if the one-parameter version of the Circle() constructor did more initialization than it does.

There is an important restriction on using this(): it can appear only as the first statement in a constructor. It may, of course, be followed by any additional initialization a particular version of the constructor needs to do. The reason for this restriction involves the automatic invocation of superclass constructor methods, which we'll explore later in this chapter.

Field Defaults and Initializers

Not every field of a class requires initialization. Unlike local variables, which have no default value and cannot be used until explicitly initialized, the fields of a class are automatically initialized to the default values shown in Table 2-2. Essentially, every field of a primitive type is initialized to a default value of false or zero, as appropriate. All fields of reference type are, by default, initialized to null. These default values are guaranteed by Java. If the default value of a field is appropriate, you can simply rely on it without explicitly initializing the field. This default initialization applies to both instance fields and class fields.

As we've seen, the syntax for declaring a field of a class is a lot like the syntax for declaring a local variable. Both class and instance field declarations can be followed by an equals sign and an initial value, as in:

```
public static final double PI = 3.14159;
public double r = 1.0;
```

As we discussed in Chapter 2, a variable declaration is a statement that appears within a Java method; the variable initialization is performed when the statement is executed. Field declarations, however, are not part of any method, so they cannot be executed as statements are. Instead, the Java compiler generates instance-field initialization code automatically and puts it in the constructor or constructors for the class. The initialization code is inserted into a constructor in the order it appears in the source code, which means that a field initializer can use the initial values of fields declared before it. Consider the following code excerpt, which shows a constructor and two instance fields of a hypothetical class:

```
public class TestClass {
  ... public int len = 10;
  public int[] table = new int[len];

  public TestClass() {
    for(int i = 0; i < len; i++) table[i] = i;
  }
```

```
// Rest of the class is omitted...
}
```

In this case, the code generated for the constructor is actually equivalent to the following:

```
public TestClass() {
  len = 10;
  table = new int[len];
  for(int i = 0; i < len; i++) table[i] = i;
}
```

If a constructor begins with a this() call to another constructor, the field initialization code does not appear in the first constructor. Instead, the initialization is handled in the constructor invoked by the this() call.

So, if instance fields are initialized in constructor methods, where are class fields initialized? These fields are associated with the class, even if no instances of the class are ever created, so they need to be initialized even before a constructor is called. To support this, the Java compiler generates a class initialization method automatically for every class. Class fields are initialized in the body of this method, which is guaranteed to be invoked exactly once before the class is first used (often when the class is first loaded). As with instance field initialization, class field initialization expressions are inserted into the class initialization method in the order they appear in the source code. This means that the initialization expression for a class field can use the class fields declared before it. The class initialization method is an internal method that is hidden from Java programmers. If you disassemble the byte codes in a Java class file, however, you'll see the class initialization code in a method named <clinit>.

Initializer blocks

So far, we've seen that objects can be initialized through the initialization expressions for their fields and by arbitrary code in their constructor methods. A class has a class initialization method, which is like a constructor, but we cannot explicitly define the body of this method as we can for a constructor. Java does allow us to write arbitrary code for the initialization of class fields, however, with a construct known as a *static initializer*. A static initializer is simply the keyword static followed by a block of code in curly braces. A static initializer can appear in a class definition anywhere a field or method definition can appear. For example, consider the following code that performs some nontrivial initialization for two class fields:

```
// We can draw the outline of a circle using trigonometric functions
// Trigonometry is slow, though, so we precompute a bunch of values
public class TrigCircle {
  // Here are our static lookup tables and their own simple initializers
  private static final int NUMPTS = 500;
  private static double sines[] = new double[NUMPTS];
  private static double cosines[] = new double[NUMPTS];

  // Here's a static initializer that fills in the arrays
  static {
    double x = 0.0;
    double delta_x = (Circle.PI/2)/(NUMPTS-1);
```

```
      for(int i = 0, x = 0.0; i < NUMPTS; i++, x += delta_x) {
        sines[i] = Math.sin(x);
        cosines[i] = Math.cos(x);
      }
    }
    // The rest of the class is omitted... }
```

A class can have any number of static initializers. The body of each initializer block is incorporated into the class initialization method, along with any static field initialization expressions. A static initializer is like a class method in that it cannot use the this keyword or any instance fields or instance methods of the class.

In Java 1.1 and later, classes are also allowed to have instance initializers. An instance initializer is like a static initializer, except that it initializes an object, not a class. A class can have any number of instance initializers, and they can appear anywhere a field or method definition can appear. The body of each instance initializer is inserted at the beginning of every constructor for the class, along with any field initialization expressions. An instance initializer looks just like a static initializer, except that it doesn't use the static keyword. In other words, an instance initializer is just a block of arbitrary Java code that appears within curly braces.

Instance initializers can initialize arrays or other fields that require complex initialization. They are sometimes useful because they locate the initialization code right next to the field, instead of separating it off in a constructor method. For example:

```
private static final int NUMPTS = 100;
private int[] data = new int[NUMPTS];
{ for(int i = 0; i < NUMPTS; i++) data[i] = i; }
```

In practice, however, this use of instance initializers is fairly rare. Instance initializers were introduced in Java to support anonymous inner classes, and that is their main utility (we'll discuss anonymous inner classes later in this chapter).

Destroying and Finalizing Objects

Now that we've seen how new objects are created and initialized in Java, we need to study the other end of the object life cycle and examine how objects are finalized and destroyed. *Finalization* is the opposite of initialization.

As I mentioned in Chapter 2, the memory occupied by an object is automatically reclaimed when the object is no longer needed. This is done through a process known as *garbage collection*. Garbage collection is not some newfangled technique; it has been around for years in languages such as Lisp. It just takes some getting used to for programmers accustomed to such languages as C and C++, in which you must call the free() function or the delete operator to reclaim memory. The fact that you don't need to remember to destroy every object you create is one of the features that makes Java a pleasant language to work with. It is also one of the features that makes programs written in Java less prone to bugs than those written in languages that don't support automatic garbage collection.

Garbage Collection

The Java interpreter knows exactly what objects and arrays it has allocated. It can also figure out which local variables refer to which objects and arrays, and which objects and arrays refer to which other objects and arrays. Thus, the interpreter is able to determine when an allocated object is no longer referred to by any other object or variable. When the interpreter finds such an object, it knows it can destroy the object safely and does so. The garbage collector can also detect and destroy cycles of objects that refer to each other, but are not referenced by any other active objects. Any such cycles are also reclaimed.

The Java garbage collector runs as a low-priority thread, so it does most of its work when nothing else is going on, such as during idle time while waiting for user input. The only time the garbage collector must run while something high-priority is going on (i.e., the only time it will actually slow down the system) is when available memory has become dangerously low. This doesn't happen very often because the low-priority thread cleans things up in the background.

This scheme may sound slow and wasteful of memory. Actually though, modern garbage collectors can be surprisingly efficient. Garbage collection will never be as efficient as well-written, explicit memory allocation and deallocation. But it does make programming a lot easier and less prone to bugs. And for most real-world programs, rapid development, lack of bugs, and easy maintenance are more important features than raw speed or memory efficiency.

Memory Leaks in Java

The fact that Java supports garbage collection dramatically reduces the incidence of a class of bugs known as *memory leaks*. A memory leak occurs when memory is allocated and never reclaimed. At first glance, it might seem that garbage collection prevents all memory leaks because it reclaims all unused objects. A memory leak can still occur in Java, however, if a valid (but unused) reference to an unused object is left hanging around. For example, when a method runs for a long time (or forever), the local variables in that method can retain object references much longer than they are actually required. The following code illustrates:

```
public static void main(String args[]) {
  int big_array[] = new int[100000];

  // Do some computations with big_array and get a result.
  int result = compute(big_array);

  // We no longer need big_array. It will get garbage collected when there
  // are no more references to it. Since big_array is a local variable,
  // it refers to the array until this method returns. But this method
  // doesn't return. So we've got to explicitly get rid of the reference
  // ourselves, so the garbage collector knows it can reclaim the array.
  big_array = null;

  // Loop forever, handling the user's input
  for(;;) handle_input(result);
}
```

Memory leaks can also occur when you use a hashtable or similar data structure to associate one object with another. Even when neither object is required anymore, the association remains in the hashtable, preventing the objects from being reclaimed until the hashtable itself is reclaimed. If the hashtable has a substantially longer lifetime than the objects it holds, this can cause memory leaks.

Object Finalization

A *finalizer* in Java is the opposite of a constructor. While a constructor method performs initialization for an object, a finalizer method performs finalization for the object. Garbage collection automatically frees up the memory resources used by objects, but objects can hold other kinds of resources, such as open files and network connections. The garbage collector cannot free these resources for you, so you need to write a finalizer method for any object that needs to perform such tasks as closing files, terminating network connections, deleting temporary files, and so on.

A finalizer is an instance method that takes no arguments and returns no value. There can be only one finalizer per class, and it must be named finalize().* A finalizer can throw any kind of exception or error, but when a finalizer is automatically invoked by the garbage collector, any exception or error it throws is ignored and serves only to cause the finalizer method to return. Finalizer methods are typically declared protected (which we have not discussed yet), but can also be declared public. An example finalizer looks like this:

```
protected void finalize() throws Throwable {
    // Invoke the finalizer of our superclass
    // We haven't discussed superclasses or this syntax yet
    super.finalize();

    // Delete a temporary file we were using
    // If the file doesn't exist or tempfile is null, this can throw
    // an exception, but that exception is ignored.
    tempfile.delete();
}
```

Here are some important points about finalizers:

- If an object has a finalizer, the finalizer method is invoked sometime after the object becomes unused (or unreachable), but before the garbage collector reclaims the object.

- Java makes no guarantees about when garbage collection will occur or in what order objects will be collected. Therefore, Java can make no guarantees about when (or even whether) a finalizer will be invoked, in what order finalizers will be invoked, or what thread will execute finalizers.

---

* C++ programmers should note that although Java constructor methods are named like C++ constructors, Java finalization methods are not named like C++ destructor methods. As we will see, they do not behave quite like C++ destructor methods, either.

- The Java interpreter can exit without garbage collecting all outstanding objects, so some finalizers may never be invoked. In this case, though, any outstanding resources are usually freed by the operating system. In Java 1.1, the `Runtime` method `runFinalizersOnExit()` can force the virtual machine to run finalizers before exiting. Unfortunately, however, this method can cause deadlock and is inherently unsafe; it has been deprecated as of Java 1.2. In Java 1.3, the `Runtime` method `addShutdownHook()` can safely execute arbitrary code before the Java interpreter exits.

- After a finalizer is invoked, objects are not freed right away. This is because a finalizer method can resurrect an object by storing the `this` pointer somewhere so that the object once again has references. Thus, after `finalize()` is called, the garbage collector must once again determine that the object is unreferenced before it can garbage-collect it. However, even if an object is resurrected, the finalizer method is never invoked more than once. Resurrecting an object is never a useful thing to do—just a strange quirk of object finalization. As of Java 1.2, the `java.lang.ref.PhantomReference` class can implement an alternative to finalization that does not allow resurrection.

In practice, it is relatively rare for an application-level class to require a `finalize()` method. Finalizer methods are more useful, however, when writing Java classes that interface to native platform code with `native` methods. In this case, the native implementation can allocate memory or other resources that are not under the control of the Java garbage collector and need to be reclaimed explicitly by a `native` `finalize()` method.

While Java supports both class and instance initialization through static initializers and constructors, it provides only a facility for instance finalization. The original Java specification called for a `classFinalize()` method that could finalize a class when the class itself became unused and was unloaded from the VM. This feature was never implemented, however, and because it has proved to be unnecessary, class finalization has been removed from the language specification.

Subclasses and Inheritance

The `Circle` defined earlier is a simple class that distinguishes circle objects only by their radii. Suppose, instead, that we want to represent circles that have both a size and a position. For example, a circle of radius 1.0 centered at point 0,0 in the Cartesian plane is different from the circle of radius 1.0 centered at point 1,2. To do this, we need a new class, which we'll call `PlaneCircle`. We'd like to add the ability to represent the position of a circle without losing any of the existing functionality of the `Circle` class. This is done by defining `PlaneCircle` as a subclass of `Circle`, so that `PlaneCircle` inherits the fields and methods of its superclass, `Circle`. The ability to add functionality to a class by subclassing, or extending, it is central to the object-oriented programming paradigm.

Extending a Class

Example 3-3 shows how we can implement PlaneCircle as a subclass of the Circle class.

Example 3-3: Extending the Circle Class

```java
public class PlaneCircle extends Circle {
    // We automatically inherit the fields and methods of Circle,
    // so we only have to put the new stuff here.
    // New instance fields that store the center point of the circle
    public double cx, cy;

    // A new constructor method to initialize the new fields
    // It uses a special syntax to invoke the Circle() constructor
    public PlaneCircle(double r, double x, double y) {
        super(r);        // Invoke the constructor of the superclass, Circle()
        this.cx = x;     // Initialize the instance field cx
        this.cy = y;     // Initialize the instance field cy
    }

    // The area() and circumference() methods are inherited from Circle
    // A new instance method that checks whether a point is inside the circle
    // Note that it uses the inherited instance field r
    public boolean isInside(double x, double y) {
        double dx = x - cx, dy = y - cy;          // Distance from center
        double distance = Math.sqrt(dx*dx + dy*dy);  // Pythagorean theorem
        return (distance < r);                    // Returns true or false
    }
}
```

Note the use of the keyword extends in the first line of Example 3-3. This keyword tells Java that PlaneCircle extends, or subclasses, Circle, meaning that it inherits the fields and methods of that class.* The definition of the isInside() method shows field inheritance; this method uses the field r (defined by the Circle class) as if it were defined right in PlaneCircle itself. PlaneCircle also inherits the methods of Circle. Thus, if we have a PlaneCircle object referenced by variable pc, we can say:

```java
double ratio = pc.circumference() / pc.area();
```

This works just as if the area() and circumference() methods were defined in PlaneCircle itself.

Another feature of subclassing is that every PlaneCircle object is also a perfectly legal Circle object. Thus, if pc refers to a PlaneCircle object, we can assign it to a Circle variable and forget all about its extra positioning capabilities:

```java
PlaneCircle pc = new PlaneCircle(1.0, 0.0, 0.0);  // Unit circle at the origin
Circle c = pc;      // Assigned to a Circle variable without casting
```

This assignment of a PlaneCircle object to a Circle variable can be done without a cast. As we discussed in Chapter 2, this is a widening conversion and is always legal. The value held in the Circle variable c is still a valid PlaneCircle object,

---

* C++ programmers should note that extends is the Java equivalent of : in C++; both are used to indicate the superclass of a class.

but the compiler cannot know this for sure, so it doesn't allow us to do the opposite (narrowing) conversion without a cast:

```
// Narrowing conversions require a cast (and a runtime check by the VM)
PlaneCircle pc2 = (PlaneCircle) c;
boolean origininside = ((PlaneCircle) c).isInside(0.0, 0.0);
```

Final classes

When a class is declared with the final modifier, it means that it cannot be extended or subclassed. java.lang.System is an example of a final class. Declaring a class final prevents unwanted extensions to the class, and it also allows the compiler to make some optimizations when invoking the methods of a class. We'll explore this in more detail later in this chapter, when we talk about method overriding.

Superclasses, Object, and the Class Hierarchy

In our example, PlaneCircle is a subclass of Circle. We can also say that Circle is the superclass of PlaneCircle. The superclass of a class is specified in its extends clause:

```
public class PlaneCircle extends Circle { ... }
```

Every class you define has a superclass. If you do not specify the superclass with an extends clause, the superclass is the class java.lang.Object. Object is a special class for a couple of reasons:

- It is the only class in Java that does not have a superclass.

- All Java classes inherit the methods of Object.

Because every class has a superclass, classes in Java form a class hierarchy, which can be represented as a tree with Object at its root. Figure 3-1 shows a class hierarchy diagram that includes our Circle and PlaneCircle classes, as well as some of the standard classes from the Java API. Every API quick-reference chapter in Part II includes a class-hierarchy diagram for the classes it documents.

Subclass Constructors

Look again at the PlaneCircle() constructor method of Example 3-3:

```
public PlaneCircle(double r, double x, double y) {
    super(r);       // Invoke the constructor of the superclass, Circle()
    this.cx = x;    // Initialize the instance field cx
    this.cy = y;    // Initialize the instance field cy
}
```

This constructor explicitly initializes the cx and cy fields newly defined by PlaneCircle, but it relies on the superclass Circle() constructor to initialize the inherited fields of the class. To invoke the superclass constructor, our constructor calls super(). super is a reserved word in Java. One of its uses is to invoke the constructor method of a superclass from within the constructor method of a subclass. This use is analogous to the use of this() to invoke one constructor method

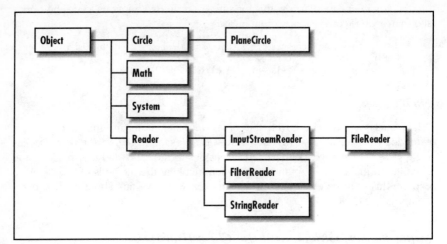

Figure 3-1: A class hierarchy diagram

of a class from within another constructor method of the same class. Using super() to invoke a constructor is subject to the same restrictions as using this() to invoke a constructor:

- super() can be used in this way only within a constructor method.

- The call to the superclass constructor must appear as the first statement within the constructor method, even before local variable declarations.

The arguments passed to super() must match the parameters of the superclass constructor. If the superclass defines more than one constructor, super() can be used to invoke any one of them, depending on the arguments passed.

Constructor Chaining and the Default Constructor

Java guarantees that the constructor method of a class is called whenever an instance of that class is created. It also guarantees that the constructor is called whenever an instance of any subclass is created. In order to guarantee this second point, Java must ensure that every constructor method calls its superclass constructor method. Thus, if the first statement in a constructor does not explicitly invoke another constructor with this() or super(), Java implicitly inserts the call super(); that is, it calls the superclass constructor with no arguments. If the superclass does not have a constructor that takes no arguments, this implicit invocation causes a compilation error.

Consider what happens when we create a new instance of the PlaneCircle class. First, the PlaneCircle constructor is invoked. This constructor explicitly calls super(r) to invoke a Circle constructor, and that Circle() constructor implicitly calls super() to invoke the constructor of its superclass, Object. The body of the Object constructor runs first. When it returns, the body of the Circle() constructor runs. Finally, when the call to super(r) returns, the remaining statements of the PlaneCircle() constructor are executed.

What all this means is that constructor calls are chained; any time an object is created, a sequence of constructor methods is invoked, from subclass to superclass on up to `Object` at the root of the class hierarchy. Because a superclass constructor is always invoked as the first statement of its subclass constructor, the body of the `Object` constructor always runs first, followed by the constructor of its subclass and on down the class hierarchy to the class that is being instantiated. There is an important implication here; when a constructor is invoked, it can count on the fields of its superclass to be initialized.

The default constructor

There is one missing piece in the previous description of constructor chaining. If a constructor does not invoke a superclass constructor, Java does so implicitly. But what if a class is declared without a constructor? In this case, Java implicitly adds a constructor to the class. This default constructor does nothing but invoke the superclass constructor. For example, if we don't declare a constructor for the `PlaneCircle` class, Java implicitly inserts this constructor:

```
public PlaneCircle() { super(); }
```

If the superclass, `Circle`, doesn't declare a no-argument constructor, the `super()` call in this automatically inserted default constructor for `PlaneCircle()` causes a compilation error. In general, if a class does not define a no-argument constructor, all its subclasses must define constructors that explicitly invoke the superclass constructor with the necessary arguments.

If a class does not declare any constructors, it is given a no-argument constructor by default. Classes declared `public` are given `public` constructors. All other classes are given a default constructor that is declared without any visibility modifier: such a constructor has default visibility. (The notion of visibility is explained later in this chapter.) If you are creating a `public` class that should not be publicly instantiated, you should declare at least one non-`public` constructor to prevent the insertion of a default `public` constructor. Classes that should never be instantiated (such as `java.lang.Math` or `java.lang.System`) should define a `private` constructor. Such a constructor can never be invoked from outside of the class, but it prevents the automatic insertion of the default constructor.

Finalizer chaining?

You might assume that, since Java chains constructor methods, it also automatically chains the finalizer methods for an object. In other words, you might assume that the finalizer method of a class automatically invokes the finalizer of its superclass, and so on. In fact, Java does *not* do this. When you write a `finalize()` method, you must explicitly invoke the superclass finalizer. (You should do this even if you know that the superclass does not have a finalizer because a future implementation of the superclass might add a finalizer.)

As we saw in our example finalizer earlier in the chapter, you can invoke a superclass method with a special syntax that uses the `super` keyword:

```
// Invoke the finalizer of our superclass.
super.finalize();
```

We'll discuss this syntax in more detail when we consider method overriding. In practice, the need for finalizer methods, and thus finalizer chaining, rarely arises.

Shadowing Superclass Fields

For the sake of example, imagine that our `PlaneCircle` class needs to know the distance between the center of the circle and the origin (0,0). We can add another instance field to hold this value:

```
public double r;
```

Adding the following line to the constructor computes the value of the field:

```
this.r = Math.sqrt(cx*cx + cy*cy);  // Pythagorean Theorem
```

But wait, this new field r has the same name as the radius field r in the `Circle` superclass. When this happens, we say that the field r of `PlaneCircle` *shadows* the field r of `Circle`. (This is a contrived example, of course: the new field should really be called `distanceFromOrigin`. Although you should attempt to avoid it, subclass fields do sometimes shadow fields of their superclass.)

With this new definition of `PlaneCircle`, the expressions r and `this.r` both refer to the field of `PlaneCircle`. How, then, can we refer to the field r of `Circle` that holds the radius of the circle? There is a special syntax for this that uses the super keyword:

```
r        // Refers to the PlaneCircle field
this.r   // Refers to the PlaneCircle field
super.r  // Refers to the Circle field
```

Another way to refer to a shadowed field is to cast `this` (or any instance of the class) to the appropriate superclass and then access the field:

```
((Circle) this).r   // Refers to field r of the Circle class
```

This casting technique is particularly useful when you need to refer to a shadowed field defined in a class that is not the immediate superclass. Suppose, for example, that classes A, B, and C all define a field named x and that C is a subclass of B, which is a subclass of A. Then, in the methods of class C, you can refer to these different fields as follows:

```
x               // Field x in class C
this.x          // Field x in class C
super.x         // Field x in class B
((B)this).x     // Field x in class B
((A)this).x     // Field x in class A
super.super.x   // Illegal; does not refer to x in class A
```

You cannot refer to a shadowed field x in the superclass of a superclass with `super.super.x`. This is not legal syntax.

Similarly, if you have an instance c of class C, you can refer to the three fields named x like this:

```
c.x             // Field x of class C
((B)c).x        // Field x of class B
((A)c).x        // Field x of class A
```

So far, we've been discussing instance fields. Class fields can also be shadowed. You can use the same super syntax to refer to the shadowed value of the field, but this is never necessary since you can always refer to a class field by prepending the name of the desired class. Suppose that the implementer of `PlaneCircle` decides that the `Circle.PI` field does not express π to enough decimal places. She can define her own class field `PI`:

```
public static final double PI = 3.14159265358979323846;
```

Now, code in `PlaneCircle` can use this more accurate value with the expressions `PI` or `PlaneCircle.PI`. It can also refer to the old, less accurate value with the expressions `super.PI` and `Circle.PI`. Note, however, that the `area()` and `circumference()` methods inherited by `PlaneCircle` are defined in the `Circle` class, so they use the value `Circle.PI`, even though that value is shadowed now by `PlaneCircle.PI`.

Overriding Superclass Methods

When a class defines an instance method using the same name, return type, and parameters as a method in its superclass, that method *overrides* the method of the superclass. When the method is invoked for an object of the class, it is the new definition of the method that is called, not the superclass's old definition.

Method overriding is an important and useful technique in object-oriented programming. `PlaneCircle` does not override either of the methods defined by `Circle`, but suppose we define another subclass of `Circle`, named `Ellipse`.* In this case, it is important for `Ellipse` to override the `area()` and `circumference()` methods of `Circle`, since the formulas used to compute the area and circumference of a circle do not work for ellipses.

The upcoming discussion of method overriding considers only instance methods. Class methods behave quite differently, and there isn't much to say. Like fields, class methods can be shadowed by a subclass, but not overridden. As I noted earlier in this chapter, it is good programming style to always prefix a class method invocation with the name of the class in which it is defined. If you consider the class name part of the class method name, the two methods have different names, so nothing is actually shadowed at all. It is, however, illegal for a class method to shadow an instance method.

Before we go any further with the discussion of method overriding, you need to be sure you understand the difference between method overriding and method overloading. As we discussed in Chapter 2, method overloading refers to the practice of defining multiple methods (in the same class) that have the same name, but different parameter lists. This is very different from method overriding, so don't get them confused.

---

* Mathematical purists may argue that since all circles are ellipses, `Ellipse` should be the superclass and `Circle` the subclass. A pragmatic engineer might counterargue that circles can be represented with fewer instance fields, so `Circle` objects should not be burdened by inheriting unnecessary fields from `Ellipse`. In any case, this is a useful example here.

Overriding is not shadowing

Although Java treats the fields and methods of a class analogously in many ways, method overriding is not like field shadowing at all. You can refer to shadowed fields simply by casting an object to an instance of the appropriate superclass, but you cannot invoke overridden instance methods with this technique. The following code illustrates this crucial difference:

```
class A {                             // Define a class named A
  int i = 1;                          // An instance field
  int f() { return i; }               // An instance method
  static char g() { return 'A'; }     // A class method
}

class B extends A {                   // Define a subclass of A
  int i = 2;                          // Shadows field i in class A
  int f() { return -i; }              // Overrides instance method f in class A
  static char g() { return 'B'; }     // Shadows class method g() in class A
}

public class OverrideTest {
  public static void main(String args[]) {
    B b = new B();                    // Creates a new object of type B
    System.out.println(b.i);          // Refers to B.i; prints 2
    System.out.println(b.f());        // Refers to B.f(); prints -2
    System.out.println(b.g());        // Refers to B.g(); prints B
    System.out.println(B.g());        // This is a better way to invoke B.g()

    A a = (A) b;                      // Casts b to an instance of class A
    System.out.println(a.i);          // Now refers to A.i; prints 1
    System.out.println(a.f());        // Still refers to B.f(); prints -2
    System.out.println(a.g());        // Refers to A.g(); prints A
    System.out.println(A.g());        // This is a better way to invoke A.g()
  }
}
```

While this difference between method overriding and field shadowing may seem surprising at first, a little thought makes the purpose clear. Suppose we have a bunch of `Circle` and `Ellipse` objects we are manipulating. To keep track of the circles and ellipses, we store them in an array of type `Circle[]`. (We can do this because `Ellipse` is a subclass of `Circle`, so all `Ellipse` objects are legal `Circle` objects.) When we loop through the elements of this array, we don't have to know or care whether the element is actually a `Circle` or an `Ellipse`. What we do care about very much, however, is that the correct value is computed when we invoke the `area()` method of any element of the array. In other words, we don't want to use the formula for the area of a circle when the object is actually an ellipse! Seen in this context, it is not surprising at all that method overriding is handled differently by Java than field shadowing.

Dynamic method lookup

If we have a `Circle[]` array that holds `Circle` and `Ellipse` objects, how does the compiler know whether to call the `area()` method of the `Circle` class or the `Ellipse` class for any given item in the array? In fact, the compiler does not know this because it cannot know it. The compiler knows that it does not know, however, and produces code that uses dynamic method lookup at runtime. When the interpreter runs the code, it looks up the appropriate area() method to call for each of the objects in the array. That is, when the interpreter interprets the expression o.area(), it checks the actual type of the object referred to by the variable o and then finds the area() method that is appropriate for that type. It does not simply use the area() method that is statically associated with the type of the variable o. This process of dynamic method lookup is sometimes also called virtual method invocation.*

Final methods and static method lookup

Virtual method invocation is fast, but method invocation is faster when no dynamic lookup is necessary at runtime. Fortunately, there are a number of situations in which Java does not need to use dynamic method lookup. In particular, if a method is declared with the final modifier, it means that the method definition is the final one; it cannot be overridden by any subclasses. If a method cannot be overridden, the compiler knows that there is only one version of the method, and dynamic method lookup is not necessary.† In addition, all methods of a final class are themselves implicitly final and cannot be overridden. As we'll discuss later in this chapter, private methods are not inherited by subclasses and, therefore, cannot be overridden (i.e., all private methods are implicitly final). Finally, class methods behave like fields (i.e., they can be shadowed by subclasses but not overridden). Taken together, this means that all methods of a class that is declared final, as well as all methods that are final, private, or static, are invoked without dynamic method lookup. These methods are also candidates for inlining at runtime by a just-in-time compiler (JIT) or similar optimization tool.

Invoking an overridden method

We've seen the important differences between method overriding and field shadowing. Nevertheless, the Java syntax for invoking an overridden method is quite similar to the syntax for accessing a shadowed field: both use the super keyword. The following code illustrates:

```
class A {
  int i = 1;              // An instance field shadowed by subclass B
  int f() { return i; }   // An instance method overridden by subclass B
}
class B extends A {
  int i;                  // This field shadows i in A
  int f() {               // This method overrides f() in A
    i = super.i + 1;      // It can retrieve A.i like this
    return super.f() + i; // It can invoke A.f() like this
  }
}
```

---

* C++ programmers should note that dynamic method lookup is what C++ does for virtual functions. An important difference between Java and C++ is that Java does not have a virtual keyword. In Java, methods are virtual by default.

† In this sense, the final modifier is the opposite of the virtual modifier in C++. All non-final methods in Java are virtual.

Recall that when you use super to refer to a shadowed field, it is the same as casting this to the superclass type and accessing the field through that. Using super to invoke an overridden method, however, is not the same as casting this. In other words, in the previous code, the expression super.f() is not the same as ((A)this).f().

When the interpreter invokes an instance method with this super syntax, a modified form of dynamic method lookup is performed. The first step, as in regular dynamic method lookup, is to determine the actual class of the object through which the method is invoked. Normally, the dynamic search for an appropriate method definition would begin with this class. When a method is invoked with the super syntax, however, the search begins at the superclass of the class. If the superclass implements the method directly, that version of the method is invoked. If the superclass inherits the method, the inherited version of the method is invoked.

Note that the super keyword invokes the most immediately overridden version of a method. Suppose class A has a subclass B that has a subclass C, and all three classes define the same method f(). Then the method C.f() can invoke the method B.f(), which it overrides directly, with super.f(). But there is no way for C.f() to invoke A.f() directly: super.super.f() is not legal Java syntax. Of course, if C.f() invokes B.f(), it is reasonable to suppose that B.f() might also invoke A.f(). This kind of chaining is relatively common when working with overridden methods: it is a way of augmenting the behavior of a method without replacing the method entirely. We saw this technique in the the example finalize() method shown earlier in the chapter: that method invoked super.finalize() to run its superclass finalization method.

Don't confuse the use of super to invoke an overridden method with the super() method call used in constructor methods to invoke a superclass constructor. Although they both use the same keyword, these are two entirely different syntaxes. In particular, you can use super to invoke an overridden method anywhere in the overriding method, while you can use super() only to invoke a superclass constructor as the very first statement of a constructor.

It is also important to remember that super can be used only to invoke an overridden method from within the class that overrides it. Given an Ellipse object e, there is no way for a program that uses an object (with or without the super syntax) to invoke the area() method defined by the Circle class on this object.

I've already explained that class methods can shadow class methods in superclasses, but cannot override them. The preferred way to invoke class methods is to include the name of the class in the invocation. If you do not do this, however, you can use the super syntax to invoke a shadowed class method, just as you would invoke an instance method or refer to a shadowed field.

Data Hiding and Encapsulation

We started this chapter by describing a class as "a collection of data and methods." One of the important object-oriented techniques we haven't discussed so far is hiding the data within the class and making it available only through the methods.

This technique is known as *encapsulation* because it seals the data (and internal methods) safely inside the "capsule" of the class, where it can be accessed only by trusted users (i.e., by the methods of the class).

Why would you want to do this? The most important reason is to hide the internal implementation details of your class. If you prevent programmers from relying on those details, you can safely modify the implementation without worrying that you will break existing code that uses the class.

Another reason for encapsulation is to protect your class against accidental or willful stupidity. A class often contains a number of interdependent fields that must be in a consistent state. If you allow a programmer (including yourself) to manipulate those fields directly, he may change one field without changing important related fields, thus leaving the class in an inconsistent state. If, instead, he has to call a method to change the field, that method can be sure to do everything necessary to keep the state consistent. Similarly, if a class defines certain methods for internal use only, hiding these methods prevents users of the class from calling them.

Here's another way to think about encapsulation: when all the data for a class is hidden, the methods define the only possible operations that can be performed on objects of that class. Once you have carefully tested and debugged your methods, you can be confident that the class will work as expected. On the other hand, if all the fields of the class can be directly manipulated, the number of possibilities you have to test becomes unmanageable.

There are other reasons to hide fields and methods of a class, as well:

*   Internal fields and methods that are visible outside the class just clutter up the API. Keeping visible fields to a minimum keeps your class tidy and therefore easier to use and understand.

*   If a field or method is visible to the users of your class, you have to document it. Save yourself time and effort by hiding it instead.

Access Control

All the fields and methods of a class can always be used within the body of the class itself. Java defines access control rules that restrict members of a class from being used outside the class. In an number of examples in this chapter, you've seen the `public` modifier used in field and method declarations. This `public` keyword, along with `protected` and `private`, are *access control modifiers*; they specify the access rules for the field or method.

Access to packages

A package is always accessible to code defined within the package. Whether it is accessible to code from other packages depends on the way the package is deployed on the host system. When the class files that comprise a package are stored in a directory, for example, a user must have read access to the directory and the files within it in order to have access to the package. Package access is not part of the Java language itself. Access control is usually done at the level of classes and members of classes instead.

Access to classes

By default, top-level classes are accessible within the package in which they are defined. However, if a top-level class is declared public, it is accessible everywhere (or everywhere that the package itself is accessible). The reason that we've restricted these statements to top-level classes is that, as we'll see later in this chapter, classes can also be defined as members of other classes. Because these inner classes are members of a class, they obey the member access-control rules.

Access to members

As I've already said, the members of a class are always accessible within the body of the class. By default, members are also accessible throughout the package in which the class is defined. This implies that classes placed in the same package should trust each other with their internal implementation details.* This default level of access is often called *package access*. It is only one of four possible levels of access. The other three levels of access are defined by the public, protected, and private modifiers. Here is some example code that uses these modifiers:

```
public class Laundromat {           // People can use this class.
    private Laundry[] dirty;        // They cannot use this internal field,
    public void wash() { ... }      // but they can use these public methods
    public void dry() { ... }       // to manipulate the internal field.
}
```

Here are the access rules that apply to members of a class:

- If a member of a class is declared with the public modifier, it means that the member is accessible anywhere the containing class is accessible. This is the least restrictive type of access control.

- If a member of a class is declared private, the member is never accessible, except within the class itself. This is the most restrictive type of access control.

- If a member of a class is declared protected, it is accessible to all classes within the package (the same as the default package accessibility) and also accessible within the body of any subclass of the class, regardless of the package in which that subclass is defined. This is more restrictive than public access, but less restrictive than package access.

- If a member of a class is not declared with any of these modifiers, it has the default package access: it is accessible to code within all classes that are defined in the same package, but inaccessible outside of the package.

protected access requires a little more elaboration. Suppose that the field r of our Circle class had been declared protected and that our PlaneCircle class had been defined in a different package. In this case, every PlaneCircle object inherits the field r, and the PlaneCircle code can use that field as it currently does. Now suppose that PlaneCircle defines the following method to compare the size of a PlaneCircle object to the size of some other Circle object:

---

* C++ programmers might say that all classes within a package are friend-ly to each other.

```
// Return true if this object is bigger than the specified circle
public boolean isBigger(Circle c) {
  return (this.r > c.r);  // If r is protected, c.r is illegal access!
}
```

In this scenario, this method does not compile. The expression `this.r` is perfectly legal, since it accesses a protected field inherited by `PlaneCircle`. Accessing `c.r` is not legal, however, since it is attempting to access a protected field it does not inherit. To make this method legal, we either have to declare `PlaneCircle` in the same package as `Circle` or change the type of the `isBigger()` parameter to be a `PlaneCircle` instead of a `Circle`.

Access control and inheritance

The Java specification states that a subclass inherits all the instance fields and instance methods of its superclass accessible to it. If the subclass is defined in the same package as the superclass, it inherits all non-`private` instance fields and methods. If the subclass is defined in a different package, however, it inherits all `protected` and `public` instance fields and methods. `private` fields and methods are never inherited; neither are class fields or class methods. Finally, constructors are not inherited; they are chained, as described earlier in this chapter.

The statement that a subclass does not inherit the inaccessible fields and methods of its superclass can be a confusing one. It would seem to imply that when you create an instance of a subclass, no memory is allocated for any `private` fields defined by the superclass. This is not the intent of the statement, however. Every instance of a subclass does, in fact, include a complete instance of the superclass within it, including all inaccessible fields and methods. It is simply a matter of terminology. Because the inaccessible fields cannot be used in the subclass, we say they are not inherited. I stated earlier in this section that the members of a class are always accessible within the body of the class. If this statement is to apply to all members of the class, including inherited members, then we have to define "inherited members" to include only those members that are accessible. If you don't care for this definition, you can think of it this way instead:

- A class inherits *all* instance fields and instance methods (but not constructors) of its superclass.

- The body of a class can always access all the fields and methods it declares itself. It can also access the *accessible* fields and members it inherits from its superclass.

Member access summary

Table 3-1 summarizes the member access rules.

Table 3-1: Class Member Accessibility

Accessible to:	Member Visibility			
	public	*protected*	*package*	*private*
Defining class	Yes	Yes	Yes	Yes
Class in same package	Yes	Yes	Yes	No
Subclass in different package	Yes	Yes	No	No
Non-subclass different package	Yes	No	No	No

Here are some simple rules of thumb for using visibility modifiers:

- Use `public` only for methods and constants that form part of the public API of the class. Certain important or frequently used fields can also be `public`, but it is common practice to make fields non-`public` and encapsulate them with `public` accessor methods.

- Use `protected` for fields and methods that aren't required by most programmers using the class, but that may be of interest to anyone creating a subclass as part of a different package. Note that `protected` members are technically part of the exported API of a class. They should be documented and cannot be changed without potentially breaking code that relies on them.

- Use the default package visibility for fields and methods that are internal implementation details, but are used by cooperating classes in the same package. You cannot take real advantage of package visibility unless you use the `package` directive to group your cooperating classes into a package.

- Use `private` for fields and methods that are used only inside the class and should be hidden everywhere else.

If you are not sure whether to use `protected`, package, or `private` accessibility, it is better to start with overly restrictive member access. You can always relax the access restrictions in future versions of your class, if necessary. Doing the reverse is not a good idea because increasing access restrictions is not a backwards-compatible change.

Data Accessor Methods

In the `Circle` example we've been using, we've declared the circle radius to be a `public` field. The `Circle` class is one in which it may well be reasonable to keep that field publicly accessible; it is a simple enough class, with no dependencies between its fields. On the other hand, our current implementation of the class allows a `Circle` object to have a negative radius, and circles with negative radii should simply not exist. As long as the radius is stored in a `public` field, however, any programmer can set the field to any value she wants, no matter how unreasonable. The only solution is to restrict the programmer's direct access to the field and define `public` methods that provide indirect access to the field. Providing `public` methods to read and write a field is not the same as making the field itself `public`. The crucial difference is that methods can perform error checking.

Example 3-4 shows how we might reimplement `Circle` to prevent circles with negative radii. This version of `Circle` declares the r field to be protected and defines accessor methods named getRadius() and setRadius() to read and write the field value while enforcing the restriction on negative radius values. Because the r field is protected, it is directly (and more efficiently) accessible to subclasses.

Example 3-4: The Circle Class Using Data Hiding and Encapsulation

```
package shapes;            // Specify a package for the class

public class Circle {      // The class is still public
  // This is a generally useful constant, so we keep it public
  public static final double PI = 3.14159;

  protected double r;      // Radius is hidden, but visible to subclasses

  // A method to enforce the restriction on the radius
  // This is an implementation detail that may be of interest to subclasses
  protected void checkRadius(double radius) {
    if (radius < 0.0)
      throw new IllegalArgumentException("radius may not be negative.");
  }

  // The constructor method
  public Circle(double r) {
    checkRadius(r);
    this.r = r;
  }

  // Public data accessor methods
  public double getRadius() { return r; }
  public void setRadius(double r) {
    checkRadius(r);
    this.r = r;
  }

  // Methods to operate on the instance field
  public double area() { return PI * r * r; }
  public double circumference() { return 2 * PI * r; }
}
```

We have defined the `Circle` class within a package named shapes. Since r is protected, any other classes in the shapes package have direct access to that field and can set it however they like. The assumption here is that all classes within the shapes package were written by the same author or a closely cooperating group of authors, and that the classes all trust each other not to abuse their privileged level of access to each other's implementation details.

Finally, the code that enforces the restriction against negative radius values is itself placed within a protected method, checkRadius(). Although users of the `Circle` class cannot call this method, subclasses of the class can call it and even override it if they want to change the restrictions on the radius.

Note particularly the getRadius() and setRadius() methods of Example 3-4. It is almost universal in Java that data accessor methods begin with the prefixes "get" and "set." If the field being accessed is of type boolean, however, the get()

method may be replaced with an equivalent method that begins with "is." For example, the accessor method for a boolean field named readable is typically called isReadable() instead of getReadable(). In the programming conventions of the JavaBeans component model (covered in Chapter 6, *JavaBeans*), a hidden field with one or more data accessor methods whose names begin with "get," "is," or "set" is called a *property*. An interesting way to study a complex class is to look at the set of properties it defines. Properties are particularly common in the AWT and Swing APIs, which are covered in *Java Foundation Classes in a Nutshell* (O'Reilly).

Abstract Classes and Methods

In Example 3-4, we declared our Circle class to be part of a package named shapes. Suppose we plan to implement a number of shape classes: Rectangle, Square, Ellipse, Triangle, and so on. We can give these shape classes our two basic area() and circumference() methods. Now, to make it easy to work with an array of shapes, it would be helpful if all our shape classes had a common superclass, Shape. If we structure our class hierarchy this way, every shape object, regardless of the actual type of shape it represents, can be assigned to variables, fields, or array elements of type Shape. We want the Shape class to encapsulate whatever features all our shapes have in common (e.g., the area() and circumference() methods). But our generic Shape class doesn't represent any real kind of shape, so it cannot define useful implementations of the methods. Java handles this situation with *abstract methods*.

Java lets us define a method without implementing it by declaring the method with the abstract modifier. An abstract method has no body; it simply has a signature definition followed by a semicolon.* Here are the rules about abstract methods and the abstract classes that contain them:

- Any class with an abstract method is automatically abstract itself and must be declared as such.

- An abstract class cannot be instantiated.

- A subclass of an abstract class can be instantiated only if it overrides each of the abstract methods of its superclass and provides an implementation (i.e., a method body) for all of them. Such a class is often called a *concrete* subclass, to emphasize the fact that it is not abstract.

- If a subclass of an abstract class does not implement all the abstract methods it inherits, that subclass is itself abstract.

- static, private, and final methods cannot be abstract, since these types of methods cannot be overridden by a subclass. Similarly, a final class cannot contain any abstract methods.

---

* An abstract method in Java is something like a pure virtual function in C++ (i.e., a virtual function that is declared = 0). In C++, a class that contains a pure virtual function is called an abstract class and cannot be instantiated. The same is true of Java classes that contain abstract methods.

- A class can be declared abstract even if it does not actually have any abstract methods. Declaring such a class abstract indicates that the implementation is somehow incomplete and is meant to serve as a superclass for one or more subclasses that will complete the implementation. Such a class cannot be instantiated.

There is an important feature of the rules of abstract methods. If we define the Shape class to have abstract area() and circumference() methods, any subclass of Shape is required to provide implementations of these methods so it can be instantiated. In other words, every Shape object is guaranteed to have implementations of these methods defined. Example 3-5 shows how this might work. It defines an abstract Shape class and two concrete subclasses of it.

Example 3-5: An Abstract Class and Concrete Subclasses

```
public abstract class Shape {
    public abstract double area();            // Abstract methods: note
    public abstract double circumference();   // semicolon instead of body.
}

class Circle extends Shape {
    public static final double PI = 3.14159265358979323846;
    protected double r;                       // Instance data
    public Circle(double r) { this.r = r; }   // Constructor
    public double getRadius() { return r; }   // Accessor
    public double area() { return PI*r*r; }   // Implementations of
    public double circumference() { return 2*PI*r; } // abstract methods.
}

class Rectangle extends Shape {
    protected double w, h;                     // Instance data
    public Rectangle(double w, double h) {     // Constructor
        this.w = w;  this.h = h;
    }
    public double getWidth() { return w; }     // Accessor method
    public double getHeight() { return h; }    // Another accessor
    public double area() { return w*h; }       // Implementations of
    public double circumference() { return 2*(w + h); } // abstract methods.
}
```

Each abstract method in Shape has a semicolon right after its parentheses. There are no curly braces, and no method body is defined. Using the classes defined in Example 3-5, we can now write code like this:

```
Shape[] shapes = new Shape[3];        // Create an array to hold shapes
shapes[0] = new Circle(2.0);          // Fill in the array
shapes[1] = new Rectangle(1.0, 3.0);
shapes[2] = new Rectangle(4.0, 2.0);

double total_area = 0;
for(int i = 0; i < shapes.length; i++)
    total_area += shapes[i].area();   // Compute the area of the shapes
```

There are two important points to notice here:

- Subclasses of Shape can be assigned to elements of an array of Shape. No cast is necessary. This is another example of a widening reference type conversion (discussed in Chapter 2).

- You can invoke the `area()` and `circumference()` methods for any `Shape` object, even though the `Shape` class does not define a body for these methods. When you do this, the method to be invoked is found using dynamic method lookup, so the area of a circle is computed using the method defined by `Circle`, and the area of a rectangle is computed using the method defined by `Rectangle`.

Interfaces

Let's extend our `shapes` package further. Suppose we now want to implement a number of shapes that not only know their sizes, but also know the position of their center point in the Cartesian coordinate plane. One way to do this is to define an abstract `CenteredShape` class and then implement various subclasses of it, such as `CenteredCircle`, `CenteredRectangle`, and so on.

But we also want these positionable shape classes to support the `area()` and `circumference()` methods we've already defined, without reimplementing these methods. So, for example, we'd like to define `CenteredCircle` as a subclass of `Circle`, so that it inherits `area()` and `circumference()`. But a class in Java can have only one immediate superclass. If `CenteredCircle` extends `Circle`, it cannot also extend the abstract `CenteredShape` class!*

Java's solution to this problem is called an interface. Although a Java class can extend only a single superclass, it can *implement* any number of interfaces.

Defining an Interface

An interface is a reference type that is closely related to a class. Almost everything you've read so far in this book about classes applies equally to interfaces. Defining an interface is a lot like defining an abstract class, except that the keywords `abstract` and `class` are replaced with the keyword `interface`. When you define an interface, you are creating a new reference type, just as you are when you define a class. As its name implies, an *interface* specifies an interface, or API, for certain functionality. It does not define any implementation of that API, however. There are a number of restrictions that apply to the members of an interface:

- An interface contains no implementation whatsoever. All methods of an interface are implicitly `abstract`, even if the `abstract` modifier is omitted. Interface methods have no implementation; a semicolon appears in place of the method body. Because interfaces can contain only `abstract` methods, and class methods cannot be abstract, the methods of an interface must all be instance methods.

- An interface defines a public API. All methods of an interface are implicitly `public`, even if the `public` modifier is omitted. It is an error to define a `protected` or `private` method in an interface.

---

* C++ allows classes to have more than one superclass, using a technique known as multiple inheritance. Multiple inheritance adds a lot of complexity to a language; Java supports what many believe is a more elegant solution.

- Although a class defines data and methods that operate on that data, an interface cannot define instance fields. Fields are an implementation detail, and an interface is a pure specification without any implementation. The only fields allowed in an interface definition are constants that are declared both `static` and `final`.

- An interface cannot be instantiated, so it does not define a constructor.

Example 3-6 shows the definition of an interface named `Centered`. This interface defines the methods a `Shape` subclass should implement if it knows the x,y coordinate of its center point.

Example 3-6: An Interface Definition

```
public interface Centered {
  public void setCenter(double x, double y);
  public double getCenterX();
  public double getCenterY();
}
```

Implementing an Interface

Just as a class uses `extends` to specify its superclass, it can use `implements` to name one or more interfaces it supports. `implements` is a Java keyword that can appear in a class declaration following the `extends` clause. `implements` should be followed by the name or names of the interface(s) the class implements, with multiple names separated by commas.

When a class declares an interface in its `implements` clause, it is saying that it provides an implementation (i.e., a body) for each method of that interface. If a class implements an interface but does not provide an implementation for every interface method, it inherits those unimplemented `abstract` methods from the interface and must itself be declared `abstract`. If a class implements more than one interface, it must implement every method of each interface it implements (or be declared `abstract`).

Example 3-7 shows how we can define a `CenteredRectangle` class that extends our `Rectangle` class and implements the `Centered` interface we defined in Example 3-6.

Example 3-7: Implementing an Interface

```
public class CenteredRectangle extends Rectangle implements Centered {
  // New instance fields
  private double cx, cy;

  // A constructor
  public CenteredRectangle(double cx, double cy, double w, double h) {
    super(w, h);
    this.cx = cx;
    this.cy = cy;
  }

  // We inherit all the methods of Rectangle, but must
  // provide implementations of all the Centered methods.
  public void setCenter(double x, double y) { cx = x; cy = y; }
```

Example 3-7: Implementing an Interface (continued)

```
public double getCenterX() { return cx; }
public double getCenterY() { return cy; }
}
```

As I noted earlier, constants can appear in an interface definition. Any class that implements the interface inherits the constants and can use them as if they were defined directly in the class. There is no need to prefix them with the name of the interface or provide any kind of implementation of the constants. When you have a set of constants used by more than one class (e.g., a port number and other protocol constants used by a client and server), it can be convenient to define the necessary constants in an interface that contains no methods. Then, any class that wants to use those constants needs only to declare that it implements the interface. `java.io.ObjectStreamConstants` is just such an interface.

Using Interfaces

Suppose we implement CenteredCircle and CenteredSquare just as we implemented CenteredRectangle in Example 3-7. Since each class extends Shape, instances of the classes can be treated as instances of the Shape class, as we saw earlier. Since each class implements Centered, instances can also be treated as instances of that type. The following code demonstrates both techniques:

```
Shape[] shapes = new Shape[3];              // Create an array to hold shapes

// Create some centered shapes, and store them in the Shape[]
// No cast necessary: these are all widening conversions
shapes[0] = new CenteredCircle(1.0, 1.0, 1.0);
shapes[1] = new CenteredSquare(2.5, 2, 3);
shapes[2] = new CenteredRectangle(2.3, 4.5, 3, 4);

// Compute average area of the shapes and average distance from the origin
double totalArea = 0;
double totalDistance = 0;
for(int i = 0; i < shapes.length; i++) {
  totalArea += shapes[i].area();          // Compute the area of the shapes
  if (shapes[i] instanceof Centered) { // The shape is a Centered shape
    // Note the required cast from Shape to Centered (no cast
    // would be required to go from CenteredSquare to Centered, however).
    Centered c = (Centered) shapes[i]; // Assign it to a Centered variable
    double cx = c.getCenterX();          // Get coordinates of the center
    double cy = c.getCenterY();          // Compute distance from origin
    totalDistance += Math.sqrt(cx*cx + cy*cy);
  }
}
System.out.println("Average area: " + totalArea/shapes.length);
System.out.println("Average distance: " + totalDistance/shapes.length);
```

This example demonstrates that interfaces are data types in Java, just like classes. When a class implements an interface, instances of that class can be assigned to variables of the interface type. Don't interpret this example, however, to imply that you must assign a CenteredRectangle object to a Centered variable before you can invoke the setCenter() method or to a Shape variable before you can invoke the area() method. CenteredRectangle defines setCenter() and inherits area() from its Rectangle superclass, so you can always invoke these methods.

When to Use Interfaces

When defining an abstract type (e.g., Shape) that you expect to have many sub-types (e.g., Circle, Rectangle, Square), you are often faced with a choice between interfaces and abstract classes. Since they have similar features, it is not always clear when to use one over the other.

An interface is useful because any class can implement it, even if that class extends some entirely unrelated superclass. But an interface is a pure API specification and contains no implementation. If an interface has numerous methods, it can become tedious to implement the methods over and over, especially when much of the implementation is duplicated by each implementing class.

On the other hand, a class that extends an abstract class cannot extend any other class, which can cause design difficulties in some situations. However, an abstract class does not need to be entirely abstract; it can contain a partial implementation that subclasses can take advantage of. In some cases, numerous subclasses can rely on default method implementations provided by an abstract class.

Another important difference between interfaces and abstract classes has to do with compatibility. If you define an interface as part of a public API and then later add a new method to the interface, you break any classes that implemented the previous version of the interface. If you use an abstract clas, however, you can safely add nonabstract methods to that class without requiring modifications to existing classes that extend the abstract class.

In some situations, it will be clear that an interface or an abstract class is the right design choice. In other cases, a common design pattern is to use both. First, define the type as a totally abstract interface. Then create an abstract class that implements the interface and provides useful default implementations subclasses can take advantage of. For example:

```
// Here is a basic interface. It represents a shape that fits inside
// of a rectangular bounding box. Any class that wants to serve as a
// RectangularShape can implement these methods from scratch.
public interface RectangularShape {
   public void setSize(double width, double height);
   public void setPosition(double x, double y);
   public void translate(double dx, double dy);
   public double area();
   public boolean isInside();
}

// Here is a partial implementation of that interface. Many
// implementations may find this a useful starting point.
public abstract class AbstractRectangularShape implements RectangularShape {
   // The position and size of the shape
   protected double x, y, w, h;

   // Default implementations of some of the interface methods
   public void setSize(double width, double height) { w = width; h = height; }
   public void setPosition(double x, double y) { this.x = x; this.y = y; }
   public void translate (double dx, double dy) { x += dx; y += dy; }
}
```

Implementing Multiple Interfaces

Suppose we want shape objects that can be positioned in terms of not only their center points, but also their upper-right corners. And suppose we also want shapes that can be scaled larger and smaller. Remember that although a class can extend only a single superclass, it can implement any number of interfaces. Assuming we have defined appropriate UpperRightCornered and Scalable interfaces, we can declare a class as follows:

```
public class SuperDuperSquare extends Shape
       implements Centered, UpperRightCornered, Scalable {
    // class members omitted here.
}
```

When a class implements more than one interface, it simply means that it must provide implementations for all abstract methods in all its interfaces.

Extending Interfaces

Interfaces can have subinterfaces, just as classes can have subclasses. A subinterface inherits all the abstract methods and constants of its superinterface and can define new abstract methods and constants. Interfaces are different from classes in one very important way, however: an interface can have an extends clause that lists more than one superinterface. For example, here are some interfaces that extend other interfaces:

```
public interface Positionable extends Centered {
  public void setUpperRightCorner(double x, double y);
  public double getUpperRightX();
  public double getUpperRightY();
}
public interface Transformable extends Scalable, Translatable, Rotatable {}
public interface SuperShape extends Positionable, Transformable {}
```

An interface that extends more than one interface inherits all the abstract methods and constants from each of those interfaces and can define its own additional abstract methods and constants. A class that implements such an interface must implement the abstract methods defined directly by the interface, as well as all the abstract methods inherited from all the superinterfaces.

Marker Interfaces

Sometimes it is useful to define an interface that is entirely empty. A class can implement this interface simply by naming it in its implements clause without having to implement any methods. In this case, any instances of the class become valid instances of the interface. Java code can check whether an object is an instance of the interface using the instanceof operator, so this technique is a useful way to provide additional information about an object. The Cloneable interface in java.lang is an example of this type of *marker interface*. It defines no methods, but identifies the class as one that allows its internal state to be cloned by the clone() method of the Object class. As of Java 1.1, java.io.Serializable is another such marker interface. Given an arbitrary object, you can determine whether it has a working clone() method with code like this:

```
Object o;      // Initialized elsewhere
Object copy;
if (o instanceof Cloneable) copy = o.clone();
else copy = null;
```

Inner Class Overview

The classes and interfaces we have seen so far in this chapter have all been top-level classes (i.e., they are direct members of packages, not nested within any other classes). Starting in Java 1.1, however, there are four other types of classes, loosely known as *inner classes*, that can be defined in a Java program. Used correctly, inner classes are an elegant and powerful feature of the Java language. These four types of classes are summarized here:

Static member classes
> A static member class is a class (or interface) defined as a static member of another class. A static method is called a class method, so, by analogy, we could call this type of inner class a "class class," but this terminology would obviously be confusing. A static member class behaves much like an ordinary top-level class, except that it can access the static members of the class that contains it. Interfaces can be defined as static members of classes.

Member classes
> A member class is also defined as a member of an enclosing class, but is not declared with the static modifier. This type of inner class is analogous to an instance method or field. An instance of a member class is always associated with an instance of the enclosing class, and the code of a member class has access to all the fields and methods (both static and non-static) of its enclosing class. There are several features of Java syntax that exist specifically to work with the enclosing instance of a member class. Interfaces can only be defined as static members of a class, not as non-static members.

Local classes
> A local class is a class defined within a block of Java code. Like a local variable, a local class is visible only within that block. Although local classes are not member classes, they are still defined within an enclosing class, so they share many of the features of member classes. Additionally, however, a local class can access any final local variables or parameters that are accessible in the scope of the block that defines the class. Interfaces cannot be defined locally.

Anonymous classes
> An anonymous class is a kind of local class that has no name; it combines the syntax for class definition with the syntax for object instantiation. While a local class definition is a Java statement, an anonymous class definition (and instantiation) is a Java expression, so it can appear as part of a larger expression, such as method invocation. Interfaces cannot be defined anonymously.

Java programmers have not reached a consensus on the appropriate names for the various kinds of inner classes. Thus, you may find them referred to by different names in different situations. In particular, static member classes are sometimes called "nested top-level" classes, and the term "nested classes" may refer to all types of inner classes. The term "inner classes" is itself overloaded and sometimes refers specifically to member classes. On other occasions, "inner classes" refers to member classes, local classes, and anonymous classes, but not static member classes. In this book, I use "inner class" to mean any class other than a standard top-level class and the names shown previously to refer to the individual types of inner classes.

Static Member Classes

A *static member class* (or interface) is much like a regular top-level class (or interface). For convenience, however, it is nested within another class or interface. Example 3-8 shows a helper interface defined as a static member of a containing class. The example also shows how this interface is used both within the class that contains it and by external classes. Note the use of its hierarchical name in the external class.

Example 3-8: Defining and Using a Static Member Interface

```
// A class that implements a stack as a linked list
public class LinkedStack {
  // This static member interface defines how objects are linked
  public static interface Linkable {
    public Linkable getNext();
    public void setNext(Linkable node);
  }

  // The head of the list is a Linkable object
  Linkable head;

  // Method bodies omitted
  public void push(Linkable node) { ... }
  public Object pop() { ... }
}

// This class implements the static member interface
class LinkableInteger implements LinkedStack.Linkable {
  // Here's the node's data and constructor
  int i;
  public LinkableInteger(int i) { this.i = i; }

  // Here are the data and methods required to implement the interface
  LinkedStack.Linkable next;
  public LinkedStack.Linkable getNext() { return next; }
  public void setNext(LinkedStack.Linkable node) { next = node; }
}
```

Features of Static Member Classes

A static member class or interface is defined as a static member of a containing class, making it analogous to the class fields and methods that are also declared static. Like a class method, a static member class is not associated with any instance of the containing class (i.e., there is no this object). A static member class does, however, have access to all the static members (including any other static member classes and interfaces) of its containing class. A static member class can use any other static member without qualifying its name with the name of the containing class.

A static member class has access to all static members of its containing class, including private members. The reverse is true as well: the methods of the containing class have access to all members of a static member class, including the private members. A static member class even has access to all the members of any other static member classes, including the private members of those classes.

Since static member classes are themselves class members, a static member class can be declared with its own access control modifiers. These modifiers have the same meanings for static member classes as they do for other members of a class. In Example 3-8, the Linkable interface is declared public, so it can be implemented by any class that is interested in being stored on a LinkedStack.

Restrictions on Static Member Classes

A static member class cannot have the same name as any of its enclosing classes. In addition, static member classes and interfaces can be defined only within top-level classes and other static member classes and interfaces. This is actually part of a larger prohibition against static members of any sort within member, local, and anonymous classes.

New Syntax for Static Member Classes

In code outside of the containing class, a static member class or interface is named by combining the name of the outer class with the name of the inner class (e.g., LinkedStack.Linkable). You can use the import directive to import a static member class:

```
import LinkedStack.Linkable;  // Import a specific inner class
import LinkedStack.*;         // Import all inner classes of LinkedStack
```

Importing inner classes is not recommended, however, because it obscures the fact that the inner class is tightly associated with its containing class.

Member Classes

A *member class* is a class that is declared as a non-static member of a containing class. If a static member class is analogous to a class field or class method, a member class is analogous to an instance field or instance method. Example 3-9 shows how a member class can be defined and used. This example extends the previous LinkedStack example to allow enumeration of the elements on the stack by defining an enumerate() method that returns an implementation of the java.util.Enumeration interface. The implementation of this interface is defined as a member class.

Example 3-9: An Enumeration Implemented as a Member Class

```
public class LinkedStack {
  // Our static member interface; body omitted here...
  public static interface Linkable { ... }
```

Example 3-9: An Enumeration Implemented as a Member Class (continued)

```
// The head of the list
private Linkable head;

// Method bodies omitted here
public void push(Linkable node) { ... }
public Linkable pop() { ... }

// This method returns an Enumeration object for this LinkedStack
public java.util.Enumeration enumerate() { return new Enumerator(); }

// Here is the implementation of the Enumeration interface,
// defined as a member class.
protected class Enumerator implements java.util.Enumeration {
  Linkable current;
  // The constructor uses the private head field of the containing class
  public Enumerator() { current = head; }
  public boolean hasMoreElements() {  return (current != null); }
  public Object nextElement() {
    if (current == null) throw new java.util.NoSuchElementException();
    Object value = current;
    current = current.getNext();
    return value;
  }
}
}
```

Notice how the Enumerator class is nested within the LinkedStack class. Since Enumerator is a helper class used only within LinkedStack, there is a real elegance to having it defined so close to where it is used by the containing class.

Features of Member Classes

Like instance fields and instance methods, every member class is associated with an instance of the class within which it is defined (i.e., every instance of a member class is associated with an instance of the containing class). This means that the code of a member class has access to all the instance fields and instance methods (as well as the static members) of the containing class, including any that are declared private.

This crucial feature is illustrated in Example 3-9. Here is the body of the Linked-Stack.Enumerator() constructor again:

```
current = head;
```

This single line of code sets the current field of the inner class to the value of the head field of the containing class. The code works as shown, even though head is declared as a private field in the containing class.

A member class, like any member of a class, can be assigned one of three visibility levels: public, protected, or private. If none of these visibility modifiers is specified, the default package visibility is used. In Example 3-9, the Enumerator class is declared protected, so it is inaccessible to code (in a different package) using the LinkedStack class, but accessible to any class that subclasses LinkedStack.

Restrictions on Member Classes

There are three important restrictions on member classes:

- A member class cannot have the same name as any containing class or package. This is an important rule, and one not shared by fields and methods.

- Member classes cannot contain any `static` fields, methods, or classes (with the exception of constant fields declared both `static` and `final`). `static` fields, methods, and classes are top-level constructs not associated with any particular object, while every member class is associated with an instance of its enclosing class. Defining a `static` top-level member within a non-top-level member class simply promotes confusion and bad programming style, so you are required to define all static members within a top-level or static member class or interface.

- Interfaces cannot be defined as member classes. An interface cannot be instantiated, so there is no object to associate with an instance of the enclosing class. If you declare an interface as a member of a class, the interface is implicitly `static`, making it a static member class.

New Syntax for Member Classes

The most important feature of a member class is that it can access the instance fields and methods in its containing object. We saw this in the `LinkedStack.Enumerator()` constructor of Example 3-9:

```
public Enumerator() { current = head; }
```

In this example, head is a field of the `LinkedStack` class, and we assign it to the current field of the `Enumerator` class. The current code works, but what if we want to make these references explicit? We could try code like this:

```
public Enumerator() { this.current = this.head; }
```

This code does not compile, however. `this.current` is fine; it is an explicit reference to the current field in the newly created `Enumerator` object. It is the `this.head` expression that causes the problem; it refers to a field named head in the `Enumerator` object. Since there is no such field, the compiler generates an error. To solve this problem, Java defines a special syntax for explicitly referring to the containing instance of the `this` object. Thus, if we want to be explicit in our constructor, we can use the following syntax:

```
public Enumerator() { this.current = LinkedStack.this.head; }
```

The general syntax is *classname*.this, where *classname* is the name of a containing class. Note that member classes can themselves contain member classes, nested to any depth. Since no member class can have the same name as any containing class, however, the use of the enclosing class name prepended to this is a perfectly general way to refer to any containing instance. This syntax is needed only when referring to a member of a containing class that is hidden by a member of the same name in the member class.

Accessing superclass members of the containing class

When a class shadows or overrides a member of its superclass, you can use the keyword super to refer to the hidden member. This super syntax can be extended to work with member classes as well. On the rare occasion when you need to refer to a shadowed field f or an overridden method m of a superclass of a containing class C, use the following expressions:

```
C.super.f
C.super.m()
```

This syntax was not implemented by Java 1.1 compilers, but it works correctly as of Java 1.2.

Specifying the containing instance

As we've seen, every instance of a member class is associated with an instance of its containing class. Look again at our definition of the enumerate() method in Example 3-9:

```
public Enumeration enumerate() { return new Enumerator(); }
```

When a member class constructor is invoked like this, the new instance of the member class is automatically associated with the this object. This is what you would expect to happen and exactly what you want to occur in most cases. Occasionally, however, you may want to specify the containing instance explicitly when instantiating a member class. You can do this by preceding the new operator with a reference to the containing instance. Thus, the enumerate() method shown above is shorthand for the following:

```
public Enumeration enumerate() { return this.new Enumerator(); }
```

Let's pretend we didn't define an enumerate() method for LinkedStack. In this case, the code to obtain an Enumerator object for a given LinkedStack object might look like this:

```
LinkedStack stack = new LinkedStack();    // Create an empty stack
Enumeration e = stack.new Enumerator();    // Create an Enumeration for it
```

The containing instance implicitly specifies the name of the containing class; it is a syntax error to explicitly specify that containing class:

```
Enumeration e = stack.new LinkedStack.Enumerator(); // Syntax error
```

There is one other special piece of Java syntax that specifies an enclosing instance for a member class explicitly. Before we consider it, however, let me point out that you should rarely, if ever, need to use this syntax. It is one of the pathological cases that snuck into the language along with all the elegant features of inner classes.

As strange as it may seem, it is possible for a top-level class to extend a member class. This means that the subclass does not have a containing instance, but its superclass does. When the subclass constructor invokes the superclass constructor, it must specify the containing instance. It does this by prepending the containing instance and a period to the super keyword. If we had not declared our

Enumerator class to be a protected member of LinkedStack, we could subclass it. Although it is not clear why we would want to do so, we could write code like the following:

```
// A top-level class that extends a member class
class SpecialEnumerator extends LinkedStack.Enumerator {
    // The constructor must explicitly specify a containing instance
    // when invoking the superclass constructor.
    public SpecialEnumerator(LinkedStack s) { s.super(); }
      // Rest of class omitted...
}
```

Scope Versus Inheritance for Member Classes

We've just noted that a top-level class can extend a member class. With the introduction of member classes, there are two separate hierarchies that must be considered for any class. The first is the *class hierarchy*, from superclass to subclass, that defines the fields and methods a member class inherits. The second is the *containment hierarchy*, from containing class to contained class, that defines a set of fields and methods that are in the scope of (and are therefore accessible to) the member class.

The two hierarchies are entirely distinct from each other; it is important that you do not confuse them. This should not be a problem if you refrain from creating naming conflicts, where a field or method in a superclass has the same name as a field or method in a containing class. If such a naming conflict does arise, however, the inherited field or method takes precedence over the field or method of the same name in the containing class. This behavior is logical: when a class inherits a field or method, that field or method effectively becomes part of that class. Therefore, inherited fields and methods are in the scope of the class that inherits them and take precedence over fields and methods by the same name in enclosing scopes.

Because this can be quite confusing, Java does not leave it to chance that you get it right. Whenever there is a naming conflict between an inherited field or method and a field or method in a containing class, Java requires that you *explicitly* specify which one you mean. For example, if a member class B inherits a field named x and is contained within a class A that also defines a field named x, you must use this.x to specify the inherited field and A.this.x to specify the field in the containing class. Any attempt to use the field x without an explicit specification of the desired instance causes a compilation error.

A good way to prevent confusion between the class hierarchy and the containment hierarchy is to avoid deep containment hierarchies. If a class is nested more than two levels deep, it is probably going to cause more confusion than it is worth. Furthermore, if a class has a deep class hierarchy (i.e., it has many superclass ancestors), consider defining it as a top-level class, rather than as a member class.

Local Classes

A *local class* is declared locally within a block of Java code, rather than as a member of a class. Typically, a local class is defined within a method, but it can also be defined within a static initializer or instance initializer of a class. Because all blocks of Java code appear within class definitions, all local classes are nested within containing classes. For this reason, local classes share many of the features of member classes. It is usually more appropriate, however, to think of them as an entirely separate kind of inner class. A local class has approximately the same relationship to a member class as a local variable has to an instance variable of a class.

The defining characteristic of a local class is that it is local to a block of code. Like a local variable, a local class is valid only within the scope defined by its enclosing block. If a member class is used only within a single method of its containing class, for example, there is usually no reason it cannot be coded as a local class, rather than a member class. Example 3-10 shows how we can modify the enumerate() method of the LinkedStack class so it defines Enumerator as a local class instead of a member class. By doing this, we move the definition of the class even closer to where it is used and hopefully improve the clarity of the code even further. For brevity, Example 3-10 shows only the enumerate() method, not the entire LinkedStack class that contains it.

Example 3-10: Defining and Using a Local Class

```
// This method creates and returns an Enumeration object
public java.util.Enumeration enumerate() {

  // Here's the definition of Enumerator as a local class
  class Enumerator implements java.util.Enumeration {
    Linkable current;
    public Enumerator() { current = head; }
    public boolean hasMoreElements() {  return (current != null); }
    public Object nextElement() {
      if (current == null) throw new java.util.NoSuchElementException();
      Object value = current;
      current = current.getNext();
      return value;
    }
  }

  // Now return an instance of the Enumerator class defined directly above
  return new Enumerator();
}
```

Features of Local Classes

Local classes have the following interesting features:

* Like member classes, local classes are associated with a containing instance, and can access any members, including private members, of the containing class.

- In addition to accessing fields defined by the containing class, local classes can access any local variables, method parameters, or exception parameters that are in the scope of the local method definition and declared final.

Restrictions on Local Classes

Local classes are subject to the following restrictions:

- A local class is visible only within the block that defines it; it can never be used outside that block.

- Local classes cannot be declared public, protected, private, or static. These modifiers are for members of classes; they are not allowed with local variable declarations or local class declarations.

- Like member classes, and for the same reasons, local classes cannot contain static fields, methods, or classes. The only exception is for constants that are declared both static and final.

- Interfaces cannot be defined locally.

- A local class, like a member class, cannot have the same name as any of its enclosing classes.

- As noted earlier, a local class can use the local variables, method parameters, and even exception parameters that are in its scope, but only if those variables or parameters are declared final. This is because the lifetime of an instance of a local class can be much longer than the execution of the method in which the class is defined. For this reason, a local class must have a private internal copy of all local variables it uses (these copies are automatically generated by the compiler). The only way to ensure that the local variable and the private copy are always the same is to insist that the local variable is final.

New Syntax for Local Classes

In Java 1.0, only fields, methods, and classes can be declared final. The addition of local classes in Java 1.1 has required a liberalization in the use of the final modifier. It can now be applied to local variables, method parameters, and even the exception parameter of a catch statement. The meaning of the final modifier remains the same in these new uses: once the local variable or parameter has been assigned a value, that value cannot be changed.

Instances of local classes, like instances of member classes, have an enclosing instance that is implicitly passed to all constructors of the local class. Local classes can use the same this syntax as member classes, to refer explicitly to members of enclosing classes. Because local classes are never visible outside the blocks that define them, however, there is never a need to use the new and super syntax used by member classes to specify the enclosing instance explicitly.

Scope of a Local Class

In discussing member classes, we saw that a member class can access any members inherited from superclasses and any members defined by its containing classes. The same is true for local classes, but local classes can also access final local variables and parameters. The following code illustrates the many fields and variables that may be accessible to a local class:

```
class A { protected char a = 'a'; }
class B { protected char b = 'b'; }

public class C extends A {
  private char c = 'c';          // Private fields visible to local class
  public static char d = 'd';
  public void createLocalObject(final char e)
  {
    final char f = 'f';
    int i = 0;                    // i not final; not usable by local class
    class Local extends B
    {
      char g = 'g';
      public void printVars()
      {
        // All of these fields and variables are accessible to this class
        System.out.println(g);   // (this.g) g is a field of this class
        System.out.println(f);   // f is a final local variable
        System.out.println(e);   // e is a final local parameter
        System.out.println(d);   // (C.this.d) d -- field of containing class
        System.out.println(c);   // (C.this.c) c -- field of containing class
        System.out.println(b);   // b is inherited by this class
        System.out.println(a);   // a is inherited by the containing class
      }
    }
    Local l = new Local();        // Create an instance of the local class
    l.printVars();                // and call its printVars() method.
  }
}
```

Local Classes and Local Variable Scope

A local variable is defined within a block of code, which defines its scope. A local variable ceases to exist outside of its scope. Java is a *lexically scoped* language, which means that its concept of scope has to do with the way the source code is written. Any code within the curly braces that define the boundaries of a block can use local variables defined in that block.*

Lexical scoping simply defines a segment of source code within which a variable can be used. It is common, however, to think of a scope as a temporal scope—to think of a local variable as existing from the time the Java interpreter begins executing the block until the time the interpreter exits the block. This is usually a reasonable way to think about local variables and their scope.

---

* This section covers advanced material; first-time readers may want to skip it for now and return to it later.

The introduction of local classes confuses the picture, however, because local classes can use local variables, and instances of a local class can have a lifetime much longer than the time it takes the interpreter to execute the block of code. In other words, if you create an instance of a local class, the instance does not automatically go away when the interpreter finishes executing the block that defines the class, as shown in the following code:

```
public class Weird {
  // A static member interface used below
  public static interface IntHolder { public int getValue(); }

  public static void main(String[] args) {
    IntHolder[] holders = new IntHolder[10];   // An array to hold 10 objects
    for(int i = 0; i < 10; i++) {              // Loop to fill the array up
      final int fi = i;                        // A final local variable
      class MyIntHolder implements IntHolder { // A local class
          public int getValue() { return fi; } // It uses the final variable
      }
      holders[i] = new MyIntHolder();          // Instantiate the local class
    }

    // The local class is now out of scope, so we can't use it. But
    // we've got ten valid instances of that class in our array. The local
    // variable fi is not in our scope here, but it is still in scope for
    // the getValue() method of each of those ten objects. So call getValue()
    // for each object and print it out. This prints the digits 0 to 9.
    for(int i = 0; i < 10; i++) System.out.println(holders[i].getValue());
  }
}
```

The behavior of the previous program is pretty surprising. To make sense of it, remember that the lexical scope of the methods of a local class has nothing to do with when the interpreter enters and exits the block of code that defines the local class. Here's another way to think about it: each instance of a local class has an automatically created private copy of each of the final local variables it uses, so, in effect, it has its own private copy of the scope that existed when it was created.

Anonymous Classes

An *anonymous class* is a local class without a name. An anonymous class is defined and instantiated in a single succinct expression using the new operator. While a local class definition is a statement in a block of Java code, an anonymous class definition is an expression, which means that it can be included as part of a larger expression, such as a method call. When a local class is used only once, consider using anonymous class syntax, which places the definition and use of the class in exactly the same place.

Consider Example 3-11, which shows the Enumeration class implemented as an anonymous class within the enumerate() method of the LinkedStack class. Compare it with Example 3-10, which shows the same class implemented as a local class.

Example 3-11: An Enumeration Implemented with an Anonymous Class

```
public java.util.Enumeration enumerate() {
  // The anonymous class is defined as part of the return statement
  return new java.util.Enumeration() {
    Linkable current;
    { current = head; } // Replace constructor with an instance initializer
    public boolean hasMoreElements() {  return (current != null); }
    public Object nextElement() {
      if (current == null) throw new java.util.NoSuchElementException();
      Object value = current;
      current = current.getNext();
      return value;
    }
  };  // Note the required semicolon: it terminates the return statement
}
```

One common use for an anonymous class is to provide a simple implementation of an adapter class. An *adapter class* is one that defines code that is invoked by some other object. Take, for example, the list() method of the java.io.File class. This method lists the files in a directory. Before it returns the list, though, it passes the name of each file to a FilenameFilter object you must supply. This FilenameFilter object accepts or rejects each file. When you implement the FilenameFilter interface, you are defining an adapter class for use with the File.list() method. Since the body of such a class is typically quite short, it is easy to define an adapter class as an anonymous class. Here's how you can define a FilenameFilter class to list only those files whose names end with .*java*:

```
File f = new File("/src");      // The directory to list

// Now call the list() method with a single FilenameFilter argument
// Define and instantiate an anonymous implementation of FilenameFilter
// as part of the method invocation expression.
String[] filelist = f.list(new FilenameFilter() {
  public boolean accept(File f, String s) { return s.endsWith(".java"); }
}); // Don't forget the parenthesis and semicolon that end the method call!
```

As you can see, the syntax for defining an anonymous class and creating an instance of that class uses the new keyword, followed by the name of a class and a class body definition in curly braces. If the name following the new keyword is the name of a class, the anonymous class is a subclass of the named class. If the name following new specifies an interface, as in the two previous examples, the anonymous class implements that interface and extends Object. The syntax does not include any way to specify an extends clause, an implements clause, or a name for the class.

Because an anonymous class has no name, it is not possible to define a constructor for it within the class body. This is one of the basic restrictions on anonymous classes. Any arguments you specify between the parentheses following the superclass name in an anonymous class definition are implicitly passed to the superclass constructor. Anonymous classes are commonly used to subclass simple classes that do not take any constructor arguments, so the parentheses in the anonymous class definition syntax are often empty. In the previous examples, each anonymous class implemented an interface and extended Object. Since the Object() constructor takes no arguments, the parentheses were empty in those examples.

Features of Anonymous Classes

One of the most elegant things about anonymous classes is that they allow you to define a one-shot class exactly where it is needed. In addition, anonymous classes have a succinct syntax that reduces clutter in your code.

Restrictions on Anonymous Classes

Because an anonymous class is just a type of local class, anonymous classes and local classes share the same restrictions. An anonymous class cannot define any `static` fields, methods, or classes, except for `static final` constants. Interfaces cannot be defined anonymously, since there is no way to implement an interface without a name. Also, like local classes, anonymous classes cannot be `public`, `private`, `protected`, or `static`.

Since an anonymous class has no name, it is not possible to define a constructor for an anonymous class. If your class requires a constructor, you must use a local class instead. However, you can often use an instance initializer as a substitute for a constructor. In fact, instance initializers were introduced into the language for this very purpose.

The syntax for defining an anonymous class combines definition with instantiation. Thus, using an anonymous class instead of a local class is not appropriate if you need to create more than a single instance of the class each time the containing block is executed.

New Syntax for Anonymous Classes

We've already seen examples of the syntax for defining and instantiating an anonymous class. We can express that syntax more formally as:

```
new class-name ( [ argument-list ] ) { class-body }
```

or:

```
new interface-name () { class-body }
```

As I already mentioned, instance initializers are another specialized piece of Java syntax that was introduced to support anonymous classes. As we discussed earlier in the chapter, an instance initializer is a block of initialization code contained within curly braces inside a class definition. The contents of an instance initializer for a class are automatically inserted into all constructors for the class, including any automatically created default constructor. An anonymous class cannot define a constructor, so it gets a default constructor. By using an instance initializer, you can get around the fact that you cannot define a constructor for an anonymous class.

When to Use an Anonymous Class

As we've discussed, an anonymous class behaves just like a local class and is distinguished from a local class merely in the syntax used to define and instantiate it. In your own code, when you have to choose between using an anonymous class

Object-Oriented

and a local class, the decision often comes down to a matter of style. You should use whichever syntax makes your code clearer. In general, you should consider using an anonymous class instead of a local class if:

- The class has a very short body.

- Only one instance of the class is needed.

- The class is used right after it is defined.

- The name of the class does not make your code any easier to understand.

Anonymous Class Indentation and Formatting

The common indentation and formatting conventions we are familiar with for block-structured languages like Java and C begin to break down somewhat once we start placing anonymous class definitions within arbitrary expressions. Based on their experience with inner classes, the engineers at Sun recommend the following formatting rules:

- The opening curly brace should not be on a line by itself; instead, it should follow the close parenthesis of the new operator. Similarly, the new operator should, when possible, appear on the same line as the assignment or other expression of which it is a part.

- The body of the anonymous class should be indented relative to the beginning of the line that contains the new keyword.

- The closing curly brace of an anonymous class should not be on a line by itself either; it should be followed by whatever tokens are required by the rest of the expression. Often this is a semicolon or a close parenthesis followed by a semicolon. This extra punctuation serves as a flag to the reader that this is not just an ordinary block of code and makes it easier to understand anonymous classes in a code listing.

How Inner Classes Work

The preceding sections have explained the features and behavior of the various types of inner classes. Strictly speaking, that should be all you need to know about inner classes. In practice, however, some programmers find it easier to understand the details of inner classes if they understand how they are implemented.

Inner classes were introduced in Java 1.1. Despite the dramatic changes to the Java language, the introduction of inner classes did not change the Java Virtual Machine or the Java class file format. As far as the Java interpreter is concerned, there is no such thing as an inner class: all classes are normal top-level classes. In order to make an inner class behave as if it is actually defined inside another class, the Java compiler ends up inserting hidden fields, methods, and constructor arguments into the classes it generates. You may want to use the *javap* disassembler to disassemble some of the class files for inner classes so you can see what tricks the compiler has used to make inner classes work. (See Chapter 8, *Java Development Tools*, for information on *javap*.)

Static Member Class Implementation

Recall our first LinkedStack example (Example 3-8), which defined a static member interface named Linkable. When you compile this LinkedStack class, the compiler actually generates two class files. The first one is *LinkedStack.class*, as expected. The second class file, however, is called *LinkedStack$Linkable.class*. The $ in this name is automatically inserted by the Java compiler. This second class file contains the implementation of the static member interface.

As we discussed earlier, a static member class can access all the static members of its containing class. If a static member class does this, the compiler automatically qualifies the member access expression with the name of the containing class. A static member class is even allowed to access the private static fields of its containing class. Since the static member class is compiled into an ordinary top-level class, however, there is no way it can directly access the private members of its container. Therefore, if a static member class uses a private member of its containing class (or vice versa), the compiler automatically generates non-private access methods and converts the expressions that access the private members into expressions that access these specially generated methods. These methods are given the default package access, which is sufficient, as the member class and its containing class are guaranteed to be in the same package.

Member Class Implementation

A member class is implemented much like a static member class. It is compiled into a separate top-level class file, and the compiler performs various code manipulations to make interclass member access work correctly.

The most significant difference between a member class and a static member class is that each instance of a member class is associated with an instance of the enclosing class. The compiler enforces this association by defining a synthetic field named this$0 in each member class. This field is used to hold a reference to the enclosing instance. Every member class constructor is given an extra parameter that initializes this field. Every time a member class constructor is invoked, the compiler automatically passes a reference to the enclosing class for this extra parameter.

As we've seen, a member class, like any member of a class, can be declared public, protected, or private, or given the default package visibility. However, as I mentioned earlier, there have been no changes to the Java Virtual Machine to support member classes. Member classes are compiled to class files just like top-level classes, but top-level classes can only have public or package access. Therefore, as far as the Java interpreter is concerned, member classes can only have public or package visibility. This means that a member class declared protected is actually treated as a public class, and a member class declared private actually has package visibility. This does not mean you should never declare a member class as protected or private. Although the interpreter cannot enforce these access control modifiers, the modifiers are noted in the class file. This allows any conforming Java compiler to enforce the access modifiers and prevent the member classes from being accessed in unintended ways.

Local and Anonymous Class Implementation

A local class is able to refer to fields and methods in its containing class for exactly the same reason that a member class can; it is passed a hidden reference to the containing class in its constructor and saves that reference away in a `private` field added by the compiler. Also, like member classes, local classes can use `private` fields and methods of their containing class because the compiler inserts any required accessor methods.

What makes local classes different from member classes is that they have the ability to refer to local variables in the scope that defines them. The crucial restriction on this ability, however, is that local classes can only reference local variables and parameters that are declared `final`. The reason for this restriction becomes apparent from the implementation. A local class can use local variables because the compiler automatically gives the class a `private` instance field to hold a copy of each local variable the class uses. The compiler also adds hidden parameters to each local class constructor to initialize these automatically created `private` fields. Thus, a local class does not actually access local variables, but merely its own private copies of them. The only way this can work correctly is if the local variables are declared `final`, so that they are guaranteed not to change. With this guarantee, the local class can be assured that its internal copies of the variables are always in sync with the real local variables.

Since anonymous classes have no names, you may wonder what the class files that represent them are named. This is an implementation detail, but the Java compiler from Sun uses numbers to provide anonymous class names. If you compile the example shown in Example 3-11, you'll find that it produces a file with a name like *LinkedStack$1.class*. This is the class file for the anonymous class.

Modifier Summary

As we've seen, classes, interfaces, and their members can be declared with one or more *modifiers*—keywords such as `public`, `static`, and `final`. This chapter has introduced the `public`, `protected`, and `private` access modifiers, as well as the `abstract`, `final`, and `static` modifiers. In addition to these six, Java defines five other less commonly used modifiers. Table 3-2 lists the Java modifiers, explains what types of Java constructs they can modify, and explains what they do.

Table 3-2: Java Modifiers

Modifier	Used on	Meaning
abstract	class	The class contains unimplemented methods and cannot be instantiated.
	interface	All interfaces are `abstract`. The modifier is optional in interface declarations.

Table 3–2: Java Modifiers (continued)

Modifier	Used on	Meaning
abstract	method	No body is provided for the method; it is provided by a subclass. The signature is followed by a semicolon. The enclosing class must also be abstract.
final	class	The class cannot be subclassed.
	method	The method cannot be overridden (and is not subject to dynamic method lookup).
	field	The field cannot have its value changed. static final fields are compile-time constants.
	variable	A local variable, method parameter, or exception parameter cannot have its value changed (Java 1.1 and later). Useful with local classes.
native	method	The method is implemented in some platform-dependent way (often in C). No body is provided; the signature is followed by a semicolon.
none (package)	class	A non-public class is accessible only in its package.
	interface	A non-public interface is accessible only in its package.
	member	A member that is not private, protected, or public has package visibility and is accessible only within its package.
private	member	The member is accessible only within the class that defines it.
protected	member	The member is accessible only within the package in which it is defined and within subclasses.
public	class	The class is accessible anywhere its package is.
	interface	The interface is accessible anywhere its package is.
	member	The member is accessible anywhere its class is.
strictfp	class	All methods of the class are implicitly strictfp (Java 1.2 and later).

Table 3-2: Java Modifiers (continued)

Modifier	Used on	Meaning
strictfp	method	All floating-point computation done by the method must be performed in a way that strictly conforms to the IEEE 754 standard. In particular, all values, including intermediate results, must be expressed as IEEE float or double values and cannot take advantage of any extra precision or range offered by native platform floating-point formats or hardware (Java 1.2 and later). This modifier is rarely used.
static	class	An inner class declared static is a top-level class, not associated with a member of the containing class (Java 1.1 and later).
	method	A static method is a class method. It is not passed an implicit this object reference. It can be invoked through the class name.
	field	A static field is a class field. There is only one instance of the field, regardless of the number of class instances created. It can be accessed through the class name.
	initializer	The initializer is run when the class is loaded, rather than when an instance is created.
synchronized	method	The method makes non-atomic modifications to the class or instance, so care must be taken to ensure that two threads cannot modify the class or instance at the same time. For a static method, a lock for the class is acquired before executing the method. For a non-static method, a lock for the specific object instance is acquired.
transient	field	The field is not part of the persistent state of the object and should not be serialized with the object. Used with object serialization; see java.io.ObjectOutputStream.
volatile	field	The field can be accessed by unsynchronized threads, so certain optimizations must not be performed on it. This modifier can sometimes be used as an alternative to synchronized. This modifier is very rarely used.

C++ Features Not Found in Java

Throughout this chapter, I've noted similarities and differences between Java and C++ in footnotes. Java shares enough concepts and features with C++ to make it an easy language for C++ programmers to pick up. There are several features of C++ that have no parallel in Java, however. In general, Java does not adopt those features of C++ that make the language significantly more complicated.

C++ supports multiple inheritance of method implementations from more than one superclass at a time. While this seems like a useful feature, it actually introduces many complexities to the language. The Java language designers chose to avoid the added complexity by using interfaces instead. Thus, a class in Java can inherit method implementations only from a single superclass, but it can inherit method declarations from any number of interfaces.

C++ supports templates that allow you, for example, to implement a Stack class and then instantiate it as Stack<int> or Stack<double> to produce two separate types: a stack of integers and a stack of floating-point values. Java does not allow this, but efforts are underway to add this feature to the language in a robust and standardized way. Furthermore, the fact that every class in Java is a subclass of Object means that every object can be cast to an instance of Object. Thus, in Java it is often sufficient to define a data structure (such as a Stack class) that operates on Object values; the objects can be cast back to their actual types whenever necessary.

C++ allows you to define operators that perform arbitrary operations on instances of your classes. In effect, it allows you to extend the syntax of the language. This is a nifty feature, called operator overloading, that makes for elegant examples. In practice, however, it tends to make code quite difficult to understand. After much debate, the Java language designers decided to omit such operator overloading from the language. Note, though, that the use of the + operator for string concatenation in Java is at least reminiscent of operator overloading.

C++ allows you to define conversion functions for a class that automatically invoke an appropriate constructor method when a value is assigned to a variable of that class. This is simply a syntactic shortcut (similar to overriding the assignment operator) and is not included in Java.

In C++, objects are manipulated by value by default; you must use & to specify a variable or function argument automatically manipulated by reference. In Java, all objects are manipulated by reference, so there is no need for this & syntax.

CHAPTER 4

The Java Platform

Chapter 2, *Java Syntax from the Ground Up*, and Chapter 3, *Object-Oriented Programming in Java*, documented the Java programming language. This chapter switches gears and covers the Java platform, which is the vast collection of predefined classes available to every Java program, regardless of the underlying host system on which it is running. The classes of the Java platform are collected into related groups, known as *packages*. This chapter begins with an overview of the packages of the Java platform that are documented in this book. It then moves on to demonstrate, in the form of short examples, the most useful classes in these packages.

Java Platform Overview

Table 4-1 summarizes the key packages of the Java platform that are covered in this book.

Table 4–1: Key Packages of the Java Platform

Package	Description
java.beans	The JavaBeans component model for reusable, embeddable software components.
java.beans.beancontext	Additional classes that define bean context objects that hold and provide services to the JavaBeans objects they contain.
java.io	Classes and interfaces for input and output. Although some of the classes in this package are for working directly with files, most are for working with streams of bytes or characters.
java.lang	The core classes of the language, such as String, Math, System, Thread, and Exception.

Table 4-1: Key Packages of the Java Platform (continued)

Package	Description
`java.lang.ref`	Classes that define weak references to objects. A weak reference is one that does not prevent the referent object from being garbage-collected.
`java.lang.reflect`	Classes and interfaces that allow Java programs to reflect on themselves by examining the constructors, methods, and fields of classes.
`java.math`	A small package that contains classes for arbitrary-precision integer and floating-point arithmetic.
`java.net`	Classes and interfaces for networking with other systems.
`java.security`	Classes and interfaces for access control and authentication. Supports cryptographic message digests and digital signatures.
`java.security.acl`	A package that supports access control lists. Deprecated and unused as of Java 1.2.
`java.security.cert`	Classes and interfaces for working with public key certificates.
`java.security.interfaces`	Interfaces used with DSA and RSA public-key encryption.
`java.security.spec`	Classes and interfaces for transparent representations of keys and parameters used in public-key cryptography.
`java.text`	Classes and interfaces for working with text in internationalized applications.
`java.util`	Various utility classes, including the powerful collections framework for working with collections of objects.
`java.util.jar`	Classes for reading and writing JAR files.
`java.util.zip`	Classes for reading and writing ZIP files.
`javax.crypto`	Classes and interfaces for encryption and decryption of data.
`javax.crypto.interfaces`	Interfaces that represent the Diffie-Hellman public/private keys used in the Diffie-Hellman key agreement protocol.
`javax.crypto.spec`	Classes that define transparent representations of keys and parameters used in cryptography.

Table 4-1 does not list all the packages in the Java platform, only those documented in this book. Java also defines numerous packages for graphics and graphical user interface programming and for distributed, or enterprise, computing. The graphics and GUI packages are `java.awt` and `javax.swing` and their many sub-packages. These packages, along with the `java.applet` package, are documented in *Java Foundation Classes in a Nutshell* (O'Reilly). The enterprise packages of Java include `java.rmi`, `java.sql`, `javax.jndi`, `org.omg.CORBA`, `org.omg.CosNaming`, and all of their subpackages. These packages, as well as several standard extensions to the Java platform, are documented in the book *Java Enterprise in a Nutshell* (O'Reilly).

Strings and Characters

Strings of text are a fundamental and commonly used data type. In Java, however, strings are not a primitive type, like `char`, `int`, and `float`. Instead, strings are represented by the `java.lang.String` class, which defines many useful methods for manipulating strings. `String` objects are *immutable*: once a `String` object has been created, there is no way to modify the string of text it represents. Thus, each method that operates on a string typically returns a new `String` object that holds the modified string.

This code shows some of the basic operations you can perform on strings:

```
// Creating strings
String s = "Now";                   // String objects have a special literal syntax
String t = s + " is the time.";     // Concatenate strings with + operator
String t1 = s + " " + 23.4;         // + converts other values to strings
t1 = String.valueOf('c');           // Get string corresponding to char value
t1 = String.valueOf(42);            // Get string version of integer or any value
t1 = Object.toString();             // Convert objects to strings with toString()

// String length
int len = t.length();               // Number of characters in the string: 16

// Substrings of a string
String sub = t.substring(4);        // Returns char 4 to end: "is the time."
sub = t.substring(4, 6);            // Returns chars 4 and 5: "is"
sub = t.substring(0, 3);            // Returns chars 0 through 2: "Now"
sub = t.substring(x, y);            // Returns chars between pos x and y-1
int numchars = sub.length();        // Length of substring is always (y-x)

// Extracting characters from a string
char c = t.charAt(2);               // Get the 3rd character of t: w
char[] ca = t.toCharArray();        // Convert string to an array of characters
t.getChars(0, 3, ca, 1);            // Put 1st 3 chars of s into ca[1]-ca[3]

// Case conversion
String caps = t.toUpperCase();      // Convert to uppercase
String lower = t.toLowerCase();     // Convert to lowercase

// Comparing strings
boolean b1 = t.equals("hello");            // Returns false: strings not equal
boolean b2 = t.equalsIgnoreCase(caps);     // Case-insensitive compare: true
boolean b3 = t.startsWith("Now");          // Returns true
boolean b4 = t.endsWith("time.");          // Returns true
int r1 = s.compareTo("Pow");               // Returns < 0: s comes before "Pow"
int r2 = s.compareTo("Now");               // Returns 0: strings are equal
int r3 = s.compareTo("Mow");               // Returns > 0: s comes after "Mow"
r1 = s.compareToIgnoreCase("pow");         // Returns < 0 (Java 1.2 and later)
```

```
// Searching for characters and substrings
int pos = t.indexOf('i');            // Position of first 'i': 4
pos = t.indexOf('i', pos+1);         // Position of the next 'i': 12
pos = t.indexOf('i', pos+1);         // No more 'i's in string, returns -1
pos = t.lastIndexOf('i');            // Position of last 'i' in string: 12
pos = t.lastIndexOf('i', pos-1);     // Search backwards for 'i' from char 11

pos = t.indexOf("is");               // Search for substring: returns 4
pos = t.indexOf("is", pos+1);        // Only appears once: returns -1
pos = t.lastIndexOf("the ");         // Search backwards for a string
String noun = t.substring(pos+4);    // Extract word following "the"

// Replace all instances of one character with another character
String exclaim = t.replace('.', '!');  // Only works with chars, not substrings

// Strip blank space off the beginning and end of a string
String noextraspaces = t.trim();

// Obtain unique instances of strings with intern()
String s1 = s.intern();              // Returns s1 equal to s
String s2 = "Now".intern();          // Returns s2 equal to "Now"
boolean equals = (s1 == s2);         // Now can test for equality with ==
```

Since String objects are immutable, you cannot manipulate the characters of a String in place. If you need to do this, use a java.lang.StringBuffer instead:

```
// Create a string buffer from a string
StringBuffer b = new StringBuffer("Mow");

// Get and set individual characters of the StringBuffer
char c = b.charAt(0);                // Returns 'M': just like String.charAt()
b.setCharAt(0, 'N');                 // b holds "Now": can't do that with a String!

// Append to a StringBuffer
b.append(' ');                       // Append a character
b.append("is the time.");            // Append a string
b.append(23);                        // Append an integer or any other value

// Insert Strings or other values into a StringBuffer
b.insert(6, "n't");                  // b now holds: "Now isn't the time.23"

// Replace a range of characters with a string (Java 1.2 and later)
b.replace(4, 9, "is");               // Back to "Now is the time.23"

// Delete characters
b.delete(16, 18);                    // Delete a range: "Now is the time"
b.deleteCharAt(2);                   // Delete 2nd character: "No is the time"
b.setLength(5);                      // Truncate by setting the length: "No is"

// Other useful operations
b.reverse();                         // Reverse characters: "si oN"
String s = b.toString();             // Convert back to an immutable string
s = b.substring(1,2);                // Or take a substring: "i"
b.setLength(0);                      // Erase buffer; now it is ready for reuse
```

In addition to the String and StringBuffer classes, there are a number of other Java classes that operate on strings. One notable class is java.util.StringTokenizer, which you can use to break a string of text into its component words:

```
String s = "Now is the time";
java.util.StringTokenizer st = new java.util.StringTokenizer(s);
while(st.hasMoreTokens()) {
  System.out.println(st.nextToken());
}
```

You can even use this class to tokenize words that are delimited by characters
other than spaces:

```
String s = "a:b:c:d";
java.util.StringTokenizer st = new java.util.StringTokenizer(s, ":");
```

As you know, individual characters are represented in Java by the primitive char
type. The Java platform also defines a Character class, which defines useful class
methods for checking the type of a character and converting the case of a character. For example:

```
char[] text;  // An array of characters, initialized somewhere else
int p = 0;    // Our current position in the array of characters
// Skip leading whitespace
while((p < text.length) && Character.isWhitespace(text[p])) p++;
// Capitalize the first word of text
while((p < text.length) && Character.isLetter(text[p])) {
  text[p] = Character.toUpperCase(text[p]);
  p++;
}
```

The compareTo() and equals() methods of the String class allow you to compare
strings. compareTo() bases its comparison on the character order defined by the
Unicode encoding, while equals() defines string equality as strict character-by-
character equality. These are not always the right methods to use, however. In
some languages, the character ordering imposed by the Unicode standard does not
match the dictionary ordering used when alphabetizing strings. In Spanish, for
example, the letters "ch" are considered a single letter that comes after "c" and
before "d." When comparing human-readable strings in an internationalized application, you should use the java.text.Collator class instead:

```
import java.text.*;

// Compare two strings; results depend on where the program is run
// Return values of Collator.compare() have same meanings as String.compareTo()
Collator c = Collator.getInstance();      // Get Collator for current locale
int result = c.compare("chica", "coche"); // Use it to compare two strings
```

Numbers and Math

Java provides the byte, short, int, long, float, and double primitive types for
representing numbers. The java.lang package includes the corresponding Byte,
Short, Integer, Long, Float, and Double classes, each of which is a subclass of
Number. These classes can be useful as object wrappers around their primitive
types, and they also define some useful constants:

```
// Integral range constants: Integer, Long, and Character also define these
Byte.MIN_VALUE      // The smallest (most negative) byte value
Byte.MAX_VALUE      // The largest byte value
Short.MIN_VALUE     // The most negative short value
```

```
Short.MAX_VALUE      // The largest short value

// Floating-point range constants: Double also defines these
Float.MIN_VALUE      // Smallest (closest to zero) positive float value
Float.MAX_VALUE      // Largest positive float value

// Other useful constants
Math.PI              // 3.14159265358979323846
Math.E               // 2.7182818284590452354
```

A Java program that operates on numbers must get its input values from some-where. Often, such a program reads a textual representation of a number and must convert it to a numeric representation. The various Number subclasses define useful conversion methods:

```
String s = "-42";
byte b = Byte.parseByte(s);              // s as a byte
short sh = Short.parseShort(s);          // s as a short
int i = Integer.parseInt(s);             // s as an int
long l = Long.parseLong(s);              // s as a long
float f = Float.parseFloat(s);           // s as a float (Java 1.2 and later)
f = Float.valueOf(s).floatValue();       // s as a float (prior to Java 1.2)
double d = Double.parseDouble(s);        // s as a double (Java 1.2 and later)
d = Double.valueOf(s).doubleValue();     // s as a double (prior to Java 1.2)

// The integer conversion routines handle numbers in other bases
byte b = Byte.parseByte("1011", 2);      // 1011 in binary is 11 in decimal
short sh = Short.parseShort("ff", 16);   // ff in base 16 is 255 in decimal

// The valueOf() method can handle arbitrary bases between 2 and 36
int i = Integer.valueOf("egg", 17).intValue();   // Base 17!

// The decode() method handles octal, decimal, or hexadecimal, depending
// on the numeric prefix of the string
short sh = Short.decode("0377").byteValue();     // Leading 0 means base 8
int i = Integer.decode("0xff").shortValue();     // Leading 0x means base 16
long l = Long.decode("255").intValue();          // Other numbers mean base 10

// Integer class can convert numbers to strings
String decimal = Integer.toString(42);
String binary = Integer.toBinaryString(42);
String octal = Integer.toOctalString(42);
String hex = Integer.toHexString(42);
String base36 = Integer.toString(42, 36);
```

Numeric values are often printed differently in different countries. For example, many European languages use a comma to separate the integral part of a floating-point value from the fractional part (instead of a decimal point). Formatting differences can diverge even further when displaying numbers that represent monetary values. When converting numbers to strings for display, therefore, it is best to use the java.text.NumberFormat class to perform the conversion in a locale-specific way:

```
import java.text.*;

// Use NumberFormat to format and parse numbers for the current locale
NumberFormat nf = NumberFormat.getNumberInstance();  // Get a NumberFormat
System.out.println(nf.format(9876543.21)); // Format number for current locale
try {
```

```
        Number n = nf.parse("1.234.567,89");      // Parse strings according to locale
    } catch (ParseException e) { /* Handle exception */ }

    // Monetary values are sometimes formatted differently than other numbers
    NumberFormat moneyFmt = NumberFormat.getCurrencyInstance();
    System.out.println(moneyFmt.format(1234.56)); // Prints $1,234.56 in U.S.
```

The Math class defines a number of methods that provide trigonometric, logarith-mic, exponential, and rounding operations, among others. This class is primarily useful with floating-point values. For the trigonometric functions, angles are expressed in radians. The logarithm and exponentiation functions are base e, not base 10. Here are some examples:

```
    double d = Math.toRadians(27);      // Convert 27 degrees to radians
    d = Math.cos(d);                    // Take the cosine
    d = Math.sqrt(d);                   // Take the square root
    d = Math.log(d);                    // Take the natural logarithm
    d = Math.exp(d);                    // Do the inverse: e to the power d
    d = Math.pow(10, d);                // Raise 10 to this power
    d = Math.atan(d);                   // Compute the arc tangent
    d = Math.toDegrees(d);              // Convert back to degrees
    double up = Math.ceil(d);           // Round to ceiling
    double down = Math.floor(d);        // Round to floor
    long nearest = Math.round(d);       // Round to nearest
```

The Math class also defines a rudimentary method for generating pseudo-random numbers, but the java.util.Random class is more flexible. If you need *very* ran-dom pseudo-random numbers, you can use the java.security.SecureRandom class:

```
    // A simple random number
    double r = Math.random();       // Returns d such that: 0.0 <= d < 1.0

    // Create a new Random object, seeding with the current time
    java.util.Random generator = new java.util.Random(System.currentTimeMillis());
    double d = generator.nextDouble();   // 0.0 <= d < 1.0
    float f = generator.nextFloat();     // 0.0 <= f < 1.0
    long l = generator.nextLong();       // Chosen from the entire range of long
    int i = generator.nextInt();         // Chosen from the entire range of int
    i = generator.nextInt(limit);        // 0 <= i < limit (Java 1.2 and later)
    boolean b = generator.nextBoolean(); // true or false (Java 1.2 and later)
    d = generator.nextGaussian();        // Mean value: 0.0; std. deviation: 1.0
    byte[] randomBytes = new byte[128];
    generator.nextBytes(randomBytes);    // Fill in array with random bytes

    // For cryptographic strength random numbers, use the SecureRandom subclass
    java.security.SecureRandom generator2 = new java.security.SecureRandom();
    // Have the generator generate its own 16-byte seed; takes a *long* time
    generator2.setSeed(generator2.generateSeed(16));  // Extra random 16-byte seed
    // Then use SecureRandom like any other Random object
    generator2.nextBytes(randomBytes);   // Generate more random bytes
```

The java.math package contains the BigInteger and BigDecimal classes. These classes allow you to work with arbitrary-size and arbitrary-precision integers and floating-point values. For example:

```
    import java.math.*;

    // Compute the factorial of 1000
```

```
BigInteger total = BigInteger.valueOf(1);
for(int i = 2; i <= 1000; i++)
  total = total.multiply(BigInteger.valueOf(i));
System.out.println(total.toString());
```

Dates and Times

Java uses several different classes for working with dates and times. The
java.util.Date class represents an instant in time (precise down to the millisecond). This class is nothing more than a wrapper around a long value that holds
the number of milliseconds since midnight GMT, January 1, 1970. Here are two
ways to determine the current time:

```
long t0 = System.currentTimeMillis();       // Current time in milliseconds
java.util.Date now = new java.util.Date(); // Basically the same thing
long t1 = now.getTime();                     // Convert a Date to a long value
```

The Date class has a number of interesting-sounding methods, but almost all of
them have been deprecated in favor of methods of the java.util.Calendar and
java.text.DateFormat classes. To print a date or a time, use the DateFormat class,
which automatically handles locale-specific conventions for date and time formatting. DateFormat even works correctly in locales that use a calendar other than the
common era (Gregorian) calendar in use in much of the world:

```
import java.util.Date;
import java.text.*;

// Display today's date using a default format for the current locale
DateFormat defaultDate = DateFormat.getDateInstance();
System.out.println(defaultDate.format(new Date()));

// Display the current time using a short time format for the current locale
DateFormat shortTime = DateFormat.getTimeInstance(DateFormat.SHORT);
System.out.println(shortTime.format(new Date()));

// Display date and time using a long format for both
DateFormat longTimestamp =
  DateFormat.getDateTimeInstance(DateFormat.FULL, DateFormat.FULL);
System.out.println(longTimestamp.format(new Date()));

// Use SimpleDateFormat to define your own formatting template
// See java.text.SimpleDateFormat for the template syntax
DateFormat myformat = new SimpleDateFormat("yyyy.MM.dd");
System.out.println(myformat.format(new Date()));
try {   // DateFormat can parse dates too
  Date leapday = myformat.parse("2000.02.29");
}
catch (ParseException e) { /* Handle parsing exception */ }
```

The Date class and its millisecond representation allow only a very simple form of
date arithmetic:

```
long now = System.currentTimeMillis();       // The current time
long anHourFromNow = now + (60 * 60 * 1000); // Add 3,600,000 milliseconds
```

To perform more sophisticated date and time arithmetic and manipulate dates in ways humans (rather than computers) typically care about, use the java.util.Calendar class:

```java
import java.util.*;

// Get a Calendar for current locale and time zone
Calendar cal = Calendar.getInstance();

// Figure out what day of the year today is
cal.setTime(new Date());                            // Set to the current time
int dayOfYear = cal.get(Calendar.DAY_OF_YEAR);  // What day of the year is it?

// What day of the week does the leap day in the year 2000 occur on?
cal.set(2000, Calendar.FEBRUARY, 29);               // Set year, month, day fields
int dayOfWeek = cal.get(Calendar.DAY_OF_WEEK);  // Query a different field

// What day of the month is the 3rd Thursday of May, 2001?
cal.set(Calendar.YEAR, 2001);                           // Set the year
cal.set(Calendar.MONTH, Calendar.MAY);                  // Set the month
cal.set(Calendar.DAY_OF_WEEK, Calendar.THURSDAY);   // Set the day of week
cal.set(Calendar.DAY_OF_WEEK_IN_MONTH, 3);              // Set the week
int dayOfMonth = cal.get(Calendar.DAY_OF_MONTH);    // Query the day in month

// Get a Date object that represents 30 days from now
Date today = new Date();                    // Current date
cal.setTime(today);                         // Set it in the Calendar object
cal.add(Calendar.DATE, 30);                 // Add 30 days
Date expiration = cal.getTime();            // Retrieve the resulting date
```

Arrays

The java.lang.System class defines an arraycopy() method that is useful for copying specified elements in one array to a specified position in a second array. The second array must be the same type as the first, and it can even be the same array:

```java
char[] text = "Now is the time".toCharArray();
char[] copy = new char[100];
// Copy 10 characters from element 4 of text into copy, starting at copy[0]
System.arraycopy(text, 4, copy, 0, 10);

// Move some of the text to later elements, making room for insertions
System.arraycopy(copy, 3, copy, 6, 7);
```

In Java 1.2 and later, the java.util.Arrays class defines useful array-manipulation methods, including methods for sorting and searching arrays:

```java
import java.util.Arrays;

int[] intarray = new int[] { 10, 5, 7, -3 }; // An array of integers
Arrays.sort(intarray);                       // Sort it in place
int pos = Arrays.binarySearch(intarray, 7);  // Value 7 is found at index 2
pos = Arrays.binarySearch(intarray, 12);     // Not found: negative return value

// Arrays of objects can be sorted and searched too
String[] strarray = new String[] { "now", "is", "the", "time" };
Arrays.sort(strarray);       // { "is", "now", "the", "time" }
```

```
// Arrays.equals() compares all elements of two arrays
String[] clone = (String[]) strarray.clone();
boolean b1 = Arrays.equals(strarray, clone);  // Yes, they're equal

// Arrays.fill() initializes array elements
byte[] data = new byte[100];            // An empty array; elements set to 0
Arrays.fill(data, (byte) -1);           // Set them all to -1
Arrays.fill(data, 5, 10, (byte) -2);   // Set elements 5, 6, 7, 8, 9 to -2
```

Arrays can be treated and manipulated as objects in Java. Given an arbitrary object o, you can use code such as the following to find out if the object is an array and, if so, what type of array it is:

```
Class type = o.getClass();
if (type.isArray()) {
  Class elementType = type.getComponentType();
}
```

Collections

The Java collection framework is a set of important utility classes and interfaces in the java.util package for working with collections of objects. The collection framework defines two fundamental types of collections. A Collection is a group of objects, while a Map is a set of mappings, or associations, between objects. A Set is a type of Collection in which there are no duplicates, and a List is a Collection in which the elements are ordered. Collection, Set, List, and Map are all interfaces, but the java.util package also defines various concrete implementations (see Chapter 23, *The java.util Package*). Other important interfaces are Iterator and ListIterator, which allow you to loop through the objects in a collection. The collection framework is new as of Java 1.2, but prior to that release you can use Vector and Hashtable, which are approximately the same as ArrayList and HashMap.

The following code demonstrates how you might create and perform basic manipulations on sets, lists, and maps:

```
import java.util.*;

Set s = new HashSet();               // Implementation based on a hash table
s.add("test");                       // Add a String object to the set
boolean b = s.contains("test2");     // Check whether a set contains an object
s.remove("test");                    // Remove a member from a set

Set ss = new TreeSet();              // TreeSet implements SortedSet
ss.add("b");                         // Add some elements
ss.add("a");
// Now iterate through the elements (in sorted order) and print them
for(Iterator i = ss.iterator(); i.hasNext();)
  System.out.println(i.next());

List l = new LinkedList();           // LinkedList implements a doubly linked list
l = new ArrayList();                 // ArrayList is more efficient, usually
Vector v = new Vector();             // Vector is an alternative in Java 1.1/1.0
l.addAll(ss);                        // Append some elements to it
l.addAll(1, ss);                     // Insert the elements again at index 1
Object o = l.get(1);                 // Get the second element
```

```
l.set(3, "new element");        // Set the fourth element
l.add("test");                  // Append a new element to the end
l.add(0, "test2");              // Insert a new element at the start
l.remove(1);                    // Remove the second element
l.remove("a");                  // Remove the element "a"
l.removeAll(ss);                // Remove elements from this set
if (!l.isEmpty())               // If list is not empty,
   System.out.println(l.size()); // print out the number of elements in it
boolean b1 = l.contains("a");   // Does it contain this value?
boolean b2 = l.containsAll(ss); // Does it contain all these values?
List sublist = l.subList(1,3);  // A sublist of the 2nd and 3rd elements
Object[] elements = l.toArray(); // Convert it to an array
l.clear();                      // Delete all elements

Map m = new HashMap();          // Hashtable an alternative in Java 1.1/1.0
m.put("key", new Integer(42));  // Associate a value object with a key object
Object value = m.get("key");    // Look up the value associated with a key
m.remove("key");                // Remove the association from the Map
Set keys = m.keySet();          // Get the set of keys held by the Map
```

Arrays of objects and collections serve similar purposes. It is possible to convert from one to the other:

```
Object[] members = set.toArray();           // Get set elements as an array
Object[] items = list.toArray();            // Get list elements as an array
Object[] keys = map.keySet().toArray();     // Get map key objects as an array
Object[] values = map.values().toArray();   // Get map value objects as an array

List l = Arrays.asList(a);                  // View array as an ungrowable list
List l = new ArrayList(Arrays.asList(a));   // Make a growable copy of it
```

Just as the java.util.Arrays class defined methods to operate on arrays, the java.util.Collections class defines methods to operate on collections. Most notable are methods to sort and search the elements of collections:

```
Collections.sort(list);
int pos = Collections.binarySearch(list, "key"); // list must be sorted first
```

Here are some other interesting Collections methods:

```
Collections.copy(list1, list2); // Copy list2 into list1, overwriting list1
Collections.fill(list, o);      // Fill list with Object o
Collections.max(c);             // Find the largest element in Collection c
Collections.min(c);             // Find the smallest element in Collection c
Collections.reverse(list);      // Reverse list
Collections.shuffle(list);      // Mix up list

Set s = Collections.singleton(o); // Return an immutable set with one element o
List ul = Collections.unmodifiableList(list); // Immutable wrapper for list
Map sm = Collections.synchronizedMap(map);    // Synchronized wrapper for map
```

One particularly useful collection class is java.util.Properties. Properties is a subclass of Hashtable that predates the collections framework of Java 1.2, making it a legacy collection. A Properties object maintains a mapping between string keys and string values, and defines methods that allow the mappings to be written to and read from a simple-format text file. This makes the Properties class ideal for configuration and user preference files. The Properties class is also used for the system properties returned by System.getProperty():

```
import java.util.*;
import java.io.*;

String homedir = System.getProperty("user.home");   // Get a system property
Properties sysprops = System.getProperties();       // Get all system properties

// Print the names of all defined system properties
for(Enumeration e = sysprops.propertyNames(); e.hasMoreElements();)
  System.out.println(e.nextElement());

sysprops.list(System.out);  // Here's an even easier way to list the properties

// Read properties from a configuration file
Properties options = new Properties();              // Empty properties list
File configfile = new File(homedir, ".config");     // The configuration file
try {
  options.load(new FileInputStream(configfile));    // Load props from the file
} catch (IOException e) { /* Handle exception here */ }

// Query a property ("color"), specifying a default ("gray") if undefined
String color = options.getProperty("color", "gray");

// Set a property named "color" to the value "green"
options.setProperty("color", "green");

// Store the contents of the Properties object back into a file
try {
  options.store(new FileOutputStream(configfile),   // Output stream
                "MyApp Config File");               // File header comment text
} catch (IOException e) { /* Handle exception */ }
```

Types, Reflection, and Dynamic Loading

The java.lang.Class class represents data types in Java and, along with the classes in the java.lang.reflect package, gives Java programs the capability of introspection (or self-reflection); a Java class can look at itself, or any other class, and determine its superclass, what methods it defines, and so on. There are several ways you can obtain a Class object in Java:

```
// Obtain the Class of an arbitrary object o
Class c = o.getClass();

// Obtain a Class object for primitive types with various predefined constants
c = Void.TYPE;          // The special "no-return-value" type
c = Byte.TYPE;          // Class object that represents a byte
c = Integer.TYPE;       // Class object that represents an int
c = Double.TYPE;        // etc. See also Short, Character, Long, Float.

// Express a class literal as a type name followed by ".class"
c = int.class;          // Same as Integer.TYPE
c = String.class;       // Same as "dummystring".getClass()
c = byte[].class;       // Type of byte arrays
c = Class[][].class;    // Type of array of arrays of Class objects
```

Once you have a Class object, you can perform some interesting reflective operations with it:

```
import java.lang.reflect.*;

Object o;                      // Some unknown object to investigate
Class c = o.getClass();        // Get its type

// If it is an array, figure out its base type
while (c.isArray()) c = c.getComponentType();

// If c is not a primitive type, print its class hierarchy
if (!c.isPrimitive()) {
  for(Class s = c; s != null; s = s.getSuperclass())
    System.out.println(s.getName() + " extends");
}

// Try to create a new instance of c; this requires a no-arg constructor
Object newobj = null;
try { newobj = c.newInstance(); }
catch (Exception e) {
  // Handle InstantiationException, IllegalAccessException
}

// See if the class has a method named setText that takes a single String
// If so, call it with a string argument
try {
  Method m = c.getMethod("setText", new Class[] { String.class });
  m.invoke(newobj, new Object[] { "My Label" });
} catch(Exception e) { /* Handle exceptions here */ }
```

Class also provides a simple mechanism for dynamic class loading in Java. For more complete control over dynamic class loading, however, you should use a java.lang.ClassLoader object, typically a java.net.URLClassLoader. This technique is useful, for example, when you want to load a class that is named in a configuration file instead of being hardcoded into your program:

```
// Dynamically load a class specified by name in a config file
String classname =                  // Look up the name of the class
  config.getProperty("filterclass",   // The property name
                     "com.davidflanagan.filters.Default"); // A default

try {
  Class c = Class.forName(classname);   // Dynamically load the class
  Object o = c.newInstance();           // Dynamically instantiate it
} catch (Exception e) { /* Handle exceptions */ }
```

Another technique:

```
// If the class to be loaded is not in the classpath, create a custom
// class loader to load it.
// Use the config file again to specify the custom path
import java.net.*;
String classdir = config.getProperty("classpath");
try {
  ClassLoader loader = new URLClassLoader(new URL[] { new URL(classdir) });
  Class c = loader.loadClass(classname);
}
catch (Exception e) { /* Handle exceptions */ }
```

Threads

Java makes it easy to define and work with multiple threads of execution within a program. java.lang.Thread is the fundamental thread class in the Java API. There are two ways to define a thread. One is to subclass Thread, override the run() method, and then instantiate your Thread subclass. The other is to define a class that implements the Runnable method (i.e., define a run() method) and then pass an instance of this Runnable object to the Thread() constructor. In either case, the result is a Thread object, where the run() method is the body of the thread. When you call the start() method of the Thread object, the interpreter creates a new thread to execute the run() method. This new thread continues to run until the run() method exits, at which point it ceases to exist. Meanwhile, the original thread continues running itself, starting with the statement following the start() method. The following code demonstrates:

```
final List list;  // Some long unsorted list of objects; initialized elsewhere

/** A Thread class for sorting a List in the background */
class BackgroundSorter extends Thread {
  List l;
  public BackgroundSorter(List l) { this.l = l; }    // Constructor
  public void run() { Collections.sort(l); }         // Thread body
}

// Create a BackgroundSorter thread
Thread sorter = new BackgroundSorter(list);
// Start it running; the new thread runs the run() method above, while
// the original thread continues with whatever statement comes next.
sorter.start();

// Here's another way to define a similar thread
Thread t = new Thread(new Runnable() {          // Create a new thread
  public void run() { Collections.sort(list); } // to sort the list of objects.
});
t.start();                                      // Start it running
```

Threads can run at different priority levels. A thread at a given priority level does not run unless there are no higher-priority threads waiting to run. Here is some code you can use when working with thread priorities:

```
// Set a thread t to lower-than-normal priority
t.setPriority(Thread.NORM_PRIORITY-1);

// Set a thread to lower priority than the current thread
t.setPriority(Thread.currentThread().getPriority() - 1);

// Threads that don't pause for I/O should explicitly yield the CPU
// to give other threads with the same priority a chance to run.
Thread t = new Thread(new Runnable() {
  public void run() {
    for(int i = 0; i < data.length; i++) {  // Loop through a bunch of data
      process(data[i]);                     // Process it
      if ((i % 10) == 0)                    // But after every 10 iterations,
        Thread.yield();                     // pause to let other threads run.
    }
  }
});
```

Often, threads are used to perform some kind of repetitive task at a fixed interval. This is particularly true when doing graphical programming that involves animation or similar effects:

```
public class Clock extends Thread {
    java.text.DateFormat f =      // How to format the time for this locale
      java.text.DateFormat.getTimeInstance(java.text.DateFormat.MEDIUM);
    volatile boolean keepRunning = true;

    public Clock() {           // The constructor
      setDaemon(true);         // Daemon thread: interpreter can exit while it runs
      start();                 // This thread starts itself
    }

    public void run() {        // The body of the thread
      while(keepRunning) {     // This thread runs until asked to stop
        String time = f.format(new java.util.Date()); // Current time
        System.out.println(time);                      // Print the time
        try { Thread.sleep(1000); }                    // Wait 1000 milliseconds
        catch (InterruptedException e) {}              // Ignore this exception
      }
    }

    // Ask the thread to stop running
    public void pleaseStop() { keepRunning = false; }
}
```

Notice the `pleaseStop()` method in the previous example. You can forcefully terminate a thread by calling its `stop()` method, but this method has been deprecated because a thread that is forcefully stopped can leave objects it is manipulating in an inconsistent state. If you need a thread that can be stopped, you should define a method such as `pleaseStop()` that stops the thread in a controlled way.

In Java 1.3, the `java.util.Timer` and `java.util.TimerTask` classes make it even easier to run repetitive tasks. Here is some code that behaves much like the previous `Clock` class:

```
import java.util.*;

// How to format the time for this locale
final java.text.DateFormat timeFmt =
  java.text.DateFormat.getTimeInstance(java.text.DateFormat.MEDIUM);
// Define the time-display task
TimerTask displayTime = new TimerTask() {
  public void run() { System.out.println(timeFmt.format(new Date())); }
};
// Create a timer object to run the task (and possibly others)
Timer timer = new Timer();
// Now schedule that task to be run every 1000 milliseconds, starting now
Timer.schedule(displayTime, 0, 1000);
// To stop the time-display task
displayTime.cancel();
```

Sometimes one thread needs to stop and wait for another thread to complete. You can accomplish this with the join() method:

```
List list;  // A long list of objects to be sorted; initialized elsewhere

// Define a thread to sort the list: lower its priority, so it only runs
// when the current thread is waiting for I/O, and then start it running.
Thread sorter = new BackgroundSorter(list);           // Defined earlier
sorter.setPriority(Thread.currentThread.getPriority()-1); // Lower priority
sorter.start();                                        // Start sorting

// Meanwhile, in this original thread, read data from a file
byte[] data = readData();  // Method defined elsewhere

// Before we can proceed, we need the list to be fully sorted, so
// we've got to wait for the sorter thread to exit, if it hasn't already.
sorter.join();
```

When using multiple threads, you must be very careful if you allow more than one thread to access the same data structure. Consider what would happen if one thread was trying to loop through the elements of a List while another thread was sorting those elements. Preventing this problem is called *thread synchronization* and is one of the central problems of multithreaded computing. The basic technique for preventing two threads from accessing the same object at the same time is to require a thread to obtain a lock on the object before the thread can modify it. While any one thread holds the lock, another thread that requests the lock has to wait until the first thread is done and releases the lock. Every Java object has the fundamental ability to provide such a locking capability.

The easiest way to keep objects thread-safe is to declare any sensitive methods synchronized. A thread must obtain a lock on an object before it can execute any of its synchronized methods, which means that no other thread can execute any other synchronized method at the same time. (If a static method is declared synchronized, the thread must obtain a lock on the class, and this works in the same manner.) To do finer-grained locking, you can specify synchronized blocks of code that hold a lock on a specified object for a short time:

```
// This method swaps two array elements in a synchronized block
 public static void swap(Object[] array, int index1, int index2) {
   synchronized(array) {
     Object tmp = array[index1];
     array[index1] = array[index2];
     array[index2] = tmp;
   }
}

// The Collection, Set, List, and Map implementations in java.util do
// not have synchronized methods (except for the legacy implementations
// Vector and Hashtable). When working with multiple threads, you can
// obtain synchronized wrapper objects.
List synclist = Collections.synchronizedList(list);
Map syncmap = Collections.synchronizedMap(map);
```

When you are synchronizing threads, you must be careful to avoid *deadlock*, which occurs when two threads end up waiting for each other to release a lock they need. Since neither can proceed, neither one can release the lock it holds, and they both stop running:

```
// When two threads try to lock two objects, deadlock can occur unless
// they always request the locks in the same order.
final Object resource1 = new Object();   // Here are two objects to lock
final Object resource2 = new Object();
Thread t1 = new Thread(new Runnable() { // Locks resource1 then resource2
  public void run() {
    synchronized(resource1) {
      synchronized(resource2) { compute(); }
    }
  }
});

Thread t2 = new Thread(new Runnable() {  // Locks resource2 then resource1
  public void run() {
    synchronized(resource2) {
      synchronized(resource1) { compute(); }
    }
  }
});

t1.start(); // Locks resource1
t2.start(); // Locks resource2 and now neither thread can progress!
```

Sometimes a thread needs to stop running and wait until some kind of event
occurs, at which point it is told to continue running. This is done with the wait()
and notify() methods. These aren't methods of the Thread class, however; they
are methods of Object. Just as every Java object has a lock associated with it,
every object can maintain a list of waiting threads. When a thread calls the wait()
method of an object, it is added to the list of waiting threads for that object and
stops running. When another thread calls the notify() method of the same object,
the object wakes up one of the waiting threads and allows it to continue running:

```
/**
 * A queue. One thread calls push() to put an object on the queue.
 * Another calls pop() to get an object off the queue. If there is no
 * data, pop() waits until there is some, using wait()/notify().
 * wait() and notify() must be used within a synchronized method or
 * block.
 */
import java.util.*;

public class Queue {
  LinkedList q = new LinkedList();  // Where objects are stored
  public synchronized void push(Object o) {
    q.add(o);        // Append the object to the end of the list
    this.notify(); // Tell waiting threads that data is ready
  }
  public synchronized Object pop() {
    while(q.size() == 0) {
      try { this.wait(); }
      catch (InterruptedException e) { /* Ignore this exception */ }
    }
    return q.remove(0);
  }
}
```

Files and Directories

The java.io.File class represents a file or a directory and defines a number of important methods for manipulating files and directories. Note, however, that none of these methods allow you to read the contents of a file; that is the job of java.io.FileInputStream, which is just one of the many types of input/output streams used in Java and discussed in the next section. Here are some things you can do with File:

```java
import java.io.*;
import java.util.*;

// Get the name of the user's home directory and represent it with a File
File homedir = new File(System.getProperty("user.home"));
// Create a File object to represent a file in that directory
File f = new File(homedir, ".configfile");

// Find out how big a file is and when it was last modified
long filelength = f.length();
Date lastModified = new java.util.Date(f.lastModified());

// If the file exists, is not a directory, and is readable,
// move it into a newly created directory.
if (f.exists() && f.isFile() && f.canRead()) {    // Check config file
  File configdir = new File(homedir, ".configdir");  // A new config directory
  configdir.mkdir();                                 // Create that directory
  f.renameTo(new File(configdir, ".config"));        // Move the file into it
}

// List all files in the home directory
String[] allfiles = homedir.list();

// List all files that have a ".java" suffix
String[] sourcecode = homedir.list(new FilenameFilter() {
  public boolean accept(File d, String name) { return name.endsWith(".java"); }
});
```

The File class provides some important additional functionality as of Java 1.2:

```java
// List all filesystem root directories; on Windows, this gives us
// File objects for all drive letters (Java 1.2 and later).
File[] rootdirs = File.listRoots();

// Atomically, create a lock file, then delete it (Java 1.2 and later)
File lock = new File(configdir, ".lock");
if (lock.createNewFile()) {
  // We successfully created the file, so do something
  ...
  // Then delete the lock file
  lock.delete();
}
else {
  // We didn't create the file; someone else has a lock
  System.err.println("Can't create lock file; exiting.");
  System.exit(0);
}

// Create a temporary file to use during processing (Java 1.2 and later)
File temp = File.createTempFile("app", ".tmp");  // Filename prefix and suffix
```

```
// Make sure file gets deleted when we're done with it (Java 1.2 and later)
temp.deleteOnExit();
```

The `java.io` package also defines a `RandomAccessFile` class that allows you to read binary data from arbitrary locations in a file. This can be a useful thing to do in certain situations, but most applications read files sequentially, using the stream classes described in the next section. Here is a short example of using `RandomAccessFile`:

```
// Open a file for read/write ("rw") access
File datafile = new File(configdir, "datafile");
RandomAccessFile f = new RandomAccessFile(datafile, "rw");
f.seek(100);                   // Move to byte 100 of the file
byte[] data = new byte[100];   // Create a buffer to hold data
f.read(data);                  // Read 100 bytes from the file
int i = f.readInt();           // Read a 4-byte integer from the file
f.seek(100);                   // Move back to byte 100
f.writeInt(i);                 // Write the integer first
f.write(data);                 // Then write the 100 bytes
f.close();                     // Close file when done with it
```

Input and Output Streams

The `java.io` package defines a large number of classes for reading and writing streaming, or sequential, data. The `InputStream` and `OutputStream` classes are for reading and writing streams of bytes, while the `Reader` and `Writer` classes are for reading and writing streams of characters. Streams can be nested, meaning you might read characters from a `FilterReader` object that reads and processes characters from an underlying `Reader` stream. This underlying `Reader` stream might read bytes from an `InputStream` and convert them to characters.

There are a number of common operations you can perform with streams. One is to read lines of input the user types at the console:

```
import java.io.*;

BufferedReader console = new BufferedReader(new InputStreamReader(System.in));
System.out.print("What is your name: ");
String name = null;
try {
  name = console.readLine();
}
catch (IOException e) { name = "<" + e + ">"; }  // This should never happen
System.out.println("Hello " + name);
```

Reading lines of text from a file is a similar operation. The following code reads an entire text file and quits when it reaches the end:

```
String filename = System.getProperty("user.home") + File.separator + ".cshrc";
try {
  BufferedReader in = new BufferedReader(new FileReader(filename));
  String line;
  while((line = in.readLine()) != null) {  // Read line, check for end-of-file
    System.out.println(line);              // Print the line
  }
  in.close();     // Always close a stream when you are done with it
}
```

```
catch (IOException e) {
  // Handle FileNotFoundException, etc. here
}
```

Throughout this book, you've seen the use of the System.out.println() method to display text on the console. System.out simply refers to an output stream. You can print text to any output stream using similar techniques. The following code shows how to output text to a file:

```
try {
  File f = new File(homedir, ".config");
  PrintWriter out = new PrintWriter(new FileWriter(f));
  out.println("## Automatically generated config file. DO NOT EDIT!");
  out.close();  // We're done writing
}
catch (IOException e) { /* Handle exceptions */ }
```

Not all files contain text, however. The following lines of code treat a file as a stream of bytes and read the bytes into a large array:

```
try {
  File f;                            // File to read; initialized elsewhere
  int filesize = (int) f.length();   // Figure out the file size
  byte[] data = new byte[filesize];  // Create an array that is big enough
  // Create a stream to read the file
  DataInputStream in = new DataInputStream(new FileInputStream(f));
  in.readFully(data);  // Read file contents into array
  in.close();
}
catch (IOException e) { /* Handle exceptions */ }
```

Various other packages of the Java platform define specialized stream classes that operate on streaming data in some useful way. The following code shows how to use stream classes from java.util.zip to compute a checksum of data and then compress the data while writing it to a file:

```
import java.io.*;
import java.util.zip.*;

try {
  File f;                            // File to write to; initialized elsewhere
  byte[] data;                       // Data to write; initialized elsewhere
  Checksum check = new Adler32();    // An object to compute a simple checksum

  // Create a stream that writes bytes to the file f
  FileOutputStream fos = new FileOutputStream(f);
  // Create a stream that compresses bytes and writes them to fos
  GZIPOutputStream gzos = new GZIPOutputStream(fos);
  // Create a stream that computes a checksum on the bytes it writes to gzos
  CheckedOutputStream cos = new CheckedOutputStream(gzos, check);

  cos.write(data);          // Now write the data to the nested streams
  cos.close();              // Close down the nested chain of streams
  long sum = check.getValue(); // Obtain the computed checksum
}
catch (IOException e) { /* Handle exceptions */ }
```

The java.util.zip package also contains a ZipFile class that gives you random access to the entries of a ZIP archive and allows you to read those entries through a stream:

```
import java.io.*;
import java.util.zip.*;

String filename;       // File to read; initialized elsewhere
String entryname;      // Entry to read from the ZIP file; initialized elsewhere
ZipFile zipfile = new ZipFile(filename);         // Open the ZIP file
ZipEntry entry = zipfile.getEntry(entryname);   // Get one entry
InputStream in = zipfile.getInputStream(entry); // A stream to read the entry
BufferedInputStream bis = new BufferedInputStream(in);  // Improves efficiency
// Now read bytes from bis...
// Print out contents of the ZIP file
for(java.util.Enumeration e = zipfile.entries(); e.hasMoreElements();) {
  ZipEntry zipentry = (ZipEntry) e.nextElement();
  System.out.println(zipentry.getName());
}
```

If you need to compute a cryptographic-strength checksum (also knows as a message digest), use one of the stream classes of the java.security package. For example:

```
import java.io.*;
import java.security.*;
import java.util.*;

File f;          // File to read and compute digest on; initialized elsewhere
List text = new ArrayList();  // We'll store the lines of text here

// Get an object that can compute an SHA message digest
MessageDigest digester = MessageDigest.getInstance("SHA");
// A stream to read bytes from the file f
FileInputStream fis = new FileInputStream(f);
// A stream that reads bytes from fis and computes an SHA message digest
DigestInputStream dis = new DigestInputStream(fis, digester);
// A stream that reads bytes from dis and converts them to characters
InputStreamReader isr = new InputStreamReader(dis);
// A stream that can read a line at a time
BufferedReader br = new BufferedReader(isr);
// Now read lines from the stream
for(String line; (line = br.readLine()) != null; text.add(line)) ;
// Close the streams
br.close();
// Get the message digest
byte[] digest = digester.digest();
```

So far, we've used a variety of stream classes to manipulate streaming data, but the data itself ultimately comes from a file or is written to the console. The java.io package defines other stream classes that can read data from and write data to arrays of bytes or strings of text:

```
import java.io.*;

// Set up a stream that uses a byte array as its destination
ByteArrayOutputStream baos = new ByteArrayOutputStream();
DataOutputStream out = new DataOutputStream(baos);
out.writeUTF("hello");              // Write some string data out as bytes
```

```
out.writeDouble(Math.PI);          // Write a floating-point value out as bytes
byte[] data = baos.toByteArray(); // Get the array of bytes we've written
out.close();                       // Close the streams

// Set up a stream to read characters from a string
Reader in = new StringReader("Now is the time!");
// Read characters from it until we reach the end
int c;
while((c = in.read()) != -1) System.out.print((char) c);
```

Other classes that operate this way include ByteArrayInputStream, StringWriter, CharArrayReader, and CharArrayWriter.

PipedInputStream and PipedOutputStream and their character-based counterparts, PipedReader and PipedWriter, are another interesting set of streams defined by java.io. These streams are used in pairs by two threads that want to communicate. One thread writes bytes to a PipedOutputStream or characters to a Piped-Writer, and another thread reads bytes or characters from the corresponding PipedInputStream or PipedReader:

```
// A pair of connected piped I/O streams forms a pipe. One thread writes
// bytes to the PipedOutputStream, and another thread reads them from the
// corresponding PipedInputStream. Or use PipedWriter/PipedReader for chars.
final PipedOutputStream writeEndOfPipe = new PipedOutputStream();
final PipedInputStream readEndOfPipe = new PipedInputStream(writeEndOfPipe);

// This thread reads bytes from the pipe and discards them
Thread devnull = new Thread(new Runnable() {
  public void run() {
    try { while(readEndOfPipe.read() != -1); }
    catch (IOException e) {}  // ignore it
  }
});
devnull.start();
```

One of the most important features of the java.io package is the ability to *serialize* objects: to convert an object into a stream of bytes that can later be deserialized back into a copy of the original object. The following code shows how to use serialization to save an object to a file and later read it back:

```
Object o;  // The object we are serializing; it must implement Serializable
File f;     // The file we are saving it to

try {
  // Serialize the object
  ObjectOutputStream oos = new ObjectOutputStream(new FileOutputStream(f));
  oos.writeObject(o);
  oos.close();

  // Read the object back in:
  ObjectInputStream ois = new ObjectInputStream(new FileInputStream(f));
  Object copy = ois.readObject();
  ois.close();
}
catch (IOException e) { /* Handle input/output exceptions */ }
catch (ClassNotFoundException cnfe) { /* readObject() can throw this */ }
```

The previous example serializes to a file, but remember, you can write serialized objects to any type of stream. Thus, you can write an object to a byte array, then read it back from the byte array, creating a deep copy of the object. You can write the object's bytes to a compression stream or even write the bytes to a stream connected across a network to another program!

Networking

The `java.net` package defines a number of classes that make writing networked applications surprisingly easy. The easiest class to use is URL, which represents a uniform resource locator. Different Java implementations may support different sets of URL protocols, but, at a minimum, you can rely on support for the `http:`, `ftp:`, and `file:` protocols. Here are some ways you can use the URL class:

```
import java.net.*;
import java.io.*;

// Create some URL objects
URL url1=null, url2=null, url3=null;
try {
  url = new URL("http://www.oreilly.com");        // An absolute URL
  url2 = new URL(url, "catalog/books/javanut3/"); // A relative URL
  url3 = new URL("http:", "www.oreilly.com", "index.html");
} catch (MalformedURLException e) { /* Ignore this exception */ }

// Read the content of a URL from an input stream:
InputStream in = url.openStream();

// For more control over the reading process, get a URLConnection object
URLConnection conn = url.openConnection();

// Now get some information about the URL
String type = conn.getContentType();
String encoding = conn.getContentEncoding();
java.util.Date lastModified = new java.util.Date(conn.getLastModified());
int len = conn.getContentLength();

// If necessary, read the contents of the URL using this stream
InputStream in = conn.getInputStream();
```

Sometimes you need more control over your networked application than is possible with the URL class. In this case, you can use a Socket to communicate directly with a server. For example:

```
import java.net.*;
import java.io.*;

// Here's a simple client program that connects to a web server,
// requests a document, and reads the document from the server.
String hostname = "java.oreilly.com";  // The server to connect to
int port = 80;                         // Standard port for HTTP
String filename = "/index.html";       // The file to read from the server
Socket s = new Socket(hostname, port); // Connect to the server

// Get I/O streams we can use to talk to the server
InputStream sin = s.getInputStream();
BufferedReader fromServer = new BufferedReader(new InputStreamReader(sin));
OutputStream sout = s.getOutputStream();
PrintWriter toServer = new PrintWriter(new OutputStreamWriter(sout));
```

```
// Request the file from the server, using the HTTP protocol
toServer.print("GET " + filename + " HTTP/1.0\n\n");
toServer.flush();

// Now read the server's response, assume it is a text file, and print it out
for(String l = null; (l = fromServer.readLine()) != null; )
  System.out.println(l);

// Close everything down when we're done
toServer.close();
fromServer.close();
s.close();
```

A client application uses a Socket to communicate with a server. The server does
the same thing: it uses a Socket object to communicate with each of its clients.
However, the server has an additional task, in that it must be able to recognize
and accept client connection requests. This is done with the ServerSocket class.
The following code shows how you might use a ServerSocket. The code implements a simple HTTP server that responds to all requests by sending back (or mir-
roring) the exact contents of the HTTP request. A dummy server like this is useful
when debugging HTTP clients:

```
import java.io.*;
import java.net.*;

public class HttpMirror {
  public static void main(String[] args) {
    try {
      int port = Integer.parseInt(args[0]);         // The port to listen on
      ServerSocket ss = new ServerSocket(port);     // Create a socket to listen
      for(;;) {                                      // Loop forever
        Socket client = ss.accept();                 // Wait for a connection
        ClientThread t = new ClientThread(client);   // A thread to handle it
        t.start();                                    // Start the thread running
      }                                               // Loop again
    }
    catch (Exception e) {
      System.err.println(e.getMessage());
      System.err.println("Usage: java HttpMirror <port>");
    }
  }

  static class ClientThread extends Thread {
    Socket client;
    ClientThread(Socket client) { this.client = client; }
    public void run() {
      try {
        // Get streams to talk to the client
        BufferedReader in =
          new BufferedReader(new InputStreamReader(client.getInputStream()));
        PrintWriter out =
          new PrintWriter(new OutputStreamWriter(client.getOutputStream()));

        // Send an HTTP response header to the client
        out.print("HTTP/1.0 200\nContent-Type: text/plain\n\n");

        // Read the HTTP request from the client and send it right back
        // Stop when we read the blank line from the client that marks
        // the end of the request and its headers.
```

```
            String line;
            while((line = in.readLine()) != null) {
              if (line.length() == 0) break;
              out.println(line);
            }

            out.close();
            in.close();
            client.close();
          }
        catch (IOException e) { /* Ignore exceptions */ }
        }
      }
    }
```

Note how elegantly both the URL and Socket classes use the input/output streams that we saw earlier in the chapter. This is one of the features that makes the Java networking classes so powerful.

Both URL and Socket perform networking on top of a stream-based network connection. Setting up and maintaining a stream across a network takes work at the network level, however. Sometimes you need a low-level way to speed a packet of data across a network, but you don't care about maintaining a stream. If, in addition, you don't need a guarantee that your data will get there or that the packets of data will arrive in the order you sent them, you may be interested in the DatagramSocket and DatagramPacket classes:

```
import java.net.*;

// Send a message to another computer via a datagram
try {
  String hostname = "host.domain.org";        // The computer to send the data to
  InetAddress address =                        // Convert the DNS hostname
    InetAddress.getByName(hostname);           // to a lower-level IP address.
  int port = 1234;                             // The port to connect to
  String message = "The eagle has landed.";    // The message to send
  byte[] data = message.getBytes();            // Convert string to bytes
  DatagramSocket s = new DatagramSocket();     // Socket to send message with
  DatagramPacket p =                           // Create the packet to send
    new DatagramPacket(data, data.length, address, port);
  s.send(p);                                   // Now send it!
  s.close();                                   // Always close sockets when done
}
catch (UnknownHostException e) {}  // Thrown by InetAddress.getByName()
catch (SocketException e) {}       // Thrown by new DatagramSocket()
catch (java.io.IOException e) {}   // Thrown by DatagramSocket.send()

// Here's how the other computer can receive the datagram
try {
  byte[] buffer = new byte[4096];              // Buffer to hold data
  DatagramSocket s = new DatagramSocket(1234); // Socket to receive it through
  DatagramPacket p =                           // The packet to receive it
    new DatagramPacket(buffer, buffer.length); // Wait for a packet to arrive
  s.receive(p);                                // Wait for a packet to arrive
  String msg =                                 // Convert the bytes from the
    new String(buffer, 0, p.getLength());      // packet back to a string.
  s.close();                                   // Always close the socket
}
```

```
catch (SocketException e) {}       // Thrown by new DatagramSocket()
catch (java.io.IOException e) {}   // Thrown by DatagramSocket.receive()
```

Processes

Earlier in the chapter, we saw how easy it is to create and manipulate multiple
threads of execution running within the same Java interpreter. Java also has a
java.lang.Process class that represents a program running externally to the interpreter. A Java program can communicate with an external process using streams in
the same way that it might communicate with a server running on some other
computer on the network. Using a Process is always platform-dependent and is
rarely portable, but it is sometimes a useful thing to do:

```java
// Maximize portability by looking up the name of the command to execute
// in a configuration file.
java.util.Properties config;
String cmd = config.getProperty("sysloadcmd");
if (cmd != null) {
  // Execute the command; Process p represents the running command
  Process p = Runtime.getRuntime().exec(cmd);          // Start the command
  InputStream pin = p.getInputStream();                // Read bytes from it
  InputStreamReader cin = new InputStreamReader(pin);  // Convert them to chars
  BufferedReader in = new BufferedReader(cin);         // Read lines of chars
  String load = in.readLine();                         // Get the command output
  in.close();                                          // Close the stream
}
```

Security

The java.security package defines quite a few classes related to the Java access-
control architecture, which is discussed in more detail in Chapter 5, *Java Security*.
These classes allow Java programs to run untrusted code in a restricted environment from which it can do no harm. While these are important classes, you rarely
need to use them.

The more interesting classes are the ones used for authentication. A *message digest*
is a value, also known as cryptographic checksum or secure hash, that is computed over a sequence of bytes. The length of the digest is typically much smaller
than the length of the data for which it is computed, but any change, no matter
how small, in the input bytes, produces a change in the digest. When transmitting
data (a message), you can transmit a message digest along with it. Then, the recipient of the message can recompute the message digest on the received data and,
by comparing the computed digest to the received digest, determine whether the
message or the digest was corrupted or tampered with during transmission. We
saw a way to compute a message digest earlier in the chapter when we discussed
streams. A similar technique can be used to compute a message digest for non-
streaming binary data:

```java
import java.security.*;

// Obtain an object to compute message digests using the "Secure Hash
// Algorithm"; this method can throw NoSuchAlgorithmException.
MessageDigest md = MessageDigest.getInstance("SHA");
```

```
byte[] data, data1, data2, secret;  // Some byte arrays initialized elsewhere

// Create a digest for a single array of bytes
byte[] digest = md.digest(data);

// Create a digest for several chunks of data
md.reset();              // Optional: automatically called by digest()
md.update(data1);        // Process the first chunk of data
md.update(data2);        // Process the second chunk of data
digest = md.digest();    // Compute the digest

// Create a keyed digest that can be verified if you know the secret bytes
md.update(data);                 // The data to be transmitted with the digest
digest = md.digest(secret);  // Add the secret bytes and compute the digest

// Verify a digest like this
byte[] receivedData, receivedDigest;  // The data and the digest we received
byte[] verifyDigest = md.digest(receivedData);  // Digest the received data
// Compare computed digest to the received digest
boolean verified = java.util.Arrays.equals(receivedDigest, verifyDigest);
```

A *digital signature* combines a message-digest algorithm with public-key cryptography. The sender of a message, Alice, can compute a digest for a message and then encrypt that digest with her private key. She then sends the message and the encrypted digest to a recipient, Bob. Bob knows Alice's public key (it is public, after all), so he can use it to decrypt the digest and verify that the message has not been tampered with. In performing this verification, Bob also learns that the digest was encrypted with Alice's private key, since he was able to decrypt the digest successfully using Alice's public key. As Alice is the only one who knows her private key, the message must have come from Alice. A digital signature is called such because, like a pen-and-paper signature, it serves to authenticate the origin of a document or message. Unlike a pen-and-paper signature, however, a digital signature is very difficult, if not impossible, to forge, and it cannot simply be cut and pasted onto another document.

Java makes creating digital signatures easy. In order to create a digital signature, however, you need a java.security.PrivateKey object. Assuming that a keystore exists on your system (see the *keytool* documentation in Chapter 8, *Java Development Tools*), you can get one with code like the following:

```
// Here is some basic data we need
File homedir = new File(System.getProperty("user.home"));
File keyfile = new File(homedir, ".keystore"); // Or read from config file
String filepass = "KeyStore password"         // Password for entire file
String signer = "david";                       // Read from config file
String password = "No one can guess this!";    // Better to prompt for this
PrivateKey key;  // This is the key we want to look up from the keystore

try {
    // Obtain a KeyStore object and then load data into it
    KeyStore keystore = KeyStore.getInstance(KeyStore.getDefaultType());
    keystore.load(new BufferedInputStream(new FileInputStream(keyfile)),
                  filepass.toCharArray());
    // Now ask for the desired key
    key = (PrivateKey) keystore.getKey(signer, password.toCharArray());
}
catch (Exception e) { /* Handle various exception types here */ }
```

Once you have a `PrivateKey` object, you create a digital signature with a `java.security.Signature` object:

```
PrivateKey key;              // Initialized as shown previously
byte[] data;                 // The data to be signed
Signature s =                // Obtain object to create and verify signatures
   Signature.getInstance("SHA1withDSA");  // Can throw NoSuchAlgorithmException
s.initSign(key);             // Initialize it; can throw InvalidKeyException
s.update(data);              // Data to sign; can throw SignatureException
/* s.update(data2); */       // Call multiple times to specify all data
byte[] signature = s.sign(); // Compute signature
```

A `Signature` object can verify a digital signature:

```
byte[] data;        // The signed data; initialized elsewhere
byte[] signature;   // The signature to be verified; initialized elsewhere
String signername;  // Who created the signature; initialized elsewhere
KeyStore keystore;  // Where certificates stored; initialize as shown earlier

// Look for a public key certificate for the signer
java.security.cert.Certificate cert = keystore.getCertificate(signername);
PublicKey publickey = cert.getPublicKey();  // Get the public key from it

Signature s = Signature.getInstance("SHA1withDSA"); // Or some other algorithm
s.initVerify(publickey);                    // Setup for verification
s.update(data);                             // Specify signed data
boolean verified = s.verify(signature);     // Verify signature data
```

The `java.security.SignedObject` class is a convenient utility for wrapping a digital signature around an object. The `SignedObject` can then be serialized and transmitted to a recipient, who can deserialize it and use the `verify()` method to verify the signature:

```
Serializable o;  // The object to be signed; must be Serializable
PrivateKey k;    // The key to sign with; initialized elsewhere
Signature s = Signature.getInstance("SHA1withDSA"); // Signature "engine"
SignedObject so = new SignedObject(o, k, s);        // Create the SignedObject

// The SignedObject encapsulates the object o; it can now be serialized
// and transmitted to a recipient.

// Here's how the recipient verifies the SignedObject
SignedObject so;           // The deserialized SignedObject
Object o;                  // The original object to extract from it
PublicKey pk;              // The key to verify with
Signature s = Signature.getInstance("SHA1withDSA"); // Verification "engine"
if (so.verify(pk,s))       // If the signature is valid,
  o = so.getObject();      // retrieve the encapsulated object.
```

Cryptography

The `java.security` package includes cryptography-based classes, but it does not contain classes for actual encryption and decryption. That is the job of the `javax.crypto` package. This package supports symmetric-key cryptography, in which the same key is used for both encryption and decryption and must be known by both the sender and the receiver of encrypted data. The `SecretKey` interface represents an encryption key; the first step of any cryptographic operation is to obtain an appropriate SecretKey. Unfortunately, the *keytool* program supplied with the Java SDK cannot generate and store secret keys, so a program must handle these tasks itself. Here is some code that shows various ways to work with SecretKey objects:

```java
import javax.crypto.*;
import javax.crypto.spec.*;

// Generate encryption keys with a KeyGenerator object
KeyGenerator desGen = KeyGenerator.getInstance("DES");        // DES algorithm
SecretKey desKey = desGen.generateKey();                      // Generate a key
KeyGenerator desEdeGen = KeyGenerator.getInstance("DESede"); // Triple DES
SecretKey desEdeKey = desEdeGen.generateKey();               // Generate a key

// SecretKey is an opaque representation of a key. Use SecretKeyFactory to
// convert to a transparent representation that can be manipulated: saved
// to a file, securely transmitted to a receiving party, etc.
SecretKeyFactory desFactory = SecretKeyFactory.getInstance("DES");
DESKeySpec desSpec = (DESKeySpec)
  desFactory.getKeySpec(desKey, javax.crypto.spec.DESKeySpec.class);
byte[] rawDesKey = desSpec.getKey();
// Do the same for a DESede key
SecretKeyFactory desEdeFactory = SecretKeyFactory.getInstance("DESede");
DESedeKeySpec desEdeSpec = (DESedeKeySpec)
  desEdeFactory.getKeySpec(desEdeKey, javax.crypto.spec.DESedeKeySpec.class);
byte[] rawDesEdeKey = desEdeSpec.getKey();

// Convert the raw bytes of a key back to a SecretKey object
DESedeKeySpec keyspec = new DESedeKeySpec(rawDesEdeKey);
SecretKey k = desEdeFactory.generateSecret(keyspec);

// For DES and DESede keys, there is an even easier way to create keys
// SecretKeySpec implements SecretKey, so use it to represent these keys
byte[] desKeyData = new byte[8];        // Read 8 bytes of data from a file
byte[] tripleDesKeyData = new byte[24]; // Read 24 bytes of data from a file
SecretKey myDesKey = new SecretKeySpec(desKeyData, "DES");
SecretKey myTripleDesKey = new SecretKeySpec(tripleDesKeyData, "DESede");
```

Once you have obtained an appropriate SecretKey object, the central class for encryption and decryption is Cipher. Use it like this:

```java
SecretKey key;     // Obtain a SecretKey as shown earlier
byte[] plaintext;  // The data to encrypt; initialized elsewhere

// Obtain an object to perform encryption or decryption
Cipher cipher = Cipher.getInstance("DESede");  // Triple-DES encryption
// Initialize the cipher object for encryption
cipher.init(Cipher.ENCRYPT_MODE, key);
// Now encrypt data
byte[] ciphertext = cipher.doFinal(plaintext);

// If we had multiple chunks of data to encrypt, we can do this
cipher.update(message1);
cipher.update(message2);
byte[] ciphertext = cipher.doFinal();

// We simply reverse things to decrypt
cipher.init(Cipher.DECRYPT_MODE, key);
byte[] decryptedMessage = cipher.doFinal(ciphertext);
```

```
// To decrypt multiple chunks of data
byte[] decrypted1 = cipher.update(ciphertext1);
byte[] decrypted2 = cipher.update(ciphertext2);
byte[] decrypted3 = cipher.doFinal(ciphertext3);
```

The Cipher class can also be used with CipherInputStream or CipherOutput-
Stream to encrypt or decrypt while reading or writing streaming data:

```
byte[] data;                                // The data to encrypt
SecretKey key;                              // Initialize as shown earlier
Cipher c = Cipher.getInstance("DESede");    // The object to perform encryption
c.init(Cipher.ENCRYPT_MODE, key);           // Initialize it

// Create a stream to write bytes to a file
FileOutputStream fos = new FileOutputStream("encrypted.data");

// Create a stream that encrypts bytes before sending them to that stream
// See also CipherInputStream to encrypt or decrypt while reading bytes
CipherOutputStream cos = new CipherOutputStream(fos, c);

cos.write(data);                            // Encrypt and write the data to the file
cos.close();                                // Always remember to close streams
java.util.Arrays.fill(data, (byte)0);       // Erase the unencrypted data
```

Finally, the javax.crypto.SealedObject class provides an especially easy way to
perform encryption. This class serializes a specified object and encrypts the resulting stream of bytes. The SealedObject can then be serialized itself and transmitted
to a recipient. The recipient is only able to retrieve the original object if she knows
the required SecretKey:

```
Serializable o;                                 // The object to be encrypted; must be Serializable
SecretKey key;                                  // The key to encrypt it with
Cipher c = Cipher.getInstance("Blowfish");      // Object to perform encryption
c.init(Cipher.ENCRYPT_MODE, key);               // Initialize it with the key
SealedObject so = new SealedObject(o, c);       // Create the sealed object

// Object so is a wrapper around an encrypted form of the original object o;
// it can now be serialized and transmitted to another party.
// Here's how the recipient decrypts the original object
Object original = so.getObject(key);            // Must use the same SecretKey
```

CHAPTER 5

Java Security

Java programs can dynamically load Java classes from a variety of sources, including untrusted sources, such as web sites reached across an insecure network. The ability to create and work with such mobile code is one of the great strengths and features of Java. To make it work successfully, however, Java puts great emphasis on a security architecture that allows untrusted code to run safely, without fear of damage to the host system.

The need for a security system in Java is most acutely demonstrated by applets— miniature Java applications designed to be embedded in web pages.* When a user visits a web page (with a Java-enabled web browser) that contains an applet, the web browser downloads the Java class files that define that applet and runs them. In the absence of a security system, an applet could wreak havoc on the user's system by deleting files, installing a virus, stealing confidential information, and so on. Somewhat more subtly, an applet could take advantage of the user's system to forge email, generate spam, or launch hacking attempts on other systems.

Java's main line of defense against such malicious code is *access control*: untrusted code is simply not given access to certain sensitive portions of the core Java API. For example, an untrusted applet is not typically allowed to read, write, or delete files on the host system or connect over the network to any computer other than the web server from which it was downloaded. This chapter describes the Java access control architecture and a few other facets of the Java security system.

Security Risks

Java has been designed from the ground up with security in mind; this gives it a great advantage over many other existing systems and platforms. Nevertheless, no system can guarantee 100% security, and Java is no exception.

---

* Applets are documented in *Java Foundation Classes in a Nutshell* (O'Reilly) and are not covered in this book. Still, they serve as good examples here.

The Java security architecture was designed by security experts and has been studied and probed by many other security experts. The consensus is that the architecture itself is strong and robust, theoretically without any security holes (at least none that have been discovered yet). The implementation of the security architecture is another matter, however, and there is a long history of security flaws being found and patched in particular implementations of Java. For example, in April 1999, a flaw was found in Sun's implementation of the class verifier in Java 1.1. Patches for Java 1.1.6 and 1.1.7 were issued and the problem was fixed in Java 1.1.8. Even more recently, in August 1999, a severe flaw was found in Microsoft's Java Virtual Machine (which is used by the Internet Explorer 4.0 and 5.0 web browsers). The flaw was a particularly dangerous one because it allowed a malicious applet to gain unrestricted access to the underlying system. Microsoft has released a new version of their VM, and (as of this writing) there have not been any known attacks that took advantage of the flaw.

In all likelihood, security flaws will continue to be discovered (and patched) in Java VM implementations. Despite this, Java remains perhaps the most secure platform currently available. There have been few, if any, reported instances of malicious Java code exploiting security holes "in the wild." For practical purposes, the Java platform appears to be adequately secure, especially when contrasted with some of the insecure and virus-ridden alternatives.

Java VM Security and Class File Verification

The lowest level of the Java security architecture involves the design of the Java Virtual Machine and the byte codes it executes. The Java VM does not allow any kind of direct access to individual memory addresses of the underlying system, which prevents Java code from interfering with the native hardware and operating system. These intentional restrictions on the VM are reflected in the Java language itself, which does not support pointers or pointer arithmetic. The language does not allow an integer to be cast to an object reference or vice versa, and there is no way whatsoever to obtain an object's address in memory. Without capabilities like these, malicious code simply cannot gain a foothold.

In addition to the secure design of the Virtual Machine instruction set, the VM goes through a process known as *byte-code verification* whenever it loads an untrusted class. This process ensures that the byte codes of a class (and their operands) are all valid; that the code never underflows or overflows the VM stack; that local variables are not used before they are initialized; that field, method, and class access control modifiers are respected; and so on. The verification step is designed to prevent the VM from executing byte codes that might crash it or put it into an undefined and untested state where it might be vulnerable to other attacks by malicious code. Byte-code verification is a defense against malicious hand-crafted Java byte codes and untrusted Java compilers that might output invalid byte codes.

Authentication and Cryptography

In Java 1.1 and later, the java.security package (and its subpackages) provides classes and interfaces for *authentication*. As described in Chapter 4, *The Java Platform*, this piece of the security architecture allows Java code to create and verify message digests and digital signatures. These technologies can ensure that any data (such as a Java class file) is authentic; that it originates from the person who claims to have originated it and has not been accidentally or maliciously modified in transit.

The Java Cryptography Extension, or JCE, consists of the javax.crypto package and its subpackages. These packages define classes for encryption and decryption of data. This is an important security-related feature for many applications, but is not directly relevant to the basic problem of preventing untrusted code from damaging the host system, so it is not discussed in this chapter.

Access Control

As I noted at the beginning of this chapter, the heart of the Java security architecture is access control: untrusted code simply must not be granted access to the sensitive parts of the Java API that would allow it to do malicious things. As we'll discuss in the following sections, the Java access-control model evolved significantly between Java 1.0 and Java 1.2. The Java 1.2 access-control model is relatively stable; it has not changed significantly in Java 1.3.

Java 1.0: The Sandbox

In this first release of Java, all Java code installed locally on the system is trusted implicitly. All code downloaded over the network, however, is untrusted and run in a restricted environment playfully called "the sandbox." The access-control policies of the sandbox are defined by the currently installed java.lang.SecurityManager object. When system code is about to perform a restricted operation, such as reading a file from the local filesystem, it first calls an appropriate method (such as checkRead()) of the currently installed SecurityManager object. If untrusted code is running, the SecurityManager throws a SecurityException that prevents the restricted operation from taking place.

The most common user of the SecurityManager class is a Java-enabled web browser, which installs a SecurityManager object to allow applets to run without damaging the host system. The precise details of the security policy are an implementation detail of the web browser, of course, but applets are typically restricted in the following ways:

- An applet cannot read, write, rename, or delete files. It cannot query the length or modification date of a file or even check whether a given file exists. Similarly, an applet cannot create, list, or delete a directory.

- An applet cannot connect to or accept a connection from any computer other than the one it was downloaded from. It cannot use any privileged ports (i.e., ports below and including port 1024).

- An applet cannot perform system-level functions, such as loading a native library, spawning a new process, or exiting the Java interpreter. An applet cannot manipulate any threads or thread groups, except for those it creates itself. In Java 1.1 and later, applets cannot use the Java Reflection API to obtain information about the non-public members of classes, except for classes that were downloaded with the applet.

- An applet cannot access certain graphics- and GUI-related facilities. It cannot initiate a print job or access the system clipboard or event queue. In addition, all windows created by an applet typically display a prominent visual indicator that they are "insecure," to prevent an applet from spoofing the appearance of some other application.

- An applet cannot read certain system properties, notably the user.home and user.dir properties, that specify the user's home directory and current working directory.

- An applet cannot circumvent these security restrictions by registering a new SecurityManager object.

How the sandbox works

Suppose that an applet (or some other untrusted code running in the sandbox) attempts to read the contents of the file */etc/passwd* by passing this filename to the FileInputStream() constructor. The programmers who wrote the FileInput-Stream class were aware that the class provides access to a system resource (a file), so use of the class should therefore be subject to access control. For this reason, they coded the FileInputStream() constructor to use the SecurityManager class.

Every time FileInputStream() is called, it checks to see if a SecurityManager object has been installed. If so, the constructor calls the checkRead() method of that SecurityManager object, passing the filename (*/etc/passwd*, in this case) as the sole argument. The checkRead() method has no return value; it either returns normally or throws a SecurityException. If the method returns, the FileInput-Stream() constructor simply proceeds with whatever initialization is necessary and returns. Otherwise, it allows the SecurityException to propagate to the caller. When this happens, no FileInputStream object is created, and the applet does not gain access to the */etc/passwd* file.

Java 1.1: Digitally Signed Classes

Java 1.1 retains the sandbox model of Java 1.0, but adds the java.security package and its digital signature capabilities. With these capabilities, Java classes can be digitally signed and verified. Thus, web browsers and other Java installations can be configured to trust downloaded code that bears a valid digital signature of a trusted entity. Such code is treated as if it were installed locally, so it is given full access to the Java APIs. In this release, the *javakey* program manages keys and digitally signs JAR files of Java code. Although Java 1.1 adds the important ability to trust digitally signed code that would otherwise be untrusted, it sticks to the basic sandbox model: trusted code gets full access and untrusted code gets totally restricted access.

Java 1.2: Permissions and Policies

Java 1.2 introduces major new access-control features into the Java security architecture. These features are implemented by new classes in the java.security package. The Policy class is one of the most important: it defines a Java security policy. A Policy object maps CodeSource objects to associated sets of Permission objects. A CodeSource object represents the source of a piece of Java code, which includes both the URL of the class file (and can be a local file) and a list of entities that have applied their digital signatures to the class file. The Permission objects associated with a CodeSource in the Policy define the permissions that are granted to code from a given source. Various Java APIs includes subclasses of Permission that represent different types of permissions. These include java.lang.RuntimePermission, java.io.FilePermission, and java.net.SocketPermission, for example.

Under this new access-control model, the SecurityManager class continues to be the central class; access-control requests are still made by invoking methods of a SecurityManager. However, the default SecurityManager implementation now delegates most of those requests to a new AccessController class that makes access decisions based on the Permission and Policy architecture.

The new Java 1.2 access-control architecture has several important features:

- Code from different sources can be given different sets of permissions. In other words, the new architecture supports fine-grained levels of trust. Even locally installed code can be treated as untrusted or partially untrusted. Under this new architecture, only system classes and standard extensions run as fully trusted.

- It is no longer necessary to define a custom subclass of SecurityManager to define a security policy. Policies can be configured by a system administrator by editing a text file or using the new *policytool* program.

- The new architecture is not limited to a fixed set of access control methods in the SecurityManager class. New Permission subclasses can be defined easily to govern access to new system resources (which might be exposed, for example, by new standard extensions that include native code).

How policies and permissions work

Let's return to the example of an applet that attempts to create a FileInputStream to read the file */etc/passwd*. In Java 1.2, the FileInputStream() constructor behaves exactly the same as it does in Java 1.0 and Java 1.1: it looks to see if a SecurityManager is installed and, if so, calls its checkRead() method, passing the name of the file to be read.

What's new in Java 1.2 is the default behavior of the checkRead() method. Unless a program has replaced the default security manager with one of its own, the default implementation creates a FilePermission object to represent the access being requested. This `FilePermission` object has a *target* of "/etc/passwd" and an *action* of "read". The `checkRead()` method passes this `FilePermission` object to the static `checkPermission()` method of the `java.security.AccessController` class.

It is the `AccessController` and its `checkPermission()` method that do the real work of access control in Java 1.2. The method determines the `CodeSource` of each calling method and uses the current `Policy` object to determine the `Permission` objects associated with it. With this information, the `AccessController` can determine whether read access to the */etc/passwd* file should be allowed.

The `Permission` class represents both the permissions granted by a `Policy` and the permissions requested by a method like the `FileInputStream()` constructor. When requesting a permission, Java typically uses a `FilePermission` (or other `Permission` subclass) with a very specific target, like "/etc/passwd". When granting a permission, however, a `Policy` commonly uses a `FilePermission` object with a wildcard target, such as "/etc/*", to represent many files. One of the key features of a `Permission` subclass such as `FilePermission` is that it defines an `implies()` method that can determine whether permission to read "/etc/*" implies permission to read "/etc/passwd".

Security for Everyone

Programmers, system administrators, and end users all have different security concerns and, thus, different roles to play in the Java 1.2 security architecture.

Security for System Programmers

System programmers are the people who define new Java APIs that allow access to sensitive system resources. These programmers are typically working with native methods that have unprotected access to the system. They need to use the Java access-control architecture to prevent untrusted code from executing those native methods. To do this, system programmers must carefully insert `Security-Manager` calls at appropriate places in their code. A system programmer may choose to use an existing `Permission` subclass to govern access to the system resources exposed by her API, or she may decide to define a specialized subclass of `Permission`.

The system programmer carries a tremendous security burden: if she does not perform appropriate access control checks in her code, she compromises the security of the entire Java platform. The details are complex and are beyond the scope of this book. Fortunately, however, system programming that involves native methods is rare in Java; almost all of us are application programmers who can simply rely on the existing APIs.

Security for Application Programmers

Programmers who use the core Java APIs and standard extensions, but do not define new extensions or write native methods, can simply rely on the security efforts of the system programmers who created those APIs. In other words, most of us Java programmers can simply use the Java APIs and need not worry about introducing security holes into the Java platform.

In fact, application programmers rarely have to use the access-control architecture. If you are writing Java code that may be run as untrusted code, you should be aware of the restrictions placed on untrusted code by typical security policies. Keep in mind that some methods (such as methods that read or write files) can throw `SecurityException` objects, but don't feel you must write your code to catch these exceptions. Often, the appropriate response to a `SecurityException` is to allow it to propagate uncaught, so that it terminates the application.

Sometimes, as an application programmer, you want to write an application (such as an applet viewer) that can load untrusted classes and run them subject to access-control checks. To do this in Java 1.2, you must first install a security manager:

```
System.setSecurityManager(new SecurityManager());
```

Then use `java.net.URLClassLoader` to load the untrusted classes. `URLClassLoader` assigns a default set of safe permissions to the classes it loads, but in some cases you may want to modify the permissions granted to the loaded code through the `Policy` and `PermissionCollection` classes.

Security for System Administrators

In Java 1.2 and later, system administrators are responsible for defining the default security policy for the computers at their site. The default policy is stored in the file *lib/security/java.policy* in the Java installation. A system administrator can edit this text file by hand or use the *policytool* program from Sun to edit the file graphically. *policytool* is the preferred way to define policies, so the syntax of the underlying policy file is not documented in this book.

The default *java.policy* file defines a policy that is much like the policy of Java 1.0 and Java 1.1: system classes and installed extensions are fully trusted, while all other code is untrusted and only allowed a few simple permissions. While this default policy is adequate for many purposes, it may not be appropriate for all sites. For example, at some organizations, it may be appropriate to grant extra permissions to code downloaded from a secure intranet.

In order to define secure and effective security policies, a system administrator must understand the various `Permission` subclasses of the Java platform, the target and action names they support, and the security implications of granting any particular permission. These topics are explained well in a document titled "Permissions in the Java 2 SDK," which is part of the Java 1.2 release and also available (at the time of this writing) online at: *http://java.sun.com/products/jdk/1.2/docs/guide/security/permissions.html*.

Security for End Users

Most end users do not have to think about security at all: their Java programs should simply run in a secure way with no intervention by them. Some sophisticated end users may want to define their own security policies, however. An end user can do this by running *policytool* himself to define personal policy files that augment the system policy. The default personal policy is stored in a file named *.java.policy* in the user's home directory. By default, Java loads this policy file and uses it to augment the system policy file.

In Java 1.2 and later, a user can specify an additional policy file to use when starting up the Java interpreter, by defining the `java.security.policy` property with the -D option. For example:

```
C:\> java -Djava.security.policy=policyfile UntrustedApp
```

This line runs the class UntrustedApp after augmenting the default system and user policies with the policy specified in the file or URL *policyfile*. To replace the system and user policies instead of augmenting them, use a double equals sign in the property specification:

```
C:\> java -Djava.security.policy==policyfile UntrustedApp
```

Note, however, that specifying a policy file is only useful if there is a Security-Manager installed. If a user doesn't trust an application, he presumably doesn't trust that application to voluntarily install its own security manager. In this case, he can define the java.security.manager system property:

```
C:\> java -Djava.security.manager -Djava.security.policy=policyfile UntrustedApp
```

The value of this property does not matter; simply defining it is enough to tell the Java interpreter to automatically install a default SecurityManager object that subjects an application to the access control policies described in the system, user, and java.security.policy policy files.

Permission Classes

Table 5-1 lists the various Permission subclasses, the target and action names they support, and the methods that require those permissions (in Java 1.2 and later).

Table 5-1: Permission Classes and the Methods They Govern

Permission	Target, Action	Methods
AWT-Permission	"accessClipboard"	Toolkit.getSystemClipboard()
	"accessEventQueue"	Toolkit.getSystemEventQueue()
	"listenToAllAWTEvents"	Toolkit.{addAWTEventListener(), removeAWTEventListener()}
	"readDisplayPixels"	Graphics2D.setComposite()
	"showWindowWithout-WarningBanner"	Window.Window() (if permission is not granted, window has an "insecure" indication)
File-Permission	*command*, "execute"	Runtime.exec()
	filename, "delete"	File.{delete(), deleteOnExit()}

Table 5-1: Permission Classes and the Methods They Govern (continued)

Permission	Target, Action	Methods

File-
Permission
	filename, "read"	`FileInputStream.FileInputStream(),`
		`File.{exists(), canRead(),`
		`isFile(), isDirectory(),`
		`isHidden(), lastModified(),`
		`length(), list(), listFiles()},`
		`RandomAccessFile.RandomAccessFile(),`
		`ZipFile.ZipFile()`

	filename, "write"	`FileOutputStream.FileOutputStream(),`
		`File.{canWrite(), createNewFile(),`
		`createTempFile(), mkdir(), mkdirs(),`
		`renameTo(), setLastModified(),`
		`setReadOnly()},`
		`RandomAccessFile.RandomAccessFile()`

Net- Permission	"requestPassword- Authentication"	`Authenticator.requestPassword-` `Authentication()`
	"setDefaultAuthenticator"	`Authenticator.setDefault()`
	"specifyStreamHandler"	`URL.URL()`

Property-
Permission
	"*", "read, write"	`Beans.{setDesignTime(),`
		`setGuiAvailable()},`
		`Introspector.setBeanInfo-`
		`SearchPath(),`
		`PropertyEditorManager.{register-`
		`Editor(), setEditorSearchPath()},`
		`System.{getProperties(),`
		`setProperties()}`

	"user.language", "write"	`Locale.setDefault()`
	prop, "read"	`System.getProperty()`
	prop, "write"	`System.setProperty()`
Reflect- Permission	"suppressAccessChecks"	`AccessibleObject.setAccessible()`

Runtime-
Permission
	"accessClassIn-
	Package.*pkgname*"
		`Class.{getClasses(),`
		`getDeclaredClasses(),`
		`getConstructor(), getConstructors(),`
		`getDeclaredFields(),`
		`getDeclaredMethods(),`
		`getDeclaredConstructors(),`
		`getDeclaredField(),`
		`getDeclaredMethod(),`
		`getDeclaredConstructor(),`

Table 5-1: *Permission Classes and the Methods They Govern (continued)*

Permission	Target, Action	Methods
Runtime-Permission		`getFields(), getMethods(),` `getField(), getMethod()}`

	"accessDeclaredMembers"	`Class.{getClasses(),`
		`getDeclaredClasses(),`
		`getDeclaredFields(),`
		`getDeclaredMethods(),`
		`getDeclaredConstructors(),`
		`getDeclaredField(),`
		`getDeclaredMethod(),`
		`getDeclaredConstructor()}`

	"createClassLoader"	`ClassLoader.Class-Loader(),`
		`URLClassLoader.URL-ClassLoader(),`
		`SecureClassLoader.Secure-ClassLoader()`

	"exitVM"	`Runtime.{exit(),`
		`runFinalizersOnExit()},`
		`System.{exit(),`
		`runFinalizersOnExit()}`

	"getClassLoader"	`Class.{forName(), getClassLoader()},`
		`ClassLoader.{getSystemClassLoader(),`
		`getParent()},`
		`Thread.getContextClassLoader()`

	"getProtectionDomain"	`Class.getProtectionDomain()`
	"loadLibrary.*libName*"	`Runtime.{load(), loadLibrary()},` `System.{load(), loadLibrary()}`

	"modifyThread"	`Thread.{checkAccess(), interrupt(),`
		`suspend(), resume(), setPriority(),`
		`setName(), setDaemon()},`
		`ThreadGroup.{interrupt(), stop()}`

	"modifyThreadGroup"	`Thread.{Thread(), enumerate()},`
		`ThreadGroup.{ThreadGroup(),`
		`enumerate(), getParent(),`
		`interrupt(), setDaemon(),`
		`setMaxPriority(), stop(), suspend(),`
		`resume(), destroy()}`

	"queuePrintJob"	`Toolkit.getPrintJob()`
	"readFileDescriptor"	`FileInputStream.File-InputStream(FileDescriptor)`
	"setContextClassLoader"	`Thread.setContextClassLoader()`

Java Security

Table 5-1: Permission Classes and the Methods They Govern (continued)

Permission	Target, Action	Methods
Runtime-Permission	"setFactory"	ServerSocket.setSocketFactory(), Socket.setSocketImplFactory(), URL.setURLStream-HandlerFactory(), URLConnection.{setContent-HandlerFactory(), setFileNameMap()}, HttpURLConnection.set-FollowRedirects(), activation.Activation-Group.{createGroup(), setSystem()}, server.RMISocketFactory.set-SocketFactory()
	"setIO"	System.{setIn(), setOut(), setErr()}
	"setSecurityManager"	System.setSecurityManager()
	"stopThread"	Thread.stop(), ThreadGroup.stop()
	"writeFileDescriptor"	FileOutputStream.File-OutputStream(FileDescriptor)
Security-Permission	"addIdentityCertificate"	Identity.addCertificate()
	"clearProvider-Properties.*provider*"	Provider.clear()
	"getPolicy"	Policy.getPolicy()
	"getProperty.*propname*"	Security.getProperty()
	"getSignerPrivateKey"	Signer.getPrivateKey()
	"insertProvider.*provider*"	Security.{addProvider(), insertProviderAt()}
	"printIdentity"	Identity.toString()
	"putProvider-Property.*provider*"	Provider.put()
	"removeIdentityCertificate"	Identity.removeCertificate()
	"removeProvider.*provider*"	Security.removeProvider()
	"removeProvider-Property.*provider*"	Provider.remove()
	"setIdentityInfo"	Identity.setInfo(String)
	"setIdentityPublicKey"	Identity.setPublicKey()
	"setPolicy"	Policy.setPolicy();
	"setProperty.*propname*"	Security.setProperty()
	"setSignerKeypair"	Signer.setKeyPair()
	"setSystemScope"	IdentityScope.setSystemScope()

Table 5–1: Permission Classes and the Methods They Govern (continued)

Permission	Target, Action	Methods
Serializable-Permission	"enableSubclass-Implementation"	ObjectInputStream.Object-InputStream(), ObjectOutputStream.Object-OutputStream()
	"enableSubstitution"	ObjectInputStream.enable-ResolveObject(), ObjectOutputStream.enable-ReplaceObject()
Socket-Permission	"localhost:*port*", "listen"	ServerSocket.ServerSocket(), DatagramSocket.DatagramSocket(), MulticastSocket.MulticastSocket()
	host, "accept, connect"	MulticastSocket.{joinGroup(), leaveGroup(), send()}
	host, "resolve"	InetAddress.{getHostName(), getAllByName(), getLocalHost()}, DatagramSocket.getLocalAddress()
	host:port, "accept"	DatagramSocket.receive(), ServerSocket.{accept(), implAccept()}
	host:port, "connect"	DatagramSocket.send(), Socket.Socket()

CHAPTER 6

JavaBeans

The JavaBeans API provides a framework for defining reusable, embeddable, modular software components. The JavaBeans specification includes the following definition of a bean: "a reusable software component that can be manipulated visually in a builder tool." As you can see, this is a rather loose definition; beans can take a variety of forms. The most common use of beans is for graphical user interface components, such as components of the java.awt and javax.swing packages, which are documented in *Java Foundation Classes in a Nutshell* (O'Reilly).* Although all beans can be manipulated visually, this does not mean every bean has its own visual representation. For example, the javax.sql.RowSet class (documented in *Java Enterprise in a Nutshell* (O'Reilly)) is a JavaBeans component that represents the data resulting from a database query. There are no limits on the simplicity or complexity of a JavaBeans component. The simplest beans are typically basic graphical interface components, such as a java.awt.Button object. But even complex systems, such as an embeddable spreadsheet application, can function as individual beans.

One of the goals of the JavaBeans model is interoperability with similar component frameworks. So, for example, a native Windows program can, with an appropriate bridge or wrapper object, use a JavaBeans component as if it were a COM or ActiveX component. The details of this sort of interoperability are beyond the scope of this chapter, however.

The JavaBeans component model consists of the java.beans and java.beans.beancontext packages and a number of important naming and API conventions to which conforming beans and bean-manipulation tools must adhere. Because JavaBeans is a framework for generic components, the JavaBeans conventions are, in many ways, more important than the actual API.

---

* JavaBeans are documented in this book instead of that one because the JavaBeans component model is not specific to AWT or Swing programming. Nevertheless, it is hardly possible to discuss beans without mentioning AWT and Swing components. You will probably get the most out of this chapter if you have some familiarity with GUI programming in Java using AWT or Swing.

Two interesting technologies related to JavaBeans are the Java Activation Framework and InfoBus. Both are standard extensions, implemented in the `javax.activation` and `javax.infobus` packages, respectively. You can read more about them at the JavaBeans web site: *http://java.sun.com/beans/*.

Beans can be used at three levels by three different categories of programmers:

- If you are writing an application that uses beans developed by other programmers or using a beanbox tool* to combine those beans into an application, you need to be familiar with general JavaBeans concepts and terminology. You also need to read the documentation for the individual beans you use in your application, but you do not need to understand the JavaBeans API. This chapter begins with an overview of JavaBeans concepts that should be sufficient for programmers using beans at this level.

- If you are writing beans, you need to understand and follow various JavaBeans naming and packaging conventions. After the introduction to general bean concepts and terminology, this chapter describes the basic bean conventions bean developers must follow. Although a JavaBeans component can be implemented without using the JavaBeans API, most beans are distributed with various auxiliary classes that make them easier to use within beanbox tools. These auxiliary classes rely heavily on the JavaBeans API so that they can interoperate with beanbox tools.

- If you are developing a GUI editor, application builder, or other beanbox tool, you use the JavaBeans API to help you manipulate beans within the tool. You also need to be intimately familiar with all the various JavaBeans programming conventions. Although this chapter describes the most important conventions, you should also refer to the primary source, the JavaBeans specification (see *http://java.sun.com/beans/*).

Bean Basics

Any object that conforms to certain basic rules can be a bean; there is no Bean class all beans are required to subclass. Many beans are AWT components, but it is also quite possible, and often useful, to write "invisible" beans that do not have an onscreen appearance. (Just because a bean does not have an onscreen appearance in a finished application does not mean it cannot be visually manipulated by a beanbox tool, however.)

A bean is characterized by the properties, events, and methods it exports. It is these properties, events, and methods an application designer manipulates in a beanbox tool. A *property* is a piece of the bean's internal state that can be programmatically set and/or queried, usually through a standard pair of get and set accessor methods.

A bean communicates with the application in which it is embedded and with other beans by generating *events*. The JavaBeans API uses the same event model AWT

---

* *beanbox* is the name of the sample bean-manipulation program provided by Sun in its Beans Development Kit (BDK). The term is a useful one, and I'll use it to describe any kind of graphical design tool or application builder that manipulates beans.

and Swing components use. This model is based on the `java.util.EventObject` class and the `java.util.EventListener` interface; it is described in detail in *Java Foundation Classes in a Nutshell* (O'Reilly). In brief, the event model works like this:

- A bean defines an event if it provides `add` and `remove` methods for registering and deregistering listener objects for that event.

- An application that wants to be notified when an event of that type occurs uses these methods to register an event listener object of the appropriate type.

- When the event occurs, the bean notifies all registered listeners by passing an event object that describes the event to a method defined by the event listener interface.

A *unicast event* is a rare kind of event for which there can be only a single registered listener object. The `add` registration method for a unicast event throws a `TooManyListenersException` if an attempt is made to register more than a single listener.

The *methods* exported by a bean are simply any `public` methods defined by the bean, excluding those methods that get and set property values and register and remove event listeners.

In addition to the regular sort of properties described earlier, the JavaBeans API also supports several specialized property subtypes. An *indexed property* is a property that has an array value, as well as getter and setter methods that access both individual elements of the array and the entire array. A *bound property* is one that sends a `PropertyChangeEvent` to any interested `PropertyChangeListener` objects whenever the value of the property changes. A *constrained property* is one that can have any changes vetoed by any interested listener. When the value of a constrained property of a bean changes, the bean must send out a `Property-ChangeEvent` to the list of interested `VetoableChangeListener` objects. If any of these objects throws a `PropertyVetoException`, the property value is not changed, and the `PropertyVetoException` is propagated back to the property setter method.

Because Java allows dynamic loading of classes, beanbox programs can load arbitrary beans. The beanbox tool uses a process called *introspection* to determine the properties, events, and methods exported by a bean. The introspection mechanism is implemented by the `java.beans.Introspector` class; it relies on both the `java.lang.reflect` reflection mechanism and a number of JavaBeans naming conventions. `Introspector` can determine the list of properties supported by a bean, for example, by scanning the class for methods that have the right names and signatures to be `get` and `set` property accessor methods.

The introspection mechanism does not rely on the reflection capabilities of Java alone, however. Any bean can define an auxiliary `BeanInfo` class that provides additional information about the bean and its properties, events, and methods. The `Introspector` automatically attempts to locate and load the `BeanInfo` class of a bean.

The `BeanInfo` class provides additional information about the bean primarily in the form of `FeatureDescriptor` objects, each one describing a single feature of the bean. Each FeatureDescriptor provides a name and brief description of the feature it documents. The beanbox tool can display the name and description to the user, making the bean essentially self-documenting and easier to use. Specific bean features, such as properties, events, and methods, are described by specific subclasses of FeatureDescriptor, such as PropertyDescriptor, EventSetDescriptor, and MethodDescriptor.

One of the primary tasks of a beanbox application is to allow the user to customize a bean by setting property values. A beanbox defines *property editors* for commonly used property types, such as numbers, strings, fonts, and colors. If a bean has a property of a more complicated type, however, it can define a PropertyEditor class that enables the beanbox to let the user set values for that property.

In addition, a complex bean may not be satisfied with the property-by-property customization mechanism provided by most beanbox tools. Such a bean can define a Customizer class to create a graphical interface that allows the user to configure a bean in some useful way. A particularly complex bean can even define customizers that serve as "wizards" that guide the user step by step through the customization process.

A *bean context* is a logical container (and often a visual container) for JavaBeans and, optionally, for other nested bean contexts. In practice, most JavaBeans are AWT or Swing components or containers. Beanbox tools recognize this and allow component beans to be nested within container beans. A bean context is a kind of heavyweight container that formalizes this nesting relationship. More importantly, however, a bean context can provide a set of services (e.g., printing services, debugging services, database connection services) to the beans it contains. Beans that are aware of their context can be written to query the context and take advantage of the services that are available. Bean contexts are implemented using the java.beans.beancontext API, which is new as of Java 1.2 and discussed in more detail later in this chapter.

JavaBeans Conventions

The JavaBeans component model relies on a number of rules and conventions bean developers must follow. These conventions are not part of the JavaBeans API itself, but in many ways, they are more important to bean developers than the API itself. The conventions are sometimes referred to as *design patterns*; they specify such things as method names and signatures for property accessor methods defined by a bean.

The reason for these design patterns is interoperability between beans and the beanbox programs that manipulate them. As we've seen, beanbox programs may rely on introspection to determine the list of properties, events, and methods a bean supports. In order for this to work, bean developers must use method names the beanbox can recognize. The JavaBeans framework facilitates this process by establishing naming conventions. One such convention, for example, is that the getter and setter accessor methods for a property should begin with get and set.

Not all the patterns are absolute requirements. If a bean has property accessor methods that do not follow the naming conventions, it is possible to use a `PropertyDescriptor` object (specified in a `BeanInfo` class) to indicate the accessor methods for the property. Although the `BeanInfo` class provides an alternative to the property-accessor-method naming convention, the property accessor method must still follow the conventions that specify the number and type of its parameters and its return value.

Beans

A bean itself must adhere to the following conventions:

Class name
> There are no restrictions on the class name of a bean.

Superclass
> A bean can extend any other class. Beans are often AWT or Swing components, but there are no restrictions.

Instantiation
> A bean must provide a no-parameter constructor or a file that contains a serialized instance the beanbox can deserialize for use as a prototype bean, so a beanbox can instantiate the bean. The file that contains the bean should have the same name as the bean, with an extension of *.ser.*

Bean name
> The name of a bean is the name of the class that implements it or the name of the file that holds the serialized instance of the bean (with the *.ser* extension removed and directory separator (/) characters converted to dot (.) characters).

Properties

A bean defines a property *p* of type *T* if it has accessor methods that follow these patterns (if *T* is `boolean`, a special form of getter method is allowed):

Getter

```
public T getP()
```

Boolean getter

```
public boolean isP()
```

Setter

```
public void setP(T)
```

Exceptions
> Property accessor methods can throw any type of checked or unchecked exceptions

Indexed Properties

An indexed property is a property of array type that provides accessor methods that get and set the entire array, as well as methods that get and set individual elements of the array. A bean defines an indexed property *p* of type *T*[] if it defines the following accessor methods:

Array getter

```
public T[] getP()
```

Element getter

```
public T getP(int)
```

Array setter

```
public void setP(T[])
```

Element setter

```
public void setP(int,T)
```

Exceptions

Indexed property accessor methods can throw any type of checked or unchecked exceptions. In particular, they should throw an `ArrayIndexOutOf-BoundsException` if the supplied index is out of bounds.

Bound Properties

A bound property is one that generates a `PropertyChangeEvent` when its value changes. Here are the conventions for a bound property:

Accessor methods

The getter and setter methods for a bound property follow the same conventions as a regular property.

Introspection

A beanbox cannot distinguish a bound property from a nonbound property through introspection alone. Therefore, you may want to implement a `Bean-Info` class that returns a `PropertyDescriptor` object for the property. The `isBound()` method of this `PropertyDescriptor` should return `true`.

Listener registration

A bean that defines one or more bound properties must define a pair of methods for the registration of listeners that are notified when any bound property value change. The methods must have these signatures:

```
public void addPropertyChangeListener(PropertyChangeListener)
public void removePropertyChangeListener(PropertyChangeListener)
```

Named property listener registration

A bean can optionally provide additional methods that allow event listeners to be registered for changes to a single bound property value. These methods are passed the name of a property and have the following signatures:

```
public void addPropertyChangeListener(String, PropertyChangeListener)
public void removePropertyChangeListener(String, PropertyChangeListener)
```

Per-property listener registration

A bean can optionally provide additional event listener registration methods that are specific to a single property. For a property *p*, these methods have the following signatures:

```
public void addPListener(PropertyChangeListener)
public void removePListener(PropertyChangeListener)
```

Methods of this type allow a beanbox to distinguish a bound property from a nonbound property.

Notification

When the value of a bound property changes, the bean should update its internal state to reflect the change and then pass a PropertyChangeEvent to the propertyChange() method of every PropertyChangeListener object registered for the bean or the specific bound property.

Support

java.beans.PropertyChangeSupport is a helpful class for implementing bound properties.

Constrained Properties

A constrained property is one for which any changes can be vetoed by registered listeners. Most constrained properties are also bound properties. Here are the conventions for a constrained property:

Getter

The getter method for a constrained property is the same as the getter method for a regular property.

Setter

The setter method of a constrained property throws a PropertyVetoException if the property change is vetoed. For a property *p* of type *T*, the signature looks like this:

```
public void setP(T) throws PropertyVetoException
```

Listener registration

A bean that defines one or more constrained properties must define a pair of methods for the registration of listeners that are notified when any constrained property value changes. The methods must have these signatures:

```
public void addVetoableChangeListener(VetoableChangeListener)
public void removeVetoableChangeListener(VetoableChangeListener)
```

Named property listener registration

A bean can optionally provide additional methods that allow event listeners to be registered for changes to a single constrained property value. These methods are passed the name of a property and have the following signatures:

```
public void addVetoableChangeListener(String, VetoableChangeListener)
public void removeVetoableChangeListener(String, VetoableChangeListener)
```

Per-property listener registration

A bean can optionally provide additional listener registration methods that are specific to a single constrained property. For a property *p*, these methods have the following signatures:

```
public void addPListener(VetoableChangeListener)
public void removePListener(VetoableChangeListener)
```

Notification

When the setter method of a constrained property is invoked, the bean must generate a `PropertyChangeEvent` that describes the requested change and pass that event to the `vetoableChange()` method of every `VetoableChange-Listener` object registered for the bean or the specific constrained property. If any listener vetos the change by throwing a `PropertyVetoException`, the bean must send out another `PropertyChangeEvent` to revert the property to its original value, and then it should throw a `PropertyVetoException` itself. If, on the other hand, the property change is not vetoed, the bean should update its internal state to reflect the change. If the constrained property is also a bound property, the bean should notify `PropertyChangeListener` objects at this point.

Support

`java.beans.VetoableChangeSupport` is a helpful class for implementing constrained properties.

Events

In addition to `PropertyChangeEvent` events generated when bound and constrained properties are changed, a bean can generate other types of events. An event named *E* should follow these conventions:

Event class

The event class should directly or indirectly extend `java.util.EventObject` and should be named *E*`Event`.

Listener interface

The event must be associated with an event listener interface that extends `java.util.EventListener` and is named *E*`Listener`.

Listener methods

The event listener interface can define any number of methods that take a single argument of type *E*`Event` and return `void`.

Listener registration

The bean must define a pair of methods for registering event listeners that want to be notified when an *E* event occurs. The methods should have the following signatures:

```
public void addEListener(EListener)
public void removeEListener(EListener)
```

Unicast events

A unicast event allows only one listener object to be registered at a single time. If *E* is a unicast event, the listener registration method should have this signature:

```
public void addEListener(EListener) throws TooManyListenersException
```

Methods

A beanbox can expose the methods of a bean to application designers. The only formal convention is that these methods must be declared `public`. The following guidelines are also useful, however:

Method name

A method can have any name that does not conflict with the property- and event-naming conventions. The name should be as descriptive as possible.

Parameters

A method can have any number and type of parameters. However, beanbox programs may work best with no-parameter methods or methods that have simple primitive parameters.

Excluding methods

A bean can explicitly specify the list of methods it exports by providing a `BeanInfo` implementation.

Documentation

A bean can provide user-friendly, human-readable localized names and descriptions for methods through `MethodDescriptor` objects returned by a `BeanInfo` implementation.

Auxiliary Classes

A bean can provide the following auxiliary classes:

`BeanInfo`

To provide additional information about a bean *B*, implement the `BeanInfo` interface in a class named *B*`BeanInfo`.

Property editor for a specific type

To enable a beanbox to work with properties of type *T*, implement the `PropertyEditor` interface in a class named *T*`Editor`. The class must have a no-parameter constructor.

Property editor for a specific property

To customize the way a beanbox allows the user to enter values for a single property, define a class that implements the `PropertyEditor` interface and has a no-parameter constructor, and register that class with a `PropertyDescriptor` object returned by the `BeanInfo` class for the bean.

Customizers

To define a customizer, or wizard, for configuring a bean *B*, define an AWT or Swing component with a no-parameter constructor that does the customization. The class is commonly called `BCustomizer`, but this is not required. Register the class with the `BeanDescriptor` object returned by the `BeanInfo` class for the bean.

Documentation

Define default documentation for a bean *B* in HTML 2.0 format and store that documentation in a file named `B.html`. Define localized translations of the documentation in files by the same name in locale-specific directories.

Bean Packaging and Distribution

Beans are distributed in JAR archive files that have the following:

Content

The class or classes that implement a bean should be included in the JAR file, along with auxiliary classes such as `BeanInfo` and `PropertyEditor` implementations. If the bean is instantiated from a serialized instance, that instance should be included in the JAR archive with a filename ending in *.ser*. The JAR file can contain HTML documentation for the bean and should also contain any resource files, such as images, required by the bean and its auxiliary classes. A single JAR file can contain more than one bean.

`Java-Bean` *attribute*

The manifest of the JAR file must mark any *.class* and *.ser* files that define a bean with the attribute:

```
Java-Bean: true
```

`Depends-On` *attribute*

The manifest of a JAR file can use the `Depends-On` attribute to specify all other files in the JAR archive on which the bean depends. A beanbox application can use this information when generating applications or repackaging beans. Each bean can have zero or more `Depends-On` attributes, each of which can list zero or more space-separated filenames. Within a JAR file, / is always used as the directory separator.

`Design-Time-Only` *attribute*

The manifest of a JAR file can optionally use the `Design-Time-Only` attribute to specify auxiliary files, such as `BeanInfo` implementations, that are used by a beanbox, but not used by applications that use the bean. The beanbox can use this information when repackaging beans for use in an application.

Bean Contexts and Services

The JavaBeans component model was introduced in Java 1.1. Java 1.2 extends that model by introducing a containment and services protocol, defined in the `java.beans.beancontext` package. A bean context is a `java.util.Collection` of beans that implements the `BeanContext` interface and provides a context for the beans it contains. Many bean contexts define one or more services, such as a printing service, that beans can query and use. These bean contexts implement the `BeanContextServices` interface. All bean contexts are also `BeanContextChild` implementations, so contexts can be nested within each other.

Many beans never need to know about the contexts that contain them. A bean that does want to take advantage of its context and the services it provides implements the `BeanContextChild` interface. When a bean context child is added to a bean context, the `setBeanContext()` method of the `BeanContextChild` interface is invoked by the bean context. The implementation of this method should store the reference to the bean context for future use. The `setBeanContext()` method is a bound and constrained property, so it must notify `VetoableChangeListener` and `PropertyChangeListener` objects. For this reason, many beans delegate these responsibilities to a `BeanContextChildSuport` object.

If a bean (or bean context) is nested within a bean context that implements `Bean-ContextServices`, the bean can use the services provided by the bean context. A service is identified by the Java class that defines it. So a printing service is identified by the `Class` object of the `java.awt.print.PrinterJob` class, for example, and the system clipboard service is represented by the `java.awt.datatrans-fer.Clipboard` class. A bean can call the `hasService()` method of its containing `BeanContextServices` object to determine whether a specified service is available. If so, it can use `getService()` to obtain an appropriate instance of the service class. If a bean context is nested within another context, it can pass these `hasService()` and `getService()` methods to its containing context.

In addition to `getService()` and `hasService()`, a `BeanContext` provides several other methods beans can rely on. `getResource()` and `getResourceAsStream()` replace the methods by the same name defined by `Class` and `ClassLoader`. The `isDesignTime()` method (from the `DesignMode` interface) allows a bean to determine whether it is being displayed within a beanbox or run in an application or applet. The `BeanContext` method is preferred to the static `Beans.isDesignTime()` method because it is context-specific rather than global.

`BeanContext` and `BeanContextServices` are large interfaces; implementations must adhere to fairly complex specifications that govern the ways they interact with the beans they contain and the contexts within which they are nested. For these reasons, bean developers do not often create custom bean contexts. Instead, they rely on the contexts provided by the vendor of their beanbox tool. Advanced bean developers who do need to create bean contexts can delegate many of their methods to the `BeanContextSupport` and `BeanContextServicesSupport` classes that implement the basic framework and protocols.

CHAPTER 7

Java Programming and Documentation Conventions

This chapter explains a number of important and useful Java programming conventions. If you follow these conventions, your Java code will be self-documenting, easier to read and maintain, and more portable.

Naming and Capitalization Conventions

The following widely adopted naming conventions apply to packages, classes, methods, fields, and constants in Java. Because these conventions are almost universally followed and because they affect the public API of the classes you define, they should be followed carefully:

Packages

Ensure that your package names are unique by prefixing them with the inverted name of your Internet domain (e.g., com.davidflanagan.utils). All package names, or at least their unique prefixes, should be lowercase.

Classes

A class name should begin with a capital letter and be written in mixed case (e.g., String). If a class name consists of more than one word, each word should begin with a capital letter (e.g., StringBuffer). If a class name, or one of the words of a class name, is an acronym, the acronym can be written in all capital letters (e.g., URL, HTMLParser).

Since classes are designed to represent objects, you should choose class names that are nouns (e.g., Thread, Teapot, FormatConverter).

Interfaces

Interface names follow the same capitalization conventions as class names. When an interface is used to provide additional information about the classes that implement it, it is common to choose an interface name that is an adjective (e.g., Runnable, Cloneable, Serializable, DataInput). When an interface works more like an abstract superclass, use a name that is a noun (e.g., Document, FileNameMap, Collection).

Methods

A method name always begins with a lowercase letter. If the name contains more than one word, every word after the first begins with a capital letter (e.g., `insert()`, `insertObject()`, `insertObjectAt()`). Method names are typically chosen so that the first word is a verb. Method names can be as long as is necessary to make their purpose clear, but choose succinct names where possible.

Fields and constants

Nonconstant field names follow the same capitalization conventions as method names. If a field is a `static final` constant, it should be written in uppercase. If the name of a constant includes more than one word, the words should be separated with underscores (e.g., `MAX_VALUE`). A field name should be chosen to best describe the purpose of the field or the value it holds.

Parameters

The names of method parameters appear in the documentation for a method, so you should choose names that make the purpose of the parameters as clear as possible. Try to keep parameter names to a single word and use them consistently. For example, if a `WidgetProcessor` class defines many methods that accept a `Widget` object as the first parameter, name this parameter `widget` or even `w` in each method.

Local variables

Local variable names are an implementation detail and never visible outside your class. Nevertheless, choosing good names makes your code easier to read, understand, and maintain. Variables are typically named following the same conventions as methods and fields.

In addition to the conventions for specific types of names, there are conventions regarding the characters you should use in your names. Java allows the $ character in any identifier, but, by convention, its use is reserved for synthetic names generated by source-code processors. (It is used by the Java compiler, for example, to make inner classes work.) Also, Java allows names to use any alphanumeric characters from the entire Unicode character set. While this can be convenient for non-English-speaking programmers, the use of Unicode characters should typically be restricted to local variables, private methods and fields, and other names that are not part of the public API of a class.

Portability Conventions and Pure Java Rules

Sun's motto, or core value proposition, for Java is "Write once, run anywhere." Java makes it easy to write portable programs, but Java programs do not automatically run successfully on any Java platform. To ensure portability, you must follow a few fairly simple rules that can be summarized as follows:

Native methods

Portable Java code can use any methods in the core Java APIs, including methods implemented as `native` methods. However, portable code must not define its own native methods. By their very nature, native methods must be ported to each new platform, so they directly subvert the "Write once, run anywhere" promise of Java.

The Runtime.exec() method

Calling the Runtime.exec() method to spawn a process and execute an external command on the native system is rarely allowed in portable code. This is because the native OS command to be executed is never guaranteed to exist or behave the same way on all platforms. The only time it is legal to use Runtime.exec() is when the user is allowed to specify the command to run, either by typing the command at runtime or by specifying the command in a configuration file or preferences dialog box.

The System.getenv() method

Using System.getenv() is nonportable, without exception. The method has actually been deprecated for this reason.

Undocumented classes

Portable Java code must use only classes and interfaces that are a documented part of the Java platform. Most Java implementations ship with additional undocumented public classes that are part of the implementation, but not of the Java platform specification. There is nothing to prevent a program from using and relying on these undocumented classes, but doing so is not portable because the classes are not guaranteed to exist in all Java implementations or on all platforms.

The java.awt.peer package

The interfaces in the java.awt.peer package are part of the Java platform, but are documented for use by AWT implementors only. Applications that use these interfaces directly are not portable.

Implementation-specific features

Portable code must not rely on features specific to a single implementation. For example, in a widely controversial move, Microsoft distributed a version of the Java runtime system that included a number of additional methods that were not part of the Java platform as defined by Sun. Legal action between Sun and Microsoft is pending because of this. Any program that depends on the Microsoft-specific extensions is obviously not portable to other platforms.

Implementation-specific bugs

Just as portable code must not depend on implementation-specific features, it must not depend on implementation-specific bugs. If a class or method behaves differently than the specification says it should, a portable program cannot rely on this behavior, which may be different on different platforms.

Implementation-specific behavior

Sometimes different platforms and different implementations may present different behaviors, all of which are legal according to the Java specification. Portable code must not depend on any one specific behavior. For example, the Java specification does not specify whether threads of equal priority share the CPU or if one long-running thread can starve another thread at the same priority. If an application assumes one behavior or the other, it may not run properly on all platforms.

Conventions

Standard extensions

Portable code can rely on standard extensions to the Java platform, but, if it does so, it should clearly specify which extensions it uses and exit cleanly with an appropriate error message when run on a system that does not have the extensions installed.

Complete programs

Any portable Java program must be complete and self-contained: it must supply all the classes it uses, except core platform and standard extension classes.

Defining system classes

Portable Java code never defines classes in any of the system or standard extension packages. Doing so violates the protection boundaries of those packages and exposes package-visible implementation details.

Hardcoded filenames

A portable program contains no hardcoded file or directory names. This is because different platforms have significantly different filesystem organizations and use different directory separator characters. If you need to work with a file or directory, have the user specify the filename, or at least the base directory beneath which the file can be found. This specification can be done at runtime, in a configuration file, or as a command-line argument to the program. When concatenating a file or directory name to a directory name, use the File() constructor or the File.separator constant.

Line separators

Different systems use different characters or sequences of characters as line separators. Do not hardcode "\n", "\r", or "\r\n" as the line separator in your program. Instead, use the println() method of PrintStream or PrintWriter, which automatically terminates a line with the line separator appropriate for the platform, or use the value of the line.separator system property.

Mixed event models

The AWT event model changed dramatically between Java 1.0 and Java 1.1. Although it is often possible to mix these two event models in a program, doing so is not technically portable.

The previous rules are the focus of Sun's "100% Pure Java" portability certification program; you can find out more about this program and read more about the "Pure Java" requirements at *http://java.sun.com/100percent/*.

Java Documentation Comments

Most ordinary comments within Java code explain the implementation details of that code. In contrast, the Java language specification defines a special type of comment known as a doc comment that serves to document the API of your code. A doc comment is an ordinary multiline comment that begins with /** (instead of the usual /*) and ends with */. A doc comment appears immediately before a class, interface, method, or field definition and contains documentation for that class, interface, method, or field. The documentation can include simple HTML formatting tags and other special keywords that provide additional information. Doc comments are ignored by the compiler, but they can be extracted and

automatically turned into online HTML documentation by the *javadoc* program.
(See Chapter 8, *Java Development Tools,* for more information about *javadoc*.)
Here is an example class that contains appropriate doc comments:

```
/**
 * This immutable class represents <i>complex
 * numbers</i>.
 *
 * @author David Flanagan
 * @version 1.0
 */
public class Complex {
  /**
   * Holds the real part of this complex number.
   * @see #y
   */
  protected double x;

  /**
   * Holds the imaginary part of this complex number.
   * @see #x
   */
  protected double y;

  /**
   * Creates a new Complex object that represents the complex number
   * x+yi.
   * @param x The real part of the complex number.
   * @param y The imaginary part of the complex number.
   */
  public Complex(double x, double y) {
    this.x = x;
    this.y = y;
  }

  /**
   * Adds two Complex objects and produces a third object that represents
   * their sum.
   * @param c1 A Complex object
   * @param c2 Another Complex object
   * @return  A new Complex object that represents the sum of
   *          <code>c1</code> and
   * <code>c2</code>.
   * @exception java.lang.NullPointerException
   *            If either argument is <code>null</code>.
   */
  public Complex add(Complex c1, Complex c2) {
    return new Complex(c1.x + c2.x, c1.y + c2.y);
  }
}
```

Structure of a Doc Comment

The body of a doc comment should begin with a one-sentence summary of the
class, interface, method, or field being documented. This sentence may be displayed by itself, as summary documentation, so it should be written to stand on its
own. The initial sentence can be followed by any number of other sentences and
paragraphs that describe the class, interface, method, or field.

After the descriptive paragraphs, a doc comment can contain any number of other paragraphs, each of which begins with a special doc-comment tag, such as @author, @param, or @returns. These tagged paragraphs provide specific information about the class, interface, method, or field that the *javadoc* program displays in a standard way. The full set of doc-comment tags is listed in the next section.

The descriptive material in a doc comment can contain simple HTML markup tags, such as such as <I> for emphasis, <CODE> for class, method, and field names, and <PRE> for multiline code examples. It can also contain <P> tags to break the description into separate paragraphs and <UL>, <LI>, and related tags to display bulleted lists and similar structures. Remember, however, that the material you write is embedded within a larger, more complex HTML document. For this reason, doc comments should not contain major structural HTML tags, such as <H2> or <HR>, that might interfere with the structure of the larger document.

Avoid the use of the <A> tag to include hyperlinks or cross references in your doc comments. Instead, use the special {@link} doc-comment tag, which, unlike the other doc-comment tags, can appear anywhere within a doc comment. As described in the next section, the {@link} tag allows you to specify hyperlinks to other classes, interfaces, methods, and fields without knowing the HTML-structuring conventions and filenames used by *javadoc*.

If you want to include an image in a doc comment, place the image file in a *doc-files* subdirectory of the source code directory. Give the image the same name as the class, with an integer suffix. For example, the second image that appears in the doc comment for a class named Circle can be included with this HTML tag:

```
<IMG src="doc-files/Circle-2.gif">
```

Because the lines of a doc comment are embedded within a Java comment, any leading spaces and asterisks (*) are stripped from each line of the comment before processing. Thus, you don't need to worry about the asterisks appearing in the generated documentation or about the indentation of the comment affecting the indentation of code examples included within the comment with a <PRE> tag.

Doc-Comment Tags

As I mentioned earlier, *javadoc* recognizes a number of special tags, each of which begins with an @ character. These doc-comment tags allow you to encode specific information into your comments in a standardized way, and they allow *javadoc* to choose the appropriate output format for that information. For example, the @param tag lets you specify the name and meaning of a single parameter for a method. *javadoc* can extract this information and display it using an HTML <DL> list, an HTML <TABLE>, or however it sees fit.

The doc-comment tags recognized by *javadoc* are the following; a doc comment should typically use these tags in the order listed here:

@author *name*
> Adds an "Author:" entry that contains the specified name. This tag should be used for every class or interface definition, but must not be used for individ-

ual methods and fields. If a class has multiple authors, use multiple @author tags on adjacent lines. For example:

```
@author David Flanagan
@author Paula Ferguson
```

List the authors in chronological order, with the original author first. If the author is unknown, you can use "unascribed". *javadoc* does not output authorship information unless the -author command-line argument is specified.

@version *text*

Inserts a "Version:" entry that contains the specified text. For example:

```
@version 1.32, 08/26/99
```

This tag should be included in every class and interface doc comment, but cannot be used for individual methods and fields. This tag is often used in conjunction with the automated version-numbering capabilities of a version-control system, such as SCCS, RCS, or CVS. *javadoc* does not output version information in its generated documentation unless the -version command-line argument is specified.

@param *parameter-name description*

Adds the specified parameter and its description to the "Parameters:" section of the current method. The doc comment for a method or constructor must contain one @param tag for each parameter the method expects. These tags should appear in the same order as the parameters specified by the method. The tag cannot be used in class, interface, or field doc comments. You are encouraged to use phrases and sentence fragments where possible, to keep the descriptions brief. However, if a parameter requires detailed documentation, the description can wrap onto multiple lines and include as much text as necessary. You can also use spaces to align the descriptions with each other. For example:

```
@param o      the object to insert
@param index  the position to insert it at
```

@return *description*

Inserts a "Returns:" section that contains the specified description. This tag should appear in every doc comment for a method, unless the method returns void or is a constructor. The tag must not appear in class, interface, or field doc comments. The description can be as long as necessary, but consider using a sentence fragment to keep it short. For example:

```
@return <code>true</code> if the insertion is successful, or
        <code>false</code> if the list already contains the
        specified object.
```

@exception *full-classname description*

Adds a "Throws:" entry that contains the specified exception name and description. A doc comment for a method or constructor should contain an @exception tag for every checked exception that appears in its throws clause. For example:

```
@exception java.io.FileNotFoundException
        If the specified file could not be found
```

The @exception tag can optionally be used to document unchecked exceptions (i.e., subclasses of RuntimeException) the method may throw, when these are exceptions that a user of the method may reasonably want to catch. If a method can throw more than one exception, use multiple @exception tags on adjacent lines and list the exceptions in alphabetical order. The description can be as short or as long as necessary to describe the significance of the exception. This doc-comment tag cannot be used in class, interface, or field comments. The @throws tag is a synonym for @exception.

@throws *full-classname description*

This tag is a synonym for @exception. It was introduced in Java 1.2.

@see *reference*

Adds a "See Also:" entry that contains the specified reference. This tag can appear in any kind of doc comment. *reference* can take three different forms. If it begins with a quote character, it is taken to be the name of a book or some other printed resource and is displayed as is. If *reference* begins with a < character, it is taken to be an arbitrary HTML hyperlink that uses the <A> tag and the hyperlink is inserted into the output documentation as is. This form of the @see tag can insert links to other online documents, such as a programmer's guide or user's manual.

If *reference* is not a quoted string or a hyperlink, the @see tag is expected to have the following form:

@see *feature label*

In this case, *javadoc* outputs the text specified by *label* and encodes it as a hyperlink to the specified *feature*. If *label* is omitted (as it usually is), *javadoc* uses the name of the specified *feature* instead.

feature can refer to a package, class, interface, method, constructor, or field, using one of the following forms:

pkgname

A reference to the named package. For example:

@see java.lang.reflect

pkgname.classname

A reference to a class or interface specified with its full package name. For example:

@see java.util.List

classname

A reference to a class or interface specified without its package name. For example:

@see List

javadoc resolves this reference by searching the current package and the list of imported classes for a class with this name.

classname#methodname

A reference to a named method or constructor within the specified class. For example:

```
@see java.io.InputStream#reset
@see InputStream#close
```

If the class is specified without its package name, it is resolved as described for *classname*. This syntax is ambiguous if the method is overloaded or the class defines a field by the same name.

classname#methodname(paramtypes)

A reference to a method or constructor with the type of its parameters explicitly specified. This form of the @see tag is useful when cross-referencing an overloaded method. For example:

```
@see InputStream#read(byte[], int, int)
```

#methodname

A reference to a non-overloaded method or constructor in the current class or interface or one of the containing classes, superclasses, or superinterfaces of the current class or interface. Use this concise form to refer to other methods in the same class. For example:

```
@see #setBackgroundColor
```

#methodname(paramtypes)

A reference to a method or constructor in the current class or interface or one of its superclasses or containing classes. This form works with overloaded methods because it lists the types of the method parameters explicitly. For example:

```
@see #setPosition(int, int)
```

classname#fieldname

A reference to a named field within the specified class. For example:

```
@see java.io.BufferedInputStream#buf
```

If the class is specified without its package name, it is resolved as described for *classname*.

#fieldname

A reference to a field in the current class or interface or one of the containing classes, superclasses, or superinterfaces of the current class or interface. For example:

```
@see #x
```

{@link *reference*}

The @link tag is like the @see tag except that, instead of placing a link to the specified *reference* in a special "See Also:" section, it inserts the link inline. A @link tag can appear anywhere that HTML text appears in a doc comment. In other words, it can appear in the initial description of the class, interface, method, or field and in the descriptions associated with the @param, @returns, @exception, and @deprecated tags. Because the @link tag can appear within arbitrary HTML text, the curly braces are required to delimit it. The *reference* for the @link tag uses the same syntax as the @see tag documented previously. For example:

```
@param regexp The regular expression to search for. This string
              argument must follow the syntax rules described for
              {@link RegExpParser}.
```

@deprecated *explanation*

As of Java 1.1, this tag specifies that the following class, interface, method, or field has been deprecated and that its use should be avoided. *javadoc* adds a prominent "Deprecated" entry to the documentation and includes the specified *explanation* text. This text should specify when the class or member was deprecated, and, if possible, suggest a replacement class or member and include a link to it. For example:

```
@deprecated As of Version 3.0, this method is replaced
            by {@link #setColor}.
```

Although the Java compiler ignores all comments, it does take note of the @deprecated tag in doc comments. When this tag appears, the compiler notes the deprecation in the class file it produces. This allows it to issue warnings for other classes that rely on the deprecated feature.

@since *version*

Used to specify when the class, interface, method, or field was added to the API. It should be followed by a version number or other version specification. For example:

```
@since JNUT 3.0
```

Every class and interface doc comment should include a @since tag, and any methods or fields added after the initial release of the class or interface should have @since tags in their doc comments.

@serial *description*

This tag should appear in the doc comment for any field that is part of the serialized state of a Serializable class. For classes that use the default serialization mechanism, this means all fields that are not declared transient, even fields declared private. The *description* should be a brief description of the field and of its purpose within a serialized object.

@serialField *name type description*

A Serializable class can define its serialized format by declaring an array of ObjectStreamField objects in a field named serialPersistentFields. For such a class, the doc comment for serialPersistentFields should include a @serialField tag for each element of the array. Each tag specifies the name, type, and description for a particular field in the serialized state of the class.

@serialData *description*

A Serializable class can define a writeObject() method to write additional data besides that written by the default serialization mechanism. An Externalizable class defines a writeExternal() method that is responsible for writing the complete state of an object to the serialization stream. The @serialData tag should be used in the doc comments for these writeObject() and `writeExternal()` methods, and the *description* should document the serialization format used by the method.

@beaninfo *info*

This nonstandard tag provides information about JavaBeans components and their methods. This tag is not used by *javadoc*, but it is apparently used by a tool internal to Sun that extracts information from @beaninfo tags for a class and outputs an appropriate java.beans.BeanInfo class. This tag appears in the source code of the Swing component classes in Java 1.2. A typical usage looks like this:

```
@beaninfo      bound: true
         description: the background color of this JavaBeans component
```

Doc Comments for Packages

Documentation comments for classes, interfaces, methods, constructors, and fields appear in Java source code immediately before the definitions of the features they document. *javadoc* can also read and display summary documentation for packages. Since a package is defined in a directory, not in a single file of source code, *javadoc* looks for the package documentation in a file named *package.html* in the directory that contains the source code for the classes of the package.

The *package.html* file should contain simple HTML documentation for the package. It can also contain @see, @link, @deprecated, and @since tags. Since *package.html* is not a file of Java source code, the documentation it contains should *not* be a Java comment (i.e., it should not be enclosed within /** and */ characters). Finally, any @see and @link tags that appear in *package.html* must use fully qualified class names.

In addition to defining a *package.html* file for each package, you can also provide high-level documentation for a group of packages by defining an *overview.html* file in the source tree for those packages. When *javadoc* is run over that source tree, it uses *overview.html* as the highest level overview it displays.

CHAPTER 8

Java Development Tools

Sun's implementation of Java includes a number of tools for Java developers. Chief among these are the Java interpreter and the Java compiler, of course, but there are a number of others as well. This chapter documents all the tools shipped with the Java 2 SDK (formerly known as the JDK), except for the RMI and IDL tools that are specific to enterprise programming. Those tools are documented in *Java Enterprise in a Nutshell* (O'Reilly).

The tools documented here are part of Sun's development kit; they are implementation details and not part of the Java specification itself. If you are using a Java development environment other than Sun's SDK (or a port of it), you should consult your vendor's tool documentation.

Some examples in this chapter use Unix conventions for file and path separators. If Windows is your development platform, change forward slashes in filenames to backward slashes, and colons in path specifications to semicolons.

appletviewer   JDK 1.0 and later
The Java Applet Viewer

Synopsis

    appletviewer [options] url | file...

Description

appletviewer reads or downloads the one or more HTML documents specified by the filename or URL on the command line. Next, it downloads any applets specified in any of those files and runs each applet in a separate window. If the specified document or documents do not contain any applets, *appletviewer* does nothing.

appletviewer recognizes applets specified with the <APPLET> tag and, in Java 1.2 and later, the <OBJECT> and <EMBED> tags.

Options
appletviewer recognizes the following options:

-debug

If this option is specified, *appletviewer* is started within *jdb* (the Java debugger). This allows you to debug the applets referenced by the document or documents.

-encodingenc

This option specifies the character encoding that *appletviewer* should use when reading the contents of the specified files or URLs. It is used in the conversion of applet parameter values to Unicode. Java 1.1 and later.

-Jjavaoption

This option passes the specified *javaoption* as a command-line argument to the Java interpreter. *javaoption* should not contain spaces. If a multiword option must be passed to the Java interpreter, multiple -J options should be used. See *java* for a list of valid Java interpreter options. Java 1.1 and later.

appletviewer also recognizes the -classic, -native, and -green options that the Java interpreter recognizes. See *java* for details on these options.

Commands

Each window displayed by *appletviewer* contains a single **Applet** menu, with the following commands available:

Restart

Stops and destroys the current applet, then reinitializes and restarts it.

Reload

Stops, destroys, and unloads the applet, then reloads, reinitializes, and restarts it.

Stop

Stops the current applet. Java 1.1 and later.

Save

Serializes the applet and saves the serialized applet in the file *Applet.ser* in the user's home directory. The applet should be stopped before selecting this option. Java 1.1 and later.

Start

Restarts a stopped applet. Java 1.1 and later.

Clone

Creates a new copy of the applet in a new *appletviewer* window.

Tag Pops up a dialog box that displays the <APPLET> tag and all associated <PARAM> tags that created the current applet.

Info

Pops up a dialog box that contains information about the applet. This information is provided by the getAppletInfo() and getParameterInfo() methods implemented by the applet.

Edit

This command is not implemented. The **Edit** menu item is disabled.

Character Encoding

Displays the current character encoding in the status line. Java 1.1 and later.

Print

Prints the applet. Java 1.1 and later.

Java Tools

Properties

Displays a dialog that allows the user to set *appletviewer* preferences, including settings for firewall and caching proxy servers.

Close

Closes the current *appletviewer* window.

Quit

Quits *appletviewer*, closing all open windows.

Environment

CLASSPATH

In Java 1.0 and Java 1.1, *appletviewer* uses the CLASSPATH environment variable in the same way the Java interpreter does. See *java* for details. In Java 1.2 and later, however, *appletviewer* ignores this environment variable to better simulate the action of a web browser.

Properties

When it starts up, *appletviewer* reads property definitions from the file ⁓/.*botjava/ properties* (Unix) or *.botjava\properties* relative to the HOME environment variable (Windows). These properties are stored in the system properties list and can specify the various error and status messages the applet viewer displays, as well as its security policies and use of proxy servers. The properties that affect security and proxies are described in the following sections. Most users of *appletviewer* do not need to use these properties.

Security Properties

The following properties specify the security restrictions *appletviewer* places on untrusted applets:

acl.read

A list of files and directories an untrusted applet is allowed to read. The elements of the list should be separated with colons on Unix systems and semicolons on Windows systems. On Unix systems, the ⁓ character is replaced with the home directory of the current user. If the plus character appears as an element in the list, it is replaced by the value of the acl.read.default property. This provides an easy way to enable read access—by simply setting acl.read to "+". By default, untrusted applets are not allowed to read any files or directories.

acl.read.default

A list of files and directories that are readable by untrusted applets if the acl.read property contains a plus character.

acl.write

A list of files and directories an untrusted applet is allowed to write to. The elements of the list should be separated with colons on Unix systems and semicolons on Windows systems. On Unix systems, the ⁓ character is replaced with the home directory of the current user. If the plus character appears as an element in the list, it is replaced by the value of the acl.write.default property. This provides an easy way to enable write access—by simply setting acl.write to "+". By default, untrusted applets are not allowed to write to any files or directories.

acl.write.default

A list of files and directories that are writable by untrusted applets if the acl.write property contains a plus character.

appletviewer.security.mode

Specifies the types of network access an untrusted applet is allowed to perform. If it is set to "none", the applet can perform no networking at all. The value "host" is the default; it specifies that the applet can connect only to the host from which it was loaded. The value "unrestricted" specifies that an applet can connect to any host without restrictions.

package.restrict.access.*package-prefix*

Properties of this form can be set to true to prevent untrusted applets from using classes in any package that has the specified package name prefix as the first component of its name. For example, to prevent applets from using any of the Sun classes (such as the Java compiler and the applet viewer itself) that are shipped with the Java SDK, you can specify the following property:

> package.restrict.access.sun=true

appletviewer sets this property to true by default for the sun.* and netscape.* packages.

package.restrict.definition.*package-prefix*

Properties of this form can be set to true to prevent untrusted applets from defining classes in a package that has the specified package name prefix as the first component of its name. For example, to prevent an applet from defining classes in any of the standard Java packages, you can specify the following property:

> package.restrict.definition.java=true

appletviewer sets this property to true by default for the java.*, sun.*, and netscape.* packages.

property.applet

When a property of this form is set to true (as of Java 1.1), it specifies that an applet should be allowed to read the property named property from the system properties list. By default, applets are allowed to read only 10 standard system properties (as detailed in *Java Foundation Classes in a Nutshell* (O'Reilly)). For example, to allow an applet to read the user.home property, specify a property of the form:

> user.home.applet=true

Proxy Properties

appletviewer uses the following properties to configure its use of firewall and caching proxy servers:

firewallHost

The firewall proxy host to connect to if firewallSet is true.

firewallPort

The port of the firewall proxy host to connect to if firewallSet is true.

firewallSet

Whether the applet viewer should use a firewall proxy. Values are true or false.

proxyHost

The caching proxy host to connect to if proxySet is true.

proxyPort

The port of the caching proxy host to connect to if proxySet is true.

Java Tools

proxySet
> Whether the applet viewer should use a caching proxy. Values are true or false.

See Also
java, javac, jdb

extcheck
JAR Version Conflict Utility

Synopsis
> extcheck -verbose *jarfile*

Description

extcheck checks to see if the extension contained in the specified *jarfile* (or a newer version of that extension) has already been installed on the system. It does this by reading the Specification-Title and Specification-Version manifest attributes from the specified *jarfile* and from all of the JAR files found in the system extensions directory.

extcheck is designed for use in automated installation scripts. Without the –verbose option, it does not print the results of its check. Instead, it sets its exit code to 0 if the specified extension does not conflict with any installed extensions and can be safely installed. It sets its exit code to a non-zero value if an extension with the same name is already installed and has a specification version number equal to or greater than the version of the specified file.

Options

-verbose
> Lists the installed extensions as they are checked and displays the results of the check.

See Also
jar

jar
Java Archive Tool

Synopsis
> jar c|t|u|x[f][m][M][0][v] [*jar*] [*manifest*] [-C *directory*] [*files*]
> jar -i [*jar*]

Description

jar is a tool that can create and manipulate Java Archive (JAR) files. A JAR file is a ZIP file that contains Java class files, auxiliary resource files required by those classes, and optional meta-information. This meta-information includes a manifest file that lists the contents of the JAR archive and provides auxiliary information about each file.

The *jar* command can create JAR files, list the contents of JAR files, and extract files from a JAR archive. In Java 1.2 and later, it can also add files to an existing archive or update the manifest file of an archive. In Java 1.3 and later, *jar* can also add an index entry to a JAR file.

Options

The syntax of the *jar* command is reminiscent of the Unix *tar* (tape archive) command. Most options to *jar* are specified as a block of concatenated letters passed as a single argument, rather than as individual command-line arguments. The first letter of the first argument specifies what action *jar* is to perform; it is required. Other letters are optional. The various file arguments depend on which letters are specified.

Command Options

The first letter of the first option to *jar* specifies the basic operation *jar* is to perform. Here are the four possible options:

c   Creates a new JAR archive. A list of input files and/or directories must be specified as the final arguments to *jar*. The newly created JAR file has a *META-INF/MANI-FEST.MF* file as its first entry. This automatically created manifest lists the contents of the JAR file and contains a message digest for each file.

t   Lists the contents of a JAR archive.

u   Updates the contents of a JAR archive. Any files listed on the command line are added to the archive. When used with the m option, this adds the specified manifest information to the JAR file. Java 1.2 and later.

x   Extracts the contents of a JAR archive. The files and directories specified on the command line are extracted and created in the current working directory. If no file or directory names are specified, all the files and directories in the JAR file are extracted.

Modifier Options

Each of the four command specifier letters can be followed by additional letters that provide further detail about the operation to be performed:

f   Indicates that *jar* is to operate on a JAR file whose name is specified on the command line. If this option is not present, *jar* reads a JAR file from standard input and/or writes a JAR file to standard output. If the f option is present, the command line must contain the name of the JAR file to operate on.

m   When *jar* creates or updates a JAR file, it automatically creates (or updates) a manifest file named *META-INF/MANIFEST.MF* in the JAR archive. This default manifest simply lists the contents of the JAR file. Many JAR files require additional information to be specified in the manifest; the m option tells the *jar* command that a manifest template is specified on the command line. *jar* reads this manifest file and stores all the information it contains into the *META-INF/MANIFEST.MF* file it creates. This m option should be used only with the c or u commands, not with the t or x commands.

M   Used with the c and u commands to tell *jar* not to create a default manifest file.

v   Tells *jar* to produce verbose output.

0   Used with the c and u commands to tell *jar* to store files in the JAR archive without compressing them. Note that this option is the digit zero, not the letter O.

Files

The first option to *jar* consists of an initial command letter and various option letters. This first option is followed by a list of files:

jar   If the first option contains the letter f, that option must be followed by the name of the JAR file to create or manipulate.

manifest
       If the first option contains the letter m, that option must be followed by the name of the file that contains manifest information. If the first option contains both the letters f and m, the JAR and manifest files should be listed in the same order the f and m options appear. In other words, if f comes before m, the JAR filename should come before the manifest filename. Otherwise, if m comes before f, the manifest filename should be specified before the JAR filename.

files The list of one or more files and/or directories to be inserted into or extracted from the JAR archive.

Additional Options

In addition to all the options listed previously, *jar* also supports the following:

-C *dir*

> Used within the list of files to process; it tells *jar* to change to the specified *dir* while processing the subsequent files and directories. The subsequent file and directory names are interpreted relative to *dir* and are inserted into the JAR archive without *dir* as a prefix. Any number of -C options can be used; each remains in effect until the next is encountered. The directory specified by a -C option is interpreted relative to the current working directory, not the directory specified by the previous -C option. Java 1.2 and later.

–i *jarfile*

> The –i option is used instead of the c, t, u, and x commands. It tells *jar* to produce an index of all JAR files referenced by the specified *jarfile*. The index is stored in a file named *META-INF/INDEX.LIST*; a Java interpreter or applet viewer can use the information in this index to optimize its class and resource lookup algorithm and avoid downloading unnecessary JAR files. Java 1.3 and later.

Examples

The *jar* command has a confusing array of options, but, in most cases, its use is quite simple. To create a simple JAR file that contains all the class files in the current directory and all files in a subdirectory called *images*, you can type:

    % jar cf my.jar *.class images

To verbosely list the contents of a JAR archive:

    % jar tvf your.jar

To extract the manifest file from a JAR file for examination or editing:

    % jar xf the.jar META-INF/MANIFEST.MF

To update the manifest of a JAR file:

    % jar ufm my.jar manifest.template

See Also

jarsigner

jarsigner   Java 2 SDK 1.2 and later

JAR Signing and Verification Tool

Synopsis

    jarsigner [options] jarfile signer
    jarsigner -verify jarfile

Description

jarsigner adds a digital signature to the specified *jarfile*, or, if the –verify option is specified, it verifies the digital signature or signatures already attached to the JAR file. The specified *signer* is a case-insensitive nickname or alias for the entity whose signature is to be used. The specified *signer* name is used to look up the private key that generates the signature.

When you apply your digital signature to a JAR file, you are implicitly vouching for the contents of the archive. You are offering your personal word that the JAR file contains only nonmalicious code, files that do not violate copyright laws, and so forth. When you verify a digitally signed JAR file, you can determine who the signer or signers of the file are and (if the verification succeeds) that the contents of the JAR file have not been changed, corrupted, or tampered with since the signature or signatures were applied. Verifying a digital signature is entirely different from deciding whether or not you trust the person or organization whose signature you verified.

jarsigner and the related *keytool* program replace the *javakey* program of Java 1.1.

Options

jarsigner defines a number of options, many of which specify how a private key is to be found for the specified *signer*. Most of these options are unnecessary when using the -verify option to verify a signed JAR file:

-certs
> If this option is specified along with either the -verify or -verbose option, it causes *jarsigner* to display details of the public-key certificates associated with the signed JAR file.

-Jjavaoption
> Passes the specified *javaoption* directly to the Java interpreter.

-keypass *password*
> Specifies the password that encrypts the private key of the specified *signer*. If this option is not specified, *jarsigner* prompts you for the password.

-keystore *url*
> A *keystore* is a file that contains keys and certificates. This option specifies the file-name or URL of the keystore in which the private- and public-key certificates of the specified *signer* are looked up. The default is the file named *.keystore* in the user's home directory (the value of the system property user.home). This is also the default location of the keystore managed by *keytool.*

-sigfile *basename*
> Specifies the base names of the *.SF* and *.DSA* files added to the *META-INF/* directory of the JAR file. If you leave this option unspecified, the base filename is chosen based on the *signer* name.

-signedjar *outputfile*
> Specifies the name for the signed JAR file created by *jarsigner.* If this option is not specified, *jarsigner* overwrites the *jarfile* specified on the command line.

-storepass *password*
> Specifies the password that verifies the integrity of the keystore (but does not encrypt the private key). If this option is omitted, *jarsigner* prompts you for the password.

-storetype *type*
> Specifies the type of keystore specified by the -keystore option. The default is the system-default keystore type, which on most systems is the Java Keystore type, known as "JKS". If you have the Java Cryptography Extension installed, you may want to use a "JCEKS" keystore instead.

-verbose
> Displays extra information about the signing or verification process.

-verify
> Specifies that *jarsigner* should verify the specified JAR file rather than sign it.

Java Tools

See Also
jar, keytool, javakey

java JDK 1.0 and later
The Java Interpreter

Synopsis

```
java [ interpreter-options ] classname [ program-arguments ]
java [ interpreter-options ] -jar jarfile [ program-arguments ]
```

Description

java is the Java byte-code interpreter; it runs Java programs. The program to be run is the class specified by *classname*. This must be a fully qualified name: it must include the package name of the class, but not the *.class* file extension. For example:

```
% java david.games.Checkers
% java Test
```

The specified class must define a main() method with exactly the following signature:

```
public static void main(String[] args)
```

This method serves as the program entry point: the interpreter begins execution here.

In Java 1.2 and later, a program can be packaged in an executable JAR file. To run a program packaged in this fashion, use the -jar option to specify the JAR file. The manifest of an executable JAR file must contain a Main-Class attribute that specifies which class within the JAR file contains the main() method at which the interpreter is to begin execution.

Any command-line options that precede the name of the class or JAR file to execute are options to the Java interpreter itself. Any options that follow the class name or JAR file-name are options to the program; they are ignored by the Java interpreter and passed as an array of strings to the main() method of the program.

The Java interpreter runs until the main() method exits, and any threads (except for threads marked as daemon threads) created by the program have also exited.

Interpreter Versions

The *java* program is the basic version of the Java interpreter. In addition to this program, however, there are several other versions of the Java interpreter. Each of these versions is similar to *java*, but has a specialized function. The various interpreter programs are the following:

java

This is the basic version of the Java interpreter; it is usually the correct one to use. The behavior and set of supported options changed between Java 1.1 and Java 1.2.

oldjava

This version of the interpreter is included in Java 1.2 and Java 1.3x for compatibility with the Java 1.1 interpreter. It loads classes using the Java 1.1 class-loading scheme. Very few Java applications need to use this version of the interpreter.

javaw

This version of the interpreter is included only on Windows platforms. Use *javaw* when you want to run a Java program (from a script, for example) without forcing a console window to appear. In Java 1.2 and Java 1.3, there is also an *oldjavaw* program that combines the features of *oldjava* and *javaw*.

java_g

In Java 1.0 and Java 1.1, *java_g* is a debugging version of the Java interpreter. It includes a few specialized command-line options, but is rarely used. Windows platforms also define a *javaw_g* program. *java_g* is not included in Java 1.2 or later versions.

Client or Classic VM

In Java 1.3, the *java* application launcher tool can run a program using either of two VM implementations. The "Client VM" uses Sun's HotSpot incremental compilation technology and is highly tuned for running client-side Java applications (as opposed to server applications). This is the default VM. The "Classic VM" is essentially the same VM used by Java 1.2. To select the "Classic VM," specify the -classic option.

Just-In-Time Compiler

In Java 1.2, and in Java 1.3 when you specify the -classic option, the Java interpreter uses a just-in-time compiler (if one is available for your platform). A JIT converts Java byte codes to native machine instructions at runtime and significantly speeds up the execution of a typical Java program. If you do not want to use the JIT, you can disable it by setting the JAVA_COMPILER environment variable to "NONE" or the java.compiler system property to "NONE" using the -D option:

```
% setenv JAVA_COMPILER NONE          // Unix csh syntax
% java -Djava.compiler=NONE MyProgram
```

If you want to use a different JIT compiler implementation, set the environment variable or system property to the name of the desired implementation.

Threading systems

On Solaris and related Unix platforms, you have a choice of the type of threads used by the Java 1.2 interpreter and the "Classic VM" of Java 1.3. To use native OS threads, specify -native. To use nonnative, or green, threads (the default), specify -green. In Java 1.3, the default "Client VM" uses native threads. Specifying -green or -native in Java 1.3 implicitly specifies -classic as well.

Options

-classic

Runs the "Classic VM" instead of the default high-performance "Client VM." Java 1.3 and later.

-classpath *path*

Specifies the directories, JAR files, and ZIP files *java* searches when trying to load a class. In Java 1.0 and 1.1, and with the *oldjava* interpreter, this option specifies the location of system classes, extension classes, and application classes. In Java 1.2 and later, this option specifies only the location of application classes. See the "Loading Classes" section for further details.

-cp   A synonym for -classpath. Java 1.2 and later.

-cs, -checksource

Both options tell *java* to check the modification times on the specified class file and its corresponding source file. If the class file cannot be found or if it is out of date, it is automatically recompiled from the source. Java 1.0 and Java 1.1 only; these options are not available in Java 1.2 and later.

-D*propertyname*=*value*

Defines *propertyname* to equal *value* in the system properties list. Your Java program can then look up the specified value by its property name. You can specify any number of -D options. For example:

    % java -Dawt.button.color=gray -Dmy.class.pointsize=14 my.class

-debug

Causes *java* to start up in a way that allows the *jdb* debugger to attach itself to the interpreter session. In Java 1.2 and later, this option has been replaced with -Xdebug.

-green

On operating systems such as Solaris that support multiple styles of threading, this option selects nonnative, or green, threads. This is the default in Java 1.2. In Java 1.3, using this option also selects the -classic option. See also -native. Java 1.2 and later.

-help, -?

Prints a usage message and exits. See also -X.

-jar *jarfile*

Runs the specified executable *jarfile*. The manifest of the specified *jarfile* must contain a Main-Class attribute that identifies the class with the main() method at which program execution is to begin. Java 1.2 and later.

-l*digit*

Sets the logging level for trace output. See -t and -tm. *java_g* only.

-ms *initmem*[k|m]

Specifies how much memory is allocated for the heap when the interpreter starts up. In Java 1.2 and later, this option has been renamed -Xms.

-mx *maxmem*[k|m]

Specifies the maximum heap size the interpreter can use for dynamically allocated objects and arrays. In Java 1.2 and later, this option has been renamed -Xmx.

-native

On operating systems such as Solaris that support multiple styles of threading, this option selects native threads, instead of the default green threads. Using native threads can be advantageous in some circumstances, such as when running on a multi-CPU computer. In Java 1.3, the default Hotspot virtual machine uses native threads. Selecting this option in Java 1.3 implicitly selects the -classic option as well. Java 1.2 and later.

-noasyncgc

Do not do garbage collection asynchronously. With this option specified, *java* performs garbage collection only when it runs out of memory or when the garbage collector is explicitly invoked. Without this option, *java* runs the garbage collector as a separate, low-priority thread. Java 1.0 and Java 1.1 only; this option has been removed in Java 1.2 and later versions.

-noclassgc

Do not garbage-collect loaded classes no longer in use. This option was added in Java 1.1; it has been renamed to -Xnoclassgc as of Java 1.2.

-noverify

Never run the byte-code verifier. Java 1.0 and Java 1.1 only; this option has been removed in Java 1.2 and later versions.

-oss *stacksize*[k | m]

Sets the size of each thread's Java code stack. By default, *stacksize* is specified in bytes. You can specify it in kilobytes by appending the letter k or in megabytes by appending the letter m. The default value is 400 KB. You must specify at least 1000 bytes. Java 1.0 and Java 1.1 only; this option has been removed in Java 1.2 and later versions.

-prof[:*file*]

Outputs profiling information to the specified *file* or to the file *java.prof* in the current directory. The format of this profiling information is not well-documented. Prior to Java 1.1, no *file* can be specified; profiling information is always output to *./java.prof.* Java 1.0 and Java 1.1 only; this option has been superseded in Java 1.2 by the -Xrunhprof option and in Java 1.3 by -Xprof.

-showversion

This option works like the -version option, except that the interpreter continues running after printing the version information. Java 1.3 and later.

-ss *stacksize*[k | m]

Sets the size of each thread's native code stack. By default, *stacksize* is specified in bytes. You can specify it in kilobytes by appending the letter k or in megabytes by appending the letter m. The default value is 128 KB. You must specify at least 1000 bytes. Java 1.0 and Java 1.1 only; this option has been removed in Java 1.2 and later versions.

-t   Outputs a trace of all byte codes executed. *java_g* only.

-tm Outputs a trace of all methods executed. *java_g* only.

-verbose, -v, -verbose:class

Prints a message each time *java* loads a class. In Java 1.0 and Java 1.1, you can use -v as a synonym. In Java 1.2 and later, you can use -verbose:class as a synonym.

-verbosegc

Prints a message when garbage collection occurs. In Java 1.2 and later, this option has been renamed -verbose:gc.

-verbose:gc

Prints a message when garbage collection occurs. Java 1.2 and later. Prior to Java 1.2, use -verbosegc.

-verbose:jni

Prints a message when native methods are called. Java 1.2 and later.

-verify

Runs the byte-code verifier on all classes that are loaded. Java 1.0 and Java 1.1 only; this option has been removed in Java 1.2 and later.

-verifyremote

Runs the byte-code verifier on all classes that are loaded through a class loader. (This generally refers to classes that are dynamically loaded from an untrusted location.) This is the default behavior for *java.* Java 1.0 and Java 1.1 only; this option has been removed in Java 1.2 and later.

−version

> Prints the version of the Java interpreter and exits.

−X Displays usage information for the nonstandard interpreter options (those beginning with −X) and exits. See also −help. Java 1.2 and later.

−Xbatch

> Tells the Hotspot VM to perform all just-in-time compilation in the foreground, regardless of the time required for compilation. Without this option, the VM compiles methods in the background while interpreting them in the foreground. Java 1.3 and later.

−Xbootclasspath:*path*

> Specifies a search path consisting of directories, ZIP files, and JAR files the *java* interpreter should use to look up system classes. With *oldjava*, use −classpath to specify this information. Use of this option is very rare. Java 1.2 and later.

−Xcheck:jni

> Performs additional checks when using Java Native Interface functions. Java 1.2 and later.

−Xdebug

> Starts the interpreter in a way that allows a debugger to communicate with it. Java 1.2 and later. Prior to Java 1.2, use −debug.

−Xfuture

> Strictly checks the format of all class files loaded. Without this option, *java* performs the same checks that were performed in Java 1.1. Java 1.2 and later.

−Xincgc

> Uses incremental garbage collection. In this mode the garbage collector runs continuously in the background, and a running program is rarely, if ever, subject to noticeable pauses while garbage collection occurs. Using this option typically results in a 10% decrease in overall performance, however. Java 1.3 and later.

−Xint

> Tells the Hotspot VM to operate in interpreted mode only, without performing any just-in-time compilation. Java 1.3 and later.

−Xmixed

> Tells the Hotspot VM to perform just-in-time compilation on frequently used methods ("hotspots") and execute other methods in interpreted mode. This is the default behavior. Java 1.3 and later.

−Xms *initmem*[k | m]

> Specifies how much memory is allocated for the heap when the interpreter starts up. By default, *initmem* is specified in bytes. You can specify it in kilobytes by appending the letter k or in megabytes by appending the letter m. The default is 1 MB. For large or memory-intensive applications (such as the Java compiler), you can improve runtime performance by starting the interpreter with a larger amount of memory. You must specify an initial heap size of at least 1000 bytes. Java 1.2 and later. Prior to Java 1.2, use −ms.

−Xmx *maxmem*[k | m]

> Specifies the maximum heap size the interpreter uses for dynamically allocated objects and arrays. *maxmem* is specified in bytes by default. You can specify *maxmem* in kilobytes by appending the letter k and in megabytes by appending the letter m.

The default is 16 MB. You cannot specify a heap size less than 1000 bytes. Java 1.2 and later. Prior to Java 1.2, use -mx.

-Xnoclassgc

> Do not garbage-collect classes. Java 1.2 and later. In Java 1.1, use -noclassgc.

-Xprof

> Prints profiling output to standard output. Java 1.3 and later. In Java 1.2, or when using the -classic option, use -Xrunhprof. Prior to Java 1.2, use -prof.

-Xrs Requests that the interpreter use fewer operating system signals. This option may improve performance on some systems. Java 1.2 and later.

-Xrunhprof:*suboptions*

> Turns on CPU, heap, or monitor profiling. *suboptions* is a comma-separated list of name=value pairs. Use -Xrunhprof:help for a list of supported options and values. Java 1.2 and later. Prior to Java 1.2, rudimentary profiling support is available with the -prof option. In Java 1.3, this option is supported if -classic is used, but is not supported by the new Hotspot VM. See -Xprof.

Loading Classes

The Java interpreter knows where to find the system classes that comprise the Java platform. In Java 1.2 and later, it also knows where to find the class files for all extensions installed in the system extensions directory. However, the interpreter must be told where to find the nonsystem classes that comprise the application to be run.

Class files are stored in directories that correspond to their package name. For example, the class com.davidflanagan.utils.Util is stored in a file *com/davidflanagan/utils/Util.class*. By default, the interpreter uses the current working directory as the root and looks for all classes in and beneath this directory.

The interpreter can also search for classes within ZIP and JAR files. To tell the interpreter where to look for classes, you specify a *classpath*: a list of directories and ZIP and JAR archives. When looking for a class, the interpreter searches each of the specified locations in the order in which they are specified.

The easiest way to specify a classpath is to set the CLASSPATH environment variable, which works much like the PATH variable used by a Unix shell or a Windows command-interpreter path. To specify a classpath in Unix, you might type a command like this:

```
% setenv CLASSPATH .:~/myclasses:/usr/lib/javautils.jar:/usr/lib/javaapps
```

On a Windows system, you might use a command like the following:

```
C:\> set CLASSPATH=.;c:\myclasses;c:\javatools\classes.zip;d:\javaapps
```

Note that Unix and Windows use different characters to separate directory and path components.

You can also specify a classpath with the -classpath or -cp options to the Java interpreter. A path specified with one of these options overrides any path specified by the CLASSPATH environment variable. In Java 1.2 and later, the -classpath option specifies only the search path for application and user classes. Prior to Java 1.2, or when using the *oldjava* interpreter, this option specifies the search path for all classes, including system classes and extension classes.

See Also

javac, jdb

javac

The Java Compiler

Synopsis

javac [*options*] *files*
oldjavac [*options*] *files*

Description

javac is the Java compiler; it compiles Java source code (in *.java* files) into Java byte codes (in *.class* files). The Java compiler is itself written in Java. The Java compiler has been completely rewritten in Java 1.3, and its performance has been substantially improved. Although the new *javac* is substantially compatible with previous versions of the compiler, the old version of the compiler is provided as *oldjavac*.

javac can be passed any number of Java source files, whose names must all end with the *.java* extension. *javac* produces a separate *.class* class file for each class defined in the source files. Each source file can contain any number of classes, although only one can be a public top-level class. The name of the source file (minus the *.java* extension) must match the name of the public class it contains.

In Java 1.2 and later, if a filename specified on the command line begins with the character @, that file is taken not as a Java source file, but as a list of Java source files. Thus, if you keep a list of Java source files for a particular project in a file named *project.list*, you can compile all those files at once with the command:

```
% javac @project.list
```

To compile a source file, *javac* must be able to find definitions of all classes used in the source file. It looks for definitions in both source-file and class-file form, automatically compiling any source files that have no corresponding class files or that have been modified since they were most recently compiled.

Options

−bootclasspath *path*

Specifies the search *path javac* uses to look up system classes. This option is handy when you are using *javac* as a cross-compiler to compile classes against different versions of the Java API. For example, you might use the Java 1.3 compiler to compile classes against the Java 1.2 runtime environment. This option does not specify the system classes used to run the compiler itself, only the system classes read by the compiler. See also −extdirs and −target. Java 1.2 and later.

−classpath *path*

Specifies the path *javac* uses to look up classes referenced in the specified source code. This option overrides any path specified by the CLASSPATH environment variable. The *path* specified is an ordered list of directories, ZIP files, and JAR archives, separated by colons on Unix systems or semicolons on Windows systems. If the −sourcepath option is not set, this option also specifies the search path for source files.

Prior to Java 1.2, this option specifies the path to system and extension classes, as well as user and application classes, and must be used carefully. In Java 1.2 and later, it specifies only the search path for application classes. See the discussion of "Loading Classes" in the documentation for the *java* command for further information.

−d *directory*

Specifies the directory in which (or beneath which) class files should be stored. By default, *javac* stores the *.class* files it generates in the same directory as the *.java* files those classes were defined in. If the −d option is specified, however, the specified *directory* is treated as the root of the class hierarchy, and *.class* files are placed in this directory or the appropriate subdirectory below it, depending on the package name of the class. Thus, the following command:

```
% javac -d /java/classes Checkers.java
```

places the file *Checkers.class* in the directory */java/classes* if the *Checkers.java* file has no package statement. On the other hand, if the source file specifies that it is in a package:

```
package com.davidflanagan.games;
```

the *.class* file is stored in */java/classes/com/davidflanagan/games*. When the −d option is specified, *javac* automatically creates any directories it needs to store its class files in the appropriate place.

−depend

Tells *javac* to recursively search for out-of-date class files in need of recompilation. This option forces a thorough compilation, but can slow the process down significantly. In Java 1.2 and later, this option has been renamed −Xdepend.

−deprecation

Tells *javac* to issue a warning for every use of a deprecated API. By default, *javac* issues only a single warning for each source file that uses deprecated APIs. Java 1.1 and later.

−extdirs *path*

Specifies a list of directories to search for extension JAR files. It is used along with −bootclasspath when doing cross-compilation for different versions of the Java runtime environment. Java 1.2 and later.

−g Tells *javac* to add line number, source file, and local variable information to the output class files, for use by debuggers. By default, *javac* generates only the line numbers.

−g:none

Tells *javac* to include no debugging information in the output class files. Java 1.2 and later.

−g:*keyword-list*

Tells *javac* to output the types of debugging information specified by the comma-separated *keyword-list*. The valid keywords are: source, which specifies source-file information; lines, which specifies line number information; and vars, which specifies local variable debugging information. Java 1.2 and later.

−J*javaoption*

Passes the argument *javaoption* directly through to the Java interpreter. For example: −J-Xmx32m. *javaoption* should not contain spaces; if multiple arguments must be passed to the interpreter, use multiple −J options. Java 1.1 and later.

−nowarn

Tells *javac* not to print warning messages. Errors are still reported as usual.

Java Tools

-nowrite

Tells *javac* not to create any class files. Source files are parsed as usual, but no output is written. This option is useful when you want to check that a file will compile without actually compiling it. Java 1.0 and Java 1.1 only; this option is not available in Java 1.2 and later.

-O Enables optimization of class files to improve their execution speed. Using this option can result in larger class files that are difficult to debug and cause longer compilation times. Prior to Java 1.2, this option is incompatible with -g; turning on -O implicitly turns off -g and turns on -depend.

-sourcepath *path*

Specifies the list of directories, ZIP files, and JAR archives that *javac* searches when looking for source files. The files found in this source path are compiled if no corresponding class files are found or if the source files are newer than the class files. By default, source files are searched for in the same places class files are searched for. Java 1.2 and later.

-target *version*

Specifies the class-file-format version to use for the generated class files. The default *version* is 1.1, which generates class files that can be read and executed by Java 1.0 and later virtual machines. If you specify *version* as 1.2, *javac* increments the class file version number, producing a class file that does not run with a Java 1.0 or Java 1.1 interpreter. There have not been any actual changes to the Java class-file format; the new version number is simply a convenient way to prevent classes that depend on the many new features of Java 1.2 from being run on out-of-date interpreters.

-verbose

Tells the compiler to display messages about what it is doing. In particular, it causes *javac* to list all the source files it compiles, including files that did not appear on the command line.

-X Tells the *javac* compiler (and, in Java 1.3, the *oldjavac* compiler) to display usage information for its nonstandard options (all of which begin with -X). Java 1.2 and *oldjavac* only.

-Xdepend

Tells *javac* to recursively search for source files that need recompilation. This causes a very thorough but time-consuming compilation process. Java 1.2 and *old-javac* only.

-Xstdout

Tells *javac* to send warning and error messages to the standard output stream instead of the standard error stream. Java 1.2 and *oldjavac* only.

-Xverbosepath

Displays verbose output explaining where various class files and source files were found. Java 1.2 and *oldjavac* only.

Environment

CLASSPATH

Specifies an ordered list (colon-separated on Unix, semicolon-separated on Windows systems) of directories, ZIP files, and JAR archives in which *javac* should look for user class files and source files. This variable is overridden by the -classpath option.

See Also
java, jdb

javadoc
JDK 1.0 and later

The Java Documentation Generator

Synopsis

> javadoc [*options*] *package... sourcefiles... @lists...*

Description

javadoc generates API documentation, in HTML format (by default), for any number of packages and classes you specify. The *javadoc* command line can list any number of package names and any number of Java source files. For convenience, when working with a large number of packages or source files, you can list them all in an auxiliary file and specify the name of that file on the command line, preceded by an @ character.

javadoc uses the *javac* compiler to process all the specified Java source files and all the Java source files in all the specified packages. It uses the information it gleans from this processing to generate detailed API documentation. Most importantly, the generated documentation includes the contents of all documentation comments included in the source files. See Chapter 7, *Java Programming and Documentation Conventions*, for information about writing doc comments in your own Java code.

When you specify a Java source file for *javadoc* to process, you must specify the name of the file that contains the source, including a complete path to the file. It is more common, however, to use *javadoc* to create documentation for entire packages of classes. When you specify a package for *javadoc* to process, you specify the package name, not the directory that contains the source code for the package. In this case, you may need to specify the -sourcepath option so that *javadoc* can find your package source code correctly if it is not stored in a location already listed in your default class-path.

javadoc creates HTML documentation by default, but you can customize its behavior by defining a doclet class that generates documentation in whatever format you desire. You can write your own doclets using the doclet API defined by the com.sun.javadoc package. Documentation for this package is included in the standard documentation bundle for Java 1.2 and later.

javadoc has significant new functionality as of Java 1.2. This reference page documents the Java 1.2 and later versions of the program, but makes no attempt to distinguish new features of the Java 1.2 version from the features that existed in previous versions.

Options

javadoc defines a large number of options. Some are standard options that are always recognized by *javadoc*. Other options are defined by the doclet that produces the documentation. The options for the standard HTML doclet are included in the following list:

-1.1

> Simulates the output style and directory structure of the Java 1.1 version of *javadoc*.

-author

> Includes authorship information specified with @author in the generated documentation. Default doclet only.

-bootclasspath

> Specifies the location of an alternate set of system classes. This can be useful when cross-compiling. See *javac* for more information on this option.

-bottom *text*

> Displays *text* at the bottom of each generated HTML file. *text* can contain HTML tags. See also -footer. Default doclet only.

-charset *encoding*

> Specifies the character encoding for the output. This depends on the encoding used in the documentation comments of your source code, of course. The *encoding* value is used in a <META> tag in the HTML output. Default doclet only.

-classpath *path*

> Specifies a path *javadoc* uses to look up both class files and, if you do not specify the -sourcepath option, source files. Because *javadoc* uses the *javac* compiler, it needs to be able to locate class files for all classes referenced by the packages being documented. See *java* and *javac* for more information about this option and the default value provided by the **CLASSPATH** environment variable.

-d *directory*

> Specifies the directory in and beneath which *javadoc* should store the HTML files it generates. If this option is omitted, the current directory is used. Default doclet only.

-docencoding *encoding*

> Specifies the encoding to be used for output HTML documents. The name of the encoding specified here may not exactly match the name of the charset specified with the -charset option. Default doclet only.

-doclet *classname*

> Specifies the name of the doclet class to use to generate the documentation. If this option is not specified, *javadoc* generates documentation using the default HTML doclet.

-docletpath *classpath*

> If the class specified by the -doclet tag is not available from the default classpath, this option specifies a path from which it can be loaded.

-doctitle *text*

> Provides a title to display at the top of the documentation overview file. This file is often the first thing readers see when they browse the generated documentation. The title can contain HTML tags. Default doclet only.

-encoding *encoding-name*

> Specifies the character encoding of the input source files and the documentation comments they contain. This can be different from the desired output encoding specified by -docencoding. The default is the platform default encoding.

-extdirs *dirlist*

> Specifies a list of directories to search for standard extensions. Only necessary when cross-compiling with -bootclasspath. See *javac* for details.

-footer *text*

> Specifies text to be displayed near the bottom of each file, to the right of the navigation bar. *text* can contain HTML tags. See also -bottom and -header. Default doclet only.

-group *title packagelist*

> *javadoc* generates a top-level overview page that lists all packages in the generated document. By default, these packages are listed in alphabetical order in a single table. You can break them into groups of related packages with this option, however. The *title* specifies the title of the package group, such as "Core Packages." The *packagelist* is a colon-separated list of package names, each of which can include a trailing * character as a wildcard. The *javadoc* command line can contain any number of -group options. For example:
>
> ```
> javadoc -group "AWT Packages" java.awt*
>          -group "Swing Packages" javax.accessibility:javax.swing*
> ```

-header *text*

> Specifies text to be displayed near the top of each file, to the right of the upper navigation bar. *text* can contain HTML tags. See also -footer, -doctitle, and -windowtitle. Default doclet only.

-help

> Displays a usage message for *javadoc*.

-helpfile *file*

> Specifies the name of an HTML file that contains help for using the generated documentation. *javadoc* includes links to this help file in all files it generates. If this option is not specified, *javadoc* creates a default help file. Default doclet only.

-Jjavaoption

> Passes the argument *javaoption* directly through to the Java interpreter. When processing a large number of packages, you may need to use this option to increase the amount of memory *javadoc* is allowed to use. For example:
>
> ```
> % javadoc -J-Xmx64m
> ```

-link *url*

> Specifies an absolute or relative URL of the top-level directory of another *javadoc*-generated document. *javadoc* uses this URL as the base URL for links from the current document to packages, classes, methods, and fields that are not documented in the current document. For example, when using *javadoc* to produce documentation for your own packages, you can use this option to link your documentation to the *javadoc* documentation for the core Java APIs. Default doclet only.
>
> The directory specified by *url* must contain a file named *package-list*, and *javadoc* must be able to read this file at runtime. This file is automatically generated by a previous run of *javadoc*; it contains a list of all packages documented at the *url*.
>
> More than one -link option can be specified, although this does not work properly in early releases of Java 1.2. If no -link option is specified, references in the generated documentation to classes and members that are external to the documentation are not hyperlinked.

-linkoffline *url packagelist*

> This option is like the -link option, except that the *packagelist* file is explicitly specified on the command line. This is useful when the directory specified by *url* does not have a *package-list* file or when that file is not available when *javadoc* is run. Default doclet only.

Java Tools

-locale *language_country_variant*

Specifies the locale to use for generated documentation. This is used to look up a resource file that contains localized messages and text for the output files.

-nodeprecated

Tells *javadoc* to omit documentation for deprecated features. This option implies -nodeprecatedlist. Default doclet only.

-nodeprecatedlist

Tells *javadoc* not to generate the *deprecated-list.html* file and not to output a link to it on the navigation bar. Default doclet only.

-nohelp

Tells *javadoc* not to generate a help file or a link to it in the navigation bar. Default doclet only.

-noindex

Tells *javadoc* not to generate index files. Default doclet only.

-nonavbar

Tells *javadoc* to omit the navigation bars from the top and bottom of every file. Also omits the text specified by -header and -footer. This is useful when generating documentation to be printed. Default doclet only.

-notree

Tells *javadoc* not to generate the *tree.html* class hierarchy diagram or a link to it in the navigation bar. Default doclet only.

-overview *filename*

Reads an overview doc comment from *filename* and uses that comment in the overview page. This file does not contain Java source code, so the doc comment should not actually appear between /** and */ delimiters.

-package

Includes package-visible classes and members in the output, as well as public and protected classes and members.

-private

Includes all classes and members, including private and package-visible classes and members, in the generated documentation.

-protected

Includes public and protected classes and members in the generated output. This is the default.

-public

Includes only public classes and members in the generated output. Omits protected, private, and package-visible classes and members.

-serialwarn

Issues warnings about serializable classes that do not adequately document their serialization format with @serial and related doc-comment tags. Default doclet only.

-sourcepath *path*

Specifies a search path for source files, typically set to a single root directory. *javadoc* uses this path when looking for the Java source files that implement a specified package.

-splitindex

> Generates multiple index files, one for each letter of the alphabet. Use this option when documenting large amounts of code. Otherwise, the single index file generated by *javadoc* will be too large to be useful. Default doclet only.

-stylesheetfile *file*

> Specifies a file to use as a CSS stylesheet for the generated HTML. *javadoc* inserts appropriate links to this file in the generated documentation. Default doclet only.

-use

> Generates and inserts links to an additional file for each class and package that lists the uses of the class or package.

-verbose

> Displays additional messages while processing source files.

-version

> Includes information from @version tags in the generated output. This option does *not* tell *javadoc* to print its own version number. Default doclet only.

-windowtitle *text*

> Specifies *text* to be output in the <TITLE> tag of each generated file. This title typically appears in the web-browser titlebar and its history and bookmarks lists. *text* should not contain HTML tags. See also -doctitle and -header. Default doclet only.

Environment

CLASSPATH

> This environment variable specifies the default classpath *javadoc* uses to find the class files and source files. It is overridden by the -classpath and -sourcepath options. See *java* and *javac* for further discussion of the classpath.

See Also
java, javac

javah   JDK 1.0 and later
Native Method C Stub Generator

Synopsis

> javah [options] classnames

Description

javah generates C header and source files (.*h* and .*c* files) that are used when implementing Java native methods in C. The preferred native method interface has changed between Java 1.0 and Java 1.1. In Java 1.1 and earlier, *javah* generates files for old-style native methods. In Java 1.1, the -jni option specifies that *javah* should generate new-style files. In Java 1.2 and later, this option becomes the default.

This reference page describes only how to use *javah*. A full description of how to implement Java native methods in C is beyond the scope of this book.

Options

-bootclasspath

> Specifies the path to search for system classes. See *javac* for further discussion. Java 1.2 and later.

Java Tools

-classpath *path*

> The path *javah* uses to look up the classes named on the command line. This option overrides any path specified by the **CLASSPATH** environment variable. Prior to Java 1.2, this option can specify the location of the system classes and extensions. In Java 1.2 and later, it specifies only the location of application classes. See -bootclasspath. See also *java* for further discussion of the classpath.

-d *directory*

> Specifies the directory into which *javah* stores the files it generates. By default, it stores them in the current directory. This option cannot be used with -o.

-force

> Always write output files, even if they contain no useful content.

-help

> Causes *javah* to display a simple usage message and exit.

-jni   Specifies that *javah* should output header files for use with the new Java Native Interface (JNI), rather than using the old JDK 1.0 native interface. This option is the default in Java 1.2 and later. See also -old. Java 1.1 and later.

-o *outputfile*

> Combines all output into a single file, *outputfile*, instead of creating separate files for each specified class.

-old   Outputs files for Java 1.0-style native methods. Prior to Java 1.2, this was the default. See also -jni. Java 1.2 and later.

-stubs

> Generates .c stub files for the class or classes, instead of header files. This option is only for the Java 1.0 native methods interface. See -old.

-td *directory*

> Specifies the directory where *javah* should store temporary files. On Unix systems, the default is */tmp*.

-trace

> Specifies that *javah* should include tracing output commands in the stub files it generates. In Java 1.2 and later, this option is obsolete and has been removed. In its place, you can use the -verbose:jni option of the Java interpreter.

-v, -verbose

> Verbose mode. Causes *javah* to print messages about what it is doing. In Java 1.2 and later, -verbose is a synonym.

-version

> Causes *javah* to display its version number.

Environment

CLASSPATH

> Specifies the default classpath *javah* searches to find the specified classes. See *java* for a further discussion of the classpath.

See Also
java, javac

javakey

Key Management and Digital Signatures

Synopsis

> javakey *options*

Description

javakey provides a command-line interface to a number of complex key and certificate generation and management tasks, including the generation of digital signatures. In Java 1.2 and later, *javakey* has been superseded by two new tools, *keytool* for managing keys and certificates and *jarsigner* for digitally signing code. Due to bugs in Java 1.1, digital signatures generated by *javakey* are not recognized in Java 1.2. Likewise, signatures generated by the new *jarsigner* tool are not recognized by Java 1.1.

javakey manages a system database of entities. Each entity can have public and private keys and/or certificates associated with it. In addition, each entity can be declared to be trusted or not. Any entity in the database can be an identity or a signer. Identities have only a public key associated with them, while signers have both a public and private key and thus can sign files.

Options

javakey defines a large number of options that perform a number of distinct operations:

-c *identity-name* [true | false]

> Creates and adds a new identity entity to the database, using the specified name. If *identity-name* is followed by true, it declares the identity to be trusted. Otherwise, it is untrusted.

-cs *signer-name* [true | false]

> Creates and adds a new signer entity to the database, using the specified name. If *signer-name* is followed by true, declares the signer to be trusted. Otherwise, it is untrusted.

-t *entity-name* true | false

> Specifies whether the named entity is trusted (true) or not (false).

-l   Lists the names of all entities in the security database.

-ld   Lists the names and other details about all entities in the security database.

-li *entity-name*

> Lists detailed information about the named entity from the security database.

-r *entity-name*

> Removes the named entity from the security database.

-ik *identity-name* *keyfile*

> Imports a key by reading a public key from the specified file and associating it with the named identity. The key must be in X.509 format.

-ikp *signer-name* *pubkeyfile* *privkeyfile*

> Imports a key pair by reading the specified public-key and private-key files and associating them with the named signer entity. The keys must be in X.509 format.

-ic *entity-name* *certificate-file*

> Imports a certificate by reading a certificate from the named certificate file and associating it with the named entity. If the entity already has a public key, compares it to the key in the certificate and issues a warning if they don't match. If the entity has no public key assigned, uses the public key from the certificate.

-ii *entity-name*

> Imports information, allowing you to enter arbitrary textual information about an entity into the database.

-gk *signer algorithm size [pubfile [privfile]]*

> Generates a public and private key and associates them with the named signer. Uses the specified algorithm. Currently, the only supported algorithm is "DSA". Generates keys of the specified number of bits, which must be between 512 and 1024. If *pubfile* is specified, writes the public key to the specified file. If *privfile* is specified, writes the private key to the specified file.

-g *signer algorithm size [pubfile [privfile]]*

> A synonym for the -gk command.

-gc *directivefile*

> Generates a certificate according to the parameters specified in the directive file. The directive file is a Properties file that must provide values for the following named properties:

issuer.name

> The name of the entity issuing the certificate

issuer.cert

> The issuer's certificate number to be used to sign the generated certificate (unless the certificate is self-signed)

subject.name

> The database name of the entity to which the certificate is being issued

subject.real.name

> The real name of the entity to which the certificate is being issued

subject.country

> The country the subject entity is in

subject.org

> The organization with which the subject entity is affiliated

subject.org.unit

> A division within the subject's organization

start.date

> The starting date (and time) of the certificate

end.date

> The ending date (and time) of the certificate

serial.number

> A serial number for the certificate; this number must be unique among all certificates generated by the issuer

out.file

> An optional filename that specifies the file to which the certificate should be written

-dc *certfile*

> Displays the contents of the certificate stored in *certfile*.

-ec *entity certificate-number file*

Exports the numbered certificate of the specified entity into the specified file. Use the -li command to inspect the certificate numbers for a given entity.

-ek *entity pubfile [privfile]*

Exports the public key of the specified entity into the specified file. If the entity is a signer and the *privfile* is specified, additionally exports the private key of the entity to that file.

-gs *directivefile jarfile*

Generates, or applies, a digital signature to the specified JAR file, using the directives in the specified directive file. The directive file is a Properties file that must provide values for the following named properties:

signer

The entity name of the signer

cert   The certificate number to use for the signature

chain

The length of a chain of certificates to include (not currently supported; specify 0)

signature.file

The basename of the signature file and signature block to be inserted into the JAR file; must be eight characters or less and should not conflict with any other digital signatures that may be inserted into the JAR file

out.file

This optional property specifies the name that should be used for the signed JAR file that is generated.

See Also
jar, jarsigner, keytool

javap JDK 1.0 and later
The Java Class Disassembler

Synopsis

javap [*options*] *classnames*

Description

javap reads the class files specified by the class names on the command line and prints a human-readable version of the API defined by those classes. *javap* can also disassemble the specified classes, displaying the Java VM byte codes for the methods they contain.

Options

-b   Enables backward compatibility with the output of the Java 1.1 version of *javap*. This option exists for program that depends on the precise output format of *javap*. Java 1.2 and later.

-bootclasspath *path*

Specifies the search path for the system classes. See *javac* for information about this rarely used option. Java 1.2 and later.

-c   Displays the code (i.e., Java VM byte codes) for each method of each specified class. This option always disassembles all methods, regardless of their visibility level.

-classpath *path*
     Specifies the path *javap* uses to look up the classes named on the command line. This option overrides the path specified by the CLASSPATH environment variable. Prior to Java 1.2, this argument specifies the path for all system classes, extensions, and application classes. In Java 1.2 and later, it specifies only the application class-path. See also -bootclasspath and -extdirs. See *java* and *javac* for more information on the classpath.

-extdirs *dirs*
     Specifies one or more directories that should be searched for extension classes. See *javac* for information about this rarely used option. Java 1.2 and later.

-l   Displays tables of line numbers and local variables, if available in the class files. This option is typically useful only when used with -c. The *javac* compiler does not include local variable information in its class files by default. See the -g and related options to *javac*.

-help
     Prints a usage message and exits.

-J*javaoption*
     Passes the specified *javaoption* directly to the Java interpreter.

-package
     Displays package-visible, protected, and public class members, but not private members. This is the default.

-private
     Displays all class members, including private members.

-protected
     Displays only protected and public members.

-public
     Displays only public members of the specified classes.

-s   Outputs the class member declarations using the internal VM type and method signature format, instead of the more readable source-code format.

-verbose
     Verbose mode. Outputs additional information (in the form of Java comments) about each member of each specified class.

-verify
     Causes *javap* to perform partial class verification on the specified class or classes and display the results. Java 1.0 and 1.1. only; this option has been removed in Java 1.2 and later because it does not perform a sufficiently thorough verification.

-version
     Causes *javap* to display its version number.

Environment

CLASSPATH

Specifies the default search path for application classes. The -classpath option overrides this environment variable. See *java* for a discussion of the classpath.

See Also

java, javac

jdb JDK 1.0 and later

The Java Debugger

Synopsis

```
jdb [ options ] class [ program options ]
jdb connect options
```

Description

jdb is a debugger for Java classes. It is text-based, command-line-oriented, and has a command syntax like that of the Unix *dbx* or *gdb* debuggers used with C and C++ programs.

jdb is written in Java, so it runs within a Java interpreter. When *jdb* is invoked with the name of a Java class, it starts another copy of the *java* interpreter, using any interpreter options specified on the command line. The new interpreter is started with special options that enable it to communicate with *jdb*. The new interpreter loads the specified class file and then stops and waits for debugging commands before executing the first byte code.

jdb can also debug a program that is already running in another Java interpreter. Doing so requires special options be passed to both the *java* interpreter and to *jdb*. The Java debugging architecture has changed dramatically with the introduction of Java 1.3, and so have the *java* and *jdb* options used to allow *jdb* to connect to a running interpreter.

jdb Expression Syntax

jdb debugging commands such as print, dump, and suspend allow you to refer to classes, objects, methods, fields, and threads in the program being debugged. You can refer to classes by name, with or without their package names. You can also refer to static class members by name. You can refer to individual objects by object ID, which is an eight-digit hexadecimal integer. Or, when the classes you are debugging contain local variable information, you can often use local variable names to refer to objects. You can use normal Java syntax to refer to the fields of an object and the elements of an array; you can also use this syntax to write quite complex expressions. In Java 1.3, *jdb* even supports method invocation using standard Java syntax.

A number of *jdb* commands require you to specify a thread. Each thread is given an integer identifier and is named using the syntax t@*n*, where *n* is the thread ID.

Options

When invoking *jdb* with a specified class file, any of the *java* interpreter options can be specified. See the *java* reference page for an explanation of these options. In addition, *jdb* supports the following options:

-attach [*host:*]*port*

Specifies that *jdb* should connect to the Java "Client VM" that is already running on the specified host (or the local host, if unspecified) and listening for debugging connections on the specified port. Java 1.3 and later.

In order to use *jdb* to connect to a running VM in this way, the VM must have been started with a command line something like this:

```
% java -Xdebug -Xrunjdwp:transport=dt_socket,address=8000,server=y,suspend=n
```

The Java 1.3 *jdb* architecture allows a complex set of interpreter-to-debugger connection options, and *java* and *jdb* provide a complex set of options and suboptions to enable it. A detailed description of those options is beyond the scope of this book.

-help

Displays a usage message listing supported options.

-host *hostname*

In Java 1.2 and earlier, this option is used to connect to an already running interpreter. It specifies the name of the host upon which the desired interpreter session is running. If omitted, the default is the local host. This option must be used with -password. In Java 1.3, this option has been replaced by the -attach option.

-launch

Starts the specified application when *jdb* starts. This avoids the need to explicitly use the run command to start it. Java 1.3 and later.

-password *password*

In Java 1.2 and earlier, this option specifies a password that uniquely identifies a Java VM on a particular host. When used in conjunction with -hostname, this option enables *jdb* to connect to a running interpreter. The interpreter must have been started with the -debug or -Xdebug option, which causes it to display an appropriate *password* for use with this option. In Java 1.3, this option has been replaced by the -attach option.

-sourcepath *path*

Specifies the locations *jdb* searches when attempting to find source files that correspond to the class files being debugged. If unspecified, *jdb* uses the classpath by default. Java 1.3 and later.

-tclassic

Tells *jdb* to invoke the "Classic VM" instead of the "Client VM" (Hotspot), which is the default VM in Java 1.3. Java 1.3 and later.

-version

Displays the *jdb* version number and exits.

Commands

jdb understands the following debugging commands:

? or help

Lists all supported commands, with a short explanation of each.

!!

A shorthand command that is replaced with the text of the last command entered. It can be followed with additional text that is appended to that previous command.

catch [*exception-class*]

Causes a breakpoint whenever the specified exception is thrown. If no exception is specified, the command lists the exceptions currently being caught. Use ignore to stop these breakpoints from occurring.

classes

Lists all classes that have been loaded.

clear
> Lists all currently set breakpoints.

clear *class.method* [(*param-type . . .*)]
> Clears the breakpoint set in the specified method of the specified class.

clear [*class:line*]
> Removes the breakpoint set at the specified line of the specified class.

cont Resumes execution. This command should be used when the current thread is stopped at a breakpoint.

down [*n*]
> Moves down *n* frames in the call stack of the current thread. If n is not specified, moves down one frame.

dump *id . . .*
> Prints the value of all fields of the specified object or objects. If you specify the name of a class, dump displays all class (static) methods and variables of the class, and also displays the superclass and list of implemented interfaces. Objects and classes can be specified by name or by their eight-digit hexadecimal ID numbers. Threads can also be specified with the shorthand *t@thread-number*.

exit or quit
> Quits *jdb*.

gc Runs the garbage collector to force unused objects to be reclaimed.

ignore *exception-class*
> Does not treat the specified exception as a breakpoint. This command turns off a catch command. This command does not cause the Java interpreter to ignore exceptions; it merely tells *jdb* to ignore them.

list [*line-number*]
> Lists the specified line of source code as well as several lines that appear before and after it. If no line number is specified, uses the line number of the current stack frame of the current thread. The lines listed are from the source file of the current stack frame of the current thread. Use the use command to tell *jdb* where to find source files.

list *method*
> Displays the source code of the specified method.

load *classname*
> Loads the specified class into *jdb*.

locals
> Displays a list of local variables for the current stack frame. Java code must be compiled with the -g option in order to contain local variable information.

memory
> Displays a summary of memory usage for the Java program being debugged.

methods *class*
> Lists all methods of the specified class. Use dump to list the instance variables of an object or the class (static) variables of a class.

print *id* . . .
>Prints the value of the specified item or items. Each item can be a class, object, field, or local variable, and can be specified by name or by eight-digit hexadecimal ID number. You can also refer to threads with the special syntax *t@thread-number*. The print command displays an object's value by invoking its toString() method.

next Executes the current line of source code, including any method calls it makes. See also step.

resume [*thread-id* . . .]
>Resumes execution of the specified thread or threads. If no threads are specified, all suspended threads are resumed. See also suspend.

run [*class*] [*args*]
>Runs the main() method of the specified class, passing the specified arguments to it. If no class or arguments are specified, uses the class and arguments specified on the *jdb* command line.

step Runs the current line of the current thread and stops again. If the line invokes a method, steps into that method and stops. See also next.

stepi
>Executes a single Java VM instruction.

step up
>Runs until the current method returns to its caller and stops again.

stop Lists current breakpoints.

stop at *class:line*
>Sets a breakpoint at the specified line of the specified class. Program execution stops when it reaches this line. Use clear to remove a breakpoint.

stop in *class.method* [(*param-type* . . .)]
>Sets a breakpoint at the beginning of the specified method of the specified class. Program execution stops when it enters the method. Use clear to remove a breakpoint.

suspend [*thread-id* . . .]
>Suspends the specified thread or threads. If no threads are specified, suspends all running threads. Use resume to restart them.

thread *thread-id*
>Sets the current thread to the specified thread. This thread is used implicitly by a number of other *jdb* commands. The thread can be specified by name or number.

threadgroup *name*
>Sets the current thread group.

threadgroups
>Lists all thread groups running in the Java interpreter session being debugged.

threads [*threadgroup*]
>Lists all threads in the named thread group. If no thread group is specified, lists all threads in the current thread group (specified by threadgroup).

up [*n*]

Moves up *n* frames in the call stack of the current thread. If n is not specified, moves up one frame.

use [*source-file-path*]

Sets the path used by *jdb* to look up source files for the classes being debugged. If no path is specified, displays the current source path.

where [*thread-id*] [all]

Displays a stack trace for the specified thread. If no thread is specified, displays a stack trace for the current thread. If all is specified, displays a stack trace for all threads.

wherei [*thread-id* x]

Displays a stack trace for the specified or current thread, including detailed program counter information.

Environment

CLASSPATH

Specifies an ordered list (colon-separated on Unix, semicolon-separated on Windows systems) of directories, ZIP files, and JAR archives in which *jdb* should look for class definitions. When a path is specified with this environment variable, *jdb* always implicitly appends the location of the system classes to the end of the path. If this environment variable is not specified, the default path is the current directory and the system classes. This variable is overridden by the -classpath option.

See Also

java

keytool   Java 2 SDK 1.2 and later
Key and Certificate Management Tool

Synopsis

keytool *command options*

Description

keytool manages and manipulates a *keystore*: a repository for public and private keys and public-key certificates. *keytool* defines various commands for generating keys, importing data into the keystore, and exporting and displaying keystore data. Keys and certificates are stored in a keystore using a case-insensitive name, or *alias*. *keytool* uses this alias to refer to a key or certificate.

The first option to *keytool* always specifies the basic command to be performed. Subsequent options provide details about how the command is to be performed. Only the command must be specified. If a command requires an option that does not have a default value, *keytool* prompts you interactively for the value.

Commands

-certreq

Generates a certificate signing request in PKCS#10 format for the specified alias. The request is written to the specified file or to the standard output stream. The request should be sent to a certificate authority (CA), which authenticates the requestor and sends back a signed certificate authenticating the requestor's public key. This signed certificate can then be imported into the keystore with the -import command. This command uses the following options: -alias, -file, -keypass, -keystore, -sigalg, -storepass, -storetype, and -v.

Java Tools

-delete

Deletes a specified alias from a specified keystore. This command uses the following options: -alias, -keystore, -storepass, -storetype, and -v.

-export

Writes the certificate associated with the specified alias to the specified file or to standard output. This command uses the following options: -alias, -file, -keystore, -rfc, -storepass, -storetype, and -v.

-genkey

Generates a public/private key pair and a self-signed X.509 certificate for the public key. Self-signed certificates are not often useful by themselves, so this command is often followed by -certreq. This command uses the following options: -alias, -dname, -keyalg, -keypass, -keysize, -keystore, -sigalg, -storepass, -storetype, -v, and -validity.

-help

Lists all available *keytool* commands and their options. This command is not used with any other options.

-identitydb

Reads keys and certificates from a Java 1.1 identity database managed with *javakey* and stores them into a keystore so they can be manipulated by *keytool*. The identity database is read from the specified file or from standard input if no file is specified. The keys and certificates are written into the specified keystore file, which is automatically created if it does not exist yet. This command uses the following options: -file, -keystore, -storepass, -storetype, and -v.

-import

Reads a certificate or PKCS#7-formatted certificate chain from a specified file or from standard input and stores it as a trusted certificate in the keystore with the specified alias. This command uses the following options: -alias, -file, -keypass, -keystore, -noprompt, -storepass, -storetype, -trustcacerts, and -v.

-keyclone

Duplicates the keystore entry of a specified alias and stores it in the keystore under a new alias. This command uses the following options: -alias, -dest, -keypass, -keystore, -new, -storepass, -storetype, and -v.

-keypasswd

Changes the password that encrypts the private key associated with a specified alias. This command uses the following options: -alias, -keypass, -new, -storetype, and -v.

-list Displays (on standard output) the fingerprint of the certificate associated with the specified alias. With the -v option, prints certificate details in human-readable format. With -rfc, prints certificate contents in a machine-readable, printable-encoding format. This command uses the following options: -alias, -keystore, -rfc, -storepass, -storetype, and -v.

-printcert

Displays the contents of a certificate read from the specified file or from standard input. Unlike most *keytool* commands, this one does not use a keystore. This command uses the following options: -file and -v.

-selfcert
> Creates a self-signed certificate for the public key associated with the specified alias and uses it to replace any certificate or certificate chain already associated with that alias. This command uses the following options: -alias, -dname, -keypass, -keystore, -sigalg, -storepass, -storetype, -v, and -validity.

-storepasswd
> Changes the password that protects the integrity of the keystore as a whole. The new password must be at least six characters long. This command uses the following options: -keystore, -new, -storepass, -storetype, and -v.

Options

The various *keytool* commands can be passed various options from the following list. Many of these options have reasonable default values. *keytool* interactively prompts for any unspecified options that do not have defaults:

-alias *name*
> Specifies the alias to be manipulated in the keystore. The default is "mykey".

-dest *newalias*
> Specifies the new alias name (the destination alias) for the -keyclone command. If not specified, *keytool* prompts for a value.

-dname *X.500-distinguished-name*
> Specifies the X.500 distinguished name to appear on the certificate generated by -selfcert or -genkey. A distinguished name is a highly qualified name intended to be globally unique. For example:
>
> CN=David Flanagan, OU=Editorial, O=OReilly, L=Cambridge, S=Massachusetts, C=US
>
> The -genkey command of *keytool* prompts for a distinguished name if none is specified. The -selfcert command uses the distinguished name of the current certificate if no replacement name is specified.

-file *file*
> Specifies the input or output file for many of the *keytool* commands. If left unspecified, *keytool* reads from the standard input or writes to the standard output.

-keyalg *algorithm-name*
> Used with -genkey to specify what type of cryptographic keys to generate. In the default Java implementation shipped from Sun, the only supported algorithm is "DSA"; this is the default if this option is omitted.

-keypass *password*
> Specifies the password that encrypts a private key in the keystore. If this option is unspecified, *keytool* first tries the -storepass password. If that does not work, it prompts for the appropriate password.

-keysize *size*
> Used with the -genkey command to specify the length in bits of the generated keys. If unspecified, the default is 1024.

-keystore *filename*
> Specifies the location of the keystore file. If unspecified, a file named *.keystore* in the user's home directory is used.

-new *new-password-or-alias*

Used with the -keyclone command to specify the new alias name and with -keypasswd and -storepasswd to specify the new password. If unspecified, *keytool* prompts for the value of this option.

-noprompt

Used with the -import command to disable interactive prompting of the user when a chain of trust cannot be established for an imported certificate. If this option is not specified, the -import command prompts the user.

-rfc   Used with the -list and -export commands to specify that certificate output should be in the printable encoding format specified by RFC-1421. If this option is not specified, -export outputs the certificate in binary format, and -list lists only the certificate fingerprint. This option cannot be combined with -v in the -list command.

-sigalg *algorithm-name*

Specifies a digital signature algorithm that signs a certificate. If omitted, the default for this option depends on the type of underlying public key. If it is a DSA key, the default algorithm is "SHA1withDSA". If the key is an RSA key, the default signature algorithm is "MD5withRSA".

-storepass *password*

Specifies a password that protects the integrity of the entire keystore file. This password also serves as a default password for any private keys that do not have their own -keypass specified. If -storepass is not specified, *keytool* prompts for it. The password must be at least six characters long.

-storetype *type*

Specifies the type of the keystore to be used. If this option is not specified, the default is taken from the system security properties file. Often, the default is Sun's "JKS" Java Keystore type.

-trustcacerts

Used with the -import command to specify that the self-signed certificate authority certificates contained in the keystore in the *jre/lib/security/cacerts* file should be considered trusted. If this option is omitted, *keytool* ignores that file.

-v   This option specifies verbose mode, if present, and makes many *keytool* commands produce additional output.

-validity *time*

Used with the -genkey and -selfcert commands to specify the period of validity (in days) of the generated certificate. If unspecified, the default is 90 days.

See Also
jarsigner, javakey, policytool

native2ascii   JDK 1.1 and later

Converts Java Source Code to ASCII

Synopsis

    native2ascii [options] [inputfile [outputfile]]

Description

javac can only process files encoded in the eight-bit Latin-1 encoding, with any other characters encoded using the \u*xxxx* Unicode notation. *native2ascii* is a simple program that reads a Java source file encoded using a local encoding and converts it to the Latin-1-plus-ASCII-encoded-Unicode form required by *javac*.

The *inputfile* and *outputfile* are optional. If unspecified, standard input and standard output are used, making *native2ascii* suitable for use in pipes.

Options

-encoding *encoding-name*
> Specifies the encoding used by source files. If this option is not specified, the encoding is taken from the file.encoding system property.

-reverse
> Specifies that the conversion should be done in reverse—from encoded \u*xxxx* characters to characters in the native encoding.

See Also
java.io.InputStreamReader, java.io.OutputStreamWriter

policytool
Java 2 SDK 1.2 and later
Policy File Creation and Management Tool

Synopsis

> policytool

Description

policytool displays a Swing user interface that makes it easy to edit security policy configuration files. The Java security architecture is based on policy files, which specify sets of permissions to be granted to code from various sources. By default, the Java security policy is defined by a system policy file stored in the *jre/lib/security/java.policy* file and a user policy file stored in the *.java.policy* file in the user's home directory. System administrators and users can edit these files with a text editor, but the syntax of the file is somewhat complex, so it is usually easier to use *policytool* to define and edit security policies.

Selecting the Policy File to Edit

When *policytool* starts up, it opens the *.java.policy* file in the user's home directory by default. Use the **New**, **Open**, and **Save** commands in the **File** menu to create a new policy file, open an existing file, and save an edited file, respectively.

Editing the Policy File

The main *policytool* window displays a list of the entries contained in the policy file. Each entry specifies a code source and the permissions that are to be granted to code from that source. The window also contains buttons that allow you to add a new entry, edit an existing entry, or delete an entry from the policy file. If you add or edit an entry, *policytool* opens a new window that displays the details of that policy entry.

Every policy file has an associated keystore, from which it obtains the certificates it needs when verifying the digital signatures of Java code. You can usually rely on the default keystore, but if you need to specify the keystore explicitly for a policy file, use the **Change Keystore** command in the **Edit** menu of the main *policytool* window.

Adding or Editing a Policy Entry

The policy entry editor window displays the code source for the policy entry and a list of permissions associated with that code source. It also contains buttons that allow you to add a new permission, delete a permission, or edit an existing permission.

When defining a new policy entry, the first step is to specify the code source. A code source is defined by a URL from which the code is downloaded and/or a list of digital signatures that must appear on the code. Specify one or both of these values by typing in a URL and/or a comma-separated list of aliases. These aliases identify trusted certificates in the keystore associated with the policy file.

*Java
Tools*

After you have defined the code source for a policy entry, you must define the permissions to be granted to code from that source. Use the **Add Permission** and **Edit Permission** buttons to add and edit permissions. These buttons bring up yet another *policytool* window.

Defining a Permission

To define a permission in the permission editor window, first select the desired permission type from the **Permission** drop-down menu. Then, select an appropriate target value from the **Target Name** menu. The choices in this menu are customized depending on the permission type you selected. For some types of permission, such as FilePermission, there is not a fixed set of possible targets, and you usually have to type in the specific target you want. For example, you might type "/tmp" to specify the directory */tmp*, "/tmp/*" to specify all the files in that directory, or "/tmp/-" to specify all the files in the directory, and, recursively, any subdirectories. See the documentation of the individual Permission classes for a description of the targets they support.

Depending on the type of permission you select, you may also have to select one or more action values from the **Actions** menu. When you have selected a permission and appropriate target and action values, click the **Okay** button to dismiss the window.

See Also
jarsigner, keytool

serialver JDK 1.1 and later
Class Version Number Generator

Synopsis

serialver [-show] *classname*...

Description

serialver displays the version number of a class or classes. This version number is used for the purposes of serialization: the version number must change each time the serialization format of the class changes.

If the specified class declares a long serialVersionUID constant, the value of that field is displayed. Otherwise, a unique version number is computed by applying the Secure Hash Algorithm (SHA) to the API defined by the class. This program is primarily useful for computing an initial unique version number for a class, which is then declared as a constant in the class. The output of *serialver* is a line of legal Java code, suitable for pasting into a class definition.

Options

-show

When the -show option is specified, *serialver* displays a simple graphical interface that allows the user to type in a single classname at a time and obtain its serialization UID. When using -show, no class names can be specified on the command-line.

Environment

CLASSPATH

serialver is written in Java, so it is sensitive to the CLASSPATH environment variable in the same way the *java* interpreter is. The specified classes are looked up relative to this classpath.

See Also
java.io.ObjectStreamClass

PART II

API Quick Reference

Part II is the real heart of this book: quick-reference material for the essential APIs of the Java platform. Please read the following section, *How To Use This Quick Reference*, to learn how to get the most out of this material.

How To Use This
Quick Reference

The quick-reference section that follows packs a lot of information into a small space. This introduction explains how to get the most out of that information. It describes how the quick reference is organized and how to read the individual quick-ref entries.

Finding a Quick-Reference Entry

The quick reference is organized into chapters, one per package. Each chapter begins with an overview of the package and includes a hierarchy diagram for the classes and interfaces in the package. Following this overview are quick-reference entries for all of the classes and interfaces in the package.

Entries are organized alphabetically by class *and* package name, so that related classes are grouped near each other. Thus, in order to look up a quick reference entry for a particular class, you must also know the name of the package that contains that class. Usually, the package name is obvious from the context, and you should have no trouble looking up the quick-reference entry you want. Use the tabs on the outside edge of the book and the dictionary-style headers on the upper outside corner of each page to help you find the package and class you are looking for.

Occasionally, you may need to look up a class for which you do not already know the package. In this case, refer to Chapter 29, *Class, Method, and Field Index.* This index allows you to look up a class by class name and find out what package it is part of.

Reading a Quick-Reference Entry

Each quick-reference entry contains quite a bit of information. The sections that follow describe the structure of a quick-reference entry, explaining what information is available, where it is found, and what it means. While reading the descriptions that follow, you will find it helpful to flip through the reference section itself to find examples of the features being described.

Class Name, Package Name, Availability, and Flags

Each quick-reference entry begins with a four-part title that specifies the name, package, and availability of the class, and may also specify various additional flags that describe the class. The class name appears in bold at the upper left of the title. The package name appears, in smaller print, in the lower left, below the class name.

The upper-right portion of the title indicates the availability of the class; it specifies the earliest release that contained the class. If a class was introduced in Java 1.1, for example, this portion of the title reads "Java 1.1". If a class was introduced in Version 1.2 of the Java 2 platform, the availability reads "Java 1.2" for simplicity's sake. The availability section of the title is also used to indicate whether a class has been deprecated, and, if so, in what release. For example, it might read "Java 1.1; Deprecated in Java 1.2".

In the lower-right corner of the title you may find a list of flags that describe the class. The possible flags and their meanings are as follows:

checked
: The class is a checked exception, which means that it extends java.lang.Exception, but not java.lang.RuntimeException. In other words, it must be declared in the throws clause of any method that may throw it.

cloneable
: The class, or a superclass, implements java.lang.Cloneable.

collection
: The class, or a superclass, implements java.util.Collection or java.util.Map.

comparable
: The class, or a superclass, implements java.lang.Comparable.

error
: The class extends java.lang.Error.

event
: The class extends java.util.EventObject.

event adapter
: The class, or a superclass, implements java.util.EventListener, and the class name ends with "Adapter".

event listener
: The class, or a superclass, implements java.util.EventListener.

PJ1.1
: The class or interface is part of the Personal Java 1.1 platform.

PJ1.1(mod)

The class or interface is supported, in modified form, by the Personal Java 1.1 platform.

PJ1.1(opt)

The class or interface is an optional part of the Personal Java 1.1 platform. Support for the class is implementation-dependent.

runnable

The class, or a superclass, implements java.lang.Runnable.

serializable

The class, or a superclass, implements java.io.Serializable and may be serialized.

unchecked

The class is an unchecked exception, which means it extends java.lang.RuntimeException and therefore does not need to be declared in the throws clause of a method that may throw it.

Description

The title of each quick-reference entry is followed by a short description of the most important features of the class or interface. This description may be anywhere from a couple of sentences to several paragraphs long.

Synopsis

The most important part of every quick-reference entry is the class synopsis, which follows the title and description. The synopsis for a class looks a lot like the source code for the class, except that the method bodies are omitted and some additional annotations are added. If you know Java syntax, you know how to read the class synopsis.

The first line of the synopsis contains information about the class itself. It begins with a list of class modifiers, such as public, abstract, and final. These modifiers are followed by the class or interface keyword and then by the name of the class. The class name may be followed by an extends clause that specifies the superclass and an implements clause that specifies any interfaces the class implements.

The class definition line is followed by a list of the fields and methods that the class defines. Once again, if you understand basic Java syntax, you should have no trouble making sense of these lines. The listing for each member includes the modifiers, type, and name of the member. For methods, the synopsis also includes the type and name of each method parameter and an optional throws clause that lists the exceptions the method can throw. The member names are in boldface, so it is easy to scan the list of members looking for the one you want. The names of method parameters are in italics to indicate that they are not to be used literally. The member listings are printed on alternating gray and white backgrounds to keep them visually separate.

Member availability and flags

Each member listing is a single line that defines the API for that member. These listings use Java syntax, so their meaning is immediately clear to any Java programmer. There is some auxiliary information associated with each member synopsis, however, that requires explanation.

Recall that each quick-reference entry begins with a title section that includes the release in which the class was first defined. When a member is introduced into a class after the initial release of the class, the version in which the member was introduced appears, in small print, to the left of the member synopsis. For example, if a class was first introduced in Java 1.1, but had a new method added in Version 1.2 of Java 2, the title contains the string "Java 1.1", and the listing for the new member is preceded by the number "1.2". Furthermore, if a member has been deprecated, that fact is indicated with a hash mark (#) to the left of the member synopsis.

The area to the right of the member synopsis is used to display a variety of flags that provide additional information about the member. Some of these flags indicate additional specification details that do not appear in the member API itself. Other flags contain implementation-specific information. This information can be quite useful in understanding the class and in debugging your code, but be aware that it may differ between implementations. The implementation-specific flags displayed in this book are based on Sun's implementation of Java for Microsoft Windows.

The following flags may be displayed to the right of a member synopsis:

native
> An implementation-specific flag that indicates that a method is implemented in native code. Although native is a Java keyword and can appear in method signatures, it is part of the method implementation, not part of its specification. Therefore, this information is included with the member flags, rather than as part of the member listing. This flag is useful as a hint about the expected performance of a method.

synchronized
> An implementation-specific flag that indicates that a method implementation is declared synchronized, meaning that it obtains a lock on the object or class before executing. Like the native keyword, the synchronized keyword is part of the method implementation, not part of the specification, so it appears as a flag, not in the method synopsis itself. This flag is a useful hint that the method is probably implemented in a thread-safe manner.

> Whether or not a method is thread-safe is part of the method specification, and this information *should* appear (although it often does not) in the method documentation. There are a number of different ways to make a method thread-safe, however, and declaring the method with the synchronized keyword is only one possible implementation. In other words, a method that does not bear the synchronized flag can still be thread-safe.

Overrides:

Indicates that a method overrides a method in one of its superclasses. The flag is followed by the name of the superclass that the method overrides. This is a specification detail, not an implementation detail. As we'll see in the next section, overriding methods are usually grouped together in their own section of the class synopsis. The Overrides: flag is only used when an overriding method is not grouped in that way.

Implements:

Indicates that a method implements a method in an interface. The flag is followed by the name of the interface that is implemented. This is a specification detail, not an implementation detail. As we'll see in the next section, methods that implement an interface are usually grouped into a special section of the class synopsis. The Implements: flag is only used for methods that are not grouped in this way.

empty

Indicates that the implementation of the method has an empty body. This can be a hint to the programmer that the method may need to be overridden in a subclass.

constant

An implementation flag that indicates that a method has a trivial implementation. Only methods with a void return type can be truly empty. Any method declared to return a value must have at least a return statement. The "constant" flag indicates that the method implementation is empty except for a return statement that returns a constant value. Such a method might have a body like return null; or return false;. Like the "empty" flag, this flag indicates that a method may need to be overridden.

default:

This flag is used with property accessor methods that read the value of a property (i.e., methods whose names begins with "get" and take no arguments). The flag is followed by the default value of the property. Strictly speaking, default property values are a specification detail. In practice, however, these defaults are not always documented, and care should be taken, because the default values may change between implementations.

Not all property accessors have a "default:" flag. A default value is determined by dynamically loading the class in question, instantiating it using a no-argument constructor, and then calling the method to find out what it returns. This technique can be used only on classes that can be dynamically loaded and instantiated and that have no-argument constructors, so default values are shown for those classes only. Furthermore, note that when a class is instantiated using a different constructor, the default values for its properties may be different.

=   For static final fields, this flag is followed by the constant value of the field. Only constants of primitive and String types and constants with the value null are displayed. Some constant values are specification details, while others are implementation details. The reason that symbolic constants are defined, however, is so you can write code that does not rely directly upon the constant value. Use this flag to help you understand the class, but do not rely upon the constant values in your own programs.

Functional grouping of members

Within a class synopsis, the members are not listed in strict alphabetical order. Instead, they are broken down into functional groups and listed alphabetically within each group. Constructors, methods, fields, and inner classes are all listed separately. Instance methods are kept separate from static (class) methods. Constants are separated from non-constant fields. Public members are listed separately from protected members. Grouping members by category breaks a class down into smaller, more comprehensible segments, making the class easier to understand. This grouping also makes it easier for you to find a desired member.

Functional groups are separated from each other in a class synopsis with Java comments, such as "// Public Constructors", "// Inner Classes", and "// Methods Implementing Servlet". The various functional categories are as follows (in the order in which they appear in a class synopsis):

Constructors
Displays the constructors for the class. Public constructors and protected constructors are displayed separately in subgroupings. If a class defines no constructor at all, the Java compiler adds a default no-argument constructor that is displayed here. If a class defines only private constructors, it cannot be instantiated, so a special, empty grouping entitled "No Constructor" indicates this fact. Constructors are listed first because the first thing you do with most classes is instantiate them by calling a constructor.

Constants
Displays all of the constants (i.e., fields that are declared static and final) defined by the class. Public and protected constants are displayed in separate subgroups. Constants are listed here, near the top of the class synopsis, because constant values are often used throughout the class as legal values for method parameters and return values.

Inner Classes
Groups all of the inner classes and interfaces defined by the class or interface. For each inner class, there is a single-line synopsis. Each inner class also has its own quick-reference entry that includes a full class synopsis for the inner class. Like constants, inner classes are listed near the top of the class synopsis because they are often used by a number of other members of the class.

Static Methods
Lists the static methods (class methods) of the class, broken down into subgroups for public static methods and protected static methods.

Event Listener Registration Methods
Lists the public instance methods that register and deregister event listener objects with the class. The names of these methods begin with the words "add" and "remove" and end in "Listener". These methods are always passed a java.util.EventListener object. The methods are typically defined in pairs, so the

pairs are listed together. The methods are listed alphabetically by event name rather than by method name.

Property Accessor Methods

Lists the public instance methods that set or query the value of a property or attribute of the class. The names of these methods begin with the words "set", "get", and "is", and their signatures follow the patterns set out in the Java-Beans specification. Although the naming conventions and method signature patterns are defined for JavaBeans, classes and interfaces throughout the Java platform define property accessor methods that follow these conventions and patterns. Looking at a class in terms of the properties it defines can be a powerful tool for understanding the class, so property methods are grouped together in this section. Property accessor methods are listed alphabetically by property name, not by method name. This means that the "set", "get", and "is" methods for a property all appear together.

Public Instance Methods

Contains all of the public instance methods that are not grouped elsewhere.

Implementing Methods

Groups the methods that implement the same interface. There is one subgroup for each interface implemented by the class. Methods that are defined by the same interface are almost always related to each other, so this is a useful functional grouping of methods.

Note that if an interface method is also an event registration method or a property accessor method, it is listed both in this group and in the event or property group. This situation does not arise often, but when it does, all of the functional groupings are important and useful enough to warrant the duplicate listing. When an interface method is listed in the event or property group, it displays an "Implements:" flag that specifies the name of the interface of which it is part.

Overriding Methods

Groups the methods that override methods of a superclass broken down into subgroups by superclass. This is typically a useful grouping, because it helps to make it clear how a class modifies the default behavior of its superclasses. In practice, it is also often true that methods that override the same superclass are functionally related to each other.

Sometimes a method that overrides a superclass is also a property accessor method or (more rarely) an event registration method. When this happens, the method is grouped with the property or event methods and displays a flag that indicates which superclass it overrides. The method is not listed with other overriding methods, however. Note that this is different from interface methods, which, because they are more strongly functionally related, may have duplicate listings in both groups.

Protected Instance Methods

Contains all of the protected instance methods that are not grouped elsewhere.

Fields

Lists all the non-constant fields of the class, breaking them down into subgroups for public and protected static fields and public and protected instance fields. Many classes do not define any publicly accessible fields. For those that do, many object-oriented programmers prefer not to use those fields directly, but instead to use accessor methods when such methods are available.

Deprecated Members

Deprecated methods and deprecated fields are grouped at the very bottom of the class synopsis. Use of these members is strongly discouraged.

Class Hierarchy

For any class or interface that has a non-trivial class hierarchy, the class synopsis is followed by a "Hierarchy" section. This section lists all of the superclasses of the class, as well as any interfaces implemented by those superclasses. It may also list any interfaces extended by an interface. In the hierarchy listing, arrows indicate superclass to subclass relationships, while the interfaces implemented by a class follow the class name in parentheses. For example, the following hierarchy indicates that java.io.DataOutputStream implements DataOutput and extends FilterOutputStream, which itself extends OutputStream, which extends Object:

Object→OutputStream→FilterOutputStream→DataOutputStream(DataOutput)

If a class has subclasses, the "Hierarchy" section is followed by a "Subclasses" section that lists those subclasses. If an interface has implementations, the "Hierarchy" section is followed by an "Implementations" section that lists those implementations. While the "Hierarchy" section shows ancestors of the class, the "Subclasses" or "Implementations" section shows descendants.

Cross References

The class hierarchy section of a quick-reference entry is followed by a number of optional "cross reference" sections that indicate other, related classes and methods that may be of interest. These sections are the following:

Passed To

This section lists all of the methods and constructors that are passed an object of this type as an argument. This is useful when you have an object of a given type and want to figure out what you can do with it.

Returned By

This section lists all of the methods (but not constructors) that return an object of this type. This is useful when you know that you want to work with an object of this type, but don't know how to obtain one.

Thrown By

For checked exception classes, this section lists all of the methods and constructors that throw exceptions of this type. This material helps you figure out when a given exception or error may be thrown. Note, however, that this section is based on the exception types listed in the throws clauses of methods and constructors. Subclasses of RuntimeException and Error do not have to be listed in

---

throws clauses, so it is not possible to generate a complete cross reference of methods that throw these types of unchecked exceptions.

Type Of

This section lists all of the fields and constants that are of this type, which can help you figure out how to obtain an object of this type.

A Note About Class Names

Throughout the quick reference, you'll notice that classes are sometimes referred to by class name alone and at other times referred to by class name and package name. If package names were always used, the class synopses would become long and hard to read. On the other hand, if package names were never used, it would sometimes be difficult to know what class was being referred to. The rules for including or omitting the package name are complex. They can be summarized approximately as follows, however:

- If the class name alone is ambiguous, the package name is always used.

- If the class is part of the java.lang package or is a very commonly used class like java.io.Serializable, the package name is omitted.

- If the class being referred to is part of the current package (and has a quick-reference entry in the current chapter), the package name is omitted. The package name is also omitted if the class being referred to is part of a package that contains the current package.

How To
Use

CHAPTER 9

The java.beans Package

The java.beans package contains classes and interfaces related to JavaBeans components. Most of the classes and interfaces are used by tools that manipulate beans, rather
than by the beans themselves. They are also used or implemented by auxiliary classes
provided by bean implementors for the benefit of bean-manipulation tools. Figure 9-1
shows the class hierarchy for this package.

The Beans class defines several generally useful static methods. Its instantiate() method is
particularly important. The Introspector class is used to obtain information about a bean
and the properties, events, and methods it exports. Most of this information is returned
using the FeatureDescriptor class and its various subclasses. The java.beans package also
defines the PropertyChangeEvent class and the PropertyChangeListener interface that are
widely used by AWT and Swing to provide notification when a bound property of a
GUI component changes.

See Chapter 6, *JavaBeans*, for a complete introduction to the JavaBeans component
model.

AppletInitializer   Java 1.2

java.beans

This interface defines general methods to initialize a newly instantiated Applet object. An
AppletInitializer can be passed to the Beans.instantiate() method so that when a bean that is
also an applet is created, it can be properly initialized. The initialize() method should
associate the applet object with an appropriate AppletContext and AppletStub, place it
within an appropriate Container, and call its init() method. The activate() method should
make the applet active by calling its start() method. This interface is typically used by
bean context implementors. Applications writers may need to use AppletInitializer objects,
but should not usually have to invoke or implement the methods directly.

```
public interface AppletInitializer {
// Public Instance Methods
    public abstract void activate(java.applet.Applet newApplet);
    public abstract void initialize(java.applet.Applet newAppletBean, java.beans.beancontext.BeanContext bCtxt);
}
```

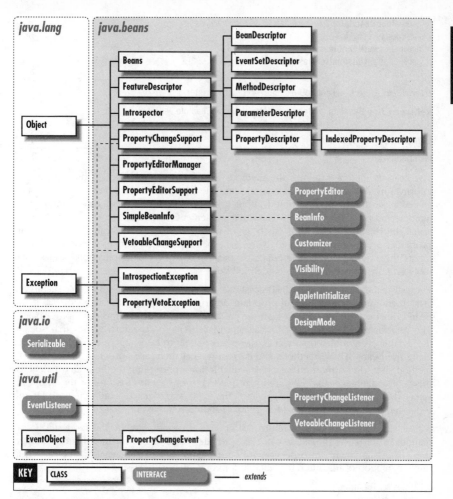

java.beans

Figure 9-1: The java.beans package

Passed To: Beans.instantiate()

BeanDescriptor
java.beans

Java 1.1

PJ1.1

A BeanDescriptor object is a type of FeatureDescriptor that describes a JavaBeans component. The BeanInfo class for a bean optionally creates and initializes a BeanDescriptor
object to describe the bean. Typically, only application builders and similar tools use
the BeanDescriptor. To create a BeanDescriptor, you must specify the class of the bean and,
optionally, the class of a Customizer for the bean. You can use the methods of Feature-
Descriptor to provide additional information about the bean.

```
public class BeanDescriptor extends FeatureDescriptor {
// Public Constructors
    public BeanDescriptor(Class beanClass);
```

```
   public BeanDescriptor(Class beanClass, Class customizerClass);
// Public Instance Methods
   public Class getBeanClass();
   public Class getCustomizerClass();
}
```

Hierarchy: Object→ FeatureDescriptor→ BeanDescriptor

Returned By: BeanInfo.getBeanDescriptor(), SimpleBeanInfo.getBeanDescriptor()

BeanInfo   Java 1.1

java.beans   PJ1.1

The BeanInfo interface defines the methods a class must implement in order to export
information about a JavaBeans component. The Introspector class knows how to obtain
all the basic information required about a bean. A bean that wants to be more pro-
grammer-friendly can provide a class that implements this interface, and provide additional information about itself (such as an icon and description strings for each of its
properties, events, and methods). Note that a bean developer defines a class that implements the methods of this interface. Typically, only builder applications and similar
tools actually invoke the methods defined here.

The getBeanDescriptor(), getEventSetDescriptors(), getPropertyDescriptors(), and getMethodDescrip-
tors() methods should return appropriate descriptor objects for the bean or null if the
bean does not provide explicit bean, event set, property, or method descriptor objects.
The getDefaultEventIndex() and getDefaultPropertyIndex() methods return values that specify
the default event and property (i.e., those most likely to be of interest to a programmer
using the bean). These methods should return −1 if there are no defaults. The getIcon()
method should return an image object suitable for representing the bean in a palette or
menu of available beans. The argument passed to this method is one of the four constants defined by the class; it specifies the type and size of icon requested. If the
requested icon cannot be provided, getIcon() should return null.

A BeanInfo class is allowed to return null or −1 if it cannot provide the requested information. In this case, the Introspector class provides basic values for the omitted information from its own introspection of the bean. See SimpleBeanInfo for a trivial
implementation of this interface suitable for convenient subclassing.

```
public interface BeanInfo {
// Public Constants
   public static final int ICON_COLOR_16x16;                                  =1
   public static final int ICON_COLOR_32x32;                                  =2
   public static final int ICON_MONO_16x16;                                   =3
   public static final int ICON_MONO_32x32;                                   =4
// Property Accessor Methods (by property name)
   public abstract BeanInfo[ ] getAdditionalBeanInfo();
   public abstract BeanDescriptor getBeanDescriptor();
   public abstract int getDefaultEventIndex();
   public abstract int getDefaultPropertyIndex();
   public abstract EventSetDescriptor[ ] getEventSetDescriptors();
   public abstract MethodDescriptor[ ] getMethodDescriptors();
   public abstract PropertyDescriptor[ ] getPropertyDescriptors();
// Public Instance Methods
   public abstract java.awt.Image getIcon(int iconKind);
}
```

Implementations: SimpleBeanInfo, java.beans.beancontext.BeanContextServiceProviderBeanInfo

Returned By: BeanInfo.getAdditionalBeanInfo(), Introspector.getBeanInfo(), SimpleBeanInfo.getAdditionalBeanInfo(), java.beans.beancontext.BeanContextServiceProviderBeanInfo.getServicesBeanInfo()

Beans   Java 1.1
java.beans   *PJ1.1*

The Beans class is not meant to be instantiated; its static methods provide miscellaneous JavaBeans features. The instantiate() method creates an instance of a bean. The specified bean name represents either a serialized bean file or a bean class file; it is interpreted relative to the specified ClassLoader object.

The setDesignTime() and isDesignTime() methods can set and query a flag that indicates whether beans are being used in a application builder environment. Similarly, set-GuiAvailable() and isGuiAvailable() set and query a flag that indicates whether the Java Virtual Machine is running in an environment in which a GUI is available. (Note that untrusted applet code cannot call setDesignTime() or setGuiAvailable().)

The isInstanceOf() method is a replacement for the Java instanceof operator to use with beans. Currently, it behaves like instanceof, but in the future it may work with beans that consist of a set of Java objects, each of which provides a different view of a bean. Similarly, the getInstanceOf() method is a replacement for the Java cast operator. This method converts a bean to a superclass or interface type, and currently, it behaves like a cast, but in the future, it will be compatible with multiclass beans.

```
public class Beans {
// Public Constructors
    public Beans();
// Public Class Methods
    public static Object getInstanceOf(Object bean, Class targetType);
    public static Object instantiate(ClassLoader cls, String beanName) throws java.io.IOException,
        ClassNotFoundException;
1.2 public static Object instantiate(ClassLoader cls, String beanName,
                            java.beans.beancontext.BeanContext beanContext) throws java.io.IOException,
        ClassNotFoundException;
1.2 public static Object instantiate(ClassLoader cls, String beanName,
                            java.beans.beancontext.BeanContext beanContext, AppletInitializer initializer)
        throws java.io.IOException, ClassNotFoundException;
    public static boolean isDesignTime();
    public static boolean isGuiAvailable();
    public static boolean isInstanceOf(Object bean, Class targetType);
    public static void setDesignTime(boolean isDesignTime) throws SecurityException;
    public static void setGuiAvailable(boolean isGuiAvailable) throws SecurityException;
}
```

Customizer   Java 1.1
java.beans   *PJ1.1*

The Customizer interface specifies the methods that must be defined by any class designed to customize a JavaBeans component. In addition to implementing this interface, a customizer class must be a subclass of java.awt.Component and have a constructor that takes no arguments so it can be instantiated by an application builder.

Customizer classes are typically used by a complex bean to allow the user to easily configure the bean and provide an alternative to a simple list of properties and their values. If a customizer class is defined for a bean, it must be associated with the bean through a BeanDescriptor object returned by a BeanInfo class for the bean. Note that while a Customizer class is created by the author of a bean, that class is instantiated and used only by application builders and similar tools.

After a Customizer class is instantiated, its setObject() method is invoked once to specify the bean object to customize. The addPropertyChangeListener() and removePropertyChangeListener() methods can be called to register and deregister PropertyChangeListener objects. The Customizer should send a PropertyChangeEvent to all registered listeners any time it changes a property of the bean it is customizing.

```
public interface Customizer {
// Event Registration Methods (by event name)
    public abstract void addPropertyChangeListener(PropertyChangeListener listener);
    public abstract void removePropertyChangeListener(PropertyChangeListener listener);
// Public Instance Methods
    public abstract void setObject(Object bean);
}
```

DesignMode   Java 1.2

java.beans

This interface defines a single boolean designTime property that specifies whether a bean is running within an interactive design tool or a standalone application or applet. This interface is typically implemented by a bean container or bean context, so that children beans can query the designTime property.

```
public interface DesignMode {
// Public Constants
    public static final String PROPERTYNAME;                            ="designTime"
// Public Instance Methods
    public abstract boolean isDesignTime();
    public abstract void setDesignTime(boolean designTime);
}
```

Implementations: java.beans.beancontext.BeanContext

EventSetDescriptor   Java 1.1

java.beans   PJ1.1

An EventSetDescriptor object is a type of FeatureDescriptor that describes a single set of events supported by a JavaBeans component. A set of events corresponds to one or more methods supported by a single EventListener interface. The BeanInfo class for a bean optionally creates EventSetDescriptor objects to describe the event sets the bean supports. Typically, only application builders and similar tools use the get and is methods of EventSetDescriptor objects to obtain the event-set description information.

To create an EventSetDescriptor object, you must specify the class of the bean that supports the event set, the base name of the event set, the class of the EventListener interface that corresponds to the event set, and the methods within this interface that are invoked when particular events within the set occur. Optionally, you can also specify the methods of the bean class that add and remove EventListener objects. The various constructors allow you to specify methods by name, as java.lang.reflect.Method objects, or as MethodDescriptor objects.

Once you have created an EventSetDescriptor, use setUnicast() to specify whether it represents a unicast event and setInDefaultEventSet() to specify whether the event set should be treated as the default event set by builder applications. The methods of the FeatureDescriptor superclass allow additional information about the property to be specified.

```
public class EventSetDescriptor extends FeatureDescriptor {
// Public Constructors
    public EventSetDescriptor(Class sourceClass, String eventSetName, Class listenerType,
                         String listenerMethodName) throws IntrospectionException;
    public EventSetDescriptor(String eventSetName, Class listenerType,
                         MethodDescriptor[ ] listenerMethodDescriptors,
                         java.lang.reflect.Method addListenerMethod,
                         java.lang.reflect.Method removeListenerMethod) throws IntrospectionException;
    public EventSetDescriptor(String eventSetName, Class listenerType, java.lang.reflect.Method[ ] listenerMethods,
                         java.lang.reflect.Method addListenerMethod,
                         java.lang.reflect.Method removeListenerMethod) throws IntrospectionException;
    public EventSetDescriptor(Class sourceClass, String eventSetName, Class listenerType,
                         String[ ] listenerMethodNames, String addListenerMethodName,
                         String removeListenerMethodName) throws IntrospectionException;
// Property Accessor Methods (by property name)
    public java.lang.reflect.Method getAddListenerMethod();
    public boolean isInDefaultEventSet();
    public void setInDefaultEventSet(boolean inDefaultEventSet);
    public MethodDescriptor[ ] getListenerMethodDescriptors();
    public java.lang.reflect.Method[ ] getListenerMethods();
    public Class getListenerType();
    public java.lang.reflect.Method getRemoveListenerMethod();
    public boolean isUnicast();
    public void setUnicast(boolean unicast);
}
```

Hierarchy: Object→ FeatureDescriptor→ EventSetDescriptor

Returned By: BeanInfo.getEventSetDescriptors(), SimpleBeanInfo.getEventSetDescriptors()

FeatureDescriptor   Java 1.1
java.beans   PJ1.1

The FeatureDescriptor class is the base class for MethodDescriptor and PropertyDescriptor, as well as other classes used by the JavaBeans introspection mechanism. It provides basic information about a feature (e.g., method, property, or event) of a bean. Typically, the methods that begin with get and is are used by application builders or other tools to query the features of a bean. The set methods, on the other hand, may be used by bean authors to define information about the bean.

setName() specifies the locale-independent, programmatic name of the feature; setDisplayName() specifies a localized, human-readable name; and setShortDescription() specifies a short localized string (about 40 characters) that describes the feature. Both the short description and the localized name default to the value of the programmatic name. setExpert() and setHidden() allow you to indicate that the feature is for use only by experts or by the builder tool and should be hidden from users of the builder. Finally, the setValue() method allows you to associate an arbitrary named value with the feature.

```
public class FeatureDescriptor {
// Public Constructors
    public FeatureDescriptor();
// Property Accessor Methods (by property name)
    public String getDisplayName();                                  default:null
    public void setDisplayName(String displayName);
    public boolean isExpert();                                       default:false
    public void setExpert(boolean expert);
    public boolean isHidden();                                       default:false
```

```
    public void setHidden(boolean hidden);
    public String getName();                                        default:null
    public void setName(String name);
1.2 public boolean isPreferred();                                   default:false
1.2 public void setPreferred(boolean preferred);
    public String getShortDescription();                            default:null
    public void setShortDescription(String text);
// Public Instance Methods
    public java.util.Enumeration attributeNames();
    public Object getValue(String attributeName);
    public void setValue(String attributeName, Object value);
}
```

Subclasses: BeanDescriptor, EventSetDescriptor, MethodDescriptor, ParameterDescriptor, PropertyDescriptor

IndexedPropertyDescriptor   Java 1.1

java.beans   PJ1.1

An IndexedPropertyDescriptor object is a type of PropertyDescriptor that describes a bean property that is (or behaves like) an array. The BeanInfo class for a bean optionally creates and initializes IndexedPropertyDescriptor objects to describe the indexed properties the bean supports. Typically, only application builders and similar tools use the descriptor objects to obtain indexed property description information.

You create an IndexedPropertyDescriptor by specifying the name of the indexed property and the Class object for the bean. If you have not followed the standard design patterns for accessor method naming, you can also specify the accessor methods for the property, either as method names or as java.lang.reflect.Method objects. Once you have created an IndexedPropertyDescriptor object, you can use the methods of PropertyDescriptor and FeatureDescriptor to provide additional information about the indexed property.

```
public class IndexedPropertyDescriptor extends PropertyDescriptor {
// Public Constructors
    public IndexedPropertyDescriptor(String propertyName, Class beanClass) throws IntrospectionException;
    public IndexedPropertyDescriptor(String propertyName, java.lang.reflect.Method getter,
                        java.lang.reflect.Method setter, java.lang.reflect.Method indexedGetter,
                        java.lang.reflect.Method indexedSetter) throws IntrospectionException;
    public IndexedPropertyDescriptor(String propertyName, Class beanClass, String getterName,
                        String setterName, String indexedGetterName, String indexedSetterName)
            throws IntrospectionException;
// Public Instance Methods
    public Class getIndexedPropertyType();
    public java.lang.reflect.Method getIndexedReadMethod();
    public java.lang.reflect.Method getIndexedWriteMethod();
1.2 public void setIndexedReadMethod(java.lang.reflect.Method getter) throws IntrospectionException;
1.2 public void setIndexedWriteMethod(java.lang.reflect.Method setter) throws IntrospectionException;
}
```

Hierarchy: Object→ FeatureDescriptor→ PropertyDescriptor→ IndexedPropertyDescriptor

IntrospectionException   Java 1.1

java.beans   serializable checked PJ1.1

Signals that introspection on a JavaBeans component cannot be completed. Typically, this indicates a bug in the way the bean or its associated BeanInfo class is defined.

```
public class IntrospectionException extends Exception {
// Public Constructors
    public IntrospectionException(String mess);
}
```

Hierarchy: Object→ Throwable(Serializable)→ Exception→ IntrospectionException

Thrown By: Too many methods to list.

Introspector   Java 1.1
java.beans   *PJ1.1*

The Introspector is a class that is never instantiated. Its static getBeanInfo() methods provide a way to obtain information about a JavaBeans component and are typically only
invoked by application builders or similar tools. getBeanInfo() first looks for a BeanInfo
class for the specified bean class. For a class named *x*, it looks for a BeanInfo class
named *x*BeanInfo, first in the current package and then in each of the packages in the
BeanInfo search path.

If no BeanInfo class is found, or if the BeanInfo class found does not provide complete
information about the bean properties, events, and methods, getBeanInfo() introspects on
the bean class by using the java.lang.reflect package to fill in the missing information.
When explicit information is provided by a BeanInfo class, getBeanInfo() treats it as definitive. When determining information through introspection, however, it examines each
of the bean's superclasses in turn, looking for a BeanInfo class at that level or using
introspection. When calling getBeanInfo(), you may optionally specify a second class
argument that specifies a superclass for which, and above which, getBeanInfo() does not
introspect.

```
public class Introspector {
// No Constructor
// Public Constants
1.2 public static final int IGNORE_ALL_BEANINFO;                          =3
1.2 public static final int IGNORE_IMMEDIATE_BEANINFO;                     =2
1.2 public static final int USE_ALL_BEANINFO;                             =1
// Public Class Methods
    public static String decapitalize(String name);
1.2 public static void flushCaches();
1.2 public static void flushFromCaches(Class clz);
    public static BeanInfo getBeanInfo(Class beanClass) throws IntrospectionException;
1.2 public static BeanInfo getBeanInfo(Class beanClass, int flags) throws IntrospectionException;
    public static BeanInfo getBeanInfo(Class beanClass, Class stopClass) throws IntrospectionException;
    public static String[ ] getBeanInfoSearchPath();                  synchronized
    public static void setBeanInfoSearchPath(String[ ] path);         synchronized
}
```

MethodDescriptor   Java 1.1
java.beans   *PJ1.1*

A MethodDescriptor object is a type of FeatureDescriptor that describes a method supported
by a JavaBeans component. The BeanInfo class for a bean optionally creates MethodDescriptor objects that describe the methods the bean exports. While a BeanInfo class creates and initializes MethodDescriptor objects, it is typically only application builders and
similar tools that use these objects to obtain information about the methods supported
by a bean.

To create a MethodDescriptor, you must specify the java.lang.reflect.Method object for the method and, optionally, an array of ParameterDescriptor objects that describe the parameters of the method. Once you have created a MethodDescriptor object, you can use FeatureDescriptor methods to provide additional information about each method.

```
public class MethodDescriptor extends FeatureDescriptor {
// Public Constructors
    public MethodDescriptor(java.lang.reflect.Method method);
    public MethodDescriptor(java.lang.reflect.Method method, ParameterDescriptor[ ] parameterDescriptors);
// Public Instance Methods
    public java.lang.reflect.Method getMethod();
    public ParameterDescriptor[ ] getParameterDescriptors();
}
```

Hierarchy: Object→ FeatureDescriptor→ MethodDescriptor

Passed To: EventSetDescriptor.EventSetDescriptor()

Returned By: BeanInfo.getMethodDescriptors(), EventSetDescriptor.getListenerMethodDescriptors(), SimpleBeanInfo.getMethodDescriptors()

ParameterDescriptor   Java 1.1
java.beans   PJ1.1

A ParameterDescriptor object is a type of FeatureDescriptor that describes an argument or parameter to a method of a JavaBeans component. The BeanInfo class for a JavaBeans component optionally creates ParameterDescriptor objects that describe the parameters of the methods the bean exports. While the BeanInfo class creates and initializes ParameterDescriptor objects, it is typically only application builders and similar tools that use these objects to obtain information about method parameters supported by the bean.

The ParameterDescriptor class is a trivial subclass of FeatureDescriptor and does not provide any new methods. Thus, you should use the methods of FeatureDescriptor to provide information about method parameters.

```
public class ParameterDescriptor extends FeatureDescriptor {
// Public Constructors
    public ParameterDescriptor();
}
```

Hierarchy: Object→ FeatureDescriptor→ ParameterDescriptor

Passed To: MethodDescriptor.MethodDescriptor()

Returned By: MethodDescriptor.getParameterDescriptors()

PropertyChangeEvent   Java 1.1
java.beans   serializable event PJ1.1

PropertyChangeEvent is a subclass of java.util.EventObject. An event of this type is sent to interested PropertyChangeListener objects whenever a JavaBeans component changes a bound property or whenever a PropertyEditor or Customizer changes a property value. A PropertyChangeEvent is also sent to registered VetoableChangeListener objects when a bean attempts to change the value of a constrained property.

When creating a PropertyChangeEvent, you normally specify the bean that generated the event, the programmatic (locale-independent) name of the property that changed, and the old and new values of the property. If the values cannot be determined, null should be passed instead. If the event is a notification that more than one property value changed, the name should also be null. While JavaBeans must generate and send PropertyChangeEvent objects, it is typically only application builders and similar tools that are interested in receiving them.

```
public class PropertyChangeEvent extends java.util.EventObject {
// Public Constructors
    public PropertyChangeEvent(Object source, String propertyName, Object oldValue, Object newValue);
// Public Instance Methods
    public Object getNewValue();
    public Object getOldValue();
    public Object getPropagationId();
    public String getPropertyName();
    public void setPropagationId(Object propagationId);
}
```

Hierarchy: Object→ java.util.EventObject(Serializable)→ PropertyChangeEvent

Passed To: PropertyChangeListener.propertyChange(), PropertyChangeSupport.firePropertyChange(), PropertyVetoException.PropertyVetoException(), VetoableChangeListener.vetoableChange(), VetoableChangeSupport.fireVetoableChange(), java.beans.beancontext.BeanContextSupport.{propertyChange(), vetoableChange()}, javax.swing.JList.AccessibleJList.propertyChange(), javax.swing.JTable.AccessibleJTable.propertyChange(), javax.swing.event.SwingPropertyChangeSupport.firePropertyChange(), javax.swing.table.DefaultTableColumnModel.propertyChange()

Returned By: PropertyVetoException.getPropertyChangeEvent()

PropertyChangeListener   Java 1.1

java.beans   *event listener PJ1.1*

This interface is an extension of java.util.EventListener; it defines the method a class must implement in order to be notified when property changes occur. A PropertyChangeEvent is sent to all registered PropertyChangeListener objects when a bean changes one of its bound properties or when a PropertyEditor or Customizer changes the value of a property.

```
public interface PropertyChangeListener extends java.util.EventListener {
// Public Instance Methods
    public abstract void propertyChange(PropertyChangeEvent evt);
}
```

Hierarchy: (PropertyChangeListener(java.util.EventListener))

Implementations: java.beans.beancontext.BeanContextSupport, javax.swing.JList.AccessibleJList, javax.swing.JTable.AccessibleJTable, javax.swing.table.DefaultTableColumnModel

Passed To: Too many methods to list.

Returned By: java.beans.beancontext.BeanContextSupport.getChildPropertyChangeListener(), javax.swing.AbstractButton.createActionPropertyChangeListener(), javax.swing.JCheckBox.createActionPropertyChangeListener(), javax.swing.JComboBox.createActionPropertyChangeListener(), javax.swing.JMenu.createActionChangeListener(), javax.swing.JMenuItem.createActionPropertyChangeListener(), javax.swing.JPopupMenu.createActionChangeListener(), javax.swing.JRadioButton.createActionPropertyChangeListener(), javax.swing.JTextField.createActionPropertyChangeListener(), javax.swing.JToolBar.createActionChangeListener()

PropertyChangeSupport

Java 1.1

java.beans

serializable PJ1.1

The PropertyChangeSupport class is a convenience class that maintains a list of registered PropertyChangeListener objects and provides the firePropertyChange() method for sending a PropertyChangeEvent object to all registered listeners. Because there are some tricky thread-synchronization issues involved in doing this correctly, it is recommended that all JavaBeans that support bound properties either extend this class or, more commonly, create an instance of this class to which they can delegate the task of maintaining the list of listeners.

```
public class PropertyChangeSupport implements Serializable {
// Public Constructors
    public PropertyChangeSupport(Object sourceBean);
// Event Registration Methods (by event name)
    public void addPropertyChangeListener(PropertyChangeListener listener);              synchronized
    public void removePropertyChangeListener(PropertyChangeListener listener);           synchronized
// Public Instance Methods
1.2 public void addPropertyChangeListener(String propertyName, PropertyChangeListener listener);   synchronized
1.2 public void firePropertyChange(PropertyChangeEvent evt);
1.2 public void firePropertyChange(String propertyName, int oldValue, int newValue);
1.2 public void firePropertyChange(String propertyName, boolean oldValue, boolean newValue);
    public void firePropertyChange(String propertyName, Object oldValue, Object newValue);
1.2 public boolean hasListeners(String propertyName);                                     synchronized
1.2 public void removePropertyChangeListener(String propertyName,                         synchronized
                                  PropertyChangeListener listener);
}
```

Hierarchy: Object → PropertyChangeSupport(Serializable)

Subclasses: javax.swing.event.SwingPropertyChangeSupport

Type Of: java.awt.Toolkit.desktopPropsSupport,
java.beans.beancontext.BeanContextChildSupport.pcSupport

PropertyDescriptor

Java 1.1

java.beans

PJ1.1

A PropertyDescriptor object is a type of FeatureDescriptor that describes a single property of a JavaBeans component. The BeanInfo class for a bean optionally creates and initializes PropertyDescriptor objects to describe the properties the bean supports. Typically, only application builders and similar tools use the get and is methods to obtain this property description information.

You create a PropertyDescriptor by specifying the name of the property and the Class object for the bean. If you have not followed the standard design patterns for accessor-method naming, you can also specify the accessor methods for the property. Once a PropertyDescriptor is created, the setBound() and setConstrained() methods allow you to specify whether the property is bound and/or constrained. setPropertyEditorClass() allows you to specify a specific property editor that should edit the value of this property (this is useful, for example, when the property is an enumerated type with a specific list of supported values). The methods of the FeatureDescriptor superclass allow additional information about the property to be specified.

```
public class PropertyDescriptor extends FeatureDescriptor {
// Public Constructors
    public PropertyDescriptor(String propertyName, Class beanClass) throws IntrospectionException;
    public PropertyDescriptor(String propertyName, java.lang.reflect.Method getter, java.lang.reflect.Method setter)
        throws IntrospectionException;
```

```
    public PropertyDescriptor(String propertyName, Class beanClass, String getterName, String setterName)
        throws IntrospectionException;
// Property Accessor Methods (by property name)
    public boolean isBound();
    public void setBound(boolean bound);
    public boolean isConstrained();
    public void setConstrained(boolean constrained);
    public Class getPropertyEditorClass();
    public void setPropertyEditorClass(Class propertyEditorClass);
    public Class getPropertyType();
    public java.lang.reflect.Method getReadMethod();
1.2 public void setReadMethod(java.lang.reflect.Method getter) throws IntrospectionException;
    public java.lang.reflect.Method getWriteMethod();
1.2 public void setWriteMethod(java.lang.reflect.Method setter) throws IntrospectionException;
}
```

Hierarchy: Object→ FeatureDescriptor→ PropertyDescriptor

Subclasses: IndexedPropertyDescriptor

Returned By: BeanInfo.getPropertyDescriptors(), SimpleBeanInfo.getPropertyDescriptors()

PropertyEditor   Java 1.1

java.beans   *PJ1.1*

The PropertyEditor interface defines the methods that must be implemented by a
JavaBeans property editor intended for use within an application builder or similar tool.
PropertyEditor is a complex interface because it defines methods to support different
ways of displaying property values to the user. It also defines methods to support different ways of allowing the user to edit the property value.

For a property of type *x*, the author of a bean typically implements a property editor of
class *x*Editor. While the editor is implemented by the bean author, it is usually instantiated or used only by application builders or similar tools (or by a Customizer class for a
bean). In addition to implementing the PropertyEditor interface, a property editor must
have a constructor that expects no arguments, so that it can be easily be instantiated by
an application builder. Also, it must accept registration and deregistration of Property-
ChangeListener objects and send a PropertyChangeEvent to all registered listeners when it
changes the value of the property being edited. The PropertyEditorSupport class is a trivial
implementation of PropertyEditor, suitable for subclassing or for supporting a list of PropertyChangeListener objects.

```
public interface PropertyEditor {
// Event Registration Methods (by event name)
    public abstract void addPropertyChangeListener(PropertyChangeListener listener);
    public abstract void removePropertyChangeListener(PropertyChangeListener listener);
// Property Accessor Methods (by property name)
    public abstract String getAsText();
    public abstract void setAsText(String text) throws IllegalArgumentException;
    public abstract java.awt.Component getCustomEditor();
    public abstract String getJavaInitializationString();
    public abstract boolean isPaintable();
    public abstract String[ ] getTags();
    public abstract Object getValue();
    public abstract void setValue(Object value);
// Public Instance Methods
    public abstract void paintValue(java.awt.Graphics gfx, java.awt.Rectangle box);
```

```
   public abstract boolean supportsCustomEditor();
}
```

Implementations: PropertyEditorSupport

Returned By: PropertyEditorManager.findEditor()

PropertyEditorManager   Java 1.1
java.beans   *PJ1.1*

The PropertyEditorManager class is not meant to be instantiated; it defines static methods for registering and looking up PropertyEditor classes for a specified property type. A bean can specify a particular PropertyEditor class for a given property by specifying it in a PropertyDescriptor object for the property. If it does not do this, the PropertyEditorManager is used to register and look up editors. A bean or an application builder tool can call the registerEditor() method to register a PropertyEditor for properties of a specified type. Application builders and bean Customizer classes can call the findEditor() method to obtain a PropertyEditor for a given property type. If no editor has been registered for a given type, the PropertyEditorManager attempts to locate one. For a type x, it looks for a class xEditor first in the same package as x, and then in each package listed in the property editor search path.

```
public class PropertyEditorManager {
// Public Constructors
   public PropertyEditorManager();
// Public Class Methods
   public static PropertyEditor findEditor(Class targetType);                    synchronized
   public static String[ ] getEditorSearchPath();                               synchronized
   public static void registerEditor(Class targetType, Class editorClass);
   public static void setEditorSearchPath(String[ ] path);                      synchronized
}
```

PropertyEditorSupport   Java 1.1
java.beans   *PJ1.1*

The PropertyEditorSupport class is a trivial implementation of the PropertyEditor interface. It provides no-op default implementations of most methods, so you can define simple PropertyEditor subclasses that override only a few required methods. In addition, PropertyEditorSupport defines working versions of addPropertyChangeListener() and removePropertyChangeListener(), along with a firePropertyChange() method that sends a PropertyChangeEvent to all registered listeners. PropertyEditor classes may choose to instantiate a PropertyEditorSupport object simply to handle the job of managing the list of listeners. When used in this way, the PropertyEditorSupport object should be instantiated with a source object specified, so that the source object can be used in the PropertyChangeEvent objects that are sent.

```
public class PropertyEditorSupport implements PropertyEditor {
// Protected Constructors
   protected PropertyEditorSupport();
   protected PropertyEditorSupport(Object source);
// Event Registration Methods (by event name)
   public void addPropertyChangeListener(                       Implements:PropertyEditor synchronized
                            PropertyChangeListener listener);
   public void removePropertyChangeListener(                    Implements:PropertyEditor synchronized
                            PropertyChangeListener listener);
```

```
// Public Instance Methods
    public void firePropertyChange();
// Methods Implementing PropertyEditor
    public void addPropertyChangeListener(PropertyChangeListener listener);         synchronized
    public String getAsText();
    public java.awt.Component getCustomEditor();                                    constant
    public String getJavaInitializationString();
    public String[ ] getTags();                                                    constant
    public Object getValue();
    public boolean isPaintable();                                                  constant
    public void paintValue(java.awt.Graphics gfx, java.awt.Rectangle box);         empty
    public void removePropertyChangeListener(PropertyChangeListener listener);     synchronized
    public void setAsText(String text) throws IllegalArgumentException;
    public void setValue(Object value);
    public boolean supportsCustomEditor();                                         constant
}
```

Hierarchy: Object→ PropertyEditorSupport(PropertyEditor)

PropertyVetoException   Java 1.1

java.beans   *serializable checked PJ1.1*

Signals that a VetoableChangeListener that received a PropertyChangeEvent for a constrained property of a bean has vetoed that proposed change. When this exception is received, the property in question should revert to its original value, and any VetoableChangeListener objects that have already been notified of the property change must be renotified to indicate that the property has reverted to its old value. The VetoableChangeSupport class handles this renotification automatically and rethrows the PropertyVetoException to notify its caller that the change was rejected.

```
public class PropertyVetoException extends Exception {
// Public Constructors
    public PropertyVetoException(String mess, PropertyChangeEvent evt);
// Public Instance Methods
    public PropertyChangeEvent getPropertyChangeEvent();
}
```

Hierarchy: Object→ Throwable(Serializable)→ Exception→ PropertyVetoException

Thrown By: VetoableChangeListener.vetoableChange(),
VetoableChangeSupport.fireVetoableChange(),
java.beans.beancontext.BeanContextChild.setBeanContext(),
java.beans.beancontext.BeanContextChildSupport.{fireVetoableChange(), setBeanContext()},
java.beans.beancontext.BeanContextSupport.{setLocale(), vetoableChange()},
javax.swing.JComponent.fireVetoableChange(), javax.swing.JInternalFrame.{setClosed(), setIcon(),
setMaximum(), setSelected()}

SimpleBeanInfo   Java 1.1

java.beans   *PJ1.1*

The SimpleBeanInfo class is a trivial implementation of the BeanInfo interface. The methods of this class all return null or –1, indicating that no bean information is available. To use this class, you need to override only the method or methods that return the particular type of bean information you want to provide. In addition, SimpleBeanInfo provides a convenience method, loadImage(), that takes a resource name as an argument and returns an Image object. This method is useful when defining the getIcon() method.

```
public class SimpleBeanInfo implements BeanInfo {
// Public Constructors
    public SimpleBeanInfo();
// Public Instance Methods
    public java.awt.Image loadImage(String resourceName);
// Methods Implementing BeanInfo
    public BeanInfo[ ] getAdditionalBeanInfo();                    constant default:null
    public BeanDescriptor getBeanDescriptor();                     constant default:null
    public int getDefaultEventIndex();                              constant default:-1
    public int getDefaultPropertyIndex();                           constant default:-1
    public EventSetDescriptor[ ] getEventSetDescriptors();          constant default:null
    public java.awt.Image getIcon(int iconKind);                            constant
    public MethodDescriptor[ ] getMethodDescriptors();              constant default:null
    public PropertyDescriptor[ ] getPropertyDescriptors();          constant default:null
}
```

Hierarchy: Object→ SimpleBeanInfo(BeanInfo)

VetoableChangeListener   Java 1.1
java.beans   *event listener PJ1.1*

This interface is an extension of java.util.EventListener. It defines the method a class must implement in order to be notified when a Java bean makes a change to a constrained property. A PropertyChangeEvent is passed to the VetoableChange() method when such a change occurs. If the VetoableChangeListener wants to prevent the change from occurring, this method should throw a PropertyVetoException.

```
public interface VetoableChangeListener extends java.util.EventListener {
// Public Instance Methods
    public abstract void vetoableChange(PropertyChangeEvent evt) throws PropertyVetoException;
}
```

Hierarchy: (VetoableChangeListener(java.util.EventListener))

Implementations: java.beans.beancontext.BeanContextSupport

Passed To: VetoableChangeSupport.{addVetoableChangeListener(), removeVetoableChangeListener()}, java.beans.beancontext.BeanContextChild.{addVetoableChangeListener(), removeVetoableChangeListener()}, java.beans.beancontext.BeanContextChildSupport.{addVetoableChangeListener(), removeVetoableChangeListener()}, javax.swing.JComponent.{addVetoableChangeListener(), removeVetoableChangeListener()}

Returned By: java.beans.beancontext.BeanContextSupport.getChildVetoableChangeListener()

VetoableChangeSupport   Java 1.1
java.beans   *serializable PJ1.1*

VetoableChangeSupport is a convenience class that maintains a list of registered VetoableChangeListener objects and provides a fireVetoableChange() method for sending a PropertyChangeEvent to all registered listeners. If any of the registered listeners veto the proposed change, fireVetoableChange() sends out another PropertyChangeEvent notifying previously notified listeners that the property has reverted to its original value. Because of the extra complexity of correctly handling veto-able changes and because of some tricky thread-synchronization issues involved in maintaining the list of listeners, it is recommended that all Java beans that support constrained events create a VetoableChangeSupport object to which they can delegate the tasks of maintaining the list of listeners and of firing events.

```
public class VetoableChangeSupport implements Serializable {
// Public Constructors
    public VetoableChangeSupport(Object sourceBean);
// Event Registration Methods (by event name)
    public void addVetoableChangeListener(VetoableChangeListener listener);          synchronized
    public void removeVetoableChangeListener(VetoableChangeListener listener);       synchronized
// Public Instance Methods
1.2 public void addVetoableChangeListener(String propertyName, VetoableChangeListener listener);   synchronized
1.2 public void fireVetoableChange(PropertyChangeEvent evt) throws PropertyVetoException;
1.2 public void fireVetoableChange(String propertyName, int oldValue, int newValue) throws PropertyVetoException;
1.2 public void fireVetoableChange(String propertyName, boolean oldValue, boolean newValue)
        throws PropertyVetoException;
    public void fireVetoableChange(String propertyName, Object oldValue, Object newValue)
        throws PropertyVetoException;
1.2 public boolean hasListeners(String propertyName);                                synchronized
1.2 public void removeVetoableChangeListener(String propertyName,                    synchronized
                                VetoableChangeListener listener);
}
```

Hierarchy: Object→ VetoableChangeSupport(Serializable)

Type Of: java.beans.beancontext.BeanContextChildSupport.vcSupport

Visibility
java.beans

Java 1.1
PJ1.1

This interface is intended to be implemented by advanced beans that can run both with and without a GUI present. The methods it defines allow a bean to specify whether it requires a GUI and allow the environment to notify the bean whether a GUI is available. If a bean absolutely requires a GUI, it should return true from needsGui(). If a bean is running without a GUI, it should return true from avoidingGui(). If no GUI is available, the bean can be notified through a call to dontUseGui(), and if a GUI is available, the bean can be notified through a call to okToUseGui().

```
public interface Visibility {
// Public Instance Methods
    public abstract boolean avoidingGui();
    public abstract void dontUseGui();
    public abstract boolean needsGui();
    public abstract void okToUseGui();
}
```

Implementations: java.beans.beancontext.BeanContext

Returned By: java.beans.beancontext.BeanContextSupport.getChildVisibility()

CHAPTER 10

The java.beans.beancontext Package

The java.beans.beancontext package extends the JavaBeans component model to add the notion of a containment hierarchy. It also supports bean containers that provide an execution context for the beans they contain and that may also provide a set of services to those beans. This package is typically used by advanced bean developers and developers of bean-manipulation tools. Application programmers who are simply using beans do not typically use this package. Figure 10-1 shows the class hierarchy.

BeanContext is the central interface of this package. It is a container for beans and also defines several methods that specify context information for beans. BeanContextServices extends BeanContext to define methods that allow a contained bean to query and request available services. A bean that wishes to be told about its containing BeanContext implements the BeanContextChild interface. BeanContext is itself a BeanContextChild, which means that contexts can be nested within other contexts.

See Chapter 6, *JavaBeans*, for more information on beans and bean contexts.

BeanContext   Java 1.2

java.beans.beancontext   *collection*

This interface defines the methods that must be implemented by any class that wants to act as a logical container for JavaBeans components. Every BeanContext is also a BeanContextChild and can therefore be nested within a higher-level bean context. BeanContext is extended by BeanContextServices; any bean context that wants to provide services to the beans it contains must implement this more specialized interface.

The BeanContext interface extends the java.util.Collection interface; the children it contains are accessed using the methods of that interface. In addition, BeanContext defines several important methods of its own. instantiateChild() instantiates a new bean, in the same manner as the standard Beans.instantiate() method, and then makes that new bean a child of the context. Calling this method is typically the same as calling the three-argument version of Beans.instantiate(). getResource() and getResourceAsStream() are the BeanContext versions of the java.lang.Class and java.lang.ClassLoader methods of the same name. Some bean-context implementations may provide special behavior for these methods; others may simply delegate to the Class or ClassLoader of the bean. The remaining two methods allow the registration and deregistration of event listeners that the BeanContext notifies when bean children are added or removed from the context.

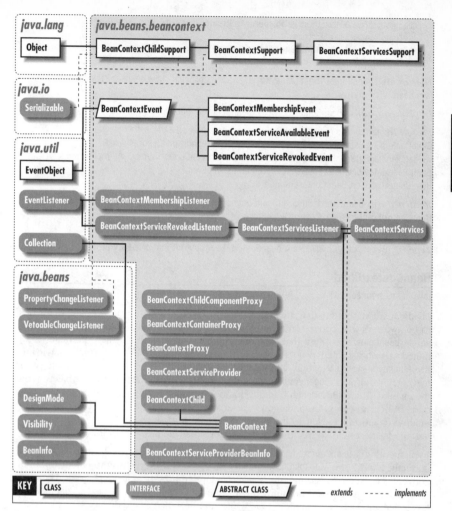

Figure 10–1: The java.beans.beancontext package

Implementing a BeanContext is a more specialized task than developing a JavaBeans component. Many bean developers will never have to implement a bean context themselves. If you do implement a bean context, you'll probably find it easier to use BeanContextSupport, either by extending it or using an instance as a proxy.

```
public interface BeanContext extends BeanContextChild, java.util.Collection, java.beans.DesignMode,
      java.beans.Visibility {
// Public Constants
   public static final Object globalHierarchyLock;
// Event Registration Methods (by event name)
   public abstract void addBeanContextMembershipListener(BeanContextMembershipListener bcml);
   public abstract void removeBeanContextMembershipListener(BeanContextMembershipListener bcml);
// Public Instance Methods
   public abstract java.net.URL getResource(String name, BeanContextChild bcc) throws IllegalArgumentException;
```

```
    public abstract java.io.InputStream getResourceAsStream(String name, BeanContextChild bcc)
        throws IllegalArgumentException;
    public abstract Object instantiateChild(String beanName) throws java.io.IOException, ClassNotFoundException;
}
```

Hierarchy: (BeanContext(BeanContextChild, java.util.Collection, java.beans.DesignMode, java.beans.Visibility))

Implementations: BeanContextServices, BeanContextSupport

Passed To: java.beans.AppletInitializer.initialize(), java.beans.Beans.instantiate(), BeanContextChild.setBeanContext(), BeanContextChildSupport.{setBeanContext(), validatePendingSetBeanContext()}, BeanContextEvent.{BeanContextEvent(), setPropagatedFrom()}, BeanContextMembershipEvent.BeanContextMembershipEvent(), BeanContextSupport.BeanContextSupport()

Returned By: BeanContextChild.getBeanContext(), BeanContextChildSupport.getBeanContext(), BeanContextEvent.{getBeanContext(), getPropagatedFrom()}, BeanContextSupport.getBeanContextPeer()

Type Of: BeanContextChildSupport.beanContext, BeanContextEvent.propagatedFrom

BeanContextChild   Java 1.2

java.beans.beancontext

JavaBeans components that are designed to be nested within a bean context and need to be aware of that context must implement this interface. BeanContextChild implements a single beanContext property that identifies the BeanContext within which the bean is contained. The beanContext property is bound and constrained, which means that it must fire PropertyChangeEvent events when setBeanContext() is called, and any call to setBeanContext() may result in a PropertyVetoException if one of the VetoableChangeListener objects vetoes the change. The setBeanContext() method is not intended for use by beans or by applications. When a bean is instantiated or deserialized, its containing bean context calls this method to introduce itself to the bean. The bean must store a reference to its BeanContext in a transient field so that the context is not serialized along with the bean itself.

Implementing a BeanContextChild from scratch can be somewhat tricky because you must correctly handle the VetoableChangeListener protocol and correctly implement important conventions, such as storing the BeanContext reference in a transient field. Therefore, most bean developers do not implement the interface directly, but instead use BeanContextSupport, either by subclassing it or by using an instance as a delegate.

```
public interface BeanContextChild {
// Public Instance Methods
    public abstract void addPropertyChangeListener(String name, java.beans.PropertyChangeListener pcl);
    public abstract void addVetoableChangeListener(String name, java.beans.VetoableChangeListener vcl);
    public abstract BeanContext getBeanContext();
    public abstract void removePropertyChangeListener(String name, java.beans.PropertyChangeListener pcl);
    public abstract void removeVetoableChangeListener(String name, java.beans.VetoableChangeListener vcl);
    public abstract void setBeanContext(BeanContext bc) throws java.beans.PropertyVetoException;
}
```

Implementations: BeanContext, BeanContextChildSupport

Passed To: BeanContext.{getResource(), getResourceAsStream()}, BeanContextChildSupport.BeanContextChildSupport(), BeanContextServices.{getService(), releaseService()}, BeanContextServicesSupport.{getService(), releaseService()}, BeanContextSupport.{getResource(), getResourceAsStream()}

Returned By: BeanContextChildSupport.getBeanContextChildPeer(),
BeanContextProxy.getBeanContextProxy(), BeanContextSupport.getChildBeanContextChild()

Type Of: BeanContextChildSupport.beanContextChildPeer

BeanContextChildComponentProxy   Java 1.2
java.beans.beancontext

If a BeanContextChild is not a Component subclass but has an associated Component object
to display its visual representation, it implements this interface to allow access to that
component.

```
public interface BeanContextChildComponentProxy {
// Public Instance Methods
   public abstract java.awt.Component getComponent();
}
```

BeanContextChildSupport   Java 1.2
java.beans.beancontext   *serializable*

This class provides support for implementing the BeanContextChild interface in a way that
correctly conforms to the details of the bean context specification. A subclass should
implement initializeBeanContextResources() and releaseBeanContextResources() to obtain and
release whatever resources the bean context child requires, such as service objects
obtained from the containing BeanContext. These methods are called when the containing bean context introduces itself by calling setBeanContext(). Any resources obtained
with these methods should be stored in transient fields so that they are not serialized
along with the bean. A bean that wants a chance to approve any call to setBeanContext()
before that call succeeds can implement validatePendingSetBeanContext(). If this method
returns false, the setBeanContext() call that triggered it fails with a PropertyVetoException.

Many beans are AWT or Swing components and cannot subclass both Component and
BeanContextChildSupport. Therefore, many bean developers find it useful to delegate to an
internal instance of BeanContextChildSupport. One way to do this is to have your bean
implement the BeanContextProxy interface and simply return an instance of BeanContextChildSupport from the getBeanContextProxy() method. Another technique is to actually
implement the BeanContextChild interface in your bean, but provide dummy methods that
call the corresponding methods of BeanContextChildSupport. If you do this, you should
pass an instance of your bean to the BeanContextChildSupport() constructor. This makes
the delegation transparent so events appear to come directly from your bean. In either
case, you can instantiate BeanContextChildSupport directly. Often, however, you want to
create a custom subclass (perhaps as an inner class) to implement methods such as initializeBeanContextResources().

```
public class BeanContextChildSupport implements BeanContextChild, BeanContextServicesListener, Serializable {
// Public Constructors
   public BeanContextChildSupport();
   public BeanContextChildSupport(BeanContextChild bcc);
// Public Instance Methods
   public void firePropertyChange(String name, Object oldValue, Object newValue);
   public void fireVetoableChange(String name, Object oldValue, Object newValue)
      throws java.beans.PropertyVetoException;
   public BeanContextChild getBeanContextChildPeer();              default:BeanContextChildSupport
   public boolean isDelegated();                                   default:false
   public boolean validatePendingSetBeanContext(BeanContext newValue);        constant
// Methods Implementing BeanContextChild
   public void addPropertyChangeListener(String name, java.beans.PropertyChangeListener pcl);
```

```
     public void addVetoableChangeListener(String name, java.beans.VetoableChangeListener vcl);
     public BeanContext getBeanContext();                                    synchronized default:null
     public void removePropertyChangeListener(String name, java.beans.PropertyChangeListener pcl);
     public void removeVetoableChangeListener(String name, java.beans.VetoableChangeListener vcl);
     public void setBeanContext(BeanContext bc) throws java.beans.PropertyVetoException;    synchronized
// Methods Implementing BeanContextServiceRevokedListener
     public void serviceRevoked(BeanContextServiceRevokedEvent bcsre);                           empty
// Methods Implementing BeanContextServicesListener
     public void serviceAvailable(BeanContextServiceAvailableEvent bcsae);                        empty
// Protected Instance Methods
     protected void initializeBeanContextResources();                                            empty
     protected void releaseBeanContextResources();                                               empty
// Public Instance Fields
     public BeanContextChild beanContextChildPeer;
// Protected Instance Fields
     protected transient BeanContext beanContext;
     protected java.beans.PropertyChangeSupport pcSupport;
     protected transient boolean rejectedSetBCOnce;
     protected java.beans.VetoableChangeSupport vcSupport;
}
```

Hierarchy: Object→ BeanContextChildSupport(BeanContextChild, BeanContextServicesListener(BeanContextServiceRevokedListener(java.util.EventListener)), Serializable)

Subclasses: BeanContextSupport

BeanContextContainerProxy   Java 1.2

java.beans.beancontext

This interface is implemented by a BeanContext that has a java.awt.Container associated with it. The getContainer() method allows any interested parties to obtain a reference to the container associated with the bean context. It is a common practice for bean contexts to be associated with containers. Unfortunately, BeanContext implements java.util.Collection, which has method-name conflicts with java.awt.Container, so no Container subclass can implement the BeanContext interface. See also BeanContextProxy, which reverses the direction of the proxy relationship.

```
public interface BeanContextContainerProxy {
// Public Instance Methods
     public abstract java.awt.Container getContainer();
}
```

BeanContextEvent   Java 1.2

java.beans.beancontext   *serializable event*

This is the abstract superclass of all bean context-related events. getBeanContext() returns the source of the event. If isPropagated() returns true, the event has been propagated through a hierarchy of bean contexts, and getPropagatedFrom() returns the most recent bean context to propagate the event.

```
public abstract class BeanContextEvent extends java.util.EventObject {
// Protected Constructors
     protected BeanContextEvent(BeanContext bc);
// Public Instance Methods
     public BeanContext getBeanContext();
     public BeanContext getPropagatedFrom();                                                 synchronized
```

```
    public boolean isPropagated();                                    synchronized
    public void setPropagatedFrom(BeanContext bc);                    synchronized
// Protected Instance Fields
    protected BeanContext propagatedFrom;
}
```

Hierarchy: Object→ java.util.EventObject(Serializable)→ BeanContextEvent

Subclasses: BeanContextMembershipEvent, BeanContextServiceAvailableEvent, BeanContextServiceRevokedEvent

BeanContextMembershipEvent   Java 1.2

java.beans.beancontext   *serializable event*

An event of this type is generated by a BeanContext when beans are added to it or removed from it. The event object contains the list of children that were added or removed and allows access to that list in several ways. The size() method returns the number of affected children. The contains() method checks whether a specified object was one of the affected children. toArray() returns the list of affected children as an array, and iterator() returns the list in the form of a java.util.Iterator.

```
public class BeanContextMembershipEvent extends BeanContextEvent {
// Public Constructors
    public BeanContextMembershipEvent(BeanContext bc, Object[ ] changes);
    public BeanContextMembershipEvent(BeanContext bc, java.util.Collection changes);
// Public Instance Methods
    public boolean contains(Object child);
    public java.util.Iterator iterator();
    public int size();
    public Object[ ] toArray();
// Protected Instance Fields
    protected java.util.Collection children;
}
```

Hierarchy: Object→ java.util.EventObject(Serializable)→ BeanContextEvent→ BeanContextMembershipEvent

Passed To: BeanContextMembershipListener.{childrenAdded(), childrenRemoved()}, BeanContextSupport.{fireChildrenAdded(), fireChildrenRemoved()}

BeanContextMembershipListener   Java 1.2

java.beans.beancontext   *event listener*

This interface should be implemented by any object that wants to be notified when children are added to or removed from a BeanContext.

```
public interface BeanContextMembershipListener extends java.util.EventListener {
// Public Instance Methods
    public abstract void childrenAdded(BeanContextMembershipEvent bcme);
    public abstract void childrenRemoved(BeanContextMembershipEvent bcme);
}
```

Hierarchy: (BeanContextMembershipListener(java.util.EventListener))

Passed To: BeanContext.{addBeanContextMembershipListener(), removeBeanContextMembershipListener()}, BeanContextSupport.{addBeanContextMembershipListener(), removeBeanContextMembershipListener()}

Returned By: BeanContextSupport.getChildBeanContextMembershipListener()

BeanContextProxy   Java 1.2

java.beans.beancontext

This interface is implemented by a JavaBeans component (often, but not always, an AWT Component or Container object) that is not itself a BeanContext or BeanContextChild, but has a BeanContext or BeanContextChild object associated with it. The getBeanContextProxy() method returns the associated object. The return type of this method is BeanContextChild. Depending on the context in which you call this method, however, the returned object may actually be a BeanContext or BeanContextServices object. You should test for this using the instanceof operator before casting the object to these more specific types.

```
public interface BeanContextProxy {
// Public Instance Methods
    public abstract BeanContextChild getBeanContextProxy();
}
```

BeanContextServiceAvailableEvent   Java 1.2

java.beans.beancontext   *serializable event*

An event of this type is generated to notify interested BeanContextServicesListener objects that a new class of service is available from a BeanContextServices object. getServiceClass() returns the class of the service, and getCurrentServiceSelectors() may return a set of additional arguments that can parameterize the service.

```
public class BeanContextServiceAvailableEvent extends BeanContextEvent {
// Public Constructors
    public BeanContextServiceAvailableEvent(BeanContextServices bcs, Class sc);
// Public Instance Methods
    public java.util.Iterator getCurrentServiceSelectors();
    public Class getServiceClass();
    public BeanContextServices getSourceAsBeanContextServices();
// Protected Instance Fields
    protected Class serviceClass;
}
```

Hierarchy: Object→ java.util.EventObject(Serializable)→ BeanContextEvent→ BeanContextServiceAvailableEvent

Passed To: BeanContextChildSupport.serviceAvailable(), BeanContextServicesListener.serviceAvailable(), BeanContextServicesSupport.{fireServiceAdded(), serviceAvailable()}

BeanContextServiceProvider   Java 1.2

java.beans.beancontext

This interface defines the methods that must be implemented by a factory class that wants to provide service objects to beans. To provide its service, a BeanContextService-Provider is passed to the addService() method of a BeanContextServices object. This creates a mapping in the BeanContextServices object between a class of service (such as java.awt.print.PrinterJob) and a BeanContextServiceProvider that can return a suitable instance of that class to provide the service.

When a BeanContextChild requests a service of a particular class from its BeanContextServices container, the BeanContextServices object finds the appropriate BeanContextService-Provider object and forwards the request to its getService() method. When the bean relinquishes the service, releaseService() is called. A getService() request may include an arbitrary object as an additional parameter or service selector. Service providers that use the service selector argument and that support a finite set of legal service selector values should implement the getCurrentServiceSelectors() method to allow the list of legal selector values to be queried.

Bean developers typically do not have to use or implement this interface. From the point of view of a bean context child, service objects are obtained from a BeanContextServices object. Developers creating BeanContextServices implementations, however, must implement appropriate BeanContextServiceProvider objects to provide the services.

```
public interface BeanContextServiceProvider {
// Public Instance Methods
    public abstract java.util.Iterator getCurrentServiceSelectors(BeanContextServices bcs, Class serviceClass);
    public abstract Object getService(BeanContextServices bcs, Object requestor, Class serviceClass,
                                Object serviceSelector);
    public abstract void releaseService(BeanContextServices bcs, Object requestor, Object service);
}
```

Implementations: BeanContextServicesSupport.BCSSProxyServiceProvider

Passed To: BeanContextServices.{addService(), revokeService()},
BeanContextServicesSupport.{addService(), createBCSSServiceProvider(), revokeService()}

Returned By: BeanContextServicesSupport.BCSSServiceProvider.getServiceProvider()

Type Of: BeanContextServicesSupport.BCSSServiceProvider.serviceProvider

BeanContextServiceProviderBeanInfo
java.beans.beancontext

Java 1.2

A BeanContextServiceProvider that wishes to provide information to a GUI builder tool about the service or services it offers should implement this BeanInfo subinterface. Following the standard BeanInfo naming conventions, the implementing class should have the same name as the service provider class, with "BeanInfo" appended. This enables a design tool to look for and dynamically load the bean info class when necessary.

getServicesBeanInfo() should return an array of BeanInfo objects, one for each class of service offered by the BeanContextServiceProvider. These BeanInfo objects enable a design tool to allow the user to visually configure the service object. This can be quite useful, since service objects may be instances of existing classes that were not designed with the standard JavaBeans naming conventions in mind.

```
public interface BeanContextServiceProviderBeanInfo extends java.beans.BeanInfo {
// Public Instance Methods
    public abstract java.beans.BeanInfo[ ] getServicesBeanInfo();
}
```

Hierarchy: (BeanContextServiceProviderBeanInfo(java.beans.BeanInfo))

BeanContextServiceRevokedEvent
java.beans.beancontext

Java 1.2

serializable event

This event class provides details about a service revocation initiated by a BeanContextServices object. getServiceClass() specifies the class of service being revoked. isCurrentServiceInvalidNow() specifies whether the currently owned service object has become invalid. If this method returns true, the bean that receives this event must stop using the service object immediately. If the method returns false, the bean can continue to use the service object, but future requests for services of this class will fail.

```
public class BeanContextServiceRevokedEvent extends BeanContextEvent {
// Public Constructors
    public BeanContextServiceRevokedEvent(BeanContextServices bcs, Class sc, boolean invalidate);
// Public Instance Methods
    public Class getServiceClass();
    public BeanContextServices getSourceAsBeanContextServices();
    public boolean isCurrentServiceInvalidNow();
    public boolean isServiceClass(Class service);
// Protected Instance Fields
    protected Class serviceClass;
}
```

Hierarchy: Object→ java.util.EventObject(Serializable)→ BeanContextEvent→
BeanContextServiceRevokedEvent

Passed To: BeanContextChildSupport.serviceRevoked(),
BeanContextServiceRevokedListener.serviceRevoked(),
BeanContextServicesSupport.{fireServiceRevoked(), serviceRevoked()},
BeanContextServicesSupport.BCSSProxyServiceProvider.serviceRevoked()

BeanContextServiceRevokedListener

Java 1.2

java.beans.beancontext

event listener

This interface defines a method that is invoked when a service object returned by a
BeanContextServices object is forcibly revoked. Unlike other types of event listeners, the
BeanContextServiceRevokedListener is not registered and deregistered with a pair of add and
remove methods. Instead, an implementation of this interface must be passed to every
getService() call on a BeanContextServices object. If the returned service is ever revoked by
the granting BeanContextServiceProvider object before the bean has relinquished the service, the serviceRevoked() method of this interface is called.

When a service is revoked, it means that future requests for the service will not succeed. But it may also mean that current service objects have become invalid and must
not be used anymore. The serviceRevoked() method should call the isCurrentServiceInvalid-
Now() method of the supplied event object to determine if this is the case. If so, it must
immediately stop using the service object.

```
public interface BeanContextServiceRevokedListener extends java.util.EventListener {
// Public Instance Methods
    public abstract void serviceRevoked(BeanContextServiceRevokedEvent bcsre);
}
```

Hierarchy: (BeanContextServiceRevokedListener(java.util.EventListener))

Implementations: BeanContextServicesListener,
BeanContextServicesSupport.BCSSProxyServiceProvider

Passed To: BeanContextServices.getService(), BeanContextServicesSupport.getService()

BeanContextServices

Java 1.2

java.beans.beancontext

collection event listener

This interface defines additional methods a bean context class must implement if it
wants to provide services to the beans it contains. A bean calls hasService() to determine
if a service of a particular type is available from its bean context. It calls getService() to
request an instance of the specified service class and then calls releaseService() when it
no longer needs the service object. A bean that wants to find the complete list of available services can call getCurrentServiceClasses(). Some services allow (or require) a service

selector object to be passed to the getService() method to provide additional information about the service object. If a service defines a fixed set of legal service selectors, getCurrentServiceSelectors() allows a bean to iterate through the set of selector objects. Beans that want to know when new services become available or when existing services are revoked should register a BeanContextServicesListener object with addBeanContextServicesListener().

If a BeanContextServices object does not provide a requested service, but is nested within another BeanContext, it should check whether any of its ancestor bean contexts can provide the service. The BeanContextServices interface extends BeanContextServicesListener. This means that every BeanContextServices object can be listening to the set of services available from its container.

The previous methods are the ones beans call to obtain services. BeanContextServices defines a different set of methods service providers use to deliver services. addService() defines a BeanContextServiceProvider for a specified Class of service. revokeService() removes this mapping between service class and service provider, and indicates that the specified service is no longer available. When a service is revoked, the BeanContextServices object must notify any beans that have been granted service objects (and have not released them yet) that the service has been revoked. It does this by notifying the BeanContextServiceRevokedListener objects passed to the getService() method.

Bean context developers may find it easier to use the BeanContextServicesSupport class, either by subclassing or by delegation, instead of implementing BeanContextServices from scratch.

```
public interface BeanContextServices extends BeanContext, BeanContextServicesListener {
// Event Registration Methods (by event name)
    public abstract void addBeanContextServicesListener(BeanContextServicesListener bcsl);
    public abstract void removeBeanContextServicesListener(BeanContextServicesListener bcsl);
// Public Instance Methods
    public abstract boolean addService(Class serviceClass, BeanContextServiceProvider serviceProvider);
    public abstract java.util.Iterator getCurrentServiceClasses();
    public abstract java.util.Iterator getCurrentServiceSelectors(Class serviceClass);
    public abstract Object getService(BeanContextChild child, Object requestor, Class serviceClass,
                            Object serviceSelector, BeanContextServiceRevokedListener bcsrl)
        throws java.util.TooManyListenersException;
    public abstract boolean hasService(Class serviceClass);
    public abstract void releaseService(BeanContextChild child, Object requestor, Object service);
    public abstract void revokeService(Class serviceClass, BeanContextServiceProvider serviceProvider,
                            boolean revokeCurrentServicesNow);
}
```

Hierarchy: (BeanContextServices(BeanContext(BeanContextChild, java.util.Collection, java.beans.DesignMode, java.beans.Visibility), BeanContextServicesListener(BeanContextServiceRevokedListener(java.util.EventListener))))

Implementations: BeanContextServicesSupport

Passed To: BeanContextServiceAvailableEvent.BeanContextServiceAvailableEvent(), BeanContextServiceProvider.{getCurrentServiceSelectors(), getService(), releaseService()}, BeanContextServiceRevokedEvent.BeanContextServiceRevokedEvent(), BeanContextServicesSupport.BeanContextServicesSupport(), BeanContextServicesSupport.BCSSProxyServiceProvider.{getCurrentServiceSelectors(), getService(), releaseService()}

Returned By: BeanContextServiceAvailableEvent.getSourceAsBeanContextServices(), BeanContextServiceRevokedEvent.getSourceAsBeanContextServices(), BeanContextServicesSupport.getBeanContextServicesPeer()

BeanContextServicesListener

Java 1.2

java.beans.beancontext

event listener

This interface adds a serviceAvailable() method to the serviceRevoked() method of BeanContextServiceRevokedListener. Listeners of this type can be registered with a BeanContextServices object and are notified when a new class of service becomes available or when an existing class of service is revoked.

```
public interface BeanContextServicesListener extends BeanContextServiceRevokedListener {
// Public Instance Methods
    public abstract void serviceAvailable(BeanContextServiceAvailableEvent bcsae);
}
```

Hierarchy: (BeanContextServicesListener(BeanContextServiceRevokedListener(java.util.EventListener)))

Implementations: BeanContextChildSupport, BeanContextServices

Passed To: BeanContextServices.{addBeanContextServicesListener(), removeBeanContextServicesListener()}, BeanContextServicesSupport.{addBeanContextServicesListener(), removeBeanContextServicesListener()}

Returned By: BeanContextServicesSupport.getChildBeanContextServicesListener()

BeanContextServicesSupport

Java 1.2

java.beans.beancontext

serializable collection

This class is a useful implementation of the BeanContextServices interface that correctly conforms to the bean context specifications and conventions. Most bean context implementors find it easier to subclass this class or delegate to an instance of this class rather than implement BeanContextServices from scratch. The most common technique is to implement the BeanContextProxy interface and return an instance of BeanContextServicesSupport from the getBeanContextProxy() method.

```
public class BeanContextServicesSupport extends BeanContextSupport implements BeanContextServices {
// Public Constructors
    public BeanContextServicesSupport();
    public BeanContextServicesSupport(BeanContextServices peer);
    public BeanContextServicesSupport(BeanContextServices peer, java.util.Locale lcle);
    public BeanContextServicesSupport(BeanContextServices peer, java.util.Locale lcle, boolean dtime);
    public BeanContextServicesSupport(BeanContextServices peer, java.util.Locale lcle, boolean dTime,
                                      boolean visible);
// Inner Classes
    protected class BCSSChild extends BeanContextSupport.BCSChild;
    protected class BCSSProxyServiceProvider implements BeanContextServiceProvider,
        BeanContextServiceRevokedListener;
    protected static class BCSSServiceProvider implements Serializable;
// Protected Class Methods
    protected static final BeanContextServicesListener getChildBeanContextServicesListener(Object child);
// Event Registration Methods (by event name)
    public void addBeanContextServicesListener(                     Implements:BeanContextServices
                                BeanContextServicesListener bcsl);
    public void removeBeanContextServicesListener(                  Implements:BeanContextServices
                                BeanContextServicesListener bcsl);
// Public Instance Methods
    public BeanContextServices getBeanContextServicesPeer();        default:BeanContextServicesSupport
// Methods Implementing BeanContextServiceRevokedListener
    public void serviceRevoked(BeanContextServiceRevokedEvent bcssre);
```

```
// Methods Implementing BeanContextServices
    public void addBeanContextServicesListener(BeanContextServicesListener bcsl);
    public boolean addService(Class serviceClass, BeanContextServiceProvider bcsp);
    public java.util.Iterator getCurrentServiceClasses();                    default:BeanContextSupport.BCSIterator
    public java.util.Iterator getCurrentServiceSelectors(Class serviceClass);
    public Object getService(BeanContextChild child, Object requestor, Class serviceClass, Object serviceSelector,
                    BeanContextServiceRevokedListener bcsrl) throws java.util.TooManyListenersException;
    public boolean hasService(Class serviceClass);                                        synchronized
    public void releaseService(BeanContextChild child, Object requestor, Object service);
    public void removeBeanContextServicesListener(BeanContextServicesListener bcsl);
    public void revokeService(Class serviceClass, BeanContextServiceProvider bcsp,
                    boolean revokeCurrentServicesNow);
// Methods Implementing BeanContextServicesListener
    public void serviceAvailable(BeanContextServiceAvailableEvent bcssae);
// Public Methods Overriding BeanContextSupport
    public void initialize();
// Protected Methods Overriding BeanContextSupport
    protected void bcsPreDeserializationHook(java.io.ObjectInputStream ois)            synchronized
        throws java.io.IOException, ClassNotFoundException;
    protected void bcsPreSerializationHook(java.io.ObjectOutputStream oos)             synchronized
        throws java.io.IOException;
    protected void childJustRemovedHook(Object child, BeanContextSupport.BCSChild bcsc);
    protected BeanContextSupport.BCSChild createBCSChild(Object targetChild, Object peer);
// Protected Methods Overriding BeanContextChildSupport
    protected void initializeBeanContextResources();                                  synchronized
    protected void releaseBeanContextResources();                                     synchronized
// Protected Instance Methods
    protected boolean addService(Class serviceClass, BeanContextServiceProvider bcsp, boolean fireEvent);
    protected BeanContextServicesSupport.BCSSServiceProvider createBCSSServiceProvider(Class sc,
                    BeanContextServiceProvider bcsp);
    protected final void fireServiceAdded(BeanContextServiceAvailableEvent bcssae);
    protected final void fireServiceAdded(Class serviceClass);
    protected final void fireServiceRevoked(BeanContextServiceRevokedEvent bcsre);
    protected final void fireServiceRevoked(Class serviceClass, boolean revokeNow);
// Protected Instance Fields
    protected transient java.util.ArrayList bcsListeners;
    protected transient BeanContextServicesSupport.BCSSProxyServiceProvider proxy;
    protected transient int serializable;
    protected transient java.util.HashMap services;
}
```

Hierarchy: Object→ BeanContextChildSupport(BeanContextChild,
BeanContextServicesListener(BeanContextServiceRevokedListener(java.util.EventListener)),
Serializable)→ BeanContextSupport(BeanContext(BeanContextChild, java.util.Collection,
java.beans.DesignMode, java.beans.Visibility),
java.beans.PropertyChangeListener(java.util.EventListener), Serializable,
java.beans.VetoableChangeListener(java.util.EventListener))→
BeanContextServicesSupport(BeanContextServices(BeanContext(BeanContextChild, java.util.Collection,
java.beans.DesignMode, java.beans.Visibility),
BeanContextServicesListener(BeanContextServiceRevokedListener(java.util.EventListener))))

BeanContextServicesSupport.BCSSChild
java.beans.beancontext

Java 1.2

serializable

This class is used internally by BeanContextServicesSupport to associate additional information with each child of the bean context. It has no public or protected method or fields, but may be customized by subclassing.

```
protected class BeanContextServicesSupport.BCSSChild extends BeanContextSupport.BCSChild {
// No Constructor
}
```

BeanContextServicesSupport.BCSSProxyServiceProvider
java.beans.beancontext

Java 1.2

This inner class is used internally by BeanContextServicesSupport to properly handle delegation to the services provided by containing bean contexts. It implements the BeanContextServiceProvider interface in terms of the methods of a containing BeanContextServices object.

```
protected class BeanContextServicesSupport.BCSSProxyServiceProvider
      implements BeanContextServiceProvider, BeanContextServiceRevokedListener {
// No Constructor
// Methods Implementing BeanContextServiceProvider
    public java.util.Iterator getCurrentServiceSelectors(BeanContextServices bcs, Class serviceClass);
    public Object getService(BeanContextServices bcs, Object requestor, Class serviceClass, Object serviceSelector);
    public void releaseService(BeanContextServices bcs, Object requestor, Object service);
// Methods Implementing BeanContextServiceRevokedListener
    public void serviceRevoked(BeanContextServiceRevokedEvent bcsre);
}
```

Type Of: BeanContextServicesSupport.proxy

BeanContextServicesSupport.BCSSServiceProvider
java.beans.beancontext

Java 1.2

serializable

This inner class is a trivial wrapper around a BeanContextServiceProvider object. Subclasses that want to associate additional information with each service provider can subclass this class and override the createBCSSServiceProvider() method of BeanContextServicesSupport.

```
protected static class BeanContextServicesSupport.BCSSServiceProvider implements Serializable {
// No Constructor
// Protected Instance Methods
    protected BeanContextServiceProvider getServiceProvider();
// Protected Instance Fields
    protected BeanContextServiceProvider serviceProvider;
}
```

Returned By: BeanContextServicesSupport.createBCSSServiceProvider()

BeanContextSupport
java.beans.beancontext

Java 1.2

serializable collection

This class provides a simple, easily customizable implementation of BeanContext. Most bean context implementors find it easier to subclass BeanContextSupport or create a BeanContextSupport delegate object rather than implement the BeanContext interface from scratch.

Bean contexts are often AWT or Swing containers and cannot (because of a method-naming conflict) implement BeanContext. Therefore, a context object implements the BeanContextProxy interface and returns a BeanContext object from its getBeanContextProxy() method. A BeanContextSupport object is a suitable object to return from this method.

Some bean contexts require customized behavior, however, and BeanContextSupport is designed to be easily customized through subclassing. Protected methods such as childJustAddedHook() and validatePendingAdd() are particularly useful when subclassing.

```
public class BeanContextSupport extends BeanContextChildSupport implements BeanContext,
    java.beans.PropertyChangeListener, Serializable, java.beans.VetoableChangeListener {
// Public Constructors
    public BeanContextSupport();
    public BeanContextSupport(BeanContext peer);
    public BeanContextSupport(BeanContext peer, java.util.Locale lcle);
    public BeanContextSupport(BeanContext peer, java.util.Locale lcle, boolean dtime);
    public BeanContextSupport(BeanContext peer, java.util.Locale lcle, boolean dTime, boolean visible);
// Inner Classes
    protected class BCSChild implements Serializable;
    protected static final class BCSIterator implements java.util.Iterator;
// Protected Class Methods
    protected static final boolean classEquals(Class first, Class second);
    protected static final BeanContextChild getChildBeanContextChild(Object child);
    protected static final BeanContextMembershipListener getChildBeanContextMembershipListener(
                                             Object child);
    protected static final java.beans.PropertyChangeListener getChildPropertyChangeListener(Object child);
    protected static final Serializable getChildSerializable(Object child);
    protected static final java.beans.VetoableChangeListener getChildVetoableChangeListener(Object child);
    protected static final java.beans.Visibility getChildVisibility(Object child);
// Event Registration Methods (by event name)
    public void addBeanContextMembershipListener(                        Implements:BeanContext
                             BeanContextMembershipListener bcml);
    public void removeBeanContextMembershipListener(                     Implements:BeanContext
                             BeanContextMembershipListener bcml);
// Property Accessor Methods (by property name)
    public BeanContext getBeanContextPeer();                             default:BeanContextSupport
    public boolean isDesignTime();           Implements:DesignMode synchronized default:false
    public void setDesignTime(boolean dTime);             Implements:DesignMode synchronized
    public boolean isEmpty();                         Implements:Collection default:true
    public java.util.Locale getLocale();                                 synchronized
    public void setLocale(java.util.Locale newLocale) throws java.beans.PropertyVetoException;  synchronized
    public boolean isSerializing();                                      default:false
// Public Instance Methods
    public boolean containsKey(Object o);
    public final void readChildren(java.io.ObjectInputStream ois) throws java.io.IOException, ClassNotFoundException;
    public final void writeChildren(java.io.ObjectOutputStream oos) throws java.io.IOException;
// Methods Implementing BeanContext
    public void addBeanContextMembershipListener(BeanContextMembershipListener bcml);
    public java.net.URL getResource(String name, BeanContextChild bcc);
    public java.io.InputStream getResourceAsStream(String name, BeanContextChild bcc);
    public Object instantiateChild(String beanName) throws java.io.IOException, ClassNotFoundException;
    public void removeBeanContextMembershipListener(BeanContextMembershipListener bcml);
// Methods Implementing Collection
    public boolean add(Object targetChild);
    public boolean addAll(java.util.Collection c);
    public void clear();
    public boolean contains(Object o);
```

```
      public boolean containsAll(java.util.Collection c);
      public boolean isEmpty();                                                          default:true
      public java.util.Iterator iterator();
      public boolean remove(Object targetChild);
      public boolean removeAll(java.util.Collection c);
      public boolean retainAll(java.util.Collection c);
      public int size();
      public Object[ ] toArray();
      public Object[ ] toArray(Object[ ] arry);
   // Methods Implementing DesignMode
      public boolean isDesignTime();                                       synchronized default:false
      public void setDesignTime(boolean dTime);                                        synchronized
   // Methods Implementing PropertyChangeListener
      public void propertyChange(java.beans.PropertyChangeEvent pce);
   // Methods Implementing VetoableChangeListener
      public void vetoableChange(java.beans.PropertyChangeEvent pce) throws java.beans.PropertyVetoException;
   // Methods Implementing Visibility
      public boolean avoidingGui();
      public void dontUseGui();                                                        synchronized
      public boolean needsGui();                                                       synchronized
      public void okToUseGui();                                                        synchronized
   // Protected Instance Methods
      protected java.util.Iterator bcsChildren();
      protected void bcsPreDeserializationHook(java.io.ObjectInputStream ois) throws java.io.IOException,   empty
         ClassNotFoundException;
      protected void bcsPreSerializationHook(java.io.ObjectOutputStream oos) throws java.io.IOException;     empty
      protected void childDeserializedHook(Object child, BeanContextSupport.BCSChild bcsc);
      protected void childJustAddedHook(Object child, BeanContextSupport.BCSChild bcsc);                     empty
      protected void childJustRemovedHook(Object child, BeanContextSupport.BCSChild bcsc);                   empty
      protected final Object[ ] copyChildren();
      protected BeanContextSupport.BCSChild createBCSChild(Object targetChild, Object peer);
      protected final void deserialize(java.io.ObjectInputStream ois, java.util.Collection coll) throws java.io.IOException,
         ClassNotFoundException;
      protected final void fireChildrenAdded(BeanContextMembershipEvent bcme);
      protected final void fireChildrenRemoved(BeanContextMembershipEvent bcme);
      protected void initialize();                                                     synchronized
      protected boolean remove(Object targetChild, boolean callChildSetBC);
      protected final void serialize(java.io.ObjectOutputStream oos, java.util.Collection coll) throws java.io.IOException;
      protected boolean validatePendingAdd(Object targetChild);                          constant
      protected boolean validatePendingRemove(Object targetChild);                       constant
   // Protected Instance Fields
      protected transient java.util.ArrayList bcmListeners;
      protected transient java.util.HashMap children;
      protected boolean designTime;
      protected java.util.Locale locale;
      protected boolean okToUseGui;
}
```

Hierarchy: Object→ BeanContextChildSupport(BeanContextChild,
BeanContextServicesListener(BeanContextServiceRevokedListener(java.util.EventListener)),
Serializable) → BeanContextSupport(BeanContext(BeanContextChild, java.util.Collection,
java.beans.DesignMode, java.beans.Visibility),
java.beans.PropertyChangeListener(java.util.EventListener), Serializable,
java.beans.VetoableChangeListener(java.util.EventListener))

Subclasses: BeanContextServicesSupport

BeanContextSupport.BCSChild

Java 1.2

java.beans.beancontext   *serializable*

This class is used internally by BeanContextSupport to keep track of additional information about its children. In particular, for children that implement the BeanContextProxy interface, it keeps track of the BeanContextChild object associated with the child. This class does not define any public or protected fields or methods. BeanContextSupport subclasses that want to associate additional information with each child can subclass this class and override the createBCSChild() method to instantiate the new subclass.

```
protected class BeanContextSupport.BCSChild implements Serializable {
// No Constructor
}
```

Subclasses: BeanContextServicesSupport.BCSSChild

Passed To: BeanContextServicesSupport.childJustRemovedHook(),
BeanContextSupport.{childDeserializedHook(), childJustAddedHook(), childJustRemovedHook()}

Returned By: BeanContextServicesSupport.createBCSChild(), BeanContextSupport.createBCSChild()

BeanContextSupport.BCSIterator

Java 1.2

java.beans.beancontext

This class implements the java.util.Iterator interface. An instance of this class is returned by the iterator() method implemented by BeanContextSupport. The remove() method has an empty implementation and does not actually remove a child of the bean context.

```
protected static final class BeanContextSupport.BCSIterator implements java.util.Iterator {
// No Constructor
// Methods Implementing Iterator
    public boolean hasNext();
    public Object next();
    public void remove();                                                    empty
}
```

CHAPTER 11

The java.io Package

The java.io package contains a relatively large number of classes, but, as you can see from Figure 11-1 and Figure 11-2, the classes form a fairly structured hierarchy. Most of the package consists of byte streams—subclasses of InputStream or OutputStream and (in Java 1.1) character streams—subclasses of Reader or Writer. Each of these stream types has a specific purpose, and, despite its size, java.io is a straightforward package to understand and to use.

Before we consider the stream classes in the package, let's examine the important non-stream classes. File represents a file or directory name in a system-independent way and provides methods for listing directories, querying file attributes, and renaming and deleting files. FilenameFilter is an interface that defines a method that accepts or rejects specified filenames. It is used by java.awt.FileDialog and File to specify what types of files should be included in directory listings. RandomAccessFile allows you to read from or write to arbitrary locations of a file. Often, though, you'll prefer sequential access to a file and should use one of the stream classes.

InputStream and OutputStream are abstract classes that define methods for reading and writing bytes. Their subclasses allow bytes to be read from and written to a variety of sources and sinks. FileInputStream and FileOutputStream read from and write to files. ByteAr-rayInputStream and ByteArrayOutputStream read from and write to an array of bytes in memory. PipedInputStream reads bytes from a PipedOutputStream, and PipedOutputStream writes bytes to a PipedInputStream. These classes work together to implement a *pipe* for communication between threads.

FilterInputStream and FilterOutputStream are special; they filter input and output bytes. When you create a FilterInputStream, you specify an InputStream for it to filter. When you call the read() method of a FilterInputStream, it calls the read() method of its InputStream, processes the bytes it reads, and returns the filtered bytes. Similarly, when you create a FilterOutputStream, you specify an OutputStream to be filtered. Calling the write() method of a FilterOutputStream causes it to process your bytes in some way and then pass those filtered bytes to the write() method of its OutputStream.

FilterInputStream and FilterOutputStream do not perform any filtering themselves; this is done by their subclasses. BufferedInputStream and BufferedOutputStream provide input and output buffering and can increase I/O efficiency. DataInputStream reads raw bytes from a stream and interprets them in various binary formats. It has various methods to read

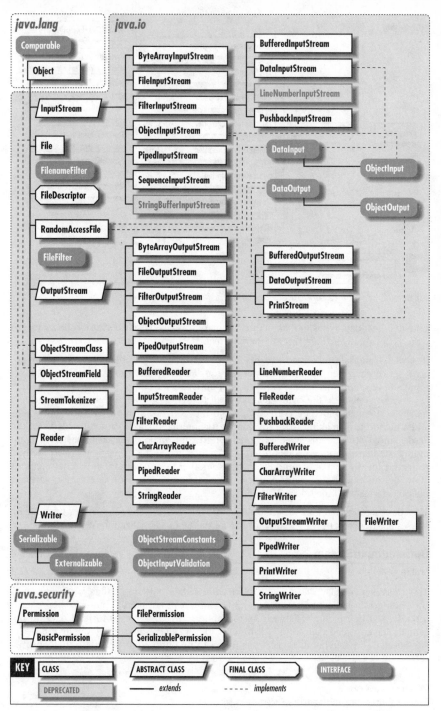

Figure 11-1: The java.io package

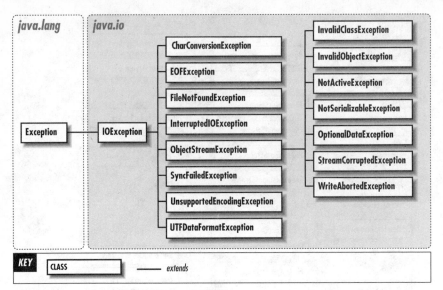

CharConversionException

EOFException

FileNotFoundException

InterruptedIOException

ObjectStreamException

SyncFailedException

UnsupportedEncodingException

UTFDataFormatException

Exception — IOException

InvalidClassException

InvalidObjectException

NotActiveException

NotSerializableException

OptionalDataException

StreamCorruptedException

WriteAbortedException

KEY   CLASS   ——— extends

Figure 11-2: The exception classes of the java.io package

primitive Java data types in their standard binary formats. DataOutputStream allows you to write Java primitive data types in binary format.

In Java 1.1 and later, the byte streams I just described are complemented by an analogous set of character input and output streams. Reader is the superclass of all character input streams, and Writer is the superclass of all character output streams. These character streams supersede the byte streams for all textual I/O. They are more efficient than the byte streams, and they correctly handle the conversion between local encodings and Unicode text, making them invaluable for internationalized programs. Most of the Reader and Writer streams have obvious byte-stream analogs. BufferedReader is a commonly used stream; it provides buffering for efficiency and also has a readLine() method to read a line of text at a time. PrintWriter is another very common stream; its methods allow output of a textual representation of any primitive Java type or of any object (via the object's toString() method).

The ObjectInputStream and ObjectOutputStream classes are special. These byte-stream classes are new as of Java 1.1 and are part of the Object Serialization API.

BufferedInputStream   Java 1.0

java.io   PJ1.1

This class is a FilterInputStream that provides input data buffering; efficiency is increased by reading in a large amount of data and storing it in an internal buffer. When data is requested, it is usually available from the buffer. Thus, most calls to read data do not actually have to read data from a disk, network, or other slow source. Create a Buffered-InputStream by specifying the InputStream that is to be buffered in the call to the constructor. See also BufferedReader.

```
public class BufferedInputStream extends FilterInputStream {
// Public Constructors
    public BufferedInputStream(java.io.InputStream in);
    public BufferedInputStream(java.io.InputStream in, int size);
```

```
// Public Methods Overriding FilterInputStream
·    public int available() throws IOException;                                          synchronized
1.2 public void close() throws IOException;
     public void mark(int readlimit);                                                    synchronized
     public boolean markSupported();                                                         constant
     public int read() throws IOException;                                              synchronized
     public int read(byte[ ] b, int off, int len) throws IOException;                  synchronized
     public void reset() throws IOException;                                            synchronized
     public long skip(long n) throws IOException;                                       synchronized
// Protected Instance Fields
     protected byte[ ] buf;
     protected int count;
     protected int marklimit;
     protected int markpos;
     protected int pos;
}
```

Hierarchy: Object→ java.io.InputStream→ FilterInputStream→ BufferedInputStream

BufferedOutputStream   Java 1.0
java.io   PJ1.1

This class is a FilterOutputStream that provides output data buffering; output efficiency is
increased by storing values to be written in a buffer and actually writing them out only
when the buffer fills up or when the flush() method is called. Create a BufferedOutput-
Stream by specifying the OutputStream that is to be buffered in the call to the constructor.
See also BufferedWriter.

```
public class BufferedOutputStream extends FilterOutputStream {
// Public Constructors
     public BufferedOutputStream(java.io.OutputStream out);
     public BufferedOutputStream(java.io.OutputStream out, int size);
// Public Methods Overriding FilterOutputStream
     public void flush() throws IOException;                                            synchronized
     public void write(int b) throws IOException;                                       synchronized
     public void write(byte[ ] b, int off, int len) throws IOException;                 synchronized
// Protected Instance Fields
     protected byte[ ] buf;
     protected int count;
}
```

Hierarchy: Object→ java.io.OutputStream→ FilterOutputStream→ BufferedOutputStream

BufferedReader   Java 1.1
java.io   PJ1.1

This class applies buffering to a character input stream, thereby improving the efficiency of character input. You create a BufferedReader by specifying some other character
input stream from which it is to buffer input. (You can also specify a buffer size at this
time, although the default size is usually fine.) Typically, you use this sort of buffering
with a FileReader or InputStreamReader. BufferedReader defines the standard set of Reader
methods and provides a readLine() method that reads a line of text (not including the
line terminator) and returns it as a String. BufferedReader is the character-stream analog of
BufferedInputStream. It also provides a replacement for the deprecated readLine() method
of DataInputStream, which did not properly convert bytes into characters.

```
public class BufferedReader extends Reader {
// Public Constructors
    public BufferedReader(Reader in);
    public BufferedReader(Reader in, int sz);
// Public Instance Methods
    public String readLine() throws IOException;
// Public Methods Overriding Reader
    public void close() throws IOException;
    public void mark(int readAheadLimit) throws IOException;
    public boolean markSupported();                                    constant
    public int read() throws IOException;
    public int read(char[] cbuf, int off, int len) throws IOException;
    public boolean ready() throws IOException;
    public void reset() throws IOException;
    public long skip(long n) throws IOException;
}
```

Hierarchy: Object→ Reader→ BufferedReader

Subclasses: LineNumberReader

Returned By: javax.servlet.ServletRequest.getReader()

BufferedWriter
java.io

Java 1.1

PJ1.1

This class applies buffering to a character output stream, improving output efficiency by coalescing many small write requests into a single larger request. You create a BufferedWriter by specifying some other character output stream to which it sends its buffered and coalesced output. (You can also specify a buffer size at this time, although the default size is usually satisfactory.) Typically, you use this sort of buffering with a FileWriter or OutputStreamWriter. BufferedWriter defines the standard write(), flush(), and close() methods all output streams define, but it adds a newLine() method that outputs the platform-dependent line separator (usually a newline character, a carriage-return character, or both) to the stream. BufferedWriter is the character-stream analog of BufferedOutputStream.

```
public class BufferedWriter extends Writer {
// Public Constructors
    public BufferedWriter(Writer out);
    public BufferedWriter(Writer out, int sz);
// Public Instance Methods
    public void newLine() throws IOException;
// Public Methods Overriding Writer
    public void close() throws IOException;
    public void flush() throws IOException;
    public void write(int c) throws IOException;
    public void write(String s, int off, int len) throws IOException;
    public void write(char[] cbuf, int off, int len) throws IOException;
}
```

Hierarchy: Object→ Writer→ BufferedWriter

ByteArrayInputStream
java.io

Java 1.0

PJ1.1

This class is a subclass of InputStream in which input data comes from a specified array of byte values. This is useful when you want to read data in memory as if it were coming from a file, pipe, or socket. Note that the specified array of bytes is not copied when a ByteArrayInputStream is created. See also CharArrayReader.

```
public class ByteArrayInputStream extends java.io.InputStream {
// Public Constructors
    public ByteArrayInputStream(byte[ ] buf);
    public ByteArrayInputStream(byte[ ] buf, int offset, int length);
// Public Methods Overriding InputStream
    public int available();                                              synchronized
1.2 public void close() throws IOException;                              synchronized
1.1 public void mark(int readAheadLimit);
1.1 public boolean markSupported();                                         constant
    public int read();                                                  synchronized
    public int read(byte[ ] b, int off, int len);                       synchronized
    public void reset();                                                synchronized
    public long skip(long n);                                           synchronized
// Protected Instance Fields
    protected byte[ ] buf;
    protected int count;
1.1 protected int mark;
    protected int pos;
}
```

Hierarchy: Object→ java.io.InputStream→ ByteArrayInputStream

ByteArrayOutputStream   Java 1.0

java.io   PJ1.1

This class is a subclass of OutputStream in which output data is stored in an internal byte array. The internal array grows as necessary and can be retrieved with toByteArray() or toString(). The reset() method discards any data currently stored in the internal array and stores data from the beginning again. See also CharArrayWriter.

```
public class ByteArrayOutputStream extends java.io.OutputStream {
// Public Constructors
    public ByteArrayOutputStream();
    public ByteArrayOutputStream(int size);
// Public Instance Methods
    public void reset();                                                synchronized
    public int size();
    public byte[ ] toByteArray();                                       synchronized
1.1 public String toString(String enc) throws UnsupportedEncodingException;
    public void writeTo(java.io.OutputStream out) throws IOException;   synchronized
// Public Methods Overriding OutputStream
1.2 public void close() throws IOException;                             synchronized
    public void write(int b);                                          synchronized
    public void write(byte[ ] b, int off, int len);                    synchronized
// Public Methods Overriding Object
    public String toString();
// Protected Instance Fields
    protected byte[ ] buf;
    protected int count;
// Deprecated Public Methods
#   public String toString(int hibyte);
}
```

Hierarchy: Object→ java.io.OutputStream→ ByteArrayOutputStream

CharArrayReader

Java 1.1

java.io

PJ1.1

This class is a character input stream that uses a character array as the source of the characters it returns. You create a CharArrayReader by specifying the character array (or portion of an array) it is to read from. CharArrayReader defines the usual Reader methods and supports the mark() and reset() methods. Note that the character array you pass to the CharArrayReader() constructor is not copied. This means that changes you make to the elements of the array after you create the input stream affect the values read from the array. CharArrayReader is the character-array analog of ByteArrayInputStream and is similar to StringReader.

```
public class CharArrayReader extends Reader {
// Public Constructors
    public CharArrayReader(char[ ] buf);
    public CharArrayReader(char[ ] buf, int offset, int length);
// Public Methods Overriding Reader
    public void close();
    public void mark(int readAheadLimit) throws IOException;
    public boolean markSupported();                                          constant
    public int read() throws IOException;
    public int read(char[ ] b, int off, int len) throws IOException;
    public boolean ready() throws IOException;
    public void reset() throws IOException;
    public long skip(long n) throws IOException;
// Protected Instance Fields
    protected char[ ] buf;
    protected int count;
    protected int markedPos;
    protected int pos;
}
```

Hierarchy: Object→ Reader→ CharArrayReader

CharArrayWriter

Java 1.1

java.io

PJ1.1

This class is a character output stream that uses an internal character array as the destination of characters written to it. When you create a CharArrayWriter, you may optionally specify an initial size for the character array, but you do not specify the character array itself; this array is managed internally by the CharArrayWriter and grows as necessary to accommodate all the characters written to it. The toString() and toCharArray() methods return a copy of all characters written to the stream, as a string and an array of characters, respectively. CharArrayWriter defines the standard write(), flush(), and close() methods all Writer subclasses define. It also defines a few other useful methods. size() returns the number of characters that have been written to the stream. reset() resets the stream to its initial state, with an empty character array; this is more efficient than creating a new CharArrayWriter. Finally, writeTo() writes the contents of the internal character array to some other specified character stream. CharArrayWriter is the character-stream analog of ByteArrayOutputStream and is quite similar to StringWriter.

```
public class CharArrayWriter extends Writer {
// Public Constructors
    public CharArrayWriter();
    public CharArrayWriter(int initialSize);
// Public Instance Methods
    public void reset();
```

```
    public int size();
    public char[ ] toCharArray();
    public void writeTo(Writer out) throws IOException;
// Public Methods Overriding Writer
    public void close();                                                    empty
    public void flush();                                                    empty
    public void write(int c);
    public void write(char[ ] c, int off, int len);
    public void write(String str, int off, int len);
// Public Methods Overriding Object
    public String toString();
// Protected Instance Fields
    protected char[ ] buf;
    protected int count;
}
```

Hierarchy: Object→ Writer→ CharArrayWriter

CharConversionException   Java 1.1
java.io   *serializable checked PJ1.1*

Signals an error when converting bytes to characters or vice versa.

```
public class CharConversionException extends IOException {
// Public Constructors
    public CharConversionException();
    public CharConversionException(String s);
}
```

Hierarchy: Object→ Throwable(Serializable)→ Exception→ IOException→
CharConversionException

DataInput   Java 1.0
java.io   *PJ1.1*

This interface defines the methods required for streams that can read Java primitive
data types in a machine-independent binary format. It is implemented by DataInput-
Stream and RandomAccessFile. See DataInputStream for more information on the methods.

```
public interface DataInput {
// Public Instance Methods
    public abstract boolean readBoolean() throws IOException;
    public abstract byte readByte() throws IOException;
    public abstract char readChar() throws IOException;
    public abstract double readDouble() throws IOException;
    public abstract float readFloat() throws IOException;
    public abstract void readFully(byte[ ] b) throws IOException;
    public abstract void readFully(byte[ ] b, int off, int len) throws IOException;
    public abstract int readInt() throws IOException;
    public abstract String readLine() throws IOException;
    public abstract long readLong() throws IOException;
    public abstract short readShort() throws IOException;
    public abstract int readUnsignedByte() throws IOException;
    public abstract int readUnsignedShort() throws IOException;
    public abstract String readUTF() throws IOException;
    public abstract int skipBytes(int n) throws IOException;
}
```

Implementations: java.io.DataInputStream, ObjectInput, RandomAccessFile

Passed To: java.io.DataInputStream.readUTF(), java.rmi.server.UID.read()

DataInputStream   Java 1.0

java.io   PJ1.1

This class is a type of FilterInputStream that allows you to read binary representations of Java primitive data types in a portable way. Create a DataInputStream by specifying the InputStream that is to be filtered in the call to the constructor. DataInputStream reads only primitive Java types; use ObjectInputStream to read object values.

Many of the methods read and return a single Java primitive type, in binary format, from the stream. readUnsignedByte() and readUnsignedShort() read unsigned values and return them as int values, since unsigned byte and short types are not supported in Java. read() reads data into an array of bytes, blocking until at least some data is available. By contrast, readFully() reads data into an array of bytes, but blocks until all requested data becomes available. skipBytes() blocks until the specified number of bytes have been read and discarded. readLine() reads characters from the stream until it encounters a newline, a carriage return, or a newline/carriage return pair. The returned string is not terminated with a newline or carriage return. This method is deprecated as of Java 1.1; see BufferedReader for an alternative. readUTF() reads a string of Unicode text encoded in a slightly modified version of the UTF-8 transformation format. UTF-8 is an ASCII-compatible encoding of Unicode characters that is often used for the transmission and storage of Unicode text. This class uses a modified UTF-8 encoding that never contains embedded null characters.

```
public class DataInputStream extends FilterInputStream implements DataInput {
// Public Constructors
     public DataInputStream(java.io.InputStream in);
// Public Class Methods
     public static final String readUTF(DataInput in) throws IOException;
// Methods Implementing DataInput
     public final boolean readBoolean() throws IOException;
     public final byte readByte() throws IOException;
     public final char readChar() throws IOException;
     public final double readDouble() throws IOException;
     public final float readFloat() throws IOException;
     public final void readFully(byte[ ] b) throws IOException;
     public final void readFully(byte[ ] b, int off, int len) throws IOException;
     public final int readInt() throws IOException;
     public final long readLong() throws IOException;
     public final short readShort() throws IOException;
     public final int readUnsignedByte() throws IOException;
     public final int readUnsignedShort() throws IOException;
     public final String readUTF() throws IOException;
     public final int skipBytes(int n) throws IOException;
// Public Methods Overriding FilterInputStream
     public final int read(byte[ ] b) throws IOException;
     public final int read(byte[ ] b, int off, int len) throws IOException;
// Deprecated Public Methods
#    public final String readLine() throws IOException;                  Implements:DataInput
}
```

Hierarchy: Object→ java.io.InputStream→ FilterInputStream→ java.io.DataInputStream(DataInput)

Passed To: javax.swing.text.html.parser.DTD.read()

DataOutput

java.io

This interface defines the methods required for streams that can write Java primitive data types in a machine-independent binary format. It is implemented by DataOutput-Stream and RandomAccessFile. See DataOutputStream for more information on the methods.

```
public interface DataOutput {
// Public Instance Methods
    public abstract void write(byte[ ] b) throws IOException;
    public abstract void write(int b) throws IOException;
    public abstract void write(byte[ ] b, int off, int len) throws IOException;
    public abstract void writeBoolean(boolean v) throws IOException;
    public abstract void writeByte(int v) throws IOException;
    public abstract void writeBytes(String s) throws IOException;
    public abstract void writeChar(int v) throws IOException;
    public abstract void writeChars(String s) throws IOException;
    public abstract void writeDouble(double v) throws IOException;
    public abstract void writeFloat(float v) throws IOException;
    public abstract void writeInt(int v) throws IOException;
    public abstract void writeLong(long v) throws IOException;
    public abstract void writeShort(int v) throws IOException;
    public abstract void writeUTF(String str) throws IOException;
}
```

Implementations: java.io.DataOutputStream, ObjectOutput, RandomAccessFile

Passed To: java.rmi.server.UID.write()

DataOutputStream

java.io

This class is a subclass of FilterOutputStream that allows you to write Java primitive data types in a portable binary format. Create a DataOutputStream by specifying the Output-Stream that is to be filtered in the call to the constructor. DataOutputStream has methods that output only primitive types; use ObjectOutputStream to output object values.

Many of this class's methods write a single Java primitive type, in binary format, to the output stream. write() writes a single byte, an array, or a subarray of bytes. flush() forces any buffered data to be output. size() returns the number of bytes written so far. writeUTF() outputs a Java string of Unicode characters using a slightly modified version of the UTF-8 transformation format. UTF-8 is an ASCII-compatible encoding of Unicode characters that is often used for the transmission and storage of Unicode text. Except for the writeUTF() method, this class is used for binary output of data. Textual output should be done with PrintWriter (or PrintStream in Java 1.0).

```
public class DataOutputStream extends FilterOutputStream implements DataOutput {
// Public Constructors
    public DataOutputStream(java.io.OutputStream out);
// Public Instance Methods
    public final int size();
// Methods Implementing DataOutput
    public void write(int b) throws IOException;                              synchronized
    public void write(byte[ ] b, int off, int len) throws IOException;        synchronized
    public final void writeBoolean(boolean v) throws IOException;
    public final void writeByte(int v) throws IOException;
    public final void writeBytes(String s) throws IOException;
    public final void writeChar(int v) throws IOException;
```

```
    public final void writeChars(String s) throws IOException;
    public final void writeDouble(double v) throws IOException;
    public final void writeFloat(float v) throws IOException;
    public final void writeInt(int v) throws IOException;
    public final void writeLong(long v) throws IOException;
    public final void writeShort(int v) throws IOException;
    public final void writeUTF(String str) throws IOException;
// Public Methods Overriding FilterOutputStream
    public void flush() throws IOException;
// Protected Instance Fields
    protected int written;
}
```

Hierarchy: Object→ java.io.OutputStream→ FilterOutputStream→
java.io.DataOutputStream(DataOutput)

EOFException

java.io

Java 1.0

serializable checked PJ1.1

An IOException that signals the end-of-file.

```
public class EOFException extends IOException {
// Public Constructors
    public EOFException();
    public EOFException(String s);
}
```

Hierarchy: Object→ Throwable(Serializable)→ Exception→ IOException→ EOFException

Externalizable

java.io

Java 1.1

serializable PJ1.1

This interface defines the methods that must be implemented by an object that wants complete control over the way it is serialized. The writeExternal() and readExternal() methods should be implemented to write and read object data in some arbitrary format, using the methods of the DataOutput and DataInput interfaces. Externalizable objects must serialize their own fields and are also responsible for serializing the fields of their superclasses. Most objects do not need to define a custom output format and can use the Serializable interface instead of Externalizable for serialization.

```
public interface Externalizable extends Serializable {
// Public Instance Methods
    public abstract void readExternal(ObjectInput in) throws IOException, ClassNotFoundException;
    public abstract void writeExternal(ObjectOutput out) throws IOException;
}
```

Hierarchy: (Externalizable(Serializable))

Implementations: java.awt.datatransfer.DataFlavor, java.rmi.server.RemoteRef

File

java.io

Java 1.0

serializable comparable PJ1.1(opt)

This class supports a platform-independent definition of file and directory names. It also provides methods to list the files in a directory; check the existence, readability, writeability, type, size, and modification time of files and directories; make new directories; rename files and directories; delete files and directories; and create and delete temporary and lock files. The constants defined by this class are the platform-dependent directory and path-separator characters, available as a String and a char.

getName() returns the name of the File with any directory names omitted. getPath() returns the full name of the file, including the directory name. getParent() and getParentFile() return the directory that contains the File; the only difference between the two methods is that one returns a String, while the other returns a File. isAbsolute() tests whether the File is an absolute specification. If not, getAbsolutePath() returns an absolute filename created by appending the relative filename to the current working directory. getAbsolute-File() returns the equivalent absolute File object. getCanonicalPath() and getCanonicalFile() are similar methods: they return an absolute filename or File object that has been converted to its system-dependent canonical form. This can be useful when comparing two File objects to see if they refer to the same file or directory.

exists(), canWrite(), canRead(), isFile(), isDirectory(), and isHidden() perform the obvious tests on the specified File. length() returns the length of the file. lastModified() returns the modification time of the file (which should be used for comparison with other file times only and not interpreted as any particular time format). setLastModified() allows the modification time to be set; setReadOnly() makes a file or directory read-only.

list() returns the names of all entries in a directory that are not rejected by an optional FilenameFilter. listFiles() returns an array of File objects that represent all entries in a directory not rejected by an optional FilenameFilter or FileFilter. listRoots() returns an array of File objects representing all root directories on the system. On Unix systems, for example, there is typically only one root, /. On Windows systems, however, there is a different root for each drive letter: *c:*, *d:*, and *e:*, for example.

mkdir() creates a directory, and mkdirs() creates all the directories in a File specification. renameTo() renames a file or directory; delete() deletes a file or directory. Prior to Java 1.2, the File class doesn't provide any way to create a file; that task is accomplished typically with FileOutputStream. As of Java 1.2, however, two special-purpose file creation methods have been added. The static createTempFile() method returns a File object that refers to a newly created empty file with a unique name that begins with the specified prefix (which must be at least three characters long) and ends with the specified suffix. One version of this method creates the file in a specified directory, and the other creates it in the system temporary directory. Applications can use temporary files for any purpose without worrying about overwriting files belonging to other applications. The other file-creation method of Java 1.2 is createNewFile(). This instance method attempts to create a new, empty file with the name specified by the File object. If it succeeds, it returns true. However, if the file already exists, it returns false. createNewFile() works atomically, and is therefore useful for file locking and other mutual-exclusion schemes. When working with createTempFile() or createNewFile(), consider using deleteOnExit() to request that the files be deleted when the Java VM exits normally.

```
public class File implements Comparable, Serializable {
// Public Constructors
    public File(String pathname);
    public File(String parent, String child);
    public File(File parent, String child);
// Public Constants
    public static final String pathSeparator;
    public static final char pathSeparatorChar;
    public static final String separator;
    public static final char separatorChar;
// Public Class Methods
1.2 public static File createTempFile(String prefix, String suffix) throws IOException;
1.2 public static File createTempFile(String prefix, String suffix, File directory) throws IOException;
```

```
1.2 public static File[ ] listRoots( );
// Property Accessor Methods (by property name)
    public boolean isAbsolute( );
1.2 public File getAbsoluteFile( );
    public String getAbsolutePath( );
1.2 public File getCanonicalFile( ) throws IOException;
1.1 public String getCanonicalPath( ) throws IOException;
    public boolean isDirectory( );
    public boolean isFile( );
1.2 public boolean isHidden( );
    public String getName( );
    public String getParent( );
1.2 public File getParentFile( );
    public String getPath( );
// Public Instance Methods
    public boolean canRead( );
    public boolean canWrite( );
1.2 public int compareTo(File pathname);
1.2 public boolean createNewFile( ) throws IOException;
    public boolean delete( );
1.2 public void deleteOnExit( );
    public boolean exists( );
    public long lastModified( );
    public long length( );
    public String[ ] list( );
    public String[ ] list(FilenameFilter filter);
1.2 public File[ ] listFiles( );
1.2 public File[ ] listFiles(java.io.FileFilter filter);
1.2 public File[ ] listFiles(FilenameFilter filter);
    public boolean mkdir( );
    public boolean mkdirs( );
    public boolean renameTo(File dest);
1.2 public boolean setLastModified(long time);
1.2 public boolean setReadOnly( );
1.2 public java.net.URL toURL( ) throws java.net.MalformedURLException;
// Methods Implementing Comparable
1.2 public int compareTo(Object o);
// Public Methods Overriding Object
    public boolean equals(Object obj);
    public int hashCode( );
    public String toString( );
}
```

Hierarchy: Object→ File(Comparable, Serializable)

Passed To: Too many methods to list.

Returned By: Too many methods to list.

FileDescriptor   Java 1.0

java.io   PJ1.1

This class is a platform-independent representation of a low-level handle to an open file or socket. The static in, out, and err variables are FileDescriptor objects that represent the standard input, output, and error streams, respectively. There is no public constructor method to create a FileDescriptor object. You can obtain one with the getFD() method of FileInputStream, FileOutputStream, or RandomAccessFile.

```
public final class FileDescriptor {
// Public Constructors
     public FileDescriptor();
// Public Constants
     public static final FileDescriptor err;
     public static final FileDescriptor in;
     public static final FileDescriptor out;
// Public Instance Methods
1.1 public void sync() throws SyncFailedException;                          native
     public boolean valid();
}
```

Passed To: FileInputStream.FileInputStream(), FileOutputStream.FileOutputStream(),
FileReader.FileReader(), FileWriter.FileWriter(), SecurityManager.{checkRead(), checkWrite()}

Returned By: FileInputStream.getFD(), FileOutputStream.getFD(), RandomAccessFile.getFD(),
java.net.DatagramSocketImpl.getFileDescriptor(), java.net.SocketImpl.getFileDescriptor()

Type Of: FileDescriptor.{err, in, out}, java.net.DatagramSocketImpl.fd, java.net.SocketImpl.fd

FileFilter   Java 1.2
java.io

This interface defines an accept() method that filters a list of files. You can list the contents of a directory by calling the listFiles() method of the File object that represents the
desired directory. If you want a filtered listing, such as a listing of files but not subdirectories or a listing of files whose names end in *.class*, you can pass a FileFilter object to
listFiles(). For each entry in the directory, a File object is passed to the accept() method. If
accept() returns true, that File is included in the return value of listFiles(). If accept() returns
false, that entry is not included in the listing. FileFilter is new in Java 1.2. Use Filename-
Filter if compatibility with previous releases of Java is required or if you prefer to filter
filenames (i.e., String objects) rather than File objects.

```
public interface FileFilter {
// Public Instance Methods
     public abstract boolean accept(File pathname);
}
```

Passed To: File.listFiles()

FileInputStream   Java 1.0
java.io   PJ1.1(opt)

This class is a subclass of InputStream that reads bytes from a file specified by name or
by a File or FileDescriptor object. read() reads a byte or array of bytes from the file. It
returns −1 when the end-of-file has been reached. To read binary data, you typically
use this class in conjunction with a BufferedInputStream and DataInputStream. To read text,
you typically use it with an InputStreamReader and BufferedReader. Call close() to close the
file when input is no longer needed.

```
public class FileInputStream extends java.io.InputStream {
// Public Constructors
     public FileInputStream(String name) throws FileNotFoundException;
     public FileInputStream(FileDescriptor fdObj);
     public FileInputStream(File file) throws FileNotFoundException;
// Public Instance Methods
     public final FileDescriptor getFD() throws IOException;
```

```
// Public Methods Overriding InputStream
    public int available() throws IOException;                                        native
    public void close() throws IOException;                                           native
    public int read() throws IOException;                                             native
    public int read(byte[ ] b) throws IOException;
    public int read(byte[ ] b, int off, int len) throws IOException;
    public long skip(long n) throws IOException;                                      native
// Protected Methods Overriding Object
    protected void finalize() throws IOException;
}
```

Hierarchy: Object→ java.io.InputStream→ FileInputStream

FilenameFilter   Java 1.0

java.io   PJ1.1(opt)

This interface defines the accept() method that must be implemented by any object that
filters filenames (i.e., selects a subset of filenames from a list of filenames). There are
no standard FilenameFilter classes implemented by Java, but objects that implement this
interface are used by the java.awt.FileDialog object and the File.list() method. A typical FilenameFilter object might check that the specified File represents a file (not a directory), is
readable (and possibly writable as well), and that its name ends with some desired
extension.

```
public interface FilenameFilter {
// Public Instance Methods
    public abstract boolean accept(File dir, String name);
}
```

Passed To: java.awt.FileDialog.setFilenameFilter(), java.awt.peer.FileDialogPeer.setFilenameFilter(),
File.{list(), listFiles()}

Returned By: java.awt.FileDialog.getFilenameFilter()

FileNotFoundException   Java 1.0

java.io   serializable checked PJ1.1(opt)

An IOException that signals that a specified file cannot be found.

```
public class FileNotFoundException extends IOException {
// Public Constructors
    public FileNotFoundException();
    public FileNotFoundException(String s);
}
```

Hierarchy: Object→ Throwable(Serializable)→ Exception→ IOException→ FileNotFoundException

Thrown By: FileInputStream.FileInputStream(), FileOutputStream.FileOutputStream(),
FileReader.FileReader(), RandomAccessFile.RandomAccessFile()

FileOutputStream   Java 1.0

java.io   PJ1.1(opt)

This class is a subclass of OutputStream that writes data to a file specified by name or by
a File or FileDescriptor object. write() writes a byte or array of bytes to the file. To write
binary data, you·typically use this class in conjunction with a BufferedOutputStream and a
DataOutputStream. To write text, you typically use it with a PrintWriter, BufferedWriter and an
OutputStreamWriter. Use close() to close a FileOutputStream when no further output will be
written to it.

```
public class FileOutputStream extends java.io.OutputStream {
// Public Constructors
   public FileOutputStream(FileDescriptor fdObj);
   public FileOutputStream(String name) throws FileNotFoundException;
   public FileOutputStream(File file) throws FileNotFoundException;
1.1 public FileOutputStream(String name, boolean append) throws FileNotFoundException;
// Public Instance Methods
   public final FileDescriptor getFD() throws IOException;
// Public Methods Overriding OutputStream
   public void close() throws IOException;                                        native
   public void write(int b) throws IOException;                                   native
   public void write(byte[] b) throws IOException;
   public void write(byte[] b, int off, int len) throws IOException;
// Protected Methods Overriding Object
   protected void finalize() throws IOException;
}
```

Hierarchy: Object→ java.io.OutputStream→ FileOutputStream

FilePermission

Java 1.2

java.io

serializable permission

This class is a java.security.Permission that governs access to the local filesystem. A FilePermission has a name, or target, which specifies what file or files it pertains to, and a comma-separated list of actions that may be performed on the file or files. The supported actions are read, write, delete, and execute. Read and write permission are required by any methods that read or write a file. Delete permission is required by File.delete(), and execute permission is required by Runtime.exec().

The name of a FilePermission may be as simple as a file or directory name. FilePermission also supports the use of certain wildcards, however, to specify a permission that applies to more than one file. If the name of the FilePermission is a directory name followed by /* (* on Windows platforms), it specifies all files in the named directory. If the name is a directory name followed by /- (\- on Windows), it specifies all files in the directory, and, recursively, all files in all subdirectories. A * alone specifies all files in the current directory, and a - alone specifies all files in or beneath the current directory. Finally, the special name <<ALL FILES>> matches all files anywhere in the filesystem.

Applications do not need to use this class directly. Programmers writing system-level code and system administrators configuring security policies may need to use it, however. Be very careful when granting any types of FilePermission. Restricting access (especially write access) to files is one of the cornerstones of the Java security model with regard to untrusted code.

```
public final class FilePermission extends java.security.Permission implements Serializable {
// Public Constructors
   public FilePermission(String path, String actions);
// Public Methods Overriding Permission
   public boolean equals(Object obj);
   public String getActions();
   public int hashCode();
   public boolean implies(java.security.Permission p);
   public java.security.PermissionCollection newPermissionCollection();
}
```

Hierarchy: Object→ java.security.Permission(java.security.Guard, Serializable)→ FilePermission(Serializable)

FileReader   Java 1.1
java.io   *PJ1.1(opt)*

FileReader is a convenience subclass of InputStreamReader that is useful when you want to read text (as opposed to binary data) from a file. You create a FileReader by specifying the file to be read in any of three possible forms. The FileReader constructor internally creates a FileInputStream to read bytes from the specified file and uses the functionality of its superclass, InputStreamReader, to convert those bytes from characters in the local encoding to the Unicode characters used by Java. Because FileReader is a trivial subclass of InputStreamReader, it does not define any read() methods or other methods of its own. Instead, it inherits all its methods from its superclass. If you want to read Unicode characters from a file that uses some encoding other than the default encoding for the locale, you must explicitly create your own InputStreamReader to perform the byte-to-character conversion.

```
public class FileReader extends InputStreamReader {
// Public Constructors
    public FileReader(FileDescriptor fd);
    public FileReader(File file) throws FileNotFoundException;
    public FileReader(String fileName) throws FileNotFoundException;
}
```

Hierarchy: Object→ Reader→ InputStreamReader→ FileReader

FileWriter   Java 1.1
java.io   *PJ1.1(opt)*

FileWriter is a convenience subclass of OutputStreamWriter that is useful when you want to write text (as opposed to binary data) to a file. You create a FileWriter by specifying the file to be written to and, optionally, whether the data should be appended to the end of an existing file instead of overwriting that file. The FileWriter class creates an internal FileOutputStream to write bytes to the specified file and uses the functionality of its superclass, OutputStreamWriter, to convert the Unicode characters written to the stream into bytes using the default encoding of the default locale. (If you want to use an encoding other than the default, you cannot use FileWriter; in that case you must create your own OutputStreamWriter and FileOutputStream.) Because FileWriter is a trivial subclass of OutputStreamWriter, it does not define any methods of its own, but simply inherits them from its superclass.

```
public class FileWriter extends OutputStreamWriter {
// Public Constructors
    public FileWriter(File file) throws IOException;
    public FileWriter(FileDescriptor fd);
    public FileWriter(String fileName) throws IOException;
    public FileWriter(String fileName, boolean append) throws IOException;
}
```

Hierarchy: Object→ Writer→ OutputStreamWriter→ FileWriter

FilterInputStream   Java 1.0
java.io   *PJ1.1*

This class provides method definitions required to filter data obtained from the Input-Stream specified when the FilterInputStream is created. It must be subclassed to perform some sort of filtering operation and cannot be instantiated directly. See the subclasses BufferedInputStream, DataInputStream, and PushbackInputStream.

```
public class FilterInputStream extends java.io.InputStream {
// Protected Constructors
    protected FilterInputStream(java.io.InputStream in);
// Public Methods Overriding InputStream
    public int available() throws IOException;
    public void close() throws IOException;
    public void mark(int readlimit);                                      synchronized
    public boolean markSupported();
    public int read() throws IOException;
    public int read(byte[ ] b) throws IOException;
    public int read(byte[ ] b, int off, int len) throws IOException;
    public void reset() throws IOException;                               synchronized
    public long skip(long n) throws IOException;
// Protected Instance Fields
    protected java.io.InputStream in;
}
```

Hierarchy: Object→ java.io.InputStream→ FilterInputStream

Subclasses: BufferedInputStream, java.io.DataInputStream, LineNumberInputStream, PushbackInputStream, java.security.DigestInputStream, java.util.zip.CheckedInputStream, java.util.zip.InflaterInputStream, javax.crypto.CipherInputStream, javax.swing.ProgressMonitorInputStream

FilterOutputStream
java.io

Java 1.0
PJ1.1

This class provides method definitions required to filter the data to be written to the OutputStream specified when the FilterOutputStream is created. It must be subclassed to perform some sort of filtering operation and may not be instantiated directly. See the subclasses BufferedOutputStream and DataOutputStream.

```
public class FilterOutputStream extends java.io.OutputStream {
// Public Constructors
    public FilterOutputStream(java.io.OutputStream out);
// Public Methods Overriding OutputStream
    public void close() throws IOException;
    public void flush() throws IOException;
    public void write(int b) throws IOException;
    public void write(byte[ ] b) throws IOException;
    public void write(byte[ ] b, int off, int len) throws IOException;
// Protected Instance Fields
    protected java.io.OutputStream out;
}
```

Hierarchy: Object→ java.io.OutputStream→ FilterOutputStream

Subclasses: BufferedOutputStream, java.io.DataOutputStream, PrintStream, java.security.DigestOutputStream, java.util.zip.CheckedOutputStream, java.util.zip.DeflaterOutputStream, javax.crypto.CipherOutputStream

FilterReader
java.io

Java 1.1
PJ1.1

This abstract class is intended to act as a superclass for character input streams that read data from some other character input stream, filter it in some way, and then return the filtered data when a read() method is called. FilterReader is declared abstract so that it cannot be instantiated. But none of its methods are themselves abstract: they all simply call the requested operation on the input stream passed to the FilterReader() constructor. If you were allowed to instantiate a FilterReader, you'd find that it is a null filter (i.e., it simply reads characters from the specified input stream and returns them without any kind of filtering).

Because FilterReader implements a null filter, it is an ideal superclass for classes that want to implement simple filters but do not want to override all the methods of Reader. In order to create your own filtered character input stream, you should subclass Filter-Reader and override both its read() methods to perform the desired filtering operation. Note that you can implement one of the read() methods in terms of the other, and thus only implement the filtration once. Recall that the other read() methods defined by Reader are implemented in terms of these methods, so you do not need to override those. In some cases, you may need to override other methods of FilterReader and provide methods or constructors that are specific to your subclass. FilterReader is the character-stream analog to FilterInputStream.

```
public abstract class FilterReader extends Reader {
// Protected Constructors
    protected FilterReader(Reader in);
// Public Methods Overriding Reader
    public void close() throws IOException;
    public void mark(int readAheadLimit) throws IOException;
    public boolean markSupported();
    public int read() throws IOException;
    public int read(char[] cbuf, int off, int len) throws IOException;
    public boolean ready() throws IOException;
    public void reset() throws IOException;
    public long skip(long n) throws IOException;
// Protected Instance Fields
    protected Reader in;
}
```

Hierarchy: Object→ Reader→ FilterReader

Subclasses: PushbackReader

FilterWriter
Java 1.1

java.io
PJ1.1

This abstract class is intended to act as a superclass for character output streams that filter the data written to them before writing it to some other character output stream. FilterWriter is declared abstract so that it cannot be instantiated. But none of its methods are themselves abstract: they all simply invoke the corresponding method on the output stream that was passed to the FilterWriter constructor. If you were allowed to instantiate a FilterWriter object, you'd find that it acts as a null filter (i.e., it simply passes the characters written to it along, without any filtration).

Because FilterWriter implements a null filter, it is an ideal superclass for classes that want to implement simple filters without having to override all of the methods of Writer. In order to create your own filtered character output stream, you should subclass Filter-Writer and override all its write() methods to perform the desired filtering operation. Note that you can implement two of the write() methods in terms of the third and thus implement your filtering algorithm only once. In some cases, you may want to override other Writer methods and add other methods or constructors that are specific to your subclass. FilterWriter is the character-stream analog of FilterOutputStream.

```
public abstract class FilterWriter extends Writer {
// Protected Constructors
     protected FilterWriter(Writer out);
// Public Methods Overriding Writer
     public void close() throws IOException;
     public void flush() throws IOException;
     public void write(int c) throws IOException;
     public void write(char[ ] cbuf, int off, int len) throws IOException;
     public void write(String str, int off, int len) throws IOException;
// Protected Instance Fields
     protected Writer out;
}
```

Hierarchy: Object→ Writer→ FilterWriter

InputStream

java.io

This abstract class is the superclass of all input streams. It defines the basic input methods all input stream classes provide. read() reads a single byte or an array (or subarray) of bytes. It returns the byte read, the number of bytes read, or −1 if the end-of-file has been reached. skip() skips a specified number of bytes of input. available() returns the number of bytes that can be read without blocking. close() closes the input stream and frees up any system resources associated with it. The stream should not be used after close() has been called.

If markSupported() returns true for a given InputStream, that stream supports mark() and reset() methods. mark() marks the current position in the input stream so that reset() can return to that position (as long as no more than the specified number of bytes have been read between the calls to mark() and reset()). See also Reader.

```
public abstract class InputStream {
// Public Constructors
     public InputStream();
// Public Instance Methods
     public int available() throws IOException;                          constant
     public void close() throws IOException;                                empty
     public void mark(int readlimit);                             synchronized empty
     public boolean markSupported();                                     constant
     public abstract int read() throws IOException;
     public int read(byte[ ] b) throws IOException;
     public int read(byte[ ] b, int off, int len) throws IOException;
     public void reset() throws IOException;                          synchronized
     public long skip(long n) throws IOException;
}
```

Subclasses: ByteArrayInputStream, FileInputStream, FilterInputStream, ObjectInputStream, PipedInputStream, SequenceInputStream, StringBufferInputStream, javax.servlet.ServletInputStream, org.omg.CORBA.portable.InputStream

Passed To: Too many methods to list.

Returned By: Too many methods to list.

Type Of: FilterInputStream.in, System.in

InputStreamReader
java.io

Java 1.1
PJ1.1

This class is a character input stream that uses a byte input stream as its data source. It reads bytes from a specified InputStream and translates them into Unicode characters according to a particular platform- and locale-dependent character encoding. This is an important internationalization feature in Java 1.1 and later. InputStreamReader supports the standard Reader methods. It also has a getEncoding() method that returns the name of the encoding being used to convert bytes to characters.

When you create an InputStreamReader, you specify an InputStream from which the Input-StreamReader is to read bytes and, optionally, the name of the character encoding used by those bytes. If you do not specify an encoding name, the InputStreamReader uses the default encoding for the default locale, which is usually the correct thing to do.

```
public class InputStreamReader extends Reader {
// Public Constructors
    public InputStreamReader(java.io.InputStream in);
    public InputStreamReader(java.io.InputStream in, String enc) throws UnsupportedEncodingException;
// Public Instance Methods
    public String getEncoding();
// Public Methods Overriding Reader
    public void close() throws IOException;
    public int read() throws IOException;
    public int read(char[] cbuf, int off, int len) throws IOException;
    public boolean ready() throws IOException;
}
```

Hierarchy: Object→ Reader→ InputStreamReader

Subclasses: FileReader

InterruptedIOException
java.io

Java 1.0
serializable checked PJ1.1

An IOException that signals that an input or output operation was interrupted. The bytes-Transferred field contains the number of bytes read or written before the operation was interrupted.

```
public class InterruptedIOException extends IOException {
// Public Constructors
    public InterruptedIOException();
    public InterruptedIOException(String s);
// Public Instance Fields
    public int bytesTransferred;
}
```

Hierarchy: Object→ Throwable(Serializable)→ Exception→ IOException→ InterruptedIOException

InvalidClassException
java.io

Java 1.1
serializable checked PJ1.1

Signals that the serialization mechanism has encountered one of several possible problems with the class of an object that is being serialized or deserialized. The classname field should contain the name of the class in question, and the getMessage() method is overridden to return this class name with the message.

```
public class InvalidClassException extends ObjectStreamException {
// Public Constructors
    public InvalidClassException(String reason);
    public InvalidClassException(String cname, String reason);
// Public Methods Overriding Throwable
    public String getMessage();
// Public Instance Fields
    public String classname;
}
```

Hierarchy: Object→ Throwable(Serializable)→ Exception→ IOException→ ObjectStreamException→ InvalidClassException

InvalidObjectException
Java 1.1

java.io
serializable checked PJ1.1

This exception should be thrown by the validateObject() method of an object that implements the ObjectInputValidation interface when a deserialized object fails an input validation test for any reason.

```
public class InvalidObjectException extends ObjectStreamException {
// Public Constructors
    public InvalidObjectException(String reason);
}
```

Hierarchy: Object→ Throwable(Serializable)→ Exception→ IOException→ ObjectStreamException→ InvalidObjectException

Thrown By: java.awt.font.TextAttribute.readResolve(), ObjectInputStream.registerValidation(), ObjectInputValidation.validateObject(), java.text.AttributedCharacterIterator.Attribute.readResolve()

IOException
Java 1.0

java.io
serializable checked PJ1.1

Signals that an exceptional condition has occurred during input or output. This class has several more specific subclasses. See EOFException, FileNotFoundException, InterruptedIOException, and UTFDataFormatException.

```
public class IOException extends Exception {
// Public Constructors
    public IOException();
    public IOException(String s);
}
```

Hierarchy: Object→ Throwable(Serializable)→ Exception→ IOException

Subclasses: CharConversionException, EOFException, FileNotFoundException, InterruptedIOException, ObjectStreamException, SyncFailedException, UnsupportedEncodingException, UTFDataFormatException, java.net.MalformedURLException, java.net.ProtocolException, java.net.SocketException, java.net.UnknownHostException, java.net.UnknownServiceException, java.rmi.RemoteException, java.util.zip.ZipException, javax.swing.text.ChangedCharSetException

Passed To: java.awt.print.PrinterIOException.PrinterIOException()

Returned By: java.awt.print.PrinterIOException.getIOException()

Thrown By: Too many methods to list.

LineNumberInputStream

Java 1.0; Deprecated in Java 1.1

java.io

PJ1.1

This class is a FilterInputStream that keeps track of the number of lines of data that have been read. getLineNumber() returns the current line number; setLineNumber() sets the line number of the current line. Subsequent lines are numbered starting from that number. This class is deprecated as of Java 1.1 because it does not properly convert bytes to characters. Use LineNumberReader instead.

```
public class LineNumberInputStream extends FilterInputStream {
// Public Constructors
    public LineNumberInputStream(java.io.InputStream in);
// Public Instance Methods
    public int getLineNumber();
    public void setLineNumber(int lineNumber);
// Public Methods Overriding FilterInputStream
    public int available() throws IOException;
    public void mark(int readlimit);
    public int read() throws IOException;
    public int read(byte[ ] b, int off, int len) throws IOException;
    public void reset() throws IOException;
    public long skip(long n) throws IOException;
}
```

Hierarchy: Object→ java.io.InputStream→ FilterInputStream→ LineNumberInputStream

LineNumberReader

Java 1.1

java.io

PJ1.1

This class is a character input stream that keeps track of the number of lines of text that have been read from it. It supports the usual Reader methods and also the readLine() method introduced by its superclass. In addition to these methods, you can call getLine-Number() to query the number of lines set so far. You can also call setLineNumber() to set the line number for the current line. Subsequent lines are numbered sequentially from this specified starting point. This class is a character-stream analog to LineNumberInput-Stream, which has been deprecated as of Java 1.1.

```
public class LineNumberReader extends BufferedReader {
// Public Constructors
    public LineNumberReader(Reader in);
    public LineNumberReader(Reader in, int sz);
// Public Instance Methods
    public int getLineNumber();
    public void setLineNumber(int lineNumber);
// Public Methods Overriding BufferedReader
    public void mark(int readAheadLimit) throws IOException;
    public int read() throws IOException;
    public int read(char[ ] cbuf, int off, int len) throws IOException;
    public String readLine() throws IOException;
    public void reset() throws IOException;
    public long skip(long n) throws IOException;
}
```

Hierarchy: Object→ Reader→ BufferedReader→ LineNumberReader

NotActiveException

Java 1.1

java.io   *serializable checked PJ1.1*

This exception is thrown in several circumstances. It indicates that the invoked method was not invoked at the right time or in the correct context. Typically, it means that an ObjectOutputStream or ObjectInputStream is not currently active and therefore the requested operation cannot be performed.

```
public class NotActiveException extends ObjectStreamException {
// Public Constructors
    public NotActiveException();
    public NotActiveException(String reason);
}
```

Hierarchy: Object→ Throwable(Serializable)→ Exception→ IOException→ ObjectStreamException→ NotActiveException

Thrown By: ObjectInputStream.{defaultReadObject(), readFields(), registerValidation()}

NotSerializableException

Java 1.1

java.io   *serializable checked PJ1.1*

Signals that an object cannot be serialized. It is thrown when serialization is attempted on an instance of a class that does not implement the Serializable interface. Note that it is also thrown when an attempt is made to serialize a Serializable object that refers to (or contains) an object that is not Serializable. A subclass of a class that is Serializable can prevent itself from being serialized by throwing this exception from its writeObject() and/or readObject() methods.

```
public class NotSerializableException extends ObjectStreamException {
// Public Constructors
    public NotSerializableException();
    public NotSerializableException(String classname);
}
```

Hierarchy: Object→ Throwable(Serializable)→ Exception→ IOException→ ObjectStreamException→ NotSerializableException

ObjectInput

Java 1.1

java.io   *PJ1.1*

This interface extends the DataInput interface and adds methods for deserializing objects and reading bytes and arrays of bytes.

```
public interface ObjectInput extends DataInput {
// Public Instance Methods
    public abstract int available() throws IOException;
    public abstract void close() throws IOException;
    public abstract int read() throws IOException;
    public abstract int read(byte[ ] b) throws IOException;
    public abstract int read(byte[ ] b, int off, int len) throws IOException;
    public abstract Object readObject() throws ClassNotFoundException, IOException;
    public abstract long skip(long n) throws IOException;
}
```

Hierarchy: (ObjectInput(DataInput))

Implementations: ObjectInputStream

Passed To: java.awt.datatransfer.DataFlavor.readExternal(), Externalizable.readExternal(), java.rmi.server.ObjID.read()

Returned By: java.rmi.server.RemoteCall.getInputStream()

ObjectInputStream

java.io

ObjectInputStream deserializes objects, arrays, and other values from a stream that was previously created with an ObjectOutputStream. The readObject() method deserializes objects and arrays (which should then be cast to the appropriate type); various other methods read primitive data values from the stream. Note that only objects that implement the Serializable or Externalizable interface can be serialized and deserialized.

A class may implement its own private readObject(ObjectInputStream) method to customize the way it is deserialized. If you define such a method, there are several ObjectInput-Stream methods you can use to help you deserialize the object. defaultReadObject() is the easiest. It reads the content of the object just as an ObjectInputStream would normally do. If you wrote additional data before or after the default object contents, you should read that data before or after calling defaultReadObject(). When working with multiple versions or implementations of a class, you may have to deserialize a set of fields that do not match the fields of your class. In this case, give your class a static field named serialPersistentFields whose value is an array of ObjectStreamField objects that describe the fields to be deserialized. If you do this, your readObject() method can call readFields() to read the specified fields from the stream and return them in a ObjectInputStream.GetField object. See ObjectStreamField and ObjectInputStream.GetField for more details. Finally, you can call registerValidation() from a custom readObject() method. This method registers an ObjectInput-Validation object (typically the object being deserialized) to be notified when a complete tree of objects has been deserialized, and the original call to the readObject() method of the ObjectInputStream is about to return to its caller.

The remaining methods include miscellaneous stream-manipulation methods and several protected methods for use by subclasses that want to customize the deserialization behavior of ObjectInputStream.

```
public class ObjectInputStream extends java.io.InputStream implements ObjectInput, ObjectStreamConstants {
// Public Constructors
     public ObjectInputStream(java.io.InputStream in) throws IOException, StreamCorruptedException;
// Protected Constructors
1.2 protected ObjectInputStream() throws IOException, SecurityException;
// Inner Classes
1.2 public abstract static class GetField;
// Public Instance Methods
     public void defaultReadObject() throws IOException, ClassNotFoundException, NotActiveException;
1.2 public ObjectInputStream.GetField readFields() throws IOException, ClassNotFoundException, NotActiveException;
     public void registerValidation(ObjectInputValidation obj, int prio) throws NotActiveException,          synchronized
          InvalidObjectException;
// Methods Implementing DataInput
     public boolean readBoolean() throws IOException;
     public byte readByte() throws IOException;
     public char readChar() throws IOException;
     public double readDouble() throws IOException;
     public float readFloat() throws IOException;
     public void readFully(byte[ ] data) throws IOException;
     public void readFully(byte[ ] data, int offset, int size) throws IOException;
     public int readInt() throws IOException;
     public long readLong() throws IOException;
```

```
     public short readShort() throws IOException;
     public int readUnsignedByte() throws IOException;
     public int readUnsignedShort() throws IOException;
     public String readUTF() throws IOException;
     public int skipBytes(int len) throws IOException;
// Methods Implementing ObjectInput
     public int available() throws IOException;
     public void close() throws IOException;
     public int read() throws IOException;
     public int read(byte[] b, int off, int len) throws IOException;
     public final Object readObject() throws OptionalDataException, ClassNotFoundException, IOException;
// Protected Instance Methods
     protected boolean enableResolveObject(boolean enable) throws SecurityException;
1.3  protected ObjectStreamClass readClassDescriptor() throws IOException, ClassNotFoundException;
1.2  protected Object readObjectOverride() throws OptionalDataException, ClassNotFoundException,       constant
        IOException;
     protected void readStreamHeader() throws IOException, StreamCorruptedException;
     protected Class resolveClass(ObjectStreamClass v) throws IOException, ClassNotFoundException;
     protected Object resolveObject(Object obj) throws IOException;
1.3  protected Class resolveProxyClass(String[] interfaces) throws IOException, ClassNotFoundException;
// Deprecated Public Methods
#    public String readLine() throws IOException;                                          Implements:DataInput
}
```

Hierarchy: Object→ java.io.InputStream→ ObjectInputStream(ObjectInput(DataInput), ObjectStreamConstants))

Passed To: java.beans.beancontext.BeanContextServicesSupport.bcsPreDeserializationHook(), java.beans.beancontext.BeanContextSupport.{bcsPreDeserializationHook(), deserialize(), readChildren()}, javax.swing.text.StyleContext.{readAttributes(), readAttributeSet()}

ObjectInputStream.GetField   Java 1.2
java.io

This class holds the values of named fields read by an ObjectInputStream. It gives the programmer precise control over the deserialization process and is typically used when implementing an object with a set of fields that do not match the set of fields (and the serialization stream format) of the original implementation of the object. This class allows the implementation of a class to change without breaking serialization compatibility.

In order to use the GetField class, your class must implement a private readObject() method that is responsible for custom deserialization. Typically, when using the GetField class, you have also specified an array of ObjectStreamField objects as the value of a private static field named serialPersistentFields. This array specifies the names and types of all fields expected to be found when reading from a serialization stream. If there is no serialPersistantField field, the array of ObjectStreamField objects is created from the actual fields (excluding static and transient fields) of the class.

Within the readObject() method of your class, call the readFields() method of ObjectInputStream(). This method reads the values of all fields from the stream and stores them in an ObjectInputStream.GetField object that it returns. This GetField object is essentially a mapping from field names to field values, and you can extract the values of whatever fields you need in order to restore the proper state of the object being deserialized. The various get() methods return the values of named fields of specified types. Each method takes a default value as an argument, in case no value for the named field was present in the serialization stream. (This can happen when deserializing an object written by an earlier version of the class, for example.) Use the defaulted() method to determine whether the GetField object contains a value for the named field. If this method returns true, the named field had no value in the stream, so the get() method of the GetField object has to return the specified default value. The getObjectStreamClass() method of a GetField object returns the ObjectStreamClass object for the object being deserialized. This ObjectStreamClass can obtain the array of ObjectStreamField objects for the class.

See also ObjectOutputStream.PutField

```
public abstract static class ObjectInputStream.GetField {
// Public Constructors
    public GetField();
// Public Instance Methods
    public abstract boolean defaulted(String name) throws IOException, IllegalArgumentException;
    public abstract boolean get(String name, boolean defvalue) throws IOException, IllegalArgumentException;
    public abstract byte get(String name, byte defvalue) throws IOException, IllegalArgumentException;
    public abstract char get(String name, char defvalue) throws IOException, IllegalArgumentException;
    public abstract short get(String name, short defvalue) throws IOException, IllegalArgumentException;
    public abstract int get(String name, int defvalue) throws IOException, IllegalArgumentException;
    public abstract long get(String name, long defvalue) throws IOException, IllegalArgumentException;
    public abstract float get(String name, float defvalue) throws IOException, IllegalArgumentException;
    public abstract double get(String name, double defvalue) throws IOException, IllegalArgumentException;
    public abstract Object get(String name, Object defvalue) throws IOException, IllegalArgumentException;
    public abstract ObjectStreamClass getObjectStreamClass();
}
```

Returned By: ObjectInputStream.readFields()

ObjectInputValidation   Java 1.1
java.io   PJ1.1

A class implements this interface and defines the validateObject() method in order to validate itself when it and all the objects it depends on have been completely deserialized from an ObjectInputStream. The validateObject() method is only invoked, however, if the object is passed to ObjectInputStream.registerValidation(); this must be done from the readObject() method of the object. Note that if an object is deserialized as part of a larger object graph, its validateObject() method is not invoked until the entire graph is read, and the original call to ObjectInputStream.readObject() is about to return. validateObject() should throw an InvalidObjectException if the object fails validation. This stops object serialization, and the original call to ObjectInputStream.readObject() terminates with the InvalidObjectException exception.

```
public interface ObjectInputValidation {
// Public Instance Methods
    public abstract void validateObject() throws InvalidObjectException;
}
```

Passed To: ObjectInputStream.registerValidation()

ObjectOutput   Java 1.1
java.io   PJ1.1

This interface extends the DataOutput interface and adds methods for serializing objects and writing bytes and arrays of bytes.

```
public interface ObjectOutput extends DataOutput {
// Public Instance Methods
    public abstract void close() throws IOException;
```

```
public abstract void flush() throws IOException;
public abstract void write(byte[ ] b) throws IOException;
public abstract void write(int b) throws IOException;
public abstract void write(byte[ ] b, int off, int len) throws IOException;
public abstract void writeObject(Object obj) throws IOException;
}
```

Hierarchy: (ObjectOutput(DataOutput))

Implementations: ObjectOutputStream

Passed To: java.awt.datatransfer.DataFlavor.writeExternal(), Externalizable.writeExternal(), ObjectOutputStream.PutField.write(), java.rmi.server.ObjID.write(), java.rmi.server.RemoteRef.getRefClass()

Returned By: java.rmi.server.RemoteCall.{getOutputStream(), getResultStream()}

ObjectOutputStream
java.io

Java 1.1
PJ1.1

The ObjectOutputStream serializes objects, arrays, and other values to a stream. The writeObject() method serializes an object or array, and various other methods write primitive data values to the stream. Note that only objects that implement the Serializable or Externalizable interface can be serialized.

A class that wants to customize the way instances are serialized should declare a private writeObject(ObjectOutputStream) method. This method is invoked when an object is being serialized and can use several additional methods of ObjectOutputStream. defaultWriteObject() performs the same serialization that would happen if no writeObject() method existed. An object can call this method to serialize itself and then use other methods of ObjectOutputStream to write additional data to the serialization stream. The class must define a matching readObject() method to read that additional data, of course. When working with multiple versions or implementations of a class, you may have to serialize a set of fields that do not precisely match the fields of your class. In this case, give your class a static field named serialPersistentFields whose value is an array of ObjectStreamField objects that describe the fields to be serialized. In your writeObject() method, call putFields() to obtain an ObjectOutputStream.PutField object. Store field names and values into this object, and then call writeFields() to write them out to the serialization stream. See ObjectStreamField and ObjectOutputStream.PutField for further details.

The remaining methods of ObjectOutputStream are miscellaneous stream-manipulation methods and protected methods for use by subclasses that want to customize its serialization behavior.

```
public class ObjectOutputStream extends java.io.OutputStream implements ObjectOutput, ObjectStreamConstants {
// Public Constructors
    public ObjectOutputStream(java.io.OutputStream out) throws IOException;
// Protected Constructors
1.2 protected ObjectOutputStream() throws IOException, SecurityException;
// Inner Classes
1.2 public abstract static class PutField;
// Public Instance Methods
    public void defaultWriteObject() throws IOException;
1.2 public ObjectOutputStream.PutField putFields() throws IOException;
    public void reset() throws IOException;
1.2 public void useProtocolVersion(int version) throws IOException;
1.2 public void writeFields() throws IOException;
```

```
// Methods Implementing DataOutput
    public void writeBoolean(boolean data) throws IOException;
    public void writeByte(int data) throws IOException;
    public void writeBytes(String data) throws IOException;
    public void writeChar(int data) throws IOException;
    public void writeChars(String data) throws IOException;
    public void writeDouble(double data) throws IOException;
    public void writeFloat(float data) throws IOException;
    public void writeInt(int data) throws IOException;
    public void writeLong(long data) throws IOException;
    public void writeShort(int data) throws IOException;
    public void writeUTF(String s) throws IOException;
// Methods Implementing ObjectOutput
    public void close() throws IOException;
    public void flush() throws IOException;
    public void write(byte[ ] b) throws IOException;
    public void write(int data) throws IOException;
    public void write(byte[ ] b, int off, int len) throws IOException;
    public final void writeObject(Object obj) throws IOException;
// Protected Instance Methods
    protected void annotateClass(Class cl) throws IOException;                         empty
1.3 protected void annotateProxyClass(Class cl) throws IOException;                    empty
    protected void drain() throws IOException;
    protected boolean enableReplaceObject(boolean enable) throws SecurityException;
    protected Object replaceObject(Object obj) throws IOException;
1.3 protected void writeClassDescriptor(ObjectStreamClass classdesc) throws IOException;
1.2 protected void writeObjectOverride(Object obj) throws IOException;                 empty
    protected void writeStreamHeader() throws IOException;
}
```

Hierarchy: Object→ java.io.OutputStream → ObjectOutputStream(ObjectOutput(DataOutput), ObjectStreamConstants)

Passed To: java.awt.AWTEventMulticaster.{save(), saveInternal()}, java.beans.beancontext.BeanContextServicesSupport.bcsPreSerializationHook(), java.beans.beancontext.BeanContextSupport.{bcsPreSerializationHook(), serialize(), writeChildren()}, javax.swing.text.StyleContext.{writeAttributes(), writeAttributeSet()}

ObjectOutputStream.PutField   Java 1.2

java.io

This class holds values of named fields and allows them to be written to an ObjectOutput-Stream during the process of object serialization. It gives the programmer precise control over the serialization process and is typically used when the set of fields defined by a class do not match the set of fields (and the serialization stream format) defined by the original implementation of the class. In other words, ObjectOutputStream.PutField allows the implementation of a class to change without breaking serialization compatibility.

In order to use the PutField class, you typically define a private static serialPersistentFields field that refers to an array of ObjectStreamField objects. This array defines the set of fields written to the ObjectOutputStream, and therefore defines the serialization format. If you do not declare a serialPersistentFields field, the set of fields is all fields of the class, excluding static and transient fields.

In addition to the serialPersistentFields field, your class must also define a private writeObject() method that is responsible for the custom serialization of your class. In this method, call the putFields() method of ObjectOutputStream to obtain an ObjectOutput-Stream.PutField object. Once you have this object, use its various put() methods to specify the names and values of the field to be written out. The set of named fields should match those specified by serialPersistentFields. You may specify the fields in any order; the PutField class is responsible for writing them out in the correct order. Once you have specified the values of all fields, call the write() method of your PutField object in order to write the field values out to the serialization stream.

To reverse this custom serialization process, see ObjectInputStream.GetField.

```
public abstract static class ObjectOutputStream.PutField {
// Public Constructors
    public PutField();
// Public Instance Methods
    public abstract void put(String name, long value);
    public abstract void put(String name, int value);
    public abstract void put(String name, float value);
    public abstract void put(String name, Object value);
    public abstract void put(String name, double value);
    public abstract void put(String name, char value);
    public abstract void put(String name, boolean value);
    public abstract void put(String name, short value);
    public abstract void put(String name, byte value);
    public abstract void write(ObjectOutput out) throws IOException;
}
```

Returned By: ObjectOutputStream.putFields()

ObjectStreamClass

Java 1.1

java.io

serializable PJ1.1

This class represents a class that is being serialized. An ObjectStreamClass object contains the name of a class, its unique version identifier, and the name and type of the fields that constitute the serialization format for the class. getSerialVersionUID() returns a unique version identifier for the class. It returns either the value of the private serialVersionUID field of the class or a computed value that is based upon the public API of the class. In Java 1.2 and later, getFields() returns an array of ObjectStreamField objects that represent the names and types of the fields of the class to be serialized. getField() returns a single ObjectStreamField object that represents a single named field. By default, these methods use all the fields of a class except those that are static or transient. However, this default set of fields can be overridden by declaring a private serialPersistentFields field in the class. The value of this field should be the desired array of ObjectStreamField objects.

ObjectStreamClass class does not have a constructor; you should use the static lookup() method to obtain an ObjectStreamClass object for a given Class object. The forClass() instance method performs the opposite operation; it returns the Class object that corresponds to a given ObjectStreamClass. Most applications never need to use this class.

```
public class ObjectStreamClass implements Serializable {
// No Constructor
// Public Constants
1.2 public static final ObjectStreamField[ ] NO_FIELDS;
// Public Class Methods
    public static ObjectStreamClass lookup(Class cl);
// Public Instance Methods
    public Class forClass();
1.2 public ObjectStreamField getField(String name);
    public ObjectStreamField[ ] getFields();
```

```
    public String getName();
    public long getSerialVersionUID();
// Public Methods Overriding Object
    public String toString();
}
```

Hierarchy: Object → ObjectStreamClass(Serializable)

Passed To: ObjectInputStream.resolveClass(), ObjectOutputStream.writeClassDescriptor()

Returned By: ObjectInputStream.readClassDescriptor(),
ObjectInputStream.GetField.getObjectStreamClass(), ObjectStreamClass.lookup()

ObjectStreamConstants   Java 1.2

java.io

This interface defines various constants used by the Java object-serialization mechanism. Two important constants are PROTOCOL_VERSION_1 and PROTOCOL_VERSION_2, which specify the version of the serialization protocol to use. In Java 1.2, you can pass either of these values to the useProtocolVersion() method of an ObjectOutputStream. By default, Java 1.2 uses Version 2 of the protocol, and Java 1.1 uses Version 1 when serializing objects. Java 1.2 can deserialize objects written using either version of the protocol, as can Java 1.1.7 and later. If you want to serialize an object so that it can be read by versions of Java prior to Java 1.1.7, use PROTOCOL_VERSION_1.

The other constants defined by this interface are low-level values used by the serialization protocol. You do not need to use them unless you are reimplementing the serialization mechanism yourself.

```
public interface ObjectStreamConstants {
// Public Constants
    public static final int baseWireHandle;                                      =8257536
    public static final int PROTOCOL_VERSION_1;                                        =1
    public static final int PROTOCOL_VERSION_2;                                        =2
    public static final byte SC_BLOCK_DATA;                                            =8
    public static final byte SC_EXTERNALIZABLE;                                        =4
    public static final byte SC_SERIALIZABLE;                                          =2
    public static final byte SC_WRITE_METHOD;                                          =1
    public static final short STREAM_MAGIC;                                       =-21267
    public static final short STREAM_VERSION;                                          =5
    public static final SerializablePermission SUBCLASS_IMPLEMENTATION_PERMISSION;
    public static final SerializablePermission SUBSTITUTION_PERMISSION;
    public static final byte TC_ARRAY;                                               =117
    public static final byte TC_BASE;                                                =112
    public static final byte TC_BLOCKDATA;                                           =119
    public static final byte TC_BLOCKDATALONG;                                       =122
    public static final byte TC_CLASS;                                               =118
    public static final byte TC_CLASSDESC;                                           =114
    public static final byte TC_ENDBLOCKDATA;                                        =120
    public static final byte TC_EXCEPTION;                                           =123
1.3 public static final byte TC_LONGSTRING;                                          =124
    public static final byte TC_MAX;                                                 =125
    public static final byte TC_NULL;                                                =112
    public static final byte TC_OBJECT;                                              =115
1.3 public static final byte TC_PROXYCLASSDESC;                                      =125
    public static final byte TC_REFERENCE;                                           =113
    public static final byte TC_RESET;                                               =121
```

```
   public static final byte TC_STRING;                                    =116
}
```

Implementations: ObjectInputStream, ObjectOutputStream

ObjectStreamException   Java 1.1
java.io   *serializable checked PJ1.1*

This class is the superclass of a number of more specific exception types that may be
raised in the process of serializing and deserializing objects with the ObjectOutputStream
and ObjectInputStream classes.

```
public abstract class ObjectStreamException extends IOException {
// Protected Constructors
   protected ObjectStreamException();
   protected ObjectStreamException(String classname);
}
```

Hierarchy: Object→ Throwable(Serializable)→ Exception→ IOException→ ObjectStreamException

Subclasses: InvalidClassException, InvalidObjectException, NotActiveException,
NotSerializableException, OptionalDataException, StreamCorruptedException, WriteAbortedException

Thrown By: java.awt.color.ICC_Profile.readResolve(), java.security.cert.Certificate.writeReplace(),
java.security.cert.Certificate.CertificateRep.readResolve()

ObjectStreamField   Java 1.2
java.io   *comparable*

This class represents a named field of a specified type (i.e., a specified Class). When a
class serializes itself by writing a set of fields that are different from the fields it uses in
its own implementation, it defines the set of fields to be written with an array of Object-
StreamField objects. This array should be the value of a private static field named serialPersistentFields. The methods of this class are used internally by the serialization
mechanism and are not typically used elsewhere. See also ObjectOutputStream.PutField and
ObjectInputStream.GetField.

```
public class ObjectStreamField implements Comparable {
// Public Constructors
   public ObjectStreamField(String n, Class clazz);
// Property Accessor Methods (by property name)
   public String getName();
   public int getOffset();
   public boolean isPrimitive();
   public Class getType();
   public char getTypeCode();
   public String getTypeString();
// Methods Implementing Comparable
   public int compareTo(Object o);
// Public Methods Overriding Object
   public String toString();
// Protected Instance Methods
   protected void setOffset(int offset);
}
```

Hierarchy: Object→ ObjectStreamField(Comparable)

Returned By: ObjectStreamClass.{getField(), getFields()}

Type Of: ObjectStreamClass.NO_FIELDS

OptionalDataException

java.io   *serializable checked PJ1.1*

Thrown by the readObject() method of an ObjectInputStream when it encounters primitive type data where it expects object data. Despite the exception name, this data is not optional, and object deserialization is stopped.

```
public class OptionalDataException extends ObjectStreamException {
// No Constructor
// Public Instance Fields
    public boolean eof;
    public int length;
}
```

Hierarchy: Object→ Throwable(Serializable)→ Exception→ IOException→ ObjectStreamException→ OptionalDataException

Thrown By: ObjectInputStream.{readObject(), readObjectOverride()}

OutputStream

java.io   *PJ1.1*

This abstract class is the superclass of all output streams. It defines the basic output methods all output stream classes provide. write() writes a single byte or an array (or subarray) of bytes. flush() forces any buffered output to be written. close() closes the stream and frees up any system resources associated with it. The stream may not be used once close() has been called. See also Writer.

```
public abstract class OutputStream {
// Public Constructors
    public OutputStream();
// Public Instance Methods
    public void close() throws IOException;                                    empty
    public void flush() throws IOException;                                    empty
    public abstract void write(int b) throws IOException;
    public void write(byte[ ] b) throws IOException;
    public void write(byte[ ] b, int off, int len) throws IOException;
}
```

Subclasses: ByteArrayOutputStream, FileOutputStream, FilterOutputStream, ObjectOutputStream, PipedOutputStream, javax.servlet.ServletOutputStream, org.omg.CORBA.portable.OutputStream

Passed To: Too many methods to list.

Returned By: Process.getOutputStream(), Runtime.getLocalizedOutputStream(), java.net.Socket.getOutputStream(), java.net.SocketImpl.getOutputStream(), java.net.URLConnection.getOutputStream(), java.rmi.server.LogStream.getOutputStream()

Type Of: FilterOutputStream.out

OutputStreamWriter

java.io   *PJ1.1*

This class is a character output stream that uses a byte output stream as the destination for its data. When characters are written to an OutputStreamWriter, it translates them into bytes according to a particular locale- and/or platform-specific character encoding and writes those bytes to the specified OutputStream. This is a very important international-ization feature in Java 1.1 and later. OutputStreamWriter supports the usual Writer methods.

It also has a getEncoding() method that returns the name of the encoding being used to convert characters to bytes.

When you create an OutputStreamWriter, specify the OutputStream to which it writes bytes and, optionally, the name of the character encoding that should be used to convert characters to bytes. If you do not specify an encoding name, the OutputStreamWriter uses the default encoding of the default locale, which is usually the correct thing to do.

```
public class OutputStreamWriter extends Writer {
// Public Constructors
    public OutputStreamWriter(java.io.OutputStream out);
    public OutputStreamWriter(java.io.OutputStream out, String enc) throws UnsupportedEncodingException;
// Public Instance Methods
    public String getEncoding();
// Public Methods Overriding Writer
    public void close() throws IOException;
    public void flush() throws IOException;
    public void write(int c) throws IOException;
    public void write(char[ ] cbuf, int off, int len) throws IOException;
    public void write(String str, int off, int len) throws IOException;
}
```

Hierarchy: Object→ Writer→ OutputStreamWriter

Subclasses: FileWriter

PipedInputStream

Java 1.0

java.io   *PJ1.1*

This class is an InputStream that implements one half of a pipe and is useful for communication between threads. A PipedInputStream must be connected to a PipedOutputStream object, which may be specified when the PipedInputStream is created or with the connect() method. Data read from a PipedInputStream object is received from the PipedOutputStream to which it is connected. See InputStream for information on the low-level methods for reading data from a PipedInputStream. A FilterInputStream can provide a higher-level interface for reading data from a PipedInputStream.

```
public class PipedInputStream extends java.io.InputStream {
// Public Constructors
    public PipedInputStream();
    public PipedInputStream(PipedOutputStream src) throws IOException;
// Protected Constants
1.1 protected static final int PIPE_SIZE;                                                   =1024
// Public Instance Methods
    public void connect(PipedOutputStream src) throws IOException;
// Public Methods Overriding InputStream
    public int available() throws IOException;                                       synchronized
    public void close() throws IOException;
    public int read() throws IOException;                                            synchronized
    public int read(byte[ ] b, int off, int len) throws IOException;                 synchronized
// Protected Instance Methods
    protected void receive(int b) throws IOException;                                synchronized
// Protected Instance Fields
    protected byte[ ] buffer;
    protected int in;
    protected int out;
}
```

Hierarchy: Object→ java.io.InputStream→ PipedInputStream

Passed To: PipedOutputStream.{connect(), PipedOutputStream()}

PipedOutputStream   Java 1.0
java.io   *PJ1.1*

This class is an OutputStream that implements one half of a pipe and is useful for communication between threads. A PipedOutputStream must be connected to a PipedInputStream, which may be specified when the PipedOutputStream is created or with the connect() method. Data written to the PipedOutputStream is available for reading on the PipedInputStream. See OutputStream for information on the low-level methods for writing data to a PipedOutputStream. A FilterOutputStream can provide a higher-level interface for writing data to a PipedOutputStream.

```
public class PipedOutputStream extends java.io.OutputStream {
// Public Constructors
    public PipedOutputStream();
    public PipedOutputStream(PipedInputStream snk) throws IOException;
// Public Instance Methods
    public void connect(PipedInputStream snk) throws IOException;                  synchronized
// Public Methods Overriding OutputStream
    public void close() throws IOException;
    public void flush() throws IOException;                                        synchronized
    public void write(int b) throws IOException;
    public void write(byte[ ] b, int off, int len) throws IOException;
}
```

Hierarchy: Object→ java.io.OutputStream→ PipedOutputStream

Passed To: PipedInputStream.{connect(), PipedInputStream()}

PipedReader   Java 1.1
java.io   *PJ1.1*

PipedReader is a character input stream that reads characters from a PipedWriter character output stream to which it is connected. PipedReader implements one half of a pipe and is useful for communication between two threads of an application. A PipedReader cannot be used until it is connected to a PipedWriter object, which may be passed to the PipedReader() constructor or to the connect() method. PipedReader inherits most of the methods of its superclass. See Reader for more information. PipedReader is the character-stream analog of PipedInputStream.

```
public class PipedReader extends Reader {
// Public Constructors
    public PipedReader();
    public PipedReader(PipedWriter src) throws IOException;
// Public Instance Methods
    public void connect(PipedWriter src) throws IOException;
// Public Methods Overriding Reader
    public void close() throws IOException;
1.2 public int read() throws IOException;                                          synchronized
    public int read(char[ ] cbuf, int off, int len) throws IOException;            synchronized
1.2 public boolean ready() throws IOException;                                     synchronized
}
```

Hierarchy: Object→ Reader→ PipedReader

Passed To: PipedWriter.{connect(), PipedWriter()}

PipedWriter

Java 1.1

java.io

PJ1.1

PipedWriter is a character output stream that writes characters to the PipedReader character input stream to which it is connected. PipedWriter implements one half of a pipe and is useful for communication between two threads of an application. A PipedWriter cannot be used until it is connected to a PipedReader object, which may be passed to the Piped-Writer() constructor, or to the connect() method. PipedWriter inherits most of the methods of its superclass. See Writer for more information. PipedWriter is the character-stream analog of PipedOutputStream.

```
public class PipedWriter extends Writer {
// Public Constructors
    public PipedWriter();
    public PipedWriter(PipedReader snk) throws IOException;
// Public Instance Methods
    public void connect(PipedReader snk) throws IOException;                          synchronized
// Public Methods Overriding Writer
    public void close() throws IOException;
    public void flush() throws IOException;                                           synchronized
1.2 public void write(int c) throws IOException;
    public void write(char[] cbuf, int off, int len) throws IOException;
}
```

Hierarchy: Object→ Writer→ PipedWriter

Passed To: PipedReader.{connect(), PipedReader()}

PrintStream

Java 1.0

java.io

PJ1.1

This class is a FilterOutputStream that implements a number of methods for displaying textual representations of Java primitive data types. The print() methods output standard textual representations of each data type. The println() methods do the same and follow the representations with newlines. Each method converts a Java primitive type to a String representation and outputs the resulting string. When an Object is passed to a print() or println(), it is converted to a String by calling its toString() method. PrintStream is the OutputStream type that makes it easiest to output text. As such, it is the most commonly used of the output streams. The System.out variable is a PrintStream.

Note that in Java 1.0 this class does not handle Unicode characters correctly; it discards the top 8 bits of all 16-bit characters and thus works only with Latin-1 (ISO8859-1) characters. Although this problem has been fixed as of Java 1.1, PrintStream has been superseded by PrintWriter as of Java 1.1. The constructors of this class have been deprecated, but the class itself has not, because it is still used by the System.out and System.err standard output streams.

PrintStream, and its PrintWriter replacement, output textual representations of Java data types. Use DataOutputStream to output binary representations of data.

```
public class PrintStream extends FilterOutputStream {
// Public Constructors
    public PrintStream(java.io.OutputStream out);
    public PrintStream(java.io.OutputStream out, boolean autoFlush);
// Public Instance Methods
    public boolean checkError();
```

```
    public void print(long l);
    public void print(int i);
    public void print(char c);
    public void print(float f);
    public void print(String s);
    public void print(Object obj);
    public void print(double d);
    public void print(char[ ] s);
    public void print(boolean b);
    public void println();
    public void println(long x);
    public void println(float x);
    public void println(char x);
    public void println(int x);
    public void println(String x);
    public void println(Object x);
    public void println(double x);
    public void println(char[ ] x);
    public void println(boolean x);
// Public Methods Overriding FilterOutputStream
    public void close();
    public void flush();
    public void write(int b);
    public void write(byte[ ] buf, int off, int len);
// Protected Instance Methods
1.1 protected void setError();
}
```

Hierarchy: Object→ java.io.OutputStream→ FilterOutputStream→ PrintStream

Subclasses: java.rmi.server.LogStream

Passed To: Too many methods to list.

Returned By: java.rmi.server.LogStream.getDefaultStream(), java.rmi.server.RemoteServer.getLog(), java.sql.DriverManager.getLogStream(), javax.swing.DebugGraphics.logStream()

Type Of: System.{err, out}

PrintWriter   Java 1.1
java.io   PJ1.1

This class is a character output stream that implements a number of print() and println() methods that output textual representations of primitive values and objects. When you create a PrintWriter object, you specify a character or byte output stream that it should write its characters to and, optionally, whether the PrintWriter stream should be automatically flushed whenever println() is called. If you specify a byte output stream as the destination, the PrintWriter() constructor automatically creates the necessary OutputStreamWriter object to convert characters to bytes using the default encoding.

PrintWriter implements the normal write(), flush(), and close() methods all Writer subclasses define. It is more common to use the higher-level print() and println() methods, each of which converts its argument to a string before outputting it. println() can also terminate the line (and optionally flush the buffer) after printing its argument.

The methods of PrintWriter never throw exceptions. Instead, when errors occur, they set an internal flag you can check by calling checkError(). checkError() first flushes the internal stream and then returns true if any exception has occurred while writing values to that stream. Once an error has occurred on a PrintWriter object, all subsequent calls to check-Error() return true; there is no way to reset the error flag.

PrintWriter is the character stream analog to PrintStream, which it supersedes. You can usually trivially replace any PrintStream objects in a program with PrintWriter objects. This is particularly important for internationalized programs. The only valid remaining use for the PrintStream class is for the System.out and System.err standard output streams. See PrintStream for details.

```
public class PrintWriter extends Writer {
// Public Constructors
    public PrintWriter(java.io.OutputStream out);
    public PrintWriter(Writer out);
    public PrintWriter(java.io.OutputStream out, boolean autoFlush);
    public PrintWriter(Writer out, boolean autoFlush);
// Public Instance Methods
    public boolean checkError();
    public void print(int i);
    public void print(long l);
    public void print(boolean b);
    public void print(char c);
    public void print(double d);
    public void print(char[] s);
    public void print(String s);
    public void print(float f);
    public void print(Object obj);
    public void println();
    public void println(int x);
    public void println(long x);
    public void println(boolean x);
    public void println(char x);
    public void println(String x);
    public void println(Object x);
    public void println(char[] x);
    public void println(float x);
    public void println(double x);
// Public Methods Overriding Writer
    public void close();
    public void flush();
    public void write(char[] buf);
    public void write(String s);
    public void write(int c);
    public void write(String s, int off, int len);
    public void write(char[] buf, int off, int len);
// Protected Instance Methods
    protected void setError();
// Protected Instance Fields
    protected Writer out;
}
```

Hierarchy: Object→ Writer→ PrintWriter

Passed To: Too many methods to list.

Returned By: java.sql.DriverManager.getLogWriter(), javax.servlet.ServletResponse.getWriter(), javax.sql.ConnectionPoolDataSource.getLogWriter(), javax.sql.DataSource.getLogWriter(), javax.sql.XADataSource.getLogWriter()

PushbackInputStream

Java 1.0

java.io

PJ1.1

This class is a FilterInputStream that implements a one-byte pushback buffer or, as of Java 1.1, a pushback buffer of a specified length. The unread() methods push bytes back into the stream; these bytes are the first ones read by the next call to a read() method. This class is sometimes useful when writing parsers. See also PushbackReader.

```
public class PushbackInputStream extends FilterInputStream {
// Public Constructors
    public PushbackInputStream(java.io.InputStream in);
1.1 public PushbackInputStream(java.io.InputStream in, int size);
// Public Instance Methods
    public void unread(int b) throws IOException;
1.1 public void unread(byte[ ] b) throws IOException;
1.1 public void unread(byte[ ] b, int off, int len) throws IOException;
// Public Methods Overriding FilterInputStream
    public int available() throws IOException;
1.2 public void close() throws IOException;                              synchronized
    public boolean markSupported();                                        constant
    public int read() throws IOException;
    public int read(byte[ ] b, int off, int len) throws IOException;
1.2 public long skip(long n) throws IOException;
// Protected Instance Fields
1.1 protected byte[ ] buf;
1.1 protected int pos;
}
```

Hierarchy: Object→ java.io.InputStream→ FilterInputStream→ PushbackInputStream

PushbackReader

Java 1.1

java.io

PJ1.1

This class is a character input stream that uses another input stream as its input source and adds the ability to push characters back onto the stream. This feature is often useful when writing parsers. When you create a PushbackReader stream, you specify the stream to be read from and, optionally, the size of the pushback buffer (i.e., the number of characters that may be pushed back onto the stream or unread). If you do not specify a size for this buffer, the default size is one character. PushbackReader inherits or overrides all standard Reader methods and adds three unread() methods that push a single character, an array of characters, or a portion of an array of characters back onto the stream. This class is the character stream analog of PushbackInputStream.

```
public class PushbackReader extends FilterReader {
// Public Constructors
    public PushbackReader(Reader in);
    public PushbackReader(Reader in, int size);
// Public Instance Methods
    public void unread(int c) throws IOException;
    public void unread(char[ ] cbuf) throws IOException;
    public void unread(char[ ] cbuf, int off, int len) throws IOException;
// Public Methods Overriding FilterReader
    public void close() throws IOException;
1.2 public void mark(int readAheadLimit) throws IOException;
    public boolean markSupported();                                        constant
    public int read() throws IOException;
    public int read(char[ ] cbuf, int off, int len) throws IOException;
```

```
    public boolean ready( ) throws IOException;
1.2 public void reset( ) throws IOException;
}
```

Hierarchy: Object→ Reader→ FilterReader→ PushbackReader

RandomAccessFile   Java 1.0

java.io   *PJ1.1(opt)*

This class allows you to read and write arbitrary bytes, text, and primitive Java data types from or to any specified location in a file. Because this class provides random, rather than sequential, access to files, it is neither a subclass of InputStream nor of Output-Stream, but provides an entirely independent method for reading and writing data from or to files. RandomAccessFile implements the same interfaces as DataInputStream and DataOutputStream, and thus defines the same methods for reading and writing data as those classes do.

The seek() method provides random access to the file; it is used to select the position in the file where data should be read or written. The *mode* argument to the constructor methods should be "r" for a file that is to be read-only or "rw" for a file that is to be written (and perhaps read as well).

```
public class RandomAccessFile implements DataInput, DataOutput {
// Public Constructors
    public RandomAccessFile(String name, String mode) throws FileNotFoundException;
    public RandomAccessFile(File file, String mode) throws FileNotFoundException;
// Public Instance Methods
    public void close( ) throws IOException;                                        native
    public final FileDescriptor getFD( ) throws IOException;
    public long getFilePointer( ) throws IOException;                              native
    public long length( ) throws IOException;                                       native
    public int read( ) throws IOException;                                          native
    public int read(byte[ ] b) throws IOException;
    public int read(byte[ ] b, int off, int len) throws IOException;
    public void seek(long pos) throws IOException;                                  native
1.2 public void setLength(long newLength) throws IOException;                       native
// Methods Implementing DataInput
    public final boolean readBoolean( ) throws IOException;
    public final byte readByte( ) throws IOException;
    public final char readChar( ) throws IOException;
    public final double readDouble( ) throws IOException;
    public final float readFloat( ) throws IOException;
    public final void readFully(byte[ ] b) throws IOException;
    public final void readFully(byte[ ] b, int off, int len) throws IOException;
    public final int readInt( ) throws IOException;
    public final String readLine( ) throws IOException;
    public final long readLong( ) throws IOException;
    public final short readShort( ) throws IOException;
    public final int readUnsignedByte( ) throws IOException;
    public final int readUnsignedShort( ) throws IOException;
    public final String readUTF( ) throws IOException;
    public int skipBytes(int n) throws IOException;
// Methods Implementing DataOutput
    public void write(int b) throws IOException;                                    native
    public void write(byte[ ] b) throws IOException;
    public void write(byte[ ] b, int off, int len) throws IOException;
```

```
    public final void writeBoolean(boolean v) throws IOException;
    public final void writeByte(int v) throws IOException;
    public final void writeBytes(String s) throws IOException;
    public final void writeChar(int v) throws IOException;
    public final void writeChars(String s) throws IOException;
    public final void writeDouble(double v) throws IOException;
    public final void writeFloat(float v) throws IOException;
    public final void writeInt(int v) throws IOException;
    public final void writeLong(long v) throws IOException;
    public final void writeShort(int v) throws IOException;
    public final void writeUTF(String str) throws IOException;
}
```

Hierarchy: Object→ RandomAccessFile(DataInput, DataOutput)

Reader   Java 1.1

java.io   *PJ1.1*

This abstract class is the superclass of all character input streams. It is an analog to
InputStream, which is the superclass of all byte input streams. Reader defines the basic
methods that all character output streams provide. read() returns a single character or an
array (or subarray) of characters, blocking if necessary; it returns –1 if the end of the
stream has been reached. ready() returns true if there are characters available for reading.
If ready() returns true, the next call to read() is guaranteed not to block. close() closes the
character input stream. skip() skips a specified number of characters in the input stream.
If markSupported() returns true, mark() marks a position in the stream and, if necessary,
creates a look-ahead buffer of the specified size. Future calls to reset() restore the
stream to the marked position if they occur within the specified look-ahead limit. Note
that not all stream types support this mark-and-reset functionality. To create a subclass
of Reader, you need only implement the three-argument version of read() and the close()
method. Most subclasses implement additional methods, however.

```
public abstract class Reader {
// Protected Constructors
    protected Reader();
    protected Reader(Object lock);
// Public Instance Methods
    public abstract void close() throws IOException;
    public void mark(int readAheadLimit) throws IOException;
    public boolean markSupported();                                           constant
    public int read() throws IOException;
    public int read(char[ ] cbuf) throws IOException;
    public abstract int read(char[ ] cbuf, int off, int len) throws IOException;
    public boolean ready() throws IOException;                                constant
    public void reset() throws IOException;
    public long skip(long n) throws IOException;
// Protected Instance Fields
    protected Object lock;
}
```

Subclasses: BufferedReader, CharArrayReader, FilterReader, InputStreamReader, PipedReader,
StringReader

Passed To: Too many methods to list.

Returned By: java.awt.datatransfer.DataFlavor.getReaderForText(),
java.sql.Clob.getCharacterStream(), java.sql.ResultSet.getCharacterStream(),
java.sql.SQLInput.readCharacterStream()

Type Of: FilterReader.in

SequenceInputStream
Java 1.0

java.io
PJ1.1

This class provides a way of seamlessly concatenating the data from two or more input streams. It provides an InputStream interface to a sequence of InputStream objects. Data is read from the streams in the order in which the streams are specified. When the end of one stream is reached, data is automatically read from the next stream. This class might be useful, for example, when implementing an include file facility for a parser of some sort.

```
public class SequenceInputStream extends java.io.InputStream {
// Public Constructors
    public SequenceInputStream(java.util.Enumeration e);
    public SequenceInputStream(java.io.InputStream s1, java.io.InputStream s2);
// Public Methods Overriding InputStream
1.1 public int available() throws IOException;
    public void close() throws IOException;
    public int read() throws IOException;
    public int read(byte[ ] b, int off, int len) throws IOException;
}
```

Hierarchy: Object → java.io.InputStream → SequenceInputStream

Serializable
Java 1.1

java.io
serializable PJ1.1

The Serializable interface defines no methods or constants. A class should implement this interface simply to indicate that it allows itself to be serialized and deserialized with ObjectOutputStream.writeObject() and ObjectInputStream.readObject().

Objects that need special handling during serialization or deserialization may implement one or both of the following methods. Note, however, that these methods are not part of the Serializable interface:

```
private void writeObject(java.io.ObjectOutputStream out) throws IOException;
private void readObject(java.io.ObjectInputStream in) throws IOException, ClassNotFoundException;
```

Typically, the writeObject() method performs any necessary cleanup or preparation for serialization, invokes the defaultWriteObject() method of the ObjectOutputStream to serialize the non-transient fields of the class, and optionally writes any additional data that is required. Similarly, the readObject() method typically invokes the defaultReadObject() method of the ObjectInputStream, reads any additional data written by the corresponding writeObject() method, and performs any extra initialization required by the object. The readObject() method may also register an ObjectInputValidation object to validate the object once it is completely deserialized.

```
public interface Serializable {
}
```

Implementations: Too many classes to list.

Passed To: java.security.SignedObject.SignedObject(), javax.crypto.SealedObject.SealedObject(), javax.jms.ObjectMessage.setObject(), javax.jms.Session.createObjectMessage(), org.omg.CORBA.Any.insert_Value(), org.omg.CORBA.DataOutputStream.write_Value(), org.omg.CORBA.DynAny.insert_val(), org.omg.CORBA.StreamingPolicy.marshal(), org.omg.CORBA.StringValueHelper.write_value(), org.omg.CORBA.ValueBaseHelper.{insert(), write()}, org.omg.CORBA.ValueBaseHolder.ValueBaseHolder(), org.omg.CORBA.WStringValueHelper.write_value(), org.omg.CORBA.portable.BoxedValueHelper.write_value()

Returned By: java.beans.beancontext.BeanContextSupport.getChildSerializable(),
javax.jms.ObjectMessage.getObject(), org.omg.CORBA.Any.extract_Value(),
org.omg.CORBA.DataInputStream.read_Value(), org.omg.CORBA.DynAny.get_val(),
org.omg.CORBA.StreamingPolicy.unmarshal(), org.omg.CORBA.StringValueHelper.read_value(),
org.omg.CORBA.ValueBaseHelper.{extract(), read()}, org.omg.CORBA.WStringValueHelper.read_value(),
org.omg.CORBA.portable.BoxedValueHelper.read_value(),
org.omg.CORBA.portable.ValueFactory.read_value()

Type Of: org.omg.CORBA.ValueBaseHolder.value

SerializablePermission   Java 1.2

java.io   *serializable permission*

This class is a java.security.Permission that governs the use of certain sensitive features of
serialization. SerializablePermission objects have a name, or target, but do not have an
action list. The name "enableSubclassImplementation" represents permission to serialize
and deserialize objects using subclasses of ObjectOutputStream and ObjectInputStream. This
capability is protected by a permission because malicious code can define object stream
subclasses that incorrectly serialize and deserialize objects.

The only other name supported by SerializablePermission is "enableSubstitution", which
represents permission for one object to be substituted for another during serialization
or deserialization. The ObjectOutputStream.enableReplaceObject() and ObjectInput-
Stream.enableResolveObject() methods require a permission of this type.

Applications never need to use this class. Programmers writing system-level code may
use it, and system adminstrators configuring security policies should be familiar with it.

```
public final class SerializablePermission extends java.security.BasicPermission {
// Public Constructors
    public SerializablePermission(String name);
    public SerializablePermission(String name, String actions);
}
```

Hierarchy: Object → java.security.Permission(java.security.Guard, Serializable) →
java.security.BasicPermission(Serializable) → SerializablePermission

Type Of: ObjectStreamConstants.{SUBCLASS_IMPLEMENTATION_PERMISSION,
SUBSTITUTION_PERMISSION}

StreamCorruptedException   Java 1.1

java.io   *serializable checked PJ1.1*

Signals that the data stream being read by an ObjectInputStream has been corrupted and
does not contain valid serialized object data.

```
public class StreamCorruptedException extends ObjectStreamException {
// Public Constructors
    public StreamCorruptedException();
    public StreamCorruptedException(String reason);
}
```

Hierarchy: Object → Throwable(Serializable) → Exception → IOException →
ObjectStreamException → StreamCorruptedException

Thrown By: ObjectInputStream.{ObjectInputStream(), readStreamHeader()},
java.rmi.server.RemoteCall.getResultStream()

StreamTokenizer

java.io

This class performs lexical analysis of a specified input stream and breaks the input into tokens. It can be extremely useful when writing simple parsers. nextToken() returns the next token in the stream; this is either one of the constants defined by the class (which represent end-of-file, end-of-line, a parsed floating-point number, and a parsed word) or a character value. pushBack() pushes the token back onto the stream, so that it is returned by the next call to nextToken(). The public variables sval and nval contain the string and numeric values (if applicable) of the most recently read token. They are applicable when the returned token is TT_WORD or TT_NUMBER. lineno() returns the current line number.

The remaining methods allow you to specify how tokens are recognized. wordChars() specifies a range of characters that should be treated as parts of words. whitespaceChars() specifies a range of characters that serve to delimit tokens. ordinaryChars() and ordinaryChar() specify characters that are never part of tokens and should be returned as-is. resetSyntax() makes all characters ordinary. eolIsSignificant() specifies whether end-of-line is significant. If so, the TT_EOL constant is returned for end-of-lines; otherwise, they are treated as whitespace. commentChar() specifies a character that begins a comment that lasts until the end of the line. No characters in the comment are returned. slashStarComments() and slashSlashComments() specify whether the StreamTokenizer should recognize C- and C++-style comments. If so, no part of the comment is returned as a token. quoteChar() specifies a character used to delimit strings. When a string token is parsed, the quote character is returned as the token value, and the body of the string is stored in the sval variable. lowerCaseMode() specifies whether TT_WORD tokens should be converted to all lowercase characters before being stored in sval. parseNumbers() specifies that the StreamTokenizer should recognize and return double-precision floating-point number tokens.

```
public class StreamTokenizer {
// Public Constructors
1.1 public StreamTokenizer(Reader r);
  # public StreamTokenizer(java.io.InputStream is);
// Public Constants
    public static final int TT_EOF;                               =-1
    public static final int TT_EOL;                               =10
    public static final int TT_NUMBER;                            =-2
    public static final int TT_WORD;                              =-3
// Public Instance Methods
    public void commentChar(int ch);
    public void eolIsSignificant(boolean flag);
    public int lineno();
    public void lowerCaseMode(boolean fl);
    public int nextToken() throws IOException;
    public void ordinaryChar(int ch);
    public void ordinaryChars(int low, int hi);
    public void parseNumbers();
    public void pushBack();
    public void quoteChar(int ch);
    public void resetSyntax();
    public void slashSlashComments(boolean flag);
    public void slashStarComments(boolean flag);
    public void whitespaceChars(int low, int hi);
    public void wordChars(int low, int hi);
```

```
// Public Methods Overriding Object
   public String toString( );
// Public Instance Fields
   public double nval;
   public String sval;
   public int ttype;
}
```

StringBufferInputStream   Java 1.0; Deprecated in Java 1.1

java.io   *PJ1.1*

This class is a subclass of InputStream in which input bytes come from the characters of
a specified String object. This class does not correctly convert the characters of a String-
Buffer into bytes and is deprecated as of Java 1.1. Use StringReader instead to convert
characters into bytes or use ByteArrayInputStream to read bytes from an array of bytes.

```
public class StringBufferInputStream extends java.io.InputStream {
// Public Constructors
   public StringBufferInputStream(String s);
// Public Methods Overriding InputStream
   public int available( );                                          synchronized
   public int read( );                                               synchronized
   public int read(byte[ ] b, int off, int len);                     synchronized
   public void reset( );                                             synchronized
   public long skip(long n);                                         synchronized
// Protected Instance Fields
   protected String buffer;
   protected int count;
   protected int pos;
}
```

Hierarchy: Object→ java.io.InputStream→ StringBufferInputStream

StringReader   Java 1.1

java.io   *PJ1.1*

This class is a character input stream that uses a String object as the source of the characters it returns. When you create a StringReader, you must specify the String to read
from. StringReader defines the normal Reader methods and supports mark() and reset(). If
reset() is called before mark() has been called, the stream is reset to the beginning of the
specified string. StringReader is a character stream analog to StringBufferInputStream, which
is deprecated as of Java 1.1. StringReader is also similar to CharArrayReader.

```
public class StringReader extends Reader {
// Public Constructors
   public StringReader(String s);
// Public Methods Overriding Reader
   public void close( );
   public void mark(int readAheadLimit) throws IOException;
   public boolean markSupported( );                                  constant
   public int read( ) throws IOException;
   public int read(char[ ] cbuf, int off, int len) throws IOException;
   public boolean ready( ) throws IOException;
   public void reset( ) throws IOException;
   public long skip(long ns) throws IOException;
}
```

Hierarchy: Object→ Reader→ StringReader

StringWriter

Java 1.1

java.io

PJ1.1

This class is a character output stream that uses an internal StringBuffer object as the destination of the characters written to the stream. When you create a StringWriter, you may optionally specify an initial size for the StringBuffer, but you do not specify the StringBuffer itself; it is managed internally by the StringWriter and grows as necessary to accommodate the characters written to it. StringWriter defines the standard write(), flush(), and close() methods all Writer subclasses define, as well as two methods to obtain the characters that have been written to the stream. toString() returns the contents of the internal buffer as a String, and getBuffer() returns the buffer itself. Note that getBuffer() returns a reference to the actual internal buffer, not a copy of it, so any changes you make to the buffer are reflected in subsequent calls to toString(). StringWriter is quite similar to CharArrayWriter, but does not have a byte-stream analog.

```
public class StringWriter extends Writer {
// Public Constructors
    public StringWriter();
    public StringWriter(int initialSize);
// Public Instance Methods
    public StringBuffer getBuffer();
// Public Methods Overriding Writer
    public void close() throws IOException;
    public void flush();
    public void write(int c);
    public void write(String str);
    public void write(String str, int off, int len);
    public void write(char[ ] cbuf, int off, int len);
// Public Methods Overriding Object
    public String toString();
}
```

Hierarchy: Object→ Writer→ StringWriter

SyncFailedException

Java 1.1

java.io

serializable checked PJ1.1

Signals that a call to FileDescriptor.sync() did not complete successfully.

```
public class SyncFailedException extends IOException {
// Public Constructors
    public SyncFailedException(String desc);
}
```

Hierarchy: Object→ Throwable(Serializable)→ Exception→ IOException→ SyncFailedException

Thrown By: FileDescriptor.sync()

UnsupportedEncodingException

Java 1.1

java.io

serializable checked PJ1.1

Signals that a requested character encoding is not supported by the current Java Virtual Machine.

```
public class UnsupportedEncodingException extends IOException {
// Public Constructors
   public UnsupportedEncodingException();
   public UnsupportedEncodingException(String s);
}
```

Hierarchy: Object→ Throwable(Serializable)→ Exception→ IOException→
UnsupportedEncodingException

Thrown By: ByteArrayOutputStream.toString(), InputStreamReader.InputStreamReader(),
OutputStreamWriter.OutputStreamWriter(), String.{getBytes(), String()}

UTFDataFormatException   Java 1.0
java.io   serializable checked PJ1.1

An IOException that signals that a malformed UTF-8 string has been encountered by a
class that implements the DataInput interface. UTF-8 is an ASCII-compatible transformation format for Unicode characters that is often used to store and transmit Unicode text.

```
public class UTFDataFormatException extends IOException {
// Public Constructors
   public UTFDataFormatException();
   public UTFDataFormatException(String s);
}
```

Hierarchy: Object→ Throwable(Serializable)→ Exception→ IOException→
UTFDataFormatException

WriteAbortedException   Java 1.1
java.io   serializable checked PJ1.1

Thrown when reading a stream of data that is incomplete because an exception was
thrown while it was being written. The detail field may contain the exception that terminated the output stream. The getMessage() method has been overridden to include the
message of this detail exception, if any.

```
public class WriteAbortedException extends ObjectStreamException {
// Public Constructors
   public WriteAbortedException(String s, Exception ex);
// Public Methods Overriding Throwable
   public String getMessage();
// Public Instance Fields
   public Exception detail;
}
```

Hierarchy: Object→ Throwable(Serializable)→ Exception→ IOException→
ObjectStreamException→ WriteAbortedException

Writer   Java 1.1
java.io   PJ1.1

This abstract class is the superclass of all character output streams. It is an analog to
OutputStream, which is the superclass of all byte output streams. Writer defines the basic
write(), flush(), and close() methods all character output streams provide. The five versions
of the write() method write a single character, a character array or subarray, or a string
or substring to the destination of the stream. The most general version of this
method—the one that writes a specified portion of a character array—is abstract and
must be implemented by all subclasses. By default, the other write() methods are

implemented in terms of this abstract one. The flush() method is another abstract method all subclasses must implement. It should force any output buffered by the stream to be written to its destination. If that destination is itself a character or byte output stream, it should invoke the flush() method of the destination stream as well. The close() method is also abstract. A subclass must implement this method so that it flushes and then closes the current stream and also closes whatever destination stream it is connected to. Once the stream is closed, any future calls to write() or flush() should throw an IOException.

```
public abstract class Writer {
// Protected Constructors
    protected Writer();
    protected Writer(Object lock);
// Public Instance Methods
    public abstract void close() throws IOException;
    public abstract void flush() throws IOException;
    public void write(String str) throws IOException;
    public void write(char[ ] cbuf) throws IOException;
    public void write(int c) throws IOException;
    public void write(String str, int off, int len) throws IOException;
    public abstract void write(char[ ] cbuf, int off, int len) throws IOException;
// Protected Instance Fields
    protected Object lock;
}
```

Subclasses: BufferedWriter, CharArrayWriter, FilterWriter, OutputStreamWriter, PipedWriter, PrintWriter, StringWriter

Passed To: Too many methods to list.

Returned By: javax.swing.text.AbstractWriter.getWriter()

Type Of: FilterWriter.out, PrintWriter.out

java.io

CHAPTER 12

The java.lang Package

The java.lang package contains the classes that are most central to the Java language. As you can see from Figure 12-1, the class hierarchy is broad rather than deep, which means that the classes are independent of each other.

Object is the ultimate superclass of all Java classes and is therefore at the top of all class hierarchies. Class is a class that describes a Java class. There is one Class object for each class that is loaded into Java.

Boolean, Character, Byte, Short, Integer, Long, Float, and Double are immutable class wrappers around each of the primitive Java data types. These classes are useful when you need to manipulate primitive types as objects. They also contain useful conversion and utility methods. String and StringBuffer are objects that represent strings. String is an immutable type, while StringBuffer can have its string changed in place. In Java 1.2 and later, all these classes (except StringBuffer) implement the Comparable interface, which enables sorting and searching algorithms. The Math class (and, in Java 1.3, the StrictMath class) defines static methods for various floating-point mathematical functions.

The Thread class provides support for multiple threads of control running within the same Java interpreter. The Runnable interface is implemented by objects that have a run() method that can serve as the body of a thread.

System provides low-level system methods. Runtime provides similar low-level methods, including an exec() method that, along with the Process class, defines an API for running external processes.

Throwable is the root class of the exception and error hierarchy. Throwable objects are used with the Java throw and catch statements. java.lang defines quite a few subclasses of Throwable. Exception and Error are the superclasses of all exceptions and errors. Figure 12-2 and Figure 12-3 show the class hierarchies for these core Java exceptions and errors.

AbstractMethodError	**Java 1.0**
java.lang	*serializable error PJ1.1*

Signals an attempt to invoke an abstract method.

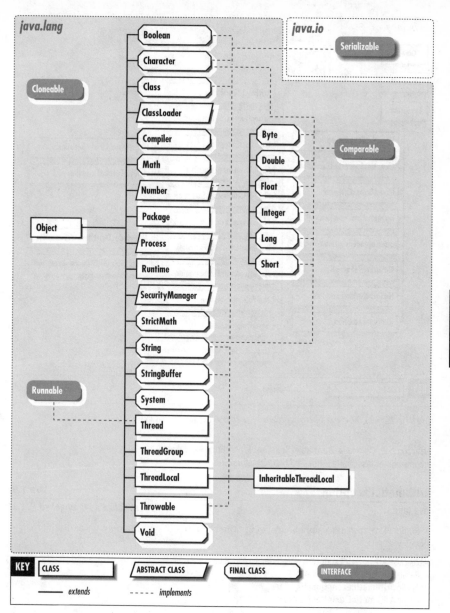

Figure 12–1: The java.lang package

```
public class AbstractMethodError extends IncompatibleClassChangeError {
// Public Constructors
    public AbstractMethodError();
    public AbstractMethodError(String s);
}
```

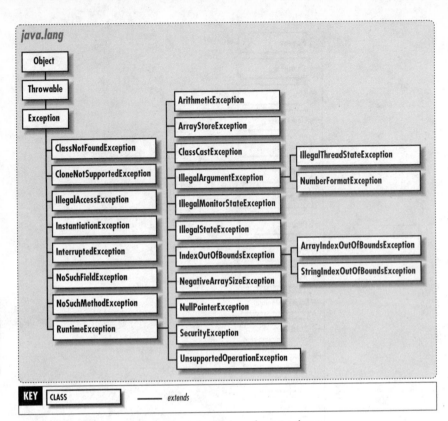

Figure 12-2: The exception classes in the java.lang package

Hierarchy: Object→ Throwable(Serializable)→ Error→ LinkageError→
IncompatibleClassChangeError→ AbstractMethodError

ArithmeticException

java.lang

Java 1.0

serializable unchecked PJ1.1

A RuntimeException that signals an exceptional arithmetic condition, such as integer division by zero.

```
public class ArithmeticException extends RuntimeException {
// Public Constructors
   public ArithmeticException();
   public ArithmeticException(String s);
}
```

Hierarchy: Object→ Throwable(Serializable)→ Exception→ RuntimeException→
ArithmeticException

ArrayIndexOutOfBoundsException

java.lang

Java 1.0

serializable unchecked PJ1.1

Signals that an array index less than zero or greater than or equal to the array size has been used.

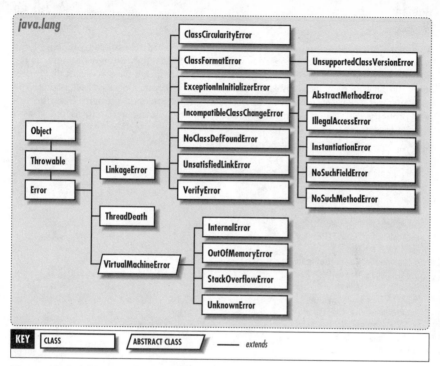

Figure 12-3: The error classes in the java.lang package

```
public class ArrayIndexOutOfBoundsException extends IndexOutOfBoundsException {
// Public Constructors
   public ArrayIndexOutOfBoundsException();
   public ArrayIndexOutOfBoundsException(String s);
   public ArrayIndexOutOfBoundsException(int index);
}
```

Hierarchy: Object→ Throwable(Serializable)→ Exception→ RuntimeException→
IndexOutOfBoundsException→ ArrayIndexOutOfBoundsException

Thrown By: Too many methods to list.

ArrayStoreException

Java 1.0

java.lang

serializable unchecked PJ1.1

Signals an attempt to store the wrong type of object into an array.

```
public class ArrayStoreException extends RuntimeException {
// Public Constructors
   public ArrayStoreException();
   public ArrayStoreException(String s);
}
```

Hierarchy: Object→ Throwable(Serializable)→ Exception→ RuntimeException→
ArrayStoreException

Boolean

java.lang

This class provides an immutable object wrapper around the boolean primitive type. Note that the TRUE and FALSE constants are Boolean objects; they are not the same as the true and false boolean values. As of Java 1.1, this class defines a Class constant that represents the boolean type. booleanValue() returns the boolean value of a Boolean object. The class method getBoolean() retrieves the boolean value of a named property from the system property list. The class method valueOf() parses a string and returns the boolean value it represents.

```
public final class Boolean implements Serializable {
// Public Constructors
    public Boolean(boolean value);
    public Boolean(String s);
// Public Constants
    public static final Boolean FALSE;
    public static final Boolean TRUE;
1.1 public static final Class TYPE;
// Public Class Methods
    public static boolean getBoolean(String name);
    public static Boolean valueOf(String s);
// Public Instance Methods
    public boolean booleanValue();
// Public Methods Overriding Object
    public boolean equals(Object obj);
    public int hashCode();
    public String toString();
}
```

Hierarchy: Object→ Boolean(Serializable)

Passed To: javax.swing.DefaultDesktopManager.setWasIcon()

Returned By: Boolean.valueOf(), javax.swing.filechooser.FileView.isTraversable()

Type Of: java.awt.font.TextAttribute.{RUN_DIRECTION_LTR, RUN_DIRECTION_RTL, STRIKETHROUGH_ON, SWAP_COLORS_ON}, Boolean.{FALSE, TRUE}

Byte

java.lang

This class provides an object wrapper around the byte primitive type. It defines useful constants for the minimum and maximum values that can be stored by the byte type and a Class object constant that represents the byte type. It also provides various methods for converting Byte values to and from strings and other numeric types.

Most of the static methods of this class can convert a String to a Byte object or a byte value: the four parseByte() and valueOf() methods parse a number from the specified string using an optionally specified radix and return it in one of these two forms. The decode() method parses a byte specified in base 10, base 8, or base 16 and returns it as a Byte. If the string begins with "0x" or "#", it is interpreted as a hexadecimal number. If it begins with "0", it is interpreted as an octal number. Otherwise, it is interpreted as a decimal number.

Note that this class has two toString() methods. One is static and converts a byte primitive value to a string; the other is the usual toString() method that converts a Byte object to a string. Most of the remaining methods convert a Byte to various primitive numeric types.

```
public final class Byte extends Number implements Comparable {
// Public Constructors
    public Byte(byte value);
    public Byte(String s) throws NumberFormatException;
// Public Constants
    public static final byte MAX_VALUE;                                    =127
    public static final byte MIN_VALUE;                                    =-128
    public static final Class TYPE;
// Public Class Methods
    public static Byte decode(String nm) throws NumberFormatException;
    public static byte parseByte(String s) throws NumberFormatException;
    public static byte parseByte(String s, int radix) throws NumberFormatException;
    public static String toString(byte b);
    public static Byte valueOf(String s) throws NumberFormatException;
    public static Byte valueOf(String s, int radix) throws NumberFormatException;
// Public Instance Methods
1.2 public int compareTo(Byte anotherByte);
// Methods Implementing Comparable
1.2 public int compareTo(Object o);
// Public Methods Overriding Number
    public byte byteValue();
    public double doubleValue();
    public float floatValue();
    public int intValue();
    public long longValue();
    public short shortValue();
// Public Methods Overriding Object
    public boolean equals(Object obj);
    public int hashCode();
    public String toString();
}
```

Hierarchy: Object→ Number(Serializable)→ Byte(Comparable)

Passed To: Byte.compareTo()

Returned By: Byte.{decode(), valueOf()}

Character

Java 1.0

java.lang

serializable comparable PJ1.1

This class provides an immutable object wrapper around the primitive char data type. charValue() returns the char value of a Character object. A number of class methods provide the Java/Unicode equivalent of the C *<ctype.h>* character macros for checking the type of characters and converting to uppercase and lowercase letters. getType() returns the character type. The return value is one of the constants defined by the class, which represents a number of broad Unicode character categories. digit() returns the integer equivalent of a given character for a given radix (e.g., radix 16 for hexadecimal). forDigit() returns the character that corresponds to the specified value for the specified radix.

```
public final class Character implements Comparable, Serializable {
// Public Constructors
    public Character(char value);
// Public Constants
1.1 public static final byte COMBINING_SPACING_MARK;                     =8
1.1 public static final byte CONNECTOR_PUNCTUATION;                      =23
```

1.1 public static final byte **CONTROL**;	=15
1.1 public static final byte **CURRENCY_SYMBOL**;	=26
1.1 public static final byte **DASH_PUNCTUATION**;	=20
1.1 public static final byte **DECIMAL_DIGIT_NUMBER**;	=9
1.1 public static final byte **ENCLOSING_MARK**;	=7
1.1 public static final byte **END_PUNCTUATION**;	=22
1.1 public static final byte **FORMAT**;	=16
1.1 public static final byte **LETTER_NUMBER**;	=10
1.1 public static final byte **LINE_SEPARATOR**;	=13
1.1 public static final byte **LOWERCASE_LETTER**;	=2
1.1 public static final byte **MATH_SYMBOL**;	=25
public static final int **MAX_RADIX**;	=36
public static final char **MAX_VALUE**;	='\uFFFF'
public static final int **MIN_RADIX**;	=2
public static final char **MIN_VALUE**;	='\0'
1.1 public static final byte **MODIFIER_LETTER**;	=4
1.1 public static final byte **MODIFIER_SYMBOL**;	=27
1.1 public static final byte **NON_SPACING_MARK**;	=6
1.1 public static final byte **OTHER_LETTER**;	=5
1.1 public static final byte **OTHER_NUMBER**;	=11
1.1 public static final byte **OTHER_PUNCTUATION**;	=24
1.1 public static final byte **OTHER_SYMBOL**;	=28
1.1 public static final byte **PARAGRAPH_SEPARATOR**;	=14
1.1 public static final byte **PRIVATE_USE**;	=18
1.1 public static final byte **SPACE_SEPARATOR**;	=12
1.1 public static final byte **START_PUNCTUATION**;	=21
1.1 public static final byte **SURROGATE**;	=19
1.1 public static final byte **TITLECASE_LETTER**;	=3
1.1 public static final Class **TYPE**;	
1.1 public static final byte **UNASSIGNED**;	=0
1.1 public static final byte **UPPERCASE_LETTER**;	=1

// Inner Classes
1.2 public static class **Subset**;
1.2 public static final class **UnicodeBlock** extends Character.Subset;
// Public Class Methods
public static int **digit**(char *ch*, int *radix*);
public static char **forDigit**(int *digit*, int *radix*);
1.1 public static int **getNumericValue**(char *ch*);
1.1 public static int **getType**(char *ch*);
public static boolean **isDefined**(char *ch*);
public static boolean **isDigit**(char *ch*);
1.1 public static boolean **isIdentifierIgnorable**(char *ch*);
1.1 public static boolean **isISOControl**(char *ch*);
1.1 public static boolean **isJavaIdentifierPart**(char *ch*);
1.1 public static boolean **isJavaIdentifierStart**(char *ch*);
public static boolean **isLetter**(char *ch*);
public static boolean **isLetterOrDigit**(char *ch*);
public static boolean **isLowerCase**(char *ch*);
1.1 public static boolean **isSpaceChar**(char *ch*);
public static boolean **isTitleCase**(char *ch*);
1.1 public static boolean **isUnicodeIdentifierPart**(char *ch*);
1.1 public static boolean **isUnicodeIdentifierStart**(char *ch*);
public static boolean **isUpperCase**(char *ch*);
1.1 public static boolean **isWhitespace**(char *ch*);
public static char **toLowerCase**(char *ch*);

```
    public static char toTitleCase(char ch);
    public static char toUpperCase(char ch);
// Public Instance Methods
    public char charValue();
1.2 public int compareTo(Character anotherCharacter);
// Methods Implementing Comparable
1.2 public int compareTo(Object o);
// Public Methods Overriding Object
    public boolean equals(Object obj);
    public int hashCode();
    public String toString();
// Deprecated Public Methods
#   public static boolean isJavaLetter(char ch);
#   public static boolean isJavaLetterOrDigit(char ch);
#   public static boolean isSpace(char ch);
}
```

Hierarchy: Object→ Character(Comparable, Serializable)

Passed To: Character.compareTo()

Character.Subset

java.lang

This class represents a named subset of the Unicode character set. The toString() method returns the name of the subset. This is a base class intended for further subclassing. Note, in particular, that it does not provide a way to list the members of the subset, nor a way to test for membership in the subset. See Character.UnicodeBlock.

```
public static class Character.Subset {
// Protected Constructors
    protected Subset(String name);
// Public Methods Overriding Object
    public final boolean equals(Object obj);
    public final int hashCode();
    public final String toString();
}
```

Subclasses: java.awt.im.InputSubset, Character.UnicodeBlock

Passed To: java.awt.im.InputContext.setCharacterSubsets(),
java.awt.im.spi.InputMethod.setCharacterSubsets()

Character.UnicodeBlock

Java 1.2

java.lang

This subclass of Character.Subset defines a number of constants that represent named subsets of the Unicode character set. The subsets and their names are the character blocks defined by the Unicode 2.0 specification (see *http://www.unicode.org/*). The static method of() takes a character and returns the Character.UnicodeBlock to which it belongs, or null if it is not part of any defined block. When presented with an unknown Unicode character, this method provides a useful way to determine what alphabet it belongs to.

```
public static final class Character.UnicodeBlock extends Character.Subset {
// No Constructor
// Public Constants
    public static final Character.UnicodeBlock ALPHABETIC_PRESENTATION_FORMS;
    public static final Character.UnicodeBlock ARABIC;
    public static final Character.UnicodeBlock ARABIC_PRESENTATION_FORMS_A;
    public static final Character.UnicodeBlock ARABIC_PRESENTATION_FORMS_B;
    public static final Character.UnicodeBlock ARMENIAN;
    public static final Character.UnicodeBlock ARROWS;
    public static final Character.UnicodeBlock BASIC_LATIN;
    public static final Character.UnicodeBlock BENGALI;
    public static final Character.UnicodeBlock BLOCK_ELEMENTS;
    public static final Character.UnicodeBlock BOPOMOFO;
    public static final Character.UnicodeBlock BOX_DRAWING;
    public static final Character.UnicodeBlock CJK_COMPATIBILITY;
    public static final Character.UnicodeBlock CJK_COMPATIBILITY_FORMS;
    public static final Character.UnicodeBlock CJK_COMPATIBILITY_IDEOGRAPHS;
    public static final Character.UnicodeBlock CJK_SYMBOLS_AND_PUNCTUATION;
    public static final Character.UnicodeBlock CJK_UNIFIED_IDEOGRAPHS;
    public static final Character.UnicodeBlock COMBINING_DIACRITICAL_MARKS;
    public static final Character.UnicodeBlock COMBINING_HALF_MARKS;
    public static final Character.UnicodeBlock COMBINING_MARKS_FOR_SYMBOLS;
    public static final Character.UnicodeBlock CONTROL_PICTURES;
    public static final Character.UnicodeBlock CURRENCY_SYMBOLS;
    public static final Character.UnicodeBlock CYRILLIC;
    public static final Character.UnicodeBlock DEVANAGARI;
    public static final Character.UnicodeBlock DINGBATS;
    public static final Character.UnicodeBlock ENCLOSED_ALPHANUMERICS;
    public static final Character.UnicodeBlock ENCLOSED_CJK_LETTERS_AND_MONTHS;
    public static final Character.UnicodeBlock GENERAL_PUNCTUATION;
    public static final Character.UnicodeBlock GEOMETRIC_SHAPES;
    public static final Character.UnicodeBlock GEORGIAN;
    public static final Character.UnicodeBlock GREEK;
    public static final Character.UnicodeBlock GREEK_EXTENDED;
    public static final Character.UnicodeBlock GUJARATI;
    public static final Character.UnicodeBlock GURMUKHI;
    public static final Character.UnicodeBlock HALFWIDTH_AND_FULLWIDTH_FORMS;
    public static final Character.UnicodeBlock HANGUL_COMPATIBILITY_JAMO;
    public static final Character.UnicodeBlock HANGUL_JAMO;
    public static final Character.UnicodeBlock HANGUL_SYLLABLES;
    public static final Character.UnicodeBlock HEBREW;
    public static final Character.UnicodeBlock HIRAGANA;
    public static final Character.UnicodeBlock IPA_EXTENSIONS;
    public static final Character.UnicodeBlock KANBUN;
    public static final Character.UnicodeBlock KANNADA;
    public static final Character.UnicodeBlock KATAKANA;
    public static final Character.UnicodeBlock LAO;
    public static final Character.UnicodeBlock LATIN_1_SUPPLEMENT;
    public static final Character.UnicodeBlock LATIN_EXTENDED_A;
    public static final Character.UnicodeBlock LATIN_EXTENDED_ADDITIONAL;
    public static final Character.UnicodeBlock LATIN_EXTENDED_B;
    public static final Character.UnicodeBlock LETTERLIKE_SYMBOLS;
    public static final Character.UnicodeBlock MALAYALAM;
    public static final Character.UnicodeBlock MATHEMATICAL_OPERATORS;
    public static final Character.UnicodeBlock MISCELLANEOUS_SYMBOLS;
```

```
    public static final Character.UnicodeBlock MISCELLANEOUS_TECHNICAL;
    public static final Character.UnicodeBlock NUMBER_FORMS;
    public static final Character.UnicodeBlock OPTICAL_CHARACTER_RECOGNITION;
    public static final Character.UnicodeBlock ORIYA;
    public static final Character.UnicodeBlock PRIVATE_USE_AREA;
    public static final Character.UnicodeBlock SMALL_FORM_VARIANTS;
    public static final Character.UnicodeBlock SPACING_MODIFIER_LETTERS;
    public static final Character.UnicodeBlock SPECIALS;
    public static final Character.UnicodeBlock SUPERSCRIPTS_AND_SUBSCRIPTS;
    public static final Character.UnicodeBlock SURROGATES_AREA;
    public static final Character.UnicodeBlock TAMIL;
    public static final Character.UnicodeBlock TELUGU;
    public static final Character.UnicodeBlock THAI;
    public static final Character.UnicodeBlock TIBETAN;
// Public Class Methods
    public static Character.UnicodeBlock of(char c);
}
```

Returned By: Character.UnicodeBlock.of()

Type Of: Too many fields to list.

Class

Java 1.0

java.lang

serializable PJ1.1

This class represents a Java class or interface, or, as of Java 1.1, any Java type. There is one Class object for each class that is loaded into the Java Virtual Machine, and, as of Java 1.1, there are special Class objects that represent the Java primitive types. The TYPE constants defined by Boolean, Integer, and the other primitive wrapper classes hold these special Class objects. Array types are also represented by Class objects in Java 1.1.

There is no constructor for this class. You can obtain a Class object by calling the getClass() method of any instance of the desired class. In Java 1.1 and later, you can also refer to a Class object by appending .class to the name of a class. Finally, and most interestingly, a class can be dynamically loaded by passing its fully qualified name (i.e., package name plus class name) to the static Class.forName() method. This method loads the named class (if it is not already loaded) into the Java interpreter and returns a Class object for it. Classes can also be loaded with a ClassLoader object.

The newInstance() method creates an instance of a given class; this allows you to create instances of dynamically loaded classes for which you cannot use the new keyword. Note that this method only works when the target class has a no-argument constructor. See newInstance() in java.lang.reflect.Constructor for a more powerful way to instantiate dynamically loaded classes.

getName() returns the name of the class. getSuperclass() returns its superclass. isInterface() tests whether the Class object represents an interface, and getInterfaces() returns an array of the interfaces that this class implements. In Java 1.2 and later, getPackage() returns a Package object that represents the package containing the class. getProtectionDomain() returns the java.security.ProtectionDomain to which this class belongs. The various other get() and is() methods return other information about the represented class; they form part of the Java Reflection API, along with the classes in java.lang.reflect.

```
public final class Class implements Serializable {
// No Constructor
// Public Class Methods
    public static Class forName(String className) throws ClassNotFoundException;
```

1.2 public static Class **forName**(String *name*, boolean *initialize*, ClassLoader *loader*) throws ClassNotFoundException;
// Property Accessor Methods (by property name)
1.1 public boolean **isArray**();   *native*
1.1 public Class[ ] **getClasses**();
public ClassLoader **getClassLoader**();
1.1 public Class **getComponentType**();   *native*
1.1 public java.lang.reflect.Constructor[ ] **getConstructors**() throws SecurityException;
1.1 public Class[ ] **getDeclaredClasses**() throws SecurityException;
1.1 public java.lang.reflect.Constructor[ ] **getDeclaredConstructors**() throws SecurityException;
1.1 public java.lang.reflect.Field[ ] **getDeclaredFields**() throws SecurityException;
1.1 public java.lang.reflect.Method[ ] **getDeclaredMethods**() throws SecurityException;
1.1 public Class **getDeclaringClass**();   *native*
1.1 public java.lang.reflect.Field[ ] **getFields**() throws SecurityException;
public boolean **isInterface**();   *native*
public Class[ ] **getInterfaces**();   *native*
1.1 public java.lang.reflect.Method[ ] **getMethods**() throws SecurityException;
1.1 public int **getModifiers**();   *native*
public String **getName**();   *native*
1.2 public Package **getPackage**();
1.1 public boolean **isPrimitive**();   *native*
1.2 public java.security.ProtectionDomain **getProtectionDomain**();
1.1 public Object[ ] **getSigners**();   *native*
public Class **getSuperclass**();   *native*
// Public Instance Methods
1.1 public java.lang.reflect.Constructor **getConstructor**(Class[ ] *parameterTypes*) throws NoSuchMethodException,
        SecurityException;
1.1 public java.lang.reflect.Constructor **getDeclaredConstructor**(Class[ ] *parameterTypes*)
        throws NoSuchMethodException, SecurityException;
1.1 public java.lang.reflect.Field **getDeclaredField**(String *name*) throws NoSuchFieldException, SecurityException;
1.1 public java.lang.reflect.Method **getDeclaredMethod**(String *name*, Class[ ] *parameterTypes*)
        throws NoSuchMethodException, SecurityException;
1.1 public java.lang.reflect.Field **getField**(String *name*) throws NoSuchFieldException, SecurityException;
1.1 public java.lang.reflect.Method **getMethod**(String *name*, Class[ ] *parameterTypes*) throws NoSuchMethodException,
        SecurityException;
1.1 public java.net.URL **getResource**(String *name*);
1.1 public java.io.InputStream **getResourceAsStream**(String *name*);
1.1 public boolean **isAssignableFrom**(Class *cls*);   *native*
1.1 public boolean **isInstance**(Object *obj*);   *native*
public Object **newInstance**() throws InstantiationException, IllegalAccessException;
// Public Methods Overriding Object
public String **toString**();
}

Hierarchy: Object→ Class(Serializable)

Passed To: Too many methods to list.

Returned By: Too many methods to list.

Type Of: java.beans.beancontext.BeanContextServiceAvailableEvent.serviceClass,
java.beans.beancontext.BeanContextServiceRevokedEvent.serviceClass, Boolean.TYPE, Byte.TYPE,
Character.TYPE, Double.TYPE, Float.TYPE, Integer.TYPE, Long.TYPE, Short.TYPE, Void.TYPE

ClassCastException   Java 1.0
java.lang   *serializable unchecked PJ1.1*

Signals an invalid cast of an object to a type of which it is not an instance.

```
public class ClassCastException extends RuntimeException {
// Public Constructors
   public ClassCastException();
   public ClassCastException(String s);
}
```

Hierarchy: Object→ Throwable(Serializable)→ Exception→ RuntimeException→ ClassCastException

ClassCircularityError
Java 1.0

java.lang   *serializable error PJ1.1*

Signals that a circular dependency has been detected while performing initialization for a class.

```
public class ClassCircularityError extends LinkageError {
// Public Constructors
   public ClassCircularityError();
   public ClassCircularityError(String s);
}
```

Hierarchy: Object→ Throwable(Serializable)→ Error→ LinkageError→ ClassCircularityError

ClassFormatError
Java 1.0

java.lang   *serializable error PJ1.1*

Signals an error in the binary format of a class file.

```
public class ClassFormatError extends LinkageError {
// Public Constructors
   public ClassFormatError();
   public ClassFormatError(String s);
}
```

Hierarchy: Object→ Throwable(Serializable)→ Error→ LinkageError→ ClassFormatError

Subclasses: UnsupportedClassVersionError

Thrown By: ClassLoader.defineClass()

ClassLoader
Java 1.0

java.lang   *PJ1.1*

This class is the abstract superclass of objects that know how to load Java classes into a Java VM. Given a ClassLoader object, you can dynamically load a class by calling the public loadClass() method, specifying the full name of the desired class. You can obtain a resource associated with a class by calling getResource(), getResources(), and getResource-AsStream(). Many applications do not need to use ClassLoader directly; these applications use the Class.forName() and Class.getResource() methods to dynamically load classes and resources using the ClassLoader object that loaded the application itself.

In order to load classes over the network or from any source other than the standard system classes, you must use a custom ClassLoader object that knows how to obtain data from that source. A java.net.URLClassLoader is suitable for this purpose for almost all applications. Only rarely should an application need to define a ClassLoader subclass of its own. When this is necessary, the subclass should typically extend java.security.Secure-ClassLoader and override the findClass() method. This method must find the bytes that comprise the named class, then pass them to the defineClass() method and return the resulting Class object. In Java 1.2 and later, the findClass() method must also define the

Package object associated with the class, if it has not already been defined. It can use getPackage() and definePackage() for this purpose. Custom subclasses of ClassLoader should also override findResource() and findResources() to enable the public getResource() and getResources() methods.

```
public abstract class ClassLoader {
// Protected Constructors
     protected ClassLoader();
1.2 protected ClassLoader(ClassLoader parent);
// Public Class Methods
1.2 public static ClassLoader getSystemClassLoader();
1.1 public static java.net.URL getSystemResource(String name);
1.1 public static java.io.InputStream getSystemResourceAsStream(String name);
1.2 public static java.util.Enumeration getSystemResources(String name) throws java.io.IOException;
// Public Instance Methods
1.2 public final ClassLoader getParent();
1.1 public java.net.URL getResource(String name);
1.1 public java.io.InputStream getResourceAsStream(String name);
1.2 public final java.util.Enumeration getResources(String name) throws java.io.IOException;
1.1 public Class loadClass(String name) throws ClassNotFoundException;
// Protected Instance Methods
1.1 protected final Class defineClass(String name, byte[ ] b, int off, int len) throws ClassFormatError;
1.2 protected final Class defineClass(String name, byte[ ] b, int off, int len,
                              java.security.ProtectionDomain protectionDomain) throws ClassFormatError;
1.2 protected Package definePackage(String name, String specTitle, String specVersion, String specVendor,
                              String implTitle, String implVersion, String implVendor, java.net.URL sealBase)
         throws IllegalArgumentException;
1.2 protected Class findClass(String name) throws ClassNotFoundException;
1.2 protected String findLibrary(String libname);                                         constant
1.1 protected final Class findLoadedClass(String name);                                     native
1.2 protected java.net.URL findResource(String name);                                     constant
1.2 protected java.util.Enumeration findResources(String name) throws java.io.IOException;
     protected Class findSystemClass(String name) throws ClassNotFoundException;
1.2 protected Package getPackage(String name);
1.2 protected Package[ ] getPackages();
     protected Class loadClass(String name, boolean resolve) throws ClassNotFoundException;   synchronized
     protected final void resolveClass(Class c);
1.1 protected final void setSigners(Class c, Object[ ] signers);
// Deprecated Protected Methods
#   protected final Class defineClass(byte[ ] b, int off, int len) throws ClassFormatError;
}
```

Subclasses: java.security.SecureClassLoader

Passed To: Too many methods to list.

Returned By: Class.getClassLoader(), ClassLoader.{getParent(), getSystemClassLoader()}, SecurityManager.currentClassLoader(), Thread.getContextClassLoader(), java.rmi.server.RMIClassLoader.getClassLoader()

ClassNotFoundException   Java 1.0

java.lang   *serializable checked PJ1.1*

Signals that a class to be loaded cannot be found.

```
public class ClassNotFoundException extends Exception {
// Public Constructors
     public ClassNotFoundException();
```

```
   public ClassNotFoundException(String s);
1.2 public ClassNotFoundException(String s, Throwable ex);
// Public Instance Methods
1.2 public Throwable getException();                                    default:null
// Public Methods Overriding Throwable
1.2 public void printStackTrace();
1.2 public void printStackTrace(java.io.PrintWriter pw);
1.2 public void printStackTrace(java.io.PrintStream ps);
}
```

Hierarchy: Object→ Throwable(Serializable)→ Exception→ ClassNotFoundException

Thrown By: Too many methods to list.

Cloneable
java.lang

Java 1.0
cloneable PJ1.1

This interface defines no methods or variables, but indicates that the class that implements it may be cloned (i.e., copied) by calling the Object method clone(). Calling clone() for an object that does not implement this interface (and does not override clone() with its own implementation) causes a CloneNotSupportedException to be thrown.

```
public interface Cloneable {
}
```

Implementations: Too many classes to list.

CloneNotSupportedException
java.lang

Java 1.0
serializable checked PJ1.1

Signals that the clone() method has been called for an object of a class that does not implement the Cloneable interface.

```
public class CloneNotSupportedException extends Exception {
// Public Constructors
   public CloneNotSupportedException();
   public CloneNotSupportedException(String s);
}
```

Hierarchy: Object→ Throwable(Serializable)→ Exception→ CloneNotSupportedException

Subclasses: java.rmi.server.ServerCloneException

Thrown By: java.awt.datatransfer.DataFlavor.clone(), Object.clone(), java.rmi.server.UnicastRemoteObject.clone(), java.security.MessageDigest.clone(), java.security.MessageDigestSpi.clone(), java.security.Signature.clone(), java.security.SignatureSpi.clone(), javax.crypto.Mac.clone(), javax.crypto.MacSpi.clone(), javax.swing.AbstractAction.clone(), javax.swing.DefaultListSelectionModel.clone(), javax.swing.tree.DefaultTreeSelectionModel.clone()

Comparable
java.lang

Java 1.2
comparable

This interface defines a single method, compareTo(), that is responsible for comparing one object to another and determining their relative order, according to some natural ordering for that class of objects. Any general-purpose class that represents a value that can be sorted or ordered should implement this interface. Any class that does implement this interface can make use of various powerful methods such as java.util.Collections.sort() and java.util.Arrays.binarySearch(). As of Java 1.2, many of the key classes in the Java API have been modified to implement this interface.

The compareTo() object compares this object to the object passed as an argument. It should assume that the supplied object is of the appropriate type; if it is not, it should throw a ClassCastException. If this object is less than the supplied object or should appear before the supplied object in a sorted list, compareTo() should return a negative number. If this object is greater than the supplied object or should come after the supplied object in a sorted list, compareTo() should return a positive integer. If the two objects are equivalent, and their relative order in a sorted list does not matter, compareTo() should return 0. If compareTo() returns 0 for two objects, the equals() method should typically return true. If this is not the case, the Comparable objects are not suitable for use in java.util.TreeSet and java.util.TreeMap classes.

See java.util.Comparator for a way to define an ordering for objects that do not implement Comparable or to define an ordering other than the natural ordering defined by a Comparable class.

```
public interface Comparable {
// Public Instance Methods
    public abstract int compareTo(Object o);
}
```

Implementations: java.io.File, java.io.ObjectStreamField, Byte, Character, Double, Float, Integer, Long, Short, String, java.math.BigDecimal, java.math.BigInteger, java.text.CollationKey, java.util.Date

Compiler   Java 1.0
java.lang   PJ1.1

The static methods of this class provide an interface to the just-in-time (JIT) byte-code-to-native code compiler in use by the Java interpreter. If no JIT compiler is in use by the VM, these methods do nothing. compileClass() asks the JIT compiler to compile the specified class. compileClasses() asks the JIT compiler to compile all classes that match the specified name. These methods return true if the compilation was successful, or false if it failed or if there is no JIT compiler on the system. enable() and disable() turn just-in-time compilation on and off. command() asks the JIT compiler to perform some compiler-specific operation; this is a hook for vendor extensions. No standard operations have been defined.

```
public final class Compiler {
// No Constructor
// Public Class Methods
    public static Object command(Object any);                              native
    public static boolean compileClass(Class clazz);                       native
    public static boolean compileClasses(String string);                   native
    public static void disable();                                          native
    public static void enable();                                           native
}
```

Double   Java 1.0
java.lang   serializable comparable PJ1.1

This class provides an immutable object wrapper around the double primitive data type. valueOf() converts a string to a Double, doubleValue() returns the primitive double value of a Double object, and there are other methods for returning a Double value as a variety of other primitive types. This class also provides some useful constants and static methods for testing double values. MIN_VALUE and MAX_VALUE are the smallest (closest to zero) and largest representable double values. isInfinite() in class and instance method forms tests whether a double or a Double has an infinite value. Similarly, isNaN() tests whether a double or Double is not-a-number; this is a comparison that cannot be done directly because the NaN constant never tests equal to any other value, including itself. doubleToLongBits() and longBitsToDouble() allow you to manipulate the bit representation of a double directly.

```
public final class Double extends Number implements Comparable {
// Public Constructors
    public Double(String s) throws NumberFormatException;
    public Double(double value);
// Public Constants
    public static final double MAX_VALUE;                                      =1.7976931348623157E308
    public static final double MIN_VALUE;                                                 =4.9E-324
    public static final double NaN;                                                            =NaN
    public static final double NEGATIVE_INFINITY;                                          =-Infinity
    public static final double POSITIVE_INFINITY;                                           =Infinity
1.1 public static final Class TYPE;
// Public Class Methods
    public static long doubleToLongBits(double value);                                        native
1.3 public static long doubleToRawLongBits(double value);                                     native
    public static boolean isInfinite(double v);
    public static boolean isNaN(double v);
    public static double longBitsToDouble(long bits);                                         native
1.2 public static double parseDouble(String s) throws NumberFormatException;
    public static String toString(double d);
    public static Double valueOf(String s) throws NumberFormatException;
// Public Instance Methods
1.2 public int compareTo(Double anotherDouble);
    public boolean isInfinite();
    public boolean isNaN();
// Methods Implementing Comparable
1.2 public int compareTo(Object o);
// Public Methods Overriding Number
1.1 public byte byteValue();
    public double doubleValue();
    public float floatValue();
    public int intValue();
    public long longValue();
1.1 public short shortValue();
// Public Methods Overriding Object
    public boolean equals(Object obj);
    public int hashCode();
    public String toString();
}
```

Hierarchy: Object→ Number(Serializable)→ Double(Comparable)

Passed To: Double.compareTo()

Returned By: Double.valueOf()

Error   Java 1.0
java.lang   serializable error PJ1.1

This class forms the root of the error hierarchy in Java. Subclasses of Error, unlike subclasses of Exception, should not be caught and generally cause termination of the program. Subclasses of Error need not be declared in the throws clause of a method definition. getMessage() returns a message associated with the error. See Throwable for other methods.

```
public class Error extends Throwable {
// Public Constructors
    public Error();
    public Error(String s);
}
```

Hierarchy: Object→ Throwable(Serializable)→ Error

Subclasses: java.awt.AWTError, LinkageError, ThreadDeath, VirtualMachineError

Passed To: java.rmi.ServerError.ServerError()

Exception   Java 1.0

java.lang   *serializable checked PJ1.1*

This class forms the root of the exception hierarchy in Java. An Exception signals an abnormal condition that must be specially handled to prevent program termination. Exceptions may be caught and handled. An exception that is not a subclass of Runtime-Exception must be declared in the throws clause of any method that can throw it. getMessage() returns a message associated with the exception. See Throwable for other methods.

```
public class Exception extends Throwable {
// Public Constructors
    public Exception();
    public Exception(String s);
}
```

Hierarchy: Object→ Throwable(Serializable)→ Exception

Subclasses: Too many classes to list.

Passed To: Too many methods to list.

Returned By: java.awt.event.InvocationEvent.getException(),
java.security.PrivilegedActionException.getException(), javax.ejb.EJBException.getCausedByException(),
javax.jms.JMSException.getLinkedException(), org.omg.CORBA.Environment.exception()

Thrown By: java.rmi.server.RemoteCall.executeCall(), java.rmi.server.RemoteRef.invoke(),
java.rmi.server.Skeleton.dispatch(), java.security.PrivilegedExceptionAction.run(),
javax.naming.spi.NamingManager.getObjectInstance(),
javax.naming.spi.ObjectFactory.getObjectInstance()

Type Of: java.io.WriteAbortedException.detail, java.rmi.server.ServerCloneException.detail

ExceptionInInitializerError   Java 1.1

java.lang   *serializable error PJ1.1*

This error is thrown by the Java Virtual Machine when an exception occurs in the static initializer of a class. You can use the getException() method to obtain the Throwable object that was thrown from the initializer.

```
public class ExceptionInInitializerError extends LinkageError {
// Public Constructors
    public ExceptionInInitializerError();
    public ExceptionInInitializerError(String s);
    public ExceptionInInitializerError(Throwable thrown);
// Public Instance Methods
    public Throwable getException();                                       default:null
// Public Methods Overriding Throwable
1.2 public void printStackTrace();
```

1.2 public void **printStackTrace**(java.io.PrintWriter *pw*);
1.2 public void **printStackTrace**(java.io.PrintStream *ps*);
}

Hierarchy: Object→ Throwable(Serializable)→ Error→ LinkageError→ ExceptionInInitializerError

Float

java.lang

This class provides an immutable object wrapper around the float primitive data type. valueOf() converts a string to a Float, floatValue() returns the primitive float value of a Float object, and there are methods for returning a Float value as a variety of other primitive types. This class also provides some useful constants and static methods for testing float values. MIN_VALUE and MAX_VALUE are the smallest (closest to zero) and largest representable double values. isInfinite() in class and instance method forms tests whether a float or a Float has an infinite value. Similarly, isNaN() tests whether a float or Float is not-a-number; this is a comparison that cannot be done directly because the NaN constant never tests equal to any other value, including itself. floatToIntBits() and intBitsToFloat() allow you to manipulate the bit representation of a float directly.

```
public final class Float extends Number implements Comparable {
// Public Constructors
    public Float(String s) throws NumberFormatException;
    public Float(float value);
    public Float(double value);
// Public Constants
    public static final float MAX_VALUE;                                   =3.4028235E38
    public static final float MIN_VALUE;                                   =1.4E-45
    public static final float NaN;                                         =NaN
    public static final float NEGATIVE_INFINITY;                           =-Infinity
    public static final float POSITIVE_INFINITY;                           =Infinity
1.1 public static final Class TYPE;
// Public Class Methods
    public static int floatToIntBits(float value);                         native
1.3 public static int floatToRawIntBits(float value);                      native
    public static float intBitsToFloat(int bits);                          native
    public static boolean isInfinite(float v);
    public static boolean isNaN(float v);
1.2 public static float parseFloat(String s) throws NumberFormatException;
    public static String toString(float f);
    public static Float valueOf(String s) throws NumberFormatException;
// Public Instance Methods
1.2 public int compareTo(Float anotherFloat);
    public boolean isInfinite();
    public boolean isNaN();
// Methods Implementing Comparable
1.2 public int compareTo(Object o);
// Public Methods Overriding Number
1.1 public byte byteValue();
    public double doubleValue();
    public float floatValue();
    public int intValue();
    public long longValue();
1.1 public short shortValue();
// Public Methods Overriding Object
    public boolean equals(Object obj);
```

```
    public int hashCode();
    public String toString();
}
```

Hierarchy: Object→ Number(Serializable)→ Float(Comparable)

Passed To: Float.compareTo()

Returned By: Float.valueOf()

Type Of: Too many fields to list.

IllegalAccessError

Java 1.0

java.lang

serializable error PJ1.1

Signals an attempted use of a class, method, or field that is not accessible.

```
public class IllegalAccessError extends IncompatibleClassChangeError {
// Public Constructors
    public IllegalAccessError();
    public IllegalAccessError(String s);
}
```

Hierarchy: Object→ Throwable(Serializable)→ Error→ LinkageError→
IncompatibleClassChangeError→ IllegalAccessError

IllegalAccessException

Java 1.0

java.lang

serializable checked PJ1.1

Signals that a class or initializer is not accessible. Thrown by Class.newInstance().

```
public class IllegalAccessException extends Exception {
// Public Constructors
    public IllegalAccessException();
    public IllegalAccessException(String s);
}
```

Hierarchy: Object→ Throwable(Serializable)→ Exception→ IllegalAccessException

Thrown By: Too many methods to list.

IllegalArgumentException

Java 1.0

java.lang

serializable unchecked PJ1.1

Signals an illegal argument to a method. See subclasses IllegalThreadStateException and
NumberFormatException.

```
public class IllegalArgumentException extends RuntimeException {
// Public Constructors
    public IllegalArgumentException();
    public IllegalArgumentException(String s);
}
```

Hierarchy: Object→ Throwable(Serializable)→ Exception→ RuntimeException→
IllegalArgumentException

Subclasses: IllegalThreadStateException, NumberFormatException,
java.security.InvalidParameterException

Thrown By: Too many methods to list.

IllegalMonitorStateException

Java 1.0

java.lang

serializable unchecked PJ1.1

Signals an illegal monitor state. It is thrown by the Object notify() and wait() methods used for thread synchronization.

```
public class IllegalMonitorStateException extends RuntimeException {
// Public Constructors
    public IllegalMonitorStateException();
    public IllegalMonitorStateException(String s);
}
```

Hierarchy: Object→ Throwable(Serializable)→ Exception→ RuntimeException→
IllegalMonitorStateException

IllegalStateException

Java 1.1

java.lang

serializable unchecked PJ1.1

Signals that a method has been invoked on an object that is not in an appropriate state to perform the requested operation.

```
public class IllegalStateException extends RuntimeException {
// Public Constructors
    public IllegalStateException();
    public IllegalStateException(String s);
}
```

Hierarchy: Object→ Throwable(Serializable)→ Exception→ RuntimeException→
java.lang.IllegalStateException

Subclasses: java.awt.IllegalComponentStateException, java.awt.dnd.InvalidDnDOperationException

Thrown By: Too many methods to list.

IllegalThreadStateException

Java 1.0

java.lang

serializable unchecked PJ1.1

Signals that a thread is not in the appropriate state for an attempted operation to succeed.

```
public class IllegalThreadStateException extends IllegalArgumentException {
// Public Constructors
    public IllegalThreadStateException();
    public IllegalThreadStateException(String s);
}
```

Hierarchy: Object→ Throwable(Serializable)→ Exception→ RuntimeException→
IllegalArgumentException→ IllegalThreadStateException

IncompatibleClassChangeError

Java 1.0

java.lang

serializable error PJ1.1

This is the superclass of a group of related error types. It signals some kind of illegal use of a legal class.

```
public class IncompatibleClassChangeError extends LinkageError {
// Public Constructors
    public IncompatibleClassChangeError();
    public IncompatibleClassChangeError(String s);
}
```

Hierarchy: Object→ Throwable(Serializable)→ Error→ LinkageError→
IncompatibleClassChangeError

Subclasses: AbstractMethodError, IllegalAccessError, InstantiationError, NoSuchFieldError,
NoSuchMethodError

IndexOutOfBoundsException   Java 1.0

java.lang   *serializable unchecked PJ1.1*

Signals that an index is out of bounds. See the subclasses ArrayIndexOutOfBoundsException
and StringIndexOutOfBoundsException.

```
public class IndexOutOfBoundsException extends RuntimeException {
// Public Constructors
    public IndexOutOfBoundsException();
    public IndexOutOfBoundsException(String s);
}
```

Hierarchy: Object→ Throwable(Serializable)→ Exception→ RuntimeException→
IndexOutOfBoundsException

Subclasses: ArrayIndexOutOfBoundsException, StringIndexOutOfBoundsException

Thrown By: java.awt.Toolkit.createCustomCursor(), java.awt.print.Book.{getPageFormat(),
getPrintable(), setPage()}, java.awt.print.Pageable.{getPageFormat(), getPrintable()}

InheritableThreadLocal   Java 1.2

java.lang

This class holds a thread-local value that is inherited by child threads. See ThreadLocal
for a discussion of thread-local values. Note that the inheritance referred to in the name
of this class is not superclass-to-subclass inheritance; instead, it is parent-thread-to-
child-thread inheritance.

This class is best understood by example. Suppose that an application has defined an
InheritableThreadLocal object and that a certain thread (the parent thread) has a threadlocal value stored in that object. Whenever that thread creates a new thread (a child
thread), the InheritableThreadLocal object is automatically updated so that the new child
thread has the same value associated with it as the parent thread. Note that the value
associated with the child thread is independent from the value associated with the parent thread. If the child thread subsequently alters its value by calling the set() method of
the InheritableThreadLocal, the value associated with the parent thread does not change.

By default, a child thread inherits a parent's values unmodified. By overriding the child-
Value() method, however, you can create a subclass of InheritableThreadLocal in which the
child thread inherits some arbitrary function of the parent thread's value.

```
public class InheritableThreadLocal extends ThreadLocal {
// Public Constructors
    public InheritableThreadLocal();
// Protected Instance Methods
    protected Object childValue(Object parentValue);
}
```

Hierarchy: Object→ ThreadLocal→ InheritableThreadLocal

InstantiationError

java.lang   *serializable error PJ1.1*

Signals an attempt to instantiate an interface or abstract class.

```
public class InstantiationError extends IncompatibleClassChangeError {
// Public Constructors
    public InstantiationError();
    public InstantiationError(String s);
}
```

Hierarchy: Object→ Throwable(Serializable)→ Error→ LinkageError→
IncompatibleClassChangeError→ InstantiationError

InstantiationException

java.lang   *serializable checked PJ1.1*

Signals an attempt to instantiate an interface or an abstract class.

```
public class InstantiationException extends Exception {
// Public Constructors
    public InstantiationException();
    public InstantiationException(String s);
}
```

Hierarchy: Object→ Throwable(Serializable)→ Exception→ InstantiationException

Thrown By: Class.newInstance(), java.lang.reflect.Constructor.newInstance(),
javax.swing.UIManager.setLookAndFeel()

Integer

java.lang   *serializable comparable PJ1.1*

This class provides an immutable object wrapper around the int primitive data type. This class also contains useful minimum and maximum constants and useful conversion methods. parseInt() and valueOf() convert a string to an int or to an Integer, respectively. Each can take a radix argument to specify the base the value is represented in. decode() also converts a String to an Integer. It assumes a hexadecimal number if the string begins with "0X" or "0x", or an octal number if the string begins with "0". Otherwise, a decimal number is assumed. toString() converts in the other direction, and the static version takes a radix argument. toBinaryString(), toOctalString(), and toHexString() convert an int to a string using base 2, base 8, and base 16. These methods treat the integer as an unsigned value. Other routines return the value of an Integer as various primitive types, and, finally, the getInteger() methods return the integer value of a named property from the system property list, or the specified default value.

```
public final class Integer extends Number implements Comparable {
// Public Constructors
    public Integer(String s) throws NumberFormatException;
    public Integer(int value);
// Public Constants
    public static final int MAX_VALUE;                          =2147483647
    public static final int MIN_VALUE;                          =-2147483648
1.1 public static final Class TYPE;
// Public Class Methods
    public static Integer decode(String nm) throws NumberFormatException;
    public static Integer getInteger(String nm);
    public static Integer getInteger(String nm, int val);
```

```
   public static Integer getInteger(String nm, Integer val);
   public static int parseInt(String s) throws NumberFormatException;
   public static int parseInt(String s, int radix) throws NumberFormatException;
   public static String toBinaryString(int i);
   public static String toHexString(int i);
   public static String toOctalString(int i);
   public static String toString(int i);
   public static String toString(int i, int radix);
   public static Integer valueOf(String s) throws NumberFormatException;
   public static Integer valueOf(String s, int radix) throws NumberFormatException;
// Public Instance Methods
1.2 public int compareTo(Integer anotherInteger);
// Methods Implementing Comparable
1.2 public int compareTo(Object o);
// Public Methods Overriding Number
1.1 public byte byteValue();
   public double doubleValue();
   public float floatValue();
   public int intValue();
   public long longValue();
1.1 public short shortValue();
// Public Methods Overriding Object
   public boolean equals(Object obj);
   public int hashCode();
   public String toString();
}
```

Hierarchy: Object→ Number(Serializable)→ Integer(Comparable)

Passed To: Integer.{compareTo(), getInteger()}, javax.swing.JInternalFrame.setLayer()

Returned By: Integer.{decode(), getInteger(), valueOf()}, javax.swing.JLayeredPane.getObjectForLayer()

Type Of: java.awt.font.TextAttribute.{SUPERSCRIPT_SUB, SUPERSCRIPT_SUPER, UNDERLINE_LOW_DASHED, UNDERLINE_LOW_DOTTED, UNDERLINE_LOW_GRAY, UNDERLINE_LOW_ONE_PIXEL, UNDERLINE_LOW_TWO_PIXEL, UNDERLINE_ON}, javax.swing.JLayeredPane.{DEFAULT_LAYER, DRAG_LAYER, FRAME_CONTENT_LAYER, MODAL_LAYER, PALETTE_LAYER, POPUP_LAYER}

InternalError   Java 1.0
java.lang   serializable error PJ1.1

Signals an internal error in the Java interpreter.

```
public class InternalError extends VirtualMachineError {
// Public Constructors
   public InternalError();
   public InternalError(String s);
}
```

Hierarchy: Object→ Throwable(Serializable)→ Error→ VirtualMachineError→ InternalError

InterruptedException   Java 1.0
java.lang   serializable checked PJ1.1

Signals that the thread has been interrupted.

```
public class InterruptedException extends Exception {
// Public Constructors
    public InterruptedException( );
    public InterruptedException(String s);
}
```

Hierarchy: Object→ Throwable(Serializable)→ Exception→ InterruptedException

Thrown By: Too many methods to list.

LinkageError   Java 1.0
java.lang   *serializable error PJ1.1*

The superclass of a group of errors that signal problems linking a class or resolving dependencies between classes.

```
public class LinkageError extends Error {
// Public Constructors
    public LinkageError( );
    public LinkageError(String s);
}
```

Hierarchy: Object→ Throwable(Serializable)→ Error→ LinkageError

Subclasses: ClassCircularityError, ClassFormatError, ExceptionInInitializerError, IncompatibleClassChangeError, NoClassDefFoundError, UnsatisfiedLinkError, VerifyError

Long   Java 1.0
java.lang   *serializable comparable PJ1.1*

This class provides an immutable object wrapper around the long primitive data type. This class also contains useful minimum and maximum constants and useful conversion methods. parseLong() and valueOf() convert a string to a long or to a Long, respectively. Each can take a radix argument to specify the base the value is represented in. toString() converts in the other direction and may also take a radix argument. toBinaryString(), toOctalString(), and toHexString() convert a long to a string using base 2, base 8, and base 16. These methods treat the long as an unsigned value. Other routines return the value of a Long as various primitive types, and, finally, the getLong() methods return the long value of a named property or the value of the specified default.

```
public final class Long extends Number implements Comparable {
// Public Constructors
    public Long(long value);
    public Long(String s) throws NumberFormatException;
// Public Constants
    public static final long MAX_VALUE;                      =9223372036854775807
    public static final long MIN_VALUE;                     =-9223372036854775808
1.1 public static final Class TYPE;
// Public Class Methods
1.2 public static Long decode(String nm) throws NumberFormatException;
    public static Long getLong(String nm);
    public static Long getLong(String nm, long val);
    public static Long getLong(String nm, Long val);
    public static long parseLong(String s) throws NumberFormatException;
    public static long parseLong(String s, int radix) throws NumberFormatException;
    public static String toBinaryString(long i);
    public static String toHexString(long i);
```

java.lang

```
    public static String toOctalString(long i);
    public static String toString(long i);
    public static String toString(long i, int radix);
    public static Long valueOf(String s) throws NumberFormatException;
    public static Long valueOf(String s, int radix) throws NumberFormatException;
// Public Instance Methods
1.2 public int compareTo(Long anotherLong);
// Methods Implementing Comparable
1.2 public int compareTo(Object o);
// Public Methods Overriding Number
1.1 public byte byteValue();
    public double doubleValue();
    public float floatValue();
    public int intValue();
    public long longValue();
1.1 public short shortValue();
// Public Methods Overriding Object
    public boolean equals(Object obj);
    public int hashCode();
    public String toString();
}
```

Hierarchy: Object→ Number(Serializable)→ Long(Comparable)

Passed To: Long.{compareTo(), getLong()}

Returned By: Long.{decode(), getLong(), valueOf()}

Math   Java 1.0
java.lang   PJ1.1

This class defines constants for the mathematical values *e* and *π* and defines static methods for floating-point trigonometry, exponentiation, and other operations. It is the equivalent of the C *<math.h>* functions. It also contains methods for computing minimum and maximum values and for generating pseudo-random numbers.

Most methods of Math operate on float and double floating-point values. Remember that these values are only approximations of actual real numbers. To allow implementations to take full advantage of the floating-point capabilities of a native platform, the methods of Math are not required to return exactly the same values on all platforms. In other words, the results returned by different implementations may differ slightly in the least-significant bits. In Java 1.3, applications that require strict platform-independence of results should use StrictMath instead.

```
public final class Math {
// No Constructor
// Public Constants
    public static final double E;                              =2.718281828459045
    public static final double PI;                             =3.141592653589793
// Public Class Methods
    public static int abs(int a);                                          strictfp
    public static long abs(long a);                                        strictfp
    public static float abs(float a);                                      strictfp
    public static double abs(double a);                                    strictfp
    public static double acos(double a);                                   strictfp
    public static double asin(double a);                                   strictfp
    public static double atan(double a);                                   strictfp
```

```
public static double atan2(double a, double b);                              strictfp
public static double ceil(double a);                                         strictfp
public static double cos(double a);                                          strictfp
public static double exp(double a);                                          strictfp
public static double floor(double a);                                        strictfp
public static double IEEEremainder(double f1, double f2);                    strictfp
public static double log(double a);                                          strictfp
public static int max(int a, int b);                                         strictfp
public static long max(long a, long b);                                      strictfp
public static float max(float a, float b);                                   strictfp
public static double max(double a, double b);                                strictfp
public static int min(int a, int b);                                         strictfp
public static long min(long a, long b);                                      strictfp
public static float min(float a, float b);                                   strictfp
public static double min(double a, double b);                                strictfp
public static double pow(double a, double b);                                strictfp
public static double random();                                               strictfp
public static double rint(double a);                                         strictfp
public static int round(float a);                                            strictfp
public static long round(double a);                                          strictfp
public static double sin(double a);                                          strictfp
public static double sqrt(double a);                                         strictfp
public static double tan(double a);                                          strictfp
1.2 public static double toDegrees(double angrad);                           strictfp
1.2 public static double toRadians(double angdeg);                           strictfp
}
```

NegativeArraySizeException   Java 1.0

java.lang   *serializable unchecked PJ1.1*

Signals an attempt to allocate an array with fewer than zero elements.

```
public class NegativeArraySizeException extends RuntimeException {
// Public Constructors
    public NegativeArraySizeException();
    public NegativeArraySizeException(String s);
}
```

Hierarchy: Object→ Throwable(Serializable)→ Exception→ RuntimeException→
NegativeArraySizeException

Thrown By: java.lang.reflect.Array.newInstance()

NoClassDefFoundError   Java 1.0

java.lang   *serializable error PJ1.1*

Signals that the definition of a specified class cannot be found.

```
public class NoClassDefFoundError extends LinkageError {
// Public Constructors
    public NoClassDefFoundError();
    public NoClassDefFoundError(String s);
}
```

Hierarchy: Object→ Throwable(Serializable)→ Error→ LinkageError→ NoClassDefFoundError

NoSuchFieldError

Java 1.0

java.lang

serializable error PJ1.1

Signals that a specified field cannot be found.

```
public class NoSuchFieldError extends IncompatibleClassChangeError {
// Public Constructors
    public NoSuchFieldError();
    public NoSuchFieldError(String s);
}
```

Hierarchy: Object→ Throwable(Serializable)→ Error→ LinkageError→
IncompatibleClassChangeError→ NoSuchFieldError

NoSuchFieldException

Java 1.1

java.lang

serializable checked PJ1.1

This exception signals that the specified field does not exist in the specified class.

```
public class NoSuchFieldException extends Exception {
// Public Constructors
    public NoSuchFieldException();
    public NoSuchFieldException(String s);
}
```

Hierarchy: Object→ Throwable(Serializable)→ Exception→ NoSuchFieldException

Thrown By: Class.{getDeclaredField(), getField()}

NoSuchMethodError

Java 1.0

java.lang

serializable error PJ1.1

Signals that a specified method cannot be found.

```
public class NoSuchMethodError extends IncompatibleClassChangeError {
// Public Constructors
    public NoSuchMethodError();
    public NoSuchMethodError(String s);
}
```

Hierarchy: Object→ Throwable(Serializable)→ Error→ LinkageError→
IncompatibleClassChangeError→ NoSuchMethodError

NoSuchMethodException

Java 1.0

java.lang

serializable checked PJ1.1

Signals that the specified method does not exist in the specified class.

```
public class NoSuchMethodException extends Exception {
// Public Constructors
    public NoSuchMethodException();
    public NoSuchMethodException(String s);
}
```

Hierarchy: Object→ Throwable(Serializable)→ Exception→ NoSuchMethodException

Thrown By: Class.{getConstructor(), getDeclaredConstructor(), getDeclaredMethod(), getMethod()}

NullPointerException

java.lang

Java 1.0

serializable unchecked PJ1.1

Signals an attempt to access a field or invoke a method of a null object.

```
public class NullPointerException extends RuntimeException {
// Public Constructors
    public NullPointerException();
    public NullPointerException(String s);
}
```

Hierarchy: Object→ Throwable(Serializable)→ Exception→ RuntimeException→
NullPointerException

Thrown By: java.awt.print.PrinterJob.setPageable()

Number

java.lang

Java 1.0

serializable PJ1.1

This is an abstract class that is the superclass of Byte, Short, Integer, Long, Float, and Double.
It defines the conversion functions those types implement.

```
public abstract class Number implements Serializable {
// Public Constructors
    public Number();
// Public Instance Methods
1.1 public byte byteValue();
    public abstract double doubleValue();
    public abstract float floatValue();
    public abstract int intValue();
    public abstract long longValue();
1.1 public short shortValue();
}
```

Hierarchy: Object→ Number(Serializable)

Subclasses: Byte, Double, Float, Integer, Long, Short, java.math.BigDecimal, java.math.BigInteger

Passed To: java.awt.Button.AccessibleAWTButton.setCurrentAccessibleValue(),
java.awt.Checkbox.AccessibleAWTCheckbox.setCurrentAccessibleValue(),
java.awt.CheckboxMenuItem.AccessibleAWTCheckboxMenuItem.setCurrentAccessibleValue(),
java.awt.MenuItem.AccessibleAWTMenuItem.setCurrentAccessibleValue(),
java.awt.Scrollbar.AccessibleAWTScrollBar.setCurrentAccessibleValue(),
javax.accessibility.AccessibleValue.setCurrentAccessibleValue(),
javax.swing.AbstractButton.AccessibleAbstractButton.setCurrentAccessibleValue(),
javax.swing.JInternalFrame.AccessibleJInternalFrame.setCurrentAccessibleValue(),
javax.swing.JInternalFrame.JDesktopIcon.AccessibleJDesktopIcon.setCurrentAccessibleValue(),
javax.swing.JProgressBar.AccessibleJProgressBar.setCurrentAccessibleValue(),
javax.swing.JScrollBar.AccessibleJScrollBar.setCurrentAccessibleValue(),
javax.swing.JSlider.AccessibleJSlider.setCurrentAccessibleValue(),
javax.swing.JSplitPane.AccessibleJSplitPane.setCurrentAccessibleValue()

Returned By: Too many methods to list.

NumberFormatException

java.lang

Java 1.0

serializable unchecked PJ1.1

Signals an illegal number format.

```
public class NumberFormatException extends IllegalArgumentException {
```

```
// Public Constructors
    public NumberFormatException();
    public NumberFormatException(String s);
}
```

Hierarchy: Object→ Throwable(Serializable)→ Exception→ RuntimeException→ IllegalArgumentException→ NumberFormatException

Thrown By: Too many methods to list.

Object   Java 1.0

java.lang   PJ1.1

This is the root class in Java. All classes are subclasses of Object, and thus all objects can invoke the public and protected methods of this class. For classes that implement the Cloneable interface, clone() makes a byte-for-byte copy of an Object. getClass() returns the Class object associated with any Object, and the notify(), notifyAll(), and wait() methods are used for thread synchronization on a given Object.

A number of these Object methods should be overridden by subclasses of Object. For example, a subclass should provide its own definition of the toString() method so that it can be used with the string concatenation operator and with the PrintWriter.println() methods. Defining the toString() method for all objects also helps with debugging.

The default implementation of the equals() method simply uses the == operator to test whether this object reference and the specified object reference refer to the same object. Many subclasses override this method to compare the individual fields of two distinct objects (i.e., they override the method to test for the equivalence of distinct objects rather than the equality of object references). Some classes, particularly those that override equals(), may also want to override the hashCode() method to provide an appropriate hashcode to be used when storing instances in a Hashtable data structure.

A class that allocates system resources other than memory (such as file descriptors or windowing system graphic contexts) should override the finalize() method to release these resources when the object is no longer referred to and is about to be garbage-collected.

```
public class Object {
// Public Constructors
    public Object();                                                          empty
// Public Instance Methods
    public boolean equals(Object obj);
    public final Class getClass();                                          native
    public int hashCode();                                                  native
    public final void notify();                                             native
    public final void notifyAll();                                          native
    public String toString();
    public final void wait() throws InterruptedException;
    public final void wait(long timeout) throws InterruptedException;       native
    public final void wait(long timeout, int nanos) throws InterruptedException;
// Protected Instance Methods
    protected Object clone() throws CloneNotSupportedException;             native
    protected void finalize() throws Throwable;                             empty
}
```

Subclasses: Too many classes to list.

Passed To: Too many methods to list.

Returned By: Too many methods to list.

Type Of: Too many fields to list.

OutOfMemoryError

Java 1.0
java.lang
serializable error PJ1.1

Signals that the interpreter has run out of memory (and that garbage collection is unable to free any memory).

```
public class OutOfMemoryError extends VirtualMachineError {
// Public Constructors
    public OutOfMemoryError();
    public OutOfMemoryError(String s);
}
```

Hierarchy: Object→ Throwable(Serializable)→ Error→ VirtualMachineError→ OutOfMemoryError

Package

Java 1.2
java.lang

This class represents a Java package. You can obtain the Package object for a given Class by calling the getPackage() method of the Class object. The static Package.getPackage() method returns a Package object for the named package, if any such package has been loaded by the current class loader. Similarly, the static Package.getPackages() returns all Package objects that have been loaded by the current class loader. Note that a Package object is not defined unless at least one class has been loaded from that package. Although you can obtain the Package of a given Class, you cannot obtain an array of Class objects contained in a specified Package.

If the classes that comprise a package are contained in a JAR file that has the appropriate attributes set in its manifest file, the Package object allows you to query the title, vendor, and version of both the package specification and the package implementation; all six values are strings. The specification version string has a special format. It consists of one or more integers, separated from each other by periods. Each integer can have leading zeros, but is not considered an octal digit. Increasing numbers indicate later versions. The isCompatibleWith() method calls getSpecificationVersion() to obtain the specification version and compares it with the version string supplied as an argument. If the package-specification version is the same as or greater than the specified string, isCompatibleWith() returns true. This allows you to test whether the version of a package (typically a standard extension) is new enough for the purposes of your application.

Packages may be sealed, which means that all classes in the package must come from the same JAR file. If a package is sealed, the no-argument version of isSealed() returns true. The one-argument version of isSealed() returns true if the specified URL represents the JAR file from which the package is loaded.

```
public class Package {
// No Constructor
// Public Class Methods
    public static Package getPackage(String name);
    public static Package[] getPackages();
// Property Accessor Methods (by property name)
    public String getImplementationTitle();
    public String getImplementationVendor();
    public String getImplementationVersion();
```

```
    public String getName();
    public boolean isSealed();
    public boolean isSealed(java.net.URL url);
    public String getSpecificationTitle();
    public String getSpecificationVendor();
    public String getSpecificationVersion();
// Public Instance Methods
    public boolean isCompatibleWith(String desired) throws NumberFormatException;
// Public Methods Overriding Object
    public int hashCode();
    public String toString();
}
```

Returned By: Class.getPackage(), ClassLoader.{definePackage(), getPackage(), getPackages()},
Package.{getPackage(), getPackages()}, java.net.URLClassLoader.definePackage()

Process   Java 1.0

java.lang   *PJ1.1*

This class describes a process that is running externally to the Java interpreter. Note that
a Process is very different from a Thread; the Process class is abstract and cannot be
instantiated. Call one of the Runtime.exec() methods to start a process and return a corresponding Process object.

waitFor() blocks until the process exits. exitValue() returns the exit code of the process.
destroy() kills the process. getErrorStream() returns an InputStream from which you can read
any bytes the process sends to its standard error stream. getInputStream() returns an Input-
Stream from which you can read any bytes the process sends to its standard output
stream. getOutputStream() returns an OutputStream you can use to send bytes to the standard input stream of the process.

```
public abstract class Process {
// Public Constructors
    public Process();
// Property Accessor Methods (by property name)
    public abstract java.io.InputStream getErrorStream();
    public abstract java.io.InputStream getInputStream();
    public abstract java.io.OutputStream getOutputStream();
// Public Instance Methods
    public abstract void destroy();
    public abstract int exitValue();
    public abstract int waitFor() throws InterruptedException;
}
```

Returned By: Runtime.exec()

Runnable   Java 1.0

java.lang   *runnable PJ1.1*

This interface specifies the run() method that is required to use with the Thread class.
Any class that implements this interface can provide the body of a thread. See Thread for
more information.

```
public interface Runnable {
// Public Instance Methods
    public abstract void run();
}
```

Implementations: java.awt.image.renderable.RenderableImageProducer, Thread, java.util.TimerTask, javax.jms.Session, javax.swing.text.AsyncBoxView.ChildState

Passed To: java.awt.EventQueue.{invokeAndWait(), invokeLater()}, java.awt.event.InvocationEvent.InvocationEvent(), Thread.Thread(), javax.swing.SwingUtilities.{invokeAndWait(), invokeLater()}, javax.swing.text.AbstractDocument.render(), javax.swing.text.Document.render(), javax.swing.text.LayoutQueue.addTask()

Returned By: javax.swing.text.LayoutQueue.waitForWork()

Type Of: java.awt.event.InvocationEvent.runnable

Runtime
Java 1.0

java.lang
PJ1.1

This class encapsulates a number of platform-dependent system functions. The static method getRuntime() returns the Runtime object for the current platform; this object can perform system functions in a platform-independent way.

exit() causes the Java interpreter to exit and return a specified return code. This method is usually invoked through System.exit(). In Java 1.3, addShutdownHook() registers an unstarted Thread object that is run when the virtual machine shuts down, either through a call to exit() or through a user interrupt (a CTRL-C, for example). The purpose of a shutdown hook is to perform necessary cleanup, such as shutting down network connections, deleting temporary files, and so on. Any number of hooks can be registered with addShutdownHook(). Before the interpreter exits, it starts all registered shutdown-hook threads and lets them run concurrently. Any hooks you write should perform their cleanup operation and exit promptly so they do not delay the shutdown process. To remove a shutdown hook before it is run, call removeShutdownHook(). To force an immediate exit that does not invoke the shutdown hooks, call halt().

exec() starts a new process running externally to the interpreter. Note that any processes run outside of Java may be system-dependent.

freeMemory() returns the approximate amount of free memory. totalMemory() returns the total amount of memory available to the Java interpreter. gc() forces the garbage collector to run synchronously; which may free up more memory. Similarly, runFinalization() forces the finalize() methods of unreferenced objects to be run immediately. This may free up system resources those objects were holding.

load() loads a dynamic library with a fully specified pathname. loadLibrary() loads a dynamic library with only the library name specified; it looks in platform-dependent locations for the specified library. These libraries generally contain native code definitions for native methods.

traceInstructions() and traceMethodCalls() enable and disable tracing by the interpreter. These methods are used for debugging or profiling an application. It is not specified how the VM emits the trace information, and VMs are not even required to support this feature.

Note that some of the Runtime methods are more commonly called via the static methods of the System class.

```
public class Runtime {
// No Constructor
// Public Class Methods
    public static Runtime getRuntime();
// Public Instance Methods
1.3 public void addShutdownHook(Thread hook);
    public Process exec(String[ ] cmdarray) throws java.io.IOException;
```

```
     public Process exec(String command) throws java.io.IOException;
     public Process exec(String command, String[ ] envp) throws java.io.IOException;
     public Process exec(String[ ] cmdarray, String[ ] envp) throws java.io.IOException;
     public void exit(int status);
     public long freeMemory();                                                              native
     public void gc();                                                                      native
1.3  public void halt(int status);
     public void load(String filename);
     public void loadLibrary(String libname);
1.3  public boolean removeShutdownHook(Thread hook);
     public void runFinalization();
     public long totalMemory();                                                             native
     public void traceInstructions(boolean on);                                             native
     public void traceMethodCalls(boolean on);                                              native
// Deprecated Public Methods
#    public java.io.InputStream getLocalizedInputStream(java.io.InputStream in);
#    public java.io.OutputStream getLocalizedOutputStream(java.io.OutputStream out);
1.1# public static void runFinalizersOnExit(boolean value);
}
```

Returned By: Runtime.getRuntime()

RuntimeException   Java 1.0
java.lang   *serializable unchecked PJ1.1*

This exception type is not used directly, but serves as a superclass of a group of runtime exceptions that need not be declared in the throws clause of a method definition.
These exceptions need not be declared because they are runtime conditions that can
generally occur in any Java method. Thus, declaring them would be unduly burden-
some, and Java does not require it.

```
public class RuntimeException extends Exception {
// Public Constructors
     public RuntimeException();
     public RuntimeException(String s);
}
```

Hierarchy: Object→ Throwable(Serializable)→ Exception→ RuntimeException

Subclasses: Too many classes to list.

RuntimePermission   Java 1.2
java.lang   *serializable permission*

This class is a java.security.Permission that represents access to various important system
facilities. A RuntimePermission has a name, or target, that represents the facility for which
permission is being sought or granted. The name "exitVM" represents permission to call
System.exit(), and the name "accessClassInPackage.java.lang" represents permission to
read classes from the java.lang package. The name of a RuntimePermission may use a ".*"
suffix as a wildcard. For example, the name "accessClassInPackage.java.*" represents
permission to read classes from any package whose name begins with "java.". RuntimePermission does not use action list strings as some Permission classes do; the name of
the permission alone is enough.

Supported RuntimePermssion names are: "accessClassInPackage.*package*", "accessDeclared-
Members", "createClassLoader", "createSecurityManager", "defineClassInPackage.*package*",
"exitVM", "getClassLoader", "getProtectionDomain", "loadLibrary.*library_name*", "modi-
fyThread", "modifyThreadGroup", "queuePrintJob", "readFileDescriptor", "set-

ContextClassLoader", "setFactory", "setIO", "setSecurityManager", "stopThread", and "writeFileDescriptor".

System administrators configuring security policies should be familiar with these permission names, the operations they govern access to, and with the risks inherent in granting any of them. Although system programmers may need to work with this class, application programmers should never need to use RuntimePermssion directly.

```
public final class RuntimePermission extends java.security.BasicPermission {
// Public Constructors
    public RuntimePermission(String name);
    public RuntimePermission(String name, String actions);
}
```

Hierarchy: Object→ java.security.Permission(java.security.Guard, Serializable)→ java.security.BasicPermission(Serializable)→ RuntimePermission

SecurityException   Java 1.0
java.lang   *serializable unchecked PJ1.1*

Signals that an operation is not permitted for security reasons.

```
public class SecurityException extends RuntimeException {
// Public Constructors
    public SecurityException();
    public SecurityException(String s);
}
```

Hierarchy: Object→ Throwable(Serializable)→ Exception→ RuntimeException→ SecurityException

Subclasses: java.rmi.RMISecurityException, java.security.AccessControlException

Thrown By: Too many methods to list.

SecurityManager   Java 1.0
java.lang   *PJ1.1*

This class defines the methods necessary to implement a security policy for the safe execution of untrusted code. Before performing potentially sensitive operations, Java calls methods of the SecurityManager object currently in effect to determine whether the operations are permitted. These methods throw a SecurityException if the operation is not permitted. Typical applications do not need to use or subclass SecurityManager. It is typically used only by web browsers, applet viewers, and other programs that need to run untrusted code in a controlled environment.

Prior to Java 1.2, this class is abstract, and the default implementation of each check() method throws a SecurityException unconditionally. The Java security mechanism has been overhauled as of Java 1.2. As part of the overhaul, this class is no longer abstract and its methods have useful default implementations, so there is rarely a need to subclass it. If so, the method returns silently; if not, it throws a SecurityException. checkPermission() operates by invoking the checkPermission() method of the system java.security.AccessController object. In Java 1.2 and later, all other check() methods of SecurityManager are now implemented on top of checkPermission().

```
public class SecurityManager {
// Public Constructors
    public SecurityManager();
// Property Accessor Methods (by property name)
    public Object getSecurityContext();                    default:AccessControlContext
1.1 public ThreadGroup getThreadGroup();
```

```
// Public Instance Methods
    public void checkAccept(String host, int port);
    public void checkAccess(Thread t);
    public void checkAccess(ThreadGroup g);
1.1 public void checkAwtEventQueueAccess();
    public void checkConnect(String host, int port);
    public void checkConnect(String host, int port, Object context);
    public void checkCreateClassLoader();
    public void checkDelete(String file);
    public void checkExec(String cmd);
    public void checkExit(int status);
    public void checkLink(String lib);
    public void checkListen(int port);
1.1 public void checkMemberAccess(Class clazz, int which);
1.1 public void checkMulticast(java.net.InetAddress maddr);
1.1 public void checkMulticast(java.net.InetAddress maddr, byte ttl);
    public void checkPackageAccess(String pkg);
    public void checkPackageDefinition(String pkg);
1.2 public void checkPermission(java.security.Permission perm);
1.2 public void checkPermission(java.security.Permission perm, Object context);
1.1 public void checkPrintJobAccess();
    public void checkPropertiesAccess();
    public void checkPropertyAccess(String key);
    public void checkRead(String file);
    public void checkRead(java.io.FileDescriptor fd);
    public void checkRead(String file, Object context);
1.1 public void checkSecurityAccess(String target);
    public void checkSetFactory();
1.1 public void checkSystemClipboardAccess();
    public boolean checkTopLevelWindow(Object window);
    public void checkWrite(String file);
    public void checkWrite(java.io.FileDescriptor fd);
// Protected Instance Methods
    protected Class[ ] getClassContext();                                            native
// Deprecated Public Methods
#   public boolean getInCheck();                                                 default:false
// Deprecated Protected Methods
#   protected int classDepth(String name);                                           native
#   protected int classLoaderDepth();
#   protected ClassLoader currentClassLoader();
1.1# protected Class currentLoadedClass();
#   protected boolean inClass(String name);
#   protected boolean inClassLoader();
// Deprecated Protected Fields
#   protected boolean inCheck;
}
```

Subclasses: java.rmi.RMISecurityManager

Passed To: System.setSecurityManager()

Returned By: System.getSecurityManager()

Short   Java 1.1

java.lang   *serializable comparable PJ1.1*

This class provides an object wrapper around the short primitive type. It defines useful
constants for the minimum and maximum values that can be stored by the short type,

and also a Class object constant that represents the short type. It also provides various methods for converting Short values to and from strings and other numeric types.

Most of the static methods of this class can convert a String to a Short object or a short value; the four parseShort() and valueOf() methods parse a number from the specified string using an optionally specified radix and return it in one of these two forms. The decode() method parses a number specified in base 10, base 8, or base 16 and returns it as a Short. If the string begins with "0x" or "#", it is interpreted as a hexadecimal number; if it begins with "0", it is interpreted as an octal number. Otherwise, it is interpreted as a decimal number.

Note that this class has two different toString() methods. One is static and converts a short primitive value to a string. The other is the usual toString() method that converts a Short object to a string. Most of the remaining methods convert a Short to various primitive numeric types.

```
public final class Short extends Number implements Comparable {
// Public Constructors
    public Short(short value);
    public Short(String s) throws NumberFormatException;
// Public Constants
    public static final short MAX_VALUE;                                           =32767
    public static final short MIN_VALUE;                                           =-32768
    public static final Class TYPE;
// Public Class Methods
    public static Short decode(String nm) throws NumberFormatException;
    public static short parseShort(String s) throws NumberFormatException;
    public static short parseShort(String s, int radix) throws NumberFormatException;
    public static String toString(short s);
    public static Short valueOf(String s) throws NumberFormatException;
    public static Short valueOf(String s, int radix) throws NumberFormatException;
// Public Instance Methods
1.2 public int compareTo(Short anotherShort);
// Methods Implementing Comparable
1.2 public int compareTo(Object o);
// Public Methods Overriding Number
    public byte byteValue();
    public double doubleValue();
    public float floatValue();
    public int intValue();
    public long longValue();
    public short shortValue();
// Public Methods Overriding Object
    public boolean equals(Object obj);
    public int hashCode();
    public String toString();
}
```

Hierarchy: Object→ Number(Serializable)→ Short(Comparable)

Passed To: Short.compareTo()

Returned By: Short.{decode(), valueOf()}

StackOverflowError   Java 1.0

java.lang   *serializable error PJ1.1*

Signals that a stack overflow has occurred within the Java interpreter.

```
public class StackOverflowError extends VirtualMachineError {
// Public Constructors
    public StackOverflowError();
    public StackOverflowError(String s);
}
```

Hierarchy: Object→ Throwable(Serializable)→ Error→ VirtualMachineError→ StackOverflowError

StrictMath   Java 1.3

java.lang

This class is identical to the Math class, but additionally requires that its methods strictly adhere to the behavior of certain published algorithms. The methods of StrictMath are intended to operate identically, down to the very least significant bit, for all possible arguments. When strict platform-independence of floating-point results is not required, use the Math class for better performance.

```
public final class StrictMath {
// No Constructor
// Public Constants
    public static final double E;                                  =2.718281828459045
    public static final double PI;                                 =3.141592653589793
// Public Class Methods
    public static int abs(int a);                                              strictfp
    public static long abs(long a);                                            strictfp
    public static float abs(float a);                                          strictfp
    public static double abs(double a);                                        strictfp
    public static double acos(double a);                                native strictfp
    public static double asin(double a);                                native strictfp
    public static double atan(double a);                                native strictfp
    public static double atan2(double a, double b);                     native strictfp
    public static double ceil(double a);                                native strictfp
    public static double cos(double a);                                 native strictfp
    public static double exp(double a);                                 native strictfp
    public static double floor(double a);                               native strictfp
    public static double IEEEremainder(double f1, double f2);           native strictfp
    public static double log(double a);                                 native strictfp
    public static int max(int a, int b);                                       strictfp
    public static long max(long a, long b);                                    strictfp
    public static float max(float a, float b);                                 strictfp
    public static double max(double a, double b);                              strictfp
    public static int min(int a, int b);                                       strictfp
    public static long min(long a, long b);                                    strictfp
    public static float min(float a, float b);                                 strictfp
    public static double min(double a, double b);                              strictfp
    public static double pow(double a, double b);                       native strictfp
    public static double random();                                             strictfp
    public static double rint(double a);                                native strictfp
    public static int round(float a);                                          strictfp
    public static long round(double a);                                        strictfp
    public static double sin(double a);                                 native strictfp
    public static double sqrt(double a);                                native strictfp
    public static double tan(double a);                                 native strictfp
    public static double toDegrees(double angrad);                             strictfp
    public static double toRadians(double angdeg);                             strictfp
}
```

String

java.lang

The String class represents a string of characters. A String object is created by the Java compiler whenever it encounters a string in double quotes; this method of creation is typically simpler than using a constructor. Some methods of this class provide useful string-manipulation functions. length() returns the number of characters in a string. charAt() extracts a character from a string. compareTo() compares two strings, while equals-IgnoreCase() tests strings for equality, ignoring case. startsWith() and endsWith() compare the start and end of a string to a specified value. indexOf() and lastIndexOf() search forward and backward in a string for a specified character or substring. substring() returns a substring of a string. replace() creates a new copy of the string with one character replaced by another. toUpperCase() and toLowerCase() convert the case of a string. trim() strips whitespace from the start and end of a string. concat() concatenates two strings, which can also be done with the + operator. The static valueOf() methods convert various Java primitive types to strings.

Note that String objects are immutable; there is no setCharAt() method to change the contents. The methods above that return a String do not modify the string they are passed, but instead return a modified copy of the string. Use a StringBuffer if you want to manipulate the contents of a string or toCharArray() to convert a string to an array of char values.

```
public final class String implements Comparable, Serializable {
// Public Constructors
     public String( );
1.1  public String(byte[ ] bytes);
     public String(StringBuffer buffer);
     public String(String value);
     public String(char[ ] value);
1.1  public String(byte[ ] bytes, String enc) throws java.io.UnsupportedEncodingException;
#    public String(byte[ ] ascii, int hibyte);
     public String(char[ ] value, int offset, int count);
1.1  public String(byte[ ] bytes, int offset, int length);
1.1  public String(byte[ ] bytes, int offset, int length, String enc) throws java.io.UnsupportedEncodingException;
#    public String(byte[ ] ascii, int hibyte, int offset, int count);
// Public Constants
1.2  public static final java.util.Comparator CASE_INSENSITIVE_ORDER;
// Public Class Methods
     public static String copyValueOf(char[ ] data);
     public static String copyValueOf(char[ ] data, int offset, int count);
     public static String valueOf(long l);
     public static String valueOf(float f);
     public static String valueOf(double d);
     public static String valueOf(int i);
     public static String valueOf(Object obj);
     public static String valueOf(char[ ] data);
     public static String valueOf(char c);
     public static String valueOf(boolean b);
     public static String valueOf(char[ ] data, int offset, int count);
// Public Instance Methods
     public char charAt(int index);
     public int compareTo(String anotherString);
1.2  public int compareToIgnoreCase(String str);
     public String concat(String str);
     public boolean endsWith(String suffix);
```

```
      public boolean equalsIgnoreCase(String anotherString);
1.1 public byte[ ] getBytes( );
1.1 public byte[ ] getBytes(String enc) throws java.io.UnsupportedEncodingException;
      public void getChars(int srcBegin, int srcEnd, char[ ] dst, int dstBegin);
      public int indexOf(String str);
      public int indexOf(int ch);
      public int indexOf(int ch, int fromIndex);
      public int indexOf(String str, int fromIndex);
      public String intern( );                                                  native
      public int lastIndexOf(int ch);
      public int lastIndexOf(String str);
      public int lastIndexOf(int ch, int fromIndex);
      public int lastIndexOf(String str, int fromIndex);
      public int length( );
      public boolean regionMatches(int toffset, String other, int ooffset, int len);
      public boolean regionMatches(boolean ignoreCase, int toffset, String other, int ooffset, int len);
      public String replace(char oldChar, char newChar);
      public boolean startsWith(String prefix);
      public boolean startsWith(String prefix, int toffset);
      public String substring(int beginIndex);
      public String substring(int beginIndex, int endIndex);
      public char[ ] toCharArray( );
      public String toLowerCase( );
1.1 public String toLowerCase(java.util.Locale locale);
      public String toUpperCase( );
1.1 public String toUpperCase(java.util.Locale locale);
      public String trim( );
// Methods Implementing Comparable
1.2 public int compareTo(Object o);
// Public Methods Overriding Object
      public boolean equals(Object anObject);
      public int hashCode( );
      public String toString( );
// Deprecated Public Methods
 #  public void getBytes(int srcBegin, int srcEnd, byte[ ] dst, int dstBegin);
}
```

Hierarchy: Object→ String(Comparable, Serializable)

Passed To: Too many methods to list.

Returned By: Too many methods to list.

Type Of: Too many fields to list.

StringBuffer   Java 1.0

java.lang   serializable PJ1.1

This class represents a mutable string of characters that can grow or shrink as necessary. Its mutability makes it suitable for processing text in place, which is not possible with the immutable String class. Its resizability and the various methods it implements make it easier to use than a char[]. You can query the character stored at a given index with charAt() and set the character with setCharAt(). Use the various append() methods to append text to the end of the buffer. Use insert() to insert text at a specified position within the buffer. Note that arguments to append() and insert() are converted to strings as necessary before they are appended or inserted. Use toString() to convert the contents of a StringBuffer to a String object. In Java 1.2 and later, use deleteCharAt() or delete() to delete a single character or a range of characters from the buffer. Use replace() to replace a range of characters with a specified String, and use substring() to convert a portion of a StringBuffer to a String.

String concatenation in Java is performed with the + operator and is implemented using the append() method of a StringBuffer. After a string is processed in a StringBuffer object, it can be efficiently converted to a String object for subsequent use. The String-Buffer.toString() method is typically implemented so that it does not copy the internal array of characters. Instead, it shares that array with the new String object, making a new copy for itself only if and when further modifications are made to the StringBuffer object.

```
public final class StringBuffer implements Serializable {
// Public Constructors
    public StringBuffer();
    public StringBuffer(int length);
    public StringBuffer(String str);
// Public Instance Methods
    public StringBuffer append(char[ ] str);                                  synchronized
    public StringBuffer append(boolean b);
    public StringBuffer append(Object obj);                                   synchronized
    public StringBuffer append(String str);                                   synchronized
    public StringBuffer append(char c);                                       synchronized
    public StringBuffer append(float f);
    public StringBuffer append(double d);
    public StringBuffer append(int i);
    public StringBuffer append(long l);
    public StringBuffer append(char[ ] str, int offset, int len);             synchronized
    public int capacity();
    public char charAt(int index);                                            synchronized
1.2 public StringBuffer delete(int start, int end);                           synchronized
1.2 public StringBuffer deleteCharAt(int index);                              synchronized
    public void ensureCapacity(int minimumCapacity);                          synchronized
    public void getChars(int srcBegin, int srcEnd, char[ ] dst, int dstBegin); synchronized
    public StringBuffer insert(int offset, char[ ] str);                      synchronized
    public StringBuffer insert(int offset, boolean b);
    public StringBuffer insert(int offset, Object obj);                       synchronized
    public StringBuffer insert(int offset, String str);                       synchronized
    public StringBuffer insert(int offset, char c);                           synchronized
    public StringBuffer insert(int offset, float f);
    public StringBuffer insert(int offset, double d);
    public StringBuffer insert(int offset, int i);
    public StringBuffer insert(int offset, long l);
1.2 public StringBuffer insert(int index, char[ ] str, int offset, int len);  synchronized
    public int length();
1.2 public StringBuffer replace(int start, int end, String str);             synchronized
    public StringBuffer reverse();                                            synchronized
    public void setCharAt(int index, char ch);                                synchronized
    public void setLength(int newLength);                                     synchronized
1.2 public String substring(int start);
1.2 public String substring(int start, int end);                             synchronized
// Public Methods Overriding Object
    public String toString();
}
```

Hierarchy: Object→ StringBuffer(Serializable)

Passed To: Too many methods to list.

Returned By: Too many methods to list.

StringIndexOutOfBoundsException
java.lang   Java 1.0

serializable unchecked PJ1.1

Signals that the index used to access a character of a String or StringBuffer is less than zero or is too large.

```
public class StringIndexOutOfBoundsException extends IndexOutOfBoundsException {
// Public Constructors
    public StringIndexOutOfBoundsException();
    public StringIndexOutOfBoundsException(int index);
    public StringIndexOutOfBoundsException(String s);
}
```

Hierarchy: Object→ Throwable(Serializable)→ Exception→ RuntimeException→ IndexOutOfBoundsException→ StringIndexOutOfBoundsException

System
java.lang   Java 1.0

PJ1.1

This class defines a platform-independent interface to system facilities, including system properties and system input and output streams. All methods and variables of this class are static, and the class cannot be instantiated. Because the methods defined by this class are low-level system methods, most require special permissions and cannot be executed by untrusted code.

getProperty() looks up a named property on the system-properties list, returning the optionally specified default value if no property definition is found. getProperties() returns the entire properties list. setProperties() sets a Properties object on the properties list. In Java 1.2 and later, setProperty() sets the value of a system property. The following table lists system properties that are always defined. Untrusted code may be unable to read some or all of these properties. Additional properties can be defined using the –D option when invoking the Java interpreter.

Property Name	Description
java.home	The directory Java is installed in
java.class.path	Where classes are loaded from
java.specification.version	Version of the Java API specification (Java 1.2)
java.specification.vendor	Vendor of the Java API specifiction (Java 1.2)
java.specification.name	Name of the Java API specification (Java 1.2)
java.version	Version of the Java API implementation
java.vendor	Vendor of this Java API implementation
java.vendor.url	URL of the vendor of this Java API implementation
java.vm.specification.version	Version of the Java VM specification (Java 1.2)
java.vm.specification.vendor	Vendor of the Java VM specification (Java 1.2)
java.vm.specification.name	Name of the Java VM specification (Java 1.2)
java.vm.version	Version of the Java VM implementation (Java 1.2)
java.vm.vendor	Vendor of the Java VM implementation (Java 1.2)
java.vm.name	Name of the Java VM implementation (Java 1.2)
java.class.version	Version of the Java class file format
os.name	Name of the host operating system

Property Name	Description
os.arch	Host operating system architecture
os.version	Version of the host operating system
file.separator	Platform directory separator character
path.separator	Platform path separator character
line.separator	Platform line separator character(s)
user.name	Current user's account name
user.home	Home directory of current user
user.dir	The current working directory

The in, out, and err fields hold the standard input, output, and error streams for the system. These fields are frequently used in calls such as System.out.println(). In Java 1.1, setIn(), setOut(), and setErr() allow these streams to be redirected.

System also defines various other useful static methods. exit() causes the Java VM to exit. arraycopy() efficiently copies an array or a portion of an array into a destination array. currentTimeMillis() returns the current time in milliseconds since midnight GMT, January 1, 1970 GMT. gc() requests that the garbage collector perform a thorough garbage-collection pass, and runFinalization() requests that the garbage collector finalize all objects that are ready for finalization. Applications do not typically need to call these garbage-collection methods, but they can be useful when benchmarking code with currentTimeMillis(). identityHashCode() computes the hashcode for an object in the same way that the default Object.hashCode() method does. It does this regardless of whether or how the hashCode() method has been overridden. load() and loadLibrary() can read libraries of native code into the system. mapLibraryName() converts a system-independent library name into a system-dependent library filename. Finally, getSecurityManager() and setSecurityManager() get and set the system SecurityManager object responsible for the system security policy.

See also Runtime, which defines several other methods that provide low-level access to system facilities.

```
public final class System {
// No Constructor
// Public Constants
    public static final java.io.PrintStream err;
    public static final java.io.InputStream in;
    public static final java.io.PrintStream out;
// Public Class Methods
    public static void arraycopy(Object src, int src_position, Object dst, int dst_position, int length);   native
    public static long currentTimeMillis();                                                                 native
    public static void exit(int status);
    public static void gc();
    public static java.util.Properties getProperties();
    public static String getProperty(String key);
    public static String getProperty(String key, String def);
    public static SecurityManager getSecurityManager();
1.1 public static int identityHashCode(Object x);                                                           native
    public static void load(String filename);
    public static void loadLibrary(String libname);
1.2 public static String mapLibraryName(String libname);                                                    native
    public static void runFinalization();
1.1 public static void setErr(java.io.PrintStream err);
1.1 public static void setIn(java.io.InputStream in);
```

```
1.1 public static void setOut(java.io.PrintStream out);
    public static void setProperties(java.util.Properties props);
1.2 public static String setProperty(String key, String value);
    public static void setSecurityManager(SecurityManager s);
// Deprecated Public Methods
#   public static String getenv(String name);
1.1# public static void runFinalizersOnExit(boolean value);
}
```

Thread   Java 1.0

java.lang   *runnable PJ1.1*

This class encapsulates all information about a single thread of control running on the
Java interpreter. To create a thread, you must either pass a Runnable object (i.e., an
object that implements the Runnable interface by defining a run() method) to the Thread
constructor or subclass Thread so that it defines its own run() method. The run() method
of the Thread or of the specified Runnable object is the body of the thread. It begins executing when the start() method of the Thread object is called. The thread runs until the
run() method returns. isAlive() returns true if a thread has been started, and the run()
method has not yet exited.

The static methods of this class operate on the currently running thread. currentThread()
returns the Thread object of the currently running code. sleep() makes the current thread
stop for a specified amount of time. yield() makes the current thread give up control to
any other threads of equal priority that are waiting to run.

The instance methods may be called by one thread to operate on a different thread.
checkAccess() checks whether the running thread has permission to modify a Thread
object and throws a SecurityException if it does not. join() waits for a thread to die. inter-
rupt() wakes up a waiting or sleeping thread (with an InterruptedException) or sets an
interrupted flag on a nonsleeping thread. A thread can test its own interrupted flag with
the static interrupted() method or can test the flag of another thread with isInterrupted().
Calling interrupted() implicitly clears the interrupted flag, but calling isInterrupted() does
not. Methods related to sleep() and interrupt() are the wait() and notify() methods defined
by the Object class. Calling wait() causes the current thread to block until the object's
notify() method is called by another thread.

setName() sets the name of a thread, which is purely optional. setPriority() sets the priority
of the thread. Higher priority threads run before lower-priority threads. Java does not
specify what happens to multiple threads of equal priority; some systems perform time-
slicing and share the CPU between such threads. On other systems, one compute-
bound thread that does not call yield() may starve another thread of the same priority.
setDaemon() sets a boolean flag that specifies whether this thread is a daemon or not.
The Java VM keeps running as long as at least one non-daemon thread is running. Call
getThreadGroup() to obtain the ThreadGroup of which a thread is part. In Java 1.2 and later,
use setContextClassLoader() to specify the ClassLoader to be used to load any classes
required by the thread.

suspend(), resume(), and stop() suspend, resume, and stop a given thread, respectively,
but all three methods are deprecated because they are inherently unsafe and can cause
deadlock. If a thread must be stoppable, have it periodically check a flag and exit if the
flag is set.

```
public class Thread implements Runnable {
// Public Constructors
    public Thread();
```

```
    public Thread(String name);
    public Thread(Runnable target);
    public Thread(Runnable target, String name);
    public Thread(ThreadGroup group, Runnable target);
    public Thread(ThreadGroup group, String name);
    public Thread(ThreadGroup group, Runnable target, String name);
// Public Constants
    public static final int MAX_PRIORITY;                                        =10
    public static final int MIN_PRIORITY;                                         =1
    public static final int NORM_PRIORITY;                                        =5
// Public Class Methods
    public static int activeCount();
    public static Thread currentThread();                                      native
    public static void dumpStack();
    public static int enumerate(Thread[ ] tarray);
    public static boolean interrupted();
    public static void sleep(long millis) throws InterruptedException;         native
    public static void sleep(long millis, int nanos) throws InterruptedException;
    public static void yield();                                                native
// Property Accessor Methods (by property name)
    public final boolean isAlive();                                   native default:false
1.2 public ClassLoader getContextClassLoader();
1.2 public void setContextClassLoader(ClassLoader cl);
    public final boolean isDaemon();                                       default:false
    public final void setDaemon(boolean on);
    public boolean isInterrupted();                                        default:false
    public final String getName();                                    default:"Thread-0"
    public final void setName(String name);
    public final int getPriority();                                           default:5
    public final void setPriority(int newPriority);
    public final ThreadGroup getThreadGroup();
// Public Instance Methods
    public final void checkAccess();
    public void destroy();
    public void interrupt();
    public final void join() throws InterruptedException;
    public final void join(long millis) throws InterruptedException;       synchronized
    public final void join(long millis, int nanos) throws InterruptedException;  synchronized
    public void start();                                           native synchronized
// Methods Implementing Runnable
    public void run();
// Public Methods Overriding Object
    public String toString();
// Deprecated Public Methods
#   public int countStackFrames();                                            native
#   public final void resume();
#   public final void stop();
#   public final void stop(Throwable obj);                                synchronized
#   public final void suspend();
}
```

Hierarchy: Object→ Thread(Runnable)

Passed To: Runtime.{addShutdownHook(), removeShutdownHook()}, SecurityManager.checkAccess(),
Thread.enumerate(), ThreadGroup.{enumerate(), uncaughtException()}

Returned By: Thread.currentThread(), javax.swing.text.AbstractDocument.getCurrentWriter()

ThreadDeath

Java 1.0

java.lang

serializable error PJ1.1

Signals that a thread should terminate. This error is thrown in a thread when the Thread.stop() method is called for that thread. This is an unusual Error type that simply causes a thread to be terminated, but does not print an error message or cause the interpreter to exit. You can catch ThreadDeath errors to do any necessary cleanup for a thread, but if you do, you must rethrow the error so that the thread actually terminates.

```
public class ThreadDeath extends Error {
// Public Constructors
    public ThreadDeath();
}
```

Hierarchy: Object→ Throwable(Serializable)→ Error→ ThreadDeath

ThreadGroup

Java 1.0

java.lang

PJ1.1

This class represents a group of threads and allows that group to be manipulated as a whole. A ThreadGroup can contain Thread objects, as well as other child ThreadGroup objects. All ThreadGroup objects are created as children of some other ThreadGroup, and thus there is a parent/child hierarchy of ThreadGroup objects. Use getParent() to obtain the parent ThreadGroup, and use activeCount(), activeGroupCount(), and the various enumerate() methods to list the child Thread and ThreadGroup objects. Most applications can simply rely on the default system thread group. System-level code and applications such as servers that need to create a large number of threads may find it convenient to create their own ThreadGroup objects, however.

interrupt() interrupts all threads in the group at once. setMaxPriority() specifies the maximum priority any thread in the group can have. checkAccess() checks whether the calling thread has permission to modify the given thread group. The method throws a SecurityException if the current thread does not have access. uncaughtException() contains the code that is run when a thread terminates because of an uncaught exception or error. You can customize this method by subclassing ThreadGroup.

```
public class ThreadGroup {
// Public Constructors
    public ThreadGroup(String name);
    public ThreadGroup(ThreadGroup parent, String name);
// Property Accessor Methods (by property name)
    public final boolean isDaemon();
    public final void setDaemon(boolean daemon);
1.1 public boolean isDestroyed();                                     synchronized
    public final int getMaxPriority();
    public final void setMaxPriority(int pri);
    public final String getName();
    public final ThreadGroup getParent();
// Public Instance Methods
    public int activeCount();
    public int activeGroupCount();
    public final void checkAccess();
    public final void destroy();
    public int enumerate(ThreadGroup[ ] list);
    public int enumerate(Thread[ ] list);
```

```
    public int enumerate(ThreadGroup[ ] list, boolean recurse);
    public int enumerate(Thread[ ] list, boolean recurse);
1.2 public final void interrupt( );
    public void list( );
    public final boolean parentOf(ThreadGroup g);
    public void uncaughtException(Thread t, Throwable e);
// Public Methods Overriding Object
    public String toString( );
// Deprecated Public Methods
1.1# public boolean allowThreadSuspension(boolean b);
#   public final void resume( );
#   public final void stop( );
#   public final void suspend( );
}
```

Passed To: SecurityManager.checkAccess(), Thread.Thread(), ThreadGroup.{enumerate(), parentOf(), ThreadGroup()}

Returned By: SecurityManager.getThreadGroup(), Thread.getThreadGroup(), ThreadGroup.getParent()

ThreadLocal   Java 1.2

java.lang

This class provides a convenient way to create thread-local variables. When you declare a static field in a class, there is only one value for that field, shared by all objects of the class. When you declare a nonstatic instance field in a class, every object of the class has its own separate copy of that variable. ThreadLocal provides an option between these two extremes. If you declare a static field to hold a ThreadLocal object, that ThreadLocal holds a different value for each thread. Objects running in the same thread see the same value when they call the get() method of the ThreadLocal object. Objects running in different threads obtain different values from get(), however.

The set() method sets the value held by the ThreadLocal object for the currently running thread. get() returns the value held for the currently running thread. Note that there is no way to obtain the value of the ThreadLocal object for any thread other than the one that calls get(). To understand the ThreadLocal class, you may find it helpful to think of a ThreadLocal object as a hashtable or java.util.Map that maps from Thread objects to arbitrary values. Calling set() creates an association between the current Thread (Thread.currentThread()) and the specified value. Calling get() first looks up the current thread, then uses the hashtable to look up the value associated with that current thread.

If a thread calls get() for the first time without having first called set() to establish a thread-local value, get() calls the protected initialValue() method to obtain the initial value to return. The default implementation of initialValue() simply returns null, but subclasses can override this if they desire.

See also InheritableThreadLocal, which allows thread-local values to be inherited from parent threads by child threads.

```
public class ThreadLocal {
// Public Constructors
    public ThreadLocal( );
// Public Instance Methods
    public Object get( );
    public void set(Object value);
```

```
// Protected Instance Methods
    protected Object initialValue();                                              constant
}
```

Subclasses: InheritableThreadLocal

Throwable   Java 1.0

java.lang   *serializable PJ1.1*

This is the root class of the Java exception and error hierarchy. All exceptions and
errors are subclasses of Throwable. The getMessage() method retrieves any error message
associated with the exception or error. printStackTrace() prints a stack trace that shows
where the exception occurred. fillInStackTrace() extends the stack trace when the exception is partially handled and then rethrown.

```
public class Throwable implements Serializable {
// Public Constructors
    public Throwable();
    public Throwable(String message);
// Public Instance Methods
    public Throwable fillInStackTrace();                                           native
1.1 public String getLocalizedMessage();                                      default:null
    public String getMessage();                                               default:null
    public void printStackTrace();
    public void printStackTrace(java.io.PrintStream s);
1.1 public void printStackTrace(java.io.PrintWriter s);
// Public Methods Overriding Object
    public String toString();
}
```

Hierarchy: Object→ Throwable(Serializable)

Subclasses: Error, Exception

Passed To: Too many methods to list.

Returned By: ClassNotFoundException.getException(), ExceptionInInitializerError.getException(),
Throwable.fillInStackTrace(), java.lang.reflect.InvocationTargetException.getTargetException(),
java.lang.reflect.UndeclaredThrowableException.getUndeclaredThrowable(),
javax.naming.NamingException.getRootCause(), javax.servlet.ServletException.getRootCause()

Thrown By: java.awt.AWTEvent.finalize(), java.awt.Font.finalize(), java.awt.Frame.finalize(),
java.awt.Window.finalize(), Object.finalize(), java.lang.reflect.InvocationHandler.invoke(),
javax.swing.text.AbstractDocument.AbstractElement.finalize()

Type Of: java.rmi.RemoteException.detail, java.rmi.activation.ActivationException.detail,
javax.naming.NamingException.rootException, org.omg.CORBA.portable.UnknownException.originalEx

UnknownError   Java 1.0

java.lang   *serializable error PJ1.1*

Signals that an unknown error has occurred at the level of the Java Virtual Machine.

```
public class UnknownError extends VirtualMachineError {
// Public Constructors
    public UnknownError();
    public UnknownError(String s);
}
```

Hierarchy: Object→ Throwable(Serializable)→ Error→ VirtualMachineError→ UnknownError

UnsatisfiedLinkError   Java 1.0
java.lang   *serializable error PJ1.1*

Signals that Java cannot satisfy all the links in a class that it has loaded.

```
public class UnsatisfiedLinkError extends LinkageError {
// Public Constructors
  public UnsatisfiedLinkError();
  public UnsatisfiedLinkError(String s);
}
```

Hierarchy: Object→ Throwable(Serializable)→ Error→ LinkageError→ UnsatisfiedLinkError

UnsupportedClassVersionError   Java 1.2
java.lang   *serializable error*

Every Java class file contains a version number that specifies the version of the class file format. This error is thrown when the Java Virtual Machine attempts to read a class file with a version number it does not support.

```
public class UnsupportedClassVersionError extends ClassFormatError {
// Public Constructors
  public UnsupportedClassVersionError();
  public UnsupportedClassVersionError(String s);
}
```

Hierarchy: Object→ Throwable(Serializable)→ Error→ LinkageError→ ClassFormatError→ UnsupportedClassVersionError

UnsupportedOperationException   Java 1.2
java.lang   *serializable unchecked*

Signals that a method you have called is not supported, and its implementation does not do anything (except throw this exception). This exception is used most often by the Java collection framework of java.util. Immutable or unmodifiable collections throw this exception when a modification method, such as add() or delete(), is called.

```
public class UnsupportedOperationException extends RuntimeException {
// Public Constructors
  public UnsupportedOperationException();
  public UnsupportedOperationException(String message);
}
```

Hierarchy: Object→ Throwable(Serializable)→ Exception→ RuntimeException→ UnsupportedOperationException

VerifyError   Java 1.0
java.lang   *serializable error PJ1.1*

Signals that a class has not passed the byte-code verification procedures.

```
public class VerifyError extends LinkageError {
// Public Constructors
  public VerifyError();
  public VerifyError(String s);
}
```

Hierarchy: Object→ Throwable(Serializable)→ Error→ LinkageError→ VerifyError

VirtualMachineError   Java 1.0

java.lang   *serializable error PJ1.1*

An abstract error type that serves as superclass for a group of errors related to the Java Virtual Machine. See InternalError, UnknownError, OutOfMemoryError, and StackOverflowError.

```
public abstract class VirtualMachineError extends Error {
// Public Constructors
    public VirtualMachineError();
    public VirtualMachineError(String s);
}
```

Hierarchy: Object→ Throwable(Serializable)→ Error→ VirtualMachineError

Subclasses: InternalError, OutOfMemoryError, StackOverflowError, UnknownError

Void   Java 1.1

java.lang   *PJ1.1*

The Void class cannot be instantiated and serves merely as a placeholder for its static TYPE field, which is a Class object constant that represents the void type.

```
public final class Void {
// No Constructor
// Public Constants
    public static final Class TYPE;
}
```

CHAPTER 13

The java.lang.ref Package

The java.lang.ref package defines classes that allow Java programs to interact with the Java garbage collector. A Reference represents an indirect reference to an arbitrary object, known as the *referent.* SoftReference, WeakReference, and PhantomReference are three concrete subclasses of Reference that interact with the garbage collector in different ways, as explained in the individual class descriptions that follow. ReferenceQueue represents a linked list of Reference objects. Any Reference object may have a ReferenceQueue associated with it. A Reference object is *enqueued* on its ReferenceQueue at some point after the garbage collector determines that the referent object has become appropriately unreachable. (The exact level of unreachability depends on the type of Reference being used.) An application can monitor a ReferenceQueue to determine when referent objects enter a new reachability status. Figure 13-1 shows the hierarchy of this package, which is new as of Java 1.2.

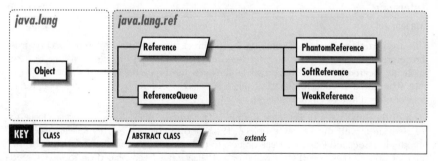

Figure 13–1: The java.lang.ref package

Using the mechanisms defined in this package, you can implement a cache that grows and shrinks in size according to the amount of available system memory. Or, you can implement a hashtable that associates auxiliary information with arbitrary objects, but does not prevent those objects from being garbage-collected if they are otherwise unused. The mechanisms provided by this package are low-level ones, however, and typical applications do not use java.lang.ref directly. Instead, they rely on higher-level utilities built on top of the package. See java.util.WeakHashMap for one example.

PhantomReference

Java 1.2

java.lang.ref

This class represents a reference to an object that does not prevent the referent object from being finalized by the garbage collector. When (or at some point after) the garbage collector determines that there are no more hard (direct) references to the referent object, that there are no SoftReference or WeakReference objects that refer to the referent, and that the referent has been finalized, it enqueues the PhantomReference object on the ReferenceQueue specified when the PhantomReference was created. This serves as notification that the object has been finalized and provides one last opportunity for any required cleanup code to be run.

To prevent a PhantomReference object from resurrecting its referent object, its get() method always returns null, both before and after the PhantomReference is enqueued. Nevertheless, a PhantomReference is not automatically cleared when it is enqueued, so when you remove a PhantomReference from a ReferenceQueue, you must call its clear() method or allow the PhantomReference object itself to be garbage-collected.

This class provides a more flexible mechanism for object cleanup than the finalize() method does. Note that in order to take advantage of it, it is necessary to subclass PhantomReference and define a method to perform the desired cleanup. Furthermore, since the get() method of a PhantomReference always returns null, such a subclass must also store whatever data is required for the cleanup operation.

```
public class PhantomReference extends java.lang.ref.Reference {
// Public Constructors
    public PhantomReference(Object referent, ReferenceQueue q);
// Public Methods Overriding Reference
    public Object get();                                            constant
}
```

Hierarchy: Object→ java.lang.ref.Reference→ PhantomReference

Reference

Java 1.2

java.lang.ref

This abstract class represents some type of indirect reference to a referent. get() returns the referent if the reference has not been explicitly cleared by the clear() method or implicitly cleared by the garbage collector. There are three concrete subclasses of Reference. The garbage collector handles these subclasses differently and clears their references under different circumstances.

Each of the subclasses of Reference defines a constructor that allows a ReferenceQueue to be associated with the Reference object. The garbage collector places Reference objects onto their associated ReferenceQueue objects to provide notification about the state of the referent object. isEnqueued() tests whether a Reference has been placed on the associated queue, and enqueue() explicitly places it on the queue. enqueue() returns false if the Reference object does not have an associated ReferenceQueue, or if it has already been enqueued.

```
public abstract class Reference {
// No Constructor
// Public Instance Methods
    public void clear();
    public boolean enqueue();
```

```
    public Object get( );
    public boolean isEnqueued( );
}
```

Subclasses: PhantomReference, SoftReference, WeakReference

Returned By: ReferenceQueue.{poll(), remove()}

ReferenceQueue
Java 1.2

java.lang.ref

This class represents a queue (or linked list) of Reference objects that have been enqueued because the garbage collector has determined that the referent objects to which they refer are no longer adequately reachable. It serves as a notification system for object-reachability changes. Use poll() to return the first Reference object on the queue; the method returns null if the queue is empty. Use remove() to return the first element on the queue, or, if the queue is empty, to wait for a Reference object to be enqueued. You can create as many ReferenceQueue objects as needed. Specify a ReferenceQueue for a Reference object by passing it to the SoftReference(), WeakReference(), or PhantomReference() constructor.

A ReferenceQueue is required to use PhantomReference objects. It is optional with SoftReference and WeakReference objects; for these classes, the get() method returns null if the referent object is no longer adequately reachable.

```
public class ReferenceQueue {
// Public Constructors
    public ReferenceQueue( );
// Public Instance Methods
    public java.lang.ref.Reference poll( );
    public java.lang.ref.Reference remove( ) throws InterruptedException;
    public java.lang.ref.Reference remove(long timeout) throws IllegalArgumentException, InterruptedException;
}
```

Passed To: PhantomReference.PhantomReference(), SoftReference.SoftReference(), WeakReference.WeakReference()

SoftReference
Java 1.2

java.lang.ref

This class represents a soft reference to an object. A SoftReference is not cleared while there are any remaining hard (direct) references to the referent. Once the referent is no longer in use (i.e., there are no remaining hard references to it), the garbage collector may clear the SoftReference to the referent at any time. However, the garbage collector does not clear a SoftReference until it determines that system memory is running low. In particular, the Java VM never throws an OutOfMemoryError without first clearing all soft references and reclaiming the memory of the referents. The VM may (but is not required to) clear soft references according to a least-recently-used ordering.

If a SoftReference has an associated ReferenceQueue, the garbage collector enqueues the SoftReference at some time after it clears the reference.

SoftReference is particularly useful for implementing object-caching systems that do not have a fixed size, but grow and shrink as available memory allows.

```
public class SoftReference extends java.lang.ref.Reference {
// Public Constructors
    public SoftReference(Object referent);
```

```
    public SoftReference(Object referent, ReferenceQueue q);
// Public Methods Overriding Reference
    public Object get();
}
```

Hierarchy: Object→ java.lang.ref.Reference→ SoftReference

WeakReference   Java 1.2
java.lang.ref

This class refers to an object in a way that does not prevent that referent object from being finalized and reclaimed by the garbage collector. When the garbage collector determines that there are no more hard (direct) references to the object, and that there are no SoftReference objects that refer to the object, it clears the WeakReference and marks the referent object for finalization. At some point after this, it also enqueues the WeakReference on its associated ReferenceQueue, if there is one, in order to provide notification that the referent has been reclaimed.

WeakReference is used by java.util.WeakHashMap to implement a hashtable that does not prevent the hashtable key object from being garbage-collected. WeakHashMap is useful when you want to associate auxiliary information with an object but do not want to prevent the object from being reclaimed.

```
public class WeakReference extends java.lang.ref.Reference {
// Public Constructors
    public WeakReference(Object referent);
    public WeakReference(Object referent, ReferenceQueue q);
}
```

Hierarchy: Object→ java.lang.ref.Reference→ WeakReference

CHAPTER 14

The java.lang.reflect Package

The java.lang.reflect package contains the classes and interfaces that, along with java.lang.Class, comprise the Java Reflection API. This package is new as of Java 1.1. Figure 14-1 shows the class hierarchy.

The Constructor, Field, and Method classes represent the constructors, fields, and methods of a class. Because these types all represent members of a class, they each implement the Member interface, which defines a simple set of methods that can be invoked for any class member. These classes allow information about the class members to be obtained, methods and constructors to be invoked, and fields to be queried and set.

Class member modifiers are represented as integers that specify a number of bit flags. The Modifer class defines static methods that help interpret the meanings of these flags. The Array class defines static methods for creating arrays, and reading and writing array elements.

In Java 1.3, the Proxy class allows the dynamic creation of new Java classes that implement a specified set of interfaces. When an interface method is invoked on an instance of such a proxy class, the invocation is delegated to an InvocationHandler object.

AccessibleObject   Java 1.2
java.lang.reflect

This class is the superclass of the Method, Constructor, and Field classes; its methods provide a mechanism for trusted applications to work with private, protected, and default visibility members that would otherwise not be accessible through the Reflection API. This class is new as of Java 1.2; in Java 1.1, the Method, Constructor, and Field classes extended Object directly.

To use the java.lang.reflect package to access a member to which your code would not normally have access, pass true to the setAccessible() method. If your code has an appropriate ReflectPermission ("suppressAccessChecks"), this allows access to the member as if it were declared public. The static version of setAccessible() is a convenience method that sets the accessible flag for an array of members, but performs only a single security check.

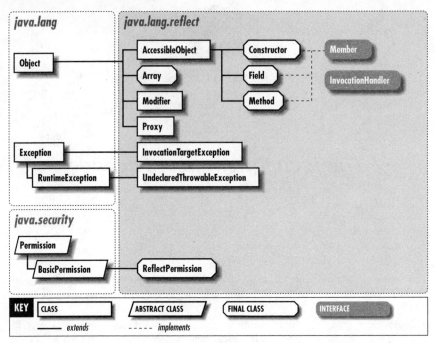

Figure 14–1: The java.lang.reflect package

```
public class AccessibleObject {
// Protected Constructors
    protected AccessibleObject();
// Public Class Methods
    public static void setAccessible(AccessibleObject[ ] array, boolean flag) throws SecurityException;
// Public Instance Methods
    public boolean isAccessible();
    public void setAccessible(boolean flag) throws SecurityException;
}
```

Subclasses: Constructor, Field, Method

Passed To: AccessibleObject.setAccessible()

Array   Java 1.1

java.lang.reflect   PJ1.1

This class contains methods that allow you to set and query the values of array elements, to determine the length of an array, and to create new instances of arrays. Note
that the Array class can manipulate only array values, not array types; Java data types,
including array types, are represented by java.lang.Class. Since the Array class represents a
Java value, unlike the Field, Method, and Constructor classes, which represent class members, the Array class is significantly different (despite some surface similarities) from
those other classes in this package. Most notably, all the methods of Array are static and
apply to all array values, not just a specific field, method, or constructor.

The get() method returns the value of the specified element of the specified array as an
Object. If the array elements are of a primitive type, the value is converted to a wrapper

object before being returned. You can also use getInt() and related methods to query array elements and return them as specific primitive types. The set() method and its primitive type variants perform the opposite operation. Also, the getLength() method returns the length of the array.

The newInstance() methods create new arrays. One version of this method is passed the number of elements in the array and the type of those elements. The other version of this method creates multidimensional arrays. Besides specifying the component type of the array, it is passed an array of numbers. The length of this array specifies the number of dimensions for the array to be created, and the values of each of the array elements specify the size of each dimension of the created array.

```
public final class Array {
// No Constructor
// Public Class Methods
    public static Object get(Object array, int index) throws IllegalArgumentException,      native
        ArrayIndexOutOfBoundsException;
    public static boolean getBoolean(Object array, int index) throws IllegalArgumentException,      native
        ArrayIndexOutOfBoundsException;
    public static byte getByte(Object array, int index) throws IllegalArgumentException,      native
        ArrayIndexOutOfBoundsException;
    public static char getChar(Object array, int index) throws IllegalArgumentException,      native
        ArrayIndexOutOfBoundsException;
    public static double getDouble(Object array, int index) throws IllegalArgumentException,      native
        ArrayIndexOutOfBoundsException;
    public static float getFloat(Object array, int index) throws IllegalArgumentException,      native
        ArrayIndexOutOfBoundsException;
    public static int getInt(Object array, int index) throws IllegalArgumentException,      native
        ArrayIndexOutOfBoundsException;
    public static int getLength(Object array) throws IllegalArgumentException;      native
    public static long getLong(Object array, int index) throws IllegalArgumentException,      native
        ArrayIndexOutOfBoundsException;
    public static short getShort(Object array, int index) throws IllegalArgumentException,      native
        ArrayIndexOutOfBoundsException;
    public static Object newInstance(Class componentType, int length) throws NegativeArraySizeException;
    public static Object newInstance(Class componentType, int[ ] dimensions) throws IllegalArgumentException,
        NegativeArraySizeException;
    public static void set(Object array, int index, Object value) throws IllegalArgumentException,      native
        ArrayIndexOutOfBoundsException;
    public static void setBoolean(Object array, int index, boolean z) throws IllegalArgumentException,      native
        ArrayIndexOutOfBoundsException;
    public static void setByte(Object array, int index, byte b) throws IllegalArgumentException,      native
        ArrayIndexOutOfBoundsException;
    public static void setChar(Object array, int index, char c) throws IllegalArgumentException,      native
        ArrayIndexOutOfBoundsException;
    public static void setDouble(Object array, int index, double d) throws IllegalArgumentException,      native
        ArrayIndexOutOfBoundsException;
    public static void setFloat(Object array, int index, float f) throws IllegalArgumentException,      native
        ArrayIndexOutOfBoundsException;
    public static void setInt(Object array, int index, int i) throws IllegalArgumentException,      native
        ArrayIndexOutOfBoundsException;
    public static void setLong(Object array, int index, long l) throws IllegalArgumentException,      native
        ArrayIndexOutOfBoundsException;
    public static void setShort(Object array, int index, short s) throws IllegalArgumentException,      native
        ArrayIndexOutOfBoundsException;
}
```

java.lang. reflect

Constructor
java.lang.reflect

Java 1.1

PJ1.1

This class represents a constructor method of a class. Instances of Constructor are obtained by calling getConstructor() and related methods of java.lang.Class. Constructor implements the Member interface, so you can use the methods of that interface to obtain the constructor name, modifiers, and declaring class. In addition, getParameterTypes() and getExceptionTypes() also return important information about the represented constructor.

In addition to these methods that return information about the constructor, the newInstance() method allows the constructor to be invoked with an array of arguments in order to create a new instance of the class that declares the constructor. If any of the arguments to the constructor are of primitive types, they must be converted to their corresponding wrapper object types to be passed to newInstance(). If the constructor causes an exception, the Throwable object it throws is wrapped within the InvocationTargetException that is thrown by newInstance(). Note that newInstance() is much more useful than the newInstance() method of java.lang.Class because it can pass arguments to the constructor.

```
public final class Constructor extends AccessibleObject implements Member {
// No Constructor
// Public Instance Methods
    public Class[ ] getExceptionTypes();
    public Class[ ] getParameterTypes();
    public Object newInstance(Object[ ] initargs) throws InstantiationException, IllegalAccessException,   native
        IllegalArgumentException, InvocationTargetException;
// Methods Implementing Member
    public Class getDeclaringClass();
    public int getModifiers();
    public String getName();
// Public Methods Overriding Object
    public boolean equals(Object obj);
    public int hashCode();
    public String toString();
}
```

Hierarchy: Object→ AccessibleObject→ Constructor(Member)

Returned By: Class.{getConstructor(), getConstructors(), getDeclaredConstructor(), getDeclaredConstructors()}

Field
java.lang.reflect

Java 1.1

PJ1.1

This class represents a field of a class. Instances of Field are obtained by calling the getField() and related methods of java.lang.Class. Field implements the Member interface, so once you have obtained a Field object, you can use getName(), getModifiers(), and getDeclaringClass() to determine the name, modifiers, and class of the field. Additionally, getType() returns the type of the field.

The set() method sets the value of the represented field for a specified object. (If the represented field is static, no object need be specified, of course.) If the field is of a primitive type, its value can be specified using a wrapper object of type Boolean, Integer, and so on, or it can be set using the setBoolean(), setInt(), and related methods. Similarly, the get() method queries the value of the represented field for a specified object and returns the field value as an Object. Various other methods query the field value and return it as various primitive types.

```
public final class Field extends AccessibleObject implements Member {
// No Constructor
// Public Instance Methods
    public Object get(Object obj) throws IllegalArgumentException, IllegalAccessException;                          native
    public boolean getBoolean(Object obj) throws IllegalArgumentException, IllegalAccessException;                  native
    public byte getByte(Object obj) throws IllegalArgumentException, IllegalAccessException;                        native
    public char getChar(Object obj) throws IllegalArgumentException, IllegalAccessException;                        native
    public double getDouble(Object obj) throws IllegalArgumentException, IllegalAccessException;                    native
    public float getFloat(Object obj) throws IllegalArgumentException, IllegalAccessException;                      native
    public int getInt(Object obj) throws IllegalArgumentException, IllegalAccessException;                          native
    public long getLong(Object obj) throws IllegalArgumentException, IllegalAccessException;                        native
    public short getShort(Object obj) throws IllegalArgumentException, IllegalAccessException;                      native
    public Class getType();
    public void set(Object obj, Object value) throws IllegalArgumentException, IllegalAccessException;              native
    public void setBoolean(Object obj, boolean z) throws IllegalArgumentException, IllegalAccessException;          native
    public void setByte(Object obj, byte b) throws IllegalArgumentException, IllegalAccessException;                native
    public void setChar(Object obj, char c) throws IllegalArgumentException, IllegalAccessException;                native
    public void setDouble(Object obj, double d) throws IllegalArgumentException, IllegalAccessException;            native
    public void setFloat(Object obj, float f) throws IllegalArgumentException, IllegalAccessException;              native
    public void setInt(Object obj, int i) throws IllegalArgumentException, IllegalAccessException;                  native
    public void setLong(Object obj, long l) throws IllegalArgumentException, IllegalAccessException;                native
    public void setShort(Object obj, short s) throws IllegalArgumentException, IllegalAccessException;              native
// Methods Implementing Member
    public Class getDeclaringClass();
    public int getModifiers();
    public String getName();
// Public Methods Overriding Object
    public boolean equals(Object obj);
    public int hashCode();
    public String toString();
}
```

Hierarchy: Object→ AccessibleObject→ Field(Member)

Passed To: javax.ejb.deployment.EntityDescriptor.setContainerManagedFields()

Returned By: Class.{getDeclaredField(), getDeclaredFields(), getField(), getFields()},
javax.ejb.deployment.EntityDescriptor.getContainerManagedFields()

InvocationHandler   Java 1.3

java.lang.reflect

This interface defines a single invoke() method that is called whenever a method is
invoked on a dynamically created Proxy object. Every Proxy object has an associated
InvocationHandler object that is specified when the Proxy is instantiated. All method invocations on the proxy object are translated into calls to the invoke() method of the Invocation-
Handler.

The first argument to invoke() is the Proxy object through which the method was invoked.
The second argument is a Method object that represents the method that was invoked.
Call the getDeclaringClass() method of this Method object to determine the interface in
which the method was declared. This may be a superinterface of one of the specified
interfaces or even java.lang.Object when the method invoked is toString(), hashCode(), or
one of the other Object methods. The third argument to invoke() is the array of method
arguments. Any primitive type arguments are wrapped in their corresponding object
wrappers (e.g., Boolean, Integer, Double).

The value returned by invoke() becomes the return value of the proxy object method invocation and must be of an appropriate type. If the proxy object method returns a primitive type, invoke() should return an instance of the corresponding wrapper class. invoke() can throw any unchecked (i.e., runtime) exceptions or any checked exceptions declared by the proxy object method. If invoke() throws a checked exception that is not declared by the proxy object, that exception is wrapped within an unchecked UndeclaredThrowableException that is thrown in its place.

```
public interface InvocationHandler {
// Public Instance Methods
    public abstract Object invoke(Object proxy, Method method, Object[ ] args) throws Throwable;
}
```

Passed To: Proxy.{newProxyInstance(), Proxy()}

Returned By: Proxy.getInvocationHandler()

Type Of: Proxy.h

InvocationTargetException   Java 1.1

java.lang.reflect   *serializable checked PJ1.1*

An object of this class is thrown by Method.invoke() and Constructor.newInstance() when an exception is thrown by the method or constructor invoked through those methods. The InvocationTargetException class serves as a wrapper around the object that was thrown; that object can be retrieved with the getTargetException() method.

```
public class InvocationTargetException extends Exception {
// Public Constructors
    public InvocationTargetException(Throwable target);
    public InvocationTargetException(Throwable target, String s);
// Protected Constructors
    protected InvocationTargetException();
// Public Instance Methods
    public Throwable getTargetException();
// Public Methods Overriding Throwable
1.2 public void printStackTrace();
1.2 public void printStackTrace(java.io.PrintWriter pw);
1.2 public void printStackTrace(java.io.PrintStream ps);
}
```

Hierarchy: Object→ Throwable(Serializable)→ Exception→ InvocationTargetException

Thrown By: java.awt.EventQueue.invokeAndWait(), Constructor.newInstance(), Method.invoke(), javax.swing.SwingUtilities.invokeAndWait()

Member   Java 1.1

java.lang.reflect   *PJ1.1*

This interface defines the methods shared by all members (fields, methods, and constructors) of a class. getName() returns the name of the member, getModifiers() returns its modifiers, and getDeclaringClass() returns the Class object that represents the class of which the member is a part.

```
public interface Member {
// Public Constants
    public static final int DECLARED;                                    =1
    public static final int PUBLIC;                                      =0
```

```
// Public Instance Methods
    public abstract Class getDeclaringClass();
    public abstract int getModifiers();
    public abstract String getName();
}
```

Implementations: Constructor, Field, Method

Method   Java 1.1
java.lang.reflect   *PJ1.1*

This class represents a method. Instances of Method are obtained by calling the get-Method() and related methods of java.lang.Class. Method implements the Member interface, so you can use the methods of that interface to obtain the method name, modifiers, and declaring class. In addition, getReturnType(), getParameterTypes(), and getExceptionTypes() also return important information about the represented method.

Perhaps most importantly, the invoke() method allows the method represented by the Method object to be invoked with a specified array of argument values. If any of the arguments are of primitive types, they must be converted to their corresponding wrapper object types in order to be passed to invoke(). If the represented method is an instance method (i.e., if it is not static), the instance on which it should be invoked must also be passed to invoke(). The return value of the represented method is returned by invoke(). If the return value is a primitive value, it is first converted to the corresponding wrapper type. If the invoked method causes an exception, the Throwable object it throws is wrapped within the InvocationTargetException that is thrown by invoke().

```
public final class Method extends AccessibleObject implements Member {
// No Constructor
// Property Accessor Methods (by property name)
    public Class getDeclaringClass();                              Implements:Member
    public Class[] getExceptionTypes();
    public int getModifiers();                                     Implements:Member
    public String getName();                                       Implements:Member
    public Class[] getParameterTypes();
    public Class getReturnType();
// Public Instance Methods
    public Object invoke(Object obj, Object[] args) throws IllegalAccessException, IllegalArgumentException,    native
        InvocationTargetException;
// Methods Implementing Member
    public Class getDeclaringClass();
    public int getModifiers();
    public String getName();
// Public Methods Overriding Object
    public boolean equals(Object obj);
    public int hashCode();
    public String toString();
}
```

Hierarchy: Object → AccessibleObject → Method(Member)

Passed To: Too many methods to list.

Returned By: java.beans.EventSetDescriptor.{getAddListenerMethod(), getListenerMethods(), getRemoveListenerMethod()}, java.beans.IndexedPropertyDescriptor.{getIndexedReadMethod(), getIndexedWriteMethod()}, java.beans.MethodDescriptor.getMethod(), java.beans.PropertyDescriptor.{getReadMethod(), getWriteMethod()}, Class.{getDeclaredMethod(), getDeclaredMethods(), getMethod(), getMethods()},

javax.ejb.deployment.AccessControlEntry.getMethod(),
javax.ejb.deployment.ControlDescriptor.getMethod()

Modifier   Java 1.1

java.lang.reflect   *PJ1.1*

This class defines a number of constants and static methods that can interpret the integer values returned by the getModifiers() methods of the Field, Method, and Constructor classes. The isPublic(), isAbstract(), and related methods return true if the modifier value includes the specified modifier; otherwise, they return false. The constants defined by this class specify the various bit flags used in the modifiers value. You can use these constants to test for modifiers if you want to perform your own boolean algebra.

```
public class Modifier {
// Public Constructors
    public Modifier();
// Public Constants
    public static final int ABSTRACT;                          =1024
    public static final int FINAL;                             =16
    public static final int INTERFACE;                         =512
    public static final int NATIVE;                            =256
    public static final int PRIVATE;                           =2
    public static final int PROTECTED;                         =4
    public static final int PUBLIC;                            =1
    public static final int STATIC;                            =8
1.2 public static final int STRICT;                            =2048
    public static final int SYNCHRONIZED;                      =32
    public static final int TRANSIENT;                         =128
    public static final int VOLATILE;                          =64
// Public Class Methods
    public static boolean isAbstract(int mod);
    public static boolean isFinal(int mod);
    public static boolean isInterface(int mod);
    public static boolean isNative(int mod);
    public static boolean isPrivate(int mod);
    public static boolean isProtected(int mod);
    public static boolean isPublic(int mod);
    public static boolean isStatic(int mod);
1.2 public static boolean isStrict(int mod);
    public static boolean isSynchronized(int mod);
    public static boolean isTransient(int mod);
    public static boolean isVolatile(int mod);
    public static String toString(int mod);
}
```

Proxy   Java 1.3

java.lang.reflect   *serializable*

This class defines a simple but powerful API for dynamically generating a *proxy class*. A proxy class implements a specified list of interfaces and delegates invocations of the methods defined by those interfaces to a separate invocation handler object.

The static getProxyClass() method dynamically creates a new Class object that implements each of the interfaces specified in the supplied Class[] array. The newly created class is defined in the context of the specified ClassLoader. The Class returned by getProxyClass() is a subclass of Proxy. Every class that is dynamically generated by getProxyClass() has a single public constructor, which expects a single argument of type InvocationHandler. You can create an instance of the dynamic proxy class by using the Constructor class to invoke this constructor. Or, more simply, you can combine the call to getProxyClass() with the constructor call by calling the static newProxyInstance() method, which both defines and instantiates a proxy class.

Every instance of a dynamic proxy class has an associated InvocationHandler object. All method calls made on a proxy class are translated into calls to the invoke() method of this InvocationHandler object, which can handle the call in any way it sees fit. The static getInvocationHandler() method returns the InvocationHandler object for a given proxy object. The static isProxyClass() method returns true if a specified Class object is a dynamically generated proxy class.

```
public class Proxy implements Serializable {
// Protected Constructors
    protected Proxy(InvocationHandler h);
// Public Class Methods
    public static InvocationHandler getInvocationHandler(Object proxy) throws IllegalArgumentException;
    public static Class getProxyClass(ClassLoader loader, Class[ ] interfaces) throws IllegalArgumentException;
    public static boolean isProxyClass(Class cl);
    public static Object newProxyInstance(ClassLoader loader, Class[ ] interfaces, InvocationHandler h)
        throws IllegalArgumentException;
// Protected Instance Fields
    protected InvocationHandler h;
}
```

Hierarchy: Object→ Proxy(Serializable)

ReflectPermission   Java 1.2
java.lang.reflect   *serializable permission*

This class is a java.security.Permission that governs access to private, protected, and default-visibility methods, constructors, and fields through the Java Reflection API. In Java 1.2, the only defined name, or target, for ReflectPermission is "suppressAccessChecks". This permission is required to call the setAccessible() method of AccessibleObject. Unlike some Permission subclasses, ReflectPermission does not use a list of actions. See also AccessibleObject.

System administrators configuring security policies should be familiar with this class, but application programmers should never need to use it directly.

```
public final class ReflectPermission extends java.security.BasicPermission {
// Public Constructors
    public ReflectPermission(String name);
    public ReflectPermission(String name, String actions);
}
```

Hierarchy: Object→ java.security.Permission(java.security.Guard, Serializable)→
java.security.BasicPermission(Serializable)→ ReflectPermission

UndeclaredThrowableException   Java 1.3
java.lang.reflect   *serializable unchecked*

Thrown by a method of a Proxy object if the invoke() method of the proxy's InvocationHandler throws a checked exception not declared by the original method. This class serves as an unchecked exception wrapper around the checked exception. Use getUndeclaredThrowable() to obtain the checked exception thrown by invoke().

```
public class UndeclaredThrowableException extends RuntimeException {
// Public Constructors
    public UndeclaredThrowableException(Throwable undeclaredThrowable);
    public UndeclaredThrowableException(Throwable undeclaredThrowable, String s);
// Public Instance Methods
    public Throwable getUndeclaredThrowable();
// Public Methods Overriding Throwable
    public void printStackTrace();
    public void printStackTrace(java.io.PrintStream ps);
    public void printStackTrace(java.io.PrintWriter pw);
}
```

Hierarchy: Object→ Throwable(Serializable)→ Exception→ RuntimeException→
UndeclaredThrowableException

CHAPTER 15

The java.math Package

The java.math package, new as of Java 1.1, contains classes for arbitrary-precision integer and floating-point arithmetic. Arbitrary-length integers are required for cryptography, and arbitrary-precision floating-point values are useful for financial applications that need to be careful about rounding errors. The class hierarchy of this extremely small package is shown in Figure 15-1.

Figure 15-1: The java.math package

BigDecimal   Java 1.1
java.math   *serializable comparable PJ1.1(opt)*

This subclass of java.lang.Number represents a floating-point number of arbitrary size and precision. Its methods duplicate the functionality of the standard Java arithmetic operators. The compareTo() method compares the value of two BigDecimal objects and returns –1, 0, or 1 to indicate the result of the comparison.

A BigDecimal object is represented as an integer of arbitrary size and an integer scale that specifies the number of decimal places in the value. When working with BigDecimal values, you can explicitly specify the amount of precision (i.e., the number of decimal places) you are interested in. Also, whenever a BigDecimal method can discard precision (e.g., in a division operation), you are required to specify what sort of rounding should be performed on the digit to the left of the discarded digit or digits. The eight constants defined by this class specify the available rounding modes. Because the BigDecimal class provides arbitrary precision and gives you explicit control over rounding and the number of decimal places you are interested in, it can be useful when dealing with quantities that represent money or in other circumstances where the tolerance for rounding errors is low.

```
public class BigDecimal extends Number implements Comparable {
// Public Constructors
    public BigDecimal(BigInteger val);
    public BigDecimal(String val);
    public BigDecimal(double val);
    public BigDecimal(BigInteger unscaledVal, int scale);
// Public Constants
    public static final int ROUND_CEILING;                              =2
    public static final int ROUND_DOWN;                                 =1
    public static final int ROUND_FLOOR;                                =3
    public static final int ROUND_HALF_DOWN;                            =5
    public static final int ROUND_HALF_EVEN;                            =6
    public static final int ROUND_HALF_UP;                              =4
    public static final int ROUND_UNNECESSARY;                          =7
    public static final int ROUND_UP;                                   =0
// Public Class Methods
    public static BigDecimal valueOf(long val);
    public static BigDecimal valueOf(long unscaledVal, int scale);
// Public Instance Methods
    public BigDecimal abs();
    public BigDecimal add(BigDecimal val);
    public int compareTo(BigDecimal val);
    public BigDecimal divide(BigDecimal val, int roundingMode);
    public BigDecimal divide(BigDecimal val, int scale, int roundingMode);
    public BigDecimal max(BigDecimal val);
    public BigDecimal min(BigDecimal val);
    public BigDecimal movePointLeft(int n);
    public BigDecimal movePointRight(int n);
    public BigDecimal multiply(BigDecimal val);
    public BigDecimal negate();
    public int scale();
    public BigDecimal setScale(int scale);
    public BigDecimal setScale(int scale, int roundingMode);
    public int signum();
    public BigDecimal subtract(BigDecimal val);
    public BigInteger toBigInteger();
1.2 public BigInteger unscaledValue();
// Methods Implementing Comparable
1.2 public int compareTo(Object o);
// Public Methods Overriding Number
    public double doubleValue();
    public float floatValue();
    public int intValue();
    public long longValue();
// Public Methods Overriding Object
    public boolean equals(Object x);
    public int hashCode();
```

```
    public String toString( );
}
```

Hierarchy: Object→ Number(Serializable)→ BigDecimal(Comparable)

Passed To: Too many methods to list.

Returned By: Too many methods to list.

Type Of: org.omg.CORBA.FixedHolder.value

BigInteger
java.math

Java 1.1

serializable comparable PJ1.1(opt)

This subclass of java.lang.Number represents integers that can be arbitrarily large (i.e., integers that are not limited to the 64 bits available with the long data type). BigInteger defines methods that duplicate the functionality of the standard Java arithmetic and bit-manipulation operators. The compareTo() method compares two BigInteger objects and returns –1, 0, or 1 to indicate the result of the comparison. The gcd(), modPow(), modInverse(), and isProbablePrime() methods perform advanced operations and are used primarily in cryptographic and related algorithms.

```
public class BigInteger extends Number implements Comparable {
// Public Constructors
    public BigInteger(String val);
    public BigInteger(byte[ ] val);
    public BigInteger(String val, int radix);
    public BigInteger(int signum, byte[ ] magnitude);
    public BigInteger(int numBits, java.util.Random rnd);
    public BigInteger(int bitLength, int certainty, java.util.Random rnd);
// Public Constants
    public static final BigInteger ONE;
    public static final BigInteger ZERO;
// Public Class Methods
    public static BigInteger valueOf(long val);
// Public Instance Methods
    public BigInteger abs( );
    public BigInteger add(BigInteger val);
    public BigInteger and(BigInteger val);
    public BigInteger andNot(BigInteger val);
    public int bitCount( );
    public int bitLength( );
    public BigInteger clearBit(int n);
    public int compareTo(BigInteger val);
    public BigInteger divide(BigInteger val);
    public BigInteger[ ] divideAndRemainder(BigInteger val);
    public BigInteger flipBit(int n);
    public BigInteger gcd(BigInteger val);
    public int getLowestSetBit( );
    public boolean isProbablePrime(int certainty);
    public BigInteger max(BigInteger val);
    public BigInteger min(BigInteger val);
    public BigInteger mod(BigInteger m);
    public BigInteger modInverse(BigInteger m);
    public BigInteger modPow(BigInteger exponent, BigInteger m);
    public BigInteger multiply(BigInteger val);
    public BigInteger negate( );
```

java.math

```
    public BigInteger not();
    public BigInteger or(BigInteger val);
    public BigInteger pow(int exponent);
    public BigInteger remainder(BigInteger val);
    public BigInteger setBit(int n);
    public BigInteger shiftLeft(int n);
    public BigInteger shiftRight(int n);
    public int signum();
    public BigInteger subtract(BigInteger val);
    public boolean testBit(int n);
    public byte[ ] toByteArray();
    public String toString(int radix);
    public BigInteger xor(BigInteger val);
// Methods Implementing Comparable
1.2 public int compareTo(Object o);
// Public Methods Overriding Number
    public double doubleValue();
    public float floatValue();
    public int intValue();
    public long longValue();
// Public Methods Overriding Object
    public boolean equals(Object x);
    public int hashCode();
    public String toString();
}
```

Hierarchy: Object→ Number(Serializable)→ BigInteger(Comparable)

Passed To: Too many methods to list.

Returned By: Too many methods to list.

Type Of: BigInteger.{ONE, ZERO}, java.security.spec.RSAKeyGenParameterSpec.{F0, F4}

CHAPTER 16

The java.net Package

The java.net package provides a powerful and flexible infrastructure for networking. Figure 16-1 and Figure 16-2 show the class hierarchy for this package. Many of the classes in this package are part of the networking infrastructure and are not used by normal applications; these complicated classes can make the package a difficult one to understand. In this overview, I describe only the classes an application might normally use.

The URL class represents an Internet uniform resource locator (URL). It provides a very simple interface to networking: the object referred to by the URL can be downloaded with a single call, or streams may be opened to read from or write to the object. At a slightly more complex level, a URLConnection object can be obtained from a given URL object. The URLConnection class provides additional methods that allow you to work with URLs in more sophisticated ways.

If you want to do more than simply download an object referenced by a URL, you can do your own networking with the Socket class. This class allows you to connect to a specified port on a specified Internet host and read and write data using the InputStream and OutputStream classes of the java.io package. If you want to implement a server to accept connections from clients, you can use the related ServerSocket class. Both Socket and ServerSocket use the InetAddress address class, which represents an Internet address.

The java.net package allows you to do low-level networking with DatagramPacket objects, which may be sent and received over the network through a DatagramSocket object. As of Java 1.1, the package has been extended to include a MulticastSocket class that supports multicast networking.

Authenticator   Java 1.2
java.net

This abstract class defines a customizable mechanism for requesting and performing password authentication. The static setDefault() method establishes the systemwide Authenticator object to use when password authentication is requested. The implementation can obtain the required authentication information from the user however it wants (e.g., through a text- or a GUI-based interface). setDefault() can be called only once; subsequent calls are ignored. Calling setDefault() requires an appropriate NetPermission.

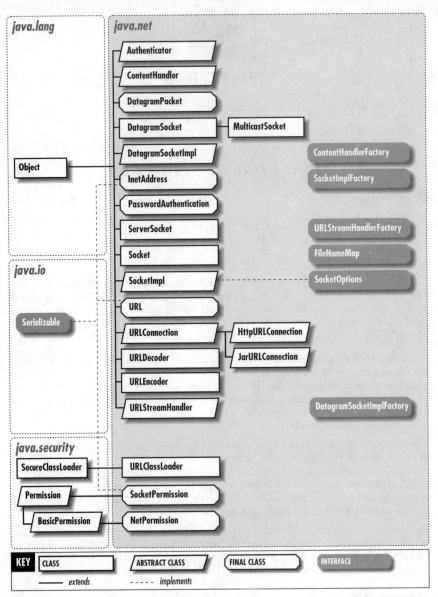

Figure 16-1: The classes of the java.net package

When an application or the Java runtime system requires password authentication (to read the contents of a specified URL, for example), it calls the static requestPasswordAuthentication() method, passing arguments that specify the host and port for which the password is required and a prompt that may be displayed to the user. This method looks up the default Authenticator for the system and calls its getPasswordAuthentication() method. Calling requestPasswordAuthentication() requires an appropriate NetPermission.

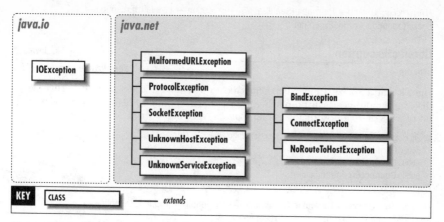

Figure 16-2: The exceptions of the java.net package

Authenticator is an abstract class; its default implementation of getPasswordAuthentication() always returns null. To create an Authenticator, you must override this method so that it prompts the user to enter a username and password and returns that information in the form of a PasswordAuthentication object. Your implementation of getPasswordAuthentication() may call the various getRequesting() methods to find who is requesting the password and what the recommended user prompt is.

```
public abstract class Authenticator {
// Public Constructors
    public Authenticator();
// Public Class Methods
    public static PasswordAuthentication requestPasswordAuthentication(InetAddress addr, int port,
                                        String protocol, String prompt, String scheme);
    public static void setDefault(Authenticator a);                                synchronized
// Protected Instance Methods
    protected PasswordAuthentication getPasswordAuthentication();                     constant
    protected final int getRequestingPort();
    protected final String getRequestingPrompt();
    protected final String getRequestingProtocol();
    protected final String getRequestingScheme();
    protected final InetAddress getRequestingSite();
}
```

Passed To: Authenticator.setDefault()

BindException   Java 1.1

java.net   *serializable checked PJ1.1*

Signals that a socket cannot be bound to a local address and port. This often means that the port is already in use.

```
public class BindException extends SocketException {
// Public Constructors
    public BindException();
    public BindException(String msg);
}
```

Hierarchy: Object→ Throwable(Serializable)→ Exception→ java.io.IOException→ SocketException→ BindException

ConnectException

java.net

serializable checked PJ1.1

Signals that a socket cannot be connected to a remote address and port. This means that the remote host can be reached, but is not responding, perhaps because there is no process on that host that is listening on the specified port.

```
public class ConnectException extends SocketException {
// Public Constructors
    public ConnectException( );
    public ConnectException(String msg);
}
```

Hierarchy: Object→ Throwable(Serializable)→ Exception→ java.io.IOException→ SocketException→ java.net.ConnectException

ContentHandler

java.net

PJ1.1

This abstract class defines a method that reads data from a URLConnection and returns an object that represents that data. Each subclass that implements this method is responsible for handling a different type of content (i.e., a different MIME type). Applications never create ContentHandler objects directly; they are created, when necessary, by the registered ContentHandlerFactory object. Applications should also never call ContentHandler methods directly; they should call URL.getContent() or URLConnection.getContent() instead. You need to subclass ContentHandler only if you are writing a web browser or similar application that needs to parse and understand some new content type.

```
public abstract class ContentHandler {
// Public Constructors
    public ContentHandler( );
// Public Instance Methods
    public abstract Object getContent(URLConnection urlc) throws java.io.IOException;
1.3 public Object getContent(URLConnection urlc, Class[ ] classes) throws java.io.IOException;
}
```

Returned By: ContentHandlerFactory.createContentHandler()

ContentHandlerFactory

java.net

PJ1.1

This interface defines a method that creates and returns an appropriate ContentHandler object for a specified MIME type. A systemwide ContentHandlerFactory interface may be specified using the URLConnection.setContentHandlerFactory() method. Normal applications never need to use or implement this interface.

```
public interface ContentHandlerFactory {
// Public Instance Methods
    public abstract ContentHandler createContentHandler(String mimetype);
}
```

Passed To: URLConnection.setContentHandlerFactory()

DatagramPacket

Java 1.0

java.net

PJ1.1

This class implements a packet of data that may be sent or received over the network through a DatagramSocket. One of the DatagramPacket constructors specifies an array of binary data to be sent with its destination address and port. A packet created with this constructor can then be sent with the send() method of a DatagramSocket. The other DatagramPacket constructor specifies an array of bytes into which data should be received. The receive() method of DatagramSocket waits for data and stores it in a DatagramPacket created in this way. The contents and sender of a received packet can be queried with the DatagramPacket instance methods.

```
public final class DatagramPacket {
// Public Constructors
    public DatagramPacket(byte[ ] buf, int length);
1.2 public DatagramPacket(byte[ ] buf, int offset, int length);
    public DatagramPacket(byte[ ] buf, int length, InetAddress address, int port);
1.2 public DatagramPacket(byte[ ] buf, int offset, int length, InetAddress address, int port);
// Property Accessor Methods (by property name)
    public InetAddress getAddress();                                              synchronized
1.1 public void setAddress(InetAddress iaddr);                                    synchronized
    public byte[ ] getData();                                                     synchronized
1.1 public void setData(byte[ ] buf);                                             synchronized
1.2 public void setData(byte[ ] buf, int offset, int length);                     synchronized
    public int getLength();                                                       synchronized
1.1 public void setLength(int length);                                            synchronized
1.2 public int getOffset();                                                       synchronized
    public int getPort();                                                         synchronized
1.1 public void setPort(int iport);                                               synchronized
}
```

Passed To: DatagramSocket.{receive(), send()}, DatagramSocketImpl.{receive(), send()}, MulticastSocket.send()

DatagramSocket

Java 1.0

java.net

PJ1.1

This class defines a socket that can receive and send unreliable datagram packets over the network using the UDP protocol. A *datagram* is a very low-level networking interface: it is simply an array of bytes sent over the network. A datagram does not implement any kind of stream-based communication protocol, and there is no connection established between the sender and the receiver. Datagram packets are called unreliable because the protocol does not make any attempt to ensure they arrive or to resend them if they don't. Thus, packets sent through a DatagramSocket are not guaranteed to arrive in the order sent or even to arrive at all. On the other hand, this low-overhead protocol makes datagram transmission very fast. See Socket and URL for higher-level interfaces to networking.

If a port is specified when the DatagramSocket is created, that port is used for sending and receiving datagrams; otherwise, the system assigns a port. getLocalPort() returns the port number in use. send() sends a DatagramPacket through the socket. The packet must contain the destination address to which it should be sent. receive() waits for data to arrive at the socket and stores it, along with the address of the sender, in the specified DatagramPacket. close() closes the socket and frees the port for reuse. Once close() has been called, the DatagramSocket should not be used again.

Each time a packet is sent or received, the system must perform a security check to ensure that the calling code has permission to send data to or receive data from the

java.net

specified host. In Java 1.2 and later, if you are sending multiple packets to or receiving multiple packets from a single host, use connect() to specify the host with which you are communicating. This causes the security check to be done a single time, but does not allow the socket to communicate with any other host until disconnect() is called. Use getInetAddress() and getPort() to obtain the host and port, if any, the socket is connected to.

setSoTimeout() specifies the number of milliseconds that receive() waits for a packet to arrive before throwing an InterruptedIOException. Specify 0 milliseconds to wait forever. setSendBufferSize() and setReceiveBufferSize() set hints as to the underlying size of the networking buffers.

```
public class DatagramSocket {
// Public Constructors
     public DatagramSocket( ) throws SocketException;
     public DatagramSocket(int port) throws SocketException;
1.1  public DatagramSocket(int port, InetAddress laddr) throws SocketException;
// Public Class Methods
1.3  public static void setDatagramSocketImplFactory(DatagramSocketImplFactory fac)          synchronized
          throws java.io.IOException;
// Property Accessor Methods (by property name)
1.2  public InetAddress getInetAddress( );                                                    default:null
1.1  public InetAddress getLocalAddress( );
     public int getLocalPort( );                                                             default:1029
1.2  public int getPort( );                                                                    default:-1
1.2  public int getReceiveBufferSize( ) throws SocketException;                     synchronized default:8192
1.2  public void setReceiveBufferSize(int size) throws SocketException;                       synchronized
1.2  public int getSendBufferSize( ) throws SocketException;                        synchronized default:8192
1.2  public void setSendBufferSize(int size) throws SocketException;                          synchronized
1.1  public int getSoTimeout( ) throws SocketException;                                synchronized default:0
1.1  public void setSoTimeout(int timeout) throws SocketException;                            synchronized
// Public Instance Methods
     public void close( );
1.2  public void connect(InetAddress address, int port);
1.2  public void disconnect( );
     public void receive(DatagramPacket p) throws java.io.IOException;                        synchronized
     public void send(DatagramPacket p) throws java.io.IOException;
}
```

Subclasses: MulticastSocket

DatagramSocketImpl
Java 1.1

java.net   *PJ1.1*

This abstract class defines the methods necessary to implement communication through datagram and multicast sockets. System programmers may create subclasses of this class when they need to implement datagram or multicast sockets in a nonstandard network environment, such as behind a firewall or on a network that uses a nonstandard transport protocol. Normal applications never need to use or subclass this class.

```
public abstract class DatagramSocketImpl implements SocketOptions {
// Public Constructors
     public DatagramSocketImpl( );
// Methods Implementing SocketOptions
     public abstract Object getOption(int optID) throws SocketException;
     public abstract void setOption(int optID, Object value) throws SocketException;
```

```
// Protected Instance Methods
    protected abstract void bind(int lport, InetAddress laddr) throws SocketException;
    protected abstract void close();
    protected abstract void create() throws SocketException;
    protected java.io.FileDescriptor getFileDescriptor();
    protected int getLocalPort();
1.2 protected abstract int getTimeToLive() throws java.io.IOException;
    protected abstract void join(InetAddress inetaddr) throws java.io.IOException;
    protected abstract void leave(InetAddress inetaddr) throws java.io.IOException;
    protected abstract int peek(InetAddress i) throws java.io.IOException;
    protected abstract void receive(DatagramPacket p) throws java.io.IOException;
    protected abstract void send(DatagramPacket p) throws java.io.IOException;
1.2 protected abstract void setTimeToLive(int ttl) throws java.io.IOException;
// Protected Instance Fields
    protected java.io.FileDescriptor fd;
    protected int localPort;
// Deprecated Protected Methods
#   protected abstract byte getTTL() throws java.io.IOException;
#   protected abstract void setTTL(byte ttl) throws java.io.IOException;
}
```

Hierarchy: Object→ DatagramSocketImpl(SocketOptions)

Returned By: DatagramSocketImplFactory.createDatagramSocketImpl()

DatagramSocketImplFactory   Java 1.3

java.net

This interface defines a method that creates DatagramSocketImpl objects. You can register an instance of this factory interface with the static setDatagramSocketImplFactory() method of DatagramSocket. Application-level code never needs to use or implement this interface.

```
public interface DatagramSocketImplFactory {
// Public Instance Methods
    public abstract DatagramSocketImpl createDatagramSocketImpl();
}
```

Passed To: DatagramSocket.setDatagramSocketImplFactory()

FileNameMap   Java 1.1

java.net   PJ1.1

This interface defines a single method that is called to obtain the MIME type of a file based on the name of the file. The fileNameMap field of the URLConnection class refers to an object that implements this interface. The filename-to-file-type map it implements is used by the static URLConnection.guessContentTypeFromName() method.

```
public interface FileNameMap {
// Public Instance Methods
    public abstract String getContentTypeFor(String fileName);
}
```

Passed To: URLConnection.setFileNameMap()

Returned By: URLConnection.getFileNameMap()

java.net

HttpURLConnection   **Java 1.1**

java.net   *PJ1.1*

This class is a specialization of URLConnection. An instance of this class is returned when the openConnection() method is called for a URL object that uses the HTTP protocol. The many constants defined by this class are the status codes returned by HTTP servers. setRequestMethod() specifies what kind of HTTP request is made. The contents of this request must be sent through the OutputStream returned by the getOutputStream() method of the superclass. Once an HTTP request has been sent, getResponseCode() returns the HTTP server's response code as an integer, and getResponseMessage() returns the server's response message. The disconnect() method closes the connection. The static setFollowRedirects() specifies whether URL connections that use the HTTP protocol should automatically follow redirect responses sent by HTTP servers. In order to successfully use this class, you need to understand the details of the HTTP protocol.

```
public abstract class HttpURLConnection extends URLConnection {
// Protected Constructors
    protected HttpURLConnection(URL u);
// Public Constants
    public static final int HTTP_ACCEPTED;                        =202
    public static final int HTTP_BAD_GATEWAY;                     =502
    public static final int HTTP_BAD_METHOD;                      =405
    public static final int HTTP_BAD_REQUEST;                     =400
    public static final int HTTP_CLIENT_TIMEOUT;                  =408
    public static final int HTTP_CONFLICT;                        =409
    public static final int HTTP_CREATED;                         =201
    public static final int HTTP_ENTITY_TOO_LARGE;                =413
    public static final int HTTP_FORBIDDEN;                       =403
    public static final int HTTP_GATEWAY_TIMEOUT;                 =504
    public static final int HTTP_GONE;                            =410
    public static final int HTTP_INTERNAL_ERROR;                  =500
    public static final int HTTP_LENGTH_REQUIRED;                 =411
    public static final int HTTP_MOVED_PERM;                      =301
    public static final int HTTP_MOVED_TEMP;                      =302
    public static final int HTTP_MULT_CHOICE;                     =300
    public static final int HTTP_NO_CONTENT;                      =204
    public static final int HTTP_NOT_ACCEPTABLE;                  =406
    public static final int HTTP_NOT_AUTHORITATIVE;               =203
    public static final int HTTP_NOT_FOUND;                       =404
1.3 public static final int HTTP_NOT_IMPLEMENTED;                 =501
    public static final int HTTP_NOT_MODIFIED;                    =304
    public static final int HTTP_OK;                              =200
    public static final int HTTP_PARTIAL;                         =206
    public static final int HTTP_PAYMENT_REQUIRED;                =402
    public static final int HTTP_PRECON_FAILED;                   =412
    public static final int HTTP_PROXY_AUTH;                      =407
    public static final int HTTP_REQ_TOO_LONG;                    =414
    public static final int HTTP_RESET;                           =205
    public static final int HTTP_SEE_OTHER;                       =303
    public static final int HTTP_UNAUTHORIZED;                    =401
    public static final int HTTP_UNAVAILABLE;                     =503
    public static final int HTTP_UNSUPPORTED_TYPE;                =415
    public static final int HTTP_USE_PROXY;                       =305
    public static final int HTTP_VERSION;                         =505
// Public Class Methods
    public static boolean getFollowRedirects();
```

```
    public static void setFollowRedirects(boolean set);
// Public Instance Methods
    public abstract void disconnect();
1.2 public java.io.InputStream getErrorStream();                                        constant
    public String getRequestMethod();
    public int getResponseCode() throws java.io.IOException;
    public String getResponseMessage() throws java.io.IOException;
    public void setRequestMethod(String method) throws ProtocolException;
    public abstract boolean usingProxy();
// Public Methods Overriding URLConnection
1.3 public long getHeaderFieldDate(String name, long Default);
1.2 public java.security.Permission getPermission() throws java.io.IOException;
// Protected Instance Fields
    protected String method;
    protected int responseCode;
    protected String responseMessage;
// Deprecated Public Fields
#   public static final int HTTP_SERVER_ERROR;                                          =500
}
```

Hierarchy: Object→ URLConnection→ HttpURLConnection

InetAddress   Java 1.0
java.net   serializable PJ1.1

This class represents an Internet address and is used when creating DatagramPacket or
Socket objects. The class does not have a public constructor function, but instead supports three static methods that return one or more instances of InetAddress. getLocalHost()
returns an InetAddress for the local host. getByName() returns the InetAddress of a host
specified by name. getAllByName() returns an array of InetAddress objects that represents
all the available addresses for a host specified by name. Instance methods are getHost-
Name(), which returns the hostname of an InetAddress, and getAddress(), which returns the
Internet IP address as an array of bytes, with the highest-order byte as the first element
of the array.

```
public final class InetAddress implements Serializable {
// No Constructor
// Public Class Methods
    public static InetAddress[ ] getAllByName(String host) throws java.net.UnknownHostException;
    public static InetAddress getByName(String host) throws java.net.UnknownHostException;
    public static InetAddress getLocalHost() throws java.net.UnknownHostException;          synchronized
// Property Accessor Methods (by property name)
    public byte[ ] getAddress();
    public String getHostAddress();
    public String getHostName();
1.1 public boolean isMulticastAddress();
// Public Methods Overriding Object
    public boolean equals(Object obj);
    public int hashCode();
    public String toString();
}
```

Hierarchy: Object→ InetAddress(Serializable)

Passed To: Too many methods to list.

Returned By: Authenticator.getRequestingSite(), DatagramPacket.getAddress(),
DatagramSocket.{getInetAddress(), getLocalAddress()}, InetAddress.{getAllByName(), getByName(),

getLocalHost()}, MulticastSocket.getInterface(), ServerSocket.getInetAddress(), Socket.{getInetAddress(), getLocalAddress()}, SocketImpl.getInetAddress(), URLStreamHandler.getHostAddress()

Type Of: SocketImpl.address

JarURLConnection

Java 1.2

java.net

This class is a specialized URLConnection that represents a connection to a jar: URL. A jar: URL is a compound URL that includes the URL of a JAR archive and, optionally, a reference to a file or directory within the JAR archive. The jar: URL syntax uses the ! character to separate the pathname of the JAR archive from the filename within the JAR archive. Note that a jar: URL contains a subprotocol that specifies the protocol that retrieves the JAR file itself. For example:

```
jar:http://my.jar.com/my.jar!/              // The whole archive
jar:file:/usr/java/lib/my.jar!/com/jar/     // A directory of the archive
jar:ftp://ftp.jar.com/pub/my.jar!/com/jar/Jar.class  // A file in the archive
```

To obtain a JarURLConnection, define a URL object for a jar: URL, open a connection to it with openConnection(), and cast the returned URLConnection object to a JarURLConnection. The various methods defined by JarURLConnection allow you to read the manifest file of the JAR archive and look up attributes from that manifest for the archive as a whole or for individual entries in the archive. These methods make use of various classes from the java.util.jar package.

```
public abstract class JarURLConnection extends URLConnection {
// Protected Constructors
    protected JarURLConnection(URL url) throws MalformedURLException;
// Property Accessor Methods (by property name)
    public java.util.jar.Attributes getAttributes() throws java.io.IOException;
    public java.security.cert.Certificate[] getCertificates() throws java.io.IOException;
    public String getEntryName();
    public java.util.jar.JarEntry getJarEntry() throws java.io.IOException;
    public abstract java.util.jar.JarFile getJarFile() throws java.io.IOException;
    public URL getJarFileURL();
    public java.util.jar.Attributes getMainAttributes() throws java.io.IOException;
    public java.util.jar.Manifest getManifest() throws java.io.IOException;
// Protected Instance Fields
    protected URLConnection jarFileURLConnection;
}
```

Hierarchy: Object→ URLConnection→ JarURLConnection

MalformedURLException

Java 1.0

java.net

serializable checked PJ1.1

Signals that an unparseable URL specification has been passed to a method.

```
public class MalformedURLException extends java.io.IOException {
// Public Constructors
    public MalformedURLException();
    public MalformedURLException(String msg);
}
```

Hierarchy: Object→ Throwable(Serializable)→ Exception→ java.io.IOException→ MalformedURLException

Thrown By: Too many methods to list.

MulticastSocket

java.net

This subclass of DatagramSocket can send and receive multicast UDP packets. It extends DatagramSocket by adding joinGroup() and leaveGroup() methods to join and leave multicast groups. The IP address specified to these methods should be a valid multicast address in the range of 224.0.0.1 to 239.255.255.255. Note that you do not have to join a group to send a packet to a multicast address, but you must join the group to receive packets sent to that address. Note that untrusted code is not allowed to use multicast sockets.

MulticastSocket defines a variant send() method that allows you to specify a time-to-live (TTL) value for the packet you send. This value specifies the number of network hops the packet can travel before it expires. You can also set a default TTL for all packets sent though a MulticastSocket with setTimeToLive(), or, prior to Java 1.2, with setTTL().

```
public class MulticastSocket extends DatagramSocket {
// Public Constructors
    public MulticastSocket() throws java.io.IOException;
    public MulticastSocket(int port) throws java.io.IOException;
// Property Accessor Methods (by property name)
    public InetAddress getInterface() throws SocketException;
    public void setInterface(InetAddress inf) throws SocketException;
1.2 public int getTimeToLive() throws java.io.IOException;                           default:1
1.2 public void setTimeToLive(int ttl) throws java.io.IOException;
// Public Instance Methods
    public void joinGroup(InetAddress mcastaddr) throws java.io.IOException;
    public void leaveGroup(InetAddress mcastaddr) throws java.io.IOException;
    public void send(DatagramPacket p, byte ttl) throws java.io.IOException;
// Deprecated Public Methods
#   public byte getTTL() throws java.io.IOException;                                 default:1
#   public void setTTL(byte ttl) throws java.io.IOException;
}
```

Hierarchy: Object→ DatagramSocket→ MulticastSocket

NetPermission

java.net

serializable permission

This class is a java.security.Permission that represents various permissions required for Java's URL-based networking system. See also SocketPermission, which represents permissions to perform lower-level networking operations. A NetPermission is defined solely by its name; no actions list is required or supported. As of Java 1.2, there are three NetPermission targets defined: "setDefaultAuthenticator" is required to call Authenticator.setDefault(); "requestPasswordAuthentication" to call Authenticator.requestPasswordAuthentication(); and "specifyStreamHandler" to explicitly pass a URLStreamHandler object to the URL() constructor. The target "*" is a wildcard that represents all defined NetPermission targets.

System administrators configuring security policies must be familiar with this class and the permissions it represents. System programmers may use this class, but application programmers never need to use it explicitly.

java.net

```
public final class NetPermission extends java.security.BasicPermission {
// Public Constructors
   public NetPermission(String name);
   public NetPermission(String name, String actions);
}
```

Hierarchy: Object→ java.security.Permission(java.security.Guard, Serializable)→
java.security.BasicPermission(Serializable)→ NetPermission

NoRouteToHostException   Java 1.1

java.net   *serializable checked PJ1.1*

This exception signals that a socket cannot be connected to a remote host because the
host cannot be contacted. Typically, this means that some link in the network between
the local machine and the remote host is down or that the host is behind a firewall.

```
public class NoRouteToHostException extends SocketException {
// Public Constructors
   public NoRouteToHostException();
   public NoRouteToHostException(String msg);
}
```

Hierarchy: Object→ Throwable(Serializable)→ Exception→ java.io.IOException→
SocketException→ NoRouteToHostException

PasswordAuthentication   Java 1.2

java.net

This simple immutable class encapsulates a username and a password. The password is
stored as a character array rather than as a String object so that the caller can erase the
contents of the array after use for increased security. Note that the PasswordAuthentica-
tion() constructor clones the specified password character array, but getPassword() returns
a reference to the object's internal array. Obtain a PasswordAuthentication object by calling
Authenticator.requestPasswordAuthentication().

```
public final class PasswordAuthentication {
// Public Constructors
   public PasswordAuthentication(String userName, char[ ] password);
// Public Instance Methods
   public char[ ] getPassword();
   public String getUserName();
}
```

Returned By: Authenticator.{getPasswordAuthentication(), requestPasswordAuthentication()}

ProtocolException   Java 1.0

java.net   *serializable checked PJ1.1*

Signals a protocol error in the Socket class.

```
public class ProtocolException extends java.io.IOException {
// Public Constructors
   public ProtocolException();
   public ProtocolException(String host);
}
```

Hierarchy: Object→ Throwable(Serializable)→ Exception→ java.io.IOException→
ProtocolException

Thrown By: HttpURLConnection.setRequestMethod()

ServerSocket   Java 1.0
java.net   PJ1.1

This class is used by servers to listen for connection requests from clients. When you create a ServerSocket, you specify the port to listen on. The accept() method begins listening on that port and blocks until a client requests a connection on the port. At that point, accept() accepts the connection, creating and returning a Socket the server can use to communicate with the client. A typical server starts a new thread to handle the communication with the client and calls accept() again to listen for another connection. If you do not want accept() to block for an indefinite amount of time, call setSoTimeout() to specify the number of milliseconds accept() should wait for a connection before throwing an InterruptedIOException.

```
public class ServerSocket {
// Public Constructors
    public ServerSocket(int port) throws java.io.IOException;
    public ServerSocket(int port, int backlog) throws java.io.IOException;
1.1 public ServerSocket(int port, int backlog, InetAddress bindAddr) throws java.io.IOException;
// Public Class Methods
    public static void setSocketFactory(SocketImplFactory fac) throws java.io.IOException;      synchronized
// Property Accessor Methods (by property name)
    public InetAddress getInetAddress();
    public int getLocalPort();
1.1 public int getSoTimeout() throws java.io.IOException;                                         synchronized
1.1 public void setSoTimeout(int timeout) throws SocketException;                                 synchronized
// Public Instance Methods
    public Socket accept() throws java.io.IOException;
    public void close() throws java.io.IOException;
// Public Methods Overriding Object
    public String toString();
// Protected Instance Methods
1.1 protected final void implAccept(Socket s) throws java.io.IOException;
}
```

Returned By: java.rmi.server.RMIServerSocketFactory.createServerSocket(), java.rmi.server.RMISocketFactory.createServerSocket()

Socket   Java 1.0
java.net   PJ1.1

This class implements a socket for stream-based interprocess communication over the network. See URL for a higher-level interface to networking and DatagramSocket for a lower-level interface.

Use the Socket() constructor to create a socket and connect it to the specified host and port. Once the socket is created, getInputStream() and getOutputStream() return InputStream and OutputStream objects you can use to communicate with the remote host, just as you would use them for file input and output. getInetAddress() and getPort() return the address and port to which the socket is connected. getLocalPort() returns the local port the socket is using. See ServerSocket for information about how a server can listen for and accept connections of this type. When you are done with a Socket, use close() to close it. In Java 1.3, you can also use shutdownInput() and shutdownOutput() to close the input and output communication channels individually.

There are several options you can specify for a Socket object to alter its behavior. setSendBufferSize() and setReceiveBufferSize() provide hints to the underlying networking system as to what buffer size is best to use with this socket. setSoTimeout() specifies the number of milliseconds a read() call on the input stream returned by getInputStream() waits for data before throwing an InterruptedIOException. The default value of 0 specifies that the stream blocks indefinitely. setSoLinger() specifies what to do when a socket is closed while there is still data waiting to be transmitted. If lingering is turned on, the close() call blocks for up to the specified number of seconds while attempting to transmit the remaining data. Calling setTcpNoDelay() with an argument of true causes data to be sent through the socket as soon as it is available, instead of waiting for the TCP packet to become more full before sending it. In Java 1.3, use setKeepAlive() to enable or disable the periodic exchange of control messages across an idle socket connection. The keepalive protocol enables a client to determine if its server has crashed without closing the socket and vice versa.

```
public class Socket {
// Public Constructors
     public Socket(String host, int port) throws java.net.UnknownHostException, java.io.IOException;
     public Socket(InetAddress address, int port) throws java.io.IOException;
#    public Socket(String host, int port, boolean stream) throws java.io.IOException;
#    public Socket(InetAddress host, int port, boolean stream) throws java.io.IOException;
1.1  public Socket(String host, int port, InetAddress localAddr, int localPort) throws java.io.IOException;
1.1  public Socket(InetAddress address, int port, InetAddress localAddr, int localPort) throws java.io.IOException;
// Protected Constructors
     protected Socket();
1.1  protected Socket(SocketImpl impl) throws SocketException;
// Public Class Methods
     public static void setSocketImplFactory(SocketImplFactory fac) throws java.io.IOException;      synchronized
// Property Accessor Methods (by property name)
     public InetAddress getInetAddress();
     public java.io.InputStream getInputStream() throws java.io.IOException;
1.3  public boolean getKeepAlive() throws SocketException;
1.3  public void setKeepAlive(boolean on) throws SocketException;
1.1  public InetAddress getLocalAddress();
     public int getLocalPort();
     public java.io.OutputStream getOutputStream() throws java.io.IOException;
     public int getPort();
1.2  public int getReceiveBufferSize() throws SocketException;                                        synchronized
1.2  public void setReceiveBufferSize(int size) throws SocketException;                               synchronized
1.2  public int getSendBufferSize() throws SocketException;                                           synchronized
1.2  public void setSendBufferSize(int size) throws SocketException;                                  synchronized
1.1  public int getSoLinger() throws SocketException;
1.1  public int getSoTimeout() throws SocketException;                                                synchronized
1.1  public void setSoTimeout(int timeout) throws SocketException;                                    synchronized
1.1  public boolean getTcpNoDelay() throws SocketException;
1.1  public void setTcpNoDelay(boolean on) throws SocketException;
// Public Instance Methods
     public void close() throws java.io.IOException;                                                  synchronized
1.1  public void setSoLinger(boolean on, int linger) throws SocketException;
1.3  public void shutdownInput() throws java.io.IOException;
1.3  public void shutdownOutput() throws java.io.IOException;
// Public Methods Overriding Object
     public String toString();
}
```

Passed To: ServerSocket.implAccept()

Returned By: ServerSocket.accept(), java.rmi.server.RMIClientSocketFactory.createSocket(), java.rmi.server.RMISocketFactory.createSocket()

SocketException

java.net   *serializable checked PJ1.1*

Signals an exceptional condition while using a socket.

```
public class SocketException extends java.io.IOException {
// Public Constructors
    public SocketException();
    public SocketException(String msg);
}
```

Hierarchy: Object→ Throwable(Serializable)→ Exception→ java.io.IOException→ SocketException

Subclasses: BindException, java.net.ConnectException, NoRouteToHostException

Thrown By: Too many methods to list.

SocketImpl

java.net   *PJ1.1*

This abstract class defines the methods necessary to implement communication through sockets. Different subclasses of this class may provide different implementations suitable in different environments (such as behind firewalls). These socket implementations are used by the Socket and ServerSocket classes. Normal applications never need to use or subclass this class.

```
public abstract class SocketImpl implements SocketOptions {
// Public Constructors
    public SocketImpl();
// Methods Implementing SocketOptions
1.1 public abstract Object getOption(int optID) throws SocketException;
1.1 public abstract void setOption(int optID, Object value) throws SocketException;
// Public Methods Overriding Object
    public String toString();
// Protected Instance Methods
    protected abstract void accept(SocketImpl s) throws java.io.IOException;
    protected abstract int available() throws java.io.IOException;
    protected abstract void bind(InetAddress host, int port) throws java.io.IOException;
    protected abstract void close() throws java.io.IOException;
    protected abstract void connect(String host, int port) throws java.io.IOException;
    protected abstract void connect(InetAddress address, int port) throws java.io.IOException;
    protected abstract void create(boolean stream) throws java.io.IOException;
    protected java.io.FileDescriptor getFileDescriptor();
    protected InetAddress getInetAddress();
    protected abstract java.io.InputStream getInputStream() throws java.io.IOException;
    protected int getLocalPort();
    protected abstract java.io.OutputStream getOutputStream() throws java.io.IOException;
    protected int getPort();
    protected abstract void listen(int backlog) throws java.io.IOException;
1.3 protected void shutdownInput() throws java.io.IOException;
1.3 protected void shutdownOutput() throws java.io.IOException;
// Protected Instance Fields
    protected InetAddress address;
    protected java.io.FileDescriptor fd;
    protected int localport;
    protected int port;
}
```

Hierarchy: Object→ SocketImpl(SocketOptions)

Passed To: Socket.Socket(), SocketImpl.accept()

Returned By: SocketImplFactory.createSocketImpl()

SocketImplFactory   Java 1.0

java.net   *PJ1.1*

This interface defines a method that creates SocketImpl objects. SocketImplFactory objects may be registered to create SocketImpl objects for the Socket and ServerSocket classes. Normal applications never need to use or implement this interface.

```
public interface SocketImplFactory {
// Public Instance Methods
    public abstract SocketImpl createSocketImpl();
}
```

Passed To: ServerSocket.setSocketFactory(), Socket.setSocketImplFactory()

SocketOptions   Java 1.2

java.net

This interface defines constants that represent low-level BSD Unix-style socket options and methods that set and query the value of those options. In Java 1.2, SocketImpl and DatagramSocketImpl implement this interface. Any custom socket implementations you define should also provide meaningful implementations for the getOption() and setOption() methods. Your implementation may support options other than those defined here. Only custom socket implementations need to use this interface. All other code can use methods defined by Socket, ServerSocket, DatagramSocket, and MulticastSocket to set specific socket options for those socket types.

```
public interface SocketOptions {
// Public Constants
    public static final int IP_MULTICAST_IF;                   =16
    public static final int SO_BINDADDR;                       =15
1.3 public static final int SO_KEEPALIVE;                       =8
    public static final int SO_LINGER;                        =128
    public static final int SO_RCVBUF;                       =4098
    public static final int SO_REUSEADDR;                       =4
    public static final int SO_SNDBUF;                       =4097
    public static final int SO_TIMEOUT;                      =4102
    public static final int TCP_NODELAY;                        =1
// Public Instance Methods
    public abstract Object getOption(int optID) throws SocketException;
    public abstract void setOption(int optID, Object value) throws SocketException;
}
```

Implementations: DatagramSocketImpl, SocketImpl

SocketPermission   Java 1.2

java.net   *serializable permission*

This class is a java.security.Permission that governs all networking operations performed with sockets. Like all permissions, a SocketPermission consists of a name, or target, and a list of actions that may be performed on that target. The target of a SocketPermission is the host and, optionally, the port or ports for which permission is being granted or requested. The target consists of a hostname optionally followed by a colon and a port specification. The host may be a DNS domain name, a numerical IP address, or the string "localhost". If you specify a host domain name, you may use * as a wildcard as the leftmost portion of the hostname. The port specification, if present, must be a single port number or a range of port numbers in the form n1-n2. If n1 is omitted, it is taken to be 0, and if n2 is omitted, it is taken to be 65535. If no port is specified, the socket permission applies to all ports of the specified host. Here are some legal SocketPermission targets:

```
java.sun.com:80
*.sun.com:1024-2000
*:1024-
localhost:-1023
```

In addition to a target, each SocketPermission must have a comma-separated list of actions, which specify the operations that may be performed on the specified host(s) and port(s). The available actions are "connect", "accept", "listen", and "resolve". "connect" represents permission to connect to the specified target. "accept" indicates permission to accept connections from the specified target. "listen" represents permission to listen on the specified ports for connection requests. This action is only valid when used for ports on "localhost". Finally, the "resolve" action indicates permission to use the DNS name service to resolve domain names into IP addresses. This action is required for and implied by all other actions.

System administrators configuring security policies must be familiar with this class and understand the risks of granting the various permissions it represents. System programmers writing new low-level networking libraries or connecting to native code that performs networking may need to use this class. Application programmers, however, should never need to use it directly.

```
public final class SocketPermission extends java.security.Permission implements Serializable {
// Public Constructors
    public SocketPermission(String host, String action);
// Public Methods Overriding Permission
    public boolean equals(Object obj);
    public String getActions();
    public int hashCode();
    public boolean implies(java.security.Permission p);
    public java.security.PermissionCollection newPermissionCollection();
}
```

Hierarchy: Object→ java.security.Permission(java.security.Guard, Serializable)→ SocketPermission(Serializable)

UnknownHostException

Java 1.0
java.net   serializable checked PJ1.1

Signals that the name of a specified host could not be resolved.

```
public class UnknownHostException extends java.io.IOException {
// Public Constructors
    public UnknownHostException();
    public UnknownHostException(String host);
}
```

Hierarchy: Object→ Throwable(Serializable)→ Exception→ java.io.IOException→ java.net.UnknownHostException

Thrown By: InetAddress.{getAllByName(), getByName(), getLocalHost()}, Socket.Socket()

UnknownServiceException
java.net

Java 1.0

serializable checked PJ1.1

Signals an attempt to use an unsupported service of a network connection.

```
public class UnknownServiceException extends java.io.IOException {
// Public Constructors
    public UnknownServiceException();
    public UnknownServiceException(String msg);
}
```

Hierarchy: Object→ Throwable(Serializable)→ Exception→ java.io.IOException→ UnknownServiceException

URL
java.net

Java 1.0

serializable PJ1.1

This class represents a uniform resource locator and allows the data referred to by the URL to be downloaded. A URL can be specified as a single string or with separate protocol, host, port, and file specifications. Relative URLs can also be specified with a String and the URL object to which it is relative. getFile(), getHost(), getPort(), getProtocol(), and getRef() return the various portions of the URL specified by a URL object. sameFile() determines whether a URL object refers to the same file as this one. The data or object referred to by a URL can be downloaded from the Internet in three ways: with a URLConnection created with openConnection(), with an InputStream created by openStream(), or with getContent(), which returns the URL contents directly if an appropriate ContentHandler can be found.

```
public final class URL implements Serializable {
// Public Constructors
    public URL(String spec) throws MalformedURLException;
    public URL(URL context, String spec) throws MalformedURLException;
1.2 public URL(URL context, String spec, URLStreamHandler handler) throws MalformedURLException;
    public URL(String protocol, String host, String file) throws MalformedURLException;
    public URL(String protocol, String host, int port, String file) throws MalformedURLException;
1.2 public URL(String protocol, String host, int port, String file, URLStreamHandler handler)
        throws MalformedURLException;
// Public Class Methods
    public static void setURLStreamHandlerFactory(URLStreamHandlerFactory fac);                synchronized
// Property Accessor Methods (by property name)
1.3 public String getAuthority();
    public final Object getContent() throws java.io.IOException;
1.3 public final Object getContent(Class[ ] classes) throws java.io.IOException;
    public String getFile();
    public String getHost();
1.3 public String getPath();
    public int getPort();
    public String getProtocol();
1.3 public String getQuery();
    public String getRef();
1.3 public String getUserInfo();
// Public Instance Methods
    public URLConnection openConnection() throws java.io.IOException;
    public final java.io.InputStream openStream() throws java.io.IOException;
    public boolean sameFile(URL other);
    public String toExternalForm();
```

```
// Public Methods Overriding Object
    public boolean equals(Object obj);
    public int hashCode();                                                              synchronized
    public String toString();
// Protected Instance Methods
    protected void set(String protocol, String host, int port, String file, String ref);
1.3 protected void set(String protocol, String host, int port, String authority, String userInfo, String path, String query,
                String ref);
}
```

Hierarchy: Object→ URL(Serializable)

Passed To: Too many methods to list.

Returned By: Too many methods to list.

Type Of: URLConnection.url

URLClassLoader   Java 1.2
java.net

This ClassLoader provides a useful way to load untrusted Java code from a search path of arbitrary URLs, where each URL represents a directory or JAR file to search. Use the inherited loadClass() method to load a named class with a URLClassLoader. Classes loaded by a URLClassLoader have whatever permissions are granted to their java.security.CodeSource by the system java.security.Policy, plus they have one additional permission that allows the class loader to read any resource files associated with the class. If the class is loaded from a local file: URL that represents a directory, the class is given permission to read all files and directories below that directory. If the class is loaded from a local file: URL that represents a JAR file, the class is given permission to read that JAR file. If the class is loaded from a URL that represents a resource on another host, that class is given permission to connect to and accept network connections from that host. Note, however, that loaded classes are not granted this additional permission if the code that created the URLClassLoader in the first place would not have had that permission.

You can obtain a URLClassLoader by calling one of the URLClassLoader() constructors or one of the static newInstance() methods. If you call newInstance(), the loadClass() method of the returned URLClassLoader performs an additional check to ensure that the caller has permission to access the specified package.

```
public class URLClassLoader extends java.security.SecureClassLoader {
// Public Constructors
    public URLClassLoader(URL[ ] urls);
    public URLClassLoader(URL[ ] urls, ClassLoader parent);
    public URLClassLoader(URL[ ] urls, ClassLoader parent, URLStreamHandlerFactory factory);
// Public Class Methods
    public static URLClassLoader newInstance(URL[ ] urls);
    public static URLClassLoader newInstance(URL[ ] urls, ClassLoader parent);
// Public Instance Methods
    public URL[ ] getURLs();
// Protected Methods Overriding SecureClassLoader
    protected java.security.PermissionCollection getPermissions(java.security.CodeSource codesource);
// Public Methods Overriding ClassLoader
    public URL findResource(String name);
    public java.util.Enumeration findResources(String name) throws java.io.IOException;
// Protected Methods Overriding ClassLoader
    protected Class findClass(String name) throws ClassNotFoundException;
```

```
// Protected Instance Methods
   protected void addURL(URL url);
   protected Package definePackage(String name, java.util.jar.Manifest man, URL url)
      throws IllegalArgumentException;
}
```

Hierarchy: Object→ ClassLoader→ java.security.SecureClassLoader→ URLClassLoader

Returned By: URLClassLoader.newInstance()

URLConnection   Java 1.0

java.net   *PJ1.1*

This abstract class defines a network connection to an object specified by a URL. URL.openConnection() returns a URLConnection instance. You should use a URLConnection object when you want more control over the downloading of data than is available through the simpler URL methods. connect() actually makes the network connection. Other methods that depend on being connected call this method. getContent() returns the data referred to by the URL, parsed into an appropriate type of Object. If the URL protocol supports read and write operations, getInputStream() and getOutputStream() return input and output streams to the object referred to by the URL, respectively. getContentLength(), getContentType(), getContentEncoding(), getExpiration(), getDate(), and getLastModified() return the appropriate information about the object referred to by the URL, if that information can be determined (e.g., from HTTP header fields). getHeaderField() returns an HTTP header field specified by name or by number. getHeaderFieldInt() and getHeaderFieldDate() return the value of a named header field parsed as an integer or a date.

There are a number of options you can specify to control how the URLConnection behaves. These options are set with the various set() methods and may be queried with corresponding get() methods. The options must be set before the connect() method is called. setDoInput() and setDoOutput() allow you to specify whether you are using the URLConnection for input and/or output (input-only by default). setAllowUserInteraction() specifies whether user interaction (such as typing a password) is allowed during the data transfer (false by default). setDefaultAllowUserInteraction() is a class method that allows you to change the default value for user interaction. setUseCaches() allows you to specify whether a cached version of the URL can be used. You can set this to false to force a URL to be reloaded. setDefaultUseCaches() sets the default value for setUseCaches(). setIfModifiedSince() allows you to specify that a URL should not be fetched unless it has been modified since a specified time (if it is possible to determine its modification date).

```
public abstract class URLConnection {
// Protected Constructors
   protected URLConnection(URL url);
// Public Class Methods
   public static boolean getDefaultAllowUserInteraction();
1.1 public static FileNameMap getFileNameMap();                                  synchronized
   public static String guessContentTypeFromStream(java.io.InputStream is) throws java.io.IOException;
   public static void setContentHandlerFactory(ContentHandlerFactory fac);        synchronized
   public static void setDefaultAllowUserInteraction(boolean defaultallowuserinteraction);
1.1 public static void setFileNameMap(FileNameMap map);
// Protected Class Methods
   protected static String guessContentTypeFromName(String fname);
// Property Accessor Methods (by property name)
   public boolean getAllowUserInteraction();
   public void setAllowUserInteraction(boolean allowuserinteraction);
```

```
   public Object getContent( ) throws java.io.IOException;
1.3 public Object getContent(Class[ ] classes) throws java.io.IOException;
   public String getContentEncoding( );
   public int getContentLength( );
   public String getContentType( );
   public long getDate( );
   public boolean getDefaultUseCaches( );
   public void setDefaultUseCaches(boolean defaultusecaches);
   public boolean getDoInput( );
   public void setDoInput(boolean doinput);
   public boolean getDoOutput( );
   public void setDoOutput(boolean dooutput);
   public long getExpiration( );
   public long getIfModifiedSince( );
   public void setIfModifiedSince(long ifmodifiedsince);
   public java.io.InputStream getInputStream( ) throws java.io.IOException;
   public long getLastModified( );
   public java.io.OutputStream getOutputStream( ) throws java.io.IOException;
1.2 public java.security.Permission getPermission( ) throws java.io.IOException;
   public URL getURL( );
   public boolean getUseCaches( );
   public void setUseCaches(boolean usecaches);
// Public Instance Methods
   public abstract void connect( ) throws java.io.IOException;
   public String getHeaderField(int n);                                        constant
   public String getHeaderField(String name);                                  constant
   public long getHeaderFieldDate(String name, long Default);
   public int getHeaderFieldInt(String name, int Default);
   public String getHeaderFieldKey(int n);                                     constant
   public String getRequestProperty(String key);
   public void setRequestProperty(String key, String value);
// Public Methods Overriding Object
   public String toString( );
// Protected Instance Fields
   protected boolean allowUserInteraction;
   protected boolean connected;
   protected boolean doInput;
   protected boolean doOutput;
   protected long ifModifiedSince;
   protected URL url;
   protected boolean useCaches;
// Deprecated Public Methods
#  public static String getDefaultRequestProperty(String key);                 constant
#  public static void setDefaultRequestProperty(String key, String value);     empty
}
```

Subclasses: HttpURLConnection, JarURLConnection

Passed To: ContentHandler.getContent( )

Returned By: URL.openConnection( ), URLStreamHandler.openConnection( )

Type Of: JarURLConnection.jarFileURLConnection

URLDecoder

Java 1.2

java.net

This class defines a static decode() method that reverses the encoding performed by URLEncoder.encode(). It decodes 8-bit text with the MIME type "x-www-form-urlencoded", which is a standard encoding used by web browsers to submit form contents to CGI scripts and other server-side programs.

```
public class URLDecoder {
// Public Constructors
    public URLDecoder();
// Public Class Methods
    public static String decode(String s);
}
```

URLEncoder

Java 1.0

java.net

PJ1.1

This class defines a single static method that converts a string to its URL-encoded form. That is, spaces are converted to +, and nonalphanumeric characters other than underscore are output as two hexadecimal digits following a percent sign. Note that this technique works only for 8-bit characters. This method canonicalizes a URL specification so that it uses only characters from an extremely portable subset of ASCII that can be correctly handled by computers around the world.

```
public class URLEncoder {
// No Constructor
// Public Class Methods
    public static String encode(String s);
}
```

URLStreamHandler

Java 1.0

java.net

PJ1.1

This abstract class defines the openConnection() method that creates a URLConnection for a given URL. A separate subclass of this class may be defined for various URL protocol types. A URLStreamHandler is created by a URLStreamHandlerFactory. Normal applications never need to use or subclass this class.

```
public abstract class URLStreamHandler {
// Public Constructors
    public URLStreamHandler();
// Protected Instance Methods
1.3 protected boolean equals(URL u1, URL u2);
1.3 protected int getDefaultPort();                                                    constant
1.3 protected InetAddress getHostAddress(URL u);                                    synchronized
1.3 protected int hashCode(URL u);
1.3 protected boolean hostsEqual(URL u1, URL u2);
    protected abstract URLConnection openConnection(URL u) throws java.io.IOException;
    protected void parseURL(URL u, String spec, int start, int limit);
1.3 protected boolean sameFile(URL u1, URL u2);
1.3 protected void setURL(URL u, String protocol, String host, int port, String authority, String userInfo, String path,
                String query, String ref);
    protected String toExternalForm(URL u);
// Deprecated Protected Methods
#   protected void setURL(URL u, String protocol, String host, int port, String file, String ref);
}
```

Passed To: URL.URL()

Returned By: URLStreamHandlerFactory.createURLStreamHandler()

URLStreamHandlerFactory   Java 1.0
java.net   *PJ1.1*

This interface defines a method that creates a URLStreamHandler object for a specified
protocol. Normal applications never need to use or implement this interface.

```
public interface URLStreamHandlerFactory {
// Public Instance Methods
    public abstract URLStreamHandler createURLStreamHandler(String protocol);
}
```

Passed To: URL.setURLStreamHandlerFactory(), URLClassLoader.URLClassLoader()

CHAPTER 17

The java.security Package

The java.security package contains the classes and interfaces that implement the Java security architecture. These classes can be divided into two broad categories. First, there are classes that implement access control and prevent untrusted code from performing sensitive operations. Second, there are authentication classes that implement message digests and digital signatures and can authenticate Java classes and other objects.

The central access control class is AccessController; it uses the currently installed Policy object to decide whether a given class has Permission to access a given system resource. The Permissions and ProtectionDomain classes are also important pieces of the Java access control architecture. Figure 17-1 shows the access control classes of this package.

The key classes for authentication are MessageDigest and Signature; they compute and verify cryptographic message digests and digital signatures. These classes use public-key cryptography techniques and rely on the PublicKey and PrivateKey classes. They also rely on an infrastructure of related classes, such as SecureRandom for producing cryptographic-strength pseudo-random numbers, KeyPairGenerator for generating pairs of public and private keys, and KeyStore for managing a collection of keys and certificates. (This package defines a Certificate interface, but it is deprecated; see the java.security.cert package for the preferred Certificate class.) Figure 17-2 shows the authentication classes of java.security, while Figure 17-3 shows the exceptions.

The CodeSource class unites the authentication classes with the access control classes. It represents the source of a Java class as a URL and a set of java.security.cert.Certificate objects that contain the digital signatures of the code. The AccessController and Policy classes look at the CodeSource of a class when making access control decisions.

All the cryptographic-authentication features of this package are provider-based, which means they are implemented by security provider modules that can be plugged easily into any Java 1.2 (or later) installation. Thus, in addition to defining a security API, this package also defines a service provider interface (SPI). Various classes with names that end in Spi are part of this SPI. Security provider implementations must subclass these Spi classes, but applications never need to use them. Each security provider is represented by a Provider class, and the Security class allows new providers to be dynamically installed.

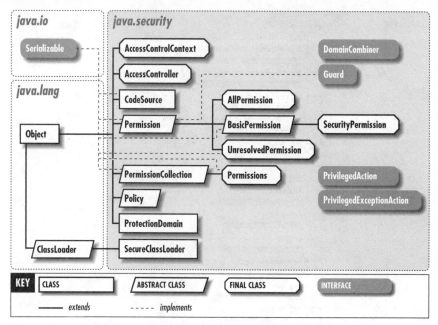

Figure 17-1: The access control classes of the java.security package

The java.security package contains several useful utility classes. For example, DigestInput-Stream and DigestOutputStream make it easy to compute message digests. GuardedObject provides customizable access control for an individual object. SignedObject protects the integrity of an arbitrary Java object by attaching a digital signature, making it easy to detect any tampering with the object. Although the java.security package contains crypto-graphic classes for authentication, it does not contain classes for encryption or decryp-tion. U.S. export control laws prevent Sun from including encryption and decryption functionality in the core Java platform. Instead, this functionality is part of the Java Cryptography Extension, or JCE. The JCE builds upon the cryptographic infrastructure of java.security; see Chapter 26, *The javax.crypto Package.*

AccessControlContext   Java 1.2

java.security

This class encapsulates the state of a call stack. The checkPermission() method can make access-control decisions based on the saved state of the call stack. Access-control checks are usually performed by the AccessController.checkPermission() method, which checks that the current call stack has the required permissions. Sometimes, however, it is necessary to make access-control decisions based on a previous state of the call stack. Call AccessController.getContext() to create an AccessControlContext for a particular call stack. In Java 1.3, this class has constructors that specify a custom context in the form of an array of ProtectionDomain objects and that associate a DomainCombiner object with an existing AccessControlContext. This class is used only by system-level code; typical appli-cations rarely need to use it.

```
public final class AccessControlContext {
// Public Constructors
    public AccessControlContext(ProtectionDomain[] context);
```

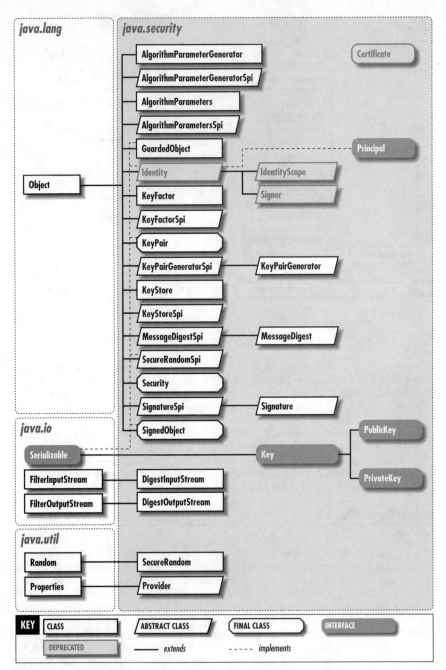

Figure 17-2: The authentication classes of the java.security package

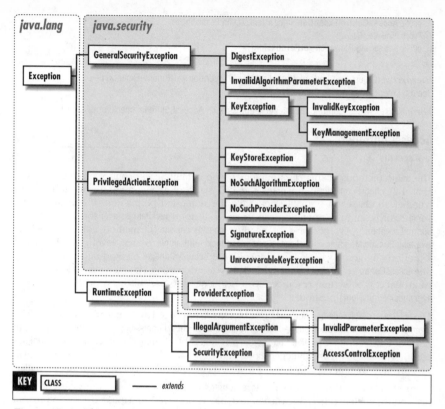

Figure 17-3: The exception classes of the java.security package

```
1.3 public AccessControlContext(AccessControlContext acc, DomainCombiner combiner);
// Public Instance Methods
   public void checkPermission(java.security.Permission perm) throws AccessControlException;
1.3 public DomainCombiner getDomainCombiner();
// Public Methods Overriding Object
   public boolean equals(Object obj);
   public int hashCode();
}
```

Passed To: AccessControlContext.AccessControlContext(), AccessController.doPrivileged()

Returned By: AccessController.getContext()

AccessControlException   Java 1.2

java.security   *serializable unchecked*

Thrown by AccessController to signal that an access request has been denied. getPermission() returns the Permission object, if any, that was involved in the denied request.

```
public class AccessControlException extends SecurityException {
// Public Constructors
   public AccessControlException(String s);
```

```
    public AccessControlException(String s, java.security.Permission p);
// Public Instance Methods
    public java.security.Permission getPermission();
}
```

Hierarchy: Object→ Throwable(Serializable)→ Exception→ RuntimeException→
SecurityException→ AccessControlException

Thrown By: AccessControlContext.checkPermission(), AccessController.checkPermission()

AccessController   Java 1.2

java.security

The static methods of this class implement the default access-control mechanism as of
Java 1.2. checkPermission() traverses the call stack of the current thread and checks
whether all classes in the call stack have the requested permission. If so, checkPermis-
sion() returns, and the operation can proceed. If not, checkPermission() throws an Access-
ControlException. As of Java 1.2, the checkPermission() method of the default
java.lang.SecurityManager calls AccessController.checkPermission(). System-level code that needs
to perform an access check should invoke the SecurityManager method rather than calling
the AccessController method directly. Unless you are writing system-level code that must
control access to system resources, you never need to use this class or the SecurityMan-
ager.checkPermission() method.

The various doPrivileged() methods run blocks of privileged code encapsulated in a PrivilegedAction or PrivilegedExceptionAction object. When checkPermission() is traversing the call
stack of a thread, it stops if it reaches a privileged block that was executed with doPrivi-
leged(). This means that privileged code can run with a full set of privileges, even if it
was invoked by untrusted or lower-privileged code. See PrivilegedAction for more details.

The getContext() method returns an AccessControlContext that represents the current security context of the caller. Such a context might be saved and passed to a future call
(perhaps a call made from a different thread). Use the two-argument version of doPrivi-
leged() to force permission checks to check the AccessControlContext as well.

```
public final class AccessController {
// No Constructor
// Public Class Methods
    public static void checkPermission(java.security.Permission perm) throws AccessControlException;
    public static Object doPrivileged(PrivilegedExceptionAction action) throws PrivilegedActionException;      native
    public static Object doPrivileged(PrivilegedAction action);                                                native
    public static Object doPrivileged(PrivilegedExceptionAction action, AccessControlContext context)          native
        throws PrivilegedActionException;
    public static Object doPrivileged(PrivilegedAction action, AccessControlContext context);                  native
    public static AccessControlContext getContext();
}
```

AlgorithmParameterGenerator   Java 1.2

java.security

This class defines a generic API for generating parameters for a cryptographic algorithm, typically a Signature or a javax.crypto.Cipher. Create an AlgorithmParameterGenerator by
calling one of the static getInstance() factory methods and specifying the name of the
algorithm and, optionally, the name of the desired provider. The default "SUN" provider
supports the "DSA" algorithm. The "SunJCE" provider shipped with the JCE supports
"DiffieHellman". Once you have obtained a generator, initialize it by calling the init()
method and specifying an algorithm-independent parameter size (in bits) or an

algorithm-dependent AlgorithmParameterSpec object. You may also specify a SecureRandom source of randomness when you call init(). Once you have created and initialized the AlgorithmParameterGenerator, call generateParameters() to generate an AlgorithmParameters object.

```
public class AlgorithmParameterGenerator {
// Protected Constructors
    protected AlgorithmParameterGenerator(AlgorithmParameterGeneratorSpi paramGenSpi, Provider provider,
                            String algorithm);
// Public Class Methods
    public static AlgorithmParameterGenerator getInstance(String algorithm) throws NoSuchAlgorithmException;
    public static AlgorithmParameterGenerator getInstance(String algorithm, String provider)
        throws NoSuchAlgorithmException, NoSuchProviderException;
// Public Instance Methods
    public final AlgorithmParameters generateParameters();
    public final String getAlgorithm();
    public final Provider getProvider();
    public final void init(java.security.spec.AlgorithmParameterSpec genParamSpec)
        throws InvalidAlgorithmParameterException;
    public final void init(int size);
    public final void init(java.security.spec.AlgorithmParameterSpec genParamSpec, SecureRandom random)
        throws InvalidAlgorithmParameterException;
    public final void init(int size, SecureRandom random);
}
```

Returned By: AlgorithmParameterGenerator.getInstance()

AlgorithmParameterGeneratorSpi   Java 1.2
java.security

This abstract class defines the service-provider interface for algorithm-parameter generation. A security provider must implement a concrete subclass of this class for each algorithm it supports. Applications never need to use or subclass this class.

```
public abstract class AlgorithmParameterGeneratorSpi {
// Public Constructors
    public AlgorithmParameterGeneratorSpi();
// Protected Instance Methods
    protected abstract AlgorithmParameters engineGenerateParameters();
    protected abstract void engineInit(java.security.spec.AlgorithmParameterSpec genParamSpec,
                            SecureRandom random) throws InvalidAlgorithmParameterException;
    protected abstract void engineInit(int size, SecureRandom random);
}
```

Passed To: AlgorithmParameterGenerator.AlgorithmParameterGenerator()

AlgorithmParameters   Java 1.2
java.security

This class is a generic, opaque representation of the parameters used by some cryptographic algorithm. You can create an instance of the class with one of the static getInstance() factory methods, specifying the desired algorithm and, optionally, the desired provider. The default "SUN" provider supports the "DSA" algorithm. The "Sun-JCE" provider shipped with the JCE supports "DES", "DESede", "PBE", "Blowfish", and "DiffieHellman". Once you have obtained an AlgorithmParameters object, initialize it by passing an algorithm-specific java.security.spec.AlgorithmParameterSpec object or the encoded parameter values as a byte array to the init() method. You can also create an AlgorithmParameters object with an AlgorithmParameterGenerator. getEncoded() returns the initialized algorithm parameters as a byte array, using either the algorithm-specific default encoding or the named encoding format you specified.

```
public class AlgorithmParameters {
// Protected Constructors
    protected AlgorithmParameters(AlgorithmParametersSpi paramSpi, Provider provider, String algorithm);
// Public Class Methods
    public static AlgorithmParameters getInstance(String algorithm) throws NoSuchAlgorithmException;
    public static AlgorithmParameters getInstance(String algorithm, String provider) throws NoSuchAlgorithmException,
        NoSuchProviderException;
// Public Instance Methods
    public final String getAlgorithm();
    public final byte[ ] getEncoded() throws java.io.IOException;
    public final byte[ ] getEncoded(String format) throws java.io.IOException;
    public final java.security.spec.AlgorithmParameterSpec getParameterSpec(Class paramSpec)
        throws java.security.spec.InvalidParameterSpecException;
    public final Provider getProvider();
    public final void init(java.security.spec.AlgorithmParameterSpec paramSpec)
        throws java.security.spec.InvalidParameterSpecException;
    public final void init(byte[ ] params) throws java.io.IOException;
    public final void init(byte[ ] params, String format) throws java.io.IOException;
// Public Methods Overriding Object
    public final String toString();
}
```

Passed To: javax.crypto.Cipher.init(), javax.crypto.CipherSpi.engineInit()

Returned By: AlgorithmParameterGenerator.generateParameters(),
AlgorithmParameterGeneratorSpi.engineGenerateParameters(), AlgorithmParameters.getInstance(),
javax.crypto.Cipher.getParameters(), javax.crypto.CipherSpi.engineGetParameters()

AlgorithmParametersSpi   Java 1.2

java.security

This abstract class defines the service-provider interface for AlgorithmParameters. A security provider must implement a concrete subclass of this class for each cryptographic algorithm it supports. Applications never need to use or subclass this class.

```
public abstract class AlgorithmParametersSpi {
// Public Constructors
    public AlgorithmParametersSpi();
// Protected Instance Methods
    protected abstract byte[ ] engineGetEncoded() throws java.io.IOException;
    protected abstract byte[ ] engineGetEncoded(String format) throws java.io.IOException;
    protected abstract java.security.spec.AlgorithmParameterSpec engineGetParameterSpec(Class paramSpec)
        throws java.security.spec.InvalidParameterSpecException;
    protected abstract void engineInit(java.security.spec.AlgorithmParameterSpec paramSpec)
        throws java.security.spec.InvalidParameterSpecException;
    protected abstract void engineInit(byte[ ] params) throws java.io.IOException;
    protected abstract void engineInit(byte[ ] params, String format) throws java.io.IOException;
    protected abstract String engineToString();
}
```

Passed To: AlgorithmParameters.AlgorithmParameters()

AllPermission

Java 1.2

serializable permission

This class is a Permission subclass whose implies() method always returns true. This means that code that has been granted AllPermission is granted all other possible permissions. This class exists to provide a convenient way to grant all permissions to completely trusted code. It should be used with care. Applications typically do not need to work directly with Permission objects.

```
public final class AllPermission extends java.security.Permission {
// Public Constructors
    public AllPermission();
    public AllPermission(String name, String actions);
// Public Methods Overriding Permission
    public boolean equals(Object obj);
    public String getActions();                                          default:"<all actions>"
    public int hashCode();                                                           constant
    public boolean implies(java.security.Permission p);                              constant
    public PermissionCollection newPermissionCollection();
}
```

Hierarchy: Object→ java.security.Permission(Guard, Serializable)→ AllPermission

BasicPermission

Java 1.2

serializable permission

This Permission class is the abstract superclass for a number of simple permission types. BasicPermission is typically subclassed to implement named permissions that have a name, or target, string, but do not support actions. The implies() method of BasicPermission defines a simple wildcarding capability. The target "*" implies permission for any target. The target "x.*" implies permission for any target that begins with "x.". Applications typically do not need to work directly with Permission objects.

```
public abstract class BasicPermission extends java.security.Permission implements Serializable {
// Public Constructors
    public BasicPermission(String name);
    public BasicPermission(String name, String actions);
// Public Methods Overriding Permission
    public boolean equals(Object obj);
    public String getActions();
    public int hashCode();
    public boolean implies(java.security.Permission p);
    public PermissionCollection newPermissionCollection();
}
```

Hierarchy: Object→ java.security.Permission(Guard, Serializable)→ BasicPermission(Serializable)

Subclasses: java.awt.AWTPermission, java.io.SerializablePermission, RuntimePermission, java.lang.reflect.ReflectPermission, java.net.NetPermission, SecurityPermission, java.sql.SQLPermission, java.util.PropertyPermission

Certificate

Java 1.1; Deprecated in Java 1.2

PJ1.1(opt)

This interface was used in Java 1.1 to represent an identity certificate. It has been deprecated as of Java 1.2 in favor of the java.security.cert package (see Chapter 19, *The java.security.cert Package*.) See also java.security.cert.Certificate.

java.security

```
public interface Certificate {
// Public Instance Methods
    public abstract void decode(java.io.InputStream stream) throws KeyException, java.io.IOException;
    public abstract void encode(java.io.OutputStream stream) throws KeyException, java.io.IOException;
    public abstract String getFormat();
    public abstract java.security.Principal getGuarantor();
    public abstract java.security.Principal getPrincipal();
    public abstract PublicKey getPublicKey();
    public abstract String toString(boolean detailed);
}
```

Passed To: Identity.{addCertificate(), removeCertificate()}

Returned By: Identity.certificates()

CodeSource   Java 1.2

java.security   *serializable*

This class represents the source of a Java class, as defined by the URL from which the class was loaded and the set of digital signatures attached to the class. A CodeSource object is created by specifying a java.net.URL and an array of java.security.cert.Certificate objects. Only applications that create custom ClassLoader objects should ever need to use or subclass this class.

When a CodeSource represents a specific piece of Java code, it includes a fully qualified URL and the actual set of certificates used to sign the code. When a CodeSource object defines a ProtectionDomain, however, the URL may include wildcards, and the array of certificates is a minimum required set of signatures. The implies() method of such a CodeSource tests whether a particular Java class comes from a matching URL and has the required set of signatures.

```
public class CodeSource implements Serializable {
// Public Constructors
    public CodeSource(java.net.URL url, java.security.cert.Certificate[ ] certs);
// Public Instance Methods
    public final java.security.cert.Certificate[ ] getCertificates();
    public final java.net.URL getLocation();
    public boolean implies(CodeSource codesource);
// Public Methods Overriding Object
    public boolean equals(Object obj);
    public int hashCode();
    public String toString();
}
```

Hierarchy: Object→ CodeSource(Serializable)

Passed To: java.net.URLClassLoader.getPermissions(), CodeSource.implies(), java.security.Policy.getPermissions(), ProtectionDomain.ProtectionDomain(), SecureClassLoader.{defineClass(), getPermissions()}

Returned By: ProtectionDomain.getCodeSource()

DigestException   Java 1.1

java.security   *serializable checked PJ1.1(opt)*

Signals a problem creating a message digest.

```
public class DigestException extends GeneralSecurityException {
```

```
// Public Constructors
    public DigestException();
    public DigestException(String msg);
}
```

Hierarchy: Object→ Throwable(Serializable)→ Exception→ GeneralSecurityException→
DigestException

Thrown By: MessageDigest.digest(), MessageDigestSpi.engineDigest()

DigestInputStream
java.security

This class is a byte input stream with an associated MessageDigest object. When bytes are
read with any of the read() methods, those bytes are automatically passed to the update()
method of the MessageDigest. When you have finished reading bytes, you can call the
digest() method of the MessageDigest to obtain a message digest. If you want to compute
a digest just for some of the bytes read from the stream, use on() to turn the digesting
function on and off. Digesting is on by default; call on(false) to turn it off. See also
DigestOutputStream and MessageDigest.

```
public class DigestInputStream extends java.io.FilterInputStream {
// Public Constructors
    public DigestInputStream(java.io.InputStream stream, MessageDigest digest);
// Public Instance Methods
    public MessageDigest getMessageDigest();
    public void on(boolean on);
    public void setMessageDigest(MessageDigest digest);
// Public Methods Overriding FilterInputStream
    public int read() throws java.io.IOException;
    public int read(byte[ ] b, int off, int len) throws java.io.IOException;
// Public Methods Overriding Object
    public String toString();
// Protected Instance Fields
    protected MessageDigest digest;
}
```

Hierarchy: Object→ java.io.InputStream→ java.io.FilterInputStream→ DigestInputStream

DigestOutputStream
java.security

This class is a byte output stream with an associated MessageDigest object. When bytes
are written to the stream with any of the write() methods, those bytes are automatically
passed to the update() method of the MessageDigest. When you have finished writing
bytes, you can call the digest() method of the MessageDigest to obtain a message digest. If
you want to compute a digest just for some of the bytes written to the stream, use on()
to turn the digesting function on and off. Digesting is on by default; call on(false) to turn
it off. See also DigestInputStream and MessageDigest.

```
public class DigestOutputStream extends java.io.FilterOutputStream {
// Public Constructors
    public DigestOutputStream(java.io.OutputStream stream, MessageDigest digest);
// Public Instance Methods
    public MessageDigest getMessageDigest();
    public void on(boolean on);
    public void setMessageDigest(MessageDigest digest);
```

```
// Public Methods Overriding FilterOutputStream
   public void write(int b) throws java.io.IOException;
   public void write(byte[ ] b, int off, int len) throws java.io.IOException;
// Public Methods Overriding Object
   public String toString( );
// Protected Instance Fields
   protected MessageDigest digest;
}
```

Hierarchy: Object→ java.io.OutputStream→ java.io.FilterOutputStream→ DigestOutputStream

DomainCombiner   Java 1.3

java.security

This interface defines a single combine() method that combines two arrays of Protection-Domain objects into a single equivalent (and perhaps optimized) array. You can associate a DomainCombiner with an existing AccessControlContext by calling the two-argument AccessControlContext() constructor. Then, when the checkPermission() method of the Access-ControlContext is called or when the AccessControlContext is passed to a doPrivileged() method of AccessController, the specified DomainCombiner merges the protection domains of the current stack frame with the protection domains encapsulated in the AccessControlContext. This class is used only by system-level code; typical applications rarely need to use it.

```
public interface DomainCombiner {
// Public Instance Methods
   public abstract ProtectionDomain[ ] combine(ProtectionDomain[ ] currentDomains,
                                   ProtectionDomain[ ] assignedDomains);
}
```

Passed To: AccessControlContext.AccessControlContext()

Returned By: AccessControlContext.getDomainCombiner()

GeneralSecurityException   Java 1.2

java.security   *serializable checked*

This class is the superclass of most of the exceptions defined by the java.security package.

```
public class GeneralSecurityException extends Exception {
// Public Constructors
   public GeneralSecurityException( );
   public GeneralSecurityException(String msg);
}
```

Hierarchy: Object→ Throwable(Serializable)→ Exception→ GeneralSecurityException

Subclasses: DigestException, InvalidAlgorithmParameterException, KeyException, KeyStoreException, NoSuchAlgorithmException, NoSuchProviderException, SignatureException, UnrecoverableKeyException, java.security.cert.CertificateException, java.security.cert.CRLException, java.security.spec.InvalidKeySpecException, java.security.spec.InvalidParameterSpecException, javax.crypto.BadPaddingException, javax.crypto.IllegalBlockSizeException, javax.crypto.NoSuchPaddingException, javax.crypto.ShortBufferException

Guard   Java 1.2

java.security

This interface guards access to an object. The checkGuard() method is passed an object to which access has been requested. If access should be granted, checkGuard() should return silently. Otherwise, if access is denied, checkGuard() should throw a java.lang.SecurityException. The Guard object is used primarily by the GuardedObject class. Note that all Permission objects implement the Guard interface.

```
public interface Guard {
// Public Instance Methods
    public abstract void checkGuard(Object object) throws SecurityException;
}
```

Implementations: java.security.Permission

Passed To: GuardedObject.GuardedObject()

GuardedObject   Java 1.2
java.security   *serializable*

This class uses a Guard object to guard against unauthorized access to an arbitrary encapsulated object. Create a GuardedObject by specifying an object and a Guard for it. The getObject() method calls the checkGuard() method of the Guard to determine whether access to the object should be allowed. If access is allowed, getObject() returns the encapsulated object. Otherwise, it throws a java.lang.SecurityException.

The Guard object used by a GuardedObject is often a Permission. In this case, access to the guarded object is granted only if the calling code is granted the specified permission by the current security policy.

```
public class GuardedObject implements Serializable {
// Public Constructors
    public GuardedObject(Object object, Guard guard);
// Public Instance Methods
    public Object getObject() throws SecurityException;
}
```

Hierarchy: Object → GuardedObject(Serializable)

Identity   Java 1.1; Deprecated in Java 1.2
java.security   *serializable PJ1.1(opt)*

This deprecated class was used in Java 1.1 to represent an entity or Principal with an associated PublicKey object. In Java 1.1, the public key for a named entity could be retrieved from the system keystore with a line like the following:

```
IdentityScope.getSystemScope().getIdentity(name).getPublicKey()
```

As of Java 1.2, the Identity class and the related IdentityScope and Signer classes have been deprecated in favor of KeyStore and java.security.cert.Certificate.

```
public abstract class Identity implements java.security.Principal, Serializable {
// Public Constructors
    public Identity(String name);
    public Identity(String name, IdentityScope scope) throws KeyManagementException;
// Protected Constructors
    protected Identity();
// Property Accessor Methods (by property name)
    public String getInfo();
    public void setInfo(String info);
    public final String getName();                               Implements:Principal
    public PublicKey getPublicKey();
    public void setPublicKey(PublicKey key) throws KeyManagementException;
    public final IdentityScope getScope();
```

```
// Public Instance Methods
    public void addCertificate(java.security.Certificate certificate) throws KeyManagementException;
    public java.security.Certificate[ ] certificates( );
    public void removeCertificate(java.security.Certificate certificate) throws KeyManagementException;
    public String toString(boolean detailed);
// Methods Implementing Principal
    public final boolean equals(Object identity);
    public final String getName( );
    public int hashCode( );
    public String toString( );
// Protected Instance Methods
    protected boolean identityEquals(Identity identity);
}
```

Hierarchy: Object→ Identity(java.security.Principal, Serializable)

Subclasses: IdentityScope, Signer

Passed To: Identity.identityEquals(), IdentityScope.{addIdentity(), removeIdentity()}, javax.ejb.EJBContext.isCallerInRole(), javax.ejb.deployment.AccessControlEntry.{AccessControlEntry(), setAllowedIdentities()}, javax.ejb.deployment.ControlDescriptor.setRunAsIdentity()

Returned By: IdentityScope.getIdentity(), javax.ejb.EJBContext.getCallerIdentity(), javax.ejb.deployment.AccessControlEntry.getAllowedIdentities(), javax.ejb.deployment.ControlDescriptor.getRunAsIdentity()

IdentityScope
Java 1.1; Deprecated in Java 1.2

java.security
serializable PJ1.1(opt)

This deprecated class was used in Java 1.1 to represent a group of Identity and Signer objects and their associated PublicKey and PrivateKey objects. As of Java 1.2, it has been replaced by the KeyStore class.

```
public abstract class IdentityScope extends Identity {
// Public Constructors
    public IdentityScope(String name);
    public IdentityScope(String name, IdentityScope scope) throws KeyManagementException;
// Protected Constructors
    protected IdentityScope( );
// Public Class Methods
    public static IdentityScope getSystemScope( );
// Protected Class Methods
    protected static void setSystemScope(IdentityScope scope);
// Public Instance Methods
    public abstract void addIdentity(Identity identity) throws KeyManagementException;
    public abstract Identity getIdentity(String name);
    public Identity getIdentity(java.security.Principal principal);
    public abstract Identity getIdentity(PublicKey key);
    public abstract java.util.Enumeration identities( );
    public abstract void removeIdentity(Identity identity) throws KeyManagementException;
    public abstract int size( );
// Public Methods Overriding Identity
    public String toString( );
}
```

Hierarchy: Object→ Identity(java.security.Principal, Serializable)→ IdentityScope

Passed To: Identity.Identity(), IdentityScope.{IdentityScope(), setSystemScope()}, Signer.Signer()

Returned By: Identity.getScope(), IdentityScope.getSystemScope()

InvalidAlgorithmParameterException   Java 1.2

java.security   *serializable checked*

Signals that one or more algorithm parameters (usually specified by a java.secu-rity.spec.AlgorithmParameterSpec object) are not valid.

```
public class InvalidAlgorithmParameterException extends GeneralSecurityException {
// Public Constructors
    public InvalidAlgorithmParameterException();
    public InvalidAlgorithmParameterException(String msg);
}
```

Hierarchy: Object → Throwable(Serializable) → Exception → GeneralSecurityException → InvalidAlgorithmParameterException

Thrown By: Too many methods to list.

InvalidKeyException   Java 1.1

java.security   *serializable checked PJ1.1(opt)*

Signals that a Key is not valid.

```
public class InvalidKeyException extends KeyException {
// Public Constructors
    public InvalidKeyException();
    public InvalidKeyException(String msg);
}
```

Hierarchy: Object → Throwable(Serializable) → Exception → GeneralSecurityException → KeyException → InvalidKeyException

Thrown By: Too many methods to list.

InvalidParameterException   Java 1.1

java.security   *serializable unchecked PJ1.1(opt)*

This subclass of java.lang.IllegalArgumentException signals that a parameter passed to a security method is not valid. This exception type is not widely used.

```
public class InvalidParameterException extends IllegalArgumentException {
// Public Constructors
    public InvalidParameterException();
    public InvalidParameterException(String msg);
}
```

Hierarchy: Object → Throwable(Serializable) → Exception → RuntimeException → IllegalArgumentException → InvalidParameterException

Thrown By: Signature.{getParameter(), setParameter()}, SignatureSpi.{engineGetParameter(), engineSetParameter()}, Signer.setKeyPair(), java.security.interfaces.DSAKeyPairGenerator.initialize()

Key   Java 1.1

java.security   *serializable PJ1.1(opt)*

This interface defines the high-level characteristics of all cryptographic keys. getAlgorithm() returns the name of the cryptographic algorithm (such as RSA) used with the key. getFormat() return the name of the external encoding (such as X.509) used with the key. getEncoded() returns the key as an array of bytes, encoded using the format specified by getFormat().

```
public interface Key extends Serializable {
// Public Constants
1.2 public static final long serialVersionUID;                         =6603384152749567654
// Public Instance Methods
    public abstract String getAlgorithm();
    public abstract byte[ ] getEncoded();
    public abstract String getFormat();
}
```

Hierarchy: (Key(Serializable))

Implementations: PrivateKey, PublicKey, javax.crypto.SecretKey

Passed To: Too many methods to list.

Returned By: KeyFactory.translateKey(), KeyFactorySpi.engineTranslateKey(), KeyStore.getKey(), KeyStoreSpi.engineGetKey(), javax.crypto.KeyAgreement.doPhase(), javax.crypto.KeyAgreementSpi.engineDoPhase()

KeyException   Java 1.1
java.security   *serializable checked PJ1.1(opt)*

Signals that something is wrong with a key. See also the subclasses InvalidKeyException and KeyManagementException.

```
public class KeyException extends GeneralSecurityException {
// Public Constructors
    public KeyException();
    public KeyException(String msg);
}
```

Hierarchy: Object→ Throwable(Serializable)→ Exception→ GeneralSecurityException→ KeyException

Subclasses: InvalidKeyException, KeyManagementException

Thrown By: java.security.Certificate.{decode(), encode()}, Signer.setKeyPair()

KeyFactory   Java 1.2
java.security

This class translates asymmetric cryptographic keys between the two representations used by the Java Security API. java.security.Key is the opaque, algorithm-independent representation of a key used by most of the Security API. java.security.spec.KeySpec is a marker interface implemented by transparent, algorithm-specific representations of keys. KeyFactory is used with public and private keys; see javax.crypto.SecretKeyFactory if you are working with symmetric or secret keys.

To convert a Key to a KeySpec or vice versa, create a KeyFactory by calling one of the static getInstance() factory methods and specifying the name of the key algorithm (e.g., DSA or RSA). Then, use generatePublic() or generatePrivate() to create a PublicKey or PrivateKey object from a corresponding KeySpec. Or use getKeySpec() to obtain a KeySpec for a given Key. Because there can be more than one KeySpec implementation used by a particular cryptographic algorithm, you must also specify the Class of the KeySpec you desire.

If you do not need to transport keys portably between applications and/or systems, you can use a KeyStore to store and retrieve keys and certificates, avoiding KeySpec and KeyFactory altogether.

```
public class KeyFactory {
// Protected Constructors
     protected KeyFactory(KeyFactorySpi keyFacSpi, Provider provider, String algorithm);
// Public Class Methods
     public static KeyFactory getInstance(String algorithm) throws NoSuchAlgorithmException;
     public static KeyFactory getInstance(String algorithm, String provider) throws NoSuchAlgorithmException,
        NoSuchProviderException;
// Public Instance Methods
     public final PrivateKey generatePrivate(java.security.spec.KeySpec keySpec)
        throws java.security.spec.InvalidKeySpecException;
     public final PublicKey generatePublic(java.security.spec.KeySpec keySpec)
        throws java.security.spec.InvalidKeySpecException;
     public final String getAlgorithm();
     public final java.security.spec.KeySpec getKeySpec(Key key, Class keySpec)
        throws java.security.spec.InvalidKeySpecException;
     public final Provider getProvider();
     public final Key translateKey(Key key) throws InvalidKeyException;
}
```

Returned By: KeyFactory.getInstance()

KeyFactorySpi

java.security

This abstract class defines the service-provider interface for KeyFactory. A security provider must implement a concrete subclass of this class for each cryptographic algorithm it supports. Applications never need to use or subclass this class.

```
public abstract class KeyFactorySpi {
// Public Constructors
     public KeyFactorySpi();
// Protected Instance Methods
     protected abstract PrivateKey engineGeneratePrivate(java.security.spec.KeySpec keySpec)
        throws java.security.spec.InvalidKeySpecException;
     protected abstract PublicKey engineGeneratePublic(java.security.spec.KeySpec keySpec)
        throws java.security.spec.InvalidKeySpecException;
     protected abstract java.security.spec.KeySpec engineGetKeySpec(Key key, Class keySpec)
        throws java.security.spec.InvalidKeySpecException;
     protected abstract Key engineTranslateKey(Key key) throws InvalidKeyException;
}
```

Passed To: KeyFactory.KeyFactory()

KeyManagementException

java.security   *serializable checked PJ1.1(opt)*

Signals an exception in a key management operation. In Java 1.2, this exception is only thrown by deprecated methods.

```
public class KeyManagementException extends KeyException {
// Public Constructors
     public KeyManagementException();
     public KeyManagementException(String msg);
}
```

Hierarchy: Object→ Throwable(Serializable)→ Exception→ GeneralSecurityException→
KeyException→ KeyManagementException

Thrown By: Identity.{addCertificate(), Identity(), removeCertificate(), setPublicKey()}, IdentityScope.{addIdentity(), IdentityScope(), removeIdentity()}, Signer.Signer()

KeyPair
java.security

Java 1.1

serializable PJ1.1(opt)

This class is a simple container for a PublicKey and a PrivateKey object. Because a KeyPair contains an unprotected private key, it must be used with as much caution as a PrivateKey object.

```
public final class KeyPair implements Serializable {
// Public Constructors
    public KeyPair(PublicKey publicKey, PrivateKey privateKey);
// Public Instance Methods
    public PrivateKey getPrivate();
    public PublicKey getPublic();
}
```

Hierarchy: Object→ KeyPair(Serializable)

Passed To: Signer.setKeyPair()

Returned By: KeyPairGenerator.{generateKeyPair(), genKeyPair()}, KeyPairGeneratorSpi.generateKeyPair()

KeyPairGenerator
java.security

Java 1.1

PJ1.1(opt)

This class generates a public/private key pair for a specified cryptographic algorithm. To create a KeyPairGenerator, call one of the static getInstance() methods, specifying the name of the algorithm and, optionally, the name of the security provider to use. The default "SUN" provider shipped with Java 1.2 supports only the "DSA" algorithm. The "SunJCE" provider of the Java Cryptography Extension (JCE) additionally supports the "DiffieHellman" algorithm.

Once you have created a KeyPairGenerator, initialize it by calling initialize(). You can perform an algorithm-independent initialization by simply specifying the desired key size in bits. Alternatively, you can do an algorithm-dependent initialization by providing an appropriate AlgorithmParameterSpec object for the key-generation algorithm. In either case, you may optionally provide your own source of randomness in the guise of a SecureRandom object. Once you have created and initialized a KeyPairGenerator, call genKeyPair() to create a KeyPair object. Remember that the KeyPair contains a PrivateKey that *must* be kept private.

For historical reasons, KeyPairGenerator extends KeyPairGeneratorSpi. Applications should not use any methods inherited from that class.

```
public abstract class KeyPairGenerator extends KeyPairGeneratorSpi {
// Protected Constructors
    protected KeyPairGenerator(String algorithm);
// Public Class Methods
    public static KeyPairGenerator getInstance(String algorithm) throws NoSuchAlgorithmException;
    public static KeyPairGenerator getInstance(String algorithm, String provider) throws NoSuchAlgorithmException,
        NoSuchProviderException;
// Public Instance Methods
1.2 public final KeyPair genKeyPair();
    public String getAlgorithm();
1.2 public final Provider getProvider();
1.2 public void initialize(java.security.spec.AlgorithmParameterSpec params)
        throws InvalidAlgorithmParameterException;
```

```
   public void initialize(int keysize);
// Public Methods Overriding KeyPairGeneratorSpi
   public KeyPair generateKeyPair( );                                                                constant
1.2 public void initialize(java.security.spec.AlgorithmParameterSpec params, SecureRandom random)     empty
       throws InvalidAlgorithmParameterException;
   public void initialize(int keysize, SecureRandom random);                                          empty
}
```

Hierarchy: Object→ KeyPairGeneratorSpi→ KeyPairGenerator

Returned By: KeyPairGenerator.getInstance()

KeyPairGeneratorSpi   Java 1.2
java.security

This abstract class defines the service-provider interface for KeyPairGenerator. A security
provider must implement a concrete subclass of this class for each cryptographic algorithm for which it can generate key pairs. Applications never need to use or subclass
this class.

```
public abstract class KeyPairGeneratorSpi {
// Public Constructors
   public KeyPairGeneratorSpi( );
// Public Instance Methods
   public abstract KeyPair generateKeyPair( );
   public void initialize(java.security.spec.AlgorithmParameterSpec params, SecureRandom random)
       throws InvalidAlgorithmParameterException;
   public abstract void initialize(int keysize, SecureRandom random);
}
```

Subclasses: KeyPairGenerator

KeyStore   Java 1.2
java.security

This class represents a mapping of names, or aliases, to Key and java.security.cert.Certificate
objects. Obtain a KeyStore object by calling one of the static getInstance() methods, specifying the desired key store type and, optionally, the desired provider. Use "JKS" to
specify the "Java Key Store" type defined by Sun. Because of U.S. export regulations,
this default KeyStore supports only weak encryption of private keys. If you have the Java
Cryptography Extension installed, use the type "JCEKS" and provider "SunJCE" to obtain
a KeyStore implementation that offers much stronger password-based encryption of keys.
Once you have created a KeyStore, use load() to read its contents from a stream, supplying an optional password that verifies the integrity of the stream data. Keystores are
typically read from a file named *.keystore* in the user's home directory.

A KeyStore may contain both public and private key entries. A public key entry is represented by a Certificate object. Use getCertificate() to look up a named public key certificate
and setCertificateEntry() to add a new public key certificate to the keystore. A private key
entry in the keystore contains both a password-protected Key and an array of Certificate
objects that represent the certificate chain for the public key that corresponds to the
private key. Use getKey() and getCertificateChain() to look up the key and certificate chain.
Use setKeyEntry() to create a new private key entry. You must provide a password when
reading or writing a private key from the keystore; this password encrypts the key data,
and each private key entry should have a different password. If you are using the JCE,
you may also store javax.crypto.SecretKey objects in a KeyStore. Secret keys are stored like
private keys, except that they do not have a certificate chain associated with them.

To delete an entry from a KeyStore, use deleteEntry(). If you modify the contents of a Key-Store, use store() to save the keystore to a specified stream. You may specify a password that is used to validate the integrity of the data, but it is not used to encrypt the key-store.

```
public class KeyStore {
// Protected Constructors
    protected KeyStore(KeyStoreSpi keyStoreSpi, Provider provider, String type);
// Public Class Methods
    public static final String getDefaultType();
    public static KeyStore getInstance(String type) throws KeyStoreException;
    public static KeyStore getInstance(String type, String provider) throws KeyStoreException,
        NoSuchProviderException;
// Public Instance Methods
    public final java.util.Enumeration aliases() throws KeyStoreException;
    public final boolean containsAlias(String alias) throws KeyStoreException;
    public final void deleteEntry(String alias) throws KeyStoreException;
    public final java.security.cert.Certificate getCertificate(String alias) throws KeyStoreException;
    public final String getCertificateAlias(java.security.cert.Certificate cert) throws KeyStoreException;
    public final java.security.cert.Certificate[] getCertificateChain(String alias) throws KeyStoreException;
    public final java.util.Date getCreationDate(String alias) throws KeyStoreException;
    public final Key getKey(String alias, char[] password) throws KeyStoreException, NoSuchAlgorithmException,
        UnrecoverableKeyException;
    public final Provider getProvider();
    public final String getType();
    public final boolean isCertificateEntry(String alias) throws KeyStoreException;
    public final boolean isKeyEntry(String alias) throws KeyStoreException;
    public final void load(java.io.InputStream stream, char[] password) throws java.io.IOException,
        NoSuchAlgorithmException, java.security.cert.CertificateException;
    public final void setCertificateEntry(String alias, java.security.cert.Certificate cert) throws KeyStoreException;
    public final void setKeyEntry(String alias, byte[] key, java.security.cert.Certificate[] chain)
        throws KeyStoreException;
    public final void setKeyEntry(String alias, Key key, char[] password, java.security.cert.Certificate[] chain)
        throws KeyStoreException;
    public final int size() throws KeyStoreException;
    public final void store(java.io.OutputStream stream, char[] password) throws KeyStoreException,
        java.io.IOException, NoSuchAlgorithmException, java.security.cert.CertificateException;
}
```

Returned By: KeyStore.getInstance()

KeyStoreException Java 1.2

java.security *serializable checked*

Signals a problem with a KeyStore.

```
public class KeyStoreException extends GeneralSecurityException {
// Public Constructors
    public KeyStoreException();
    public KeyStoreException(String msg);
}
```

Hierarchy: Object→ Throwable(Serializable)→ Exception→ GeneralSecurityException→ KeyStoreException

Thrown By: Too many methods to list.

KeyStoreSpi

java.security

This abstract class defines the service-provider interface for KeyStore. A security provider must implement a concrete subclass of this class for each KeyStore type it supports. Applications never need to use or subclass this class.

```
public abstract class KeyStoreSpi {
// Public Constructors
    public KeyStoreSpi();
// Public Instance Methods
    public abstract java.util.Enumeration engineAliases();
    public abstract boolean engineContainsAlias(String alias);
    public abstract void engineDeleteEntry(String alias) throws KeyStoreException;
    public abstract java.security.cert.Certificate engineGetCertificate(String alias);
    public abstract String engineGetCertificateAlias(java.security.cert.Certificate cert);
    public abstract java.security.cert.Certificate[ ] engineGetCertificateChain(String alias);
    public abstract java.util.Date engineGetCreationDate(String alias);
    public abstract Key engineGetKey(String alias, char[ ] password) throws NoSuchAlgorithmException,
        UnrecoverableKeyException;
    public abstract boolean engineIsCertificateEntry(String alias);
    public abstract boolean engineIsKeyEntry(String alias);
    public abstract void engineLoad(java.io.InputStream stream, char[ ] password) throws java.io.IOException,
        NoSuchAlgorithmException, java.security.cert.CertificateException;
    public abstract void engineSetCertificateEntry(String alias, java.security.cert.Certificate cert)
        throws KeyStoreException;
    public abstract void engineSetKeyEntry(String alias, byte[ ] key, java.security.cert.Certificate[ ] chain)
        throws KeyStoreException;
    public abstract void engineSetKeyEntry(String alias, Key key, char[ ] password,
                            java.security.cert.Certificate[ ] chain) throws KeyStoreException;
    public abstract int engineSize();
    public abstract void engineStore(java.io.OutputStream stream, char[ ] password) throws java.io.IOException,
        NoSuchAlgorithmException, java.security.cert.CertificateException;
}
```

Passed To: KeyStore.KeyStore()

MessageDigest

java.security

This class computes a message digest (also known as a cryptographic checksum) for an arbitrary sequence of bytes. Obtain a MessageDigest object by calling one of the static getInstance() factory methods and specifying the desired algorithm (e.g., SHA or MD5) and, optionally, the desired provider. Next, specify the data to be digested by calling any of the update() methods one or more times. Finally, call digest(), which computes the message digest and returns it as an array of bytes. If you have only one array of bytes to be digested, you can pass it directly to digest() and skip the update() step. When you call digest(), the MessageDigest() object is reset and is then ready to compute a new digest. You can also explicitly reset a MessageDigest without computing the digest by calling reset(). To compute a digest for part of a message without resetting the MessageDigest, clone the MessageDigest and call digest() on the cloned copy. Note that not all implementations are cloneable, so the clone() method may throw an exception.

The MessageDigest class is often used in conjunction with DigestInputStream and DigestOutputStream, which automate the update() calls for you.

```
public abstract class MessageDigest extends MessageDigestSpi {
// Protected Constructors
     protected MessageDigest(String algorithm);
// Public Class Methods
     public static MessageDigest getInstance(String algorithm) throws NoSuchAlgorithmException;
     public static MessageDigest getInstance(String algorithm, String provider) throws NoSuchAlgorithmException,
          NoSuchProviderException;
     public static boolean isEqual(byte[ ] digesta, byte[ ] digestb);
// Public Instance Methods
     public byte[ ] digest();
     public byte[ ] digest(byte[ ] input);
1.2  public int digest(byte[ ] buf, int offset, int len) throws DigestException;
     public final String getAlgorithm();
1.2  public final int getDigestLength();
1.2  public final Provider getProvider();
     public void reset();
     public void update(byte input);
     public void update(byte[ ] input);
     public void update(byte[ ] input, int offset, int len);
// Public Methods Overriding MessageDigestSpi
     public Object clone() throws CloneNotSupportedException;
// Public Methods Overriding Object
     public String toString();
}
```

Hierarchy: Object→ MessageDigestSpi→ MessageDigest

Passed To: DigestInputStream.{DigestInputStream(), setMessageDigest()},
DigestOutputStream.{DigestOutputStream(), setMessageDigest()}

Returned By: DigestInputStream.getMessageDigest(), DigestOutputStream.getMessageDigest(),
MessageDigest.getInstance()

Type Of: DigestInputStream.digest, DigestOutputStream.digest

MessageDigestSpi   Java 1.2

java.security

This abstract class defines the service-provider interface for MessageDigest. A security
provider must implement a concrete subclass of this class for each message-digest algorithm it supports. Applications never need to use or subclass this class.

```
public abstract class MessageDigestSpi {
// Public Constructors
     public MessageDigestSpi();
// Public Methods Overriding Object
     public Object clone() throws CloneNotSupportedException;
// Protected Instance Methods
     protected abstract byte[ ] engineDigest();
     protected int engineDigest(byte[ ] buf, int offset, int len) throws DigestException;
     protected int engineGetDigestLength();                                          constant
     protected abstract void engineReset();
     protected abstract void engineUpdate(byte input);
     protected abstract void engineUpdate(byte[ ] input, int offset, int len);
}
```

Subclasses: MessageDigest

NoSuchAlgorithmException

Java 1.1

java.security *serializable checked PJ1.1(opt)*

Signals that a requested cryptographic algorithm is not available. Thrown by getInstance() factory methods throughout the java.security package.

```
public class NoSuchAlgorithmException extends GeneralSecurityException {
// Public Constructors
    public NoSuchAlgorithmException();
    public NoSuchAlgorithmException(String msg);
}
```

Hierarchy: Object→ Throwable(Serializable)→ Exception→ GeneralSecurityException→ NoSuchAlgorithmException

Thrown By: Too many methods to list.

NoSuchProviderException

Java 1.1

java.security *serializable checked PJ1.1(opt)*

Signals that a requested cryptographic service provider is not available. Thrown by getInstance() factory methods throughout the java.security package.

```
public class NoSuchProviderException extends GeneralSecurityException {
// Public Constructors
    public NoSuchProviderException();
    public NoSuchProviderException(String msg);
}
```

Hierarchy: Object→ Throwable(Serializable)→ Exception→ GeneralSecurityException→ NoSuchProviderException

Thrown By: Too many methods to list.

Permission

Java 1.2

java.security *serializable permission*

This abstract class represents a system resource, such as a file in the filesystem, or a system capability, such as the ability to accept network connections. Concrete subclasses of Permission, such as java.io.FilePermission and java.net.SocketPermission, represent specific types of resources. Permission objects are used by system code that is requesting access to a resource. They are also used by Policy objects that grant access to resources. The AccessController.checkPermission() method considers the source of the currently running Java code, determines the set of permissions that are granted to that code by the current Policy, and then checks to see whether a specified Permission object is included in that set. With the introduction of Java 1.2, this is the fundamental Java access-control mechanism.

Each permission has a name (sometimes called the *target*) and, optionally, a comma-separated list of actions. For example, the name of a FilePermission is the name of the file or directory for which permission is being granted. The actions associated with this permission might be "read"; "write"; or "read,write". The interpretation of the name and action strings is entirely up to the implementation of Permission. A number of implementations support the use of wildcards; for example, a FilePermission can have a name of "/tmp/*", which represents access to any files in a */tmp* directory. Permission objects must be immutable, so an implementation must never define a setName() or setActions() method.

One of the most important abstract methods defined by Permission is implies(). This method must return true if this Permission implies another Permission. For example, if an application requests a FilePermission with name "/tmp/test" and action "read", and the current security Policy grants a FilePermission with name "/tmp/*" and actions "read,write", the request is granted because the requested permission is implied by the granted one.

In general, only system-level code needs to work directly with Permission and its concrete subclasses. System administrators who are configuring security policies need to understand the various Permission subclasses. Applications that want to extend the Java access-control mechanism to provide customized access control to their own resources should subclass Permission to define custom permission types.

```
public abstract class Permission implements Guard, Serializable {
// Public Constructors
    public Permission(String name);
// Public Instance Methods
    public abstract String getActions();
    public final String getName();
    public abstract boolean implies(java.security.Permission permission);
    public PermissionCollection newPermissionCollection();                          constant
// Methods Implementing Guard
    public void checkGuard(Object object) throws SecurityException;
// Public Methods Overriding Object
    public abstract boolean equals(Object obj);
    public abstract int hashCode();
    public String toString();
}
```

Hierarchy: Object→ java.security.Permission(Guard, Serializable)

Subclasses: java.io.FilePermission, java.net.SocketPermission, AllPermission, BasicPermission, UnresolvedPermission

Passed To: Too many methods to list.

Returned By: java.net.HttpURLConnection.getPermission(), java.net.URLConnection.getPermission(), AccessControlException.getPermission()

PermissionCollection   Java 1.2
java.security   *serializable*

This class is used by Permissions to store a collection of Permission objects that are all the same type. Like the Permission class itself, PermissionCollection defines an implies() method that can determine whether a requested Permission is implied by any of the Permission objects in the collection. Some Permission types may require a custom PermissionCollection type in order to correctly implement the implies() method. In this case, the Permission subclass should override newPermissionCollection() to return a Permission of the appropriate type. PermissionCollection is used by system code that manages security policies. Applications rarely need to use it.

```
public abstract class PermissionCollection implements Serializable {
// Public Constructors
    public PermissionCollection();
// Public Instance Methods
    public abstract void add(java.security.Permission permission);
    public abstract java.util.Enumeration elements();
    public abstract boolean implies(java.security.Permission permission);
    public boolean isReadOnly();
    public void setReadOnly();
```

```
// Public Methods Overriding Object
    public String toString( );
}
```

Hierarchy: Object → PermissionCollection(Serializable)

Subclasses: Permissions

Passed To: ProtectionDomain.ProtectionDomain()

Returned By: java.io.FilePermission.newPermissionCollection(),
java.net.SocketPermission.newPermissionCollection(), java.net.URLClassLoader.getPermissions(),
AllPermission.newPermissionCollection(), BasicPermission.newPermissionCollection(),
java.security.Permission.newPermissionCollection(), java.security.Policy.getPermissions(),
ProtectionDomain.getPermissions(), SecureClassLoader.getPermissions(),
UnresolvedPermission.newPermissionCollection(),
java.util.PropertyPermission.newPermissionCollection()

Permissions   Java 1.2

java.security   *serializable*

This class stores an arbitrary collection of Permission objects. When Permission objects are
added with the add() method, they are grouped into an internal set of PermissionCollection
objects that contain only a single type of Permission. Use the elements() method to obtain
an Enumeration of the Permission objects in the collection. Use implies() to determine if a
specified Permission is implied by any of the Permission objects in the collection. Permissions is used by system code that manages security policies. Applications rarely need to
use it.

```
public final class Permissions extends PermissionCollection implements Serializable {
// Public Constructors
    public Permissions( );
// Public Methods Overriding PermissionCollection
    public void add(java.security.Permission permission);
    public java.util.Enumeration elements( );
    public boolean implies(java.security.Permission permission);
}
```

Hierarchy: Object → PermissionCollection(Serializable) → Permissions(Serializable)

Policy   Java 1.2

java.security

This class provides a mapping from CodeSource objects to PermissionCollection objects; it
defines a security policy by specifying what permissions are granted to what code.
There is only a single Policy in effect at any one time. Obtain the system policy by calling the static getPolicy() method. Code that has appropriate permissions can specify a
new system policy by calling setPolicy(). getPermissions() is the central Policy method; it
evaluates the Policy for a given CodeSource and returns an appropriate PermissionCollection.
The refresh() method is a request to a Policy object to update its state (for example, by
rereading its configuration file). The Policy class is used primarily by system-level code.
Applications should not need to use this class unless they implement some kind of custom access-control mechanism.

```
public abstract class Policy {
// Public Constructors
    public Policy( );
```

```
// Public Class Methods
   public static java.security.Policy getPolicy();
   public static void setPolicy(java.security.Policy policy);
// Public Instance Methods
   public abstract PermissionCollection getPermissions(CodeSource codesource);
   public abstract void refresh();
}
```

Passed To: java.security.Policy.setPolicy()

Returned By: java.security.Policy.getPolicy()

Principal   Java 1.1
java.security   *PJ1.1(opt)*

This interface represents any entity that may serve as a principal in a cryptographic
transaction of any kind. A Principal may represent an individual, a computer, or an organization, for example.

```
public interface Principal {
// Public Instance Methods
   public abstract boolean equals(Object another);
   public abstract String getName();
   public abstract int hashCode();
   public abstract String toString();
}
```

Implementations: Identity, java.security.acl.Group

Passed To: IdentityScope.getIdentity(), java.security.acl.Acl.{addEntry(), checkPermission(),
getPermissions(), removeEntry(), setName()}, java.security.acl.AclEntry.setPrincipal(),
java.security.acl.Group.{addMember(), isMember(), removeMember()},
java.security.acl.Owner.{addOwner(), deleteOwner(), isOwner()}

Returned By: java.security.Certificate.{getGuarantor(), getPrincipal()},
java.security.acl.AclEntry.getPrincipal(), java.security.cert.X509Certificate.{getIssuerDN(),
getSubjectDN()}, java.security.cert.X509CRL.getIssuerDN()

PrivateKey   Java 1.1
java.security   *serializable PJ1.1(opt)*

This interface represents a private cryptographic key. It extends the Key interface, but
does not add any new methods. The interface exists in order to create a strong distinction between private and public keys. See also PublicKey.

```
public interface PrivateKey extends Key {
// Public Constants
1.2 public static final long serialVersionUID;                    =6034044314589513430
}
```

Hierarchy: (PrivateKey(Key(Serializable)))

Implementations: java.security.interfaces.DSAPrivateKey, java.security.interfaces.RSAPrivateKey,
javax.crypto.interfaces.DHPrivateKey

Passed To: KeyPair.KeyPair(), Signature.initSign(), SignatureSpi.engineInitSign(),
SignedObject.SignedObject()

Returned By: KeyFactory.generatePrivate(), KeyFactorySpi.engineGeneratePrivate(),
KeyPair.getPrivate(), Signer.getPrivateKey()

PrivilegedAction

java.security

This interface defines a block of code (the run() method) that is to be executed as privileged code by the AccessController.doPrivileged() method. When privileged code is run in this way, the AccessController looks only at the permissions of the immediate caller, not the permissions of the entire call stack. The immediate caller is typically fully trusted system code that has a full set of permissions, and therefore the privileged code runs with that full set of permissions, even if the system code is invoked by untrusted code with no permissions whatsoever.

Privileged code is typically required only when you are writing a trusted system library (such as a Java extension package) that must read local files or perform other restricted actions, even when called by untrusted code. For example, a class that must call System.loadLibrary() to load native methods should make the call to loadLibrary() within the run() method of a PrivilegedAction. If your privileged code may throw a checked exception, implement it in the run() method of a PrivilegedExceptionAction instead.

Be very careful when implementing this interface. To minimize the possibility of security holes, keep the body of the run() method as short as possible.

```
public interface PrivilegedAction {
// Public Instance Methods
   public abstract Object run();
}
```

Passed To: AccessController.doPrivileged()

PrivilegedActionException

java.security   *serializable checked*

This exception class is a wrapper around an arbitrary Exception thrown by a PrivilegedExceptionAction executed by the AccessController.doPrivileged() method. Use getException() to obtain the wrapped Exception object.

```
public class PrivilegedActionException extends Exception {
// Public Constructors
   public PrivilegedActionException(Exception exception);
// Public Instance Methods
   public Exception getException();
// Public Methods Overriding Throwable
   public void printStackTrace();
   public void printStackTrace(java.io.PrintWriter pw);
   public void printStackTrace(java.io.PrintStream ps);
1.3 public String toString();
}
```

Hierarchy: Object→ Throwable(Serializable)→ Exception→ PrivilegedActionException

Thrown By: AccessController.doPrivileged()

PrivilegedExceptionAction

java.security

This interface is like PrivilegedAction, except that its run() method may throw an exception. See PrivilegedAction for details.

```
public interface PrivilegedExceptionAction {
// Public Instance Methods
    public abstract Object run() throws Exception;
}
```

Passed To: AccessController.doPrivileged()

ProtectionDomain   Java 1.2
java.security

This class represents a CodeSource and the associated PermissionCollection granted to that CodeSource by a Policy object. The implies() method checks to see whether the specified Permission is implied by any of the permissions granted to this ProtectionDomain. In Java 1.2, every class has an associated ProtectionDomain, which can be obtained with the get-ProtectionDomain() method of the Class object. Only applications that implement a custom ClassLoader should need to use this class.

```
public class ProtectionDomain {
// Public Constructors
    public ProtectionDomain(CodeSource codesource, PermissionCollection permissions);
// Public Instance Methods
    public final CodeSource getCodeSource();
    public final PermissionCollection getPermissions();
    public boolean implies(java.security.Permission permission);
// Public Methods Overriding Object
    public String toString();
}
```

Passed To: ClassLoader.defineClass(), AccessControlContext.AccessControlContext(), DomainCombiner.combine()

Returned By: Class.getProtectionDomain(), DomainCombiner.combine()

Provider   Java 1.1
java.security   *cloneable serializable collection PJ1.1(opt)*

This class represents a security provider. It specifies class names for implementations of one or more algorithms for message digests, digital signatures, key generation, key conversion, key management, secure random number generation, certificate conversion, and algorithm parameter management. The getName(), getVersion(), and getInfo() methods return information about the provider. Provider inherits from Properties and maintains a mapping of property names to property values. These name/value pairs specify the capabilities of the Provider implementation. Each property name has the form:

> service_type.algorithm_name

The corresponding property value is the name of the class that implements the named algorithm. For example, say a Provider defines properties named "Signature.DSA", "MessageDigest.MD5", and "KeyStore.JKS". The values of these properties are the class names of SignatureSpi, MessageDigestSpi, and KeyStoreSpi implementations. Other properties defined by a Provider are used to provide aliases for algorithm names. For example, the property Alg.Alias.MessageDigest.SHA1 might have the value "SHA", meaning that the algorithm name "SHA1" is an alias for "SHA".

Security providers are installed for a Java system in an implementation-dependent way. For Sun's implementation, the *${java.home}/lib/security/java.security* file specifies the class names of all installed Provider implementations. An application can also install its own custom Provider with the addProvider() and insertProviderAt() methods of the Security class. Most applications do not need to use the Provider class directly. Typically, only security-provider implementors need to use the Provider class. Some applications may explicitly specify the name of a desired Provider when calling a static getInstance() factory method, however. Only applications with the most demanding cryptographic needs need to install custom providers.

```
public abstract class Provider extends java.util.Properties {
// Protected Constructors
    protected Provider(String name, double version, String info);
// Public Instance Methods
    public String getInfo();
    public String getName();
    public double getVersion();
// Public Methods Overriding Properties
1.2 public void load(java.io.InputStream inStream) throws java.io.IOException;          synchronized
// Public Methods Overriding Hashtable
1.2 public void clear();                                                                synchronized
1.2 public java.util.Set entrySet();                                                    synchronized
1.2 public java.util.Set keySet();
1.2 public Object put(Object key, Object value);                                        synchronized
1.2 public void putAll(java.util.Map t);                                                synchronized
1.2 public Object remove(Object key);                                                   synchronized
    public String toString();
1.2 public java.util.Collection values();
}
```

Hierarchy: Object→ java.util.Dictionary→ java.util.Hashtable(Cloneable, java.util.Map, Serializable)→ java.util.Properties→ Provider

Passed To: AlgorithmParameterGenerator.AlgorithmParameterGenerator(), AlgorithmParameters.AlgorithmParameters(), KeyFactory.KeyFactory(), KeyStore.KeyStore(), SecureRandom.SecureRandom(), Security.{addProvider(), insertProviderAt()}, java.security.cert.CertificateFactory.CertificateFactory(), javax.crypto.Cipher.Cipher(), javax.crypto.KeyAgreement.KeyAgreement(), javax.crypto.KeyGenerator.KeyGenerator(), javax.crypto.Mac.Mac(), javax.crypto.SecretKeyFactory.SecretKeyFactory()

Returned By: Too many methods to list.

ProviderException   Java 1.1

java.security   *serializable unchecked PJ1.1(opt)*

Signals that an exception has occurred inside a cryptographic service provider. Note that ProviderException extends RuntimeException and is therefore an unchecked exception that may be thrown from any method without being declared.

```
public class ProviderException extends RuntimeException {
// Public Constructors
    public ProviderException();
    public ProviderException(String s);
}
```

Hierarchy: Object→ Throwable(Serializable)→ Exception→ RuntimeException→ ProviderException

PublicKey   Java 1.1

java.security   *serializable PJ1.1(opt)*

This interface represents a public cryptographic key. It extends the Key interface, but does not add any new methods. The interface exists in order to create a strong distinction between public and private keys. See also PrivateKey.

```
public interface PublicKey extends Key {
// Public Constants
1.2 public static final long serialVersionUID;                                    =7187392471159151072
}
```

Hierarchy: (PublicKey(Key(Serializable)))

Implementations: java.security.interfaces.DSAPublicKey, java.security.interfaces.RSAPublicKey, javax.crypto.interfaces.DHPublicKey

Passed To: Identity.setPublicKey(), IdentityScope.getIdentity(), KeyPair.KeyPair(), Signature.initVerify(), SignatureSpi.engineInitVerify(), SignedObject.verify(), java.security.cert.Certificate.verify(), java.security.cert.X509CRL.verify()

Returned By: java.security.Certificate.getPublicKey(), Identity.getPublicKey(), KeyFactory.generatePublic(), KeyFactorySpi.engineGeneratePublic(), KeyPair.getPublic(), java.security.cert.Certificate.getPublicKey()

SecureClassLoader   Java 1.2
java.security

This class adds two protected methods to those defined by ClassLoader. The defineClass() method is passed a CodeSource object that represents the source of the class being loaded. It calls the getPermissions() method to obtain a PermissionCollection for that CodeSource. It then uses the CodeSource and PermissionCollection to create a ProtectionDomain, which is passed to the defineClass() method of its superclass.

The default implementation of the getPermissions() method uses the default Policy to determine the appropriate set of permissions for a given code source. The value of SecureClassLoader is that subclasses can use its defineClass() method to load classes without having to work explicitly with the ProtectionDomain and Policy classes. A subclass of SecureClassLoader can define its own security policy by overriding getPermissions(). In Java 1.2 and later, any application that implements a custom class loader should do so by extending SecureClassLoader, instead of subclassing ClassLoader directly. Most applications can use java.net.URLClassLoader, however, and never have to subclass this class.

```
public class SecureClassLoader extends ClassLoader {
// Protected Constructors
    protected SecureClassLoader();
    protected SecureClassLoader(ClassLoader parent);
// Protected Instance Methods
    protected final Class defineClass(String name, byte[ ] b, int off, int len, CodeSource cs);
    protected PermissionCollection getPermissions(CodeSource codesource);
}
```

Hierarchy: Object→ ClassLoader→ SecureClassLoader

Subclasses: java.net.URLClassLoader

SecureRandom   Java 1.1
java.security   serializable PJ1.1(opt)

This class generates cryptographic-quality pseudo-random bytes. Although SecureRandom defines public constructors, the preferred technique for obtaining a SecureRandom object is to call one of the static getInstance() factory methods, specifying the desired pseudo-random number-generation algorithm, and, optionally, the desired provider of that algorithm. Sun's implementation of Java ships with an algorithm named "SHA1PRNG" in the "SUN" provider.

Once you have obtained a SecureRandom object, call nextBytes() to fill an array with pseudo-random bytes. You can also call any of the methods defined by the Random superclass to obtain random numbers. The first time one of these methods is called, the SecureRandom() method uses its generateSeed() method to seed itself. If you have a source of random or very high-quality pseudo-random bytes, you may provide your own seed by calling setSeed(). Repeated calls to setSeed() augment the existing seed instead of replacing it. You can also call generateSeed() to generate seeds for use with other pseudo-random generators. generateSeed() may use a different algorithm than nextBytes() and may produce higher-quality randomness, usually at the expense of increased computation time.

```
public class SecureRandom extends java.util.Random {
// Public Constructors
    public SecureRandom();
    public SecureRandom(byte[] seed);
// Protected Constructors
1.2 protected SecureRandom(SecureRandomSpi secureRandomSpi, Provider provider);
// Public Class Methods
1.2 public static SecureRandom getInstance(String algorithm) throws NoSuchAlgorithmException;
1.2 public static SecureRandom getInstance(String algorithm, String provider) throws NoSuchAlgorithmException,
        NoSuchProviderException;
    public static byte[] getSeed(int numBytes);
// Public Instance Methods
1.2 public byte[] generateSeed(int numBytes);
1.2 public final Provider getProvider();                                          default:Sun
    public void setSeed(byte[] seed);                                            synchronized
// Public Methods Overriding Random
    public void nextBytes(byte[] bytes);                                         synchronized
    public void setSeed(long seed);
// Protected Methods Overriding Random
    protected final int next(int numBits);
}
```

Hierarchy: Object→ java.util.Random(Serializable)→ SecureRandom

Passed To: Too many methods to list.

Returned By: SecureRandom.getInstance()

Type Of: SignatureSpi.appRandom

SecureRandomSpi
java.security

Java 1.2
serializable

This abstract class defines the service-provider interface for SecureRandom. A security provider must implement a concrete subclass of this class for each pseudo-random number-generation algorithm it supports. Applications never need to use or subclass this class.

```
public abstract class SecureRandomSpi implements Serializable {
// Public Constructors
    public SecureRandomSpi();
// Protected Instance Methods
    protected abstract byte[] engineGenerateSeed(int numBytes);
    protected abstract void engineNextBytes(byte[] bytes);
    protected abstract void engineSetSeed(byte[] seed);
}
```

Hierarchy: Object → SecureRandomSpi(Serializable)

Passed To: SecureRandom.SecureRandom()

Security
java.security

Java 1.1

PJ1.1(opt)

This class defines static methods both for managing the list of installed security providers and for reading and setting the values of various properties used by the Java 1.2 security system. It is essentially an interface to the *$[java.home]/lib/security/ java.security* file that is included in Sun's implementation of Java. getProviders() is the most generally useful method; it returns an array of installed Provider objects. In Java 1.3, two new versions of getProviders() return an array of installed providers that implement the algorithm or algorithms specified by the String or Map argument.

```
public final class Security {
// No Constructor
// Public Class Methods
    public static int addProvider(Provider provider);
    public static String getProperty(String key);
    public static Provider getProvider(String name);                                    synchronized
    public static Provider[ ] getProviders( );                                          synchronized
1.3 public static Provider[ ] getProviders(String filter);
1.3 public static Provider[ ] getProviders(java.util.Map filter);
    public static int insertProviderAt(Provider provider, int position);                synchronized
    public static void removeProvider(String name);                                     synchronized
    public static void setProperty(String key, String datum);
// Deprecated Public Methods
#   public static String getAlgorithmProperty(String algName, String propName);
}
```

SecurityPermission
java.security

Java 1.2

serializable permission

This class is a Permission subclass that represents access to various methods of the Policy, Security, Provider, Signer, and Identity objects. SecurityPermission objects are defined by a name only; they do not use a list of actions. Important SecurityPermission names are "get-Policy" and "setPolicy", which represent the ability query and set the system security policy by invoking the Policy.getPolicy() and Policy.setPolicy() methods. Applications do not typically need to use this class.

```
public final class SecurityPermission extends BasicPermission {
// Public Constructors
    public SecurityPermission(String name);
    public SecurityPermission(String name, String actions);
}
```

Hierarchy: Object → java.security.Permission(Guard, Serializable) → BasicPermission(Serializable) → SecurityPermission

Signature
java.security

Java 1.1

PJ1.1(opt)

This class computes or verifies a digital signature. Obtain a Signature object by calling one of the static getInstance() factory methods and specifying the desired digital signature algorithm and, optionally, the desired provider of that algorithm. A *digital signature* is essentially a message digest encrypted by a public-key encryption algorithm. Thus, to specify a digital signature algorithm, you must specify both the digest algorithm and the encryption algorithm. The only algorithm supported by the default "SUN" provider is "SHA1withDSA".

Once you have obtained a Signature object, you must initialize it before you can create or verify a digital signature. To initialize a digital signature for creation, call initSign() and specify the private key to be used to create the signature. To initialize a signature for verification, call initVerify() and specify the public key of the signer. Once the Signature object has been initialized, call update() one or more times to specify the bytes to be signed or verified. Finally, to create a digital signature, call sign(), passing a byte array into which the signature is stored. Or, pass the bytes of the digital signature to verify(), which returns true if the signature is valid or false otherwise. After calling either sign() or verify(), the Signature object is reset internally and can be used to create or verify another signature.

```
public abstract class Signature extends SignatureSpi {
// Protected Constructors
    protected Signature(String algorithm);
// Protected Constants
    protected static final int SIGN;                                              =2
    protected static final int UNINITIALIZED;                                     =0
    protected static final int VERIFY;                                            =3
// Public Class Methods
    public static Signature getInstance(String algorithm) throws NoSuchAlgorithmException;
    public static Signature getInstance(String algorithm, String provider) throws NoSuchAlgorithmException,
        NoSuchProviderException;
// Public Instance Methods
    public final String getAlgorithm();
1.2 public final Provider getProvider();
    public final void initSign(PrivateKey privateKey) throws InvalidKeyException;
1.2 public final void initSign(PrivateKey privateKey, SecureRandom random) throws InvalidKeyException;
    public final void initVerify(PublicKey publicKey) throws InvalidKeyException;
1.3 public final void initVerify(java.security.cert.Certificate certificate) throws InvalidKeyException;
1.2 public final void setParameter(java.security.spec.AlgorithmParameterSpec params)
        throws InvalidAlgorithmParameterException;
    public final byte[ ] sign() throws SignatureException;
1.2 public final int sign(byte[ ] outbuf, int offset, int len) throws SignatureException;
    public final void update(byte b) throws SignatureException;
    public final void update(byte[ ] data) throws SignatureException;
    public final void update(byte[ ] data, int off, int len) throws SignatureException;
    public final boolean verify(byte[ ] signature) throws SignatureException;
// Public Methods Overriding SignatureSpi
    public Object clone() throws CloneNotSupportedException;
// Public Methods Overriding Object
    public String toString();
// Protected Instance Fields
    protected int state;
// Deprecated Public Methods
#   public final Object getParameter(String param) throws InvalidParameterException;
#   public final void setParameter(String param, Object value) throws InvalidParameterException;
}
```

Hierarchy: Object→ SignatureSpi→ Signature

Passed To: SignedObject.{SignedObject(), verify()}

Returned By: Signature.getInstance()

SignatureException

Java 1.1

java.security

serializable checked PJ1.1(opt)

Signals a problem while creating or verifying a digital signature.

```
public class SignatureException extends GeneralSecurityException {
// Public Constructors
    public SignatureException();
    public SignatureException(String msg);
}
```

Hierarchy: Object→ Throwable(Serializable)→ Exception→ GeneralSecurityException→ SignatureException

Thrown By: Too many methods to list.

SignatureSpi

Java 1.2

java.security

This abstract class defines the service-provider interface for Signature. A security provider must implement a concrete subclass of this class for each digital signature algorithm it supports. Applications never need to use or subclass this class.

```
public abstract class SignatureSpi {
// Public Constructors
    public SignatureSpi();
// Public Methods Overriding Object
    public Object clone() throws CloneNotSupportedException;
// Protected Instance Methods
    protected abstract void engineInitSign(PrivateKey privateKey) throws InvalidKeyException;
    protected void engineInitSign(PrivateKey privateKey, SecureRandom random) throws InvalidKeyException;
    protected abstract void engineInitVerify(PublicKey publicKey) throws InvalidKeyException;
    protected void engineSetParameter(java.security.spec.AlgorithmParameterSpec params)
        throws InvalidAlgorithmParameterException;
    protected abstract byte[ ] engineSign() throws SignatureException;
    protected int engineSign(byte[ ] outbuf, int offset, int len) throws SignatureException;
    protected abstract void engineUpdate(byte b) throws SignatureException;
    protected abstract void engineUpdate(byte[ ] b, int off, int len) throws SignatureException;
    protected abstract boolean engineVerify(byte[ ] sigBytes) throws SignatureException;
// Protected Instance Fields
    protected SecureRandom appRandom;
// Deprecated Protected Methods
#   protected abstract Object engineGetParameter(String param) throws InvalidParameterException;
#   protected abstract void engineSetParameter(String param, Object value) throws InvalidParameterException;
}
```

Subclasses: Signature

SignedObject

Java 1.2

java.security

serializable

This class applies a digital signature to any serializable Java object. Create a SignedObject by specifying the object to be signed, the PrivateKey to use for the signature, and the Signature object to create the signature. The SignedObject() constructor serializes the specified object into an array of bytes and creates a digital signature for those bytes.

After creation, a SignedObject is itself typically serialized for storage or transmission to another Java thread or process. Once the SignedObject is reconstituted, the integrity of the object it contains can be verified by calling verify() and supplying the PublicKey of the signer and a Signature that performs the verification. Whether or not verification is performed or is successful, getObject() can be called to deserialize and return the wrapped object.

```
public final class SignedObject implements Serializable {
// Public Constructors
    public SignedObject(Serializable object, PrivateKey signingKey, Signature signingEngine)
        throws java.io.IOException, InvalidKeyException, SignatureException;
// Public Instance Methods
    public String getAlgorithm();
    public Object getObject() throws java.io.IOException, ClassNotFoundException;
    public byte[ ] getSignature();
    public boolean verify(PublicKey verificationKey, Signature verificationEngine) throws InvalidKeyException,
        SignatureException;
}
```

Hierarchy: Object → SignedObject(Serializable)

Signer
Java 1.1; Deprecated in Java 1.2

java.security
serializable PJ1.1(opt)

This deprecated class was used in Java 1.1 to represent an entity or Principal that has an associated PrivateKey that enables it to create digital signatures. As of Java 1.2, this class and the related Identity and IdentityScope classes have been replaced by KeyStore and java.security.cert.Certificate. See also Identity.

```
public abstract class Signer extends Identity {
// Public Constructors
    public Signer(String name);
    public Signer(String name, IdentityScope scope) throws KeyManagementException;
// Protected Constructors
    protected Signer();
// Public Instance Methods
    public PrivateKey getPrivateKey();
    public final void setKeyPair(KeyPair pair) throws InvalidParameterException, KeyException;
// Public Methods Overriding Identity
    public String toString();
}
```

Hierarchy: Object → Identity(java.security.Principal, Serializable) → Signer

UnrecoverableKeyException
Java 1.2

java.security
serializable checked

This exception is thrown if a Key cannot be retrieved from a KeyStore. This commonly occurs when an incorrect password is used.

```
public class UnrecoverableKeyException extends GeneralSecurityException {
// Public Constructors
    public UnrecoverableKeyException();
    public UnrecoverableKeyException(String msg);
}
```

Hierarchy: Object → Throwable(Serializable) → Exception → GeneralSecurityException → UnrecoverableKeyException

Thrown By: KeyStore.getKey(), KeyStoreSpi.engineGetKey()

UnresolvedPermission

java.security

Java 1.2

serializable permission

This class is used internally to provide a mechanism for delayed resolution of permissions. An UnresolvedPermission holds a textual representation of a Permission object that can later be used to create the actual Permission object. Applications never need to use this class.

```
public final class UnresolvedPermission extends java.security.Permission implements Serializable {
// Public Constructors
    public UnresolvedPermission(String type, String name, String actions, java.security.cert.Certificate[ ] certs);
// Public Methods Overriding Permission
    public boolean equals(Object obj);
    public String getActions();
    public int hashCode();
    public boolean implies(java.security.Permission p);                                          constant
    public PermissionCollection newPermissionCollection();
    public String toString();
}
```

Hierarchy: Object→ java.security.Permission(Guard, Serializable)→
UnresolvedPermission(Serializable)

CHAPTER 18

The java.security.acl Package

The java.security.acl package defines, but does not implement, an incomplete framework for working with access control lists (ACLs). This package was added in Java 1.1, but has been superseded in Java 1.2 by the access-control mechanisms of the java.security package. In particular, see the Permission and Policy classes of that package. The use of this package is not recommended. Figure 18-1 shows the class hierarchy of this package.

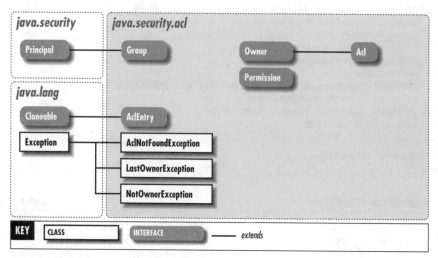

Figure 18–1: The java.security.acl package

Acl

java.security.acl

This interface represents an *access control list*, or ACL. An ACL is a list of AclEntry objects; most of the methods of this class manage that list. The exception is the checkPermission() method that tests whether this ACL grants a specified java.security.acl.Permission to a specified java.security.Principal. Note that Acl extends Owner. The methods of the Owner interface maintain a list of ACL owners. Only owners are allowed to modify an ACL.

```
public interface Acl extends Owner {
// Public Instance Methods
    public abstract boolean addEntry(java.security.Principal caller, AclEntry entry) throws NotOwnerException;
    public abstract boolean checkPermission(java.security.Principal principal,
                                            java.security.acl.Permission permission);
    public abstract java.util.Enumeration entries();
    public abstract String getName();
    public abstract java.util.Enumeration getPermissions(java.security.Principal user);
    public abstract boolean removeEntry(java.security.Principal caller, AclEntry entry) throws NotOwnerException;
    public abstract void setName(java.security.Principal caller, String name) throws NotOwnerException;
    public abstract String toString();
}
```

Hierarchy: (Acl(Owner))

AclEntry
Java 1.1

java.security.acl
cloneable

This interface defines a single entry of an ACL. Each AclEntry represents a set of java.security.acl.Permission objects either granted or denied to a given java.security.Principal. By default, an AclEntry represents permissions granted to the principal. Call setNegativePermissions() if you want the AclEntry to represent a set of permissions to be denied.

```
public interface AclEntry extends Cloneable {
// Public Instance Methods
    public abstract boolean addPermission(java.security.acl.Permission permission);
    public abstract boolean checkPermission(java.security.acl.Permission permission);
    public abstract Object clone();
    public abstract java.security.Principal getPrincipal();
    public abstract boolean isNegative();
    public abstract java.util.Enumeration permissions();
    public abstract boolean removePermission(java.security.acl.Permission permission);
    public abstract void setNegativePermissions();
    public abstract boolean setPrincipal(java.security.Principal user);
    public abstract String toString();
}
```

Hierarchy: (AclEntry(Cloneable))

Passed To: Acl.{addEntry(), removeEntry()}

AclNotFoundException
Java 1.1

java.security.acl
serializable checked

Signals that the specified Acl could not be found. Note that none of the interfaces in java.security.acl throw this exception; it is provided for the benefit of Acl implementations.

```
public class AclNotFoundException extends Exception {
// Public Constructors
    public AclNotFoundException();
}
```

Hierarchy: Object → Throwable(Serializable) → Exception → AclNotFoundException

Group
java.security.acl

This interface represents a set, or group, of java.security.Principal objects. The methods of the interface serve to manage the membership of the group. Note that Group extends the Principal interface, and, therefore, you can use a Group object wherever you would use a Principal object in this package.

```
public interface Group extends java.security.Principal {
// Public Instance Methods
    public abstract boolean addMember(java.security.Principal user);
    public abstract boolean isMember(java.security.Principal member);
    public abstract java.util.Enumeration members();
    public abstract boolean removeMember(java.security.Principal user);
}
```

Hierarchy: (Group(java.security.Principal))

LastOwnerException
java.security.acl

serializable checked

Signals that an Acl or Owner has only one Principal remaining in its ownership list and that this single owner cannot be removed.

```
public class LastOwnerException extends Exception {
// Public Constructors
    public LastOwnerException();
}
```

Hierarchy: Object→ Throwable(Serializable)→ Exception→ LastOwnerException

Thrown By: Owner.deleteOwner()

NotOwnerException
java.security.acl

serializable checked

Thrown by various methods of Acl and Owner when they are called by a Principal that is not an owner.

```
public class NotOwnerException extends Exception {
// Public Constructors
    public NotOwnerException();
}
```

Hierarchy: Object→ Throwable(Serializable)→ Exception→ NotOwnerException

Thrown By: Acl.{addEntry(), removeEntry(), setName()}, Owner.{addOwner(), deleteOwner()}

Owner
java.security.acl

This interface represents the owner or owners of an ACL. The interface defines methods for managing and checking membership in the list of owners.

```
public interface Owner {
// Public Instance Methods
    public abstract boolean addOwner(java.security.Principal caller, java.security.Principal owner)
        throws NotOwnerException;
    public abstract boolean deleteOwner(java.security.Principal caller, java.security.Principal owner)
        throws NotOwnerException, LastOwnerException;
```

```
    public abstract boolean isOwner(java.security.Principal owner);
}
```

Implementations: Acl

Permission

Java 1.1

java.security.acl

This interface represents a permission. The meaning of the permission is entirely up to the implementation. Do not confuse this interface with the newer java.security.Permission class. Also note that this interface does not have the implies() method of java.security.Permission and is therefore significantly less versatile.

```
public interface Permission {
// Public Instance Methods
    public abstract boolean equals(Object another);
    public abstract String toString();
}
```

Passed To: Acl.checkPermission(), AclEntry.{addPermission(), checkPermission(), removePermission()}

## CHAPTER 19

The java.security.cert Package

The java.security.cert package contains classes for working with identity certificates and certificate revocation lists (CRLs). It defines generic Certificate and CRL classes and X509Certificate and X509CRL classes that provide full support for standard X.509 certificates and CRLs. The CertificateFactory class serves as a certificate parser, providing the ability to convert a stream of bytes into a Certificate or CRL object. This package replaces the deprecated java.security.Certificate interface. Figure 19-1 shows the class hierarchy of this package.

Certificate   Java 1.2

java.security.cert   *serializable*

This abstract class represents an identity certificate. A *certificate* is an object that contains the name of an entity and a public key for that entity. Certificates are issued by, and bear the digital signature of,x a (presumably trusted) third party, typically a *certificate authority* (CA). By issuing and signing the certificate, the CA is certifying that, based on their research, the entity named on the certificate really is who they say they are and that the public key in the certificate really does belong to that entity.

Use a CertificateFactory to parse a stream of bytes into a Certificate object; getEncoded() reverses this process. Use verify() to verify the digital signature of the entity that issued the certificate. If the signature cannot be verified, the certificate should not be trusted. Call getPublicKey() to obtain the java.security.PublicKey of the subject of the certificate. Note that this class does not define a method for obtaining the Principal that is associated with the PublicKey. That functionality is dependent on the type of the certificate. See X509Certificate.getSubjectDN(), for example.

Do not confuse this class with the java.security.Certificate interface that was defined in Java 1.1 and has been deprecated in Java 1.2.

```
public abstract class Certificate implements Serializable {
// Protected Constructors
    protected Certificate(String type);
// Inner Classes
1.3 protected static class CertificateRep implements Serializable;
// Public Instance Methods
    public abstract byte[ ] getEncoded() throws CertificateEncodingException;
```

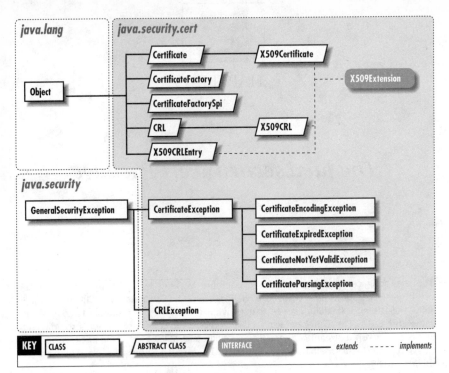

Figure 19–1: The java.security.cert package

```
    public abstract java.security.PublicKey getPublicKey();
    public final String getType();
    public abstract void verify(java.security.PublicKey key) throws CertificateException,
        java.security.NoSuchAlgorithmException, java.security.InvalidKeyException,
        java.security.NoSuchProviderException, java.security.SignatureException;
    public abstract void verify(java.security.PublicKey key, String sigProvider) throws CertificateException,
        java.security.NoSuchAlgorithmException, java.security.InvalidKeyException,
        java.security.NoSuchProviderException, java.security.SignatureException;
// Public Methods Overriding Object
    public boolean equals(Object other);
    public int hashCode();
    public abstract String toString();
// Protected Instance Methods
1.3 protected Object writeReplace() throws java.io.ObjectStreamException;
}
```

Hierarchy: Object→ java.security.cert.Certificate(Serializable)

Subclasses: X509Certificate

Passed To: java.security.CodeSource.CodeSource(), java.security.KeyStore.{getCertificateAlias(), setCertificateEntry(), setKeyEntry()}, java.security.KeyStoreSpi.{engineGetCertificateAlias(), engineSetCertificateEntry(), engineSetKeyEntry()}, java.security.Signature.initVerify(), java.security.UnresolvedPermission.UnresolvedPermission(), CRL.isRevoked()

Returned By: java.net.JarURLConnection.getCertificates(), java.security.CodeSource.getCertificates(), java.security.KeyStore.{getCertificate(), getCertificateChain()}, java.security.KeyStoreSpi.{engineGetCertificate(), engineGetCertificateChain()}, CertificateFactory.generateCertificate(), CertificateFactorySpi.engineGenerateCertificate(), java.util.jar.JarEntry.getCertificates()

Certificate.CertificateRep   Java 1.3
java.security.cert   *serializable*

This protected inner class provides an alternate representation of a certificate that can be used for serialization purposes by the writeReplace() method of some Certificate implementations. Applications do not typically need this class.

```
protected static class Certificate.CertificateRep implements Serializable {
// Protected Constructors
    protected CertificateRep(String type, byte[ ] data);
// Protected Instance Methods
    protected Object readResolve() throws java.io.ObjectStreamException;
}
```

CertificateEncodingException   Java 1.2
java.security.cert   *serializable checked*

Signals an error while attempting to encode a certificate.

```
public class CertificateEncodingException extends CertificateException {
// Public Constructors
    public CertificateEncodingException();
    public CertificateEncodingException(String message);
}
```

Hierarchy: Object→ Throwable(Serializable)→ Exception→ java.security.GeneralSecurityException→ CertificateException→ CertificateEncodingException

Thrown By: java.security.cert.Certificate.getEncoded(), X509Certificate.getTBSCertificate()

CertificateException   Java 1.2
java.security.cert   *serializable checked*

This class is the superclass of several more specific exception types that may be thrown when working with certificates.

```
public class CertificateException extends java.security.GeneralSecurityException {
// Public Constructors
    public CertificateException();
    public CertificateException(String msg);
}
```

Hierarchy: Object→ Throwable(Serializable)→ Exception→ java.security.GeneralSecurityException→ CertificateException

Subclasses: CertificateEncodingException, CertificateExpiredException, CertificateNotYetValidException, CertificateParsingException

Thrown By: java.security.KeyStore.{load(), store()}, java.security.KeyStoreSpi.{engineLoad(), engineStore()}, java.security.cert.Certificate.verify(), CertificateFactory.{generateCertificate(), generateCertificates(), getInstance()}, CertificateFactorySpi.{engineGenerateCertificate(), engineGenerateCertificates()}

CertificateExpiredException

java.security.cert

Signals that a certificate has expired or will have expired by a specified date.

```
public class CertificateExpiredException extends CertificateException {
// Public Constructors
    public CertificateExpiredException();
    public CertificateExpiredException(String message);
}
```

Hierarchy: Object→ Throwable(Serializable)→ Exception→
java.security.GeneralSecurityException→ CertificateException→ CertificateExpiredException

Thrown By: X509Certificate.checkValidity()

CertificateFactory

Java 1.2

java.security.cert

This class defines methods for parsing CRLs from byte streams. Obtain a CertificateFactory by calling one of the static getInstance() factory methods and specifying the type of certificate or CRL to be parsed, and, optionally, the desired service provider to perform the parsing. The default "SUN" provider defines only a single "X.509" certificate type. Once you have obtained a CertificateFactory for the desired type of certificate, call generateCertificate() or generateCRL() to parse a single certificate or CRL from a stream. Or call generateCertificates() or generateCRLs() to parse a Collection of certificates or CRLs from the stream. These CertificateFactory methods read to the end of the specified stream. If the stream supports mark() and reset(), however, the CertificateFactory resets the stream to the position after the end of the last certificate or CRL read.

If you specified a certificate type of "X.509", the Certificate and CRL objects returned by a CertificateFactory can be cast safely to X509Certificate and X509CRL. The X.509 certificate factory can parse certificates encoded in binary or printable hexadecimal form. If the certificate is in hexadecimal form, it must begin with the string "-----BEGIN CERTIFICATE-----" and end with the string "-----END CERTIFICATE-----".

```
public class CertificateFactory {
// Protected Constructors
    protected CertificateFactory(CertificateFactorySpi certFacSpi, java.security.Provider provider, String type);
// Public Class Methods
    public static final CertificateFactory getInstance(String type) throws CertificateException;
    public static final CertificateFactory getInstance(String type, String provider) throws CertificateException,
        java.security.NoSuchProviderException;
// Public Instance Methods
    public final java.security.cert.Certificate generateCertificate(java.io.InputStream inStream)
        throws CertificateException;
    public final java.util.Collection generateCertificates(java.io.InputStream inStream) throws CertificateException;
    public final CRL generateCRL(java.io.InputStream inStream) throws CRLException;
    public final java.util.Collection generateCRLs(java.io.InputStream inStream) throws CRLException;
    public final java.security.Provider getProvider();
    public final String getType();
}
```

Returned By: CertificateFactory.getInstance()

CertificateFactorySpi

Java 1.2

java.security.cert

This abstract class defines the service provider interface, or SPI, for the CertificateFactory class. A security provider must implement this class for each type of certificate it wishes to support. Applications never need to use or subclass this class.

```
public abstract class CertificateFactorySpi {
// Public Constructors
     public CertificateFactorySpi();
// Public Instance Methods
     public abstract java.security.cert.Certificate engineGenerateCertificate(java.io.InputStream inStream)
          throws CertificateException;
     public abstract java.util.Collection engineGenerateCertificates(java.io.InputStream inStream)
          throws CertificateException;
     public abstract CRL engineGenerateCRL(java.io.InputStream inStream) throws CRLException;
     public abstract java.util.Collection engineGenerateCRLs(java.io.InputStream inStream) throws CRLException;
}
```

Passed To: CertificateFactory.CertificateFactory()

CertificateNotYetValidException

Java 1.2

java.security.cert

serializable checked

Signals that a certificate is not yet valid or will not yet be valid on a specified date.

```
public class CertificateNotYetValidException extends CertificateException {
// Public Constructors
     public CertificateNotYetValidException();
     public CertificateNotYetValidException(String message);
}
```

Hierarchy: Object→ Throwable(Serializable)→ Exception→
java.security.GeneralSecurityException→ CertificateException→ CertificateNotYetValidException

Thrown By: X509Certificate.checkValidity()

CertificateParsingException

Java 1.2

java.security.cert

serializable checked

Signals an error or other problem while parsing a certificate.

```
public class CertificateParsingException extends CertificateException {
// Public Constructors
     public CertificateParsingException();
     public CertificateParsingException(String message);
}
```

Hierarchy: Object→ Throwable(Serializable)→ Exception→
java.security.GeneralSecurityException→ CertificateException→ CertificateParsingException

CRL

Java 1.2

java.security.cert

This abstract class represents a *certificate revocation list* (CRL). A CRL is an object issued by a certificate authority (or other certificate signer) that lists certificates that have been revoked, meaning that they are now invalid and should be rejected. Use a CertificateFactory to parse a CRL from a byte stream. Use the isRevoked() method to test whether a specified Certificate is listed on the CRL. Note that type-specific CRL subclasses, such as X509CRL, may provide access to substantially more information about the revocation list.

```
public abstract class CRL {
// Protected Constructors
    protected CRL(String type);
// Public Instance Methods
    public final String getType();
    public abstract boolean isRevoked(java.security.cert.Certificate cert);
// Public Methods Overriding Object
    public abstract String toString();
}
```

Subclasses: X509CRL

Returned By: CertificateFactory.generateCRL(), CertificateFactorySpi.engineGenerateCRL()

CRLException   Java 1.2

java.security.cert   *serializable checked*

Signals an error or other problem while working with a CRL.

```
public class CRLException extends java.security.GeneralSecurityException {
// Public Constructors
    public CRLException();
    public CRLException(String message);
}
```

Hierarchy: Object→ Throwable(Serializable)→ Exception→
java.security.GeneralSecurityException→ CRLException

Thrown By: CertificateFactory.{generateCRL(), generateCRLs()},
CertificateFactorySpi.{engineGenerateCRL(), engineGenerateCRLs()}, X509CRL.{getEncoded(),
getTBSCertList(), verify()}, X509CRLEntry.getEncoded()

X509Certificate   Java 1.2

java.security.cert   *serializable*

This class represents an X.509 certificate. Its various methods provide complete access to the contents of the certificate. For example, verify() checks the digital signature of the certificate to verify that it is not a forged certificate, while checkValidity() checks whether the certificate has expired or has not yet gone into effect. getSubjectDN() returns the Principal to whom this certificate applies, and getPublicKey() returns the PublicKey for that Principal. Note that verify() and getPublicKey() are inherited from Certificate.

Obtain an X509Certificate object by creating a CertificateFactory for certificate type "X.509" and then using generateCertificate() to parse an X.509 certificate from a stream of bytes. Finally, cast the Certificate returned by this method to an X509Certificate.

```
public abstract class X509Certificate extends java.security.cert.Certificate implements X509Extension {
// Protected Constructors
    protected X509Certificate();
// Property Accessor Methods (by property name)
    public abstract int getBasicConstraints();
    public abstract java.util.Set getCriticalExtensionOIDs();                  Implements:X509Extension
    public abstract java.security.Principal getIssuerDN();
    public abstract boolean[] getIssuerUniqueID();
    public abstract boolean[] getKeyUsage();
    public abstract java.util.Set getNonCriticalExtensionOIDs();               Implements:X509Extension
```

```
    public abstract java.util.Date getNotAfter();
    public abstract java.util.Date getNotBefore();
    public abstract java.math.BigInteger getSerialNumber();
    public abstract String getSigAlgName();
    public abstract String getSigAlgOID();
    public abstract byte[ ] getSigAlgParams();
    public abstract byte[ ] getSignature();
    public abstract java.security.Principal getSubjectDN();
    public abstract boolean[ ] getSubjectUniqueID();
    public abstract byte[ ] getTBSCertificate() throws CertificateEncodingException;
    public abstract int getVersion();
// Public Instance Methods
    public abstract void checkValidity() throws CertificateExpiredException, CertificateNotYetValidException;
    public abstract void checkValidity(java.util.Date date) throws CertificateExpiredException,
        CertificateNotYetValidException;
// Methods Implementing X509Extension
    public abstract java.util.Set getCriticalExtensionOIDs();
    public abstract byte[ ] getExtensionValue(String oid);
    public abstract java.util.Set getNonCriticalExtensionOIDs();
    public abstract boolean hasUnsupportedCriticalExtension();
}
```

Hierarchy: Object→ java.security.cert.Certificate(Serializable)→ X509Certificate(X509Extension)

X509CRL

java.security.cert

This class represents an X.509 CRL, which consists primarily of a set of X509CRLEntry objects. The various methods of this class provide access to all the details of the CRL. Use verify() to check the digital signature of the CRL to ensure that it does indeed originate from the the source it specifies. Use the inherited isRevoked() method to determine whether a given certificate has been revoked. If you are curious about the revocation date for a revoked certificate, obtain the X509CRLEntry for that certificate by calling getRevokedCertificate(). Call getThisUpdate() to obtain the date this CRL was issued. Use getNextUpdate() to find if the CRL has been superseded by a newer version.

Obtain an X509CRL object by creating a CertificateFactory for certificate type "X.509" and then using the generateCRL() to parse an X.509 CRL from a stream of bytes. Finally, cast the CRL returned by this method to an X509CRL.

```
public abstract class X509CRL extends CRL implements X509Extension {
// Protected Constructors
    protected X509CRL();
// Property Accessor Methods (by property name)
    public abstract java.util.Set getCriticalExtensionOIDs();              Implements:X509Extension
    public abstract byte[ ] getEncoded() throws CRLException;
    public abstract java.security.Principal getIssuerDN();
    public abstract java.util.Date getNextUpdate();
    public abstract java.util.Set getNonCriticalExtensionOIDs();           Implements:X509Extension
    public abstract java.util.Set getRevokedCertificates();
    public abstract String getSigAlgName();
    public abstract String getSigAlgOID();
    public abstract byte[ ] getSigAlgParams();
    public abstract byte[ ] getSignature();
    public abstract byte[ ] getTBSCertList() throws CRLException;
    public abstract java.util.Date getThisUpdate();
```

```
    public abstract int getVersion();
// Public Instance Methods
    public abstract X509CRLEntry getRevokedCertificate(java.math.BigInteger serialNumber);
    public abstract void verify(java.security.PublicKey key) throws CRLException, java.security.NoSuchAlgorithmException,
        java.security.InvalidKeyException, java.security.NoSuchProviderException, java.security.SignatureException;
    public abstract void verify(java.security.PublicKey key, String sigProvider) throws CRLException,
        java.security.NoSuchAlgorithmException, java.security.InvalidKeyException,
        java.security.NoSuchProviderException, java.security.SignatureException;
// Methods Implementing X509Extension
    public abstract java.util.Set getCriticalExtensionOIDs();
    public abstract byte[ ] getExtensionValue(String oid);
    public abstract java.util.Set getNonCriticalExtensionOIDs();
    public abstract boolean hasUnsupportedCriticalExtension();
// Public Methods Overriding Object
    public boolean equals(Object other);
    public int hashCode();
}
```

Hierarchy: Object→ CRL→ X509CRL(X509Extension)

X509CRLEntry   Java 1.2

java.security.cert

This class represents a single entry in an X509CRL. It contains the serial number and revocation date for a revoked certificate.

```
public abstract class X509CRLEntry implements X509Extension {
// Public Constructors
    public X509CRLEntry();
// Property Accessor Methods (by property name)
    public abstract java.util.Set getCriticalExtensionOIDs();               Implements:X509Extension
    public abstract byte[] getEncoded() throws CRLException;
    public abstract java.util.Set getNonCriticalExtensionOIDs();            Implements:X509Extension
    public abstract java.util.Date getRevocationDate();
    public abstract java.math.BigInteger getSerialNumber();
// Public Instance Methods
    public abstract boolean hasExtensions();
// Methods Implementing X509Extension
    public abstract java.util.Set getCriticalExtensionOIDs();
    public abstract byte[] getExtensionValue(String oid);
    public abstract java.util.Set getNonCriticalExtensionOIDs();
    public abstract boolean hasUnsupportedCriticalExtension();
// Public Methods Overriding Object
    public boolean equals(Object other);
    public int hashCode();
    public abstract String toString();
}
```

Hierarchy: Object→ X509CRLEntry(X509Extension)

Returned By: X509CRL.getRevokedCertificate()

X509Extension   Java 1.2

java.security.cert

This interface defines methods for handling a set of extensions to X.509 certificates and CRLs. Each extension has a name, or OID (object identifier), that identifies the type of the extension. An extension may be marked critical or noncritical. Noncritical extensions whose OIDs are not recognized can safely be ignored. However, if a critical exception is not recognized, the Certificate or CRL should be rejected. Each extension in the set has a byte array of data as its value. The interpretation of these bytes depends on the OID of the extension, of course.

```
public interface X509Extension {
// Public Instance Methods
    public abstract java.util.Set getCriticalExtensionOIDs( );
    public abstract byte[ ] getExtensionValue(String oid);
    public abstract java.util.Set getNonCriticalExtensionOIDs( );
    public abstract boolean hasUnsupportedCriticalExtension( );
}
```

Implementations: X509Certificate, X509CRL, X509CRLEntry

CHAPTER 20

The java.security.interfaces Package

As its name implies, the java.security.interfaces package contains only interfaces. These interfaces define methods that provide algorithm-specific information (such as key values and initialization parameter values) about DSA and RSA public and private keys. If you are using the RSA algorithm, for example, and working with a java.security.PublicKey object, you can cast that PublicKey to an RSAPublicKey object and use the RSA-specific methods defined by RSAPublicKey to query the key value directly. Figure 20-1 shows the class hierarchy of this package.

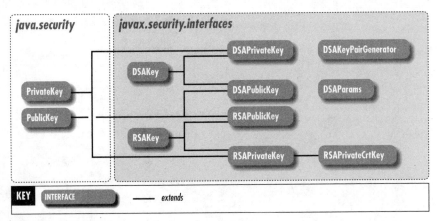

Figure 20–1: The java.security.interfaces package

The java.security.interfaces package was introduced in Java 1.1. In Java 1.2, the java.security.spec package is the preferred way for obtaining algorithm-specific information about keys and algorithm parameters. This package remains useful in Java 1.2, however, for identifying the type of a given PublicKey or PrivateKey object.

The interfaces in this package are typically of interest only to programmers who are implementing a security provider or who want to implement cryptographic algorithms themselves. Use of this package typically requires some familiarity with the mathematics underlying DSA and RSA public-key cryptography.

DSAKey
Java 1.1

java.security.interfaces   *PJ1.1(opt)*

This interface defines a method that must be implemented by both public and private DSA keys.

```
public interface DSAKey {
// Public Instance Methods
    public abstract DSAParams getParams();
}
```

Implementations: DSAPrivateKey, DSAPublicKey

DSAKeyPairGenerator
Java 1.1

java.security.interfaces   *PJ1.1(opt)*

This interface defines algorithm-specific KeyPairGenerator initialization methods for DSA keys. To generate a pair of DSA keys, use the static getInstance() factory method of java.security.KeyPairGenerator and specify "DSA" as the desired algorithm name. If you wish to perform DSA-specific initialization, cast the returned KeyPairGenerator to a DSAKeyPairGenerator and call one of the initialize() methods defined by this interface. Finally, generate the keys by calling generateKeyPair() on the KeyPairGenerator.

```
public interface DSAKeyPairGenerator {
// Public Instance Methods
    public abstract void initialize(DSAParams params, java.security.SecureRandom random)
        throws java.security.InvalidParameterException;
    public abstract void initialize(int modlen, boolean genParams, java.security.SecureRandom random)
        throws java.security.InvalidParameterException;
}
```

DSAParams
Java 1.1

java.security.interfaces   *PJ1.1(opt)*

This interface defines methods for obtaining the DSA parameters g, p, and q. These methods are useful only if you wish to perform cryptographic computation yourself. Using these methods requires a detailed understanding of the mathematics underlying DSA public-key cryptography.

```
public interface DSAParams {
// Public Instance Methods
    public abstract java.math.BigInteger getG();
    public abstract java.math.BigInteger getP();
    public abstract java.math.BigInteger getQ();
}
```

Implementations: java.security.spec.DSAParameterSpec

Passed To: DSAKeyPairGenerator.initialize()

Returned By: DSAKey.getParams()

DSAPrivateKey

Java 1.1

java.security.interfaces

serializable PJ1.1(opt)

This interface represents a DSA private key and provides direct access to the underlying key value. If you are working with a private key you know is a DSA key, you can cast the PrivateKey to a DSAPrivateKey.

```
public interface DSAPrivateKey extends DSAKey, java.security.PrivateKey {
// Public Constants
1.2 public static final long serialVersionUID;                              =7776497482533790279
// Public Instance Methods
    public abstract java.math.BigInteger getX();
}
```

Hierarchy: (DSAPrivateKey(DSAKey, java.security.PrivateKey(java.security.Key(Serializable))))

DSAPublicKey

Java 1.1

java.security.interfaces

serializable PJ1.1(opt)

This interface represents a DSA public key and provides direct access to the underlying key value. If you are working with a public key you know is a DSA key, you can cast the PublicKey to a DSAPublicKey.

```
public interface DSAPublicKey extends DSAKey, java.security.PublicKey {
// Public Constants
1.2 public static final long serialVersionUID;                              =1234526332779022332
// Public Instance Methods
    public abstract java.math.BigInteger getY();
}
```

Hierarchy: (DSAPublicKey(DSAKey, java.security.PublicKey(java.security.Key(Serializable))))

RSAKey

Java 1.3

java.security.interfaces

This is a superinterface for RSAPublicKey and RSAPrivateKey; it defines a method shared by both classes. Prior to Java 1.3, the getModulus() method was defined independently by RSAPublicKey and RSAPrivateKey.

```
public interface RSAKey {
// Public Instance Methods
    public abstract java.math.BigInteger getModulus();
}
```

Implementations: RSAPrivateKey, RSAPublicKey

RSAPrivateCrtKey

Java 1.2

java.security.interfaces

serializable

This interface extends RSAPrivateKey and provides a decomposition (based on the Chinese remainder theorem) of the private-key value into the various pieces that comprise it. This interface is useful only if you plan to implement your own cryptographic algorithms. To use this interface, you must have a detailed understanding of the mathematics underlying RSA public-key cryptography. Given a java.security.PrivateKey object, you can use the instanceof operator to determine whether you can safely cast it to an RSAPrivateCrtKey.

```
public interface RSAPrivateCrtKey extends RSAPrivateKey {
// Property Accessor Methods (by property name)
```

```
    public abstract java.math.BigInteger getCrtCoefficient( );
    public abstract java.math.BigInteger getPrimeExponentP( );
    public abstract java.math.BigInteger getPrimeExponentQ( );
    public abstract java.math.BigInteger getPrimeP( );
    public abstract java.math.BigInteger getPrimeQ( );
    public abstract java.math.BigInteger getPublicExponent( );
}
```

Hierarchy: (RSAPrivateCrtKey(RSAPrivateKey(java.security.PrivateKey(java.security.Key(Serializable)), RSAKey)))

RSAPrivateKey   Java 1.2
java.security.interfaces   *serializable*

This interface represents an RSA private key and provides direct access to the underlying key values. If you are working with a private key you know is an RSA key, you can cast the PrivateKey to an RSAPrivateKey.

```
public interface RSAPrivateKey extends java.security.PrivateKey, RSAKey {
// Public Instance Methods
    public abstract java.math.BigInteger getPrivateExponent( );
}
```

Hierarchy: (RSAPrivateKey(java.security.PrivateKey(java.security.Key(Serializable)), RSAKey))

Implementations: RSAPrivateCrtKey

RSAPublicKey   Java 1.2
java.security.interfaces   *serializable*

This interface represents an RSA public key and provides direct access to the underlying key values. If you are working with a public key you know is an RSA key, you can cast the PublicKey to an RSAPublicKey.

```
public interface RSAPublicKey extends java.security.PublicKey, RSAKey {
// Public Instance Methods
    public abstract java.math.BigInteger getPublicExponent( );
}
```

Hierarchy: (RSAPublicKey(java.security.PublicKey(java.security.Key(Serializable)), RSAKey))

CHAPTER 21

The java.security.spec Package

The java.security.spec package contains classes that define transparent representations for DSA and RSA public and private keys and for X.509 and PKCS#8 encodings of those keys. It also defines a transparent representation for DSA algorithm parameters. The classes in this package are used in conjunction with java.security.KeyFactory and java.security.AlgorithmParameters for converting opaque Key and AlgorithmParameters objects to and from transparent representations. Figure 21-1 shows the class hierarchy of this package.

This package is not frequently used. To make use of it, you must be somewhat familiar with the mathematics that underlies DSA and RSA public-key encryption and the encoding standards that specify how keys are encoded as byte streams.

AlgorithmParameterSpec   Java 1.2
java.security.spec

This interface defines no methods; it marks classes that define a transparent representation of cryptographic parameters. You can use an AlgorithmParameterSpec object to initialize an opaque java.security.AlgorithmParameters object.

```
public interface AlgorithmParameterSpec {
}
```

Implementations: DSAParameterSpec, RSAKeyGenParameterSpec, javax.crypto.spec.DHGenParameterSpec, javax.crypto.spec.DHParameterSpec, javax.crypto.spec.IvParameterSpec, javax.crypto.spec.PBEParameterSpec, javax.crypto.spec.RC2ParameterSpec, javax.crypto.spec.RC5ParameterSpec

Passed To: Too many methods to list.

Returned By: java.security.AlgorithmParameters.getParameterSpec(), java.security.AlgorithmParametersSpi.engineGetParameterSpec()

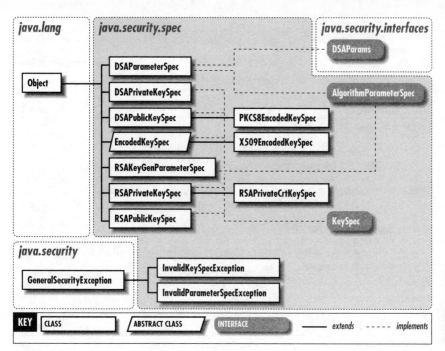

Figure 21-1: The java.security.spec package

DSAParameterSpec

java.security.spec

This class represents algorithm parameters used with DSA public-key cryptography.

```
public class DSAParameterSpec implements AlgorithmParameterSpec, java.security.interfaces.DSAParams {
// Public Constructors
    public DSAParameterSpec(java.math.BigInteger p, java.math.BigInteger q, java.math.BigInteger g);
// Methods Implementing DSAParams
    public java.math.BigInteger getG();
    public java.math.BigInteger getP();
    public java.math.BigInteger getQ();
}
```

Hierarchy: Object→ DSAParameterSpec(AlgorithmParameterSpec,
java.security.interfaces.DSAParams)

DSAPrivateKeySpec

java.security.spec

This class is a transparent representation of a DSA private key.

```
public class DSAPrivateKeySpec implements KeySpec {
// Public Constructors
    public DSAPrivateKeySpec(java.math.BigInteger x, java.math.BigInteger p, java.math.BigInteger q,
                             java.math.BigInteger g);
// Public Instance Methods
    public java.math.BigInteger getG();
```

```
   public java.math.BigInteger getP();
   public java.math.BigInteger getQ();
   public java.math.BigInteger getX();
}
```

Hierarchy: Object→ DSAPrivateKeySpec(KeySpec)

DSAPublicKeySpec   Java 1.2

java.security.spec

This class is a transparent representation of a DSA public key.

```
public class DSAPublicKeySpec implements KeySpec {
// Public Constructors
   public DSAPublicKeySpec(java.math.BigInteger y, java.math.BigInteger p, java.math.BigInteger q,
                          java.math.BigInteger g);
// Public Instance Methods
   public java.math.BigInteger getG();
   public java.math.BigInteger getP();
   public java.math.BigInteger getQ();
   public java.math.BigInteger getY();
}
```

Hierarchy: Object→ DSAPublicKeySpec(KeySpec)

EncodedKeySpec   Java 1.2

java.security.spec

This abstract class represents a public or private key in an encoded format. It serves as the superclass for encoding-specific classes.

```
public abstract class EncodedKeySpec implements KeySpec {
// Public Constructors
   public EncodedKeySpec(byte[ ] encodedKey);
// Public Instance Methods
   public byte[ ] getEncoded();
   public abstract String getFormat();
}
```

Hierarchy: Object→ EncodedKeySpec(KeySpec)

Subclasses: PKCS8EncodedKeySpec, X509EncodedKeySpec

InvalidKeySpecException   Java 1.2

java.security.spec   *serializable checked*

Signals a problem with a KeySpec.

```
public class InvalidKeySpecException extends java.security.GeneralSecurityException {
// Public Constructors
   public InvalidKeySpecException();
   public InvalidKeySpecException(String msg);
}
```

Hierarchy: Object→ Throwable(Serializable)→ Exception→
java.security.GeneralSecurityException→ InvalidKeySpecException

Thrown By: java.security.KeyFactory.{generatePrivate(), generatePublic(), getKeySpec()},
java.security.KeyFactorySpi.{engineGeneratePrivate(), engineGeneratePublic(), engineGetKeySpec()},
javax.crypto.SecretKeyFactory.{generateSecret(), getKeySpec()},
javax.crypto.SecretKeyFactorySpi.{engineGenerateSecret(), engineGetKeySpec()}

InvalidParameterSpecException   Java 1.2

java.security.spec   *serializable checked*

Signals a problem with an AlgorithmParameterSpec.

```
public class InvalidParameterSpecException extends java.security.GeneralSecurityException {
// Public Constructors
     public InvalidParameterSpecException();
     public InvalidParameterSpecException(String msg);
}
```

Hierarchy: Object→ Throwable(Serializable)→ Exception→
java.security.GeneralSecurityException→ InvalidParameterSpecException

Thrown By: java.security.AlgorithmParameters.{getParameterSpec(), init()},
java.security.AlgorithmParametersSpi.{engineGetParameterSpec(), engineInit()}

KeySpec   Java 1.2

java.security.spec

This interface defines no methods; it marks classes that define a transparent representation of a cryptographic key. Use a java.security.KeyFactory to convert a KeySpec to and from an opaque java.security.Key.

```
public interface KeySpec {
}
```

Implementations: DSAPrivateKeySpec, DSAPublicKeySpec, EncodedKeySpec, RSAPrivateKeySpec,
RSAPublicKeySpec, javax.crypto.spec.DESedeKeySpec, javax.crypto.spec.DESKeySpec,
javax.crypto.spec.DHPrivateKeySpec, javax.crypto.spec.DHPublicKeySpec,
javax.crypto.spec.PBEKeySpec, javax.crypto.spec.SecretKeySpec

Passed To: java.security.KeyFactory.{generatePrivate(), generatePublic()},
java.security.KeyFactorySpi.{engineGeneratePrivate(), engineGeneratePublic()},
javax.crypto.SecretKeyFactory.generateSecret(),
javax.crypto.SecretKeyFactorySpi.engineGenerateSecret()

Returned By: java.security.KeyFactory.getKeySpec(), java.security.KeyFactorySpi.engineGetKeySpec(),
javax.crypto.SecretKeyFactory.getKeySpec(), javax.crypto.SecretKeyFactorySpi.engineGetKeySpec()

PKCS8EncodedKeySpec   Java 1.2

java.security.spec

This class represents a private key, encoded according to the PKCS#8 standard.

```
public class PKCS8EncodedKeySpec extends EncodedKeySpec {
// Public Constructors
     public PKCS8EncodedKeySpec(byte[ ] encodedKey);
// Public Methods Overriding EncodedKeySpec
     public byte[ ] getEncoded();
     public final String getFormat();
}
```

Hierarchy: Object→ EncodedKeySpec(KeySpec)→ PKCS8EncodedKeySpec

java.security. spec

RSAKeyGenParameterSpec

java.security.spec

This class represents parameters that generate public/private key pairs for RSA cryptography.

```
public class RSAKeyGenParameterSpec implements AlgorithmParameterSpec {
// Public Constructors
    public RSAKeyGenParameterSpec(int keysize, java.math.BigInteger publicExponent);
// Public Constants
    public static final java.math.BigInteger F0;
    public static final java.math.BigInteger F4;
// Public Instance Methods
    public int getKeysize();
    public java.math.BigInteger getPublicExponent();
}
```

Hierarchy: Object→ RSAKeyGenParameterSpec(AlgorithmParameterSpec)

RSAPrivateCrtKeySpec

java.security.spec

This class is a transparent representation of an RSA private key including, for convenience, the Chinese remainder theorem values associated with the key.

```
public class RSAPrivateCrtKeySpec extends RSAPrivateKeySpec {
// Public Constructors
    public RSAPrivateCrtKeySpec(java.math.BigInteger modulus, java.math.BigInteger publicExponent,
                                java.math.BigInteger privateExponent, java.math.BigInteger primeP,
                                java.math.BigInteger primeQ, java.math.BigInteger primeExponentP,
                                java.math.BigInteger primeExponentQ, java.math.BigInteger crtCoefficient);
// Property Accessor Methods (by property name)
    public java.math.BigInteger getCrtCoefficient();
    public java.math.BigInteger getPrimeExponentP();
    public java.math.BigInteger getPrimeExponentQ();
    public java.math.BigInteger getPrimeP();
    public java.math.BigInteger getPrimeQ();
    public java.math.BigInteger getPublicExponent();
}
```

Hierarchy: Object→ RSAPrivateKeySpec(KeySpec)→ RSAPrivateCrtKeySpec

RSAPrivateKeySpec

java.security.spec

This class is a transparent representation of an RSA private key.

```
public class RSAPrivateKeySpec implements KeySpec {
// Public Constructors
    public RSAPrivateKeySpec(java.math.BigInteger modulus, java.math.BigInteger privateExponent);
// Public Instance Methods
    public java.math.BigInteger getModulus();
    public java.math.BigInteger getPrivateExponent();
}
```

Hierarchy: Object→ RSAPrivateKeySpec(KeySpec)

Subclasses: RSAPrivateCrtKeySpec

RSAPublicKeySpec

java.security.spec

This class is a transparent representation of an RSA public key.

Java 1.2

```
public class RSAPublicKeySpec implements KeySpec {
// Public Constructors
    public RSAPublicKeySpec(java.math.BigInteger modulus, java.math.BigInteger publicExponent);
// Public Instance Methods
    public java.math.BigInteger getModulus();
    public java.math.BigInteger getPublicExponent();
}
```

Hierarchy: Object→ RSAPublicKeySpec(KeySpec)

X509EncodedKeySpec

java.security.spec

This class represents a public or private key encoded according to the X.509 standard.

Java 1.2

```
public class X509EncodedKeySpec extends EncodedKeySpec {
// Public Constructors
    public X509EncodedKeySpec(byte[ ] encodedKey);
// Public Methods Overriding EncodedKeySpec
    public byte[ ] getEncoded();
    public final String getFormat();
}
```

Hierarchy: Object→ EncodedKeySpec(KeySpec)→ X509EncodedKeySpec

java.security. spec

CHAPTER 22

The java.text Package

The java.text package consists of classes and interfaces that are useful for writing internationalized programs that handle local customs, such as date and time formatting and string alphabetization, correctly. This package is new as of Java 1.1. Figure 22-1 shows its class hierarchy.

The NumberFormat class formats numbers, monetary quantities, and percentages as appropriate for the default or specified locale. DateFormat formats dates and times in a locale-specific way. The concrete DecimalFormat and SimpleDateFormat subclasses of these classes can be used for customized number, date, and time formatting. MessageFormat allows substitution of dynamic values, including formatted numbers and dates, into static message strings. ChoiceFormat formats a number using an enumerated set of string values. Collator compares strings according to the customary sorting order for a locale. BreakIterator scans text to find word, line, and sentence boundaries following locale-specific rules.

Annotation   Java 1.2
java.text

This class is a wrapper for a the value of a text attribute that represents an annotation. Annotations differ from other types of text attributes in two ways. First, annotations are linked to the text they are applied to, so changing the text invalidates or corrupts the meaning of the annotation. Second, annotations cannot be merged with adjacent annotations, even if they have the same value. Putting an annotation value in an Annotation wrapper serves to indicate these special characteristics. Note that two of the attribute keys defined by AttributedCharaterIterator.Attribute, READING and INPUT_METHOD_SEGMENT, must be used with Annotation objects.

```
public class Annotation {
// Public Constructors
    public Annotation(Object value);
// Public Instance Methods
    public Object getValue();
// Public Methods Overriding Object
    public String toString();
}
```

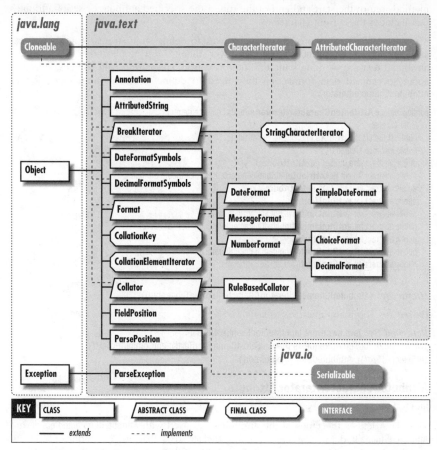

Figure 22–1: The java.text package

AttributedCharacterIterator

java.text

cloneable

This interface extends CharacterIterator for working with text that is marked up with attributes in some way. It defines an inner class, AttributedCharaterIterator.Attribute, that represents attribute keys. AttributedCharacterIterator defines methods for querying the attribute keys, values, and runs for the text being iterated over. getAllAttributeKeys() returns the Set of all attribute keys that appear anywhere in the text. getAttributes() returns a Map that contains the attribute keys and values that apply to the current character. getAttribute() returns the value associated with the specified attribute key for the current character.

getRunStart() and getRunLimit() return the index of the first and last characters in a run. A *run* is a string of adjacent characters for which an attribute has the same value or is undefined (i.e., has a value of null). A run can also be defined for a set of attributes, in which case it is a set of adjacent characters for which all attributes in the set hold a constant value (which may include null). Programs that process or display attributed text must usually work with it one run at a time. The no-argument versions of getRunStart() and getRunLimit() return the start and end of the run that includes the current character and all attributes that are applied to the current character. The other versions of these methods return the start and end of the run of the specified attribute or set of attributes that includes the current character.

The AttributedString class provides a simple way to define short strings of attributed text and obtain an AttributedCharacterIterator over them. Most applications that process attributed text are working with attributed text from specialized data sources, stored in some specialized data format, so they need to define a custom implementation of AttributedCharacterIterator.

```
public interface AttributedCharacterIterator extends CharacterIterator {
// Inner Classes
    public static class Attribute implements Serializable;
// Public Instance Methods
    public abstract java.util.Set getAllAttributeKeys();
    public abstract Object getAttribute(AttributedCharacterIterator.Attribute attribute);
    public abstract java.util.Map getAttributes();
    public abstract int getRunLimit();
    public abstract int getRunLimit(java.util.Set attributes);
    public abstract int getRunLimit(AttributedCharacterIterator.Attribute attribute);
    public abstract int getRunStart();
    public abstract int getRunStart(AttributedCharacterIterator.Attribute attribute);
    public abstract int getRunStart(java.util.Set attributes);
}
```

Hierarchy: (AttributedCharacterIterator(CharacterIterator(Cloneable)))

Passed To: Too many methods to list.

Returned By: java.awt.event.InputMethodEvent.getText(),
java.awt.im.InputMethodRequests.{cancelLatestCommittedText(), getCommittedText(),
getSelectedText()}, AttributedString.getIterator()

AttributedCharacterIterator.Attribute   Java 1.2

java.text   *serializable*

This class defines the types of the attribute keys used with AttributedCharacterIterator and AttributedString. It defines several constant Attribute keys that are commonly used with multilingual text and input methods. The LANGUAGE key represents the language of the underlying text. The value of this key should be a Locale object. The READING key represents arbitrary reading information associated with text. The value must be an Annotation object. The INPUT_METHOD_SEGMENT key serves to define text segments (usually words) that an input method operates on. The value of this attribute should be an Annotation object that contains null. Other classes may subclass this class and define other attribute keys that are useful in other circumstances or problem domains. See, for example, java.awt.font.TextAttribute in *Java Foundation Classes in a Nutshell* (O'Reilly).

```
public static class AttributedCharacterIterator.Attribute implements Serializable {
// Protected Constructors
    protected Attribute(String name);
// Public Constants
    public static final AttributedCharacterIterator.Attribute INPUT_METHOD_SEGMENT;
    public static final AttributedCharacterIterator.Attribute LANGUAGE;
    public static final AttributedCharacterIterator.Attribute READING;
// Public Methods Overriding Object
    public final boolean equals(Object obj);
    public final int hashCode();
    public String toString();
// Protected Instance Methods
```

```
    protected String getName();
    protected Object readResolve() throws java.io.InvalidObjectException;
}
```

Subclasses: java.awt.font.TextAttribute

Passed To: java.awt.im.InputMethodRequests.{cancelLatestCommittedText(), getCommittedText(), getSelectedText()}, AttributedCharacterIterator.{getAttribute(), getRunLimit(), getRunStart()}, AttributedString.{addAttribute(), AttributedString(), getIterator()}

Returned By: java.awt.Font.getAvailableAttributes()

Type Of: AttributedCharacterIterator.Attribute.{INPUT_METHOD_SEGMENT, LANGUAGE, READING}

AttributedString

Java 1.2

java.text

This class represents text and associated attributes. An AttributedString can be defined in terms of an underlying AttributedCharacterIterator or an underlying String. Additional attributes can be specified with the addAttribute() and addAttributes() methods. getIterator() returns an AttributedCharacterIterator over the AttributedString or over a specified portion of the string. Note that two of the getIterator() methods take an array of Attribute keys as an argument. These methods return an AttributedCharacterIterator that ignores all attributes that are not in the specified array. If the array argument is null, however, the returned iterator contains all attributes.

```
public class AttributedString {
// Public Constructors
    public AttributedString(String text);
    public AttributedString(AttributedCharacterIterator text);
    public AttributedString(String text, java.util.Map attributes);
    public AttributedString(AttributedCharacterIterator text, int beginIndex, int endIndex);
    public AttributedString(AttributedCharacterIterator text, int beginIndex, int endIndex,
                            AttributedCharacterIterator.Attribute[ ] attributes);
// Public Instance Methods
    public void addAttribute(AttributedCharacterIterator.Attribute attribute, Object value);
    public void addAttribute(AttributedCharacterIterator.Attribute attribute, Object value, int beginIndex, int endIndex);
    public void addAttributes(java.util.Map attributes, int beginIndex, int endIndex);
    public AttributedCharacterIterator getIterator();
    public AttributedCharacterIterator getIterator(AttributedCharacterIterator.Attribute[ ] attributes);
    public AttributedCharacterIterator getIterator(AttributedCharacterIterator.Attribute[ ] attributes, int beginIndex,
                            int endIndex);
}
```

BreakIterator

Java 1.1

java.text   *cloneable PJ1.1*

This class determines character, word, sentence, and line breaks in a block of text in a way that is independent of locale and text encoding. As an abstract class, BreakIterator cannot be instantiated directly. Instead, you must use one of the class methods getCharacterInstance(), getWordInstance(), getSentenceInstance(), or getLineInstance() to return an instance of a nonabstract subclass of BreakIterator. These various factory methods return a BreakIterator object that is configured to locate the requested boundary types and is localized to work for the optionally specified locale.

Once you have obtained an appropriate BreakIterator object, use setText() to specify the text in which to locate boundaries. To locate boundaries in a Java String object, simply specify the string. To locate boundaries in text that uses some other encoding, you must specify a CharacterIterator object for that text so that the BreakIterator object can locate the individual characters of the text. Having set the text to be searched, you can determine the character positions of characters, words, sentences, or line breaks with the first(), last(), next(), previous(), current(), and following() methods, which perform the obvious functions. Note that these methods do not return text itself, but merely the position of the appropriate word, sentence, or line break.

```
public abstract class BreakIterator implements Cloneable {
// Protected Constructors
    protected BreakIterator();
// Public Constants
    public static final int DONE;                                              =-1
// Public Class Methods
    public static java.util.Locale[ ] getAvailableLocales();            synchronized
    public static BreakIterator getCharacterInstance();
    public static BreakIterator getCharacterInstance(java.util.Locale where);
    public static BreakIterator getLineInstance();
    public static BreakIterator getLineInstance(java.util.Locale where);
    public static BreakIterator getSentenceInstance();
    public static BreakIterator getSentenceInstance(java.util.Locale where);
    public static BreakIterator getWordInstance();
    public static BreakIterator getWordInstance(java.util.Locale where);
// Public Instance Methods
    public abstract int current();
    public abstract int first();
    public abstract int following(int offset);
    public abstract CharacterIterator getText();
1.2 public boolean isBoundary(int offset);
    public abstract int last();
    public abstract int next();
    public abstract int next(int n);
1.2 public int preceding(int offset);
    public abstract int previous();
    public abstract void setText(CharacterIterator newText);
    public void setText(String newText);
// Public Methods Overriding Object
    public Object clone();
}
```

Hierarchy: Object→ BreakIterator(Cloneable)

Passed To: java.awt.font.LineBreakMeasurer.LineBreakMeasurer()

Returned By: BreakIterator.{getCharacterInstance(), getLineInstance(), getSentenceInstance(), getWordInstance()}

CharacterIterator   Java 1.1

java.text   *cloneable PJ1.1*

This interface defines an API for portably iterating through the characters that make up a string of text, regardless of the encoding of that text. Such an API is necessary because the number of bytes per character is different for different encodings, and some encodings even use variable-width characters within the same string of text. In addition to allowing iteration, a class that implements the CharacterIterator interface for non-Unicode text also performs translation of characters from their native encoding to standard Java Unicode characters.

CharacterIterator is similar to java.util.Enumeration, but is somewhat more complex than that interface. The first() and last() methods return the first and last characters in the text, and the next() and prev() methods allow you to loop forward or backwards through the characters of the text. These methods return the DONE constant when they go beyond the first or last character in the text; a test for this constant can be used to terminate a loop. The CharacterIterator interface also allows random access to the characters in a string of text. The getBeginIndex() and getEndIndex() methods return the character positions for the start and end of the string, and setIndex() sets the current position. getIndex() returns the index of the current position, and current() returns the character at that position.

```
public interface CharacterIterator extends Cloneable {
// Public Constants
    public static final char DONE;                                    ='\uFFFF'
// Public Instance Methods
    public abstract Object clone();
    public abstract char current();
    public abstract char first();
    public abstract int getBeginIndex();
    public abstract int getEndIndex();
    public abstract int getIndex();
    public abstract char last();
    public abstract char next();
    public abstract char previous();
    public abstract char setIndex(int position);
}
```

Hierarchy: (CharacterIterator(Cloneable))

Implementations: AttributedCharacterIterator, StringCharacterIterator, javax.swing.text.Segment

Passed To: java.awt.Font.{canDisplayUpTo(), createGlyphVector(), getLineMetrics(), getStringBounds()}, java.awt.FontMetrics.{getLineMetrics(), getStringBounds()}, BreakIterator.setText(), CollationElementIterator.setText(), RuleBasedCollator.getCollationElementIterator()

Returned By: BreakIterator.getText()

ChoiceFormat   Java 1.1
java.text   *cloneable serializable PJ1.1*

This class is a subclass of Format that converts a number to a String in a way reminiscent of a switch statement or an enumerated type. Each ChoiceFormat object has an array of doubles known as its *limits* and an array of strings known as its *formats*. When the format() method is called to format a number x, the ChoiceFormat finds an index i such that:

    limits[i] <= x < limits[i+1]

If x is less than the first element of the array, the first element is used, and if it is greater than the last, the last element is used. Once the index i has been determined, it is used as the index into the array of strings, and the indexed string is returned as the result of the format() method.

A ChoiceFormat object may also be created by encoding its limits and formats into a single string known as its *pattern*. A typical pattern looks like the one below, used to return the singular or plural form of a word based on the numeric value passed to the format() method:

    ChoiceFormat cf = new ChoiceFormat("0#errors|1#error|2#errors");

A ChoiceFormat object created in this way returns the string "errors" when it formats the number 0 or any number greater than or equal to 2. It returns "error" when it formats the number 1. In the syntax shown here, note the pound sign (#) used to separate the limit number from the string that corresponds to that case and the vertical bar (|) used to separate the individual cases. You can use the applyPattern() method to change the pattern used by a ChoiceFormat object; use toPattern() to query the pattern it uses.

```
public class ChoiceFormat extends NumberFormat {
// Public Constructors
    public ChoiceFormat(String newPattern);
    public ChoiceFormat(double[ ] limits, String[ ] formats);
// Public Class Methods
    public static final double nextDouble(double d);
    public static double nextDouble(double d, boolean positive);
    public static final double previousDouble(double d);
// Public Instance Methods
    public void applyPattern(String newPattern);
    public Object[ ] getFormats();
    public double[ ] getLimits();
    public void setChoices(double[ ] limits, String[ ] formats);
    public String toPattern();
// Public Methods Overriding NumberFormat
    public Object clone();
    public boolean equals(Object obj);
    public StringBuffer format(long number, StringBuffer toAppendTo, FieldPosition status);
    public StringBuffer format(double number, StringBuffer toAppendTo, FieldPosition status);
    public int hashCode();
    public Number parse(String text, ParsePosition status);
}
```

Hierarchy: Object→ Format(Cloneable, Serializable)→ NumberFormat→ ChoiceFormat

CollationElementIterator   Java 1.1
java.text   PJ1.1

A CollationElementIterator object is returned by the getCollationElementIterator() method of the RuleBasedCollator object. The purpose of this class is to allow a program to iterate (with the next() method) through the characters of a string, returning ordering values for each of the collation keys in the string. Note that collation keys are not exactly the same as characters. In the traditional Spanish collation order, for example, the two-character sequence "ch" is treated as a single collation key that comes alphabetically between the letters "c" and "d". The value returned by the next() method is the collation order of the next collation key in the string. This numeric value can be directly compared to the value returned by next() for other CollationElementIterator objects. The value returned by next() can also be decomposed into primary, secondary, and tertiary ordering values with the static methods of this class. This class is used by RuleBasedCollator to implement its compare() method and to create CollationKey objects. Few applications ever need to use it directly.

```
public final class CollationElementIterator {
// No Constructor
// Public Constants
    public static final int NULLORDER;                                    =-1
// Public Class Methods
    public static final int primaryOrder(int order);
    public static final short secondaryOrder(int order);
    public static final short tertiaryOrder(int order);
// Public Instance Methods
1.2 public int getMaxExpansion(int order);
    public int getOffset();
    public int next();
```

```
1.2 public int previous();
    public void reset();
    public void setOffset(int newOffset);
1.2 public void setText(CharacterIterator source);
    public void setText(String source);
}
```

Returned By: RuleBasedCollator.getCollationElementIterator()

CollationKey   Java 1.1
java.text   comparable PJ1.1

CollationKey objects compare strings more quickly than is possible with Collation.compare().
Objects of this class are returned by Collation.getCollationKey(). To compare two CollationKey
objects, invoke the compareTo() method of key A, passing the key B as an argument
(both CollationKey objects must be created through the same Collation object). The return
value of this method is less than zero if the key A is collated before the key B, equal to
zero if they are equivalent for the purposes of collation, or greater than zero if the key
A is collated after the key B. Use getSourceString() to obtain the string represented by a
CollationKey.

```
public final class CollationKey implements Comparable {
// No Constructor
// Public Instance Methods
    public int compareTo(CollationKey target);
    public String getSourceString();
    public byte[ ] toByteArray();
// Methods Implementing Comparable
1.2 public int compareTo(Object o);
// Public Methods Overriding Object
    public boolean equals(Object target);
    public int hashCode();
}
```

Hierarchy: Object→ CollationKey(Comparable)

Passed To: CollationKey.compareTo()

Returned By: Collator.getCollationKey(), RuleBasedCollator.getCollationKey()

Collator   Java 1.1
java.text   cloneable PJ1.1

This class compares, orders, and sorts strings in a way appropriate for the default locale
or some other specified locale. Because it is an abstract class, it cannot be instantiated
directly. Instead, you must use the static getInstance() method to obtain an instance of a
Collator subclass that is appropriate for the default or specified locale. You can use
getAvailableLocales() to determine whether a Collator object is available for a desired
locale.

Once an appropriate Collator object has been obtained, you can use the compare()
method to compare strings. The possible return values of this method are −1, 0, and 1,
which indicate, respectively, that the first string is collated before the second, that the
two are equivalent for collation purposes, and that the first string is collated after the
second. The equals() method is a convenient shortcut for testing two strings for collation
equivalence.

When sorting an array of strings, each string in the array is typically compared more
than once. Using the compare() method in this case is inefficient. A more efficient

method for comparing strings multiple times is to use getCollationKey() for each string to create CollationKey objects. These objects can then be compared to each other more quickly than the strings themselves can be compared.

You can customize the way the Collator object performs comparisons by calling set-Strength(). If you pass the constant PRIMARY to this method, the comparison looks only at primary differences in the strings; it compares letters but ignores accents and case differences. If you pass the constant SECONDARY, it ignores case differences but does not ignore accents. And if you pass TERTIARY (the default), the Collator object takes both accents and case differences into account in its comparison.

```
public abstract class Collator implements Cloneable, java.util.Comparator {
// Protected Constructors
    protected Collator();
// Public Constants
    public static final int CANONICAL_DECOMPOSITION;                        =1
    public static final int FULL_DECOMPOSITION;                             =2
    public static final int IDENTICAL;                                      =3
    public static final int NO_DECOMPOSITION;                               =0
    public static final int PRIMARY;                                        =0
    public static final int SECONDARY;                                      =1
    public static final int TERTIARY;                                       =2
// Public Class Methods
    public static java.util.Locale[ ] getAvailableLocales();        synchronized
    public static Collator getInstance();                           synchronized
    public static Collator getInstance(java.util.Locale desiredLocale);  synchronized
// Public Instance Methods
    public abstract int compare(String source, String target);
    public boolean equals(String source, String target);
    public abstract CollationKey getCollationKey(String source);
    public int getDecomposition();                                  synchronized
    public int getStrength();                                       synchronized
    public void setDecomposition(int decompositionMode);            synchronized
    public void setStrength(int newStrength);                       synchronized
// Methods Implementing Comparator
1.2 public int compare(Object o1, Object o2);
    public boolean equals(Object that);
// Public Methods Overriding Object
    public Object clone();
    public abstract int hashCode();
}
```

Hierarchy: Object→ Collator(Cloneable, java.util.Comparator)

Subclasses: RuleBasedCollator

Returned By: Collator.getInstance()

DateFormat

Java 1.1

java.text

cloneable serializable PJ1.1

This class formats and parses dates and times in a locale-specific way. As an abstract class, it cannot be instantiated directly, but it provides a number of static methods that return instances of a concrete subclass you can use to format dates in a variety of ways. The getDateInstance() methods return a DateFormat object suitable for formatting dates in either the default locale or a specified locale. A formatting style may also optionally be specified; the constants FULL, LONG, MEDIUM, SHORT, and DEFAULT specify this style. Similarly, the getTimeInstance() methods return a DateFormat object that formats and parses times, and the getDateTimeInstance() methods return a DateFormat object that formats both dates and times. These methods also optionally take a format style constant and a Locale. Finally, getInstance() returns a default DateFormat object that formats both dates and times in the SHORT format.

Once you have created a DateFormat object, you can use the setCalendar() and setTime-Zone() methods if you want to format the date using a calendar or time zone other than the default. The various format() methods convert java.util.Date objects to strings using whatever format is encapsulated in the DateFormat object. The parse() and parseObject() methods perform the reverse operation; they parse a string formatted according to the rules of the DateFormat object and convert it into to a Date object. The DEFAULT, FULL, MEDIUM, LONG, and SHORT constants specify how verbose or compact the formatted date or time should be. The remaining constants, which all end with _FIELD, specify various fields of formatted dates and times and are used with the FieldPosition object that is optionally passed to format().

```
public abstract class DateFormat extends Format {
// Protected Constructors
    protected DateFormat();
// Public Constants
    public static final int AM_PM_FIELD;                                      =14
    public static final int DATE_FIELD;                                        =3
    public static final int DAY_OF_WEEK_FIELD;                                 =9
    public static final int DAY_OF_WEEK_IN_MONTH_FIELD;                       =11
    public static final int DAY_OF_YEAR_FIELD;                                =10
    public static final int DEFAULT;                                           =2
    public static final int ERA_FIELD;                                         =0
    public static final int FULL;                                              =0
    public static final int HOUR0_FIELD;                                      =16
    public static final int HOUR1_FIELD;                                      =15
    public static final int HOUR_OF_DAY0_FIELD;                                =5
    public static final int HOUR_OF_DAY1_FIELD;                                =4
    public static final int LONG;                                              =1
    public static final int MEDIUM;                                            =2
    public static final int MILLISECOND_FIELD;                                 =8
    public static final int MINUTE_FIELD;                                      =6
    public static final int MONTH_FIELD;                                       =2
    public static final int SECOND_FIELD;                                      =7
    public static final int SHORT;                                             =3
    public static final int TIMEZONE_FIELD;                                   =17
    public static final int WEEK_OF_MONTH_FIELD;                              =13
    public static final int WEEK_OF_YEAR_FIELD;                               =12
    public static final int YEAR_FIELD;                                        =1
// Public Class Methods
    public static java.util.Locale[ ] getAvailableLocales();
    public static final DateFormat getDateInstance();
    public static final DateFormat getDateInstance(int style);
    public static final DateFormat getDateInstance(int style, java.util.Locale aLocale);
    public static final DateFormat getDateTimeInstance();
    public static final DateFormat getDateTimeInstance(int dateStyle, int timeStyle);
    public static final DateFormat getDateTimeInstance(int dateStyle, int timeStyle, java.util.Locale aLocale);
    public static final DateFormat getInstance();
    public static final DateFormat getTimeInstance();
    public static final DateFormat getTimeInstance(int style);
    public static final DateFormat getTimeInstance(int style, java.util.Locale aLocale);
// Property Accessor Methods (by property name)
    public java.util.Calendar getCalendar();
    public void setCalendar(java.util.Calendar newCalendar);
```

java.text

```
    public boolean isLenient( );
    public void setLenient(boolean lenient);
    public NumberFormat getNumberFormat( );
    public void setNumberFormat(NumberFormat newNumberFormat);
    public java.util.TimeZone getTimeZone( );
    public void setTimeZone(java.util.TimeZone zone);
// Public Instance Methods
    public final String format(java.util.Date date);
    public abstract StringBuffer format(java.util.Date date, StringBuffer toAppendTo, FieldPosition fieldPosition);
    public java.util.Date parse(String text) throws ParseException;
    public abstract java.util.Date parse(String text, ParsePosition pos);
// Public Methods Overriding Format
    public Object clone( );
    public final StringBuffer format(Object obj, StringBuffer toAppendTo, FieldPosition fieldPosition);
    public Object parseObject(String source, ParsePosition pos);
// Public Methods Overriding Object
    public boolean equals(Object obj);
    public int hashCode( );
// Protected Instance Fields
    protected java.util.Calendar calendar;
    protected NumberFormat numberFormat;
}
```

Hierarchy: Object→ Format(Cloneable, Serializable)→ DateFormat

Subclasses: SimpleDateFormat

Returned By: DateFormat.{getDateInstance(), getDateTimeInstance(), getInstance(), getTimeInstance()}

DateFormatSymbols
Java 1.1

java.text
cloneable serializable PJ1.1

This class defines accessor methods for the various pieces of data, such as names of months and days, used by SimpleDateFormat to format and parse dates and times. You do not typically need to use this class unless you are formatting dates for an unsupported locale or in some highly customized way.

```
public class DateFormatSymbols implements Cloneable, Serializable {
// Public Constructors
    public DateFormatSymbols( );
    public DateFormatSymbols(java.util.Locale locale);
// Property Accessor Methods (by property name)
    public String[ ] getAmPmStrings( );
    public void setAmPmStrings(String[ ] newAmpms);
    public String[ ] getEras( );
    public void setEras(String[ ] newEras);
    public String getLocalPatternChars( );
    public void setLocalPatternChars(String newLocalPatternChars);
    public String[ ] getMonths( );
    public void setMonths(String[ ] newMonths);
    public String[ ] getShortMonths( );
    public void setShortMonths(String[ ] newShortMonths);
    public String[ ] getShortWeekdays( );
    public void setShortWeekdays(String[ ] newShortWeekdays);
    public String[ ] getWeekdays( );
    public void setWeekdays(String[ ] newWeekdays);
```

```
  public String[ ][ ] getZoneStrings();
  public void setZoneStrings(String[ ][ ] newZoneStrings);
// Public Methods Overriding Object
  public Object clone();
  public boolean equals(Object obj);
  public int hashCode();
}
```

Hierarchy: Object→ DateFormatSymbols(Cloneable, Serializable)

Passed To: SimpleDateFormat.{setDateFormatSymbols(), SimpleDateFormat()}

Returned By: SimpleDateFormat.getDateFormatSymbols()

DecimalFormat   Java 1.1

java.text   *cloneable serializable PJ1.1*

This is the concrete Format class used by NumberFormat for all locales that use base 10 numbers. Most applications do not need to use this class directly; they can use the static methods of NumberFormat to obtain a default NumberFormat object for a desired locale and then perform minor locale-independent customizations on that object.

Applications that require highly customized number formatting and parsing may create custom DecimalFormat objects by passing a suitable pattern to the DecimalFormat() constructor method. The applyPattern() method can change this pattern. A pattern consists of a string of characters from the table below. For example:

"$#,##0.00;($#,##0.00)"

Character	Meaning
#	A digit; zeros show as absent
0	A digit; zeros show as 0
.	The locale-specific decimal separator
,	The locale-specific grouping separator (comma)
-	The locale-specific negative prefix
%	Shows value as a percentage
;	Separates positive number format (on left) from optional negative number format (on right)
'	Quotes a reserved character, so it appears literally in the output (apostrophe)
other	Appears literally in output

A DecimalFormatSymbols object can be specified optionally when creating a DecimalFormat object. If one is not specified, a DecimalFormatSymbols object suitable for the default locale is used.

```
public class DecimalFormat extends NumberFormat {
// Public Constructors
  public DecimalFormat();
  public DecimalFormat(String pattern);
  public DecimalFormat(String pattern, DecimalFormatSymbols symbols);
// Property Accessor Methods (by property name)
  public DecimalFormatSymbols getDecimalFormatSymbols();
  public void setDecimalFormatSymbols(DecimalFormatSymbols newSymbols);
  public boolean isDecimalSeparatorAlwaysShown();                default:false
  public void setDecimalSeparatorAlwaysShown(boolean newValue);
```

public int **getGroupingSize**( );	*default:3*
public void **setGroupingSize**(int *newValue*);	
1.2 public void **setMaximumFractionDigits**(int *newValue*);	*Overrides:NumberFormat*
1.2 public void **setMaximumIntegerDigits**(int *newValue*);	*Overrides:NumberFormat*
1.2 public void **setMinimumFractionDigits**(int *newValue*);	*Overrides:NumberFormat*
1.2 public void **setMinimumIntegerDigits**(int *newValue*);	*Overrides:NumberFormat*
public int **getMultiplier**( );	*default:1*
public void **setMultiplier**(int *newValue*);	
public String **getNegativePrefix**( );	*default:"-"*
public void **setNegativePrefix**(String *newValue*);	
public String **getNegativeSuffix**( );	*default:""*
public void **setNegativeSuffix**(String *newValue*);	
public String **getPositivePrefix**( );	*default:""*
public void **setPositivePrefix**(String *newValue*);	
public String **getPositiveSuffix**( );	*default:""*
public void **setPositiveSuffix**(String *newValue*);	
// *Public Instance Methods*	
public void **applyLocalizedPattern**(String *pattern*);	
public void **applyPattern**(String *pattern*);	
public String **toLocalizedPattern**( );	
public String **toPattern**( );	
// *Public Methods Overriding NumberFormat*	
public Object **clone**( );	
public boolean **equals**(Object *obj*);	
public StringBuffer **format**(long *number*, StringBuffer *result*, FieldPosition *fieldPosition*);	
public StringBuffer **format**(double *number*, StringBuffer *result*, FieldPosition *fieldPosition*);	
public int **hashCode**( );	
public Number **parse**(String *text*, ParsePosition *parsePosition*);	
}	

Hierarchy: Object→ Format(Cloneable, Serializable)→ NumberFormat→ DecimalFormat

DecimalFormatSymbols   Java 1.1

java.text   *cloneable serializable PJ1.1*

This class defines the various characters and strings, such as the decimal point, percent sign, and thousands separator, used by DecimalFormat when formatting numbers. You do not typically use this class directly unless you are formatting dates for an unsupported locale or in some highly customized way.

public final class **DecimalFormatSymbols** implements Cloneable, Serializable {	
// *Public Constructors*	
public **DecimalFormatSymbols**( );	
public **DecimalFormatSymbols**(java.util.Locale *locale*);	
// *Property Accessor Methods (by property name)*	
public String **getCurrencySymbol**( );	*default:"$"*
public void **setCurrencySymbol**(String *currency*);	
public char **getDecimalSeparator**( );	*default:.*
public void **setDecimalSeparator**(char *decimalSeparator*);	
public char **getDigit**( );	*default:#*
public void **setDigit**(char *digit*);	
public char **getGroupingSeparator**( );	*default:,*
public void **setGroupingSeparator**(char *groupingSeparator*);	
public String **getInfinity**( );	*default:"\u221E"*
public void **setInfinity**(String *infinity*);	
public String **getInternationalCurrencySymbol**( );	*default:"USD"*

```
    public void setInternationalCurrencySymbol(String currency);
    public char getMinusSign();                                              default:-
    public void setMinusSign(char minusSign);
    public char getMonetaryDecimalSeparator();                               default:.
    public void setMonetaryDecimalSeparator(char sep);
    public String getNaN();                                                  default:"\uFFFD"
    public void setNaN(String NaN);
    public char getPatternSeparator();                                       default:;
    public void setPatternSeparator(char patternSeparator);
    public char getPercent();                                                default:%
    public void setPercent(char percent);
    public char getPerMill();                                                default:\u2030
    public void setPerMill(char perMill);
    public char getZeroDigit();                                              default:0
    public void setZeroDigit(char zeroDigit);
// Public Methods Overriding Object
    public Object clone();
    public boolean equals(Object obj);
    public int hashCode();
}
```

Hierarchy: Object→ DecimalFormatSymbols(Cloneable, Serializable)

Passed To: DecimalFormat.{DecimalFormat(), setDecimalFormatSymbols()}

Returned By: DecimalFormat.getDecimalFormatSymbols()

FieldPosition

Java 1.1

java.text

PJ1.1

FieldPosition objects are optionally passed to the format() methods of the Format class and its subclasses to return additional information about the formatting that has been performed. The getBeginIndex() and getEndIndex() methods of this class return the starting and ending character positions of some field of the formatted string. The integer value passed to the FieldPosition() constructor specifies what field of the returned string should have its bounds returned. The NumberFormat and DateFormat classes define various constants (which end with the string _FIELD) that can be used here. Typically, this bounds information is useful for aligning formatted strings in columns—for example, aligning the decimal points in a column of numbers.

```
public class FieldPosition {
// Public Constructors
    public FieldPosition(int field);
// Public Instance Methods
    public int getBeginIndex();
    public int getEndIndex();
    public int getField();
    public void setBeginIndex(int bi);
    public void setEndIndex(int ei);
// Public Methods Overriding Object
1.2 public boolean equals(Object obj);
1.2 public int hashCode();
1.2 public String toString();
}
```

Passed To: ChoiceFormat.format(), DateFormat.format(), DecimalFormat.format(), Format.format(), MessageFormat.format(), NumberFormat.format(), SimpleDateFormat.format()

Format
java.text

Java 1.1

cloneable serializable PJ1.1

This abstract class is the base class for all number, date, and string formatting classes in the java.text package. It defines two abstract methods that are implemented by subclasses. format() converts an object to a string using the formatting rules encapsulated by the Format subclass and optionally appends the resulting string to an existing StringBuffer. parseObject() performs the reverse operation; it parses a formatted string and returns the corresponding object. Status information for these two operations is returned in FieldPosition and ParsePosition objects. The nonabstract methods of this class are simple shortcuts that rely on implementations of the abstract methods. See ChoiceFormat, DateFormat, MessageFormat, and NumberFormat.

```
public abstract class Format implements Cloneable, Serializable {
// Public Constructors
    public Format();
// Public Instance Methods
    public final String format(Object obj);
    public abstract StringBuffer format(Object obj, StringBuffer toAppendTo, FieldPosition pos);
    public Object parseObject(String source) throws ParseException;
    public abstract Object parseObject(String source, ParsePosition status);
// Public Methods Overriding Object
    public Object clone();
}
```

Hierarchy: Object→ Format(Cloneable, Serializable)

Subclasses: DateFormat, MessageFormat, NumberFormat

Passed To: MessageFormat.{setFormat(), setFormats()}

Returned By: MessageFormat.getFormats()

MessageFormat
java.text

Java 1.1

cloneable serializable PJ1.1

This class formats and substitutes objects into specified positions in a message string (also known as the pattern string). It provides the closest Java equivalent to the printf() function of the C programming language. If a message is to be displayed only a single time, the simplest way to use the MessageFormat class is through the static format() method. This method is passed a message or pattern string and an array of argument objects to be formatted and substituted into the string. If the message is to be displayed several times, it makes more sense to create a MessageFormat object, supplying the pattern string, and then call the format() instance method of this object, supplying the array of objects to be formatted into the message.

The message or pattern string used by the MessageFormat contains digits enclosed in curly braces to indicate where each argument should be substituted. The sequence "{0}" indicates that the first object should be converted to a string (if necessary) and inserted at that point, while the sequence "{3}" indicates that the fourth object should be inserted. If the object to be inserted is not a string, MessageFormat checks to see if it is a Date or a subclass of Number. If so, it uses a default DateFormat or NumberFormat object to convert the value to a string. If not, it simply invokes the object's toString() method to convert it.

A digit within curly braces in a pattern string may be followed optionally by a comma, and one of the words "date", "time", "number", or "choice", to indicate that the corresponding argument should be formatted as a date, time, number, or choice before being substituted into the pattern string. Any of these keywords can additionally be followed by a comma and additional pattern information to be used in formatting the date, time, number, or choice. (See SimpleDateFormat, DecimalFormat, and ChoiceFormat for more information.)

You can use the setLocale() method to specify a nondefault Locale that the MessageFormat should use when obtaining DateFormat and NumberFormat objects to format dates, time, and numbers inserted into the pattern. You can change the Format object used at a particular position in the pattern with the setFormat() method. You can set a new pattern for the MessageFormat object by calling applyPattern(), and you can obtain a string that represents the current formatting pattern by calling toPattern(). MessageFormat also supports a parse() method that can parse an array of objects out of a specified string, according to the specified pattern.

```
public class MessageFormat extends Format {
// Public Constructors
    public MessageFormat(String pattern);
// Public Class Methods
    public static String format(String pattern, Object[ ] arguments);
// Public Instance Methods
    public void applyPattern(String newPattern);
    public final StringBuffer format(Object[ ] source, StringBuffer result, FieldPosition ignore);
    public Format[ ] getFormats( );
    public java.util.Locale getLocale( );
    public Object[ ] parse(String source) throws ParseException;
    public Object[ ] parse(String source, ParsePosition status);
    public void setFormat(int variable, Format newFormat);
    public void setFormats(Format[ ] newFormats);
    public void setLocale(java.util.Locale theLocale);
    public String toPattern( );
// Public Methods Overriding Format
    public Object clone( );
    public final StringBuffer format(Object source, StringBuffer result, FieldPosition ignore);
    public Object parseObject(String text, ParsePosition status);
// Public Methods Overriding Object
    public boolean equals(Object obj);
    public int hashCode( );
}
```

Hierarchy: Object→ Format(Cloneable, Serializable)→ MessageFormat

NumberFormat

Java 1.1

java.text

cloneable serializable PJ1.1

This class formats and parses numbers in a locale-specific way. As an abstract class, it cannot be instantiated directly, but it provides a number of static methods that return instances of a concrete subclass you can use for formatting. The getInstance() method returns a NumberFormat object suitable for normal formatting of numbers in either the default locale or in a specified locale. getCurrencyInstance() and getPercentInstance() return NumberFormat objects for formatting numbers that represent monetary amounts and percentages, in either the default locale or in a specified locale. getAvailableLocales() returns an array of locales for which NumberFormat objects are available.

Once you have created a suitable NumberFormat object, you can customize its locale-independent behavior with setMaximumFractionDigits(), setGroupingUsed(), and similar set methods. In order to customize the locale-dependent behavior, you can use instanceof to test if the NumberFormat object is an instance of DecimalFormat, and, if so, cast it to that type. The DecimalFormat class provides complete control over number formatting. Note, however, that a NumberFormat customized in this way may no longer be appropriate for the desired locale.

After creating and customizing a NumberFormat object, you can use the various format() methods to convert numbers to strings or string buffers, and you can use the parse() or parseObject() methods to convert strings to numbers. The constants defined by this class are to be used by the FieldPosition object. The NumberFormat class in not intended for the display of very large or very small numbers that require exponential notation, and it may not gracefully handle infinite or NaN (not-a-number) values.

```
public abstract class NumberFormat extends Format {
// Public Constructors
    public NumberFormat();
// Public Constants
    public static final int FRACTION_FIELD;                                              =1
    public static final int INTEGER_FIELD;                                               =0
// Public Class Methods
    public static java.util.Locale[ ] getAvailableLocales();
    public static final NumberFormat getCurrencyInstance();
    public static NumberFormat getCurrencyInstance(java.util.Locale inLocale);
    public static final NumberFormat getInstance();
    public static NumberFormat getInstance(java.util.Locale inLocale);
    public static final NumberFormat getNumberInstance();
    public static NumberFormat getNumberInstance(java.util.Locale inLocale);
    public static final NumberFormat getPercentInstance();
    public static NumberFormat getPercentInstance(java.util.Locale inLocale);
// Property Accessor Methods (by property name)
    public boolean isGroupingUsed();
    public void setGroupingUsed(boolean newValue);
    public int getMaximumFractionDigits();
    public void setMaximumFractionDigits(int newValue);
    public int getMaximumIntegerDigits();
    public void setMaximumIntegerDigits(int newValue);
    public int getMinimumFractionDigits();
    public void setMinimumFractionDigits(int newValue);
    public int getMinimumIntegerDigits();
    public void setMinimumIntegerDigits(int newValue);
    public boolean isParseIntegerOnly();
    public void setParseIntegerOnly(boolean value);
// Public Instance Methods
    public final String format(long number);
    public final String format(double number);
    public abstract StringBuffer format(long number, StringBuffer toAppendTo, FieldPosition pos);
    public abstract StringBuffer format(double number, StringBuffer toAppendTo, FieldPosition pos);
    public Number parse(String text) throws ParseException;
    public abstract Number parse(String text, ParsePosition parsePosition);
// Public Methods Overriding Format
    public Object clone();
    public final StringBuffer format(Object number, StringBuffer toAppendTo, FieldPosition pos);
    public final Object parseObject(String source, ParsePosition parsePosition);
// Public Methods Overriding Object
    public boolean equals(Object obj);
    public int hashCode();
}
```

Hierarchy: Object→ Format(Cloneable, Serializable)→ NumberFormat

Subclasses: ChoiceFormat, DecimalFormat

Passed To: DateFormat.setNumberFormat()

Returned By: DateFormat.getNumberFormat(), NumberFormat.{getCurrencyInstance(), getInstance(), getNumberInstance(), getPercentInstance()}

Type Of: DateFormat.numberFormat

ParseException
Java 1.1

java.text
serializable checked PJ1.1

Signals that a string has an incorrect format and cannot be parsed. It is typically thrown by the parse() or parseObject() methods of Format and its subclasses, but is also thrown by certain methods in the java.text package that are passed patterns or other rules in string form. The getErrorOffset() method of this class returns the character position at which the parsing error occurred in the offending string.

```
public class ParseException extends Exception {
// Public Constructors
    public ParseException(String s, int errorOffset);
// Public Instance Methods
    public int getErrorOffset();
}
```

Hierarchy: Object→ Throwable(Serializable)→ Exception→ ParseException

Thrown By: DateFormat.parse(), Format.parseObject(), MessageFormat.parse(), NumberFormat.parse(), RuleBasedCollator.RuleBasedCollator()

ParsePosition
Java 1.1

java.text
PJ1.1

ParsePosition objects are passed to the parse() and parseObject() methods of Format and its subclasses. The ParsePosition class represents the position in a string at which parsing should begin or at which parsing stopped. Before calling a parse() method, you can specify the starting position of parsing by passing the desired index to the ParsePosition() constructor or by calling the setIndex() of an existing ParsePosition object. When parse() returns, you can determine where parsing ended by calling getIndex(). When parsing multiple objects or values from a string, a single ParsePosition object can be used sequentially.

```
public class ParsePosition {
// Public Constructors
    public ParsePosition(int index);
// Public Instance Methods
1.2 public int getErrorIndex();
    public int getIndex();
1.2 public void setErrorIndex(int ei);
    public void setIndex(int index);
// Public Methods Overriding Object
1.2 public boolean equals(Object obj);
1.2 public int hashCode();
1.2 public String toString();
}
```

Passed To: ChoiceFormat.parse(), DateFormat.{parse(), parseObject()}, DecimalFormat.parse(), Format.parseObject(), MessageFormat.{parse(), parseObject()}, NumberFormat.{parse(), parseObject()}, SimpleDateFormat.parse()

java.text

RuleBasedCollator

java.text

This class is a concrete subclass of the abstract Collator class. It performs collations using a table of rules that are specified in textual form. Most applications do not use this class directly; instead they call Collator.getInstance() to obtain a Collator object (typically a Rule-BasedCollator object) that implements the default collation order for a specified or default locale. You should need to use this class only if you are collating strings for a locale that is not supported by default or if you need to implement a highly customized collation order.

```
public class RuleBasedCollator extends Collator {
// Public Constructors
    public RuleBasedCollator(String rules) throws ParseException;
// Public Instance Methods
1.2 public CollationElementIterator getCollationElementIterator(CharacterIterator source);
    public CollationElementIterator getCollationElementIterator(String source);
    public String getRules();
// Public Methods Overriding Collator
    public Object clone();
    public int compare(String source, String target);                              synchronized
    public boolean equals(Object obj);
    public CollationKey getCollationKey(String source);                            synchronized
    public int hashCode();
}
```

Hierarchy: Object→ Collator(Cloneable, java.util.Comparator)→ RuleBasedCollator

SimpleDateFormat

java.text

This is the concrete Format subclass used by DateFormat to handle the formatting and parsing of dates. Most applications should not use this class directly; instead, they should obtain a localized DateFormat object by calling one of the static methods of Date-Format.

SimpleDateFormat formats dates and times according to a pattern, which specifies the positions of the various fields of the date, and a DateFormatSymbols object, which specifies important auxiliary data, such as the names of months. Applications that require highly customized date or time formatting can create a custom SimpleDateFormat object by specifying the desired pattern. This creates a SimpleDateFormat object that uses the DateFormatSymbols object for the default locale. You may also specify an locale explicitly, to use the DateFormatSymbols object for that locale. You can even provide an explicit DateFormatSymbols object of your own if you need to format dates and times for an unsupported locale.

You can use the applyPattern() method of a SimpleDateFormat to change the formatting pattern used by the object. The syntax of this pattern is described in the table below. Any characters in the format string that do not appear in this table appear literally in the formatted date.

Field	Full Form	Short Form
Year	yyyy (4 digits)	yy (2 digits)
Month	MMM (name)	MM (2 digits), M (1 or 2 digits)
Day of week	EEEE	EE
Day of month	dd (2 digits)	d (1 or 2 digits)

Field	Full Form	Short Form
Hour (1–12)	hh (2 digits)	h (1 or 2 digits)
Hour (0–23)	HH (2 digits)	H (1 or 2 digits)
Hour (0–11)	KK	K
Hour (1–24)	kk	k
Minute	mm	
Second	ss	
Millisecond	SSS	
AM/PM	a	
Time zone	zzzz	zz
Day of week in month	F (e.g., 3rd Thursday)	
Day in year	DDD (3 digits)	D (1, 2, or 3 digits)
Week in year	ww	
Era (e.g., BC/AD)	G	

```
public class SimpleDateFormat extends DateFormat {
// Public Constructors
    public SimpleDateFormat();
    public SimpleDateFormat(String pattern);
    public SimpleDateFormat(String pattern, DateFormatSymbols formatData);
    public SimpleDateFormat(String pattern, java.util.Locale loc);
// Public Instance Methods
    public void applyLocalizedPattern(String pattern);
    public void applyPattern(String pattern);
1.2 public java.util.Date get2DigitYearStart();
    public DateFormatSymbols getDateFormatSymbols();
1.2 public void set2DigitYearStart(java.util.Date startDate);
    public void setDateFormatSymbols(DateFormatSymbols newFormatSymbols);
    public String toLocalizedPattern();
    public String toPattern();
// Public Methods Overriding DateFormat
    public Object clone();
    public boolean equals(Object obj);
    public StringBuffer format(java.util.Date date, StringBuffer toAppendTo, FieldPosition pos);
    public int hashCode();
    public java.util.Date parse(String text, ParsePosition pos);
}
```

Hierarchy: Object→ Format(Cloneable, Serializable)→ DateFormat→ SimpleDateFormat

StringCharacterIterator

Java 1.1

java.text

cloneable PJ1.1

This class is a trivial implementation of the CharacterIterator interface that works for text stored in Java String objects. See CharacterIterator for details.

```
public final class StringCharacterIterator implements CharacterIterator {
// Public Constructors
    public StringCharacterIterator(String text);
    public StringCharacterIterator(String text, int pos);
    public StringCharacterIterator(String text, int begin, int end, int pos);
// Public Instance Methods
1.2 public void setText(String text);
```

```
// Methods Implementing CharacterIterator
    public Object clone( );
    public char current( );
    public char first( );
    public int getBeginIndex( );
    public int getEndIndex( );
    public int getIndex( );
    public char last( );
    public char next( );
    public char previous( );
    public char setIndex(int p);
// Public Methods Overriding Object
    public boolean equals(Object obj);
    public int hashCode( );
}
```

Hierarchy: Object→ StringCharacterIterator(CharacterIterator(Cloneable))

CHAPTER 23

The java.util Package

The java.util package defines a number of useful classes, primarily collections classes that are useful for working with groups of objects. This package should not be considered merely a utility package that is separate from the rest of the language; in fact, Java depends directly on several of the classes in this package. Figure 23-1 shows the collection classes of this package, while Figure 23-2 shows the other classes.

The most important classes in java.util are the collections classes. Prior to Java 1.2, these were Vector, a growable list of objects, and Hashtable, a mapping between arbitrary key and value objects. Java 1.2 adds an entire collections framework consisting of the Collection, Map, Set, List, SortedMap, and SortedSet interfaces and the classes that implement them. Other important classes and interfaces of the collections framework are Comparator, Collections, Arrays, Iterator, and ListIterator.

The other classes of the package are also useful. Date, Calendar, and TimeZone work with dates and times. ResourceBundle and its subclasses represent a bundle of localized resources that are read in by an internationalized program at runtime. BitSet implements an arbitrary-size array of bits. Random generates and returns pseudo-random numbers in a variety of forms. StringTokenizer parses a string into tokens. Finally, in Java 1.3, Timer and TimerTask provide a powerful API for scheduling code to be run by a background thread, once or repetitively, at a specified time in the future.

java.util

AbstractCollection   Java 1.2
java.util   *collection*

This abstract class is a partial implementation of Collection that makes it easy to define custom Collection implementations. To create an unmodifiable collection, simply override size() and iterator(). The Iterator object returned by iterator() has to support only the hasNext() and next() methods. To define a modifiable collection, you must additionally override the add() method of AbstractCollection and make sure the Iterator returned by iterator() supports the remove() method. Some subclasses may choose to override other methods to tune performance. In addition, it is conventional that all subclasses provide two constructors: one that takes no arguments and one that accepts a Collection argument that specifies the initial contents of the collection.

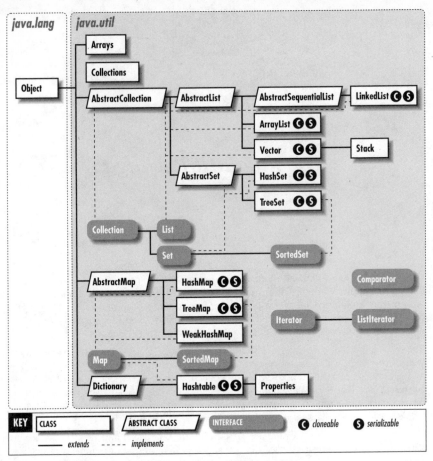

Figure 23–1: The collection classes of the java.util package

Note that if you subclass AbstractCollection directly, you are implementing a *bag*—an unordered collection that allows duplicate elements. If your add() method rejects duplicate elements, you should subclass AbstractSet instead. See also AbstractList.

```
public abstract class AbstractCollection implements Collection {
// Protected Constructors
    protected AbstractCollection();
// Methods Implementing Collection
    public boolean add(Object o);
    public boolean addAll(Collection c);
    public void clear();
    public boolean contains(Object o);
    public boolean containsAll(Collection c);
    public boolean isEmpty();
    public abstract Iterator iterator();
    public boolean remove(Object o);
    public boolean removeAll(Collection c);
    public boolean retainAll(Collection c);
    public abstract int size();
```

Figure 23-2: Other classes of the java.util package

```
   public Object[ ] toArray();
   public Object[ ] toArray(Object[ ] a);
// Public Methods Overriding Object
   public String toString();
}
```

Hierarchy: Object→ AbstractCollection(Collection)

Subclasses: AbstractList, AbstractSet

AbstractList

Java 1.2

java.util

collection

This abstract class is a partial implementation of the List interface that makes it easy to define custom List implementations based on random-access list elements (such as objects stored in an array). If you want to base a List implementation on a sequential-access data model (such as a linked list), subclass AbstractSequentialList instead.

To create an unmodifiable List, simply subclass AbstractList and override the (inherited) size() and get() methods. To create a modifiable list, you must also override set() and, optionally, add() and remove(). These three methods are optional, so unless you override them, they simply throw an UnsupportedOperationException. All other methods of the List interface are implemented in terms of size(), get(), set(), add(), and remove(). In some cases, you may want to override these other methods to improve performance. By convention, all List implementations should define two constructors: one that accepts no arguments and another that accepts a Collection of initial elements for the list.

```
public abstract class AbstractList extends AbstractCollection implements java.util.List {
// Protected Constructors
    protected AbstractList();
// Methods Implementing List
    public boolean add(Object o);
    public void add(int index, Object element);
    public boolean addAll(int index, Collection c);
    public void clear();
    public boolean equals(Object o);
    public abstract Object get(int index);
    public int hashCode();
    public int indexOf(Object o);
    public Iterator iterator();
    public int lastIndexOf(Object o);
    public ListIterator listIterator();
    public ListIterator listIterator(int index);
    public Object remove(int index);
    public Object set(int index, Object element);
    public java.util.List subList(int fromIndex, int toIndex);
// Protected Instance Methods
    protected void removeRange(int fromIndex, int toIndex);
// Protected Instance Fields
    protected transient int modCount;
}
```

Hierarchy: Object→ AbstractCollection(Collection)→ AbstractList(java.util.List(Collection))

Subclasses: AbstractSequentialList, ArrayList, Vector

AbstractMap

Java 1.2

java.util

collection

This abstract class is a partial implementation of the Map interface that makes it easy to define simple custom Map implementations. To define an unmodifiable map, subclass AbstractMap and override the entrySet() method so that it returns a set of Map.Entry objects. (Note that you must also implement Map.Entry, of course.) The returned set should not support add() or remove(), and its iterator should not support remove(). In order to define a modifiable Map, you must additionally override the put() method and provide support for the remove() method of the iterator returned by entrySet().iterator(). In addition, it is conventional that all Map implementations define two constructors: one that accepts no arguments and another that accepts a Map of initial mappings.

AbstractMap defines all Map methods in terms of its entrySet() and put() methods and the remove() method of the entry set iterator. Note, however, that the implementation is based on a linear search of the Set returned by entrySet() and is not efficient when the Map contains more than a handful of entries. Some subclasses may want to override additional AbstractMap methods to improve performance. HashMap and TreeMap use different algorithms are are substantially more efficient.

```
public abstract class AbstractMap implements Map {
// Protected Constructors
    protected AbstractMap();
// Methods Implementing Map
    public void clear();
    public boolean containsKey(Object key);
    public boolean containsValue(Object value);
    public abstract Set entrySet();
    public boolean equals(Object o);
    public Object get(Object key);
    public int hashCode();
    public boolean isEmpty();
    public Set keySet();
    public Object put(Object key, Object value);
    public void putAll(Map t);
    public Object remove(Object key);
    public int size();
    public Collection values();
// Public Methods Overriding Object
    public String toString();
}
```

Hierarchy: Object → AbstractMap(Map)

Subclasses: HashMap, TreeMap, WeakHashMap

AbstractSequentialList

Java 1.2

java.util

collection

This abstract class is a partial implementation of the List interface that makes it easy to define List implementations based on a sequential-access data model, as is the case with the LinkedList subclass. To implement a List based on an array or other random-access model, subclass AbstractList instead.

To implement an unmodifiable list, subclass this class and override the size() and listIterator() methods. listIterator() must return a ListIterator that defines the hasNext(), hasPrevious(), next(), previous(), and index() methods. If you want to allow the list to be modified, the ListIterator should also support the set() method and, optionally, the add() and remove() methods. AbstractSequentialList implements all other List methods in terms of these methods. Some subclasses may want to override additional methods to improve performance. In addition, it is conventional that all List implementations define two constructors: one that accepts no arguments and another that accepts a Collection of initial elements for the list.

```
public abstract class AbstractSequentialList extends AbstractList {
// Protected Constructors
    protected AbstractSequentialList();
```

```
// Public Methods Overriding AbstractList
    public void add(int index, Object element);
    public boolean addAll(int index, Collection c);
    public Object get(int index);
    public Iterator iterator();
    public abstract ListIterator listIterator(int index);
    public Object remove(int index);
    public Object set(int index, Object element);
}
```

Hierarchy: Object→ AbstractCollection(Collection)→ AbstractList(java.util.List(Collection))→ AbstractSequentialList

Subclasses: LinkedList

AbstractSet

Java 1.2

java.util

collection

This abstract class is a partial implementation of the Set interface that makes it easy to create custom Set implementations. Since Set defines the same methods as Collection, you can subclass AbstractSet exactly as you would subclass AbstractCollection. See Abstract-Collection for details. Note, however, that when subclassing AbstractSet, you should be sure that your add() method and your constructors do not allow duplicate elements to be added to the set. See also AbstractList.

```
public abstract class AbstractSet extends AbstractCollection implements Set {
// Protected Constructors
    protected AbstractSet();
// Methods Implementing Set
    public boolean equals(Object o);
    public int hashCode();
}
```

Hierarchy: Object→ AbstractCollection(Collection)→ AbstractSet(Set(Collection))

Subclasses: HashSet, TreeSet

ArrayList

Java 1.2

java.util

cloneable serializable collection

This class is a List implementation based on an array (that is recreated as necessary as the list grows or shrinks). ArrayList implements all optional List and Collection methods and allows list elements of any type (including null). Because ArrayList is based on an array, the get() and set() methods are very efficient. (This is not the case for the LinkedList implementation, for example.) ArrayList is a general-purpose implementation of List and is quite commonly used. ArrayList is very much like the Vector class, except that its methods are not synchronized. If you are using an ArrayList in a multithreaded environment, you should explicitly synchronize any modifications to the list, or wrap the list with Collections.synchronizedList(). See List and Collection for details on the methods of ArrayList. See also LinkedList.

An ArrayList has a *capacity*, which is the number of elements in the internal array that contains the elements of the list. When the number of elements exceeds the capacity, a new array, with a larger capacity, must be created. In addition to the List and Collection methods, ArrayList defines a couple of methods that help you manage this capacity. If you know in advance how many elements an ArrayList will contain, you can call ensure-Capacity(), which can increase efficiency by avoiding incremental reallocation of the internal array. You can also pass an initial capacity value to the ArrayList() constructor.

Finally, if an ArrayList has reached its final size and will not change in the future, you can call trimToSize() to reallocate the internal array with a capacity that matches the list size exactly. When the ArrayList will have a long lifetime, this can be a useful technique to reduce memory usage.

```
public class ArrayList extends AbstractList implements Cloneable, java.util.List, Serializable {
// Public Constructors
    public ArrayList( );
    public ArrayList(int initialCapacity);
    public ArrayList(Collection c);
// Public Instance Methods
    public void ensureCapacity(int minCapacity);
    public void trimToSize( );
// Methods Implementing List
    public boolean add(Object o);
    public void add(int index, Object element);
    public boolean addAll(Collection c);
    public boolean addAll(int index, Collection c);
    public void clear( );
    public boolean contains(Object elem);
    public Object get(int index);
    public int indexOf(Object elem);
    public boolean isEmpty( );                                          default:true
    public int lastIndexOf(Object elem);
    public Object remove(int index);
    public Object set(int index, Object element);
    public int size( );
    public Object[ ] toArray( );
    public Object[ ] toArray(Object[ ] a);
// Protected Methods Overriding AbstractList
    protected void removeRange(int fromIndex, int toIndex);
// Public Methods Overriding Object
    public Object clone( );
}
```

Hierarchy: Object → AbstractCollection(Collection) → AbstractList(java.util.List(Collection)) → ArrayList(Cloneable, java.util.List(Collection), Serializable)

Type Of: java.awt.dnd.DragGestureRecognizer.events, java.beans.beancontext.BeanContextServicesSupport.bcsListeners, java.beans.beancontext.BeanContextSupport.bcmListeners

Arrays

Java 1.2

java.util

This class defines static methods for sorting, searching, and performing other useful operations on arrays. It also defines the asList() method, which returns a List wrapper around a specified array of objects. Any changes made to the List are also made to the underlying array. This is a powerful method that allows any array of objects to be manipulated in any of the ways a List can be manipulated. It provides a link between arrays and the Java collections framework.

The various sort() methods sort an array (or a specified portion of an array) in place. Variants of the method are defined for arrays of each primitive type and for arrays of Object. For arrays of primitive types, the sorting is done according to the natural ordering of the type. For arrays of objects, the sorting is done according to the specified Comparator, or, if the array contains only java.lang.Comparable objects, according to the ordering defined by that interface. When sorting an array of objects, a stable sorting algorithm is used so that the relative ordering of equal objects is not disturbed. (This allows repeated sorts to order objects by key and subkey, for example.)

The binarySearch() methods perform an efficient search (in logarithmic time) of a sorted array for a specified value. If a match is found in the array, binarySearch() returns the index of the match. If no match is found, the method returns a negative number. For a negative return value r, the index -(r+1) specifies the array index at which the specified value can be inserted to maintain the sorted order of the array. When the array to be searched is an array of objects, the elements of the array must all implement java.lang.Comparable, or you must provide a Comparator object to compare them.

The equals() methods test whether two arrays are equal. Two arrays of primitive type are equal if they contain the same number of elements and if corresponding pairs of elements are equal according to the == operator. Two arrays of objects are equal if they contain the same number of elements and if corresponding pairs of elements are equal according to the equals() method defined by those objects. The fill() methods fill an array or a specified range of an array with the specified value.

```
public class Arrays {
// No Constructor
// Public Class Methods
    public static java.util.List asList(Object[ ] a);
    public static int binarySearch(short[ ] a, short key);
    public static int binarySearch(Object[ ] a, Object key);
    public static int binarySearch(long[ ] a, long key);
    public static int binarySearch(int[ ] a, int key);
    public static int binarySearch(double[ ] a, double key);
    public static int binarySearch(byte[ ] a, byte key);
    public static int binarySearch(char[ ] a, char key);
    public static int binarySearch(float[ ] a, float key);
    public static int binarySearch(Object[ ] a, Object key, Comparator c);
    public static boolean equals(boolean[ ] a, boolean[ ] a2);
    public static boolean equals(byte[ ] a, byte[ ] a2);
    public static boolean equals(float[ ] a, float[ ] a2);
    public static boolean equals(double[ ] a, double[ ] a2);
    public static boolean equals(int[ ] a, int[ ] a2);
    public static boolean equals(long[ ] a, long[ ] a2);
    public static boolean equals(char[ ] a, char[ ] a2);
    public static boolean equals(short[ ] a, short[ ] a2);
    public static boolean equals(Object[ ] a, Object[ ] a2);
    public static void fill(double[ ] a, double val);
    public static void fill(char[ ] a, char val);
    public static void fill(short[ ] a, short val);
    public static void fill(Object[ ] a, Object val);
    public static void fill(float[ ] a, float val);
    public static void fill(byte[ ] a, byte val);
    public static void fill(int[ ] a, int val);
    public static void fill(long[ ] a, long val);
    public static void fill(boolean[ ] a, boolean val);
    public static void fill(Object[ ] a, int fromIndex, int toIndex, Object val);
    public static void fill(boolean[ ] a, int fromIndex, int toIndex, boolean val);
    public static void fill(byte[ ] a, int fromIndex, int toIndex, byte val);
    public static void fill(float[ ] a, int fromIndex, int toIndex, float val);
    public static void fill(short[ ] a, int fromIndex, int toIndex, short val);
    public static void fill(int[ ] a, int fromIndex, int toIndex, int val);
    public static void fill(long[ ] a, int fromIndex, int toIndex, long val);
    public static void fill(double[ ] a, int fromIndex, int toIndex, double val);
```

```
    public static void fill(char[ ] a, int fromIndex, int toIndex, char val);
    public static void sort(char[ ] a);
    public static void sort(short[ ] a);
    public static void sort(int[ ] a);
    public static void sort(byte[ ] a);
    public static void sort(double[ ] a);
    public static void sort(float[ ] a);
    public static void sort(long[ ] a);
    public static void sort(Object[ ] a);
    public static void sort(Object[ ] a, Comparator c);
    public static void sort(short[ ] a, int fromIndex, int toIndex);
    public static void sort(Object[ ] a, int fromIndex, int toIndex);
    public static void sort(byte[ ] a, int fromIndex, int toIndex);
    public static void sort(char[ ] a, int fromIndex, int toIndex);
    public static void sort(float[ ] a, int fromIndex, int toIndex);
    public static void sort(double[ ] a, int fromIndex, int toIndex);
    public static void sort(int[ ] a, int fromIndex, int toIndex);
    public static void sort(long[ ] a, int fromIndex, int toIndex);
    public static void sort(Object[ ] a, int fromIndex, int toIndex, Comparator c);
}
```

BitSet

java.util

Java 1.0

cloneable serializable PJ1.1

This class defines an arbitrarily large set of bits. Instance methods allow you to set, clear, and query individual bits in the set. You can also perform bitwise boolean arithmetic on the bits in BitSet objects. This class can be used as an extremely compact array of boolean values, although reading and writing those values is slower than normal array access.

```
public class BitSet implements Cloneable, Serializable {
// Public Constructors
    public BitSet( );
    public BitSet(int nbits);
// Public Instance Methods
    public void and(BitSet set);
1.2 public void andNot(BitSet set);
    public void clear(int bitIndex);
    public boolean get(int bitIndex);
1.2 public int length( );
    public void or(BitSet set);
    public void set(int bitIndex);
    public int size( );
    public void xor(BitSet set);
// Public Methods Overriding Object
    public Object clone( );
    public boolean equals(Object obj);
    public int hashCode( );
    public String toString( );
}
```

Hierarchy: Object→ BitSet(Cloneable, Serializable)

Passed To: BitSet.{and(), andNot(), or(), xor()}, javax.swing.text.html.parser.DTD.defineElement()

Type Of: javax.swing.text.html.parser.Element.{exclusions, inclusions}

Calendar   Java 1.1

java.util   *cloneable serializable PJ1.1*

This abstract class defines methods that perform date and time arithmetic. It also includes methods that convert dates and times to and from the machine-usable millisecond format used by the Date class and units such as minutes, hours, days, weeks, months, and years that are more useful to humans. As an abstract class, Calendar cannot be directly instantiated. Instead, it provides static getInstance() methods that return instances of a Calendar subclass suitable for use in a specified or default locale with a specified or default time zone. See also Date, DateFormat, and TimeZone.

Calendar defines a number of useful constants. Some of these are values that represent days of the week and months of the year. Other constants, such as HOUR and DAY_OF_WEEK, represent various fields of date and time information. These field constants are passed to a number of Calendar methods, such as get() and set(), in order to indicate what particular date or time field is desired.

setTime() and the various set() methods set the date represented by a Calendar object. The add() method adds (or subtracts) values to a calendar field, incrementing the next larger field when the field being set rolls over. roll() does the same, without modifying anything but the specified field. before() and after() compare two Calendar objects. Many of the methods of the Calendar class are replacements for methods of Date that have been deprecated as of Java 1.1. While the Calendar class converts a time value to its various hour, day, month, and other fields, it is not intended to present those fields in a form suitable for display to the end user. That function is performed by the java.text.DateFormat class, which handles internationalization issues.

```
public abstract class Calendar implements Cloneable, Serializable {
// Protected Constructors
    protected Calendar();
    protected Calendar(TimeZone zone, Locale aLocale);
// Public Constants
    public static final int AM;                                    =0
    public static final int AM_PM;                                 =9
    public static final int APRIL;                                 =3
    public static final int AUGUST;                                =7
    public static final int DATE;                                  =5
    public static final int DAY_OF_MONTH;                          =5
    public static final int DAY_OF_WEEK;                           =7
    public static final int DAY_OF_WEEK_IN_MONTH;                  =8
    public static final int DAY_OF_YEAR;                           =6
    public static final int DECEMBER;                              =11
    public static final int DST_OFFSET;                            =16
    public static final int ERA;                                   =0
    public static final int FEBRUARY;                              =1
    public static final int FIELD_COUNT;                           =17
    public static final int FRIDAY;                                =6
    public static final int HOUR;                                  =10
    public static final int HOUR_OF_DAY;                           =11
    public static final int JANUARY;                               =0
    public static final int JULY;                                  =6
    public static final int JUNE;                                  =5
    public static final int MARCH;                                 =2
    public static final int MAY;                                   =4
    public static final int MILLISECOND;                           =14
    public static final int MINUTE;                                =12
    public static final int MONDAY;                                =2
```

```
    public static final int MONTH;                                              =2
    public static final int NOVEMBER;                                           =10
    public static final int OCTOBER;                                            =9
    public static final int PM;                                                 =1
    public static final int SATURDAY;                                           =7
    public static final int SECOND;                                             =13
    public static final int SEPTEMBER;                                          =8
    public static final int SUNDAY;                                             =1
    public static final int THURSDAY;                                           =5
    public static final int TUESDAY;                                            =3
    public static final int UNDECIMBER;                                         =12
    public static final int WEDNESDAY;                                          =4
    public static final int WEEK_OF_MONTH;                                       =4
    public static final int WEEK_OF_YEAR;                                        =3
    public static final int YEAR;                                               =1
    public static final int ZONE_OFFSET;                                        =15
// Public Class Methods
    public static Locale[ ] getAvailableLocales();                      synchronized
    public static Calendar getInstance();                              synchronized
    public static Calendar getInstance(Locale aLocale);                synchronized
    public static Calendar getInstance(TimeZone zone);                 synchronized
    public static Calendar getInstance(TimeZone zone, Locale aLocale); synchronized
// Property Accessor Methods (by property name)
    public int getFirstDayOfWeek();
    public void setFirstDayOfWeek(int value);
    public boolean isLenient();
    public void setLenient(boolean lenient);
    public int getMinimalDaysInFirstWeek();
    public void setMinimalDaysInFirstWeek(int value);
    public final java.util.Date getTime();
    public final void setTime(java.util.Date date);
    public TimeZone getTimeZone();
    public void setTimeZone(TimeZone value);
// Public Instance Methods
    public abstract void add(int field, int amount);
    public boolean after(Object when);
    public boolean before(Object when);
    public final void clear();
    public final void clear(int field);
    public final int get(int field);
1.2 public int getActualMaximum(int field);
1.2 public int getActualMinimum(int field);
    public abstract int getGreatestMinimum(int field);
    public abstract int getLeastMaximum(int field);
    public abstract int getMaximum(int field);
    public abstract int getMinimum(int field);
    public final boolean isSet(int field);
1.2 public void roll(int field, int amount);
    public abstract void roll(int field, boolean up);
    public final void set(int field, int value);
    public final void set(int year, int month, int date);
    public final void set(int year, int month, int date, int hour, int minute);
    public final void set(int year, int month, int date, int hour, int minute, int second);
// Public Methods Overriding Object
    public Object clone();
```

```
    public boolean equals(Object obj);
1.2 public int hashCode();
    public String toString();
// Protected Instance Methods
    protected void complete();
    protected abstract void computeFields();
    protected abstract void computeTime();
    protected long getTimeInMillis();
    protected final int internalGet(int field);
    protected void setTimeInMillis(long millis);
// Protected Instance Fields
    protected boolean areFieldsSet;
    protected int[ ] fields;
    protected boolean[ ] isSet;
    protected boolean isTimeSet;
    protected long time;
}
```

Hierarchy: Object→ Calendar(Cloneable, Serializable)

Subclasses: GregorianCalendar

Passed To: Too many methods to list.

Returned By: java.text.DateFormat.getCalendar(), Calendar.getInstance()

Type Of: java.text.DateFormat.calendar

Collection   Java 1.2

java.util   *collection*

This interface represents a group, or collection, of objects. The objects may or may not be ordered, and the collection may or may not contain duplicate objects. Collection is not often implemented directly. Instead, most collection classes implement one of the more specific subinterfaces: Set, an unordered collection that does not allow duplicates, or List, an ordered collection that does allow duplicates.

The Collection type provides a general way to refer to any set, list, or other collection of objects; it defines generic methods that work with any collection. contains() and containsAll() test whether the Collection contains a specified object or all the objects in a given collection. isEmpty() returns true if the Collection has no elements, or false otherwise. size() returns the number of elements in the Collection. iterator() returns an Iterator object that allows you to iterate through the objects in the collection. toArray() returns the objects in the Collection in a new array of type Object. Another version of toArray() takes an array as an argument and stores all elements of the Collection (which must all be compatible with the array) into that array. If the array is not big enough, the method allocates a new, larger array of the same type. If the array is too big, the method stores null into the first empty element of the array. This version of toArray() returns the array that was passed in or the new array, if one was allocated.

The previous methods all query or extract the contents of a collection. The Collection interface also defines methods for modifying the contents of the collection. add() and addAll() add an object or a collection of objects to a Collection. remove() and removeAll() remove an object or collection. retainAll() is a variant that removes all objects except those in a specified Collection. clear() removes all objects from the collection. All these modification methods except clear() return true if the collection was modified as a result of the call. An interface cannot specify constructors, but it is conventional that all implementations of Collection provide at least two standard constructors: one that takes no arguments and creates an empty collection, and a copy constructor that accepts a Collection object that specifies the initial contents of the new Collection.

Implementations of Collection and its subinterfaces are not required to support all operations defined by the Collection interface. All modification methods listed above are optional; an implementation (such as an immutable Set implementation) that does not support them simply throws java.lang.UnsupportedOperationException for these methods. Furthermore, implementations are free to impose restrictions on the types of objects that can be members of a collection. Some implementations might require elements to be of a particular type, for example, and others might not allow null as an element.

See also Set, List, Map, and Collections.

```
public interface Collection {
// Public Instance Methods
    public abstract boolean add(Object o);
    public abstract boolean addAll(Collection c);
    public abstract void clear();
    public abstract boolean contains(Object o);
    public abstract boolean containsAll(Collection c);
    public abstract boolean equals(Object o);
    public abstract int hashCode();
    public abstract boolean isEmpty();
    public abstract Iterator iterator();
    public abstract boolean remove(Object o);
    public abstract boolean removeAll(Collection c);
    public abstract boolean retainAll(Collection c);
    public abstract int size();
    public abstract Object[ ] toArray();
    public abstract Object[ ] toArray(Object[ ] a);
}
```

Implementations: java.beans.beancontext.BeanContext, AbstractCollection, java.util.List, Set

Passed To: Too many methods to list.

Returned By: java.awt.RenderingHints.values(), java.security.Provider.values(), java.security.cert.CertificateFactory.{generateCertificates(), generateCRLs()}, java.security.cert.CertificateFactorySpi.{engineGenerateCertificates(), engineGenerateCRLs()}, AbstractMap.values(), Collections.{synchronizedCollection(), unmodifiableCollection()}, HashMap.values(), Hashtable.values(), Map.values(), TreeMap.values(), java.util.jar.Attributes.values()

Type Of: java.beans.beancontext.BeanContextMembershipEvent.children

java.util

Collections

Java 1.2

java.util

This class defines static methods and constants that are useful for working with collections and maps. One of the most commonly used methods is sort(), which sorts a List in place (the list cannot be immutable, of course). The sorting algorithm is stable, which means that equal elements retain the same relative order. One version of sort() uses a specified Comparator to perform the sort; the other relies on the natural ordering of the list elements and requires all the elements to implement java.lang.Comparable.

A related method is binarySearch(). It efficiently (in logarithmic time) searches a sorted List for a specified object and returns the index at which a matching object is found. If no match is found, it returns a negative number. For a negative return value r, the value -(r+1) specifies the index at which the specified object can be inserted into the list to maintain the sorted order of the list. As with sort(), binarySearch() can be passed a Comparator that defines the order of the sorted list. If no Comparator is specified, the list elements must all implement Comparable, and the list is assumed to be sorted according to the natural ordering defined by this interface.

The various methods whose names begin with synchronized return a thread-safe collection object wrapped around the specified collection. Vector and Hashtable are the only two collection objects thread-safe by default. Use these methods to obtain a synchronized wrapper object if you are using any other type of Collection or Map in a multithreaded environment where more than one thread can modify it.

The various methods whose names begin with unmodifiable function like synchronized methods. They return a Collection or Map object wrapped around the specified collection. The returned object is unmodifiable, however, so its add(), remove(), set(), put(), etc., methods all throw java.lang.UnsupportedOperationException.

The Collections class also defines a number of miscellanous methods. copy() copies elements of a source list into a destination list. enumeration() returns an Enumeration for a Collection, which is useful when working with code that uses the old Enumeration interface instead of the newer Iterator interface. fill() replaces all elements of the specified list with the specified object. The min() and max() methods search an unordered Collection for the minimum and maximum elements, according either to a specified Comparator or to the natural order defined by the Comparable elements themselves. nCopies() creates a new immutable List that contains a specified number of copies of a specified object. reverse() reverses the order of the elements in a list. This method operates in place and therefore does not work for immutable lists. reverseOrder() returns a convenient predefined Comparator object that can order Comparable objects into the reverse of their natural ordering. shuffle() randomizes the order of elements in a list, using either an internal source of randomness or the Random pseudo-random number generator you provide. singleton() returns an unmodifiable set that contains only the specified object. The Collections class also defines two related constants, EMPTY_LIST and EMPTY_SET, which are immutable List and Set objects that contain no elements. In Java 1.3, singletonList() and singletonMap() return an immutable list and an immutable map, respectively, each of which contains only a single entry. The Collections class also defines related constants, EMPTY_LIST, EMPTY_SET, and EMPTY_MAP (in Java 1.3), which are immutable List, Set, and Map objects that contain no elements.

See Arrays for methods that perform sorting and searching operations on arrays instead of collections.

```
public class Collections {
// No Constructor
// Public Constants
    public static final java.util.List EMPTY_LIST;
1.3 public static final Map EMPTY_MAP;
    public static final Set EMPTY_SET;
// Public Class Methods
    public static int binarySearch(java.util.List list, Object key);
    public static int binarySearch(java.util.List list, Object key, Comparator c);
    public static void copy(java.util.List dest, java.util.List src);
    public static Enumeration enumeration(Collection c);
    public static void fill(java.util.List list, Object o);
    public static Object max(Collection coll);
    public static Object max(Collection coll, Comparator comp);
    public static Object min(Collection coll);
    public static Object min(Collection coll, Comparator comp);
    public static java.util.List nCopies(int n, Object o);
    public static void reverse(java.util.List l);
    public static Comparator reverseOrder();
```

```
    public static void shuffle(java.util.List list);
    public static void shuffle(java.util.List list, Random rnd);
    public static Set singleton(Object o);
1.3 public static java.util.List singletonList(Object o);
1.3 public static Map singletonMap(Object key, Object value);
    public static void sort(java.util.List list);
    public static void sort(java.util.List list, Comparator c);
    public static Collection synchronizedCollection(Collection c);
    public static java.util.List synchronizedList(java.util.List list);
    public static Map synchronizedMap(Map m);
    public static Set synchronizedSet(Set s);
    public static SortedMap synchronizedSortedMap(SortedMap m);
    public static SortedSet synchronizedSortedSet(SortedSet s);
    public static Collection unmodifiableCollection(Collection c);
    public static java.util.List unmodifiableList(java.util.List list);
    public static Map unmodifiableMap(Map m);
    public static Set unmodifiableSet(Set s);
    public static SortedMap unmodifiableSortedMap(SortedMap m);
    public static SortedSet unmodifiableSortedSet(SortedSet s);
}
```

Comparator   Java 1.2

java.util

This interface defines a compare() method that specifies a total ordering for a set of objects, allowing those objects to be sorted. The Comparator is used when the objects to be ordered do not have a natural ordering defined by the Comparable interface, or when you want to order them using something other than their natural ordering.

The compare() method is passed two objects. If the first argument is less than the second argument or should be placed before the second argument in a sorted list, compare() should return a negative integer. If the first argument is greater than the second argument or should be placed after the second argument in a sorted list, compare() should return a positive integer. If the two objects are equivalent or if their relative position in a sorted list does not matter, compare() should return 0. Comparator implementations may assume that both Object arguments are of appropriate types and cast them as desired. If either argument is not of the expected type, the compare() method throws a ClassCastException.

Note that the magnitude of the numbers returned by compare() does not matter, only whether they are less than, equal to, or greater than zero. In most cases, you should implement a Comparator so that compare(o1,o2) returns 0 if and only if o1.equals(o2) returns true. This is particularly important when using a Comparator to impose an ordering on a TreeSet or a TreeMap.

See Collections and Arrays for various methods that use Comparator objects for sorting and searching. See also the related java.lang.Comparable interface.

```
public interface Comparator {
// Public Instance Methods
    public abstract int compare(Object o1, Object o2);
    public abstract boolean equals(Object obj);
}
```

Implementations: java.text.Collator

Passed To: Arrays.{binarySearch(), sort()}, Collections.{binarySearch(), max(), min(), sort()}, TreeMap.TreeMap(), TreeSet.TreeSet()

Returned By: Collections.reverseOrder(), SortedMap.comparator(), SortedSet.comparator(), TreeMap.comparator(), TreeSet.comparator()

Type Of: String.CASE_INSENSITIVE_ORDER

ConcurrentModificationException   Java 1.2

java.util   *serializable unchecked*

Signals that a modification has been made to a data structure at the same time some other operation is in progress and that, as a result, the correctness of the ongoing operation cannot be guaranteed. It is typically thrown by an Iterator or ListIterator object to stop an iteration if it detects that the underlying collection has been modified while the iteration is in progress.

```
public class ConcurrentModificationException extends RuntimeException {
// Public Constructors
    public ConcurrentModificationException();
    public ConcurrentModificationException(String message);
}
```

Hierarchy: Object→ Throwable(Serializable)→ Exception→ RuntimeException→ ConcurrentModificationException

Date   Java 1.0

java.util   *cloneable serializable comparable PJ1.1*

This class represents dates and times and lets you work with them in a system-independent way. You can create a Date by specifying the number of milliseconds from the epoch (midnight GMT, January 1st, 1970) or the year, month, date, and, optionally, the hour, minute, and second. Years are specified as the number of years since 1900. If you call the Date constructor with no arguments, the Date is initialized to the current time and date. The instance methods of the class allow you to get and set the various date and time fields, to compare dates and times, and to convert dates to and from string representations. As of Java 1.1, many of the date methods have been deprecated in favor of the methods of the Calendar class.

```
public class Date implements Cloneable, Comparable, Serializable {
// Public Constructors
    public Date();
#   public Date(String s);
    public Date(long date);
#   public Date(int year, int month, int date);
#   public Date(int year, int month, int date, int hrs, int min);
#   public Date(int year, int month, int date, int hrs, int min, int sec);
// Property Accessor Methods (by property name)
    public long getTime();
    public void setTime(long time);
// Public Instance Methods
    public boolean after(java.util.Date when);
    public boolean before(java.util.Date when);
1.2 public int compareTo(java.util.Date anotherDate);
// Methods Implementing Comparable
1.2 public int compareTo(Object o);
// Public Methods Overriding Object
1.2 public Object clone();
    public boolean equals(Object obj);
    public int hashCode();
```

```
    public String toString();
// Deprecated Public Methods
#   public int getDate();
#   public int getDay();
#   public int getHours();
#   public int getMinutes();
#   public int getMonth();
#   public int getSeconds();
#   public int getTimezoneOffset();
#   public int getYear();
#   public static long parse(String s);
#   public void setDate(int date);
#   public void setHours(int hours);
#   public void setMinutes(int minutes);
#   public void setMonth(int month);
#   public void setSeconds(int seconds);
#   public void setYear(int year);
#   public String toGMTString();
#   public String toLocaleString();
#   public static long UTC(int year, int month, int date, int hrs, int min, int sec);
}
```

Hierarchy: Object → java.util.Date(Cloneable, Comparable, Serializable)

Subclasses: java.sql.Date, java.sql.Time, java.sql.Timestamp

Passed To: java.security.cert.X509Certificate.checkValidity(), java.text.DateFormat.format(), java.text.SimpleDateFormat.{format(), set2DigitYearStart()}, Calendar.setTime(), java.util.Date.{after(), before(), compareTo()}, GregorianCalendar.setGregorianChange(), SimpleTimeZone.inDaylightTime(), java.util.Timer.{schedule(), scheduleAtFixedRate()}, TimeZone.inDaylightTime()

Returned By: java.security.KeyStore.getCreationDate(), java.security.KeyStoreSpi.engineGetCreationDate(), java.security.cert.X509Certificate.{getNotAfter(), getNotBefore()}, java.security.cert.X509CRL.{getNextUpdate(), getThisUpdate()}, java.security.cert.X509CRLEntry.getRevocationDate(), java.text.DateFormat.parse(), java.text.SimpleDateFormat.{get2DigitYearStart(), parse()}, Calendar.getTime(), GregorianCalendar.getGregorianChange()

Dictionary   Java 1.0

java.util   PJ1.1

This abstract class is the superclass of Hashtable. Other hashtable-like data structures might also extend this class. See Hashtable for more information. In Java 1.2, the Map interface replaces the functionality of this class.

```
public abstract class Dictionary {
// Public Constructors
    public Dictionary();
// Public Instance Methods
    public abstract Enumeration elements();
    public abstract Object get(Object key);
    public abstract boolean isEmpty();
    public abstract Enumeration keys();
    public abstract Object put(Object key, Object value);
    public abstract Object remove(Object key);
    public abstract int size();
}
```

Subclasses: Hashtable

Passed To: javax.swing.JSlider.setLabelTable(),
javax.swing.text.AbstractDocument.setDocumentProperties()

Returned By: javax.swing.JSlider.getLabelTable(),
javax.swing.text.AbstractDocument.getDocumentProperties()

EmptyStackException   Java 1.0
java.util   *serializable unchecked PJ1.1*

Signals that a Stack object is empty.

```
public class EmptyStackException extends RuntimeException {
// Public Constructors
    public EmptyStackException();
}
```

Hierarchy: Object→ Throwable(Serializable)→ Exception→ RuntimeException→
EmptyStackException

Thrown By: java.awt.EventQueue.pop()

Enumeration   Java 1.0
java.util   *PJ1.1*

This interface defines the methods necessary to enumerate, or iterate, through a set of
values, such as the set of values contained in a hashtable or binary tree. It is particularly useful for data structures, like hashtables, for which elements cannot simply be
looked up by index, as they can in arrays. An Enumeration is usually not instantiated
directly, but instead is created by the object that is to have its values enumerated. A
number of classes, such as Vector and Hashtable, have methods that return Enumeration
objects. In Java 1.2, the new Iterator interface is preferred over Enumeration.

To use an Enumeration object, you use its two methods in a loop. hasMoreElements()
returns true if there are more values to be enumerated and can determine whether a
loop should continue. Within a loop, a call to nextElement() returns a value from the
enumeration. An Enumeration makes no guarantees about the order in which the values
are returned. The values in an Enumeration can be iterated through only once; there is
no way to reset it to the beginning.

```
public interface Enumeration {
// Public Instance Methods
    public abstract boolean hasMoreElements();
    public abstract Object nextElement();
}
```

Implementations: StringTokenizer, javax.naming.NamingEnumeration

Passed To: java.io.SequenceInputStream.SequenceInputStream(),
javax.naming.CompositeName.CompositeName(), javax.naming.CompoundName.CompoundName(),
javax.swing.JTree.removeDescendantToggledPaths(),
javax.swing.text.AbstractDocument.AbstractElement.removeAttributes(),
javax.swing.text.AbstractDocument.AttributeContext.removeAttributes(),
javax.swing.text.MutableAttributeSet.removeAttributes(),
javax.swing.text.SimpleAttributeSet.removeAttributes(), javax.swing.text.StyleContext.removeAttributes(),
javax.swing.text.StyleContext.NamedStyle.removeAttributes(),
javax.swing.text.html.StyleSheet.removeAttributes()

Returned By: Too many methods to list.

Type Of: javax.swing.tree.DefaultMutableTreeNode.EMPTY_ENUMERATION

EventListener

java.util   *event listener PJ1.1*

EventListener is a base interface for the event model that is used by AWT and Swing in Java 1.1 and later. This interface defines no methods or constants; it serves simply as a tag that identifies objects that act as event listeners. The event listener interfaces in the java.awt.event, java.beans, and javax.swing.event packages extend this interface.

```
public interface EventListener {
}
```

Implementations: Too many classes to list.

Passed To: java.awt.AWTEventMulticaster.{addInternal(), AWTEventMulticaster(), remove(), removeInternal(), save()}, javax.swing.event.EventListenerList.{add(), remove()}

Returned By: Too many methods to list.

Type Of: java.awt.AWTEventMulticaster.{a, b}

EventObject

java.util   *serializable event PJ1.1*

EventObject serves as the superclass for all event objects used by the event model introduced in Java 1.1 for AWT and JavaBeans and also used by Swing in Java 1.2. This class defines a generic type of event; it is extended by the more specific event classes in the java.awt, java.awt.event, java.beans, and javax.swing.event packages. The only common feature shared by all events is a source object, which is the object that, in some way, generated the event. The source object is passed to the EventObject() constructor and is returned by the getSource() method.

```
public class EventObject implements Serializable {
// Public Constructors
    public EventObject(Object source);
// Public Instance Methods
    public Object getSource();
// Public Methods Overriding Object
    public String toString();
// Protected Instance Fields
    protected transient Object source;
}
```

Hierarchy: Object→ EventObject(Serializable)

Subclasses: Too many classes to list.

Passed To: javax.swing.AbstractCellEditor.{isCellEditable(), shouldSelectCell()}, javax.swing.CellEditor.{isCellEditable(), shouldSelectCell()}, javax.swing.DefaultCellEditor.{isCellEditable(), shouldSelectCell()}, javax.swing.DefaultCellEditor.EditorDelegate.{isCellEditable(), shouldSelectCell(), startCellEditing()}, javax.swing.JTable.editCellAt(), javax.swing.tree.DefaultTreeCellEditor.{canEditImmediately(), isCellEditable(), shouldSelectCell(), shouldStartEditingTimer()}

java.util

GregorianCalendar

java.util

Java 1.1

cloneable serializable PJ1.1

This concrete subclass of Calendar implements the standard solar calendar with years numbered from the birth of Christ that is used is most locales throughout the world. You do not typically use this class directly, but instead obtain a Calendar object suitable for the default locale by calling Calendar.getInstance(). See Calendar for details on working with Calendar objects. There is a discontinuity in the Gregorian calendar that represents the historical switch from the Julian calendar to the Gregorian calendar. By default, GregorianCalendar assumes that this switch occurs on October 15, 1582. Most programs need not be concerned with the switch.

```
public class GregorianCalendar extends Calendar {
// Public Constructors
    public GregorianCalendar();
    public GregorianCalendar(TimeZone zone);
    public GregorianCalendar(Locale aLocale);
    public GregorianCalendar(TimeZone zone, Locale aLocale);
    public GregorianCalendar(int year, int month, int date);
    public GregorianCalendar(int year, int month, int date, int hour, int minute);
    public GregorianCalendar(int year, int month, int date, int hour, int minute, int second);
// Public Constants
    public static final int AD;                                              =1
    public static final int BC;                                              =0
// Public Instance Methods
    public final java.util.Date getGregorianChange();
    public boolean isLeapYear(int year);
    public void setGregorianChange(java.util.Date date);
// Public Methods Overriding Calendar
    public void add(int field, int amount);
    public boolean equals(Object obj);
1.2 public int getActualMaximum(int field);
1.2 public int getActualMinimum(int field);
    public int getGreatestMinimum(int field);
    public int getLeastMaximum(int field);
    public int getMaximum(int field);
    public int getMinimum(int field);
    public int hashCode();
    public void roll(int field, boolean up);
    public void roll(int field, int amount);
// Protected Methods Overriding Calendar
    protected void computeFields();
    protected void computeTime();
}
```

Hierarchy: Object → Calendar(Cloneable, Serializable) → GregorianCalendar

HashMap

java.util

Java 1.2

cloneable serializable collection

This class implements the Map interface using an internal hashtable. It supports all optional Map methods, allows key and value objects of any types, and allows null to be used as a key or a value. Because HashMap is based on a hashtable data structure, the get() and put() methods are very efficient. HashMap is much like the Hashtable class, except that the HashMap methods are not synchronized (and are therefore faster), and HashMap allows null to be used as a key or a value. If you are working in a multithreaded environment, or if compatibility with previous versions of Java is a concern, use Hashtable. Otherwise, use HashMap.

If you know in advance approximately how many mappings a HashMap will contain, you can improve efficiency by specifying *initialCapacity* when you call the HashMap() constructor. The *initialCapacity* argument times the *loadFactor* argument should be greater than the number of mappings the HashMap will contain. A good value for *loadFactor* is 0.75; this is also the default value. See Map for details on the methods of HashMap. See also TreeMap and HashSet.

```
public class HashMap extends AbstractMap implements Cloneable, Map, Serializable {
// Public Constructors
    public HashMap( );
    public HashMap(int initialCapacity);
    public HashMap(Map t);
    public HashMap(int initialCapacity, float loadFactor);
// Methods Implementing Map
    public void clear( );
    public boolean containsKey(Object key);
    public boolean containsValue(Object value);
    public Set entrySet( );
    public Object get(Object key);
    public boolean isEmpty( );                                          default:true
    public Set keySet( );
    public Object put(Object key, Object value);
    public void putAll(Map t);
    public Object remove(Object key);
    public int size( );
    public Collection values( );
// Public Methods Overriding Object
    public Object clone( );
}
```

Hierarchy: Object→ AbstractMap(Map)→ HashMap(Cloneable, Map, Serializable)

Type Of: java.beans.beancontext.BeanContextServicesSupport.services, java.beans.beancontext.BeanContextSupport.children

HashSet   Java 1.2

java.util   *cloneable serializable collection*

This class implements Set using an internal hashtable. It supports all optional Set and Collection methods and allows any type of object or null to be a member of the set. Because HashSet is based on a hashtable, the basic add(), remove(), and contains() methods are all quite efficient. HashSet makes no guarantee about the order in which the set elements are enumerated by the Iterator returned by iterator(). The methods of HashSet are not synchronized. If you are using it in a multithreaded environment, you must explicitly synchronize all code that modifies the set or obtain a synchronized wrapper for it by calling Collections.synchronizedSet().

If you know in advance approximately how many mappings a HashSet will contain, you can improve efficiency by specifying *initialCapacity* when you call the HashSet() constructor. The *initialCapacity* argument times the *loadFactor* argument should be greater than the number of mappings the HashSet will contain. A good value for *loadFactor* is 0.75; this is also the default value. See Set and Collection for details on the methods of HashSet. See also TreeSet and HashMap.

```
public class HashSet extends AbstractSet implements Cloneable, Serializable, Set {
// Public Constructors
    public HashSet();
    public HashSet(int initialCapacity);
    public HashSet(Collection c);
    public HashSet(int initialCapacity, float loadFactor);
// Methods Implementing Set
    public boolean add(Object o);
    public void clear();
    public boolean contains(Object o);
    public boolean isEmpty();                                                   default:true
    public Iterator iterator();
    public boolean remove(Object o);
    public int size();
// Public Methods Overriding Object
    public Object clone();
}
```

Hierarchy: Object→ AbstractCollection(Collection)→ AbstractSet(Set(Collection))→
HashSet(Cloneable, Serializable, Set(Collection))

Hashtable   Java 1.0

java.util   *cloneable serializable collection PJ1.1*

This class implements a hashtable data structure, which maps key objects to value
objects and allows the efficient lookup of the value associated with a given key. put()
associates a value with a key in a Hashtable. get() retrieves a value for a specified key.
remove() deletes a key/value association. keys() and elements() return Enumeration objects
that allow you to iterate through the complete set of keys and values stored in the
table. Objects used as keys in a Hashtable must have valid equals() and hashCode() methods (the versions inherited from Object are okay). null is not legal as a key or value in a
Hashtable.

Hashtable is a commonly used class and has been a part of the Java API since Java 1.0.
In Java 1.2, it has been enhanced to implement the Map interface, which defines some
functionality in addition to the Java 1.0 Hashtable methods. Hashtable is very similar to
the HashMap class, but has synchronized methods, which make it thread-safe but increase
the overhead associated with it. If you need thread safety or require compatibility with
Java 1.0 or Java 1.1, use Hashtable. Otherwise, use HashMap.

```
public class Hashtable extends Dictionary implements Cloneable, Map, Serializable {
// Public Constructors
    public Hashtable();
1.2 public Hashtable(Map t);
    public Hashtable(int initialCapacity);
    public Hashtable(int initialCapacity, float loadFactor);
// Public Instance Methods
    public boolean contains(Object value);                                       synchronized
// Methods Implementing Map
    public void clear();                                                         synchronized
    public boolean containsKey(Object key);                                      synchronized
1.2 public boolean containsValue(Object value);
1.2 public Set entrySet();
1.2 public boolean equals(Object o);                                             synchronized
    public Object get(Object key);                                               synchronized
1.2 public int hashCode();                                                       synchronized
```

public boolean **isEmpty**( );	*default:true*
1.2 public Set **keySet**( );	
public Object **put**(Object *key*, Object *value*);	*synchronized*
1.2 public void **putAll**(Map *t*);	*synchronized*
public Object **remove**(Object *key*);	*synchronized*
public int **size**( );	
1.2 public Collection **values**( );	
// Public Methods Overriding Dictionary	
public Enumeration **elements**( );	*synchronized*
public Enumeration **keys**( );	*synchronized*
// Public Methods Overriding Object	
public Object **clone**( );	*synchronized*
public String **toString**( );	*synchronized*
// Protected Instance Methods	
protected void **rehash**( );	
}	

Hierarchy: Object→ Dictionary→ Hashtable(Cloneable, Map, Serializable)

Subclasses: Properties, javax.swing.UIDefaults

Passed To: Too many methods to list.

Returned By: javax.naming.CannotProceedException.getEnvironment(),
javax.naming.Context.getEnvironment(), javax.naming.InitialContext.getEnvironment(),
javax.servlet.http.HttpUtils.{parsePostData(), parseQueryString()},
javax.swing.JLayeredPane.getComponentToLayer(), javax.swing.JSlider.createStandardLabels()

Type Of: java.awt.GridBagLayout.comptable, javax.naming.CannotProceedException.environment,
javax.naming.InitialContext.myProps, javax.swing.JTable.{defaultEditorsByColumnClass,
defaultRenderersByColumnClass}, javax.swing.text.html.parser.DTD.{elementHash, entityHash},
javax.swing.undo.StateEdit.{postState, preState}

Iterator

java.util

This interface defines methods for iterating, or enumerating, the elements of a collection. The hasNext() method returns true if there are more elements to be enumerated or false if all elements have already been returned. The next() method returns the next element. These two methods make it easy to loop through an iterator with code such as the following:

```
for(Iterator i = c.iterator(); i.hasNext(); )
    processObject(i.next());
```

The Iterator interface is much like the Enumeration interface. In Java 1.2, Iterator is preferred over Enumeration because it provides a well-defined way to safely remove elements from a collection while the iteration is in progress. The remove() method removes the object most recently returned by next() from the collection that is being iterated through. Note, however, that support for remove() is optional; if an Iterator does not support remove(), it throws a java.lang.UnsupportedOperationException when you call it. While you are iterating through a collection, you are allowed to modify the collection only by calling the remove() method of the Iterator. If the collection is modified in any other way while an iteration is ongoing, the Iterator may fail to operate correctly, or it may throw a ConcurrentModificationException.

```
public interface Iterator {
// Public Instance Methods
    public abstract boolean hasNext();
    public abstract Object next();
    public abstract void remove();
}
```

Implementations: java.beans.beancontext.BeanContextSupport.BCSIterator, ListIterator

Returned By: Too many methods to list.

LinkedList   Java 1.2

java.util   *cloneable serializable collection*

This class implements the List interface in terms of a doubly linked list. It supports all
optional methods of List and Collection and allows list elements of any type, including
null. Because LinkedList is implemented with a linked list data structure, the get() and set()
methods are substantially less efficient than the same methods for an ArrayList. However,
a LinkedList may be more efficient when the add() and remove() methods are used frequently. The methods of LinkedList are not synchronized. If you are using a LinkedList in a
multithreaded environment, you must explicitly synchronize any code that modifies the
list or obtain a synchronized wrapper object with Collections.synchronizedList().

In addition to the methods defined by the List interface, LinkedList defines methods to get
the first and last elements of the list, to add an element to the beginning or end of the
list, and to remove the first or last element of the list. These convenient and efficient
methods make LinkedList well-suited for use as a stack or queue. See List and Collection
for details on the methods of LinkedList. See also ArrayList.

```
public class LinkedList extends AbstractSequentialList implements Cloneable, java.util.List, Serializable {
// Public Constructors
    public LinkedList();
    public LinkedList(Collection c);
// Public Instance Methods
    public void addFirst(Object o);
    public void addLast(Object o);
    public Object getFirst();
    public Object getLast();
    public Object removeFirst();
    public Object removeLast();
// Methods Implementing List
    public boolean add(Object o);
    public void add(int index, Object element);
    public boolean addAll(Collection c);
    public boolean addAll(int index, Collection c);
    public void clear();
    public boolean contains(Object o);
    public Object get(int index);
    public int indexOf(Object o);
    public int lastIndexOf(Object o);
    public ListIterator listIterator(int index);
    public boolean remove(Object o);
    public Object remove(int index);
    public Object set(int index, Object element);
    public int size();
    public Object[] toArray();
    public Object[] toArray(Object[] a);
```

```
// Public Methods Overriding Object
    public Object clone();
}
```

Hierarchy: Object→ AbstractCollection(Collection)→ AbstractList(java.util.List(Collection))→
AbstractSequentialList→ LinkedList(Cloneable, java.util.List(Collection), Serializable)

List

java.util

collection

This interface represents an ordered collection of objects. Each element in a List has an index, or position, in the list, and elements can be inserted, queried, and removed by index. The first element of a List has an index of 0. The last element in a list has index size()-1.

In addition to the methods defined by the superinterface, Collection, List defines a number of methods for working with its indexed elements. get() and set() query and set the object at a particular index, respectively. Versions of add() and addAll() that take an *index* argument insert an object or Collection of objects at a specified index. The versions of add() and addAll() that do not take an *index* argument insert an object or collection of objects at the end of the list. List defines a version of remove() that removes the object at a specified index.

The iterator() method is just like the iterator() method of Collection, except that the Iterator it returns is guaranteed to enumerate the elements of the List in order. listIterator() returns a ListIterator object, which is more powerful than a regular Iterator and allows the list to be modified while iteration proceeds. listIterator() can take an index argument to specify where in the list iteration should begin.

indexOf() and lastIndexOf() perform linear searches from the beginning and end, respectively, of the list, searching for a specified object. Each method returns the index of the first matching object it finds, or −1 if it does not find a match. Finally, subList() returns a List that contains only a specified contiguous range of list elements. The returned list is simply a view into the original list, so changes in the original List are visible in the returned List. This subList() method is particularly useful if you want to sort, search, clear(), or otherwise manipulate only a partial range of a larger list.

An interface cannot specify constructors, but it is conventional that all implementations of List provide at least two standard constructors: one that takes no arguments and creates an empty list; and a copy constructor that accepts an arbitrary Collection object that specifies the initial contents of the new List.

As with Collection, all List methods that change the contents of the list are optional, and implementations that do not support them simply throw java.lang.UnsupportedOperationException. Different implementations of List may have significantly different efficiency characteristics. For example, the get() and set() methods of an ArrayList are much more efficient than those of a LinkedList. On the other hand, the add() and remove() methods of a LinkedList can be more efficient than those of an ArrayList. See also Collection, Set, Map, ArrayList, and LinkedList.

```
public interface List extends Collection {
// Public Instance Methods
    public abstract boolean add(Object o);
    public abstract void add(int index, Object element);
    public abstract boolean addAll(Collection c);
    public abstract boolean addAll(int index, Collection c);
    public abstract void clear();
```

java.util

```
  public abstract boolean contains(Object o);
  public abstract boolean containsAll(Collection c);
  public abstract boolean equals(Object o);
  public abstract Object get(int index);
  public abstract int hashCode();
  public abstract int indexOf(Object o);
  public abstract boolean isEmpty();
  public abstract Iterator iterator();
  public abstract int lastIndexOf(Object o);
  public abstract ListIterator listIterator();
  public abstract ListIterator listIterator(int index);
  public abstract boolean remove(Object o);
  public abstract Object remove(int index);
  public abstract boolean removeAll(Collection c);
  public abstract boolean retainAll(Collection c);
  public abstract Object set(int index, Object element);
  public abstract int size();
  public abstract java.util.List subList(int fromIndex, int toIndex);
  public abstract Object[ ] toArray();
  public abstract Object[ ] toArray(Object[ ] a);
}
```

Hierarchy: (java.util.List(Collection))

Implementations: AbstractList, ArrayList, LinkedList, Vector

Passed To: java.awt.dnd.DragGestureEvent.DragGestureEvent(), Collections.{binarySearch(), copy(), fill(), reverse(), shuffle(), sort(), synchronizedList(), unmodifiableList()}

Returned By: java.awt.dnd.DropTargetContext.getCurrentDataFlavorsAsList(), java.awt.dnd.DropTargetDragEvent.getCurrentDataFlavorsAsList(), java.awt.dnd.DropTargetDropEvent.getCurrentDataFlavorsAsList(), AbstractList.subList(), Arrays.asList(), Collections.{nCopies(), singletonList(), synchronizedList(), unmodifiableList()}, java.util.List.subList(), Vector.subList()

Type Of: Collections.EMPTY_LIST

ListIterator

java.util

Java 1.2

This interface is an extension of Iterator for use with ordered collections, or lists. It defines methods to iterate forward and backward through a list, to determine the list index of the elements being iterated, and, for mutable lists, to safely insert, delete, and edit elements in the list while the iteration is in progress. For some lists, notably LinkedList, using an iterator to enumerate the list's elements may be substantially more efficient than looping through the list by index and calling get() repeatedly.

hasNext() and next() are the most commonly used methods of ListIterator; they iterate forward through the list. See Iterator for details. In addition to these two methods, however, ListIterator also defines hasPrevious() and previous() that allow you to iterate backward through the list. previous() returns the previous element on the list or throws a NoSuchElementException if there is no previous element. hasPrevious() returns true if a subsequent call to previous() returns an object. nextIndex() and previousIndex() return the index of the object that would be returned by a subsequent call to next() or previous(). If next() or previous() throw a NoSuchElementException, nextIndex() returns the size of the list, and previousIndex() returns −1.

ListIterator defines three optionally supported methods that provide a safe way to modify the contents of the underlying list while the iteration is in progress. add() inserts a new object into the list, immediately before the object that would be returned by a subsequent call to next(). Calling add() does not affect the value that is returned by next(), however. If you call previous() immediately after calling add(), the method returns the object you just added. remove() deletes from the list the object most recently returned by next() or previous(). You can only call remove() once per call to next() or previous(). If you have called add(), you must call next() or previous() again before calling remove(). set() replaces the object most recently returned by next() or previous() with the specified object. If you have called add() or remove(), you must call next() or previous() again before calling set(). Remember that support for the add(), remove(), and set() methods is optional. Iterators for immutable lists never support them, of course. An unsupported method throws a java.lang.UnsupportedOperationException when called. Also, when an iterator is in use, all modifications should be made through the iterator rather than to the list itself. If the underlying list is modified while an iteration is ongoing, the ListIterator may fail to operate correctly or may throw a ConcurrentModificationException.

```
public interface ListIterator extends Iterator {
// Public Instance Methods
    public abstract void add(Object o);
    public abstract boolean hasNext();
    public abstract boolean hasPrevious();
    public abstract Object next();
    public abstract int nextIndex();
    public abstract Object previous();
    public abstract int previousIndex();
    public abstract void remove();
    public abstract void set(Object o);
}
```

Hierarchy: (ListIterator(Iterator))

Returned By: AbstractList.listIterator(), AbstractSequentialList.listIterator(), LinkedList.listIterator(), java.util.List.listIterator()

ListResourceBundle
Java 1.1

java.util
PJ1.1

This abstract class provides a simple way to define a ResourceBundle. You may find it easier to subclass ListResourceBundle than to subclass ResourceBundle directly. ListResource-Bundle provides implementations for the abstract handleGetObject() and getKeys() methods defined by ResourceBundle and adds its own abstract getContents() method a subclass must override. getContents() returns an Object[][]—an array of arrays of objects. This array can have any number of elements. Each element of this array must itself be an array with two elements: the first element of each subarray should be a String that specifies the name of a resource, and the corresponding second element should be the value of that resource; this value can be an Object of any desired type. See also ResourceBundle and PropertyResourceBundle.

```
public abstract class ListResourceBundle extends ResourceBundle {
// Public Constructors
    public ListResourceBundle();
// Public Methods Overriding ResourceBundle
    public Enumeration getKeys();
    public final Object handleGetObject(String key);
// Protected Instance Methods
    protected abstract Object[][] getContents();
}
```

Hierarchy: Object→ ResourceBundle→ ListResourceBundle

Subclasses: java.text.resources.DateFormatZoneData, java.text.resources.DateFormatZoneData_en, java.text.resources.LocaleElements, java.text.resources.LocaleElements_en, java.text.resources.LocaleElements_en_US, javax.accessibility.AccessibleResourceBundle

Locale

java.util

Java 1.1

cloneable serializable PJ1.1

The Locale class represents a locale: a political, geographical, or cultural region that typically has a distinct language and distinct customs and conventions for such things as formatting dates, times, and numbers. The Locale class defines a number of constants that represent commonly used locales. Locale also defines a static getDefault() method that returns the default Locale object, which represents a locale value inherited from the host system. getAvailableLocales() returns the list of all locales supported by the underlying system. If none of these methods for obtaining a Locale object are suitable, you can explicitly create your own Locale object. To do this, you must specify a language code, a country code, and an optional variant string. getISOCountries() and getISOLanguages() return the list of supported country codes and language codes.

The Locale class does not implement any internationalization behavior itself; it merely serves as a locale identifier for those classes that can localize their behavior. Given a Locale object, you can invoke the various getDisplay methods to obtain a description of the locale suitable for display to a user. These methods may themselves take a Locale argument, so the names of languages and countries can be localized as appropriate.

```
public final class Locale implements Cloneable, Serializable {
// Public Constructors
    public Locale(String language, String country);
    public Locale(String language, String country, String variant);
// Public Constants
    public static final Locale CANADA;
    public static final Locale CANADA_FRENCH;
    public static final Locale CHINA;
    public static final Locale CHINESE;
    public static final Locale ENGLISH;
    public static final Locale FRANCE;
    public static final Locale FRENCH;
    public static final Locale GERMAN;
    public static final Locale GERMANY;
    public static final Locale ITALIAN;
    public static final Locale ITALY;
    public static final Locale JAPAN;
    public static final Locale JAPANESE;
    public static final Locale KOREA;
    public static final Locale KOREAN;
    public static final Locale PRC;
    public static final Locale SIMPLIFIED_CHINESE;
    public static final Locale TAIWAN;
    public static final Locale TRADITIONAL_CHINESE;
    public static final Locale UK;
    public static final Locale US;
// Public Class Methods
1.2 public static Locale[ ] getAvailableLocales();
    public static Locale getDefault();
1.2 public static String[ ] getISOCountries();
1.2 public static String[ ] getISOLanguages();
```

```
    public static void setDefault(Locale newLocale);                              synchronized
// Property Accessor Methods (by property name)
    public String getCountry();
    public final String getDisplayCountry();
    public String getDisplayCountry(Locale inLocale);
    public final String getDisplayLanguage();
    public String getDisplayLanguage(Locale inLocale);
    public final String getDisplayName();
    public String getDisplayName(Locale inLocale);
    public final String getDisplayVariant();
    public String getDisplayVariant(Locale inLocale);
    public String getISO3Country() throws MissingResourceException;
    public String getISO3Language() throws MissingResourceException;
    public String getLanguage();
    public String getVariant();
// Public Methods Overriding Object
    public Object clone();
    public boolean equals(Object obj);
    public int hashCode();                                                        synchronized
    public final String toString();
}
```

Hierarchy: Object→ Locale(Cloneable, Serializable)

Passed To: Too many methods to list.

Returned By: Too many methods to list.

Type Of: Too many fields to list.

Map   Java 1.2

java.util   *collection*

This interface represents a collection of mappings, or associations, between key objects and value objects. Hashtables and associative arrays are examples of maps. The set of key objects in a Map must not have any duplicates; the collection of value objects is under no such constraint. The key objects should usually be immutable objects, or, if they are not, care should be taken that they do not change while in use in a Map. As of Java 1.2, the Map interface replaces the abstract Dictionary class. Although a Map is not a Collection, the Map interface is still considered an integral part, along with Set, List, and others, of the Java collections framework.

You can add a key/value association to a Map with the put() method. Use putAll() to copy all mappings from one Map to another. Call get() to look up the value object associated with a specified key object. Use remove() to delete the mapping between a specified key and its value, or use clear() to delete all mappings from a Map. size() returns the number of mappings in a Map, and isEmpty() tests whether the Map contains no mappings. containsKey() tests whether a Map contains the specified key object, and containsValue() tests whether it contains the specified value. (For most implementations, containsValue() is a much more expensive operation than containsKey(), however.) keySet() returns a Set of all key objects in the Map. values() returns a Collection (not a Set, since it may contain duplicates) of all value objects in the map. entrySet() returns a Set of all mappings in a Map. The elements of this returned Set are Map.Entry objects. The collections returned by values(), keySet(), and entrySet() are based on the Map itself, so changes to the Map are reflected in the collections.

An interface cannot specify constructors, but it is conventional that all implementations of Map provide at least two standard constructors: one that takes no arguments and creates an empty map, and a copy constructor that accepts a Map object that specifies the initial contents of the new Map.

Implementations are required to support all methods that query the contents of a Map, but support for methods that modify the contents of a Map is optional. If an implementation does not support a particular method, the implementation of that method simply throws a java.lang.UnsupportedOperationException. See also Collection, Set, List, HashMap, Hashtable, WeakHashMap, SortedMap, and TreeMap.

```
public interface Map {
// Inner Classes
    public static interface Entry;
// Public Instance Methods
    public abstract void clear();
    public abstract boolean containsKey(Object key);
    public abstract boolean containsValue(Object value);
    public abstract Set entrySet();
    public abstract boolean equals(Object o);
    public abstract Object get(Object key);
    public abstract int hashCode();
    public abstract boolean isEmpty();
    public abstract Set keySet();
    public abstract Object put(Object key, Object value);
    public abstract void putAll(Map t);
    public abstract Object remove(Object key);
    public abstract int size();
    public abstract Collection values();
}
```

Implementations: java.awt.RenderingHints, AbstractMap, HashMap, Hashtable, SortedMap, WeakHashMap, java.util.jar.Attributes

Passed To: Too many methods to list.

Returned By: java.awt.Font.getAttributes(), java.awt.Toolkit.mapInputMethodHighlight(), java.awt.datatransfer.FlavorMap.{getFlavorsForNatives(), getNativesForFlavors()}, java.awt.datatransfer.SystemFlavorMap.{getFlavorsForNatives(), getNativesForFlavors()}, java.awt.im.InputMethodHighlight.getStyle(), java.sql.Connection.getTypeMap(), java.text.AttributedCharacterIterator.getAttributes(), Collections.{singletonMap(), synchronizedMap(), unmodifiableMap()}, java.util.jar.Manifest.getEntries(), javax.sql.RowSet.getTypeMap()

Type Of: java.awt.Toolkit.desktopProperties, Collections.EMPTY_MAP, java.util.jar.Attributes.map

Map.Entry

java.util

This interface represents a single mapping, or association, between a key object and a value object in a Map. The entrySet() method of a Map returns a Set of Map.Entry objects that represent the set of mappings in the map. Use the iterator() method of that Set to enumerate these Map.Entry objects. Use getKey() and getValue() to obtain the key and value objects for the entry. Use the optionally supported setValue() method to change the value of an entry. This method throws a java.lang.UnsupportedOperationException if it is not supported by the implementation.

```
public static interface Map.Entry {
// Public Instance Methods
    public abstract boolean equals(Object o);
    public abstract Object getKey();
    public abstract Object getValue();
```

```
    public abstract int hashCode();
    public abstract Object setValue(Object value);
}
```

MissingResourceException

java.util   *serializable unchecked PJ1.1*

Signals that no ResourceBundle can be located for the desired locale or that a named resource cannot be found within a given ResourceBundle. getClassName() returns the name of the ResourceBundle class in question, and getKey() returns the name of the resource that cannot be located.

```
public class MissingResourceException extends RuntimeException {
// Public Constructors
    public MissingResourceException(String s, String className, String key);
// Public Instance Methods
    public String getClassName();
    public String getKey();
}
```

Hierarchy: Object→ Throwable(Serializable)→ Exception→ RuntimeException→ MissingResourceException

Thrown By: Locale.{getISO3Country(), getISO3Language()}, ResourceBundle.{getBundle(), getObject(), getString(), getStringArray(), handleGetObject()}

NoSuchElementException

java.util   *serializable unchecked PJ1.1*

Signals that there are no elements in an object (such as a Vector) or that there are no more elements in an object (such as an Enumeration).

```
public class NoSuchElementException extends RuntimeException {
// Public Constructors
    public NoSuchElementException();
    public NoSuchElementException(String s);
}
```

Hierarchy: Object→ Throwable(Serializable)→ Exception→ RuntimeException→ NoSuchElementException

Observable

java.util   *PJ1.1*

This class is the superclass of all observable objects to be used in an object-oriented model/view paradigm. The class methods allow you to add and delete Observer objects on the list maintained by an Observable object and to notify all of the Observer objects on the list. Observer objects are notified by invoking their update() methods. Observable also maintains an internal changed flag that can be set and cleared by the Observable itself and queried with hasChanged() by any interested observer.

```
public class Observable {
// Public Constructors
    public Observable();
// Public Instance Methods
    public void addObserver(Observer o);                         synchronized
    public int countObservers();                                synchronized
```

3

```
    public void deleteObserver(Observer o);                                          synchronized
    public void deleteObservers();                                                   synchronized
    public boolean hasChanged();                                                     synchronized
    public void notifyObservers();
    public void notifyObservers(Object arg);
// Protected Instance Methods
    protected void clearChanged();                                                   synchronized
    protected void setChanged();                                                     synchronized
}
```

Passed To: Observer.update()

Observer   Java 1.0
java.util   PJ1.1

This interface defines the update() method required for an object to observe subclasses
of Observable. An Observer registers interest in an Observable object by calling the addOb-
server() method of Observable. Observer objects that have been registered in this way have
their update() methods invoked by the Observable when that object has changed.

```
public interface Observer {
// Public Instance Methods
    public abstract void update(Observable o, Object arg);
}
```

Passed To: Observable.{addObserver(), deleteObserver()}

Properties   Java 1.0
java.util   cloneable serializable collection PJ1.1

This class is an extension of Hashtable that allows key/value pairs to be read from and
written to a stream. The Properties class implements the system properties list, which
supports user customization by allowing programs to look up the values of named
resources. Because the load() and store() methods provide an easy way to read and write
properties from and to a text stream, this class provides a convenient way to implement
an application configuration file.

When you create a Properties object, you may specify another Properties object that contains default values. Keys (property names) and values are associated in a Properties
object with the Hashtable method put(). Values are looked up with getProperty(); if this
method does not find the key in the current Properties object, it looks in the default Properties object that was passed to the constructor method. A default value can also be
specified, in case the key is not found at all. Use setProperty() to add a property name/
value pair to the Properties object. This Java 1.2 method is preferred over the inherited
put() method because it enforces the constraint that property names and values be
strings.

propertyNames() returns an enumeration of all property names (keys) stored in the Properties object and (recursively) all property names stored in the default Properties object
associated with it. list() prints the properties stored in a Properties object, which can be
useful for debugging. store() writes a Properties object to a stream, writing one property
per line, in name=value format. As of Java 1.2, store() is preferred over the deprecated
save() method, which writes properties in the same way but suppresses any I/O exceptions that may be thrown in the process. The second argument to both store() and save()
is a comment that is written out at the beginning of the property file. Finally, load()
reads key/value pairs from a stream and stores them in a Properties object. It is suitable
for reading both properties written with store() and hand-edited properties files.

```
public class Properties extends Hashtable {
// Public Constructors
    public Properties( );
    public Properties(Properties defaults);
// Public Instance Methods
    public String getProperty(String key);
    public String getProperty(String key, String defaultValue);
    public void list(java.io.PrintStream out);
1.1 public void list(java.io.PrintWriter out);
    public void load(java.io.InputStream inStream) throws java.io.IOException;         synchronized
    public Enumeration propertyNames( );
1.2 public Object setProperty(String key, String value);                              synchronized
1.2 public void store(java.io.OutputStream out, String header) throws java.io.IOException;   synchronized
// Protected Instance Fields
    protected Properties defaults;
// Deprecated Public Methods
#   public void save(java.io.OutputStream out, String header);                        synchronized
}
```

Hierarchy: Object→ Dictionary→ Hashtable(Cloneable, Map, Serializable)→ Properties

Subclasses: java.security.Provider

Passed To: java.awt.Toolkit.getPrintJob(), System.setProperties(),
java.rmi.activation.ActivationGroupDesc.ActivationGroupDesc(), java.sql.Driver.{connect(),
getPropertyInfo()}, java.sql.DriverManager.getConnection(), Properties.Properties(),
javax.ejb.deployment.DeploymentDescriptor.setEnvironmentProperties(),
javax.naming.CompoundName.CompoundName(), org.omg.CORBA.ORB.{init(), set_parameters()}

Returned By: System.getProperties(), java.rmi.activation.ActivationGroupDesc.getPropertyOverrides(),
javax.ejb.EJBContext.getEnvironment(),
javax.ejb.deployment.DeploymentDescriptor.getEnvironmentProperties()

Type Of: Properties.defaults, javax.naming.CompoundName.mySyntax

PropertyPermission   Java 1.2

java.util   *serializable permission*

This class is a java.security.Permission that governs read and write access to system properties with System.getProperty() and System.setProperty(). A PropertyPermission object has a
name, or target, and a comma-separated list of actions. The name of the permission is
the name of the property of interest. The action string can be "read" for getProperty()
access, "write" for setProperty() access, or "read,write" for both types of access.
PropertyPermission extends java.security.BasicPermission, so the name of the property supports simple wildcards. The name "*" represents any property name. If a name ends
with ".*", it represents any property names that share the specified prefix. For example,
the name "java.*" represents "java.version", "java.vendor", "java.vendor.url", and all
other properties that begin with "java".

Granting access to system properties is not overtly dangerous, but caution is still necessary. Some properties, such as "user.home", reveal details about the host system that
malicious code can use to mount an attack. Programmers writing system-level code and
system administrators configuring security policies may need to use this class, but applications never need to use it.

```
public final class PropertyPermission extends java.security.BasicPermission {
// Public Constructors
    public PropertyPermission(String name, String actions);
```

```
// Public Methods Overriding BasicPermission
    public boolean equals(Object obj);
    public String getActions();
    public int hashCode();
    public boolean implies(java.security.Permission p);
    public java.security.PermissionCollection newPermissionCollection();
}
```

Hierarchy: Object→ java.security.Permission(java.security.Guard, Serializable) →
java.security.BasicPermission(Serializable)→ PropertyPermission

PropertyResourceBundle
java.util

Java 1.1
PJ1.1

This class is a concrete subclass of ResourceBundle. It reads a Properties file from a specified InputStream and implements the ResourceBundle API for looking up named resources from the resulting Properties object. A Properties file contains lines of the form:

> name=value

Each such line defines a named property with the specified String value. Although you can instantiate a PropertyResourceBundle yourself, it is more common to simply define a Properties file and then allow ResourceBundle.getBundle() to look up that file and return the necessary PropertyResourceBundle object. See also Properties and ResourceBundle.

```
public class PropertyResourceBundle extends ResourceBundle {
// Public Constructors
    public PropertyResourceBundle(java.io.InputStream stream) throws java.io.IOException;
// Public Methods Overriding ResourceBundle
    public Enumeration getKeys();
    public Object handleGetObject(String key);
}
```

Hierarchy: Object→ ResourceBundle→ PropertyResourceBundle

Random
java.util

Java 1.0
serializable PJ1.1

This class implements a pseudo-random number generator suitable for games and similar applications. If you need a cryptographic-strength source of pseudo-randomness, see java.security.SecureRandom. nextDouble() and nextFloat() return a value between 0.0 and 1.0. nextLong() and the no-argument version of nextInt() return long and int values distributed across the range of those data types. In Java 1.2, if you pass an argument to nextInt(), it returns a value between zero (inclusive) and the specified number (exclusive). nextGaussian() returns pseudo-random floating-point values with a Gaussian distribution; the mean of the values is 0.0 and the standard deviation is 1.0. nextBoolean() returns a pseudo-random boolean value, and nextBytes() fills in the specified byte array with pseudo-random bytes. You can use the setSeed() method or the optional constructor argument to initialize the pseudo-random number generator with some variable seed value other than the current time (the default) or with a constant to ensure a repeatable sequence of pseudo-randomness.

```
public class Random implements Serializable {
// Public Constructors
    public Random();
    public Random(long seed);
```

```
// Public Instance Methods
1.2 public boolean nextBoolean();
1.1 public void nextBytes(byte[ ] bytes);
    public double nextDouble();
    public float nextFloat();
    public double nextGaussian();                                        synchronized
    public int nextInt();
1.2 public int nextInt(int n);
    public long nextLong();
    public void setSeed(long seed);                                      synchronized
// Protected Instance Methods
    protected int next(int bits);                                        synchronized
}
```

Hierarchy: Object→ Random(Serializable)

Subclasses: java.security.SecureRandom

Passed To: java.math.BigInteger.BigInteger(), Collections.shuffle()

ResourceBundle   Java 1.1

java.util   PJ1.1

This abstract class allows subclasses to define sets of localized resources that can then be dynamically loaded as needed by internationalized programs. Such resources may include user-visible text and images that appear in an application, as well as more complex things such as Menu objects. Use getBundle() to load a ResourceBundle subclass that is appropriate for the default or specified locale. Use getObject(), getString(), and getStringArray() to look up a named resource in a bundle. To define a bundle, provide implementations of handleGetObject() and getKeys(). It is often easier, however, to subclass ListResourceBundle or provide a Properties file that is used by PropertyResourceBundle. The name of any localized ResourceBundle class you define should include the locale language code, and, optionally, the locale country code.

```
public abstract class ResourceBundle {
// Public Constructors
    public ResourceBundle();
// Public Class Methods
    public static final ResourceBundle getBundle(String baseName) throws MissingResourceException;
    public static final ResourceBundle getBundle(String baseName, Locale locale);
    public static ResourceBundle getBundle(String baseName, Locale locale, ClassLoader loader)
        throws MissingResourceException;
// Public Instance Methods
    public abstract Enumeration getKeys();
1.2 public Locale getLocale();
    public final Object getObject(String key) throws MissingResourceException;
    public final String getString(String key) throws MissingResourceException;
    public final String[ ] getStringArray(String key) throws MissingResourceException;
// Protected Instance Methods
    protected abstract Object handleGetObject(String key) throws MissingResourceException;
    protected void setParent(ResourceBundle parent);
// Protected Instance Fields
    protected ResourceBundle parent;
}
```

Subclasses: ListResourceBundle, PropertyResourceBundle

Passed To: java.awt.ComponentOrientation.getOrientation(), java.awt.Window.applyResourceBundle(), ResourceBundle.setParent()

Returned By: ResourceBundle.getBundle()

Type Of: ResourceBundle.parent

Set

Java 1.2

java.util

collection

This interface represents an unordered Collection of objects that contains no duplicate elements. That is, a Set cannot contain two elements e1 and e2 where e1.equals(e2), and it can contain at most one null element. The Set interface defines the same methods as its superinterface, Collection. It constrains the add() and addAll() methods from adding duplicate elements to the Set.

An interface cannot specify constructors, but it is conventional that all implementations of Set provide at least two standard constructors: one that takes no arguments and creates an empty set, and a copy constructor that accepts a Collection object that specifies the initial contents of the new Set. This copy constructor must ensure that duplicate elements are not added to the Set, of course.

As with Collection, the Set methods that modify the contents of the set are optional, and implementations that do not support these methods simply throw java.lang.Unsupported-OperationException. See also Collection, List, Map, SortedSet, HashSet, and TreeSet.

```
public interface Set extends Collection {
// Public Instance Methods
    public abstract boolean add(Object o);
    public abstract boolean addAll(Collection c);
    public abstract void clear();
    public abstract boolean contains(Object o);
    public abstract boolean containsAll(Collection c);
    public abstract boolean equals(Object o);
    public abstract int hashCode();
    public abstract boolean isEmpty();
    public abstract Iterator iterator();
    public abstract boolean remove(Object o);
    public abstract boolean removeAll(Collection c);
    public abstract boolean retainAll(Collection c);
    public abstract int size();
    public abstract Object[ ] toArray();
    public abstract Object[ ] toArray(Object[ ] a);
}
```

Hierarchy: (Set(Collection))

Implementations: AbstractSet, HashSet, SortedSet

Passed To: java.text.AttributedCharacterIterator.{getRunLimit(), getRunStart()}, Collections.{synchronizedSet(), unmodifiableSet()}

Returned By: Too many methods to list.

Type Of: Collections.EMPTY_SET

SimpleTimeZone

Java 1.1

java.util

cloneable serializable PJ1.1

This concrete subclass of TimeZone is a simple implementation of that abstract class that is suitable for use in locales that use the Gregorian calendar. Programs do not normally need to instantiate this class directly; instead, they use one of the static factory methods of TimeZone to obtain a suitable TimeZone subclass. The only reason to instantiate this class directly is if you need to support a time zone with non-standard-daylight-savings-time rules. In that case, you can call setStartRule() and setEndRule() to specify the starting and ending dates of daylight-savings time for the time zone.

```
public class SimpleTimeZone extends TimeZone {
// Public Constructors
    public SimpleTimeZone(int rawOffset, String ID);
    public SimpleTimeZone(int rawOffset, String ID, int startMonth, int startDay, int startDayOfWeek, int startTime,
                          int endMonth, int endDay, int endDayOfWeek, int endTime);
    public SimpleTimeZone(int rawOffset, String ID, int startMonth, int startDay, int startDayOfWeek, int startTime,
                          int endMonth, int endDay, int endDayOfWeek, int endTime, int dstSavings);
// Public Instance Methods
1.2 public int getDSTSavings();
1.2 public void setDSTSavings(int millisSavedDuringDST);
1.2 public void setEndRule(int month, int dayOfMonth, int time);
    public void setEndRule(int month, int dayOfWeekInMonth, int dayOfWeek, int time);
1.2 public void setEndRule(int month, int dayOfMonth, int dayOfWeek, int time, boolean after);
1.2 public void setStartRule(int month, int dayOfMonth, int time);
    public void setStartRule(int month, int dayOfWeekInMonth, int dayOfWeek, int time);
1.2 public void setStartRule(int month, int dayOfMonth, int dayOfWeek, int time, boolean after);
    public void setStartYear(int year);
// Public Methods Overriding TimeZone
    public Object clone();
    public int getOffset(int era, int year, int month, int day, int dayOfWeek, int millis);
    public int getRawOffset();
1.2 public boolean hasSameRules(TimeZone other);
    public boolean inDaylightTime(java.util.Date date);
    public void setRawOffset(int offsetMillis);
    public boolean useDaylightTime();
// Public Methods Overriding Object
    public boolean equals(Object obj);
    public int hashCode();                                                     synchronized
    public String toString();
}
```

Hierarchy: Object→ TimeZone(Cloneable, Serializable)→ SimpleTimeZone

SortedMap   Java 1.2
java.util   *collection*

This interface represents a Map object that keeps its set of key objects in sorted order. As with Map, it is conventional that all implementations of this interface define a no-argument constructor to create an empty map and a copy constructor that accepts a Map object that specifies the initial contents of the SortedMap. Furthermore, when creating a SortedMap, there should be a way to specify a Comparator object to sort the key objects of the map. If no Comparator is specified, all key objects must implement the java.lang.Comparable interface so they can be sorted in their natural order. See also Map, TreeMap, and SortedSet.

The inherited keySet(), values(), and entrySet() methods return collections that can be iterated in the sorted order. firstKey() and lastKey() return the lowest and highest key values in the SortedMap. subMap() returns a SortedMap that contains only mappings for keys from (and including) the first specified key up to (but not including) the second specified key. headMap() returns a SortedMap that contains mappings whose keys are less than (but not equal to) the specified key. tailMap() returns a SortedMap that contains mappings whose keys are greater than or equal to the specified key. subMap(), headMap(), and tailMap() return SortedMap objects that are simply views of the original SortedMap; any changes in the original map are reflected in the returned map and vice versa.

```
public interface SortedMap extends Map {
// Public Instance Methods
    public abstract Comparator comparator();
    public abstract Object firstKey();
    public abstract SortedMap headMap(Object toKey);
    public abstract Object lastKey();
    public abstract SortedMap subMap(Object fromKey, Object toKey);
    public abstract SortedMap tailMap(Object fromKey);
}
```

Hierarchy: (SortedMap(Map))

Implementations: TreeMap

Passed To: Collections.{synchronizedSortedMap(), unmodifiableSortedMap()}, TreeMap.TreeMap()

Returned By: Collections.{synchronizedSortedMap(), unmodifiableSortedMap()}, SortedMap.{headMap(), subMap(), tailMap()}, TreeMap.{headMap(), subMap(), tailMap()}

SortedSet   Java 1.2

java.util   *collection*

This interface is a Set that sorts its elements and guarantees that its iterator() method returns an Iterator that enumerates the elements of the set in sorted order. As with the Set interface, it is conventional for all implementations of SortedSet to provide a no-argument constructor that creates an empty set and a copy constructor that expects a Collection object specifying the initial (unsorted) contents of the set. Furthermore, when creating a SortedSet, there should be a way to specify a Comparator object that compares and sorts the elements of the set. If no Comparator is specified, the elements of the set must all implement java.lang.Comparable so they can be sorted in their natural order. See also Set, TreeSet, and SortedMap.

SortedSet defines a few methods in addition to those it inherits from the Set interface. first() and last() return the lowest and highest objects in the set. headSet() returns all elements from the beginning of the set up to (but not including) the specified element. tailSet() returns all elements between (and including) the specified element and the end of the set. subSet() returns all elements of the set from (and including) the first specified element up to (but excluding) the second specified element. Note that all three methods return a SortedSet that is implemented as a view onto the original SortedSet. Changes in the original set are visible through the returned set and vice versa.

```
public interface SortedSet extends Set {
// Public Instance Methods
    public abstract Comparator comparator();
    public abstract Object first();
    public abstract SortedSet headSet(Object toElement);
    public abstract Object last();
    public abstract SortedSet subSet(Object fromElement, Object toElement);
    public abstract SortedSet tailSet(Object fromElement);
}
```

Hierarchy: (SortedSet(Set(Collection)))

Implementations: TreeSet

Passed To: Collections.{synchronizedSortedSet(), unmodifiableSortedSet()}, TreeSet.TreeSet()

Returned By: Collections.{synchronizedSortedSet(), unmodifiableSortedSet()}, SortedSet.{headSet(), subSet(), tailSet()}, TreeSet.{headSet(), subSet(), tailSet()}

Stack   Java 1.0

java.util   *cloneable serializable collection PJ1.1*

This class implements a last-in-first-out (LIFO) stack of objects. push() puts an object on the top of the stack. pop() removes and returns the top object from the stack. peek() returns the top object without removing it. In Java 1.2, you can instead use a LinkedList as a stack.

```
public class Stack extends Vector {
// Public Constructors
    public Stack( );
// Public Instance Methods
    public boolean empty( );
    public Object peek( );                                         synchronized
    public Object pop( );                                          synchronized
    public Object push(Object item);
    public int search(Object o);                                   synchronized
}
```

Hierarchy: Object→ AbstractCollection(Collection)→ AbstractList(java.util.List(Collection))→ Vector(Cloneable, java.util.List(Collection), Serializable)→ Stack

StringTokenizer   Java 1.0

java.util   *PJ1.1*

When a StringTokenizer is instantiated with a String, it breaks the string up into tokens separated by any of the characters in the specified string of delimiters. (For example, words separated by space and tab characters are tokens.) The hasMoreTokens() and nextToken() methods obtain the tokens in order. countTokens() returns the number of tokens in the string. StringTokenizer implements the Enumeration interface, so you may also access the tokens with the familiar hasMoreElements() and nextElement() methods. When you create a StringTokenizer, you can specify a string of delimiter characters to use for the entire string, or you can rely on the default whitespace delimiters. You can also specify whether the delimiters themselves should be returned as tokens. Finally, you can optionally specify a new string of delimiter characters when you call nextToken().

```
public class StringTokenizer implements Enumeration {
// Public Constructors
    public StringTokenizer(String str);
    public StringTokenizer(String str, String delim);
    public StringTokenizer(String str, String delim, boolean returnDelims);
// Public Instance Methods
    public int countTokens( );
    public boolean hasMoreTokens( );
    public String nextToken( );
    public String nextToken(String delim);
// Methods Implementing Enumeration
    public boolean hasMoreElements( );
    public Object nextElement( );
}
```

Hierarchy: Object→ StringTokenizer(Enumeration)

java.util

Timer

java.util

This class implements a timer: its methods allow you to schedule one or more runnable TimerTask objects to be executed (once or repetitively) by a background thread at a specified time in the future. You can create a timer with the Timer() constructor. The no-argument version of this constructor creates a regular non-daemon background thread, which means that the Java VM will not terminate while the timer thread is running. Pass true to the constructor if you want the background thread to be a daemon thread.

Once you have created a Timer, you can schedule TimerTask objects to be run in the future with the various schedule() and scheduleAtFixedRate() methods. To schedule a task for a single execution, use one of the two-argument schedule() methods and specify the desired execution time either as a number of milliseconds in the future or as an absolute Date. If the number of milliseconds is 0, or if the Date object represents a time already passed, the task is scheduled for immediate execution.

To schedule a repeating task, use one of the three-argument versions of schedule() or scheduleAtFixedRate(). These methods are passed an argument that specifies the time (either as a number of milliseconds or as a Date object) of the first execution of the task and another argument, *period*, that specifies the number of milliseconds between repeated executions of the task. The schedule() methods schedule the task for *fixed-interval* execution. That is, each execution is scheduled for *period* milliseconds after the previous execution *ends*. Use schedule() for tasks such as animation, where it is important to have a relatively constant interval between executions. The scheduleAtFixedRate() methods, on the other hand, schedule tasks for *fixed-rate* execution. That is, each repetition of the task is scheduled for *period* milliseconds after the previous execution *begins*. Use scheduleAtFixedRate() for tasks, such as updating a clock display, that must occur at specific absolute times rather than at fixed intervals.

A single Timer object can comfortably schedule many TimerTask objects. Note, however, that all tasks scheduled by a single Timer share a single thread. If you are scheduling many rapidly repeating tasks, or if some tasks take a long time to execute, other tasks may have their scheduled executions delayed.

When you are done with a Timer, call cancel() to stop its associated thread from running. This is particularly important when you are using a timer whose associated thread is not a daemon thread, because otherwise the timer thread can prevent the Java VM from exiting. To cancel the execution of a particular task, use the cancel() method of TimerTask.

```
public class Timer {
// Public Constructors
    public Timer();
    public Timer(boolean isDaemon);
// Public Instance Methods
    public void cancel();
    public void schedule(TimerTask task, long delay);
    public void schedule(TimerTask task, java.util.Date time);
    public void schedule(TimerTask task, java.util.Date firstTime, long period);
    public void schedule(TimerTask task, long delay, long period);
    public void scheduleAtFixedRate(TimerTask task, long delay, long period);
    public void scheduleAtFixedRate(TimerTask task, java.util.Date firstTime, long period);
}
```

TimerTask

java.util

This abstract Runnable class represents a task that is scheduled with a Timer object for one-time or repeated execution in the future. You can define a task by subclassing TimerTask and implementing the abstract run() method. Schedule the task for future execution by passing an instance of your subclass to one of the schedule() or scheduleAtFixedRate() methods of Timer. The Timer object will then invoke the run() method at the scheduled time or times.

Call cancel() to cancel the one-time or repeated execution of a TimerTask(). This method returns true if a pending execution was actually canceled. It returns false if the task has already been canceled, was never scheduled, or was scheduled for one-time execution and has already been executed. scheduledExecutionTime() returns the time in milliseconds at which the most recent execution of the TimerTask was scheduled to occur. When the host system is heavily loaded, the run() method may not be invoked exactly when scheduled. Some tasks may choose to do nothing if they are not invoked on time. The run() method can compare the return values of scheduledExecutionTime() and System.currentTimeMillis() to determine whether the current invocation is sufficiently timely.

```
public abstract class TimerTask implements Runnable {
// Protected Constructors
    protected TimerTask();
// Public Instance Methods
    public boolean cancel();
    public long scheduledExecutionTime();
// Methods Implementing Runnable
    public abstract void run();
}
```

Hierarchy: Object→ TimerTask(Runnable)

Passed To: java.util.Timer.{schedule(), scheduleAtFixedRate()}

TimeZone

java.util

The TimeZone class represents a time zone; it is used with the Calendar and DateFormat classes. As an abstract class, TimeZone cannot be directly instantiated. Instead, you should call the static getDefault() method to obtain a TimeZone object that represents the time zone inherited from the host operating system. Or you can call the static getTimeZone() method with the name of the desired zone. You can obtain a list of the supported time-zone names by calling the static getAvailableIDs() method.

Once you have a TimeZone object, you can call inDaylightTime() to determine whether, for a given Date, daylight-savings time is in effect for that time zone. Call getID() to obtain the name of the time zone. Call getOffset() for a given date to determine the number of milliseconds to add to GMT to convert to the time zone.

```
public abstract class TimeZone implements Cloneable, Serializable {
// Public Constructors
    public TimeZone();
// Public Constants
1.2 public static final int LONG;                                               =1
1.2 public static final int SHORT;                                              =0
// Public Class Methods
    public static String[ ] getAvailableIDs();                         synchronized
    public static String[ ] getAvailableIDs(int rawOffset);            synchronized
```

java.util

```
    public static TimeZone getDefault();                                                     synchronized
    public static TimeZone getTimeZone(String ID);                                           synchronized
    public static void setDefault(TimeZone zone);                                            synchronized
// Property Accessor Methods (by property name)
1.2 public final String getDisplayName();
1.2 public final String getDisplayName(Locale locale);
1.2 public final String getDisplayName(boolean daylight, int style);
1.2 public String getDisplayName(boolean daylight, int style, Locale locale);
    public String getID();
    public void setID(String ID);
    public abstract int getRawOffset();
    public abstract void setRawOffset(int offsetMillis);
// Public Instance Methods
    public abstract int getOffset(int era, int year, int month, int day, int dayOfWeek, int milliseconds);
1.2 public boolean hasSameRules(TimeZone other);
    public abstract boolean inDaylightTime(java.util.Date date);
    public abstract boolean useDaylightTime();
// Public Methods Overriding Object
    public Object clone();
}
```

Hierarchy: Object→ TimeZone(Cloneable, Serializable)

Subclasses: SimpleTimeZone

Passed To: java.text.DateFormat.setTimeZone(), Calendar.{Calendar(), getInstance(), setTimeZone()}, GregorianCalendar.GregorianCalendar(), SimpleTimeZone.hasSameRules(), TimeZone.{hasSameRules(), setDefault()}

Returned By: java.text.DateFormat.getTimeZone(), Calendar.getTimeZone(), TimeZone.{getDefault(), getTimeZone()}

TooManyListenersException   Java 1.1

java.util   *serializable checked PJ1.1*

Signals that an AWT component, JavaBeans component, or Swing component can have only one EventListener object registered for some specific type of event. That is, it signals that a particular event is a unicast event rather than a multicast event. This exception type serves a formal purpose in the Java event model; its presence in the throws clause of an EventListener registration method (even if the method never actually throws the exception) signals that an event is a unicast event.

```
public class TooManyListenersException extends Exception {
// Public Constructors
    public TooManyListenersException();
    public TooManyListenersException(String s);
}
```

Hierarchy: Object→ Throwable(Serializable)→ Exception→ TooManyListenersException

Thrown By: java.awt.dnd.DragGestureRecognizer.addDragGestureListener(), java.awt.dnd.DragSourceContext.addDragSourceListener(), java.awt.dnd.DropTarget.addDropTargetListener(), java.beans.beancontext.BeanContextServices.getService(), java.beans.beancontext.BeanContextServicesSupport.getService()

TreeMap

java.util

This class implements the SortedMap interface using an internal Red-Black tree data structure and guarantees that the keys and values of the mapping can be enumerated in ascending order of keys. TreeMap supports all optional Map methods. The objects used as keys in a TreeMap must all be mutually Comparable, or an appropriate Comparator must be provided when the TreeMap is created. Because TreeMap is based on a binary tree data structure, the get(), put(), remove(), and containsKey() methods operate in relatively efficient logarithmic time. If you do not need the sorting capability of TreeMap, however, use HashMap instead, as it is even more efficient. See Map and SortedMap for details on the methods of TreeMap. See also the related TreeSet class.

In order for a TreeMap to work correctly, the comparison method from the Comparable or Comparator interface must be consistent with the equals() method. That is, the equals() method must compare two objects as equal if and only if the comparison method also indicates those two objects are equal.

The methods of TreeMap are not synchronized. If you are working in a multithreaded environment, you must explicitly synchronize all code that modifies the TreeMap, or obtain a synchronized wrapper with Collections.synchronizedMap().

```
public class TreeMap extends AbstractMap implements Cloneable, Serializable, SortedMap {
// Public Constructors
    public TreeMap( );
    public TreeMap(Map m);
    public TreeMap(SortedMap m);
    public TreeMap(Comparator c);
// Methods Implementing Map
    public void clear( );
    public boolean containsKey(Object key);
    public boolean containsValue(Object value);
    public Set entrySet( );
    public Object get(Object key);
    public Set keySet( );
    public Object put(Object key, Object value);
    public void putAll(Map map);
    public Object remove(Object key);
    public int size( );
    public Collection values( );
// Methods Implementing SortedMap
    public Comparator comparator( );
    public Object firstKey( );
    public SortedMap headMap(Object toKey);
    public Object lastKey( );
    public SortedMap subMap(Object fromKey, Object toKey);
    public SortedMap tailMap(Object fromKey);
// Public Methods Overriding Object
    public Object clone( );
}
```

Hierarchy: Object→ AbstractMap(Map)→ TreeMap(Cloneable, Serializable, SortedMap(Map))

TreeSet

java.util

This class implements SortedSet, provides support for all optional methods, and guarantees that the elements of the set can be enumerated in ascending order. In order to be sorted, the elements of the set must all be mutually Comparable objects, or they must all be compatible with a Comparator object that is specified when the TreeSet is created. TreeSet is implemented on top of a TreeMap, so its add(), remove(), and contains() methods all operate in relatively efficient logarithmic time. If you do not need the sorting capability of TreeSet, however, use HashSet instead, as it is significantly more efficient. See Set, SortedSet, and Collection for details on the methods of TreeSet.

In order for a TreeSet to operate correctly, the Comparable or Comparator comparison method must be consistent with the equals() method. That is, the equals() method must compare two objects as equal if and only if the comparison method also indicates those two objects are equal.

The methods of TreeSet are not synchronized. If you are working in a multithreaded environment, you must explicitly synchronize code that modifies the contents of the set,x or obtain a synchronized wrapper with Collections.synchronizedSet().

```
public class TreeSet extends AbstractSet implements Cloneable, Serializable, SortedSet {
// Public Constructors
    public TreeSet( );
    public TreeSet(SortedSet s);
    public TreeSet(Comparator c);
    public TreeSet(Collection c);
// Methods Implementing Set
    public boolean add(Object o);
    public boolean addAll(Collection c);
    public void clear( );
    public boolean contains(Object o);
    public boolean isEmpty( );                                                 default:true
    public Iterator iterator( );
    public boolean remove(Object o);
    public int size( );
// Methods Implementing SortedSet
    public Comparator comparator( );
    public Object first( );
    public SortedSet headSet(Object toElement);
    public Object last( );
    public SortedSet subSet(Object fromElement, Object toElement);
    public SortedSet tailSet(Object fromElement);
// Public Methods Overriding Object
    public Object clone( );
}
```

Hierarchy: Object → AbstractCollection(Collection) → AbstractSet(Set(Collection)) → TreeSet(Cloneable, Serializable, SortedSet(Set(Collection)))

Vector   Java 1.0
java.util   *cloneable serializable collection PJ1.1*

This class implements an ordered collection—essentially an array—of objects that can grow or shrink as necessary. Vector is useful when you need to keep track of a number of objects, but do not know in advance how many there will be. Use setElementAt() to set the object at a given index of a Vector. Use elementAt() to retrieve the object stored at a specified index. Note that you typically must cast the Object returned by elementAt() to the desired type. Call add() to append an object to the end of the Vector or to insert an object at any specified position. Use removeElementAt() to delete the element at a specified index or removeElement() to remove a specified object from the vector. size() returns the number of objects currently in the Vector. elements() returns an Enumeration that allows you to iterate through those objects. capacity() is not the same as size(); it returns the maximum number of objects a Vector can hold before its internal storage must be resized. Vector automatically resizes its internal storage for you, but if you know in advance how many objects a Vector will contain, you can increase its efficiency by pre-allocating this many elements with ensureCapacity().

Vector has been part of the java.util package since Java 1.0, but in Java 1.2 it has been enhanced to implement the List interface. List defines new names for many of the methods already present in Vector; see List for details on those methods. Vector is quite similar to the ArrayList class, except that the methods of Vector are synchronized, which makes them thread-safe but increases the overhead of calling them. If you need thread safety or need to be compatible with Java 1.0 or Java 1.1, use Vector; otherwise, use ArrayList.

```
public class Vector extends AbstractList implements Cloneable, java.util.List, Serializable {
// Public Constructors
     public Vector();
1.2  public Vector(Collection c);
     public Vector(int initialCapacity);
     public Vector(int initialCapacity, int capacityIncrement);
// Public Instance Methods
     public void addElement(Object obj);                                                synchronized
     public int capacity();
     public void copyInto(Object[ ] anArray);                                           synchronized
     public Object elementAt(int index);                                                synchronized
     public Enumeration elements();
     public void ensureCapacity(int minCapacity);                                       synchronized
     public Object firstElement();                                                      synchronized
     public int indexOf(Object elem, int index);                                        synchronized
     public void insertElementAt(Object obj, int index);                                synchronized
     public Object lastElement();                                                       synchronized
     public int lastIndexOf(Object elem, int index);                                    synchronized
     public void removeAllElements();                                                   synchronized
     public boolean removeElement(Object obj);                                          synchronized
     public void removeElementAt(int index);                                            synchronized
     public void setElementAt(Object obj, int index);                                   synchronized
     public void setSize(int newSize);                                                  synchronized
     public void trimToSize();                                                          synchronized
// Methods Implementing List
1.2  public boolean add(Object o);                                                      synchronized
1.2  public void add(int index, Object element);
1.2  public boolean addAll(Collection c);                                              synchronized
1.2  public boolean addAll(int index, Collection c);                                   synchronized
1.2  public void clear();
     public boolean contains(Object elem);
1.2  public boolean containsAll(Collection c);                                         synchronized
1.2  public boolean equals(Object o);                                                  synchronized
1.2  public Object get(int index);                                                     synchronized
1.2  public int hashCode();                                                            synchronized
     public int indexOf(Object elem);
     public boolean isEmpty();                                                         default:true
     public int lastIndexOf(Object elem);
1.2  public boolean remove(Object o);
1.2  public Object remove(int index);                                                  synchronized
1.2  public boolean removeAll(Collection c);                                           synchronized
1.2  public boolean retainAll(Collection c);                                           synchronized
1.2  public Object set(int index, Object element);                                     synchronized
     public int size();
1.2  public java.util.List subList(int fromIndex, int toIndex);
```

```
1.2 public Object[ ] toArray();                                         synchronized
1.2 public Object[ ] toArray(Object[ ] a);                              synchronized
// Protected Methods Overriding AbstractList
1.2 protected void removeRange(int fromIndex, int toIndex);
// Public Methods Overriding AbstractCollection
    public String toString();                                          synchronized
// Public Methods Overriding Object
    public Object clone();                                             synchronized
// Protected Instance Fields
    protected int capacityIncrement;
    protected int elementCount;
    protected Object[ ] elementData;
}
```

Hierarchy: Object→ AbstractCollection(Collection)→ AbstractList(java.util.List(Collection))→
Vector(Cloneable, java.util.List(Collection), Serializable)

Subclasses: Stack

Passed To: Too many methods to list.

Returned By: java.awt.image.BufferedImage.getSources(),
java.awt.image.RenderedImage.getSources(),
java.awt.image.renderable.ParameterBlock.{getParameters(), getSources()},
java.awt.image.renderable.RenderableImage.getSources(),
java.awt.image.renderable.RenderableImageOp.getSources(),
javax.swing.table.DefaultTableModel.{convertToVector(), getDataVector()},
javax.swing.text.GapContent.getPositionsInRange(), javax.swing.text.StringContent.getPositionsInRange()

Type Of: Too many fields to list.

WeakHashMap   Java 1.2

java.util   *collection*

This class implements Map using an internal hashtable. It is similar in features and performance to HashMap, except that it uses the capabilities of the java.lang.ref package, so
that the key-to-value mappings it maintains do not prevent the key objects from being
reclaimed by the garbage collector. When there are no more references to a key object
except for the weak reference maintained by the WeakHashMap, the garbage collector
reclaims the object, and the WeakHashMap deletes the mapping between the reclaimed
key and its associated value. If there are no references to the value object except for
the one maintained by the WeakHashMap, the value object also becomes available for
garbage collection. Thus, you can use a WeakHashMap to associate an auxiliary value
with an object without preventing either the object (the key) or the auxiliary value from
being reclaimed. See HashMap for a discussion of the implementation features of this
class. See Map for a description of the methods it defines.

WeakHashMap is primarily useful with objects whose equals() methods use the == operator for comparison. It is less useful with key objects of type String, for example, because
there can be multiple String objects that are equal to one another and, even if the original key value has been reclaimed by the garbage collector, it is always possible to pass
a String with the same value to the get() method.

```
public class WeakHashMap extends AbstractMap implements Map {
// Public Constructors
    public WeakHashMap();
1.3 public WeakHashMap(Map t);
    public WeakHashMap(int initialCapacity);
```

```
    public WeakHashMap(int initialCapacity, float loadFactor);
// Methods Implementing Map
    public void clear( );
    public boolean containsKey(Object key);
    public Set entrySet( );
    public Object get(Object key);
    public boolean isEmpty( );                                              default:true
    public Object put(Object key, Object value);
    public Object remove(Object key);
    public int size( );
}
```

Hierarchy: Object→ AbstractMap(Map)→ WeakHashMap(Map)

CHAPTER 24

The java.util.jar Package

The java.util.jar package contains classes for reading and writing Java archive, or JAR, files. A JAR file is nothing more than a ZIP file whose first entry is a specially named manifest file that contains attributes and digital signatures for the ZIP file entries that follow it. Many of the classes in this package are relatively simple extensions of classes from the java.util.zip package. Figure 24-1 shows the class hierarchy of this package.

The easiest way to read a JAR file is with the random-access JarFile class. This class allows you to obtain the JarEntry that describes any named file within the JAR archive. It also allows you to obtain an enumeration of all entries in the archive and an InputStream for reading the bytes of a specific JarEntry. Each JarEntry describes a single entry in the archive and allows access to the Attributes and the digital signatures associated with the entry. The JarFile also provides access to the Manifest object for the JAR archive; this object contains Attributes for all entries in the JAR file. Attributes is a mapping of attribute name/value pairs, of course, and the inner class Attributes.Name defines constants for various standard attribute names.

You can also read a JAR file with JarInputStream. This class requires to you read each entry of the file sequentially, however. JarOutputStream allows you to write out a JAR file sequentially. Finally, you can also read an entry within a JAR file and manifest attributes for that entry with a java.net.JarURLConnection object.

Attributes   Java 1.2

java.util.jar   cloneable collection

This class is a java.util.Map that maps the attribute names of a JAR file manifest to arbitrary string values. The JAR manifest format specifies that attribute names can contain only the ASCII characters A to Z (uppercase and lowercase), the digits 0 through 9, and the hyphen and underscore characters. Thus, this class uses Attributes.Name as the type of attribute names, in addition to the more general String class. Although you can create your own Attributes objects, you more commonly obtain Attributes objects from a Manifest.

```
public class Attributes implements Cloneable, java.util.Map {
// Public Constructors
    public Attributes();
    public Attributes(java.util.jar.Attributes attr);
    public Attributes(int size);
```

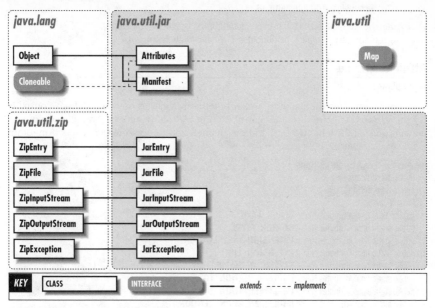

Figure 24–1: The java.util.jar package

```
// Inner Classes
   public static class Name;
// Public Instance Methods
   public String getValue(Attributes.Name name);
   public String getValue(String name);
   public String putValue(String name, String value);
// Methods Implementing Map
   public void clear();
   public boolean containsKey(Object name);
   public boolean containsValue(Object value);
   public java.util.Set entrySet();
   public boolean equals(Object o);
   public Object get(Object name);
   public int hashCode();
   public boolean isEmpty();                                          default:true
   public java.util.Set keySet();
   public Object put(Object name, Object value);
   public void putAll(java.util.Map attr);
   public Object remove(Object name);
   public int size();
   public java.util.Collection values();
// Public Methods Overriding Object
   public Object clone();
// Protected Instance Fields
   protected java.util.Map map;
}
```

Hierarchy: Object→ java.util.jar.Attributes(Cloneable, java.util.Map)

Passed To: java.util.jar.Attributes.Attributes()

Returned By: java.net.JarURLConnection.{getAttributes(), getMainAttributes()},
JarEntry.getAttributes(), Manifest.{getAttributes(), getMainAttributes()}

Attributes.Name   Java 1.2
java.util.jar

This class represents the name of an attribute in an Attributes object. It defines constants
for the various standard attribute names used in JAR file manifests. Attribute names can
contain only ASCII letters, digits, and the hyphen and underscore characters. Any other
Unicode characters are illegal.

```
public static class Attributes.Name {
// Public Constructors
    public Name(String name);
// Public Constants
    public static final Attributes.Name CLASS_PATH;
    public static final Attributes.Name CONTENT_TYPE;
1.3 public static final Attributes.Name EXTENSION_INSTALLATION;
1.3 public static final Attributes.Name EXTENSION_LIST;
1.3 public static final Attributes.Name EXTENSION_NAME;
    public static final Attributes.Name IMPLEMENTATION_TITLE;
1.3 public static final Attributes.Name IMPLEMENTATION_URL;
    public static final Attributes.Name IMPLEMENTATION_VENDOR;
1.3 public static final Attributes.Name IMPLEMENTATION_VENDOR_ID;
    public static final Attributes.Name IMPLEMENTATION_VERSION;
    public static final Attributes.Name MAIN_CLASS;
    public static final Attributes.Name MANIFEST_VERSION;
    public static final Attributes.Name SEALED;
    public static final Attributes.Name SIGNATURE_VERSION;
    public static final Attributes.Name SPECIFICATION_TITLE;
    public static final Attributes.Name SPECIFICATION_VENDOR;
    public static final Attributes.Name SPECIFICATION_VERSION;
// Public Methods Overriding Object
    public boolean equals(Object o);
    public int hashCode();
    public String toString();
}
```

Passed To: java.util.jar.Attributes.getValue()

Type Of: Too many fields to list.

JarEntry   Java 1.2
java.util.jar   *cloneable*

This class extends java.util.zip.ZipEntry; it represents a single file in a JAR archive and the
manifest attributes and digital signatures associated with that file. JarEntry objects can be
read from a JAR file with JarFile or JarInputStream, and they can be written to a JAR file
with JarOutputStream. Use getAttributes() to obtain the Attributes for the entry. Use getCertifi-
cates() to obtain a java.security.cert.Certificate array that contains the certificate chains for all
digital signatures associated with the file.

```
public class JarEntry extends java.util.zip.ZipEntry {
// Public Constructors
    public JarEntry(JarEntry je);
    public JarEntry(String name);
```

```
    public JarEntry(java.util.zip.ZipEntry ze);
// Public Instance Methods
    public java.util.jar.Attributes getAttributes() throws java.io.IOException;
    public java.security.cert.Certificate[ ] getCertificates();
}
```

Hierarchy: Object→ java.util.zip.ZipEntry(Cloneable, java.util.zip.ZipConstants)→ JarEntry

Passed To: JarEntry.JarEntry()

Returned By: java.net.JarURLConnection.getJarEntry(), JarFile.getJarEntry(),
JarInputStream.getNextJarEntry()

JarException   Java 1.2

java.util.jar   *serializable checked*

Signals an error while reading or writing a JAR file.

```
public class JarException extends java.util.zip.ZipException {
// Public Constructors
    public JarException();
    public JarException(String s);
}
```

Hierarchy: Object→ Throwable(Serializable)→ Exception→ java.io.IOException→
java.util.zip.ZipException→ JarException

JarFile   Java 1.2

java.util.jar

This class represents a JAR file and allows the manifest, file list, and individual files to
be read from the JAR file. It extends java.util.zip.ZipFile, and its use is similar to that of its
superclass. Create a JarFile by specifying a filename or File object. If you do not want
JarFile to attempt to verify any digital signatures contained in the JarFile, pass an optional
boolean argument of false to the JarFile() constructor. In Java 1.3, temporary JAR files can
be automatically deleted when they are closed. To take advantage of this feature, pass
ZipFile.OPEN_READ|ZipFile.OPEN_DELETE as the *mode* argument to the JarFile() constructor.

Once you have created a JarFile object, obtain the JAR Manifest with getManifest(). Obtain
an enumeration of the java.util.zip.ZipEntry objects in the file with entries(). Get the JarEntry
for a specified file in the JAR file with getJarEntry(). To read the contents of a specific
entry in the JAR file, obtain the JarEntry or ZipEntry object that represents that entry, pass
it to getInputStream(), and then read until the end of that stream. JarFile does not support
the creation of new JAR files or the modification of existing files.

```
public class JarFile extends java.util.zip.ZipFile {
// Public Constructors
    public JarFile(java.io.File file) throws java.io.IOException;
    public JarFile(String name) throws java.io.IOException;
    public JarFile(java.io.File file, boolean verify) throws java.io.IOException;
    public JarFile(String name, boolean verify) throws java.io.IOException;
1.3 public JarFile(java.io.File file, boolean verify, int mode) throws java.io.IOException;
// Public Constants
    public static final String MANIFEST_NAME;                      ="META-INF/MANIFEST.MF"
// Public Instance Methods
    public JarEntry getJarEntry(String name);
    public Manifest getManifest() throws java.io.IOException;
```

```
// Public Methods Overriding ZipFile
    public java.util.Enumeration entries();
    public java.util.zip.ZipEntry getEntry(String name);
    public java.io.InputStream getInputStream(java.util.zip.ZipEntry ze) throws java.io.IOException;    synchronized
}
```

Hierarchy: Object→ java.util.zip.ZipFile(java.util.zip.ZipConstants)→ JarFile

Returned By: java.net.JarURLConnection.getJarFile()

JarInputStream   Java 1.2

java.util.jar

This class allows a JAR file to be read from an input stream. It extends java.util.ZipInput-Stream and is used much like that class is used. To create a JarInputStream, simply specify the InputStream from which to read. If you do not want the JarInputStream to attempt to verify any digital signatures contained in the JAR file, pass false as the second argument to the JarInputStream() constructor. The JarInputStream() constructor first reads the JAR manifest entry, if one exists. The manifest must be the first entry in the JAR file. getMani-fest() returns the Manifest object for the JAR file.

Once you have created a JarInputStream, call getNextJarEntry() or getNextEntry() to obtain the JarEntry or java.util.zip.ZipEntry object that describes the next entry in the JAR file. Then, call a read() method (including the inherited versions) to read the contents of that entry. When the stream reaches the end of file, call getNextJarEntry() again to start reading the next entry in the file. When all entries have been read from the JAR file, getNextJarEntry() and getNextEntry() return null.

```
public class JarInputStream extends java.util.zip.ZipInputStream {
// Public Constructors
    public JarInputStream(java.io.InputStream in) throws java.io.IOException;
    public JarInputStream(java.io.InputStream in, boolean verify) throws java.io.IOException;
// Public Instance Methods
    public Manifest getManifest();
    public JarEntry getNextJarEntry() throws java.io.IOException;
// Public Methods Overriding ZipInputStream
    public java.util.zip.ZipEntry getNextEntry() throws java.io.IOException;
    public int read(byte[ ] b, int off, int len) throws java.io.IOException;
// Protected Methods Overriding ZipInputStream
    protected java.util.zip.ZipEntry createZipEntry(String name);
}
```

Hierarchy: Object→ java.io.InputStream→ java.io.FilterInputStream→
java.util.zip.InflaterInputStream→ java.util.zip.ZipInputStream(java.util.zip.ZipConstants)→
JarInputStream

JarOutputStream   Java 1.2

java.util.jar

This class can write a JAR file to an arbitrary OutputStream. JarOutputStream extends java.util.zip.ZipOutputStream and is used much like that class is used. Create a JarOutput-Stream by specifying the stream to write to and, optionally, the Manifest object for the JAR file. The JarOutputStream() constructor starts by writing the contents of the Manifest object into an appropriate JAR file entry. It is the programmer's responsibility to ensure that the contents of the JAR entries written subsequently match those specified in the Manifest object. This class provides no explicit support for attaching digital signatures to entries in the JAR file.

After creating a JarOutputStream, call putNextEntry() to specify the JarEntry or java.util.zip.ZipEntry to be written to the stream. Then, call any of the inherited write() methods to write the contents of the entry to the stream. When that entry is finished, call putNextEntry() again to begin writing the next entry. When you have written all JAR file entries in this way, call close(). Before writing any entry, you may call the inherited setMethod() and setLevel() methods to specify how the entry should be compressed. See java.util.zip.ZipOutputStream.

```
public class JarOutputStream extends java.util.zip.ZipOutputStream {
// Public Constructors
    public JarOutputStream(java.io.OutputStream out) throws java.io.IOException;
    public JarOutputStream(java.io.OutputStream out, Manifest man) throws java.io.IOException;
// Public Methods Overriding ZipOutputStream
    public void putNextEntry(java.util.zip.ZipEntry ze) throws java.io.IOException;
}
```

Hierarchy: Object→ java.io.OutputStream→ java.io.FilterOutputStream→ java.util.zip.DeflaterOutputStream→ java.util.zip.ZipOutputStream(java.util.zip.ZipConstants)→ JarOutputStream

Manifest   Java 1.2
java.util.jar   *cloneable*

This class represents the manifest entry of a JAR file. getMainAttributes() returns an Attributes object that represents the manifest attributes that apply to the entire JAR file. getAttributes() returns an Attributes object that represents the manifest attributes specified for a single file in the JAR file. getEntries() returns a java.util.Map that maps the names of entries in the JAR file to the Attributes objects associated with those entries. getEntries() returns the Map object used internally by the Manifest. You can edit the contents of the Manifest by adding, deleting, or editing entries in the Map. read() reads manifest entries from an input stream, merging them into the current set of entries. write() writes the Manifest out to the specified output stream.

```
public class Manifest implements Cloneable {
// Public Constructors
    public Manifest();
    public Manifest(Manifest man);
    public Manifest(java.io.InputStream is) throws java.io.IOException;
// Public Instance Methods
    public void clear();
    public java.util.jar.Attributes getAttributes(String name);
    public java.util.Map getEntries();                                  default:HashMap
    public java.util.jar.Attributes getMainAttributes();
    public void read(java.io.InputStream is) throws java.io.IOException;
    public void write(java.io.OutputStream out) throws java.io.IOException;
// Public Methods Overriding Object
    public Object clone();
    public boolean equals(Object o);
    public int hashCode();
}
```

Hierarchy: Object→ Manifest(Cloneable)

Passed To: java.net.URLClassLoader.definePackage(), JarOutputStream.JarOutputStream(), Manifest.Manifest()

Returned By: java.net.JarURLConnection.getManifest(), JarFile.getManifest(), JarInputStream.getManifest()

CHAPTER 25

The java.util.zip Package

The java.util.zip package contains classes for data compression and decompression. It is new as of Java 1.1. Figure 25-1 shows the class hierarchy of the package. The Deflater and Inflater classes perform data compression and decompression. DeflaterOutputStream and InflaterInputStream apply that functionality to byte streams; the subclasses of these streams implement both the GZIP and ZIP compression formats. The Adler32 and CRC32 classes implement the Checksum interface and compute the checksums required for data compression.

Adler32   Java 1.1
java.util.zip   *PJ1.1(opt)*

This class implements the Checksum interface and computes a checksum on a stream of data using the Adler-32 algorithm. This algorithm is significantly faster than the CRC-32 algorithm and is almost as reliable. The CheckedInputStream and CheckedOutputStream classes provide a higher-level interface to computing checksums on streams of data.

```
public class Adler32 implements Checksum {
// Public Constructors
    public Adler32();
// Public Instance Methods
    public void update(byte[ ] b);
// Methods Implementing Checksum
    public long getValue();                                                default:1
    public void reset();
    public void update(int b);
    public void update(byte[ ] b, int off, int len);
}
```

Hierarchy: Object→ Adler32(Checksum)

CheckedInputStream   Java 1.1
java.util.zip   *PJ1.1*

This class is a subclass of java.io.FilterInputStream; it allows a stream to be read and a checksum computed on its contents at the same time. This is useful when you want to

Figure 25–1: The java.util.zip package

check the integrity of a stream of data against a published checksum value. To create a CheckedInputStream, you must specify both the stream it should read and a Checksum object, such as CRC32, that implements the particular checksum algorithm you desire. The read() and skip() methods are the same as those of other input streams. As bytes are read, they are incorporated into the checksum that is being computed. The getCheck-sum() method does not return the checksum value itself, but rather the Checksum object. You must call the getValue() method of this object to obtain the checksum value.

```
public class CheckedInputStream extends java.io.FilterInputStream {
// Public Constructors
    public CheckedInputStream(java.io.InputStream in, Checksum cksum);
// Public Instance Methods
    public Checksum getChecksum();
// Public Methods Overriding FilterInputStream
    public int read() throws java.io.IOException;
    public int read(byte[ ] buf, int off, int len) throws java.io.IOException;
    public long skip(long n) throws java.io.IOException;
}
```

Hierarchy: Object→ java.io.InputStream→ java.io.FilterInputStream→ CheckedInputStream

CheckedOutputStream
java.util.zip

Java 1.1
PJ1.1

This class is a subclass of java.io.FilterOutputStream that allows data to be written to a stream and a checksum computed on that data at the same time. To create a CheckedOut-putStream, you must specify both the output stream to write its data to and a Checksum object, such as an instance of Adler32, that implements the particular checksum algorithm you desire. The write() methods are similar to those of other OutputStream classes. The getChecksum() method returns the Checksum object. You must call getValue() on this object in order to obtain the actual checksum value.

```
public class CheckedOutputStream extends java.io.FilterOutputStream {
// Public Constructors
    public CheckedOutputStream(java.io.OutputStream out, Checksum cksum);
// Public Instance Methods
    public Checksum getChecksum();
// Public Methods Overriding FilterOutputStream
    public void write(int b) throws java.io.IOException;
    public void write(byte[ ] b, int off, int len) throws java.io.IOException;
}
```

Hierarchy: Object→ java.io.OutputStream→ java.io.FilterOutputStream→ CheckedOutputStream

Checksum   Java 1.1
java.util.zip   PJ1.1

This interface defines the methods required to compute a checksum on a stream of data. The checksum is computed based on the bytes of data supplied by the update() methods; the current value of the checksum can be obtained at any time with the getValue() method. reset() resets the checksum to its default value; use this method before beginning a new stream of data. The checksum value computed by a Checksum object and returned through the getValue() method must fit into a long value. Therefore, this interface is not suitable for the cryptographic checksum algorithms used in cryptography and security. The classes CheckedInputStream and CheckedOutputStream provide a higher-level API for computing a checksum on a stream of data. See also java.security.MessageDigest.

```
public interface Checksum {
// Public Instance Methods
    public abstract long getValue();
    public abstract void reset();
    public abstract void update(int b);
    public abstract void update(byte[ ] b, int off, int len);
}
```

Implementations: Adler32, CRC32

Passed To: CheckedInputStream.CheckedInputStream(),
CheckedOutputStream.CheckedOutputStream()

Returned By: CheckedInputStream.getChecksum(), CheckedOutputStream.getChecksum()

CRC32   Java 1.1
java.util.zip   PJ1.1

This class implements the Checksum interface and computes a checksum on a stream of data using the CRC-32 algorithm. The CheckedInputStream and CheckedOutputStream classes provide a higher-level interface to computing checksums on streams of data.

```
public class CRC32 implements Checksum {
// Public Constructors
    public CRC32();
// Public Instance Methods
    public void update(byte[ ] b);
```

```
// Methods Implementing Checksum
    public long getValue( );                                                    default:0
    public void reset( );
    public void update(int b);
    public void update(byte[ ] b, int off, int len);
}
```

Hierarchy: Object→ CRC32(Checksum)

Type Of: GZIPInputStream.crc, GZIPOutputStream.crc

DataFormatException   Java 1.1

java.util.zip   *serializable checked PJ1.1*

Signals that invalid or corrupt data has been encountered while uncompressing data.

```
public class DataFormatException extends Exception {
// Public Constructors
    public DataFormatException( );
    public DataFormatException(String s);
}
```

Hierarchy: Object→ Throwable(Serializable)→ Exception→ DataFormatException

Thrown By: Inflater.inflate()

Deflater   Java 1.1

java.util.zip   *PJ1.1(opt)*

This class implements the general ZLIB data-compression algorithm used by the *gzip*
and *PKZip* compression programs. The constants defined by this class are used to specify the compression strategy and the compression speed/strength tradeoff level to be
used. If you set the *nowrap* argument to the constructor to true, the ZLIB header and
checksum data are omitted from the compressed output, which is the format both *gzip*
and *PKZip* use.

The important methods of this class are setInput(), which specifies input data to be compressed, and deflate(), which compresses the data and returns the compressed output.
The remaining methods exist so that Deflater can be used for stream-based compression,
as it is in higher-level classes, such as GZIPOutputStream and ZipOutputStream. These stream
classes are sufficient in most cases. Most applications do not need to use Deflater
directly. The Inflater class uncompresses data compressed with a Deflater object.

```
public class Deflater {
// Public Constructors
    public Deflater( );
    public Deflater(int level);
    public Deflater(int level, boolean nowrap);
// Public Constants
    public static final int BEST_COMPRESSION;                               =9
    public static final int BEST_SPEED;                                     =1
    public static final int DEFAULT_COMPRESSION;                            =-1
    public static final int DEFAULT_STRATEGY;                               =0
    public static final int DEFLATED;                                       =8
    public static final int FILTERED;                                       =1
    public static final int HUFFMAN_ONLY;                                   =2
    public static final int NO_COMPRESSION;                                 =0
```

```
// Property Accessor Methods (by property name)
    public int getAdler();                                              synchronized default:1
    public int getTotalIn();                                           synchronized default:0
    public int getTotalOut();                                          synchronized default:0
// Public Instance Methods
    public int deflate(byte[ ] b);
    public int deflate(byte[ ] b, int off, int len);                          synchronized
    public void end();                                                        synchronized
    public void finish();                                                     synchronized
    public boolean finished();                                                synchronized
    public boolean needsInput();
    public void reset();                                                      synchronized
    public void setDictionary(byte[ ] b);
    public void setDictionary(byte[ ] b, int off, int len);                   synchronized
    public void setInput(byte[ ] b);
    public void setInput(byte[ ] b, int off, int len);                        synchronized
    public void setLevel(int level);                                          synchronized
    public void setStrategy(int strategy);                                    synchronized
// Protected Methods Overriding Object
    protected void finalize();
}
```

Passed To: DeflaterOutputStream.DeflaterOutputStream()

Type Of: DeflaterOutputStream.def

DeflaterOutputStream   Java 1.1

java.util.zip   PJ1.1(opt)

This class is a subclass of java.io.FilterOutputStream; it filters a stream of data by compressing (deflating) it and then writing the compressed data to another output stream. To create a DeflaterOutputStream, you must specify both the stream it is to write to and a Deflater object to perform the compression. You can set various options on the Deflater object to specify just what type of compression is to be performed. Once a DeflaterOutputStream is created, its write() and close() methods are the same as those of other output streams. The InflaterInputStream class can read data written with a DeflaterOutputStream. A DeflaterOutputStream writes raw compressed data; applications often prefer one of its subclasses, GZIPOutputStream or ZipOutputStream, that wraps the raw compressed data within a standard file format.

```
public class DeflaterOutputStream extends java.io.FilterOutputStream {
// Public Constructors
    public DeflaterOutputStream(java.io.OutputStream out);
    public DeflaterOutputStream(java.io.OutputStream out, Deflater def);
    public DeflaterOutputStream(java.io.OutputStream out, Deflater def, int size);
// Public Instance Methods
    public void finish() throws java.io.IOException;
// Public Methods Overriding FilterOutputStream
    public void close() throws java.io.IOException;
    public void write(int b) throws java.io.IOException;
    public void write(byte[ ] b, int off, int len) throws java.io.IOException;
```

```
// Protected Instance Methods
   protected void deflate( ) throws java.io.IOException;
// Protected Instance Fields
   protected byte[ ] buf;
   protected Deflater def;
}
```

Hierarchy: Object→ java.io.OutputStream→ java.io.FilterOutputStream→ DeflaterOutputStream

Subclasses: GZIPOutputStream, ZipOutputStream

GZIPInputStream
java.util.zip

Java 1.1

PJ1.1

This class is a subclass of InflaterInputStream that reads and uncompresses data compressed in *gzip* format. To create a GZIPInputStream, simply specify the InputStream to read compressed data from and, optionally, a buffer size for the internal decompression buffer. Once a GZIPInputStream is created, you can use the read() and close() methods as you would with any input stream.

```
public class GZIPInputStream extends InflaterInputStream {
// Public Constructors
   public GZIPInputStream(java.io.InputStream in) throws java.io.IOException;
   public GZIPInputStream(java.io.InputStream in, int size) throws java.io.IOException;
// Public Constants
   public static final int GZIP_MAGIC;                                          =35615
// Public Methods Overriding InflaterInputStream
   public void close( ) throws java.io.IOException;
   public int read(byte[ ] buf, int off, int len) throws java.io.IOException;
// Protected Instance Fields
   protected CRC32 crc;
   protected boolean eos;
}
```

Hierarchy: Object→ java.io.InputStream→ java.io.FilterInputStream→ InflaterInputStream→ GZIPInputStream

GZIPOutputStream
java.util.zip

Java 1.1

PJ1.1(opt)

This class is a subclass of DeflaterOutputStream that compresses and writes data using the *gzip* file format. To create a GZIPOutputStream, specify the OutputStream to write to and, optionally, a size for the internal compression buffer. Once the GZIPOutputStream is created, you can use the write() and close() methods as you would any output stream.

```
public class GZIPOutputStream extends DeflaterOutputStream {
// Public Constructors
   public GZIPOutputStream(java.io.OutputStream out) throws java.io.IOException;
   public GZIPOutputStream(java.io.OutputStream out, int size) throws java.io.IOException;
// Public Methods Overriding DeflaterOutputStream
   public void close( ) throws java.io.IOException;
   public void finish( ) throws java.io.IOException;
   public void write(byte[ ] buf, int off, int len) throws java.io.IOException;      synchronized
// Protected Instance Fields
   protected CRC32 crc;
}
```

java.util.zip

java.util.zip.GZIPOutputStream

Hierarchy: Object→ java.io.OutputStream→ java.io.FilterOutputStream→ DeflaterOutputStream→ GZIPOutputStream

Inflater
Java 1.1

java.util.zip
PJ1.1(mod)

This class implements the general ZLIB data-decompression algorithm used by *gzip*, *PKZip*, and other data-compression applications. It decompresses or inflates data compressed through the Deflater class. The important methods of this class are setInput(), which specifies input data to be decompressed, and inflate(), which decompresses the input data into an output buffer. A number of other methods exist so that this class can be used for stream-based decompression, as it is in the higher-level classes, such as GZIPInputStream and ZipInputStream. These stream-based classes are sufficient in most cases. Most applications do not need to use Inflater directly.

```
public class Inflater {
// Public Constructors
    public Inflater();
    public Inflater(boolean nowrap);
// Property Accessor Methods (by property name)
    public int getAdler();                                              synchronized default:1
    public int getRemaining();                                          synchronized default:0
    public int getTotalIn();                                            synchronized default:0
    public int getTotalOut();                                           synchronized default:0
// Public Instance Methods
    public void end();                                                  synchronized
    public boolean finished();                                          synchronized
    public int inflate(byte[ ] b) throws DataFormatException;
    public int inflate(byte[ ] b, int off, int len) throws DataFormatException;   synchronized
    public boolean needsDictionary();                                   synchronized
    public boolean needsInput();                                        synchronized
    public void reset();                                                synchronized
    public void setDictionary(byte[ ] b);
    public void setDictionary(byte[ ] b, int off, int len);             synchronized
    public void setInput(byte[ ] b);
    public void setInput(byte[ ] b, int off, int len);                  synchronized
// Protected Methods Overriding Object
    protected void finalize();
}
```

Passed To: InflaterInputStream.InflaterInputStream()

Type Of: InflaterInputStream.inf

InflaterInputStream
Java 1.1

java.util.zip
PJ1.1

This class is a subclass of java.io.FilterInputStream; it reads a specified stream of compressed input data (typically one that was written with DeflaterOutputStream or a subclass) and filters that data by uncompressing (inflating) it. To create an InflaterInputStream, specify both the input stream to read from and an Inflater object to perform the decompression. Once an InflaterInputStream is created, the read() and skip() methods are the same as those of other input streams. The InflaterInputStream uncompresses raw data. Applications often prefer one of its subclasses, GZIPInputStream or ZipInputStream, that work with compressed data written in the standard *gzip* and *PKZip* file formats.

```
public class InflaterInputStream extends java.io.FilterInputStream {
// Public Constructors
     public InflaterInputStream(java.io.InputStream in);
     public InflaterInputStream(java.io.InputStream in, Inflater inf);
     public InflaterInputStream(java.io.InputStream in, Inflater inf, int size);
// Public Methods Overriding FilterInputStream
1.2 public int available() throws java.io.IOException;
1.2 public void close() throws java.io.IOException;
     public int read() throws java.io.IOException;
     public int read(byte[ ] b, int off, int len) throws java.io.IOException;
     public long skip(long n) throws java.io.IOException;
// Protected Instance Methods
     protected void fill() throws java.io.IOException;
// Protected Instance Fields
     protected byte[ ] buf;
     protected Inflater inf;
     protected int len;
}
```

Hierarchy: Object→ java.io.InputStream→ java.io.FilterInputStream→ InflaterInputStream

Subclasses: GZIPInputStream, ZipInputStream

ZipEntry
java.util.zip

Java 1.1

cloneable PJ1.1

This class describes a single entry (typically a compressed file) stored within a ZIP file. The various methods get and set various pieces of information about the entry. The ZipEntry class is used by ZipFile and ZipInputStream, which read ZIP files, and by ZipOutputStream, which writes ZIP files.

When you are reading a ZIP file, a ZipEntry object returned by ZipFile or ZipInputStream contains the name, size, modification time, and other information about an entry in the file. When writing a ZIP file, on the other hand, you must create your own ZipEntry objects and initialize them to contain the entry name and other appropriate information before writing the contents of the entry.

```
public class ZipEntry implements Cloneable {
// Public Constructors
1.2 public ZipEntry(ZipEntry e);
     public ZipEntry(String name);
// Public Constants
     public static final int DEFLATED;                                              =8
     public static final int STORED;                                                =0
// Property Accessor Methods (by property name)
     public String getComment();
     public void setComment(String comment);
     public long getCompressedSize();
1.2 public void setCompressedSize(long csize);
     public long getCrc();
     public void setCrc(long crc);
     public boolean isDirectory();
     public byte[ ] getExtra();
     public void setExtra(byte[ ] extra);
     public int getMethod();
     public void setMethod(int method);
     public String getName();
```

```
    public long getSize();
    public void setSize(long size);
    public long getTime();
    public void setTime(long time);
// Public Methods Overriding Object
1.2 public Object clone();
1.2 public int hashCode();
    public String toString();
}
```

Hierarchy: Object → ZipEntry(Cloneable, ZipConstants)

Subclasses: java.util.jar.JarEntry

Passed To: java.util.jar.JarEntry.JarEntry(), java.util.jar.JarFile.getInputStream(), java.util.jar.JarOutputStream.putNextEntry(), ZipEntry.ZipEntry(), ZipFile.getInputStream(), ZipOutputStream.putNextEntry()

Returned By: java.util.jar.JarFile.getEntry(), java.util.jar.JarInputStream.{createZipEntry(), getNextEntry()}, ZipFile.getEntry(), ZipInputStream.{createZipEntry(), getNextEntry()}

ZipException   Java 1.1

java.util.zip   *serializable checked PJ1.1*

Signals that an error has occurred in reading or writing a ZIP file.

```
public class ZipException extends java.io.IOException {
// Public Constructors
    public ZipException();
    public ZipException(String s);
}
```

Hierarchy: Object → Throwable(Serializable) → Exception → java.io.IOException → ZipException

Subclasses: java.util.jar.JarException

Thrown By: ZipFile.ZipFile()

ZipFile   Java 1.1

java.util.zip   *PJ1.1(opt)*

This class reads the contents of ZIP files. It uses a random-access file internally so that the entries of the ZIP file do not have to be read sequentially, as they do with the ZipInputStream class. A ZipFile object can be created by specifying the ZIP file to be read either as a String filename or as a File object. In Java 1.3, temporary ZIP files can be marked for automatic deletion when they are closed. To take advantage of this feature, pass ZipFile.OPEN_READ|ZipFile.OPEN_DELETE as the *mode* argument to the ZipFile() constructor.

Once a ZipFile is created, the getEntry() method returns a ZipEntry object for a named entry, and the entries() method returns an Enumeration object that allows you to loop through all the ZipEntry objects for the file. To read the contents of a specific ZipEntry within the ZIP file, pass the ZipEntry to getInputStream(); this returns an InputStream object from which you can read the entry's contents.

```
public class ZipFile {
// Public Constructors
    public ZipFile(String name) throws java.io.IOException;
    public ZipFile(java.io.File file) throws ZipException, java.io.IOException;
```

```
1.3 public ZipFile(java.io.File file, int mode) throws java.io.IOException;
// Public Constants
1.3 public static final int OPEN_DELETE;                                           =4
1.3 public static final int OPEN_READ;                                             =1
// Public Instance Methods
    public void close() throws java.io.IOException;
    public java.util.Enumeration entries();
    public ZipEntry getEntry(String name);
    public java.io.InputStream getInputStream(ZipEntry entry) throws java.io.IOException;
    public String getName();
1.2 public int size();
}
```

Hierarchy: Object→ ZipFile(ZipConstants)

Subclasses: java.util.jar.JarFile

ZipInputStream   Java 1.1

java.util.zip   PJ1.1

This class is a subclass of InflaterInputStream that reads the entries of a ZIP file in sequential order. Create a ZipInputStream by specifying the InputStream from which it is to read the contents of the ZIP file. Once the ZipInputStream is created, you can use getNextEntry() to begin reading data from the next entry in the ZIP file. This method must be called before read() is called to begin reading the first entry. getNextEntry() returns a ZipEntry object that describes the entry being read, or null when there are no more entries to be read from the ZIP file.

The read() methods of ZipInputStream read until the end of the current entry and then return −1, indicating that there is no more data to read. To continue with the next entry in the ZIP file, you must call getNextEntry() again. Similarly, the skip() method only skips bytes within the current entry. closeEntry() can be called to skip the remaining data in the current entry, but it is usually easier simply to call getNextEntry() to begin the next entry.

```
public class ZipInputStream extends InflaterInputStream {
// Public Constructors
    public ZipInputStream(java.io.InputStream in);
// Public Instance Methods
    public void closeEntry() throws java.io.IOException;
    public ZipEntry getNextEntry() throws java.io.IOException;
// Public Methods Overriding InflaterInputStream
1.2 public int available() throws java.io.IOException;
    public void close() throws java.io.IOException;
    public int read(byte[ ] b, int off, int len) throws java.io.IOException;
    public long skip(long n) throws java.io.IOException;
// Protected Instance Methods
1.2 protected ZipEntry createZipEntry(String name);
}
```

Hierarchy: Object→ java.io.InputStream→ java.io.FilterInputStream→ InflaterInputStream→ ZipInputStream(ZipConstants)

Subclasses: java.util.jar.JarInputStream

java.util. zip

ZipOutputStream

Java 1.1

java.util.zip

PJ1.1(opt)

This class is a subclass of DeflaterOutputStream that writes data in ZIP file format to an output stream. Before writing any data to the ZipOutputStream, you must begin an entry within the ZIP file with putNextEntry(). The ZipEntry object passed to this method should specify at least a name for the entry. Once you have begun an entry with putNextEntry(), you can write the contents of that entry with the write() methods. When you reach the end of an entry, you can begin a new one by calling putNextEntry() again, you can close the current entry with closeEntry(), or you can close the stream itself with close().

Before beginning an entry with putNextEntry(), you can set the compression method and level with setMethod() and setLevel(). The constants DEFLATED and STORED are the two legal values for setMethod(). If you use STORED, the entry is stored in the ZIP file without any compression. If you use DEFLATED, you can also specify the compression speed/strength tradeoff by passing a number from 1 to 9 to setLevel(), where 9 gives the strongest and slowest level of compression. You can also use the constants Deflater.BEST_SPEED, Deflater.BEST_COMPRESSION, and Deflater.DEFAULT_COMPRESSION with the setLevel() method.

If you are storing an entry without compression, the ZIP file format requires that you specify, in advance, the entry size and CRC-32 checksum in the ZipEntry object for the entry. An exception is thrown if these values are not specified or specified incorrectly.

```
public class ZipOutputStream extends DeflaterOutputStream {
// Public Constructors
    public ZipOutputStream(java.io.OutputStream out);
// Public Constants
    public static final int DEFLATED;                                           =8
    public static final int STORED;                                             =0
// Public Instance Methods
    public void closeEntry() throws java.io.IOException;
    public void putNextEntry(ZipEntry e) throws java.io.IOException;
    public void setComment(String comment);
    public void setLevel(int level);
    public void setMethod(int method);
// Public Methods Overriding DeflaterOutputStream
    public void close() throws java.io.IOException;
    public void finish() throws java.io.IOException;
    public void write(byte[ ] b, int off, int len) throws java.io.IOException;   synchronized
}
```

Hierarchy: Object→ java.io.OutputStream→ java.io.FilterOutputStream→ DeflaterOutputStream→ ZipOutputStream(ZipConstants)

Subclasses: java.util.jar.JarOutputStream

CHAPTER 26

The javax.crypto Package

The javax.crypto package defines classes and interfaces for various cryptographic operations. Figure 26-1 shows the class hierarchy of this package. The central class is Cipher, which is used to encrypt and decrypt data. CipherInputStream and CipherOutputStream are utility classes that use a Cipher object to encrypt or decrypt streaming data. SealedObject is another important utility class that uses a Cipher object to encrypt an arbitrary serializable Java object.

The KeyGenerator class creates the SecretKey objects used by Cipher for encryption and decryption. SecretKeyFactory encodes and decodes SecretKey objects. The KeyAgreement class enables two or more parties to agree on a SecretKey in such a way that an eavesdropper cannot determine the key. The Mac class computes a message authentication code (MAC) that can ensure the integrity of a transmission between two parties who share a SecretKey. A MAC is akin to a digital signature, except that it is based on a secret key instead of a public/private key pair.

Like the java.security package, the javax.crypto package is provider-based, so that arbitrary cryptographic implémentations may be plugged into any Java installation. Various classes in this package have names that end in Spi. These classes define a service-provider interface and must be implemented by each cryptographic provider that wishes to provide an implementation of a particular cryptographic service or algorithm.

This package is part of the Java Cryptography Extension (JCE). Sun distributes the JCE within the United States and Canada, but, unfortunately, U.S. export regulations prohibit the export of cryptographic technology to other countries. If you are not a resident of the United States or Canada, you have to obtain and use a third-party implementation of the JCE developed outside of the United States. The JCE is distributed with a cryptographic provider named "SunJCE" that includes a robust set of implementations for Cipher, KeyAgreement, Mac, and other classes. Installing the JCE extension is not the same, however, as installing the SunJCE provider. To make the SunJCE provider permanently available on a Java installation, you must edit the *${java.home}/lib/security/java.security* file in the Java installation to add a line such as the following:

```
security.provider.2=com.sun.crypto.provider.SunJCE
```

The digit 2 in the line above specifies the preference order of the provider; you can use a different number.

javax.crypto

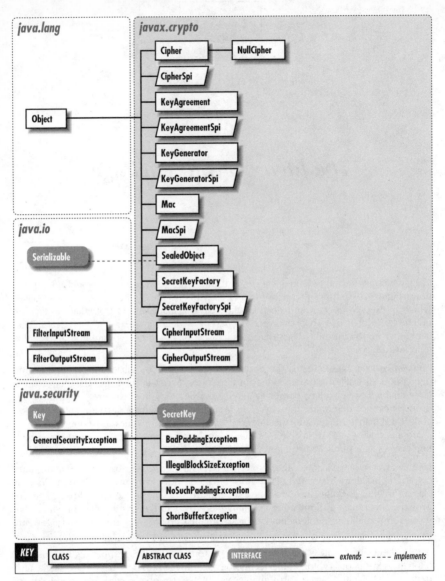

Figure 26-1: The javax.crypto package

If the SunJCE provider is not statically installed as above, you can dynamically install it in an application with code such as the following:

```
import java.security.*;
Provider sunjce = new com.sun.crypto.provider.SunJCE();
Security.addProvider(sunjce);
```

A full tutorial on cryptography is beyond the scope of this chapter and of this book. In order to use this package, you need to have a basic understanding of cryptographic algorithms such as DES. In order to take full advantage of this package, you also need to have a detailed understanding of things like feedback modes, padding schemes, the Diffie-Hellman key-agreement protocol, and so on. For a good introduction to modern cryptography in Java, see *Java Cryptography* by Jonathan Knudsen (O'Reilly). For more in-depth coverage, not specific to Java, see *Applied Cryptography* by Bruce Schneier (Wiley).

BadPaddingException   JCE 1.2
javax.crypto   *serializable checked*

Signals that input data to a Cipher is not padded correctly.

```
public class BadPaddingException extends java.security.GeneralSecurityException {
// Public Constructors
    public BadPaddingException();
    public BadPaddingException(String msg);
}
```

Hierarchy: Object→ Throwable(Serializable)→ Exception→ java.security.GeneralSecurityException→ BadPaddingException

Thrown By: Cipher.doFinal(), CipherSpi.engineDoFinal(), SealedObject.getObject()

Cipher   JCE 1.2
javax.crypto

This class performs encryption and decryption of byte arrays. Cipher is provider-based, so to obtain a Cipher object, you must call the static getInstance() factory method. The arguments to this method are a string that describes the type of encryption desired and, optionally, the name of the provider whose implementation should be used. To specify the desired type of encryption, you can simply specify the name of an encryption algorithm, such as "DES". Or you can specify a three-part name that includes the encryption algorithm, the algorithm operating mode, and the padding scheme. These three parts are separated by slash characters, as in "DES/CBC/PKCS5Padding". Finally, if you are requesting a block cipher algorithm in a stream mode, you can specify the number of bits to be processed at a time by following the name of the feedback mode with a number of bits. For example: "DES/CFB8/NoPadding".

The "SunJCE" provider supports the following cryptographic algorithms:

"DES"
    The Digital Encryption Standard.

"DESede"
    Triple DES encryption, also known as "TripleDES".

"Blowfish"
    The Blowfish block cipher designed by Bruce Schneier.

"PBEWithMD5AndDES"
    A password-based encryption scheme specified in PKCS#5. This algorithm implicitly uses "CBC" mode and the "PKCS5Padding" padding; it cannot be used with other modes or padding schemes.

"PBEWithMD5AndTripleDES"
    Password-based encryption as above, but using DESede instead of DES.

SunJCE supports the following operating modes:

"ECB"
>   Electronic Codebook mode

"CBC"
>   Cipher Block Chaining mode

"CFB"
>   Cipher Feedback mode

"OFB"
>   Output Feedback mode

"PCBC"
>   Plaintext Cipher Block Chaining mode

Finally, the "SunJCE" provider also supports two padding schemes: "NoPadding" and "PKCS5Padding". The name "SSL3Padding" is reserved, but this padding scheme is not implemented in the current release of "SunJCE".

Once you have obtained a Cipher object for the desired cryptographic algorithm, mode, and padding scheme, you must initialize it by calling one of the init() methods. The first argument to init() is one of the constants ENCRYPT_MODE or DECRYPT_MODE. The second argument is a java.security.Key object that performs the encryption or decryption. If you use one of the symmetric (i.e., non-public key) encryption algorithms supported by the "SunJCE" provider, this Key object is a SecretKey implementation. You can optionally pass a java.security.SecureRandom object to init() to provide a source of randomness. If you do not, the Cipher implementation provides its own pseudo-random number generator.

Some cryptographic algorithms require additional initialization parameters; these can be passed to init() as a java.security.AlgorithmParameters object or as a java.security.spec.Algorithm-ParameterSpec object. When encrypting, you can omit these parameters, and the Cipher implementation uses default values or generates appropriate random parameters for you. In this case, you should call getParameters() after performing encryption to obtain the AlgorithmParameters used to encrypt. These parameters are required in order to decrypt, and must therefore be saved or transferred along with the encrypted data. Of the algorithms supported by the "SunJCE" provider, the block ciphers "DES", "DESede", and "Blowfish" all require an initialization vector when they are used in "CBC", "CFB", "OFB", or "PCBC" mode. You can represent an initialization vector with a javax.crypto.spec.IvParameterSpec object and obtain the raw bytes of the initialization vector used by a Cipher with the getIV() method. The "PBEWithMD5AndDES" algorithm requires a salt and iteration count as parameters. These can be specified with a javax.crypto.spec.PBEParameterSpec object.

Once you have obtained and initialized a Cipher object, you are ready to use it for encryption or decryption. If you have only a single array of bytes to encrypt or decrypt, pass that input array to one of the doFinal() methods. Some versions of this method return the encrypted or decrypted bytes as the return value of the function. Other versions store the encrypted or decrypted bytes to another byte array you specify. If you choose to use one of these latter methods, you should first call getOutputSize() to determine the required size of the output array. If you want to encrypt or decrypt data from a streaming source or have more than one array of data, pass the data to one of the update() methods, calling it as many times as necessary. Then pass the last array of data to one of the doFinal() methods. If you are working with streaming data, consider using the CipherInputStream and CipherOutputStream classes instead.

```
public class Cipher {
// Protected Constructors
     protected Cipher(CipherSpi cipherSpi, java.security.Provider provider, String transformation);
// Public Constants
     public static final int DECRYPT_MODE;                                                    =2
     public static final int ENCRYPT_MODE;                                                    =1
// Public Class Methods
     public static final Cipher getInstance(String transformation) throws java.security.NoSuchAlgorithmException,
          NoSuchPaddingException;
     public static final Cipher getInstance(String transformation, String provider)
          throws java.security.NoSuchAlgorithmException, java.security.NoSuchProviderException,
          NoSuchPaddingException;
// Property Accessor Methods (by property name)
     public final String getAlgorithm();
     public final int getBlockSize();
     public final byte[] getIV();
     public final java.security.AlgorithmParameters getParameters();
     public final java.security.Provider getProvider();
// Public Instance Methods
     public final byte[] doFinal() throws java.lang.IllegalStateException, IllegalBlockSizeException,
          BadPaddingException;
     public final byte[] doFinal(byte[] input) throws java.lang.IllegalStateException, IllegalBlockSizeException,
          BadPaddingException;
     public final int doFinal(byte[] output, int outputOffset) throws java.lang.IllegalStateException,
          IllegalBlockSizeException, ShortBufferException, BadPaddingException;
     public final byte[] doFinal(byte[] input, int inputOffset, int inputLen) throws java.lang.IllegalStateException,
          IllegalBlockSizeException, BadPaddingException;
     public final int doFinal(byte[] input, int inputOffset, int inputLen, byte[] output)
          throws java.lang.IllegalStateException, ShortBufferException, IllegalBlockSizeException, BadPaddingException;
     public final int doFinal(byte[] input, int inputOffset, int inputLen, byte[] output, int outputOffset)
          throws java.lang.IllegalStateException, ShortBufferException, IllegalBlockSizeException, BadPaddingException;
     public final int getOutputSize(int inputLen) throws java.lang.IllegalStateException;
     public final void init(int opmode, java.security.Key key) throws java.security.InvalidKeyException;
     public final void init(int opmode, java.security.Key key, java.security.SecureRandom random)
          throws java.security.InvalidKeyException;
     public final void init(int opmode, java.security.Key key, java.security.spec.AlgorithmParameterSpec params)
          throws java.security.InvalidKeyException, java.security.InvalidAlgorithmParameterException;
     public final void init(int opmode, java.security.Key key, java.security.AlgorithmParameters params)
          throws java.security.InvalidKeyException, java.security.InvalidAlgorithmParameterException;
     public final void init(int opmode, java.security.Key key, java.security.spec.AlgorithmParameterSpec params,
               java.security.SecureRandom random) throws java.security.InvalidKeyException,
          java.security.InvalidAlgorithmParameterException;
     public final void init(int opmode, java.security.Key key, java.security.AlgorithmParameters params,
               java.security.SecureRandom random) throws java.security.InvalidKeyException,
          java.security.InvalidAlgorithmParameterException;
     public final byte[] update(byte[] input) throws java.lang.IllegalStateException;
     public final byte[] update(byte[] input, int inputOffset, int inputLen) throws java.lang.IllegalStateException;
     public final int update(byte[] input, int inputOffset, int inputLen, byte[] output)
          throws java.lang.IllegalStateException, ShortBufferException;
     public final int update(byte[] input, int inputOffset, int inputLen, byte[] output, int outputOffset)
          throws java.lang.IllegalStateException, ShortBufferException;
}
```

Subclasses: NullCipher

Passed To: CipherInputStream.CipherInputStream(), CipherOutputStream.CipherOutputStream(), SealedObject.{getObject(), SealedObject()}

Returned By: Cipher.getInstance()

CipherInputStream   JCE 1.2

javax.crypto

This class is an input stream that uses a Cipher object to encrypt or decrypt the bytes it reads from another stream. You must initialize the Cipher object before passing it to the CipherInputStream() constructor.

```
public class CipherInputStream extends java.io.FilterInputStream {
// Public Constructors
    public CipherInputStream(java.io.InputStream is, Cipher c);
// Protected Constructors
    protected CipherInputStream(java.io.InputStream is);
// Public Methods Overriding FilterInputStream
    public int available() throws java.io.IOException;
    public void close() throws java.io.IOException;
    public boolean markSupported();                                      constant
    public int read() throws java.io.IOException;
    public int read(byte[ ] b) throws java.io.IOException;
    public int read(byte[ ] b, int off, int len) throws java.io.IOException;
    public long skip(long n) throws java.io.IOException;
}
```

Hierarchy: Object→ java.io.InputStream→ java.io.FilterInputStream→ CipherInputStream

CipherOutputStream   JCE 1.2

javax.crypto

This class is an output stream that uses a Cipher object to encrypt or decrypt bytes before passing them to another output stream. You must initialize the Cipher object before passing it to the CipherOutputStream() constructor. If you are using a Cipher with any kind of padding, you must not call flush() until you are done writing all data to the stream; otherwise decryption fails.

```
public class CipherOutputStream extends java.io.FilterOutputStream {
// Public Constructors
    public CipherOutputStream(java.io.OutputStream os, Cipher c);
// Protected Constructors
    protected CipherOutputStream(java.io.OutputStream os);
// Public Methods Overriding FilterOutputStream
    public void close() throws java.io.IOException;
    public void flush() throws java.io.IOException;
    public void write(byte[ ] b) throws java.io.IOException;
    public void write(int b) throws java.io.IOException;
    public void write(byte[ ] b, int off, int len) throws java.io.IOException;
}
```

Hierarchy: Object→ java.io.OutputStream→ java.io.FilterOutputStream→ CipherOutputStream

CipherSpi   JCE 1.2

javax.crypto

This abstract class defines the service-provider interface for Cipher. A cryptographic provider must implement a concrete subclass of this class for each encryption algorithm it supports. A provider can implement a separate class for each combination of algorithm, mode, and padding scheme it supports or implement more general classes and leave the mode and/or padding scheme to be specified in calls to engineSetMode() and engineSetPadding(). Applications never need to use or subclass this class.

```
public abstract class CipherSpi {
// Public Constructors
    public CipherSpi();
// Protected Instance Methods
    protected abstract byte[] engineDoFinal(byte[] input, int inputOffset, int inputLen)
        throws IllegalBlockSizeException, BadPaddingException;
    protected abstract int engineDoFinal(byte[] input, int inputOffset, int inputLen, byte[] output, int outputOffset)
        throws ShortBufferException, IllegalBlockSizeException, BadPaddingException;
    protected abstract int engineGetBlockSize();
    protected abstract byte[] engineGetIV();
    protected abstract int engineGetOutputSize(int inputLen);
    protected abstract java.security.AlgorithmParameters engineGetParameters();
    protected abstract void engineInit(int opmode, java.security.Key key, java.security.SecureRandom random)
        throws java.security.InvalidKeyException;
    protected abstract void engineInit(int opmode, java.security.Key key,
                            java.security.spec.AlgorithmParameterSpec params,
                            java.security.SecureRandom random) throws java.security.InvalidKeyException,
        java.security.InvalidAlgorithmParameterException;
    protected abstract void engineInit(int opmode, java.security.Key key, java.security.AlgorithmParameters params,
                            java.security.SecureRandom random) throws java.security.InvalidKeyException,
        java.security.InvalidAlgorithmParameterException;
    protected abstract void engineSetMode(String mode) throws java.security.NoSuchAlgorithmException;
    protected abstract void engineSetPadding(String padding) throws NoSuchPaddingException;
    protected abstract byte[] engineUpdate(byte[] input, int inputOffset, int inputLen);
    protected abstract int engineUpdate(byte[] input, int inputOffset, int inputLen, byte[] output, int outputOffset)
        throws ShortBufferException;
}
```

Passed To: Cipher.Cipher()

IllegalBlockSizeException JCE 1.2

javax.crypto *serializable checked*

Signals that the length of data provided to a block cipher (as implemented, for example, by Cipher and SealedObject) does not match the block size for the cipher.

```
public class IllegalBlockSizeException extends java.security.GeneralSecurityException {
// Public Constructors
    public IllegalBlockSizeException();
    public IllegalBlockSizeException(String msg);
}
```

Hierarchy: Object→ Throwable(Serializable)→ Exception→
java.security.GeneralSecurityException→ IllegalBlockSizeException

Thrown By: Cipher.doFinal(), CipherSpi.engineDoFinal(), SealedObject.{getObject(), SealedObject()}

KeyAgreement JCE 1.2

javax.crypto

This class provides an API to a key-agreement protocol that allows two or more parties to agree on a secret key without exchanging any secrets and in such a way that an eavesdropper listening in on the communication between those parties cannot determine the secret key. The KeyAgreement class is algorithm-independent and provider-based, so you must obtain a KeyAgreement object by calling one of the static getInstance()

factory methods and specifying the name of the desired key agreement algorithm and, optionally, the name of the desired provider of that algorithm. The "SunJCE" provider implements a single key-agreement algorithm named "DiffieHellman".

To use a KeyAgreement object, each party first calls the init() method and supplies a Key object of its own. Then, each party obtains a Key object from one of the other parties to the agreement and calls doPhase(). Each party obtains an intermediate Key object as the return value of doPhase(), and these keys are again exchanged and passed to doPhase(). This process typically repeats n–1 times, where n is the number of parties, but the actual number of repetitions is algorithm-dependent. When doPhase() is called the last time, the second argument must be true to indicate that it is the last phase of the agreement. After all calls to doPhase() have been made, each party calls generateSecret() to obtain an array of bytes or a SecretKey object for a named algorithm type. All parties obtain the same bytes or SecretKey from this method. The KeyAgreement class is not responsible for the transfer of Key objects between parties or for mutual authentication among the parties. These tasks must be accomplished through some external mechanism.

The most common type of key agreement is "DiffieHellman" key agreement between two parties. It proceeds as follows. First, both parties obtain a java.security.KeyPairGenerator for the "DiffieHellman" algorithm and use it to generate a java.security.KeyPair of Diffie-Hellman public and private keys. Each party passes its private key to the init() method of its KeyAgreement object. (The init() method can be passed a java.security.spec.AlgorithmPa-rameterSpec object, but the Diffie-Hellman protocol does not require any additional parameters.) Next, the two parties exchange public keys, typically through some kind of networking mechanism (the KeyAgreement class is not responsible for the actual exchange of keys). Each party passes the public key of the other party to the doPhase() method of its KeyAgreement object. There are only two parties to this agreement, so only one phase is required, and the second argument to doPhase() is true. At this point, both parties call generateSecret() to obtain the shared secret key.

A three-party Diffie-Hellman key agreement requires two phases and is slightly more complicated. Let's call the three parties Alice, Bob, and Carol. Each generates a key pair and uses its private key to initialize its KeyAgreement object, as before. Then Alice passes her public key to Bob, Bob passes his to Carol, and Carol passes hers to Alice. Each party passes this public key to doPhase(). Since this is not the final doPhase(), the second argument is false, and doPhase() returns an intermediate Key object. The three parties exchange these intermediate keys again in the same way: Alice to Bob, Bob to Carol, and Carol to Alice. Now each party passes the intermediate key it has received to doPhase() a second time, passing true to indicate that this is the final phase. Finally, all three can call generateSecret() to obtain a shared key to encrypt future communication.

```
public class KeyAgreement {
// Protected Constructors
    protected KeyAgreement(KeyAgreementSpi keyAgreeSpi, java.security.Provider provider, String algorithm);
// Public Class Methods
    public static final KeyAgreement getInstance(String algorithm) throws java.security.NoSuchAlgorithmException;
    public static final KeyAgreement getInstance(String algorithm, String provider)
        throws java.security.NoSuchAlgorithmException, java.security.NoSuchProviderException;
// Public Instance Methods
    public final java.security.Key doPhase(java.security.Key key, boolean lastPhase)
        throws java.security.InvalidKeyException, java.lang.IllegalStateException;
    public final byte[ ] generateSecret( ) throws java.lang.IllegalStateException;
    public final SecretKey generateSecret(String algorithm) throws java.lang.IllegalStateException,
        java.security.NoSuchAlgorithmException, java.security.InvalidKeyException;
    public final int generateSecret(byte[ ] sharedSecret, int offset) throws java.lang.IllegalStateException,
        ShortBufferException;
```

```
  public final String getAlgorithm( );
  public final java.security.Provider getProvider( );
  public final void init(java.security.Key key) throws java.security.InvalidKeyException;
  public final void init(java.security.Key key, java.security.spec.AlgorithmParameterSpec params)
        throws java.security.InvalidKeyException, java.security.InvalidAlgorithmParameterException;
  public final void init(java.security.Key key, java.security.SecureRandom random)
        throws java.security.InvalidKeyException;
  public final void init(java.security.Key key, java.security.spec.AlgorithmParameterSpec params,
                    java.security.SecureRandom random) throws java.security.InvalidKeyException,
        java.security.InvalidAlgorithmParameterException;
}
```

Returned By: KeyAgreement.getInstance()

KeyAgreementSpi   JCE 1.2

javax.crypto

This abstract class defines the service-provider interface for KeyAgreement. A cryptographic provider must implement a concrete subclass of this class for each encryption
algorithm it supports. Applications never need to use or subclass this class.

```
public abstract class KeyAgreementSpi {
// Public Constructors
  public KeyAgreementSpi( );
// Protected Instance Methods
  protected abstract java.security.Key engineDoPhase(java.security.Key key, boolean lastPhase)
        throws java.security.InvalidKeyException, java.lang.IllegalStateException;
  protected abstract byte[ ] engineGenerateSecret() throws java.lang.IllegalStateException;
  protected abstract SecretKey engineGenerateSecret(String algorithm) throws java.lang.IllegalStateException,
        java.security.NoSuchAlgorithmException, java.security.InvalidKeyException;
  protected abstract int engineGenerateSecret(byte[ ] sharedSecret, int offset)
        throws java.lang.IllegalStateException, ShortBufferException;
  protected abstract void engineInit(java.security.Key key, java.security.SecureRandom random)
        throws java.security.InvalidKeyException;
  protected abstract void engineInit(java.security.Key key, java.security.spec.AlgorithmParameterSpec params,
                    java.security.SecureRandom random) throws java.security.InvalidKeyException,
        java.security.InvalidAlgorithmParameterException;
}
```

Passed To: KeyAgreement.KeyAgreement()

KeyGenerator   JCE 1.2

javax.crypto

This class provides an API for generating secret keys for symmetric cryptography. It is
similar to java.security.KeyPairGenerator, which generates public/private key pairs for asymmetric or public-key cryptography. KeyGenerator is algorithm-independent and provider-
based, so you must obtain a KeyGenerator instance by calling one of the static getInstance()
factory methods and specifying the name of the cryptographic algorithm for which a
key is desired and, optionally, the name of the security provider whose key-generation
implementation is to be used. The "SunJCE" provider includes KeyGenerator implementations for the "DES", "DESede", and "Blowfish" encryption algorithms, and also for the
"HmacMD5" and "HmacSHA1" message authentication (MAC) algorithms.

Once you have obtained a KeyGenerator, you initialize it with the init() method. You can
provide a java.security.spec.AlgorithmParameterSpec object to provide algorithm-specific initialization parameters or simply specify the desired size (in bits) of the key to be

generated. In either case, you can also specify a source of randomness in the form of a SecureRandom object. If you do not specify a SecureRandom, the KeyGenerator instantiates one of its own. None of the algorithms supported by the "SunJCE" provider require algorithm-specific parameters.

After calling getInstance() to obtain a KeyGenerator and init() to initialize it, simply call generateKey() to create a new SecretKey. Remember that the SecretKey must be kept secret. Take precautions when storing or transmitting the key, so that it does not fall into the wrong hands. You may want to use a java.security.KeyStore object to store the key in a password-protected form.

```
public class KeyGenerator {
// Protected Constructors
      protected KeyGenerator(KeyGeneratorSpi keyGenSpi, java.security.Provider provider, String algorithm);
// Public Class Methods
      public static final KeyGenerator getInstance(String algorithm) throws java.security.NoSuchAlgorithmException;
      public static final KeyGenerator getInstance(String algorithm, String provider)
            throws java.security.NoSuchAlgorithmException, java.security.NoSuchProviderException;
// Public Instance Methods
      public final SecretKey generateKey();
      public final String getAlgorithm();
      public final java.security.Provider getProvider();
      public final void init(java.security.spec.AlgorithmParameterSpec params)
            throws java.security.InvalidAlgorithmParameterException;
      public final void init(java.security.SecureRandom random);
      public final void init(int keysize);
      public final void init(java.security.spec.AlgorithmParameterSpec params, java.security.SecureRandom random)
            throws java.security.InvalidAlgorithmParameterException;
      public final void init(int keysize, java.security.SecureRandom random);
}
```

Returned By: KeyGenerator.getInstance()

KeyGeneratorSpi   JCE 1.2

javax.crypto

This abstract class defines the service-provider interface for KeyGenerator. A cryptographic provider must implement a concrete subclass of this class for each key-generation algorithm it supports. Applications never need to use or subclass this class.

```
public abstract class KeyGeneratorSpi {
// Public Constructors
      public KeyGeneratorSpi();
// Protected Instance Methods
      protected abstract SecretKey engineGenerateKey();
      protected abstract void engineInit(java.security.SecureRandom random);
      protected abstract void engineInit(java.security.spec.AlgorithmParameterSpec params,
                                java.security.SecureRandom random)
            throws java.security.InvalidAlgorithmParameterException;
      protected abstract void engineInit(int keysize, java.security.SecureRandom random);
}
```

Passed To: KeyGenerator.KeyGenerator()

Mac   JCE 1.2

javax.crypto   *cloneable*

This class defines an API for computing a *message authentication code* (MAC) that can check the integrity of information transmitted between two parties that share a secret key. A MAC is similar to a digital signature, except that it is generated with a secret key rather than with a public/private key pair. The Mac class is algorithm-independent and provider-based. Obtain a Mac object by calling one of the static getInstance() factory methods and specifying the name of the desired MAC algorithm and, optionally, the name of the provider of the desired implementation. The "SunJCE" provider implements two algorithms: "HmacMD5" and "HmacSHA1". These are MAC algorithms based on the MD5 and SHA-1 cryptographic hash functions.

After obtaining a Mac object, initialize it by calling the init() method and specifying a SecretKey and, optionally, a java.security.spec.AlgorithmParameterSpec object. The "HmacMD5" and "HmacSHA1" algorithms can use any kind of SecretKey; they are not restricted to a particular cryptographic algorithm. And neither algorithm requires an AlgorithmParameter-Spec object.

After obtaining and initializing a Mac object, specify the data for which the MAC is to be computed. If the data is contained in a single byte array, simply pass it to doFinal(). If the data is streaming or is stored in various locations, you can supply the data in multiple calls to update(). End the series of update() calls with a single call to doFinal(). Note that some versions of doFinal() return the MAC data as the function return value. Another version stores the MAC data in a byte array you supply. If you use this version of doFinal(), be sure to call getMacLength() to instantiate an array of the correct length.

A call to doFinal() resets the internal state of a Mac object. If you want to compute a MAC for part of your data and then proceed to compute the MAC for the full data, you should clone() the Mac object before calling doFinal(). Note, however, that Mac implementations are not required to implement Cloneable.

```
public class Mac implements Cloneable {
// Protected Constructors
    protected Mac(MacSpi macSpi, java.security.Provider provider, String algorithm);
// Public Class Methods
    public static final Mac getInstance(String algorithm) throws java.security.NoSuchAlgorithmException;
    public static final Mac getInstance(String algorithm, String provider)
        throws java.security.NoSuchAlgorithmException, java.security.NoSuchProviderException;
// Public Instance Methods
    public final byte[ ] doFinal() throws java.lang.IllegalStateException;
    public final byte[ ] doFinal(byte[ ] input) throws java.lang.IllegalStateException;
    public final void doFinal(byte[ ] output, int outOffset) throws ShortBufferException, java.lang.IllegalStateException;
    public final String getAlgorithm();
    public final int getMacLength();
    public final java.security.Provider getProvider();
    public final void init(java.security.Key key) throws java.security.InvalidKeyException;
    public final void init(java.security.Key key, java.security.spec.AlgorithmParameterSpec params)
        throws java.security.InvalidKeyException, java.security.InvalidAlgorithmParameterException;
    public final void reset();
    public final void update(byte[ ] input) throws java.lang.IllegalStateException;
    public final void update(byte input) throws java.lang.IllegalStateException;
    public final void update(byte[ ] input, int offset, int len) throws java.lang.IllegalStateException;
// Public Methods Overriding Object
    public final Object clone() throws CloneNotSupportedException;
}
```

Hierarchy: Object→ Mac(Cloneable)

Returned By: Mac.getInstance()

MacSpi

JCE 1.2

javax.crypto

This abstract class defines the service-provider interface for Mac. A cryptographic provider must implement a concrete subclass of this class for each MAC algorithm it supports. Applications never need to use or subclass this class.

```
public abstract class MacSpi {
// Public Constructors
    public MacSpi();
// Public Methods Overriding Object
    public Object clone() throws CloneNotSupportedException;
// Protected Instance Methods
    protected abstract byte[ ] engineDoFinal();
    protected abstract int engineGetMacLength();
    protected abstract void engineInit(java.security.Key key, java.security.spec.AlgorithmParameterSpec params)
        throws java.security.InvalidKeyException, java.security.InvalidAlgorithmParameterException;
    protected abstract void engineReset();
    protected abstract void engineUpdate(byte input);
    protected abstract void engineUpdate(byte[ ] input, int offset, int len);
}
```

Passed To: Mac.Mac()

NoSuchPaddingException

JCE 1.2

javax.crypto   *serializable checked*

Signals that no implementation of the requested padding scheme can be found.

```
public class NoSuchPaddingException extends java.security.GeneralSecurityException {
// Public Constructors
    public NoSuchPaddingException();
    public NoSuchPaddingException(String msg);
}
```

Hierarchy: Object→ Throwable(Serializable)→ Exception→
java.security.GeneralSecurityException→ NoSuchPaddingException

Thrown By: Cipher.getInstance(), CipherSpi.engineSetPadding()

NullCipher

JCE 1.2

javax.crypto

This trivial subclass of Cipher implements an identity cipher that does not transform plain text in any way. Unlike Cipher objects returned by Cipher.getInstance(), a NullCipher must be created with the NullCipher() constructor.

```
public class NullCipher extends Cipher {
// Public Constructors
    public NullCipher();
}
```

Hierarchy: Object→ Cipher→ NullCipher

SealedObject

JCE 1.2

javax.crypto   *serializable*

This class is a wrapper around a serializable object. It serializes the object and encrypts the resulting data stream, thereby protecting the confidentiality of the object. Create a SealedObject by specifying the object to be sealed and a Cipher object to perform the encryption. Retrieve the sealed object by calling getObject() and specifying the Cipher or java.security.Key to use for decryption. The SealedObject keeps track of the encryption algorithm and parameters so that a Key object alone can decrypt the object.

```
public class SealedObject implements Serializable {
// Public Constructors
    public SealedObject(Serializable object, Cipher c) throws java.io.IOException, IllegalBlockSizeException;
// Public Instance Methods
    public final String getAlgorithm();
    public final Object getObject(java.security.Key key) throws java.io.IOException, ClassNotFoundException,
        java.security.NoSuchAlgorithmException, java.security.InvalidKeyException;
    public final Object getObject(Cipher c) throws java.io.IOException, ClassNotFoundException,
        IllegalBlockSizeException, BadPaddingException;
    public final Object getObject(java.security.Key key, String provider) throws java.io.IOException,
        ClassNotFoundException, java.security.NoSuchAlgorithmException, java.security.NoSuchProviderException,
        java.security.InvalidKeyException;
}
```

Hierarchy: Object → SealedObject(Serializable)

SecretKey

JCE 1.2

javax.crypto   *serializable*

This interface represents a secret key used for symmetric cryptographic algorithms that depend on both the sender and receiver knowing the same secret. SecretKey extends the java.security.Key interface, but does not add any new methods. The interface exists in order to keep secret keys distinct from the public and private keys used in public-key, or asymmetric, cryptography. See also java.security.PublicKey and java.security.PrivateKey.

A secret key is nothing more than arrays of bytes and does not require a specialized encoding format. Therefore, an implementation of this interface should return the format name "RAW" from getFormat() and should return the bytes of the key from getEncoded(). (These two methods are defined by the java.security.Key interface that SecretKey extends.)

```
public abstract interface SecretKey extends java.security.Key {
}
```

Hierarchy: (SecretKey(java.security.Key(Serializable)))

Implementations: javax.crypto.spec.SecretKeySpec

Passed To: SecretKeyFactory.{getKeySpec(), translateKey()},
SecretKeyFactorySpi.{engineGetKeySpec(), engineTranslateKey()}

Returned By: KeyAgreement.generateSecret(), KeyAgreementSpi.engineGenerateSecret(),
KeyGenerator.generateKey(), KeyGeneratorSpi.engineGenerateKey(),
SecretKeyFactory.{generateSecret(), translateKey()}, SecretKeyFactorySpi.{engineGenerateSecret(),
engineTranslateKey()}

SecretKeyFactory

JCE 1.2

javax.crypto

This class defines an API for translating a secret key between its opaque SecretKey representation and its transparent javax.crypto.SecretKeySpec representation. It is much like java.security.KeyFactory, except that it works with secret (or symmetric) keys rather than with public and private (asymmetric) keys. SecretKeyFactory is algorithm-independent and provider-based, so you must obtain a SecretKeyFactory object by calling one of the static getInstance() factory methods and specifying the name of the desired secret-key algorithm and, optionally, the name of the provider whose implementation is desired. The

"SunJCE" provider provides SecretKeyFactory implementations for the "DES", "DESede", and "PBEWithMD5AndDES" algorithms.

Once you have obtained a SecretKeyFactory, use generateSecret() to create a SecretKey from a java.security.spec.KeySpec (or its subclass, javax.crypto.spec.SecretKeySpec). Or call getKeySpec() to obtain a KeySpec for a Key object. Because there can be more than one suitable type of KeySpec, getKeySpec() requires a Class object to specify the type of the KeySpec to be created. See also DESKeySpec, DESedeKeySpec, and PBEKeySpec in the javax.crypto.spec package.

```
public class SecretKeyFactory {
// Protected Constructors
    protected SecretKeyFactory(SecretKeyFactorySpi keyFacSpi, java.security.Provider provider, String algorithm);
// Public Class Methods
    public static final SecretKeyFactory getInstance(String algorithm) throws java.security.NoSuchAlgorithmException;
    public static final SecretKeyFactory getInstance(String algorithm, String provider)
        throws java.security.NoSuchAlgorithmException, java.security.NoSuchProviderException;
// Public Instance Methods
    public final SecretKey generateSecret(java.security.spec.KeySpec keySpec)
        throws java.security.spec.InvalidKeySpecException;
    public final String getAlgorithm();
    public final java.security.spec.KeySpec getKeySpec(SecretKey key, Class keySpec)
        throws java.security.spec.InvalidKeySpecException;
    public final java.security.Provider getProvider();
    public final SecretKey translateKey(SecretKey key) throws java.security.InvalidKeyException;
}
```

Returned By: SecretKeyFactory.getInstance()

SecretKeyFactorySpi   JCE 1.2

javax.crypto

This abstract class defines the service-provider interface for SecretKeyFactory. A cryptographic provider must implement a concrete subclass of this class for each type of secret key it supports. Applications never need to use or subclass this class.

```
public abstract class SecretKeyFactorySpi {
// Public Constructors
    public SecretKeyFactorySpi();
// Protected Instance Methods
    protected abstract SecretKey engineGenerateSecret(java.security.spec.KeySpec keySpec)
        throws java.security.spec.InvalidKeySpecException;
    protected abstract java.security.spec.KeySpec engineGetKeySpec(SecretKey key, Class keySpec)
        throws java.security.spec.InvalidKeySpecException;
    protected abstract SecretKey engineTranslateKey(SecretKey key) throws java.security.InvalidKeyException;
}
```

Passed To: SecretKeyFactory.SecretKeyFactory()

ShortBufferException   JCE 1.2

javax.crypto   *serializable checked*

Signals that an output buffer is too short to hold the results of an operation.

```
public class ShortBufferException extends java.security.GeneralSecurityException {
// Public Constructors
    public ShortBufferException();
    public ShortBufferException(String msg);
}
```

Hierarchy: Object→ Throwable(Serializable)→ Exception→
java.security.GeneralSecurityException→ ShortBufferException

Thrown By: Cipher.{doFinal(), update()}, CipherSpi.{engineDoFinal(), engineUpdate()},
KeyAgreement.generateSecret(), KeyAgreementSpi.engineGenerateSecret(), Mac.doFinal()

CHAPTER 27

The javax.crypto.interfaces Package

The interfaces in the javax.crypto.interfaces package define the methods that must be supported by the Diffie-Hellman public/private key pairs used in the Diffie-Hellman key-agreement protocol. These interfaces are typically of interest only to programmers who are implementing a cryptographic provider or who want to implement cryptographic algorithms themselves. Use of this package requires basic familiarity with the Diffie-Hellman key-agreement algorithm and the mathematics that underlie it. Figure 27-1 shows the class hierarchy of this package. Note that the javax.crypto.spec package also contains classes that provide algorithm-specific details about Diffie-Hellman keys.

Figure 27–1: The javax.crypto.interfaces package

DHKey   JCE 1.2
javax.crypto.interfaces

This interface represents a Diffie-Hellman key. The javax.crypto.spec.DHParameterSpec returned by getParams() specifies the parameters that generate the key; they define a key family. See the subinterfaces DHPublicKey and DHPrivateKey for the actual key values.

```
public abstract interface DHKey {
// Public Instance Methods
    public abstract javax.crypto.spec.DHParameterSpec getParams( );
}
```

Implementations: DHPrivateKey, DHPublicKey

DHPrivateKey   JCE 1.2

javax.crypto.interfaces   *serializable*

This interface represents a Diffie-Hellman private key. Note that it extends two interfaces: DHKey and java.security.PrivateKey. getX() returns the private-key value. If you are working with a PrivateKey you know is a Diffie-Hellman key, you can cast your PrivateKey to a DHPrivateKey.

```
public abstract interface DHPrivateKey extends DHKey, java.security.PrivateKey {
// Public Instance Methods
    public abstract java.math.BigInteger getX( );
}
```

Hierarchy: (DHPrivateKey(DHKey, java.security.PrivateKey(java.security.Key(Serializable))))

DHPublicKey   JCE 1.2

javax.crypto.interfaces   *serializable*

This interface represents a Diffie-Hellman public key. Note that it extends two interfaces: DHKey and java.security.PublicKey. getY() returns the public-key value. If you are working with a PublicKey you know is a Diffie-Hellman key, you can cast your PublicKey to a DHPublicKey.

```
public abstract interface DHPublicKey extends DHKey, java.security.PublicKey {
// Public Instance Methods
    public abstract java.math.BigInteger getY( );
}
```

Hierarchy: (DHPublicKey(DHKey, java.security.PublicKey(java.security.Key(Serializable))))

CHAPTER 28

The javax.crypto.spec Package

The javax.crypto.spec package contains classes that define transparent java.security.spec.KeySpec and java.security.spec.AlgorithmParameterSpec representations of secret keys, Diffie-Hellman public and private keys, and parameters used by various cryptographic algorithms. The classes in this package are used in conjunction with java.security.KeyFactory, javax.crypto.SecretKeyFactory and java.security.AlgorithmParameters for converting opaque Key, and AlgorithmParameters objects to and from transparent representations. Figure 28-1 shows the class hierarchy of this package. In order to make good use of this package, you must be familiar with the specifications of the various cryptographic algorithms it supports and the basic mathematics that underlie those algorithms.

DESedeKeySpec   JCE 1.2

javax.crypto.spec

This class is a transparent representation of a DESede (triple-DES) key. The key is 24 bytes long.

```
public class DESedeKeySpec implements java.security.spec.KeySpec {
// Public Constructors
    public DESedeKeySpec(byte[ ] key) throws java.security.InvalidKeyException;
    public DESedeKeySpec(byte[ ] key, int offset) throws java.security.InvalidKeyException;
// Public Constants
    public static final int DES_EDE_KEY_LEN;                                        =24
// Public Class Methods
    public static boolean isParityAdjusted(byte[ ] key, int offset) throws java.security.InvalidKeyException;
// Public Instance Methods
    public byte[ ] getKey( );
}
```

Hierarchy: Object → DESedeKeySpec(java.security.spec.KeySpec)

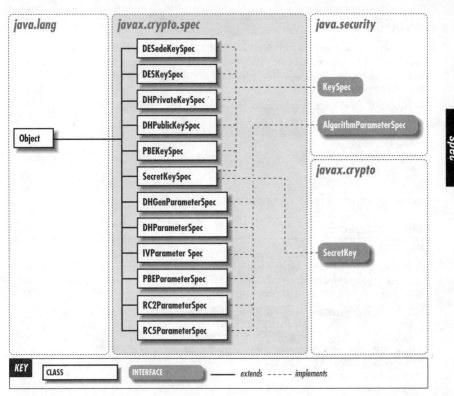

Figure 28-1: The javax.crypto.spec package

DESKeySpec

javax.crypto.spec

This class is a transparent representation of a DES key. The key is eight bytes long.

```
public class DESKeySpec implements java.security.spec.KeySpec {
// Public Constructors
    public DESKeySpec(byte[ ] key) throws java.security.InvalidKeyException;
    public DESKeySpec(byte[ ] key, int offset) throws java.security.InvalidKeyException;
// Public Constants
    public static final int DES_KEY_LEN;                                          =8
// Public Class Methods
    public static boolean isParityAdjusted(byte[ ] key, int offset) throws java.security.InvalidKeyException;
    public static boolean isWeak(byte[ ] key, int offset) throws java.security.InvalidKeyException;
// Public Instance Methods
    public byte[ ] getKey( );
}
```

Hierarchy: Object→ DESKeySpec(java.security.spec.KeySpec)

DHGenParameterSpec   JCE 1.2
javax.crypto.spec

This class is a transparent representation of the values needed to generate a set of
Diffie-Hellman parameters (see DHParameterSpec). An instance of this class can be
passed to the init() method of a java.security.AlgorithmParameterGenerator that computes
Diffie-Hellman parameters.

```
public class DHGenParameterSpec implements java.security.spec.AlgorithmParameterSpec {
// Public Constructors
    public DHGenParameterSpec(int primeSize, int exponentSize);
// Public Instance Methods
    public int getExponentSize();
    public int getPrimeSize();
}
```

Hierarchy: Object→ DHGenParameterSpec(java.security.spec.AlgorithmParameterSpec)

DHParameterSpec   JCE 1.2
javax.crypto.spec

This class is a transparent representation of the set of parameters required by the Diffie-
Hellman key-agreement algorithm. All parties to the key agreement must share these
parameters and use them to generate a Diffie-Hellman public/private key pair.

```
public class DHParameterSpec implements java.security.spec.AlgorithmParameterSpec {
// Public Constructors
    public DHParameterSpec(java.math.BigInteger p, java.math.BigInteger g);
    public DHParameterSpec(java.math.BigInteger p, java.math.BigInteger g, int l);
// Public Instance Methods
    public java.math.BigInteger getG();
    public int getL();
    public java.math.BigInteger getP();
}
```

Hierarchy: Object→ DHParameterSpec(java.security.spec.AlgorithmParameterSpec)

Returned By: javax.crypto.interfaces.DHKey.getParams()

DHPrivateKeySpec   JCE 1.2
javax.crypto.spec

This java.security.spec.KeySpec is a transparent representation of a Diffie-Hellman private
key.

```
public class DHPrivateKeySpec implements java.security.spec.KeySpec {
// Public Constructors
    public DHPrivateKeySpec(java.math.BigInteger x, java.math.BigInteger p, java.math.BigInteger g);
// Public Instance Methods
    public java.math.BigInteger getG();
    public java.math.BigInteger getP();
    public java.math.BigInteger getX();
}
```

Hierarchy: Object→ DHPrivateKeySpec(java.security.spec.KeySpec)

DHPublicKeySpec
JCE 1.2

javax.crypto.spec

This java.security.spec.KeySpec is a transparent representation of a Diffie-Hellman public key.

```
public class DHPublicKeySpec implements java.security.spec.KeySpec {
// Public Constructors
    public DHPublicKeySpec(java.math.BigInteger y, java.math.BigInteger p, java.math.BigInteger g);
// Public Instance Methods
    public java.math.BigInteger getG();
    public java.math.BigInteger getP();
    public java.math.BigInteger getY();
}
```

Hierarchy: Object→ DHPublicKeySpec(java.security.spec.KeySpec)

IvParameterSpec
JCE 1.2

javax.crypto.spec

This java.security.spec.AlgorithmParameterSpec is a transparent representation of an *initialization vector* or IV. An IV is required for block ciphers used in feedback mode, such as DES in CBC mode.

```
public class IvParameterSpec implements java.security.spec.AlgorithmParameterSpec {
// Public Constructors
    public IvParameterSpec(byte[ ] iv);
    public IvParameterSpec(byte[ ] iv, int offset, int len);
// Public Instance Methods
    public byte[ ] getIV();
}
```

Hierarchy: Object→ IvParameterSpec(java.security.spec.AlgorithmParameterSpec)

PBEKeySpec
JCE 1.2

javax.crypto.spec

This class is a transparent representation of a password used in password-based encryption (PBE). The password is stored as a char array rather than as a String, so that the characters of the password can be overwritten when they are no longer needed (for increased security).

```
public class PBEKeySpec implements java.security.spec.KeySpec {
// Public Constructors
    public PBEKeySpec(char[ ] password);
// Public Instance Methods
    public final char[ ] getPassword();
}
```

Hierarchy: Object→ PBEKeySpec(java.security.spec.KeySpec)

PBEParameterSpec
JCE 1.2

javax.crypto.spec

This class is a transparent representation of the parameters used with the password-based encryption algorithm defined by PKCS#5.

```
public class PBEParameterSpec implements java.security.spec.AlgorithmParameterSpec {
// Public Constructors
    public PBEParameterSpec(byte[ ] salt, int iterationCount);
// Public Instance Methods
    public int getIterationCount( );
    public byte[ ] getSalt( );
}
```

Hierarchy: Object→ PBEParameterSpec(java.security.spec.AlgorithmParameterSpec)

RC2ParameterSpec   JCE 1.2

javax.crypto.spec

This class is a transparent representation of the parameters used by the RC2 encryption algorithm. An object of this class initializes a Cipher object that implements RC2. Note that the "SunJCE" provider supplied by Sun does not implement RC2.

```
public class RC2ParameterSpec implements java.security.spec.AlgorithmParameterSpec {
// Public Constructors
    public RC2ParameterSpec(int effectiveKeyBits);
    public RC2ParameterSpec(int effectiveKeyBits, byte[ ] iv);
    public RC2ParameterSpec(int effectiveKeyBits, byte[ ] iv, int offset);
// Public Instance Methods
    public int getEffectiveKeyBits( );
    public byte[ ] getIV( );
}
```

Hierarchy: Object→ RC2ParameterSpec(java.security.spec.AlgorithmParameterSpec)

RC5ParameterSpec   JCE 1.2

javax.crypto.spec

This class is a transparent representation of the parameters used by the RC5 encryption algorithm. An object of this class initializes a Cipher object that implements RC5. Note that the "SunJCE" provider supplied by Sun does not implement RC5.

```
public class RC5ParameterSpec implements java.security.spec.AlgorithmParameterSpec {
// Public Constructors
    public RC5ParameterSpec(int version, int rounds, int wordSize);
    public RC5ParameterSpec(int version, int rounds, int wordSize, byte[ ] iv);
    public RC5ParameterSpec(int version, int rounds, int wordSize, byte[ ] iv, int offset);
// Public Instance Methods
    public byte[ ] getIV( );
    public int getRounds( );
    public int getVersion( );
    public int getWordSize( );
}
```

Hierarchy: Object→ RC5ParameterSpec(java.security.spec.AlgorithmParameterSpec)

SecretKeySpec   JCE 1.2

javax.crypto.spec   *serializable*

This class is a transparent and algorithm-independent representation of a secret key. This class is useful only for encryption algorithms (such as DES and DESede) whose secret keys can be represented as arbitrary byte arrays and do not require auxiliary parameters. Note that SecretKeySpec implements the javax.crypto.SecretKey interface directly, so no algorithm-specific javax.crypto.SecretKeyFactory object is required.

```
public class SecretKeySpec implements java.security.spec.KeySpec, javax.crypto.SecretKey {
// Public Constructors
    public SecretKeySpec(byte[ ] key, String algorithm);
    public SecretKeySpec(byte[ ] key, int offset, int len, String algorithm);
// Methods Implementing Key
    public String getAlgorithm();
    public byte[ ] getEncoded();
    public String getFormat();
// Public Methods Overriding Object
    public boolean equals(Object obj);
    public int hashCode();
}
```

Hierarchy: Object → SecretKeySpec(java.security.spec.KeySpec, javax.crypto.SecretKey(java.security.Key(Serializable)))

CHAPTER 29

Class, Method, and Field Index

The following index allows you to look up a class or interface and find what package it is defined in. It also allows you to look up a method or field and find what class it is defined in. Use it when you want to look up a class but don't know its package, or when you want to look up a method but don't know its class.

address: SocketImpl

addService(): BeanContextServices, BeanContextServicesSupport

addShutdownHook(): Runtime

addURL(): URLClassLoader

addVetoableChangeListener(): BeanContextChild, BeanContextChildSupport, VetoableChangeSupport

Adler32: java.util.zip

after(): Calendar, Date

AlgorithmParameterGenerator: java.security

AlgorithmParameterGeneratorSpi: java.security

AlgorithmParameters: java.security

AlgorithmParameterSpec: java.security.spec

AlgorithmParametersSpi: java.security

aliases(): KeyStore

allowThreadSuspension(): ThreadGroup

allowUserInteraction: URLConnection

AllPermission: java.security

ALPHABETIC_PRESENTATION_FORMS: UnicodeBlock

AM: Calendar

AM_PM: Calendar

AM_PM_FIELD: DateFormat

and(): BigInteger, BitSet

andNot(): BigInteger, BitSet

annotateClass(): ObjectOutputStream

annotateProxyClass(): ObjectOutputStream

Annotation: java.text

append(): StringBuffer

AppletInitializer: java.beans

applyLocalizedPattern(): DecimalFormat, SimpleDateFormat

applyPattern(): ChoiceFormat, DecimalFormat, MessageFormat, SimpleDateFormat

appRandom: SignatureSpi

APRIL: Calendar

ARABIC: UnicodeBlock

ARABIC_PRESENTATION_FORMS_A: UnicodeBlock

ARABIC_PRESENTATION_FORMS_B: UnicodeBlock

areFieldsSet: Calendar

ArithmeticException: java.lang

ARMENIAN: UnicodeBlock

Array: java.lang.reflect

arraycopy(): System

ArrayIndexOutOfBoundsException: java.lang

ArrayList: java.util

Arrays: java.util

ArrayStoreException: java.lang

ARROWS: UnicodeBlock

asin(): Math, StrictMath

asList(): Arrays

atan(): Math, StrictMath

atan2(): Math, StrictMath

Attribute: java.text.AttributedCharacterIterator

AttributedCharacterIterator: java.text

AttributedCharacterIterator.Attribute: java.text

AttributedString: java.text

attributeNames(): FeatureDescriptor

Attributes: java.util.jar

Attributes.Name: java.util.jar

AUGUST: Calendar

Authenticator: java.net

available(): BufferedInputStream, ByteArrayInputStream, CipherInputStream, FileInputStream, FilterInputStream, InflaterInputStream, InputStream, LineNumberInputStream, ObjectInput, ObjectInputStream, PipedInputStream, PushbackInputStream, SequenceInputStream, SocketImpl, StringBufferInputStream, ZipInputStream

avoidingGui(): BeanContextSupport, Visibility

B

BadPaddingException: javax.crypto

baseWireHandle: ObjectStreamConstants

BASIC_LATIN: UnicodeBlock

BasicPermission: java.security

BC: GregorianCalendar

bcmListeners: BeanContextSupport

BCSChild: java.beans.beancontext.BeanContextSupport

bcsChildren(): BeanContextSupport

BCSIterator: java.beans.beancontext.BeanContextSupport

bcsListeners: BeanContextServicesSupport

bcsPreDeserializationHook(): BeanContextServicesSupport, BeanContextSupport

bcsPreSerializationHook(): BeanContextServicesSupport, BeanContextSupport

BCSSChild: java.beans.beancontext.BeanContextServicesSupport

BCSSProxyServiceProvider: java.beans.beancontext.BeanContextServicesSupport

BCSSServiceProvider: java.beans.beancontext.BeanContextServicesSupport

beanContext: BeanContextChildSupport

BeanContext: java.beans.beancontext

BeanContextChild: java.beans.beancontext

BeanContextChildComponentProxy: java.beans.beancontext

beanContextChildPeer: BeanContextChildSupport

BeanContextChildSupport: java.beans.beancontext
BeanContextContainerProxy: java.beans.beancontext
BeanContextEvent: java.beans.beancontext
BeanContextMembershipEvent: java.beans.beancontext
BeanContextMembershipListener: java.beans.beancontext
BeanContextProxy: java.beans.beancontext
BeanContextServiceAvailableEvent: java.beans.beancontext
BeanContextServiceProvider: java.beans.beancontext
BeanContextServiceProviderBeanInfo: java.beans.beancontext
BeanContextServiceRevokedEvent: java.beans.beancontext
BeanContextServiceRevokedListener: java.beans.beancontext
BeanContextServices: java.beans.beancontext
BeanContextServicesListener: java.beans.beancontext
BeanContextServicesSupport: java.beans.beancontext
BeanContextServicesSupport.BCSSChild: java.beans.beancontext
BeanContextServicesSupport.BCSSProxyServiceProvider: java.beans.beancontext
BeanContextServicesSupport.BCSSServiceProvider: java.beans.beancontext
BeanContextSupport: java.beans.beancontext
BeanContextSupport.BCSChild: java.beans.beancontext
BeanContextSupport.BCSIterator: java.beans.beancontext
BeanDescriptor: java.beans
BeanInfo: java.beans
Beans: java.beans
before(): Calendar, Date
BENGALI: UnicodeBlock
BEST_COMPRESSION: Deflater
BEST_SPEED: Deflater
BigDecimal: java.math
BigInteger: java.math
binarySearch(): Arrays, Collections
bind(): DatagramSocketImpl, SocketImpl
BindException: java.net
bitCount(): BigInteger
bitLength(): BigInteger
BitSet: java.util
BLOCK_ELEMENTS: UnicodeBlock
Boolean: java.lang

booleanValue(): Boolean
BOPOMOFO: UnicodeBlock
BOX_DRAWING: UnicodeBlock
BreakIterator: java.text
buf: BufferedInputStream, BufferedOutputStream, ByteArrayInputStream, ByteArrayOutputStream, CharArrayReader, CharArrayWriter, DeflaterOutputStream, InflaterInputStream, PushbackInputStream
buffer: PipedInputStream, StringBufferInputStream
BufferedInputStream: java.io
BufferedOutputStream: java.io
BufferedReader: java.io
BufferedWriter: java.io
Byte: java.lang
ByteArrayInputStream: java.io
ByteArrayOutputStream: java.io
bytesTransferred: InterruptedIOException
byteValue(): Byte, Double, Float, Integer, Long, Number, Short

C

Calendar: java.util
calendar: DateFormat
CANADA: Locale
CANADA_FRENCH: Locale
cancel(): Timer, TimerTask
CANONICAL_DECOMPOSITION: Collator
canRead(): File
canWrite(): File
capacity(): StringBuffer, Vector
capacityIncrement: Vector
CASE_INSENSITIVE_ORDER: String
ceil(): Math, StrictMath
Certificate: java.security, java.security.cert
Certificate.CertificateRep: java.security.cert
CertificateEncodingException: java.security.cert
CertificateException: java.security.cert
CertificateExpiredException: java.security.cert
CertificateFactory: java.security.cert
CertificateFactorySpi: java.security.cert
CertificateNotYetValidException: java.security.cert
CertificateParsingException: java.security.cert
CertificateRep: java.security.cert.Certificate
certificates(): Identity
Character: java.lang
Character.Subset: java.lang
Character.UnicodeBlock: java.lang
CharacterIterator: java.text

CharArrayReader: java.io
CharArrayWriter: java.io
charAt(): String, StringBuffer
CharConversionException: java.io
charValue(): Character
checkAccept(): SecurityManager
checkAccess(): SecurityManager, Thread, Thread-
Group
checkAwtEventQueueAccess(): SecurityManager
checkConnect(): SecurityManager
checkCreateClassLoader(): SecurityManager
checkDelete(): SecurityManager
CheckedInputStream: java.util.zip
CheckedOutputStream: java.util.zip
checkError(): PrintStream, PrintWriter
checkExec(): SecurityManager
checkExit(): SecurityManager
checkGuard(): Guard, Permission
checkLink(): SecurityManager
checkListen(): SecurityManager
checkMemberAccess(): SecurityManager
checkMulticast(): SecurityManager
checkPackageAccess(): SecurityManager
checkPackageDefinition(): SecurityManager
checkPermission(): AccessControlContext, Access-
Controller, Acl, AclEntry, SecurityManager
checkPrintJobAccess(): SecurityManager
checkPropertiesAccess(): SecurityManager
checkPropertyAccess(): SecurityManager
checkRead(): SecurityManager
checkSecurityAccess(): SecurityManager
checkSetFactory(): SecurityManager
Checksum: java.util.zip
checkSystemClipboardAccess(): SecurityManager
checkTopLevelWindow(): SecurityManager
checkValidity(): X509Certificate
checkWrite(): SecurityManager
childDeserializedHook(): BeanContextSupport
childJustAddedHook(): BeanContextSupport
childJustRemovedHook(): BeanContextServicesSupport, BeanContextSupport
children: BeanContextMembershipEvent, BeanContextSupport
childrenAdded(): BeanContextMembershipListener
childrenRemoved(): BeanContextMembershipListener
childValue(): InheritableThreadLocal
CHINA: Locale
CHINESE: Locale
ChoiceFormat: java.text
Cipher: javax.crypto

CipherInputStream: javax.crypto
CipherOutputStream: javax.crypto
CipherSpi: javax.crypto
CJK_COMPATIBILITY: UnicodeBlock
CJK_COMPATIBILITY_FORMS: UnicodeBlock
CJK_COMPATIBILITY_IDEOGRAPHS: UnicodeBlock
CJK_SYMBOLS_AND_PUNCTUATION: UnicodeBlock
CJK_UNIFIED_IDEOGRAPHS: UnicodeBlock
Class: java.lang
CLASS_PATH: Name
ClassCastException: java.lang
ClassCircularityError: java.lang
classDepth(): SecurityManager
classEquals(): BeanContextSupport
ClassFormatError: java.lang
ClassLoader: java.lang
classLoaderDepth(): SecurityManager
classname: InvalidClassException
ClassNotFoundException: java.lang
clear(): AbstractCollection, AbstractList, AbstractMap,
ArrayList, Attributes, BeanContextSupport, BitSet,
Calendar, Collection, HashMap, HashSet,
Hashtable, LinkedList, List, Manifest, Map,
Provider, Reference, Set, TreeMap, TreeSet, Vector,
WeakHashMap
clearBit(): BigInteger
clearChanged(): Observable
clone(): AclEntry, ArrayList, Attributes, BitSet, BreakIt-
erator, Calendar, CharacterIterator, ChoiceFormat,
Collator, Date, DateFormat, DateFormatSymbols,
DecimalFormat, DecimalFormatSymbols, Format,
HashMap, HashSet, Hashtable, LinkedList, Locale,
Mac, MacSpi, Manifest, MessageDigest, Mes-
sageDigestSpi, MessageFormat, NumberFormat,
Object, RuleBasedCollator, Signature, Signa-
tureSpi, SimpleDateFormat, SimpleTimeZone,
StringCharacterIterator, TimeZone, TreeMap,
TreeSet, Vector, ZipEntry
Cloneable: java.lang
CloneNotSupportedException: java.lang
close(): BufferedInputStream, BufferedReader,
BufferedWriter, ByteArrayInputStream, ByteArray-
OutputStream, CharArrayReader, CharArrayWriter,
CipherInputStream, CipherOutputStream, Data-
gramSocket, DatagramSocketImpl, DeflaterOut-
putStream, FileInputStream, FileOutputStream,
FilterInputStream, FilterOutputStream, Filter-
Reader, FilterWriter, GZIPInputStream, GZIPOutput-
Stream, InflaterInputStream, InputStream,
InputStreamReader, ObjectInput,

ObjectInputStream, ObjectOutput, ObjectOutputStream, OutputStream, OutputStreamWriter, PipedInputStream, PipedOutputStream, PipedReader, PipedWriter, PrintStream, PrintWriter, PushbackInputStream, PushbackReader, RandomAccessFile, Reader, SequenceInputStream, ServerSocket, Socket, SocketImpl, StringReader, StringWriter, Writer, ZipFile, ZipInputStream, ZipOutputStream

closeEntry(): ZipInputStream, ZipOutputStream
CodeSource: java.security
CollationElementIterator: java.text
CollationKey: java.text
Collator: java.text
Collection: java.util
Collections: java.util
combine(): DomainCombiner
COMBINING_DIACRITICAL_MARKS: UnicodeBlock
COMBINING_HALF_MARKS: UnicodeBlock
COMBINING_MARKS_FOR_SYMBOLS: UnicodeBlock
COMBINING_SPACING_MARK: Character
command(): Compiler
commentChar(): StreamTokenizer
CompactShortArray.Iterator: java.text
Comparable: java.lang
Comparator: java.util
comparator(): SortedMap, SortedSet, TreeMap, TreeSet
compare(): Collator, Comparator, RuleBasedCollator
compareTo(): BigDecimal, BigInteger, Byte, Character, CollationKey, Comparable, Date, Double, File, Float, Integer, Long, ObjectStreamField, Short, String
compareToIgnoreCase(): String
compileClass(): Compiler
compileClasses(): Compiler
Compiler: java.lang
complete(): Calendar
computeFields(): Calendar, GregorianCalendar
computeTime(): Calendar, GregorianCalendar
concat(): String
ConcurrentModificationException: java.util
connect(): DatagramSocket, PipedInputStream, PipedOutputStream, PipedReader, PipedWriter, SocketImpl, URLConnection
connected: URLConnection
ConnectException: java.net
CONNECTOR_PUNCTUATION: Character
Constructor: java.lang.reflect
contains(): AbstractCollection, ArrayList,

BeanContextMembershipEvent, BeanContextSupport, Collection, HashSet, Hashtable, LinkedList, List, Set, TreeSet, Vector
containsAlias(): KeyStore
containsAll(): AbstractCollection, BeanContextSupport, Collection, List, Set, Vector
containsKey(): AbstractMap, Attributes, BeanContextSupport, HashMap, Hashtable, Map, TreeMap, WeakHashMap
containsValue(): AbstractMap, Attributes, HashMap, Hashtable, Map, TreeMap
CONTENT_TYPE: Name
ContentHandler: java.net
ContentHandlerFactory: java.net
CONTROL: Character
CONTROL_PICTURES: UnicodeBlock
copy(): Collections
copyChildren(): BeanContextSupport
copyInto(): Vector
copyValueOf(): String
cos(): Math, StrictMath
count: BufferedInputStream, BufferedOutputStream, ByteArrayInputStream, ByteArrayOutputStream, CharArrayReader, CharArrayWriter, StringBufferInputStream
countObservers(): Observable
countStackFrames(): Thread
countTokens(): StringTokenizer
crc: GZIPInputStream, GZIPOutputStream
CRC32: java.util.zip
create(): DatagramSocketImpl, SocketImpl
createBCSChild(): BeanContextServicesSupport, BeanContextSupport
createBCSSServiceProvider(): BeanContextServicesSupport
createContentHandler(): ContentHandlerFactory
createDatagramSocketImpl(): DatagramSocketImplFactory
createNewFile(): File
createSocketImpl(): SocketImplFactory
createTempFile(): File
createURLStreamHandler(): URLStreamHandlerFactory
createZipEntry(): JarInputStream, ZipInputStream
CRL: java.security.cert
CRLException: java.security.cert
CURRENCY_SYMBOL: Character
CURRENCY_SYMBOLS: UnicodeBlock
current(): BreakIterator, CharacterIterator, StringCharacterIterator

currentClassLoader(): SecurityManager
currentLoadedClass(): SecurityManager
currentThread(): Thread
currentTimeMillis(): System
Customizer: java.beans
CYRILLIC: UnicodeBlock

D

DASH_PUNCTUATION: Character
DataFormatException: java.util.zip
DatagramPacket: java.net
DatagramSocket: java.net
DatagramSocketImpl: java.net
DatagramSocketImplFactory: java.net
DataInput: java.io
DataInputStream: java.io
DataOutput: java.io
DataOutputStream: java.io
Date: java.util
DATE: Calendar
DATE_FIELD: DateFormat
DateFormat: java.text
DateFormatSymbols: java.text
DAY_OF_MONTH: Calendar
DAY_OF_WEEK: Calendar
DAY_OF_WEEK_FIELD: DateFormat
DAY_OF_WEEK_IN_MONTH: Calendar
DAY_OF_WEEK_IN_MONTH_FIELD: DateFormat
DAY_OF_YEAR: Calendar
DAY_OF_YEAR_FIELD: DateFormat
decapitalize(): Introspector
DECEMBER: Calendar
DECIMAL_DIGIT_NUMBER: Character
DecimalFormat: java.text
DecimalFormatSymbols: java.text
DECLARED: Member
decode(): Byte, Certificate, Integer, Long, Short,
  URLDecoder
DECRYPT_MODE: Cipher
def: DeflaterOutputStream
DEFAULT: DateFormat
DEFAULT_COMPRESSION: Deflater
DEFAULT_STRATEGY: Deflater
defaulted(): GetField
defaultReadObject(): ObjectInputStream
defaults: Properties
defaultWriteObject(): ObjectOutputStream
defineClass(): ClassLoader, SecureClassLoader
definePackage(): ClassLoader, URLClassLoader

deflate(): Deflater, DeflaterOutputStream
DEFLATED: Deflater, ZipEntry, ZipOutputStream
Deflater: java.util.zip
DeflaterOutputStream: java.util.zip
delete(): File, StringBuffer
deleteCharAt(): StringBuffer
deleteEntry(): KeyStore
deleteObserver(): Observable
deleteObservers(): Observable
deleteOnExit(): File
deleteOwner(): Owner
DES_EDE_KEY_LEN: DESedeKeySpec
DES_KEY_LEN: DESKeySpec
DESedeKeySpec: javax.crypto.spec
deserialize(): BeanContextSupport
DesignMode: java.beans
designTime: BeanContextSupport
DESKeySpec: javax.crypto.spec
destroy(): Process, Thread, ThreadGroup
detail: WriteAbortedException
DEVANAGARI: UnicodeBlock
DHGenParameterSpec: javax.crypto.spec
DHKey: javax.crypto.interfaces
DHParameterSpec: javax.crypto.spec
DHPrivateKey: javax.crypto.interfaces
DHPrivateKeySpec: javax.crypto.spec
DHPublicKey: javax.crypto.interfaces
DHPublicKeySpec: javax.crypto.spec
Dictionary: java.util
digest: DigestInputStream, DigestOutputStream
digest(): MessageDigest
DigestException: java.security
DigestInputStream: java.security
DigestOutputStream: java.security
digit(): Character
DINGBATS: UnicodeBlock
disable(): Compiler
disconnect(): DatagramSocket, HttpURLConnection
divide(): BigDecimal, BigInteger
divideAndRemainder(): BigInteger
doFinal(): Cipher, Mac
doInput: URLConnection
DomainCombiner: java.security
DONE: BreakIterator, CharacterIterator
dontUseGui(): BeanContextSupport, Visibility
doOutput: URLConnection
doPhase(): KeyAgreement
doPrivileged(): AccessController
Double: java.lang
doubleToLongBits(): Double

doubleToRawLongBits(): Double
doubleValue(): BigDecimal, BigInteger, Byte, Double, Float, Integer, Long, Number, Short
drain(): ObjectOutputStream
DSAKey: java.security.interfaces
DSAKeyPairGenerator: java.security.interfaces
DSAParameterSpec: java.security.spec
DSAParams: java.security.interfaces
DSAPrivateKey: java.security.interfaces
DSAPrivateKeySpec: java.security.spec
DSAPublicKey: java.security.interfaces
DSAPublicKeySpec: java.security.spec
DST_OFFSET: Calendar
dumpStack(): Thread

E

E: Math, StrictMath
elementAt(): Vector
elementCount: Vector
elementData: Vector
elements(): Dictionary, Hashtable, PermissionCollection, Permissions, Vector
empty(): Stack
EMPTY_LIST: Collections
EMPTY_MAP: Collections
EMPTY_SET: Collections
EmptyStackException: java.util
enable(): Compiler
enableReplaceObject(): ObjectOutputStream
enableResolveObject(): ObjectInputStream
ENCLOSED_ALPHANUMERICS: UnicodeBlock
ENCLOSED_CJK_LETTERS_AND_MONTHS: UnicodeBlock
ENCLOSING_MARK: Character
encode(): Certificate, URLEncoder
EncodedKeySpec: java.security.spec
ENCRYPT_MODE: Cipher
end(): Deflater, Inflater
END_PUNCTUATION: Character
endsWith(): String
engineAliases(): KeyStoreSpi
engineContainsAlias(): KeyStoreSpi
engineDeleteEntry(): KeyStoreSpi
engineDigest(): MessageDigestSpi
engineDoFinal(): CipherSpi, MacSpi
engineDoPhase(): KeyAgreementSpi
engineGenerateCertificate(): CertificateFactorySpi
engineGenerateCertificates(): CertificateFactorySpi
engineGenerateCRL(): CertificateFactorySpi

engineGenerateCRLs(): CertificateFactorySpi
engineGenerateKey(): KeyGeneratorSpi
engineGenerateParameters(): AlgorithmParameterGeneratorSpi
engineGeneratePrivate(): KeyFactorySpi
engineGeneratePublic(): KeyFactorySpi
engineGenerateSecret(): KeyAgreementSpi, SecretKeyFactorySpi
engineGenerateSeed(): SecureRandomSpi
engineGetBlockSize(): CipherSpi
engineGetCertificate(): KeyStoreSpi
engineGetCertificateAlias(): KeyStoreSpi
engineGetCertificateChain(): KeyStoreSpi
engineGetCreationDate(): KeyStoreSpi
engineGetDigestLength(): MessageDigestSpi
engineGetEncoded(): AlgorithmParametersSpi
engineGetIV(): CipherSpi
engineGetKey(): KeyStoreSpi
engineGetKeySpec(): KeyFactorySpi, SecretKeyFactorySpi
engineGetMacLength(): MacSpi
engineGetOutputSize(): CipherSpi
engineGetParameter(): SignatureSpi
engineGetParameters(): CipherSpi
engineGetParameterSpec(): AlgorithmParametersSpi
engineInit(): AlgorithmParameterGeneratorSpi, AlgorithmParametersSpi, CipherSpi, KeyAgreementSpi, KeyGeneratorSpi, MacSpi
engineInitSign(): SignatureSpi
engineInitVerify(): SignatureSpi
engineIsCertificateEntry(): KeyStoreSpi
engineIsKeyEntry(): KeyStoreSpi
engineLoad(): KeyStoreSpi
engineNextBytes(): SecureRandomSpi
engineReset(): MacSpi, MessageDigestSpi
engineSetCertificateEntry(): KeyStoreSpi
engineSetKeyEntry(): KeyStoreSpi
engineSetMode(): CipherSpi
engineSetPadding(): CipherSpi
engineSetParameter(): SignatureSpi
engineSetSeed(): SecureRandomSpi
engineSign(): SignatureSpi
engineSize(): KeyStoreSpi
engineStore(): KeyStoreSpi
engineToString(): AlgorithmParametersSpi
engineTranslateKey(): KeyFactorySpi, SecretKeyFactorySpi
engineUpdate(): CipherSpi, MacSpi, MessageDigestSpi, SignatureSpi
engineVerify(): SignatureSpi

ENGLISH: Locale
enqueue(): Reference
ensureCapacity(): ArrayList, StringBuffer, Vector
entries(): Acl, JarFile, ZipFile
Entry: java.util.Map
entrySet(): AbstractMap, Attributes, HashMap,
    Hashtable, Map, Provider, TreeMap,
    WeakHashMap
enumerate(): Thread, ThreadGroup
Enumeration: java.util
enumeration(): Collections
eof: OptionalDataException
EOFException: java.io
eolIsSignificant(): StreamTokenizer
eos: GZIPInputStream
equals(): AbstractList, AbstractMap, AbstractSet,
    AccessControlContext, AllPermission, Arrays,
    Attribute, Attributes, BasicPermission, BigDecimal,
    BigInteger, BitSet, Boolean, Byte, Calendar, Certifi-
    cate, Character, ChoiceFormat, CodeSource, Colla-
    tionKey, Collator, Collection, Comparator,
    Constructor, Date, DateFormat, DateFormatSym-
    bols, DecimalFormat, DecimalFormatSymbols,
    Double, Entry, Field, FieldPosition, File, FilePermis-
    sion, Float, GregorianCalendar, Hashtable, Iden-
    tity, InetAddress, Integer, List, Locale, Long,
    Manifest, Map, MessageFormat, Method, Name,
    NumberFormat, Object, ParsePosition, Permission,
    Principal, PropertyPermission, RuleBasedCollator,
    SecretKeySpec, Set, Short, SimpleDateFormat,
    SimpleTimeZone, SocketPermission, String,
    StringCharacterIterator, Subset, UnresolvedPermis-
    sion, URL, URLStreamHandler, Vector, X509CRL,
    X509CRLEntry
equalsIgnoreCase(): String
ERA: Calendar
ERA_FIELD: DateFormat
err: FileDescriptor, System
Error: java.lang
EventListener: java.util
EventObject: java.util
EventSetDescriptor: java.beans
Exception: java.lang
ExceptionInInitializerError: java.lang
exec(): Runtime
exists(): File
exit(): Runtime, System
exitValue(): Process
exp(): Math, StrictMath
EXTENSION_INSTALLATION: Name

EXTENSION_LIST: Name
EXTENSION_NAME: Name
Externalizable: java.io

F

F0: RSAKeyGenParameterSpec
F4: RSAKeyGenParameterSpec
FALSE: Boolean
fd: DatagramSocketImpl, SocketImpl
FeatureDescriptor: java.beans
FEBRUARY: Calendar
Field: java.lang.reflect
FIELD_COUNT: Calendar
FieldPosition: java.text
fields: Calendar
File: java.io
FileDescriptor: java.io
FileFilter: java.io
FileInputStream: java.io
FilenameFilter: java.io
FileNameMap: java.net
FileNotFoundException: java.io
FileOutputStream: java.io
FilePermission: java.io
FileReader: java.io
FileWriter: java.io
fill(): Arrays, Collections, InflaterInputStream
fillInStackTrace(): Throwable
FILTERED: Deflater
FilterInputStream: java.io
FilterOutputStream: java.io
FilterReader: java.io
FilterWriter: java.io
FINAL: Modifier
finalize(): Deflater, FileInputStream, FileOutput-
    Stream, Inflater, Object
findClass(): ClassLoader, URLClassLoader
findEditor(): PropertyEditorManager
findLibrary(): ClassLoader
findLoadedClass(): ClassLoader
findResource(): ClassLoader, URLClassLoader
findResources(): ClassLoader, URLClassLoader
findSystemClass(): ClassLoader
finish(): Deflater, DeflaterOutputStream, GZIPOutput-
    Stream, ZipOutputStream
finished(): Deflater, Inflater
fireChildrenAdded(): BeanContextSupport
fireChildrenRemoved(): BeanContextSupport
firePropertyChange(): BeanContextChildSupport,

PropertyChangeSupport, PropertyEditorSupport

fireServiceAdded(): BeanContextServicesSupport

fireServiceRevoked(): BeanContextServicesSupport

fireVetoableChange(): BeanContextChildSupport, VetoableChangeSupport

first(): BreakIterator, CharacterIterator, SortedSet, StringCharacterIterator, TreeSet

firstElement(): Vector

firstKey(): SortedMap, TreeMap

flipBit(): BigInteger

Float: java.lang

floatToIntBits(): Float

floatToRawIntBits(): Float

floatValue(): BigDecimal, BigInteger, Byte, Double, Float, Integer, Long, Number, Short

floor(): Math, StrictMath

flush(): BufferedOutputStream, BufferedWriter, CharArrayWriter, CipherOutputStream, DataOutputStream, FilterOutputStream, FilterWriter, ObjectOutput, ObjectOutputStream, OutputStream, OutputStreamWriter, PipedOutputStream, PipedWriter, PrintStream, PrintWriter, StringWriter, Writer

flushCaches(): Introspector

flushFromCaches(): Introspector

following(): BreakIterator

forClass(): ObjectStreamClass

forDigit(): Character

FORMAT: Character

Format: java.text

format(): ChoiceFormat, DateFormat, DecimalFormat, Format, MessageFormat, NumberFormat, SimpleDateFormat

forName(): Class

FRACTION_FIELD: NumberFormat

FRANCE: Locale

freeMemory(): Runtime

FRENCH: Locale

FRIDAY: Calendar

FULL: DateFormat

FULL_DECOMPOSITION: Collator

G

gc(): Runtime, System

gcd(): BigInteger

GENERAL_PUNCTUATION: UnicodeBlock

GeneralSecurityException: java.security

generateCertificate(): CertificateFactory

generateCertificates(): CertificateFactory

generateCRL(): CertificateFactory

generateCRLs(): CertificateFactory

generateKey(): KeyGenerator

generateKeyPair(): KeyPairGenerator, KeyPairGeneratorSpi

generateParameters(): AlgorithmParameterGenerator

generatePrivate(): KeyFactory

generatePublic(): KeyFactory

generateSecret(): KeyAgreement, SecretKeyFactory

generateSeed(): SecureRandom

genKeyPair(): KeyPairGenerator

GEOMETRIC_SHAPES: UnicodeBlock

GEORGIAN: UnicodeBlock

GERMAN: Locale

GERMANY: Locale

get(): AbstractList, AbstractMap, AbstractSequentialList, Array, ArrayList, Attributes, BitSet, Calendar, Dictionary, Field, GetField, HashMap, Hashtable, LinkedList, List, Map, PhantomReference, Reference, SoftReference, ThreadLocal, TreeMap, Vector, WeakHashMap

get2DigitYearStart(): SimpleDateFormat

getAbsoluteFile(): File

getAbsolutePath(): File

getActions(): AllPermission, BasicPermission, FilePermission, Permission, PropertyPermission, SocketPermission, UnresolvedPermission

getActualMaximum(): Calendar, GregorianCalendar

getActualMinimum(): Calendar, GregorianCalendar

getAdditionalBeanInfo(): BeanInfo, SimpleBeanInfo

getAddListenerMethod(): EventSetDescriptor

getAddress(): DatagramPacket, InetAddress

getAdler(): Deflater, Inflater

getAlgorithm(): AlgorithmParameterGenerator, AlgorithmParameters, Cipher, Key, KeyAgreement, KeyFactory, KeyGenerator, KeyPairGenerator, Mac, MessageDigest, SealedObject, SecretKeyFactory, SecretKeySpec, Signature, SignedObject

getAlgorithmProperty(): Security

getAllAttributeKeys(): AttributedCharacterIterator

getAllByName(): InetAddress

getAllowUserInteraction(): URLConnection

getAmPmStrings(): DateFormatSymbols

getAsText(): PropertyEditor, PropertyEditorSupport

getAttribute(): AttributedCharacterIterator

getAttributes(): AttributedCharacterIterator, JarEntry, JarURLConnection, Manifest

getAuthority(): URL

getAvailableIDs(): TimeZone

getAvailableLocales(): BreakIterator, Calendar,

Collator, DateFormat, Locale, NumberFormat

getBasicConstraints(): X509Certificate

getBeanClass(): BeanDescriptor

getBeanContext(): BeanContextChild, BeanContextChildSupport, BeanContextEvent

getBeanContextChildPeer(): BeanContextChildSupport

getBeanContextPeer(): BeanContextSupport

getBeanContextProxy(): BeanContextProxy

getBeanContextServicesPeer(): BeanContextServicesSupport

getBeanDescriptor(): BeanInfo, SimpleBeanInfo

getBeanInfo(): Introspector

getBeanInfoSearchPath(): Introspector

getBeginIndex(): CharacterIterator, FieldPosition, StringCharacterIterator

getBlockSize(): Cipher

getBoolean(): Array, Boolean, Field

getBuffer(): StringWriter

getBundle(): ResourceBundle

getByName(): InetAddress

getByte(): Array, Field

getBytes(): String

getCalendar(): DateFormat

getCanonicalFile(): File

getCanonicalPath(): File

getCertificate(): KeyStore

getCertificateAlias(): KeyStore

getCertificateChain(): KeyStore

getCertificates(): CodeSource, JarEntry, JarURLConnection

getChar(): Array, Field

getCharacterInstance(): BreakIterator

getChars(): String, StringBuffer

getChecksum(): CheckedInputStream, CheckedOutputStream

getChildBeanContextChild(): BeanContextSupport

getChildBeanContextMembershipListener(): BeanContextSupport

getChildBeanContextServicesListener(): BeanContextServicesSupport

getChildPropertyChangeListener(): BeanContextSupport

getChildSerializable(): BeanContextSupport

getChildVetoableChangeListener(): BeanContextSupport

getChildVisibility(): BeanContextSupport

getClass(): Object

getClassContext(): SecurityManager

getClasses(): Class

getClassLoader(): Class

getClassName(): MissingResourceException

getCodeSource(): ProtectionDomain

getCollationElementIterator(): RuleBasedCollator

getCollationKey(): Collator, RuleBasedCollator

getComment(): ZipEntry

getComponent(): BeanContextChildComponentProxy

getComponentType(): Class

getCompressedSize(): ZipEntry

getConstructor(): Class

getConstructors(): Class

getContainer(): BeanContextContainerProxy

getContent(): ContentHandler, URL, URLConnection

getContentEncoding(): URLConnection

getContentLength(): URLConnection

getContents(): ListResourceBundle

getContentType(): URLConnection

getContentTypeFor(): FileNameMap

getContext(): AccessController

getContextClassLoader(): Thread

getCountry(): Locale

getCrc(): ZipEntry

getCreationDate(): KeyStore

getCriticalExtensionOIDs(): X509Certificate, X509CRL, X509CRLEntry, X509Extension

getCrtCoefficient(): RSAPrivateCrtKey, RSAPrivateCrtKeySpec

getCurrencyInstance(): NumberFormat

getCurrencySymbol(): DecimalFormatSymbols

getCurrentServiceClasses(): BeanContextServices, BeanContextServicesSupport

getCurrentServiceSelectors(): BCSSProxyServiceProvider, BeanContextServiceAvailableEvent, BeanContextServiceProvider, BeanContextServices, BeanContextServicesSupport

getCustomEditor(): PropertyEditor, PropertyEditorSupport

getCustomizerClass(): BeanDescriptor

getData(): DatagramPacket

getDate(): Date, URLConnection

getDateFormatSymbols(): SimpleDateFormat

getDateInstance(): DateFormat

getDateTimeInstance(): DateFormat

getDay(): Date

getDecimalFormatSymbols(): DecimalFormat

getDecimalSeparator(): DecimalFormatSymbols

getDeclaredClasses(): Class

getDeclaredConstructor(): Class

getDeclaredConstructors(): Class

getDeclaredField(): Class

getDeclaredFields(): Class
getDeclaredMethod(): Class
getDeclaredMethods(): Class
getDeclaringClass(): Class, Constructor, Field, Member, Method
getDecomposition(): Collator
getDefault(): Locale, TimeZone
getDefaultAllowUserInteraction(): URLConnection
getDefaultEventIndex(): BeanInfo, SimpleBeanInfo
getDefaultPort(): URLStreamHandler
getDefaultPropertyIndex(): BeanInfo, SimpleBeanInfo
getDefaultRequestProperty(): URLConnection
getDefaultType(): KeyStore
getDefaultUseCaches(): URLConnection
getDigestLength(): MessageDigest
getDigit(): DecimalFormatSymbols
getDisplayCountry(): Locale
getDisplayLanguage(): Locale
getDisplayName(): FeatureDescriptor, Locale, TimeZone
getDisplayVariant(): Locale
getDoInput(): URLConnection
getDomainCombiner(): AccessControlContext
getDoOutput(): URLConnection
getDouble(): Array, Field
getDSTSavings(): SimpleTimeZone
getEditorSearchPath(): PropertyEditorManager
getEffectiveKeyBits(): RC2ParameterSpec
getEncoded(): AlgorithmParameters, Certificate, EncodedKeySpec, Key, PKCS8EncodedKeySpec, SecretKeySpec, X509CRL, X509CRLEntry, X509EncodedKeySpec
getEncoding(): InputStreamReader, OutputStreamWriter
getEndIndex(): CharacterIterator, FieldPosition, StringCharacterIterator
getEntries(): Manifest
getEntry(): JarFile, ZipFile
getEntryName(): JarURLConnection
getenv(): System
getEras(): DateFormatSymbols
getErrorIndex(): ParsePosition
getErrorOffset(): ParseException
getErrorStream(): HttpURLConnection, Process
getEventSetDescriptors(): BeanInfo, SimpleBeanInfo
getException(): ClassNotFoundException, ExceptionInInitializerError, PrivilegedActionException
getExceptionTypes(): Constructor, Method
getExpiration(): URLConnection
getExponentSize(): DHGenParameterSpec

getExtensionValue(): X509Certificate, X509CRL, X509CRLEntry, X509Extension
getExtra(): ZipEntry
getFD(): FileInputStream, FileOutputStream, RandomAccessFile
GetField: java.io.ObjectInputStream
getField(): Class, FieldPosition, ObjectStreamClass
getFields(): Class, ObjectStreamClass
getFile(): URL
getFileDescriptor(): DatagramSocketImpl, SocketImpl
getFileNameMap(): URLConnection
getFilePointer(): RandomAccessFile
getFirst(): LinkedList
getFirstDayOfWeek(): Calendar
getFloat(): Array, Field
getFollowRedirects(): HttpURLConnection
getFormat(): Certificate, EncodedKeySpec, Key, PKCS8EncodedKeySpec, SecretKeySpec, X509EncodedKeySpec
getFormats(): ChoiceFormat, MessageFormat
getG(): DHParameterSpec, DHPrivateKeySpec, DHPublicKeySpec, DSAParameterSpec, DSAParams, DSAPrivateKeySpec, DSAPublicKeySpec
getGreatestMinimum(): Calendar, GregorianCalendar
getGregorianChange(): GregorianCalendar
getGroupingSeparator(): DecimalFormatSymbols
getGroupingSize(): DecimalFormat
getGuarantor(): Certificate
getHeaderField(): URLConnection
getHeaderFieldDate(): HttpURLConnection, URLConnection
getHeaderFieldInt(): URLConnection
getHeaderFieldKey(): URLConnection
getHost(): URL
getHostAddress(): InetAddress, URLStreamHandler
getHostName(): InetAddress
getHours(): Date
getIcon(): BeanInfo, SimpleBeanInfo
getID(): TimeZone
getIdentity(): IdentityScope
getIfModifiedSince(): URLConnection
getImplementationTitle(): Package
getImplementationVendor(): Package
getImplementationVersion(): Package
getInCheck(): SecurityManager
getIndex(): CharacterIterator, ParsePosition, StringCharacterIterator
getIndexedPropertyType(): IndexedPropertyDescriptor

getIndexedReadMethod(): IndexedPropertyDescriptor

getIndexedWriteMethod(): IndexedPropertyDescriptor

getInetAddress(): DatagramSocket, ServerSocket, Socket, SocketImpl

getInfinity(): DecimalFormatSymbols

getInfo(): Identity, Provider

getInputStream(): JarFile, Process, Socket, SocketImpl, URLConnection, ZipFile

getInstance(): AlgorithmParameterGenerator, AlgorithmParameters, Calendar, CertificateFactory, Cipher, Collator, DateFormat, KeyAgreement, KeyFactory, KeyGenerator, KeyPairGenerator, KeyStore, Mac, MessageDigest, NumberFormat, SecretKeyFactory, SecureRandom, Signature

getInstanceOf(): Beans

getInt(): Array, Field

getInteger(): Integer

getInterface(): MulticastSocket

getInterfaces(): Class

getInternationalCurrencySymbol(): DecimalFormatSymbols

getInvocationHandler(): Proxy

getISO3Country(): Locale

getISO3Language(): Locale

getISOCountries(): Locale

getISOLanguages(): Locale

getIssuerDN(): X509Certificate, X509CRL

getIssuerUniqueID(): X509Certificate

getIterationCount(): PBEParameterSpec

getIterator(): AttributedString

getIV(): Cipher, IvParameterSpec, RC2ParameterSpec, RC5ParameterSpec

getJarEntry(): JarFile, JarURLConnection

getJarFile(): JarURLConnection

getJarFileURL(): JarURLConnection

getJavaInitializationString(): PropertyEditor, PropertyEditorSupport

getKeepAlive(): Socket

getKey(): DESedeKeySpec, DESKeySpec, Entry, KeyStore, MissingResourceException

getKeys(): ListResourceBundle, PropertyResourceBundle, ResourceBundle

getKeysize(): RSAKeyGenParameterSpec

getKeySpec(): KeyFactory, SecretKeyFactory

getKeyUsage(): X509Certificate

getL(): DHParameterSpec

getLanguage(): Locale

getLast(): LinkedList

getLastModified(): URLConnection

getLeastMaximum(): Calendar, GregorianCalendar

getLength(): Array, DatagramPacket

getLimits(): ChoiceFormat

getLineInstance(): BreakIterator

getLineNumber(): LineNumberInputStream, LineNumberReader

getListenerMethodDescriptors(): EventSetDescriptor

getListenerMethods(): EventSetDescriptor

getListenerType(): EventSetDescriptor

getLocalAddress(): DatagramSocket, Socket

getLocale(): BeanContextSupport, MessageFormat, ResourceBundle

getLocalHost(): InetAddress

getLocalizedInputStream(): Runtime

getLocalizedMessage(): Throwable

getLocalizedOutputStream(): Runtime

getLocalPatternChars(): DateFormatSymbols

getLocalPort(): DatagramSocket, DatagramSocketImpl, ServerSocket, Socket, SocketImpl

getLocation(): CodeSource

getLong(): Array, Field, Long

getLowestSetBit(): BigInteger

getMacLength(): Mac

getMainAttributes(): JarURLConnection, Manifest

getManifest(): JarFile, JarInputStream, JarURLConnection

getMaxExpansion(): CollationElementIterator

getMaximum(): Calendar, GregorianCalendar

getMaximumFractionDigits(): NumberFormat

getMaximumIntegerDigits(): NumberFormat

getMaxPriority(): ThreadGroup

getMessage(): InvalidClassException, Throwable, WriteAbortedException

getMessageDigest(): DigestInputStream, DigestOutputStream

getMethod(): Class, MethodDescriptor, ZipEntry

getMethodDescriptors(): BeanInfo, SimpleBeanInfo

getMethods(): Class

getMinimalDaysInFirstWeek(): Calendar

getMinimum(): Calendar, GregorianCalendar

getMinimumFractionDigits(): NumberFormat

getMinimumIntegerDigits(): NumberFormat

getMinusSign(): DecimalFormatSymbols

getMinutes(): Date

getModifiers(): Class, Constructor, Field, Member, Method

getModulus(): RSAKey, RSAPrivateKeySpec, RSAPublicKeySpec

getMonetaryDecimalSeparator(): DecimalFormatSymbols

getMonth(): Date

getMonths(): DateFormatSymbols

getMultiplier(): DecimalFormat

getName(): Acl, Attribute, Class, Constructor, Feature-Descriptor, Field, File, Identity, Member, Method, ObjectStreamClass, ObjectStreamField, Package, Permission, Principal, Provider, Thread, Thread-Group, ZipEntry, ZipFile

getNaN(): DecimalFormatSymbols

getNegativePrefix(): DecimalFormat

getNegativeSuffix(): DecimalFormat

getNewValue(): PropertyChangeEvent

getNextEntry(): JarInputStream, ZipInputStream

getNextJarEntry(): JarInputStream

getNextUpdate(): X509CRL

getNonCriticalExtensionOIDs(): X509Certificate, X509CRL, X509CRLEntry, X509Extension

getNotAfter(): X509Certificate

getNotBefore(): X509Certificate

getNumberFormat(): DateFormat

getNumberInstance(): NumberFormat

getNumericValue(): Character

getObject(): GuardedObject, ResourceBundle, Sealed-Object, SignedObject

getObjectStreamClass(): GetField

getOffset(): CollationElementIterator, Datagram-Packet, ObjectStreamField, SimpleTimeZone, TimeZone

getOldValue(): PropertyChangeEvent

getOption(): DatagramSocketImpl, SocketImpl, SocketOptions

getOutputSize(): Cipher

getOutputStream(): Process, Socket, SocketImpl, URLConnection

getP(): DHParameterSpec, DHPrivateKeySpec, DHPublicKeySpec, DSAParameterSpec, DSAParams, DSAPrivateKeySpec, DSAPublicKeySpec

getPackage(): Class, ClassLoader, Package

getPackages(): ClassLoader, Package

getParameter(): Signature

getParameterDescriptors(): MethodDescriptor

getParameters(): Cipher

getParameterSpec(): AlgorithmParameters

getParameterTypes(): Constructor, Method

getParams(): DHKey, DSAKey

getParent(): ClassLoader, File, ThreadGroup

getParentFile(): File

getPassword(): PasswordAuthentication, PBEKeySpec

getPasswordAuthentication(): Authenticator

getPath(): File, URL

getPatternSeparator(): DecimalFormatSymbols

getPercent(): DecimalFormatSymbols

getPercentInstance(): NumberFormat

getPerMill(): DecimalFormatSymbols

getPermission(): AccessControlException, HttpURL-Connection, URLConnection

getPermissions(): Acl, Policy, ProtectionDomain, SecureClassLoader, URLClassLoader

getPolicy(): Policy

getPort(): DatagramPacket, DatagramSocket, Socket, SocketImpl, URL

getPositivePrefix(): DecimalFormat

getPositiveSuffix(): DecimalFormat

getPrimeExponentP(): RSAPrivateCrtKey, RSAPrivate-CrtKeySpec

getPrimeExponentQ(): RSAPrivateCrtKey, RSAPrivate-CrtKeySpec

getPrimeP(): RSAPrivateCrtKey, RSAPrivateCrtKeySpec

getPrimeQ(): RSAPrivateCrtKey, RSAPrivateCrtKeySpec

getPrimeSize(): DHGenParameterSpec

getPrincipal(): AclEntry, Certificate

getPriority(): Thread

getPrivate(): KeyPair

getPrivateExponent(): RSAPrivateKey, RSAPri-vateKeySpec

getPrivateKey(): Signer

getPropagatedFrom(): BeanContextEvent

getPropagationId(): PropertyChangeEvent

getProperties(): System

getProperty(): Properties, Security, System

getPropertyChangeEvent(): PropertyVetoException

getPropertyDescriptors(): BeanInfo, SimpleBeanInfo

getPropertyEditorClass(): PropertyDescriptor

getPropertyName(): PropertyChangeEvent

getPropertyType(): PropertyDescriptor

getProtectionDomain(): Class

getProtocol(): URL

getProvider(): AlgorithmParameterGenerator, Algo-rithmParameters, CertificateFactory, Cipher, Key-Agreement, KeyFactory, KeyGenerator, KeyPairGenerator, KeyStore, Mac, MessageDigest, SecretKeyFactory, SecureRandom, Security, Signature

getProviders(): Security

getProxyClass(): Proxy

getPublic(): KeyPair

getPublicExponent(): RSAKeyGenParameterSpec, RSAPrivateCrtKey, RSAPrivateCrtKeySpec, RSAPub-licKey, RSAPublicKeySpec

getPublicKey(): Certificate, Identity

getQ(): DSAParameterSpec, DSAParams, DSAPrivateKeySpec, DSAPublicKeySpec

getQuery(): URL

getRawOffset(): SimpleTimeZone, TimeZone

getReadMethod(): PropertyDescriptor

getReceiveBufferSize(): DatagramSocket, Socket

getRef(): URL

getRemaining(): Inflater

getRemoveListenerMethod(): EventSetDescriptor

getRequestingPort(): Authenticator

getRequestingPrompt(): Authenticator

getRequestingProtocol(): Authenticator

getRequestingScheme(): Authenticator

getRequestingSite(): Authenticator

getRequestMethod(): HttpURLConnection

getRequestProperty(): URLConnection

getResource(): BeanContext, BeanContextSupport, Class, ClassLoader

getResourceAsStream(): BeanContext, BeanContextSupport, Class, ClassLoader

getResources(): ClassLoader

getResponseCode(): HttpURLConnection

getResponseMessage(): HttpURLConnection

getReturnType(): Method

getRevocationDate(): X509CRLEntry

getRevokedCertificate(): X509CRL

getRevokedCertificates(): X509CRL

getRounds(): RC5ParameterSpec

getRules(): RuleBasedCollator

getRunLimit(): AttributedCharacterIterator

getRunStart(): AttributedCharacterIterator

getRuntime(): Runtime

getSalt(): PBEParameterSpec

getScope(): Identity

getSeconds(): Date

getSecurityContext(): SecurityManager

getSecurityManager(): System

getSeed(): SecureRandom

getSendBufferSize(): DatagramSocket, Socket

getSentenceInstance(): BreakIterator

getSerialNumber(): X509Certificate, X509CRLEntry

getSerialVersionUID(): ObjectStreamClass

getService(): BCSSProxyServiceProvider, BeanContextServiceProvider, BeanContextServices, BeanContextServicesSupport

getServiceClass(): BeanContextServiceAvailableEvent, BeanContextServiceRevokedEvent

getServiceProvider(): BCSSServiceProvider

getServicesBeanInfo(): BeanContextServiceProviderBeanInfo

getShort(): Array, Field

getShortDescription(): FeatureDescriptor

getShortMonths(): DateFormatSymbols

getShortWeekdays(): DateFormatSymbols

getSigAlgName(): X509Certificate, X509CRL

getSigAlgOID(): X509Certificate, X509CRL

getSigAlgParams(): X509Certificate, X509CRL

getSignature(): SignedObject, X509Certificate, X509CRL

getSigners(): Class

getSize(): ZipEntry

getSoLinger(): Socket

getSoTimeout(): DatagramSocket, ServerSocket, Socket

getSource(): EventObject

getSourceAsBeanContextServices(): BeanContextServiceAvailableEvent, BeanContextServiceRevokedEvent

getSourceString(): CollationKey

getSpecificationTitle(): Package

getSpecificationVendor(): Package

getSpecificationVersion(): Package

getStrength(): Collator

getString(): ResourceBundle

getStringArray(): ResourceBundle

getSubjectDN(): X509Certificate

getSubjectUniqueID(): X509Certificate

getSuperclass(): Class

getSystemClassLoader(): ClassLoader

getSystemResource(): ClassLoader

getSystemResourceAsStream(): ClassLoader

getSystemResources(): ClassLoader

getSystemScope(): IdentityScope

getTags(): PropertyEditor, PropertyEditorSupport

getTargetException(): InvocationTargetException

getTBSCertificate(): X509Certificate

getTBSCertList(): X509CRL

getTcpNoDelay(): Socket

getText(): BreakIterator

getThisUpdate(): X509CRL

getThreadGroup(): SecurityManager, Thread

getTime(): Calendar, Date, ZipEntry

getTimeInMillis(): Calendar

getTimeInstance(): DateFormat

getTimeToLive(): DatagramSocketImpl, MulticastSocket

getTimeZone(): Calendar, DateFormat, TimeZone

getTimezoneOffset(): Date

getTotalIn(): Deflater, Inflater

getTotalOut(): Deflater, Inflater

getTTL(): DatagramSocketImpl, MulticastSocket

getType(): Certificate, CertificateFactory, Character, CRL, Field, KeyStore, ObjectStreamField

getTypeCode(): ObjectStreamField

getTypeString(): ObjectStreamField

getUndeclaredThrowable(): UndeclaredThrowableException

getURL(): URLConnection

getURLs(): URLClassLoader

getUseCaches(): URLConnection

getUserInfo(): URL

getUserName(): PasswordAuthentication

getValue(): Adler32, Annotation, Attributes, Checksum, CRC32, Entry, FeatureDescriptor, PropertyEditor, PropertyEditorSupport

getVariant(): Locale

getVersion(): Provider, RC5ParameterSpec, X509Certificate, X509CRL

getWeekdays(): DateFormatSymbols

getWordInstance(): BreakIterator

getWordSize(): RC5ParameterSpec

getWriteMethod(): PropertyDescriptor

getX(): DHPrivateKey, DHPrivateKeySpec, DSAPrivateKey, DSAPrivateKeySpec

getY(): DHPublicKey, DHPublicKeySpec, DSAPublicKey, DSAPublicKeySpec

getYear(): Date

getZeroDigit(): DecimalFormatSymbols

getZoneStrings(): DateFormatSymbols

globalHierarchyLock: BeanContext

GREEK: UnicodeBlock

GREEK_EXTENDED: UnicodeBlock

GregorianCalendar: java.util

Group: java.security.acl

Guard: java.security

GuardedObject: java.security

guessContentTypeFromName(): URLConnection

guessContentTypeFromStream(): URLConnection

GUJARATI: UnicodeBlock

GURMUKHI: UnicodeBlock

GZIP_MAGIC: GZIPInputStream

GZIPInputStream: java.util.zip

GZIPOutputStream: java.util.zip

H

h: Proxy

HALFWIDTH_AND_FULLWIDTH_FORMS: UnicodeBlock

halt(): Runtime

handleGetObject(): ListResourceBundle, PropertyResourceBundle, ResourceBundle

HANGUL_COMPATIBILITY_JAMO: UnicodeBlock

HANGUL_JAMO: UnicodeBlock

HANGUL_SYLLABLES: UnicodeBlock

hasChanged(): Observable

hasExtensions(): X509CRLEntry

hashCode(): AbstractList, AbstractMap, AbstractSet, AccessControlContext, AllPermission, Attribute, Attributes, BasicPermission, BigDecimal, BigInteger, BitSet, Boolean, Byte, Calendar, Certificate, Character, ChoiceFormat, CodeSource, CollationKey, Collator, Collection, Constructor, Date, DateFormat, DateFormatSymbols, DecimalFormat, DecimalFormatSymbols, Double, Entry, Field, FieldPosition, File, FilePermission, Float, GregorianCalendar, Hashtable, Identity, InetAddress, Integer, List, Locale, Long, Manifest, Map, MessageFormat, Method, Name, NumberFormat, Object, Package, ParsePosition, Permission, Principal, PropertyPermission, RuleBasedCollator, SecretKeySpec, Set, Short, SimpleDateFormat, SimpleTimeZone, SocketPermission, String, StringCharacterIterator, Subset, UnresolvedPermission, URL, URLStreamHandler, Vector, X509CRL, X509CRLEntry, ZipEntry

HashMap: java.util

HashSet: java.util

Hashtable: java.util

hasListeners(): PropertyChangeSupport, VetoableChangeSupport

hasMoreElements(): Enumeration, StringTokenizer

hasMoreTokens(): StringTokenizer

hasNext(): BCSIterator, Iterator, ListIterator

hasPrevious(): ListIterator

hasSameRules(): SimpleTimeZone, TimeZone

hasService(): BeanContextServices, BeanContextServicesSupport

hasUnsupportedCriticalExtension(): X509Certificate, X509CRL, X509CRLEntry, X509Extension

headMap(): SortedMap, TreeMap

headSet(): SortedSet, TreeSet

HEBREW: UnicodeBlock

HIRAGANA: UnicodeBlock

InheritableThreadLocal: java.lang

init(): AlgorithmParameterGenerator, AlgorithmParameters, Cipher, KeyAgreement, KeyGenerator, Mac

initialize(): AppletInitializer, BeanContextServicesSupport, BeanContextSupport, DSAKeyPairGenerator, KeyPairGenerator, KeyPairGeneratorSpi

initializeBeanContextResources(): BeanContextChildSupport, BeanContextServicesSupport

initialValue(): ThreadLocal

initSign(): Signature

initVerify(): Signature

INPUT_METHOD_SEGMENT: Attribute

InputStream: java.io

InputStreamReader: java.io

insert(): StringBuffer

insertElementAt(): Vector

insertProviderAt(): Security

instantiate(): Beans

instantiateChild(): BeanContext, BeanContextSupport

InstantiationError: java.lang

InstantiationException: java.lang

intBitsToFloat(): Float

Integer: java.lang

INTEGER_FIELD: NumberFormat

INTERFACE: Modifier

intern(): String

InternalError: java.lang

internalGet(): Calendar

interrupt(): Thread, ThreadGroup

interrupted(): Thread

InterruptedException: java.lang

InterruptedIOException: java.io

IntrospectionException: java.beans

Introspector: java.beans

intValue(): BigDecimal, BigInteger, Byte, Double, Float, Integer, Long, Number, Short

InvalidAlgorithmParameterException: java.security

InvalidClassException: java.io

InvalidKeyException: java.security

InvalidKeySpecException: java.security.spec

InvalidObjectException: java.io

InvalidParameterException: java.security

InvalidParameterSpecException: java.security.spec

InvocationHandler: java.lang.reflect

InvocationTargetException: java.lang.reflect

invoke(): InvocationHandler, Method

IOException: java.io

IP_MULTICAST_IF: SocketOptions

IPA_EXTENSIONS: UnicodeBlock

isAbsolute(): File

isAbstract(): Modifier

isAccessible(): AccessibleObject

isAlive(): Thread

isArray(): Class

isAssignableFrom(): Class

isBound(): PropertyDescriptor

isBoundary(): BreakIterator

isCertificateEntry(): KeyStore

isCompatibleWith(): Package

isConstrained(): PropertyDescriptor

isCurrentServiceInvalidNow(): BeanContextServiceRevokedEvent

isDaemon(): Thread, ThreadGroup

isDecimalSeparatorAlwaysShown(): DecimalFormat

isDefined(): Character

isDelegated(): BeanContextChildSupport

isDesignTime(): BeanContextSupport, Beans, DesignMode

isDestroyed(): ThreadGroup

isDigit(): Character

isDirectory(): File, ZipEntry

isEmpty(): AbstractCollection, AbstractMap, ArrayList, Attributes, BeanContextSupport, Collection, Dictionary, HashMap, HashSet, Hashtable, List, Map, Set, TreeSet, Vector, WeakHashMap

isEnqueued(): Reference

isEqual(): MessageDigest

isExpert(): FeatureDescriptor

isFile(): File

isFinal(): Modifier

isGroupingUsed(): NumberFormat

isGuiAvailable(): Beans

isHidden(): FeatureDescriptor, File

isIdentifierIgnorable(): Character

isInDefaultEventSet(): EventSetDescriptor

isInfinite(): Double, Float

isInstance(): Class

isInstanceOf(): Beans

isInterface(): Class, Modifier

isInterrupted(): Thread

isISOControl(): Character

isJavaIdentifierPart(): Character

isJavaIdentifierStart(): Character

isJavaLetter(): Character

isJavaLetterOrDigit(): Character

isKeyEntry(): KeyStore

isLeapYear(): GregorianCalendar

isLenient(): Calendar, DateFormat

isLetter(): Character

isLetterOrDigit(): Character

isLowerCase(): Character
isMember(): Group
isMulticastAddress(): InetAddress
isNaN(): Double, Float
isNative(): Modifier
isNegative(): AclEntry
isOwner(): Owner
isPaintable(): PropertyEditor, PropertyEditorSupport
isParityAdjusted(): DESedeKeySpec, DESKeySpec
isParseIntegerOnly(): NumberFormat
isPreferred(): FeatureDescriptor
isPrimitive(): Class, ObjectStreamField
isPrivate(): Modifier
isProbablePrime(): BigInteger
isPropagated(): BeanContextEvent
isProtected(): Modifier
isProxyClass(): Proxy
isPublic(): Modifier
isReadOnly(): PermissionCollection
isRevoked(): CRL
isSealed(): Package
isSerializing(): BeanContextSupport
isServiceClass(): BeanContextServiceRevokedEvent
isSet: Calendar
isSet(): Calendar
isSpace(): Character
isSpaceChar(): Character
isStatic(): Modifier
isStrict(): Modifier
isSynchronized(): Modifier
isTimeSet: Calendar
isTitleCase(): Character
isTransient(): Modifier
isUnicast(): EventSetDescriptor
isUnicodeIdentifierPart(): Character
isUnicodeIdentifierStart(): Character
isUpperCase(): Character
isVolatile(): Modifier
isWeak(): DESKeySpec
isWhitespace(): Character
ITALIAN: Locale
ITALY: Locale
Iterator: java.text.CompactShortArray, java.util
iterator(): AbstractCollection, AbstractList, Abstract-
    SequentialList, BeanContextMembershipEvent,
    BeanContextSupport, Collection, HashSet, List,
    Set, TreeSet
IvParameterSpec: javax.crypto.spec

J

JANUARY: Calendar
JAPAN: Locale
JAPANESE: Locale
JarEntry: java.util.jar
JarException: java.util.jar
JarFile: java.util.jar
jarFileURLConnection: JarURLConnection
JarInputStream: java.util.jar
JarOutputStream: java.util.jar
JarURLConnection: java.net
join(): DatagramSocketImpl, Thread
joinGroup(): MulticastSocket
JULY: Calendar
JUNE: Calendar

K

KANBUN: UnicodeBlock
KANNADA: UnicodeBlock
KATAKANA: UnicodeBlock
Key: java.security
KeyAgreement: javax.crypto
KeyAgreementSpi: javax.crypto
KeyException: java.security
KeyFactory: java.security
KeyFactorySpi: java.security
KeyGenerator: javax.crypto
KeyGeneratorSpi: javax.crypto
KeyManagementException: java.security
KeyPair: java.security
KeyPairGenerator: java.security
KeyPairGeneratorSpi: java.security
keys(): Dictionary, Hashtable
keySet(): AbstractMap, Attributes, HashMap,
    Hashtable, Map, Provider, TreeMap
KeySpec: java.security.spec
KeyStore: java.security
KeyStoreException: java.security
KeyStoreSpi: java.security
KOREA: Locale
KOREAN: Locale

L

LANGUAGE: Attribute
LAO: UnicodeBlock
last(): BreakIterator, CharacterIterator, SortedSet,
    StringCharacterIterator, TreeSet

lastElement(): Vector

lastIndexOf(): AbstractList, ArrayList, LinkedList, List, String, Vector

lastKey(): SortedMap, TreeMap

lastModified(): File

LastOwnerException: java.security.acl

LATIN_1_SUPPLEMENT: UnicodeBlock

LATIN_EXTENDED_A: UnicodeBlock

LATIN_EXTENDED_ADDITIONAL: UnicodeBlock

LATIN_EXTENDED_B: UnicodeBlock

leave(): DatagramSocketImpl

leaveGroup(): MulticastSocket

len: InflaterInputStream

length: OptionalDataException

length(): BitSet, File, RandomAccessFile, String, StringBuffer

LETTER_NUMBER: Character

LETTERLIKE_SYMBOLS: UnicodeBlock

LINE_SEPARATOR: Character

lineno(): StreamTokenizer

LineNumberInputStream: java.io

LineNumberReader: java.io

LinkageError: java.lang

LinkedList: java.util

List: java.util

list(): File, Properties, ThreadGroup

listen(): SocketImpl

listFiles(): File

ListIterator: java.util

listIterator(): AbstractList, AbstractSequentialList, LinkedList, List

ListResourceBundle: java.util

listRoots(): File

load(): KeyStore, Properties, Provider, Runtime, System

loadClass(): ClassLoader

loadImage(): SimpleBeanInfo

loadLibrary(): Runtime, System

Locale: java.util

locale: BeanContextSupport

localport: SocketImpl

localPort: DatagramSocketImpl

lock: Reader, Writer

log(): Math, StrictMath

LONG: DateFormat, TimeZone

Long: java.lang

longBitsToDouble(): Double

longValue(): BigDecimal, BigInteger, Byte, Double, Float, Integer, Long, Number, Short

lookup(): ObjectStreamClass

LOWERCASE_LETTER: Character

lowerCaseMode(): StreamTokenizer

M

Mac: javax.crypto

MacSpi: javax.crypto

MAIN_CLASS: Name

MALAYALAM: UnicodeBlock

MalformedURLException: java.net

Manifest: java.util.jar

MANIFEST_NAME: JarFile

MANIFEST_VERSION: Name

Map: java.util

map: Attributes

Map.Entry: java.util

mapLibraryName(): System

MARCH: Calendar

mark: ByteArrayInputStream

mark(): BufferedInputStream, BufferedReader, ByteArrayInputStream, CharArrayReader, FilterInputStream, FilterReader, InputStream, LineNumberInputStream, LineNumberReader, PushbackReader, Reader, StringReader

markedPos: CharArrayReader

marklimit: BufferedInputStream

markpos: BufferedInputStream

markSupported(): BufferedInputStream, BufferedReader, ByteArrayInputStream, CharArrayReader, CipherInputStream, FilterInputStream, FilterReader, InputStream, PushbackInputStream, PushbackReader, Reader, StringReader

Math: java.lang

MATH_SYMBOL: Character

MATHEMATICAL_OPERATORS: UnicodeBlock

max(): BigDecimal, BigInteger, Collections, Math, StrictMath

MAX_PRIORITY: Thread

MAX_RADIX: Character

MAX_VALUE: Byte, Character, Double, Float, Integer, Long, Short

MAY: Calendar

MEDIUM: DateFormat

Member: java.lang.reflect

members(): Group

MessageDigest: java.security

MessageDigestSpi: java.security

MessageFormat: java.text

method: HttpURLConnection

Method: java.lang.reflect

MethodDescriptor: java.beans
MILLISECOND: Calendar
MILLISECOND_FIELD: DateFormat
min(): BigDecimal, BigInteger, Collections, Math, StrictMath
MIN_PRIORITY: Thread
MIN_RADIX: Character
MIN_VALUE: Byte, Character, Double, Float, Integer, Long, Short
MINUTE: Calendar
MINUTE_FIELD: DateFormat
MISCELLANEOUS_SYMBOLS: UnicodeBlock
MISCELLANEOUS_TECHNICAL: UnicodeBlock
MissingResourceException: java.util
mkdir(): File
mkdirs(): File
mod(): BigInteger
modCount: AbstractList
Modifier: java.lang.reflect
MODIFIER_LETTER: Character
MODIFIER_SYMBOL: Character
modInverse(): BigInteger
modPow(): BigInteger
MONDAY: Calendar
MONTH: Calendar
MONTH_FIELD: DateFormat
movePointLeft(): BigDecimal
movePointRight(): BigDecimal
MulticastSocket: java.net
multiply(): BigDecimal, BigInteger

N

Name: java.util.jar.Attributes
NaN: Double, Float
NATIVE: Modifier
nCopies(): Collections
needsDictionary(): Inflater
needsGui(): BeanContextSupport, Visibility
needsInput(): Deflater, Inflater
negate(): BigDecimal, BigInteger
NEGATIVE_INFINITY: Double, Float
NegativeArraySizeException: java.lang
NetPermission: java.net
newInstance(): Array, Class, Constructor, URLClassLoader
newLine(): BufferedWriter
newPermissionCollection(): AllPermission, BasicPermission, FilePermission, Permission, PropertyPermission, SocketPermission, UnresolvedPermission

newProxyInstance(): Proxy
next(): BCSIterator, BreakIterator, CharacterIterator, CollationElementIterator, Iterator, ListIterator, Random, SecureRandom, StringCharacterIterator
nextBoolean(): Random
nextBytes(): Random, SecureRandom
nextDouble(): ChoiceFormat, Random
nextElement(): Enumeration, StringTokenizer
nextFloat(): Random
nextGaussian(): Random
nextIndex(): ListIterator
nextInt(): Random
nextLong(): Random
nextToken(): StreamTokenizer, StringTokenizer
NO_COMPRESSION: Deflater
NO_DECOMPOSITION: Collator
NO_FIELDS: ObjectStreamClass
NoClassDefFoundError: java.lang
NON_SPACING_MARK: Character
NORM_PRIORITY: Thread
NoRouteToHostException: java.net
NoSuchAlgorithmException: java.security
NoSuchElementException: java.util
NoSuchFieldError: java.lang
NoSuchFieldException: java.lang
NoSuchMethodError: java.lang
NoSuchMethodException: java.lang
NoSuchPaddingException: javax.crypto
NoSuchProviderException: java.security
not(): BigInteger
NotActiveException: java.io
notify(): Object
notifyAll(): Object
notifyObservers(): Observable
NotOwnerException: java.security.acl
NotSerializableException: java.io
NOVEMBER: Calendar
NullCipher: javax.crypto
NULLORDER: CollationElementIterator
NullPointerException: java.lang
Number: java.lang
NUMBER_FORMS: UnicodeBlock
NumberFormat: java.text
numberFormat: DateFormat
NumberFormatException: java.lang
nval: StreamTokenizer

O

Object: java.lang
ObjectInput: java.io
ObjectInputStream: java.io
ObjectInputStream.GetField: java.io
ObjectInputValidation: java.io
ObjectOutput: java.io
ObjectOutputStream: java.io
ObjectOutputStream.PutField: java.io
ObjectStreamClass: java.io
ObjectStreamConstants: java.io
ObjectStreamException: java.io
ObjectStreamField: java.io
Observable: java.util
Observer: java.util
OCTOBER: Calendar
of(): UnicodeBlock
okToUseGui: BeanContextSupport
okToUseGui(): BeanContextSupport, Visibility
on(): DigestInputStream, DigestOutputStream
ONE: BigInteger
OPEN_DELETE: ZipFile
OPEN_READ: ZipFile
openConnection(): URL, URLStreamHandler
openStream(): URL
OPTICAL_CHARACTER_RECOGNITION: UnicodeBlock
OptionalDataException: java.io
or(): BigInteger, BitSet
ordinaryChar(): StreamTokenizer
ordinaryChars(): StreamTokenizer
ORIYA: UnicodeBlock
OTHER_LETTER: Character
OTHER_NUMBER: Character
OTHER_PUNCTUATION: Character
OTHER_SYMBOL: Character
out: FileDescriptor, FilterOutputStream, FilterWriter, PipedInputStream, PrintWriter, System
OutOfMemoryError: java.lang
OutputStream: java.io
OutputStreamWriter: java.io
Owner: java.security.acl

P

Package: java.lang
paintValue(): PropertyEditor, PropertyEditorSupport
PARAGRAPH_SEPARATOR: Character
ParameterDescriptor: java.beans
parent: ResourceBundle

parentOf(): ThreadGroup
parse(): ChoiceFormat, Date, DateFormat, Decimal-Format, MessageFormat, NumberFormat, Simple-DateFormat
parseByte(): Byte
parseDouble(): Double
ParseException: java.text
parseFloat(): Float
parseInt(): Integer
parseLong(): Long
parseNumbers(): StreamTokenizer
parseObject(): DateFormat, Format, MessageFormat, NumberFormat
ParsePosition: java.text
parseShort(): Short
parseURL(): URLStreamHandler
PasswordAuthentication: java.net
pathSeparator: File
pathSeparatorChar: File
PBEKeySpec: javax.crypto.spec
PBEParameterSpec: javax.crypto.spec
pcSupport: BeanContextChildSupport
peek(): DatagramSocketImpl, Stack
Permission: java.security, java.security.acl
PermissionCollection: java.security
Permissions: java.security
permissions(): AclEntry
PhantomReference: java.lang.ref
PI: Math, StrictMath
PIPE_SIZE: PipedInputStream
PipedInputStream: java.io
PipedOutputStream: java.io
PipedReader: java.io
PipedWriter: java.io
PKCS8EncodedKeySpec: java.security.spec
PM: Calendar
Policy: java.security
poll(): ReferenceQueue
pop(): Stack
port: SocketImpl
pos: BufferedInputStream, ByteArrayInputStream, CharArrayReader, PushbackInputStream, String-BufferInputStream
POSITIVE_INFINITY: Double, Float
pow(): BigInteger, Math, StrictMath
PRC: Locale
preceding(): BreakIterator
previous(): BreakIterator, CharacterIterator, Colla-tionElementIterator, ListIterator, StringCharacterIt-erator

previousDouble(): ChoiceFormat
previousIndex(): ListIterator
PRIMARY: Collator
primaryOrder(): CollationElementIterator
Principal: java.security
print(): PrintStream, PrintWriter
println(): PrintStream, PrintWriter
printStackTrace(): ClassNotFoundException, ExceptionInInitializerError, InvocationTargetException, PrivilegedActionException, Throwable, UndeclaredThrowableException
PrintStream: java.io
PrintWriter: java.io
PRIVATE: Modifier
PRIVATE_USE: Character
PRIVATE_USE_AREA: UnicodeBlock
PrivateKey: java.security
PrivilegedAction: java.security
PrivilegedActionException: java.security
PrivilegedExceptionAction: java.security
Process: java.lang
propagatedFrom: BeanContextEvent
Properties: java.util
propertyChange(): BeanContextSupport, PropertyChangeListener
PropertyChangeEvent: java.beans
PropertyChangeListener: java.beans
PropertyChangeSupport: java.beans
PropertyDescriptor: java.beans
PropertyEditor: java.beans
PropertyEditorManager: java.beans
PropertyEditorSupport: java.beans
PROPERTYNAME: DesignMode
propertyNames(): Properties
PropertyPermission: java.util
PropertyResourceBundle: java.util
PropertyVetoException: java.beans
PROTECTED: Modifier
ProtectionDomain: java.security
PROTOCOL_VERSION_1: ObjectStreamConstants
PROTOCOL_VERSION_2: ObjectStreamConstants
ProtocolException: java.net
Provider: java.security
ProviderException: java.security
proxy: BeanContextServicesSupport
Proxy: java.lang.reflect
PUBLIC: Member, Modifier
PublicKey: java.security
push(): Stack
pushBack(): StreamTokenizer

PushbackInputStream: java.io
PushbackReader: java.io
put(): AbstractMap, Attributes, Dictionary, HashMap, Hashtable, Map, Provider, PutField, TreeMap, WeakHashMap
putAll(): AbstractMap, Attributes, HashMap, Hashtable, Map, Provider, TreeMap
PutField: java.io.ObjectOutputStream
putFields(): ObjectOutputStream
putNextEntry(): JarOutputStream, ZipOutputStream
putValue(): Attributes

Q

quoteChar(): StreamTokenizer

R

Random: java.util
random(): Math, StrictMath
RandomAccessFile: java.io
RC2ParameterSpec: javax.crypto.spec
RC5ParameterSpec: javax.crypto.spec
read(): BufferedInputStream, BufferedReader, ByteArrayInputStream, CharArrayReader, CheckedInputStream, CipherInputStream, DataInputStream, DigestInputStream, FileInputStream, FilterInputStream, FilterReader, GZIPInputStream, InflaterInputStream, InputStream, InputStreamReader, JarInputStream, LineNumberInputStream, LineNumberReader, Manifest, ObjectInput, ObjectInputStream, PipedInputStream, PipedReader, PushbackInputStream, PushbackReader, RandomAccessFile, Reader, SequenceInputStream, StringBufferInputStream, StringReader, ZipInputStream
readBoolean(): DataInput, DataInputStream, ObjectInputStream, RandomAccessFile
readByte(): DataInput, DataInputStream, ObjectInputStream, RandomAccessFile
readChar(): DataInput, DataInputStream, ObjectInputStream, RandomAccessFile
readChildren(): BeanContextSupport
readClassDescriptor(): ObjectInputStream
readDouble(): DataInput, DataInputStream, ObjectInputStream, RandomAccessFile
Reader: java.io
readExternal(): Externalizable
readFields(): ObjectInputStream
readFloat(): DataInput, DataInputStream, ObjectInputStream, RandomAccessFile

readFully(): DataInput, DataInputStream, ObjectInputStream, RandomAccessFile

READING: Attribute

readInt(): DataInput, DataInputStream, ObjectInputStream, RandomAccessFile

readLine(): BufferedReader, DataInput, DataInputStream, LineNumberReader, ObjectInputStream, RandomAccessFile

readLong(): DataInput, DataInputStream, ObjectInputStream, RandomAccessFile

readObject(): ObjectInput, ObjectInputStream

readObjectOverride(): ObjectInputStream

readResolve(): Attribute, CertificateRep

readShort(): DataInput, DataInputStream, ObjectInputStream, RandomAccessFile

readStreamHeader(): ObjectInputStream

readUnsignedByte(): DataInput, DataInputStream, ObjectInputStream, RandomAccessFile

readUnsignedShort(): DataInput, DataInputStream, ObjectInputStream, RandomAccessFile

readUTF(): DataInput, DataInputStream, ObjectInputStream, RandomAccessFile

ready(): BufferedReader, CharArrayReader, FilterReader, InputStreamReader, PipedReader, PushbackReader, Reader, StringReader

receive(): DatagramSocket, DatagramSocketImpl, PipedInputStream

Reference: java.lang.ref

ReferenceQueue: java.lang.ref

ReflectPermission: java.lang.reflect

refresh(): Policy

regionMatches(): String

registerEditor(): PropertyEditorManager

registerValidation(): ObjectInputStream

rehash(): Hashtable

rejectedSetBCOnce: BeanContextChildSupport

releaseBeanContextResources(): BeanContextChildSupport, BeanContextServicesSupport

releaseService(): BCSSProxyServiceProvider, BeanContextServiceProvider, BeanContextServices, BeanContextServicesSupport

remainder(): BigInteger

remove(): AbstractCollection, AbstractList, AbstractMap, AbstractSequentialList, ArrayList, Attributes, BCSIterator, BeanContextSupport, Collection, Dictionary, HashMap, HashSet, Hashtable, Iterator, LinkedList, List, ListIterator, Map, Provider, ReferenceQueue, Set, TreeMap, TreeSet, Vector, WeakHashMap

removeAll(): AbstractCollection, BeanContextSupport, Collection, List, Set, Vector

removeAllElements(): Vector

removeBeanContextMembershipListener(): BeanContext, BeanContextSupport

removeBeanContextServicesListener(): BeanContextServices, BeanContextServicesSupport

removeCertificate(): Identity

removeElement(): Vector

removeElementAt(): Vector

removeEntry(): Acl

removeFirst(): LinkedList

removeIdentity(): IdentityScope

removeLast(): LinkedList

removeMember(): Group

removePermission(): AclEntry

removePropertyChangeListener(): BeanContextChild, BeanContextChildSupport, Customizer, PropertyChangeSupport, PropertyEditor, PropertyEditorSupport

removeProvider(): Security

removeRange(): AbstractList, ArrayList, Vector

removeShutdownHook(): Runtime

removeVetoableChangeListener(): BeanContextChild, BeanContextChildSupport, VetoableChangeSupport

renameTo(): File

replace(): String, StringBuffer

replaceObject(): ObjectOutputStream

requestPasswordAuthentication(): Authenticator

reset(): Adler32, BufferedInputStream, BufferedReader, ByteArrayInputStream, ByteArrayOutputStream, CharArrayReader, CharArrayWriter, Checksum, CollationElementIterator, CRC32, Deflater, FilterInputStream, FilterReader, Inflater, InputStream, LineNumberInputStream, LineNumberReader, Mac, MessageDigest, ObjectOutputStream, PushbackReader, Reader, StringBufferInputStream, StringReader

resetSyntax(): StreamTokenizer

resolveClass(): ClassLoader, ObjectInputStream

resolveObject(): ObjectInputStream

resolveProxyClass(): ObjectInputStream

ResourceBundle: java.util

responseCode: HttpURLConnection

responseMessage: HttpURLConnection

resume(): Thread, ThreadGroup

retainAll(): AbstractCollection, BeanContextSupport, Collection, List, Set, Vector

reverse(): Collections, StringBuffer

reverseOrder(): Collections

revokeService(): BeanContextServices,

BeanContextServicesSupport

rint(): Math, StrictMath
roll(): Calendar, GregorianCalendar
round(): Math, StrictMath
ROUND_CEILING: BigDecimal
ROUND_DOWN: BigDecimal
ROUND_FLOOR: BigDecimal
ROUND_HALF_DOWN: BigDecimal
ROUND_HALF_EVEN: BigDecimal
ROUND_HALF_UP: BigDecimal
ROUND_UNNECESSARY: BigDecimal
ROUND_UP: BigDecimal
RSAKey: java.security.interfaces
RSAKeyGenParameterSpec: java.security.spec
RSAPrivateCrtKey: java.security.interfaces
RSAPrivateCrtKeySpec: java.security.spec
RSAPrivateKey: java.security.interfaces
RSAPrivateKeySpec: java.security.spec
RSAPublicKey: java.security.interfaces
RSAPublicKeySpec: java.security.spec
RuleBasedCollator: java.text
run(): PrivilegedAction, PrivilegedExceptionAction,
  Runnable, Thread, TimerTask
runFinalization(): Runtime, System
runFinalizersOnExit(): Runtime, System
Runnable: java.lang
Runtime: java.lang
RuntimeException: java.lang
RuntimePermission: java.lang

S

sameFile(): URL, URLStreamHandler
SATURDAY: Calendar
save(): Properties
SC_BLOCK_DATA: ObjectStreamConstants
SC_EXTERNALIZABLE: ObjectStreamConstants
SC_SERIALIZABLE: ObjectStreamConstants
SC_WRITE_METHOD: ObjectStreamConstants
scale(): BigDecimal
schedule(): Timer
scheduleAtFixedRate(): Timer
SEALED: Name
SealedObject: javax.crypto
search(): Stack
SECOND: Calendar
SECOND_FIELD: DateFormat
SECONDARY: Collator
secondaryOrder(): CollationElementIterator
SecretKey: javax.crypto

SecretKeyFactory: javax.crypto
SecretKeyFactorySpi: javax.crypto
SecretKeySpec: javax.crypto.spec
SecureClassLoader: java.security
SecureRandom: java.security
SecureRandomSpi: java.security
Security: java.security
SecurityException: java.lang
SecurityManager: java.lang
SecurityPermission: java.security
seek(): RandomAccessFile
send(): DatagramSocket, DatagramSocketImpl, Multi-
  castSocket
separator: File
separatorChar: File
SEPTEMBER: Calendar
SequenceInputStream: java.io
Serializable: java.io
serializable: BeanContextServicesSupport
SerializablePermission: java.io
serialize(): BeanContextSupport
serialVersionUID: DSAPrivateKey, DSAPublicKey, Key,
  PrivateKey, PublicKey
ServerSocket: java.net
serviceAvailable(): BeanContextChildSupport, Bean-
  ContextServicesListener, BeanContextServicesSupport
serviceClass: BeanContextServiceAvailableEvent,
  BeanContextServiceRevokedEvent
serviceProvider: BCSSServiceProvider
serviceRevoked(): BCSSProxyServiceProvider, Bean-
  ContextChildSupport, BeanContextServiceRevokedListener, BeanContextServicesSupport
services: BeanContextServicesSupport
Set: java.util
set(): AbstractList, AbstractSequentialList, Array,
  ArrayList, BitSet, Calendar, Field, LinkedList, List,
  ListIterator, ThreadLocal, URL, Vector
set2DigitYearStart(): SimpleDateFormat
setAccessible(): AccessibleObject
setAddress(): DatagramPacket
setAllowUserInteraction(): URLConnection
setAmPmStrings(): DateFormatSymbols
setAsText(): PropertyEditor, PropertyEditorSupport
setBeanContext(): BeanContextChild, BeanContextChildSupport
setBeanInfoSearchPath(): Introspector
setBeginIndex(): FieldPosition
setBit(): BigInteger
setBoolean(): Array, Field

setBound(): PropertyDescriptor
setByte(): Array, Field
setCalendar(): DateFormat
setCertificateEntry(): KeyStore
setChanged(): Observable
setChar(): Array, Field
setCharAt(): StringBuffer
setChoices(): ChoiceFormat
setComment(): ZipEntry, ZipOutputStream
setCompressedSize(): ZipEntry
setConstrained(): PropertyDescriptor
setContentHandlerFactory(): URLConnection
setContextClassLoader(): Thread
setCrc(): ZipEntry
setCurrencySymbol(): DecimalFormatSymbols
setDaemon(): Thread, ThreadGroup
setData(): DatagramPacket
setDatagramSocketImplFactory(): DatagramSocket
setDate(): Date
setDateFormatSymbols(): SimpleDateFormat
setDecimalFormatSymbols(): DecimalFormat
setDecimalSeparator(): DecimalFormatSymbols
setDecimalSeparatorAlwaysShown(): DecimalFormat
setDecomposition(): Collator
setDefault(): Authenticator, Locale, TimeZone
setDefaultAllowUserInteraction(): URLConnection
setDefaultRequestProperty(): URLConnection
setDefaultUseCaches(): URLConnection
setDesignTime(): BeanContextSupport, Beans, DesignMode
setDictionary(): Deflater, Inflater
setDigit(): DecimalFormatSymbols
setDisplayName(): FeatureDescriptor
setDoInput(): URLConnection
setDoOutput(): URLConnection
setDouble(): Array, Field
setDSTSavings(): SimpleTimeZone
setEditorSearchPath(): PropertyEditorManager
setElementAt(): Vector
setEndIndex(): FieldPosition
setEndRule(): SimpleTimeZone
setEras(): DateFormatSymbols
setErr(): System
setError(): PrintStream, PrintWriter
setErrorIndex(): ParsePosition
setExpert(): FeatureDescriptor
setExtra(): ZipEntry
setFileNameMap(): URLConnection
setFirstDayOfWeek(): Calendar
setFloat(): Array, Field

setFollowRedirects(): HttpURLConnection
setFormat(): MessageFormat
setFormats(): MessageFormat
setGregorianChange(): GregorianCalendar
setGroupingSeparator(): DecimalFormatSymbols
setGroupingSize(): DecimalFormat
setGroupingUsed(): NumberFormat
setGuiAvailable(): Beans
setHidden(): FeatureDescriptor
setHours(): Date
setID(): TimeZone
setIfModifiedSince(): URLConnection
setIn(): System
setInDefaultEventSet(): EventSetDescriptor
setIndex(): CharacterIterator, ParsePosition, StringCharacterIterator
setIndexedReadMethod(): IndexedPropertyDescriptor
setIndexedWriteMethod(): IndexedPropertyDescriptor
setInfinity(): DecimalFormatSymbols
setInfo(): Identity
setInput(): Deflater, Inflater
setInt(): Array, Field
setInterface(): MulticastSocket
setInternationalCurrencySymbol(): DecimalFormatSymbols
setKeepAlive(): Socket
setKeyEntry(): KeyStore
setKeyPair(): Signer
setLastModified(): File
setLength(): DatagramPacket, RandomAccessFile, StringBuffer
setLenient(): Calendar, DateFormat
setLevel(): Deflater, ZipOutputStream
setLineNumber(): LineNumberInputStream, LineNumberReader
setLocale(): BeanContextSupport, MessageFormat
setLocalPatternChars(): DateFormatSymbols
setLong(): Array, Field
setMaximumFractionDigits(): DecimalFormat, NumberFormat
setMaximumIntegerDigits(): DecimalFormat, NumberFormat
setMaxPriority(): ThreadGroup
setMessageDigest(): DigestInputStream, DigestOutputStream
setMethod(): ZipEntry, ZipOutputStream
setMinimalDaysInFirstWeek(): Calendar
setMinimumFractionDigits(): DecimalFormat, NumberFormat
setMinimumIntegerDigits(): DecimalFormat,

SignatureException: java.security
SignatureSpi: java.security
SignedObject: java.security
Signer: java.security
signum(): BigDecimal, BigInteger
SimpleBeanInfo: java.beans
SimpleDateFormat: java.text
SimpleTimeZone: java.util
SIMPLIFIED_CHINESE: Locale
sin(): Math, StrictMath
singleton(): Collections
singletonList(): Collections
singletonMap(): Collections
size(): AbstractCollection, AbstractMap, ArrayList,
    Attributes, BeanContextMembershipEvent, Bean-
    ContextSupport, BitSet, ByteArrayOutputStream,
    CharArrayWriter, Collection, DataOutputStream,
    Dictionary, HashMap, HashSet, Hashtable, Identi-
    tyScope, KeyStore, LinkedList, List, Map, Set,
    TreeMap, TreeSet, Vector, WeakHashMap, ZipFile
skip(): BufferedInputStream, BufferedReader, ByteAr-
    rayInputStream, CharArrayReader, CheckedInput-
    Stream, CipherInputStream, FileInputStream,
    FilterInputStream, FilterReader, InflaterInput-
    Stream, InputStream, LineNumberInputStream,
    LineNumberReader, ObjectInput, PushbackInput-
    Stream, Reader, StringBufferInputStream,
    StringReader, ZipInputStream
skipBytes(): DataInput, DataInputStream, ObjectIn-
    putStream, RandomAccessFile
slashSlashComments(): StreamTokenizer
slashStarComments(): StreamTokenizer
sleep(): Thread
SMALL_FORM_VARIANTS: UnicodeBlock
SO_BINDADDR: SocketOptions
SO_KEEPALIVE: SocketOptions
SO_LINGER: SocketOptions
SO_RCVBUF: SocketOptions
SO_REUSEADDR: SocketOptions
SO_SNDBUF: SocketOptions
SO_TIMEOUT: SocketOptions
Socket: java.net
SocketException: java.net
SocketImpl: java.net
SocketImplFactory: java.net
SocketOptions: java.net
SocketPermission: java.net
SoftReference: java.lang.ref
sort(): Arrays, Collections
SortedMap: java.util

SortedSet: java.util
source: EventObject
SPACE_SEPARATOR: Character
SPACING_MODIFIER_LETTERS: UnicodeBlock
SPECIALS: UnicodeBlock
SPECIFICATION_TITLE: Name
SPECIFICATION_VENDOR: Name
SPECIFICATION_VERSION: Name
sqrt(): Math, StrictMath
Stack: java.util
StackOverflowError: java.lang
start(): Thread
START_PUNCTUATION: Character
startsWith(): String
state: Signature
STATIC: Modifier
stop(): Thread, ThreadGroup
store(): KeyStore, Properties
STORED: ZipEntry, ZipOutputStream
STREAM_MAGIC: ObjectStreamConstants
STREAM_VERSION: ObjectStreamConstants
StreamCorruptedException: java.io
StreamTokenizer: java.io
STRICT: Modifier
StrictMath: java.lang
String: java.lang
StringBuffer: java.lang
StringBufferInputStream: java.io
StringCharacterIterator: java.text
StringIndexOutOfBoundsException: java.lang
StringReader: java.io
StringTokenizer: java.util
StringWriter: java.io
SUBCLASS_IMPLEMENTATION_PERMISSION:
    ObjectStreamConstants
subList(): AbstractList, List, Vector
subMap(): SortedMap, TreeMap
Subset: java.lang.Character
subSet(): SortedSet, TreeSet
SUBSTITUTION_PERMISSION: ObjectStreamCon-
    stants
substring(): String, StringBuffer
subtract(): BigDecimal, BigInteger
SUNDAY: Calendar
SUPERSCRIPTS_AND_SUBSCRIPTS: UnicodeBlock
supportsCustomEditor(): PropertyEditor, PropertyEdi-
    torSupport
SURROGATE: Character
SURROGATES_AREA: UnicodeBlock
suspend(): Thread, ThreadGroup

sval: StreamTokenizer
sync(): FileDescriptor
SyncFailedException: java.io
SYNCHRONIZED: Modifier
synchronizedCollection(): Collections
synchronizedList(): Collections
synchronizedMap(): Collections
synchronizedSet(): Collections
synchronizedSortedMap(): Collections
synchronizedSortedSet(): Collections
System: java.lang

T

tailMap(): SortedMap, TreeMap
tailSet(): SortedSet, TreeSet
TAIWAN: Locale
TAMIL: UnicodeBlock
tan(): Math, StrictMath
TC_ARRAY: ObjectStreamConstants
TC_BASE: ObjectStreamConstants
TC_BLOCKDATA: ObjectStreamConstants
TC_BLOCKDATALONG: ObjectStreamConstants
TC_CLASS: ObjectStreamConstants
TC_CLASSDESC: ObjectStreamConstants
TC_ENDBLOCKDATA: ObjectStreamConstants
TC_EXCEPTION: ObjectStreamConstants
TC_LONGSTRING: ObjectStreamConstants
TC_MAX: ObjectStreamConstants
TC_NULL: ObjectStreamConstants
TC_OBJECT: ObjectStreamConstants
TC_PROXYCLASSDESC: ObjectStreamConstants
TC_REFERENCE: ObjectStreamConstants
TC_RESET: ObjectStreamConstants
TC_STRING: ObjectStreamConstants
TCP_NODELAY: SocketOptions
TELUGU: UnicodeBlock
TERTIARY: Collator
tertiaryOrder(): CollationElementIterator
testBit(): BigInteger
THAI: UnicodeBlock
Thread: java.lang
ThreadDeath: java.lang
ThreadGroup: java.lang
ThreadLocal: java.lang
Throwable: java.lang
THURSDAY: Calendar
TIBETAN: UnicodeBlock
time: Calendar
Timer: java.util

TimerTask: java.util
TimeZone: java.util
TIMEZONE_FIELD: DateFormat
TITLECASE_LETTER: Character
toArray(): AbstractCollection, ArrayList, BeanContextMembershipEvent, BeanContextSupport, Collection, LinkedList, List, Set, Vector
toBigInteger(): BigDecimal
toBinaryString(): Integer, Long
toByteArray(): BigInteger, ByteArrayOutputStream, CollationKey
toCharArray(): CharArrayWriter, String
toDegrees(): Math, StrictMath
toExternalForm(): URL, URLStreamHandler
toGMTString(): Date
toHexString(): Integer, Long
toLocaleString(): Date
toLocalizedPattern(): DecimalFormat, SimpleDateFormat
toLowerCase(): Character, String
toOctalString(): Integer, Long
TooManyListenersException: java.util
toPattern(): ChoiceFormat, DecimalFormat, MessageFormat, SimpleDateFormat
toRadians(): Math, StrictMath
toString(): AbstractCollection, AbstractMap, Acl, AclEntry, AlgorithmParameters, Annotation, Attribute, BigDecimal, BigInteger, BitSet, Boolean, Byte, ByteArrayOutputStream, Calendar, Certificate, Character, CharArrayWriter, Class, CodeSource, Constructor, CRL, Date, DigestInputStream, DigestOutputStream, Double, EventObject, Field, FieldPosition, File, Float, Hashtable, Identity, IdentityScope, InetAddress, Integer, Locale, Long, MessageDigest, Method, Modifier, Name, Object, ObjectStreamClass, ObjectStreamField, Package, ParsePosition, Permission, PermissionCollection, Principal, PrivilegedActionException, ProtectionDomain, Provider, ServerSocket, Short, Signature, Signer, SimpleTimeZone, Socket, SocketImpl, StreamTokenizer, String, StringBuffer, StringWriter, Subset, Thread, ThreadGroup, Throwable, UnresolvedPermission, URL, URLConnection, Vector, X509CRLEntry, ZipEntry
totalMemory(): Runtime
toTitleCase(): Character
toUpperCase(): Character, String
toURL(): File
traceInstructions(): Runtime

traceMethodCalls(): Runtime
TRADITIONAL_CHINESE: Locale
TRANSIENT: Modifier
translateKey(): KeyFactory, SecretKeyFactory
TreeMap: java.util
TreeSet: java.util
trim(): String
trimToSize(): ArrayList, Vector
TRUE: Boolean
TT_EOF: StreamTokenizer
TT_EOL: StreamTokenizer
TT_NUMBER: StreamTokenizer
TT_WORD: StreamTokenizer
ttype: StreamTokenizer
TUESDAY: Calendar
TYPE: Boolean, Byte, Character, Double, Float, Integer, Long, Short, Void

U

UK: Locale
UNASSIGNED: Character
uncaughtException(): ThreadGroup
UNDECIMBER: Calendar
UndeclaredThrowableException: java.lang.reflect
UnicodeBlock: java.lang.Character
UNINITIALIZED: Signature
UnknownError: java.lang
UnknownHostException: java.net
UnknownServiceException: java.net
unmodifiableCollection(): Collections
unmodifiableList(): Collections
unmodifiableMap(): Collections
unmodifiableSet(): Collections
unmodifiableSortedMap(): Collections
unmodifiableSortedSet(): Collections
unread(): PushbackInputStream, PushbackReader
UnrecoverableKeyException: java.security
UnresolvedPermission: java.security
UnsatisfiedLinkError: java.lang
unscaledValue(): BigDecimal
UnsupportedClassVersionError: java.lang
UnsupportedEncodingException: java.io
UnsupportedOperationException: java.lang
update(): Adler32, Checksum, Cipher, CRC32, Mac, MessageDigest, Observer, Signature
UPPERCASE_LETTER: Character
url: URLConnection
URL: java.net
URLClassLoader: java.net

URLConnection: java.net
URLDecoder: java.net
URLEncoder: java.net
URLStreamHandler: java.net
URLStreamHandlerFactory: java.net
US: Locale
USE_ALL_BEANINFO: Introspector
useCaches: URLConnection
useDaylightTime(): SimpleTimeZone, TimeZone
useProtocolVersion(): ObjectOutputStream
usingProxy(): HttpURLConnection
UTC(): Date
UTFDataFormatException: java.io

V

valid(): FileDescriptor
validateObject(): ObjectInputValidation
validatePendingAdd(): BeanContextSupport
validatePendingRemove(): BeanContextSupport
validatePendingSetBeanContext(): BeanContextChild-Support
valueOf(): BigDecimal, BigInteger, Boolean, Byte, Double, Float, Integer, Long, Short, String
values(): AbstractMap, Attributes, HashMap, Hashtable, Map, Provider, TreeMap
vcSupport: BeanContextChildSupport
Vector: java.util
VERIFY: Signature
verify(): Certificate, Signature, SignedObject, X509CRL
VerifyError: java.lang
vetoableChange(): BeanContextSupport, VetoableChangeListener
VetoableChangeListener: java.beans
VetoableChangeSupport: java.beans
VirtualMachineError: java.lang
Visibility: java.beans
Void: java.lang
VOLATILE: Modifier

W

wait(): Object
waitFor(): Process
WeakHashMap: java.util
WeakReference: java.lang.ref
WEDNESDAY: Calendar
WEEK_OF_MONTH: Calendar
WEEK_OF_MONTH_FIELD: DateFormat

WEEK_OF_YEAR: Calendar
WEEK_OF_YEAR_FIELD: DateFormat
whitespaceChars(): StreamTokenizer
wordChars(): StreamTokenizer
write(): BufferedOutputStream, BufferedWriter, ByteArrayOutputStream, CharArrayWriter, CheckedOutputStream, CipherOutputStream, DataOutput, DataOutputStream, DeflaterOutputStream, DigestOutputStream, FileOutputStream, FilterOutputStream, FilterWriter, GZIPOutputStream, Manifest, ObjectOutput, ObjectOutputStream, OutputStream, OutputStreamWriter, PipedOutputStream, PipedWriter, PrintStream, PrintWriter, PutField, RandomAccessFile, StringWriter, Writer, ZipOutputStream
WriteAbortedException: java.io
writeBoolean(): DataOutput, DataOutputStream, ObjectOutputStream, RandomAccessFile
writeByte(): DataOutput, DataOutputStream, ObjectOutputStream, RandomAccessFile
writeBytes(): DataOutput, DataOutputStream, ObjectOutputStream, RandomAccessFile
writeChar(): DataOutput, DataOutputStream, ObjectOutputStream, RandomAccessFile
writeChars(): DataOutput, DataOutputStream, ObjectOutputStream, RandomAccessFile
writeChildren(): BeanContextSupport
writeClassDescriptor(): ObjectOutputStream
writeDouble(): DataOutput, DataOutputStream, ObjectOutputStream, RandomAccessFile
writeExternal(): Externalizable
writeFields(): ObjectOutputStream
writeFloat(): DataOutput, DataOutputStream, ObjectOutputStream, RandomAccessFile
writeInt(): DataOutput, DataOutputStream, ObjectOutputStream, RandomAccessFile
writeLong(): DataOutput, DataOutputStream, ObjectOutputStream, RandomAccessFile
writeObject(): ObjectOutput, ObjectOutputStream
writeObjectOverride(): ObjectOutputStream
Writer: java.io
writeReplace(): Certificate
writeShort(): DataOutput, DataOutputStream, ObjectOutputStream, RandomAccessFile
writeStreamHeader(): ObjectOutputStream
writeTo(): ByteArrayOutputStream, CharArrayWriter
writeUTF(): DataOutput, DataOutputStream, ObjectOutputStream, RandomAccessFile
written: DataOutputStream

X

X509Certificate: java.security.cert
X509CRL: java.security.cert
X509CRLEntry: java.security.cert
X509EncodedKeySpec: java.security.spec
X509Extension: java.security.cert
xor(): BigInteger, BitSet

Y

YEAR: Calendar
YEAR_FIELD: DateFormat
yield(): Thread

Z

ZERO: BigInteger
ZipEntry: java.util.zip
ZipException: java.util.zip
ZipFile: java.util.zip
ZipInputStream: java.util.zip
ZipOutputStream: java.util.zip
ZONE_OFFSET: Calendar

Class Index

Index

Symbols

?: (conditional) operator, 41
> greater than operator, 37
>= greater than/equal to operator, 37
>> (right shift) operator, signed, 40
>>= (right-shift assignment) operator, 41
>>> (right shift) operator, unsigned, 40
>>>= (right-shift unsigned assignment) operator, 41
; (semicolon)
   for empty statements, 45
   in program lines, 10
   separating statements, 13
/ division operator, 34
/* */ (multiline comments), 11, 20
/** */ (doc comments), 21
/= (division assignment) operator, 41
// (single-line comments), 10–11, 20
˜ (bitwise NOT) operator, 39
˜ (bitwise complement) operator, 39
(_) underscore, 21
| (Boolean OR) operator, 38–39
| (bitwise OR) operator, 39
|= (bitwise OR assignment) operator, 41
|| (conditional OR) operator, 38

A

<A> HTML tag, 194
abstract classes, 110–112
   InstantiationError, 349
   InstantiationException, 349
   interfaces vs., 112
abstract methods, 110–112
   AbstractMethodError, 328
abstract modifier, 132
AbstractCollection class, 497
AbstractList class, 500
AbstractMap class, 500
AbstractSequentialList class, 501
AbstractSet class, 502
accept()
   FileFilter interface, 293
   FilenameFilter interface, 294
   ServerSocket class, 407
access control, 105–108, 166, 168–171
   classes, 418
   inheritance and, 107
   java.security package, 161

java.security.acl package, 453–456
lists, package for, 137
member accessibility, list of, 108
modifiers, 105
   package for, 137
AccessControlContext class, 419
AccessControlException, 421
AccessController class, 170–171, 418, 422
AccessibleObject class, 381
ACL (Access Control List), 453
   Acl interface, 453
   AclEntry interface, 454
   AclNotFoundException, 454
actions, 171
activeCount() (ThreadGroup), 372
activeGroupCount() (ThreadGroup), 372
add(), 502
   AbstractCollection class, 497
   AbstractList class, 500
   Calendar class, 506
   Collection interface, 508
   HashSet class, 517
   LinkedList class, 520
   List interface, 521
   ListIterator interface, 522
   Permissions class, 441
   Set interface, 532
   TreeSet class, 539
   Vector class, 540
addAll()
   Collection interface, 508
   List interface, 521
addAttribute() (AttributedString), 479
addAttributes() (AttributedString), 479
addition (+) operator, 34
addObserver() (Observable), 528
addPropertyChangeListener(), 252, 260
addProvider() (Security), 444
addService() (BeanContextServices), 273
addShutdownHook(), 359
Adler32 class, 550
after(), 506
AlgorithmParameterGenerator class, 422

C

C programming language, vs. Java, 8, 80

C++ programming language
features of not found in Java, 135
vs. Java, 8, 80, 82
virtual functions, 103

CA (certificate authority), 457

Calendar class, 143, 497, 506
GregorianCalendar class, 516

cancel()
Timer class, 536
TimerTask class, 537

canRead() (File), 291

canWrite() (File), 291

capacity()
ArrayList class, 502
Vector class, 540

capitalization conventions, 189

case labels (switch), 49

case sensitivity, 10

casts, 27

catch clause, 58

certificate authority (CA), 457

Certificate class, 457, 462
Certificate interface (java.security package) vs., 457
CertificateRep class, 459
(see also X509Certificate class)

Certificate interface, 418, 425, 429, 451
Certificate class (java.security.cert) vs., 457

certificate revocation lists (see CRLs)

CertificateException, 459

CertificateExpiredException, 460

CertificateFactory class, 460

CertificateFactorySpi class, 461

CertificateNotYetValidException, 461

CertificateParsingException, 461

CertificateRep class, 459

certificates (identity), 457–465

characters, 138–140
char data type, 23, 333
Character class, 24, 140, 328, 333
Subset class, 335
UnicodeBlock class, 335
character sets, 8
CharacterIterator interface, 480
CharArrayReader class, 157, 286

CharArrayWriter class, 157, 286

CharConversionException, 287
streams of, 154
UnsupportedEncodingException, 325

charAt(), 365
StringBuffer class, 366

charValue(), 333

checkAccess()
Thread class, 370
ThreadGroup class, 372

checked exceptions, 56

CheckedInputStream class, 550

CheckedOutputStream class, 551

checkError(), 316

checkGuard() (Guard), 428

checkPermission()
AccessControlContext class, 419
AccessController class, 422
Acl interface, 453
SecurityManager class, 361

checkRead() method, 170

checkRead(), 168

checksum
computing, 155
cryptographic-strength, 156

Checksum interface, 552

checkValidity() (X509Certificate), 462

childJustAddedHook() (BeanContextSupport), 277

childValue() (InheritableThreadLocal), 348

ChoiceFormat class, 476, 481

Cipher class, 164, 561, 563
NullCipher class, 572

CipherInputStream class, 165, 566

CipherOutputStream class, 165, 566

CipherSpi class, 566

circular dependency, 339

Class class, 147

class fields, 83

class files, 79
verification of, 167

class hierarchy, 97, 123

class methods, 84

Class objects, obtaining, 147

classes, 7, 28, 61
abstract, 110–112, 132
access to, 106

files (cont'd)
   FileNotFoundException, 294
   FileOutputStream class, 280, 294
   FilePermission class, 295
   FileReader class, 296
   FileWriter class, 296
   RandomAccessFile class, 280, 319
   text, reading, 154
   ZipFile class, 558
fill()
   Arrays class, 504
   Collections class, 510
fillInStackTrace(), 374
FilterInputStream class, 280
   CheckedInputStream class, 550
FilterOutputStream class, 280, 297
FilterReader class, 297
FilterWriter class, 298
final classes, 97
final methods, static method lookup
    and, 103
final modifier, 83, 133
   in variable declarations, 46
finalization, 92–95
finalizers, 94
   chaining and, 99
finalize() (Object), 356
finally clause, 58
findClass() (ClassLoader), 339
findEditor (PropertyEditorManager),
    260
findResource() (ClassLoader), 340
findResources() (ClassLoader), 340
firePropertyChange(), 258, 260
fireVetoableChange(), 262
first()
   BreakIterator class, 480
   CharacterIterator interface, 480
   SortedSet interface, 534
firstKey() (SortedMap), 533
floating-point data types, 25, 137, 141,
    323, 391
   Double class, 26
   Float class, 26, 140, 328, 345
   strictfp modifier, 133
floatToIntBits(), 345
floatValue(), 345
flush(), 326
   BufferedOutputStream class, 283
   BufferedWriter class, 284

CharArrayWriter class, 286
CipherOutputStream class, 566
DataOutputStream class, 289
OutputStream class, 312
PrintWriter class, 316
StringWriter class, 325
following() (BreakIterator), 480
for statements, 51
forClass() (ObjectStreamClass), 309
forDigit(), 333
format()
   ChoiceFormat class, 481
   DateFormat class, 485
   Format class, 490
   MessageFormat class, 490
   NumberFormat class, 492
Format class, 490
forName() (Class), 337, 339
freeMemory(), 359
ftp: protocol, 158
functions (see methods)

G

garbage collection, 74, 80, 92
   OutOfMemoryError, 357
   system, 369
   WeakHashMap class, 542
garbage collector, Java programs and,
    377
gcd(), 393
gc(), 359
   System class, 369
GeneralSecurityException, 428
generateCertificate() (CertificateFac-
    tory), 460, 462
generateCertificates() (CertificateFac-
    tory), 460
generateCRL() (CertificateFactory),
    460, 463
generateCRLs() (CertificateFactory),
    460
generateKey() (KeyGenerator), 570
generateKeyPair() (KeyPairGenerator),
    467
generateParameters() (AlgorithmPara-
    meterGenerator), 422
generatePrivate() (KeyFactory), 432
generatePublic() (KeyFactory), 432

iterator( ), 534
  AbstractCollection class, 497
  BeanContextMembershipEvent
    class, 269
  List interface, 521
  Set interface, 526
Iterator interface, 145, 497, 519
IvParameterSpec class, 581

J

J2EE (Java 2 Platform, Enterprise Edition), 6
JAR files, 169
  archive, conventions for, 187
  classes for reading and writing,
    544–549
  manifest, format of, 544
  package for, 137
  retrieving, 404
  running programs by specifying, 79
  tools for, 204–208
JarEntry class, 544, 546
JarException, 547
JarFile class, 544, 547
JarInputStream class, 544, 548
JarOutputStream class, 544, 548
jarsigner tool, 206–208
JarURLConnection class, 404, 544
Java, 3–8
  benefits of, 6–8
  vs. C programming language, 8, 80
  vs. C++ programming language, 8,
    80, 82
  case sensitivity, 10
  files, 153–154
  learning, 20
  object-oriented programming in,
    82–135
  performance, 8
  programmers and, 4
  resources for further information,
    19
  version 1.0, 5
    access control, 168
  version 1.1, 5
    classes, digitally signed, 169
    security and, 167
  version 1.2, 5
    access-control architecture, 170

array-manipulation methods,
    144
  collections, 145
  File class, 153
  permissions/policies, 170
  policy file, additional, 173
  programs, running, 79
  version 1.3, 5
Java 2 Platform, 5
  Enterprise Edition, 6
  Micro Edition, 6
  security, 7
Java Activation Framework standard
    extension, 179
Java API, 14, 166
Java Cryptography Extension (JCE),
    168, 419, 561
Java Development Kit (see SDK)
.java file extension, 78
Java in a Nutshell, companion books,
    xi
Java interpreter, 4, 208–213
  InternalError, 350
  OutOfMemoryError, 357
  running programs, 79
  StackOverflowError, 363
Java platform, 4, 136–165
  Standard Edition, 6
Java Plug-in, 6
Java programming
  commercial products for, 9
  conventions for, 189–199
  example program, 9–18
  language, 3
  online resources, xiv
  online tutorial, 17
  programs
    classes and, 11
    compiling, 10
    running, 10
  related books on, xiii
  syntax, 19–81
Java Runtime Environment (see JRE)
Java VM (Java Virtual Machine), 4
  Microsoft implementation, security
    and, 167
  security, 167
  UnknownError, 374
  VirtualMachineError, 376

methods (cont'd)
MethodDescriptor class, 255
modifiers for, 60
naming, 60
native, 133
NoSuchMethodError, 354
NoSuchMethodException, 354
overloaded, references to, 197
overloading, 61, 81
defining multiple constructors
for a class, 89
overriding vs., 101
overriding, 101–104
invoking overridden, 103
parameters for, 12, 61
signatures, 60
static, 134
synchronized, 134, 151
unsupported, error, 375
void, 53
Microsoft Windows (95/98/NT), SDK
for, 9
MIME types, 398, 401
min() (Collections), 510
MissingResourceException, 527
mkdir() (File), 291
mkdirs() (File), 291
Modifer class, 381
modifiers, 11
list of, 132–134
for methods, 60
Modifier class, 388
modInverse(), 393
modPow(), 393
modulo (%) operator, 34
MS-DOS window, 10
MulticastSocket class, 395, 405
multidimensional arrays, 68
multiline comments (/* */), 11, 20
multiple interfaces, 116
multiplication (*) operator, 34

N

Name class, 546
namespace, 76–78
naming conventions, 189
narrowing conversions, 27

native methods, 133
conventions/rules for, 190
tool for, 221
native2ascii program, 234
nCopies() (Collections), 510
needsGui(), 263
NegativeArraySizeException, 353
NetPermission class, 405
network-centric programming, 7
networking, 158–161
java.net package, 395–417
package for, 137
new operator for object creation, 43
newInstance(), 337
Array class, 383
Constructor class, 384
URLClassLoader class, 413
newLine() (BufferedWriter), 284
newPermissionCollection() (Permission), 440
newProxyInstance() (Proxy), 389
next(), 501
CharacterIterator interface, 480
CollationElementIterator class, 482
Iterator class, 497
Iterator interface, 519
ListIterator interface, 522
nextBoolean() (Random), 530
nextBytes()
Random class, 530
SecureRandom class, 447
nextDouble(), 530
nextElement()
Enumeration class, 514
StringTokenizer class, 535
nextFloat(), 530
nextGaussian(), 530
nextIndex() (ListIterator), 522
nextInt(), 530
nextLong(), 530
nextToken(), 323
StringTokenizer class, 535
NoClassDefFoundError, 353
NoRouteToHostException, 406
NoSuchAlgorithmException, 439
NoSuchElementException, 522, 527
NoSuchFieldError, 354
NoSuchFieldException, 354
NoSuchMethodError, 354

NoSuchMethodException, 354
NoSuchPaddingException, 572
NoSuchProviderException, 439
not equals (!=) operator, 36
NotActiveException, 303
Notepad, 10
notify() (Object), 152, 347, 356, 370
notifyAll() (Object), 356
NotOwnerException, 455
NotSerializableException, 303
null value, 74
    default, reference fields, 90
    representing absence of an object,
        64
NullCipher class, 572
NullPointerException, 355
NumberFormat class, 476
numbers, 140–143, 530
    comparing (Comparator class), 511
    DateFormat class, 484
    DecimalFormat class, 487
    Enumeration class, 514
    Number class, 355
    NumberFormat class, 491
    NumberFormatException, 355
    SimpleDateFormat class, 494
numeric values, 141

O

Object class, 328, 356
object classes, 97
object creation, operator for, 43
object identifier (OID), 464
object literals, 63
object member access (.) operator, 42
object serialization
    Externalizable interface, 290
    NotSerializableException, 303
    ObjectInput interface, 303
    ObjectInputStream class, 282, 304
        GetField class, 305
    ObjectInputValidation class, 306
    ObjectOutput interface, 306
    ObjectOutputStream class, 282, 307
        PutField class, 308
    ObjectStreamConstants interface,
        310
    ObjectStreamException, 311
    ObjectStreamField class, 311

SealedObject class, 572
    Serializable interface, 321
object-oriented programming, 82–135
objects, 61–64
    AccessibleObject class, 381
    arrays of, converting to collections,
        146
    collections of, 145
        package for, 137
    comparing, 73
    copying, 71
    creating, 62, 88–92
    destroying, 92–95
    finalizing, 92–95
    initializing, 88–92
    InvalidObjectException, 301
    NullPointerException, 355
    Object class, 328, 356
    serializing/deserializing, 157
    threads and, 151
    using, 64
ObjectStreamClass class, 309
Observable class, 527
Observer interface, 528
octal numbers, 24
of() (UnicodeBlock), 335
OID (object identifier), 464
okToUseGui(), 263
on()
    DigestInputStream class, 427
    DigestOutputStream class, 427
openConnection()
    HttpURLConnection class, 402
    URL class, 412
    URLStreamHandler class, 416
openStream() (URL), 412
operands, 17
    list of, 30
    number/type, 32
operators, 16, 29–34
    arithmetic, 34
    list of, 30
    special, 42
OptionalDataException, 312
order of evaluation, 33
ordinaryChar(), 323
ordinaryChars(), 323
OutOfMemoryError, 357
output, displaying, 14

readLine()
    BufferedReader class, 282–283
    DataInputStream class, 288
    LineNumberReader class, 302
readObject()
    ObjectInputStream class, 304–306,
        321
    OptionalDataException, 312
    Serializable interface, 303
readUnsignedByte() (DataInput-
        Stream), 288
readUnsignedShort() (DataInput-
        Stream), 288
readUTF() (DataInputStream), 288
ready() (Reader), 320
receive() (DatagramSocket), 399
rectangular arrays, 69
Reference class, 377–378
reference types, 70–76
    conversions, 75
ReferenceQueue class, 377, 379
references, 70
    null, 74
referent, 377
reflection, 147
    package for, 137
ReflectPermission class, 389
refresh() (Policy), 441
registerEditor (PropertyEditorMan-
        ager), 260
registerValidation() (ObjectInput-
        Stream), 304, 306
relational operators, 36
releaseBeanContextResources()
        (BeanContextChildSupport),
        267
releaseService()
    BeanContextServiceProvider inter-
        face, 270
    BeanContextServices interface, 272
remove()
    AbstractList class, 500
    AbstractMap class, 500
    BCSIterator class, 279
    Collection interface, 508
    HashSet class, 517
    Hashtable class, 518
    Iterator class, 497
    Iterator interface, 519
    LinkedList class, 520

List interface, 521
ListIterator interface, 522
Map interface, 525
ReferenceQueue class, 379
TreeMap class, 539
TreeSet class, 539
removeElementAt() (Vector), 540
removeAll() (Collection), 508
removePropertyChangeListener(), 252,
        260
removeShutdownHook(), 359
renameTo() (File), 291
repetitive tasks, threads for, 150
replace(), 365
    StringBuffer class, 366
requestPasswordAuthentication()
        (Authenticator), 396, 405
reserved words, 22
reset()
    ByteArrayOutputStream class, 285
    CertificateFactory class, 460
    CharArrayReader class, 286
    CharArrayWriter class, 286
    Checksum interface, 552
    InputStream class, 299
    MessageDigest class, 437
    Reader class, 320
    StringReader class, 324
resetSyntax(), 323
ResourceBundle class, 497, 531
resources for further information
    enterprise packages, 137
    examples in this book, xv
    Java programming
        tutorial, 17
        web sites, xiv
    quick reference material, generat-
        ing, xvi
restrictions
    on anonymous classes, 129
    on local classes, 125
    on member classes, 121
    on static member classes, 119
resume() (Thread), 370
retainAll() (Collection), 508
@return doc-comment tag, 195
return statements, 49, 53
return types, 33
return values, 12

returning results, 17
reverse( ) (Collections), 510
reverseOrder( ) (Collections), 510
revokeService( ) (BeanContextServices), 273
right-to-left associativity, 31
roll( ), 506
root directories, listing, 291
RSA and DSA public and private keys, 466
    representing and encoding, 470–475
RSAKey interface, 468
RSAKeyGenParameterSpec interface, 474
RSAPrivateCrtKey interface, 468
RSAPrivateCrtKeySpec interface, 474
RSAPrivateKey interface, 469
RSAPrivateKeySpec interface, 474
RSAPublicKey interface, 466, 469
RSAPublicKeySpec interface, 475
RuleBasedCollator class, 494
rules, 181
    pure Java, 190–192
    (see also conventions)
run( )
    PrivilegedAction interface, 443
    PrivilegedExceptionAction, 443
    Runnable interface, 358
    Thread class, 370
    TimerTask class, 537
runFinalization( ), 359
    System class, 369
Runnable interface, 149, 358
running programs, 10
Runtime class, 328, 359
RuntimeException, 360
Runtime.exec( ) method, conventions/rules for, 191
RuntimePermission class, 360
run( ), 149

S

sameFile( ) (URL), 412
"sandbox", 168
save( ) (Properties), 528
schedule( ) (Timer), 536
scheduleAtFixedRate( ) (Timer), 536

scheduledExecutionTime( ) (TimerTask), 537
scope, 15, 46
    vs. inheritance for member classes, 123
    of local classes, 126
SDK (Software Development Kit), 6
    downloads, 9
    tools, 200–236
SealedObject class, 165, 572
searching arrays, 144
SecretKey interface, 163, 573
SecretKeyFactory class, 573
SecretKeyFactorySpi class, 574
SecretKeySpec class, 582
secure hash (see message digests)
SecureClassLoader class, 446
SecureRandom class, 418, 446
SecureRandomSpi class, 447
security, 7, 161–163, 166–177
    access control lists (ACLs), working with, 453–456
    architecture, 167
    certificates, working with, 457–465
    default, 172
    DSA and RSA public and private key representations, 470–475
    GeneralSecurityException, 428
    interfaces package, 466–469
    java.security package, 418–452
    NetPermission class, 405
    packets, sending/receiving, 399
    permission to access files, 295
    permissions, further information on, 172
    ReflectPermission class, 389
    risks, 166
    RunTimePermission class, 361
    Security class, 448
    SecurityException, 361
    SecurityManager class, 361
    SecurityPermission class, 448
    socket permissions, 410
    system properties, granting access to, 529
    tool for policy configuration files, 235
    URLClassLoader class, 413
    users, 171–173

sleep() (Thread), 370
sockets
    BindException, 397
    ConnectException, 398
    DatagramSocket class, 395, 399
    DatagramSocketImpl class, 400
    MulticastSocket class, 395, 405
    ServerSocket class, 407
    Socket class, 158, 395, 407
    SocketException, 409
    SocketImpl class, 409
    SocketImplFactory interface, 410
    SocketOptions interface, 410
    SocketPermission class, 410
    unable to connect to remote host,
        406
SoftReference class, 377, 379
software components
    package for, 136
    reusable, 178
Software Development Kit (see SDK)
Solaris operating system, SDK for, 9
SortedMap interface, 497, 533
SortedSet interface, 497, 534
sorting arrays, 144
sort()
    Arrays class, 503
    Collections class, 509
spaces, 15
    in doc comments, 194
special effects, threads for, 150
SPI (see service provider interface)
Stack class, 535
    EmptyStackException, 514
StackOverflowError, 363
stacks, LinkedList, 520
standard extensions, 6
    additional information about, 137
    conventions/rules for, 192
start() (Thread), 370
start() method, 149
startsWith(), 365
statements, 13, 43–59
    break, 52
    compound, 44
    continue, 53
    do/while, 50
    empty, 45
    expression, 44
    for, 51

    if/else, 46
    labeled, 45
    local variable declaration, 45
    return, 53
    switch, 48
    synchronized, 54
    throw, 55
    try/catch/finally, 57
    types, list of, 43
    while, 50
static
    class fields, 83
    methods, 84
static member classes, 117–118
    implementation, 131
static method lookup, 103
static modifier, 134
stop(), 150
    Thread class, 370
store()
    KeyStore class, 436
    Properties class, 528
StreamCorruptedException, 322
streaming data, 154
    (see also input streams; output
        streams)
StreamTokenizer class, 323
strictfp modifier, 133
StrictMath class, 364
StringBuffer class, 366
strings, 26, 138–140
    concatenation, 367
    String class, 138, 328, 365
    StringBuffer class, 139
    StringBufferInputStream class, 324
    StringCharacterIterator class, 495
    StringIndexOutOfBoundsException,
        368
    StringReader class, 324
    StringTokenizer class, 139, 497, 535
    StringWriter class, 157, 325
strongly typed languages, 13
subclasses, 95–104
    constructors, 97
    Permission, 173–177
subList() (List), 521
subMap() (SortedMap), 533
subroutines (see methods)
Subset class, 335

About the Author

David Flanagan is a computer programmer who spends most of his time writing about Java. His other books with O'Reilly & Associates include *Java Foundation Classes in a Nutshell*, *Java Enterprise in a Nutshell*, *JavaScript: The Definitive Guide*, *Java Examples in a Nutshell*, *Java Power Reference*, and *JavaScript Pocket Reference*. David has a degree in computer science and engineering from the Massachusetts Institute of Technology. He lives with his partner Christie in the U.S. Pacific Northwest between the cities of Seattle, Washington and Vancouver, British Columbia.

Colophon

Our look is the result of reader comments, our own experimentation, and feedback from distribution channels. Distinctive covers complement our distinctive approach to technical topics, breathing personality and life into potentially dry subjects.

The animal appearing on the cover of *Java in a Nutshell, Third Edition,* is a Javan tiger. It is the smallest of the eight subspecies of tiger, and has the longest cheek whiskers, forming a short mane across the neck. The encroachment of the growing human population, along with increases in poaching, led to the near-extinction of the Javan tiger. The Indonesian government has become involved in trying to preserve the tiger. It is to be hoped that the remaining subspecies of tiger will be helped by increasing awareness and stricter protections.

Tigers are the largest of all cats, weighing up to 660 pounds and with a body length of up to 9 feet. They are solitary animals, and, unlike lions, hunt alone. Tigers prefer large prey, such as wild pigs, cattle, or deer. Tigers rarely attack humans, although attacks on humans have increased as the increasing human population more frequently comes into contact with tigers. Tiger attacks usually occur when the tiger feels that it or its young are being threatened. In such cases, the tiger almost never eats its human victim. There are some tigers, however, who have developed a taste for human flesh. This is a particularly bad problem in an area of India and Bangladesh called the Sunderbans.

Mary Anne Weeks Mayo was the production editor and copyeditor for *Java in a Nutshell, Third Edition*; Ellie Cutler, Maureen Dempsey, and Jane Ellin provided quality control, and Ellie Fountain Maden proofread the book. Anna Kim Snow provided production assistance. Lenny Muellner and Chris Maden provided SGML support. Ellen Troutman Zaig and Brenda Miller wrote the index.

Edie Freedman designed the cover of this book, using a 19th-century engraving from the Dover Pictorial Archive. Whenever possible, our books use RepKover™, a durable and flexible lay-flat binding. If the page count exceeds RepKover's limit, perfect binding is used.

Kathleen Wilson produced the cover layout with Quark XPress 3.3 using Adobe's ITC Garamond font. The interior layouts were designed by Edie Freedman and Nancy Priest, with modifications by Alicia Cech, and Lenny Muellner implemented the layout in *gtroff*. Interior fonts are Adobe ITC Garamond and Adobe ITC Franklin

Gothic. The illustrations that appear in the book were produced by Robert Romano and Rhon Porter using Macromedia FreeHand 8 and Adobe Photoshop 5. This colophon was written by Clairemarie Fisher O'Leary.

How to stay in touch with O'Reilly

1. Visit Our Award-Winning Site

http://www.oreilly.com/

★ "Top 100 Sites on the Web" —*PC Magazine*
★ "Top 5% Web sites" —*Point Communications*
★ "3-Star site" —*The McKinley Group*

Our web site contains a library of comprehensive product information (including book excerpts and tables of contents), downloadable software, background articles, interviews with technology leaders, links to relevant sites, book cover art, and more. File us in your Bookmarks or Hotlist!

2. Join Our Email Mailing Lists

New Product Releases

To receive automatic email with brief descriptions of all new O'Reilly products as they are released, send email to:
listproc@online.oreilly.com
Put the following information in the first line of your message (*not* in the Subject field):
subscribe oreilly-news

O'Reilly Events

If you'd also like us to send information about trade show events, special promotions, and other O'Reilly events, send email to:
listproc@online.oreilly.com
Put the following information in the first line of your message (*not* in the Subject field):
subscribe oreilly-events

3. Get Examples from Our Books via FTP

There are two ways to access an archive of example files from our books:

Regular FTP

- ftp to:
  ftp.oreilly.com
  (login: anonymous
  password: your email address)
- Point your web browser to:
  ftp://ftp.oreilly.com/

FTPMAIL

- Send an email message to:
  ftpmail@online.oreilly.com
  (Write "help" in the message body)

4. Contact Us via Email

order@oreilly.com
To place a book or software order online. Good for North American and international customers.

subscriptions@oreilly.com
To place an order for any of our newsletters or periodicals.

books@oreilly.com
General questions about any of our books.

software@oreilly.com
For general questions and product information about our software. Check out O'Reilly Software Online at **http://software.oreilly.com/** for software and technical support information. Registered O'Reilly software users send your questions to:
website-support@oreilly.com

cs@oreilly.com
For answers to problems regarding your order or our products.

booktech@oreilly.com
For book content technical questions or corrections.

proposals@oreilly.com
To submit new book or software proposals to our editors and product managers.

international@oreilly.com
For information about our international distributors or translation queries. For a list of our distributors outside of North America check out:
http://www.oreilly.com/www/order/country.html

5. Work with Us

Check out our website for current employment opportunites:
www.jobs@oreilly.com
Click on "Work with Us"

O'Reilly & Associates, Inc.
101 Morris Street, Sebastopol, CA 95472 USA
TEL   707-829-0515 or 800-998-9938
          (6am to 5pm PST)
FAX   707-829-0104

O'REILLY®

International Distributors

http://international.oreilly.com/distributors.html

UK, EUROPE, MIDDLE EAST AND AFRICA (EXCEPT FRANCE, GERMANY, AUSTRIA, SWITZERLAND, LUXEMBOURG, AND LIECHTENSTEIN)

INQUIRIES
O'Reilly UK Limited
4 Castle Street
Farnham
Surrey, GU9 7HS
United Kingdom
Telephone: 44-1252-711776
Fax: 44-1252-734211
Email: information@oreilly.co.uk

ORDERS
Wiley Distribution Services Ltd.
1 Oldlands Way
Bognor Regis
West Sussex PO22 9SA
United Kingdom
Telephone: 44-1243-843294
UK Freephone: 0800-243207
Fax: 44-1243-843302 (Europe/EU orders)
or 44-1243-843274 (Middle East/Africa)
Email: cs-books@wiley.co.uk

GERMANY, SWITZERLAND, AUSTRIA, LUXEMBOURG, AND LIECHTENSTEIN

INQUIRIES & ORDERS
O'Reilly Verlag
Balthasarstr. 81
D-50670 Köln, Germany
Telephone: 49-221-973160-91
Fax: 49-221-973160-8
Email: anfragen@oreilly.de (inquiries)
Email: order@oreilly.de (orders)

FRANCE

INQUIRIES & ORDERS
Éditions O'Reilly
18 rue Séguier
75006 Paris, France
Tel: 33-1-40-51-52-30
Fax: 33-1-40-51-52-31
Email: france@oreilly.fr

CANADA (FRENCH LANGUAGE BOOKS)
Les Éditions Flammarion ltée
375, Avenue Laurier Ouest
Montréal (Québec) H2V 2K3
Tel: 00-1-514-277-8807
Fax: 00-1-514-278-2085
Email: info@flammarion.qc.ca

HONG KONG
City Discount Subscription Service, Ltd.
Unit A, 6th Floor, Yan's Tower
27 Wong Chuk Hang Road
Aberdeen, Hong Kong
Tel: 852-2580-3539
Fax: 852-2580-6463
Email: citydis@ppn.com.hk

KOREA
Hanbit Media, Inc.
Chungmu Bldg. 210
Yonnam-dong 568-33
Mapo-gu
Seoul, Korea
Tel: 822-325-0397
Fax: 822-325-9697
Email: hant93@chollian.dacom.co.kr

PHILIPPINES
Global Publishing
G/F Benavides Garden
1186 Benavides St.
Manila, Philippines
Tel: 632-254-8949/632-252-2582
Fax: 632-734-5060/632-252-2733
Email: globalp@pacific.net.ph

TAIWAN
O'Reilly Taiwan
1st Floor, No. 21, Lane 295
Section 1, Fu-Shing South Road
Taipei, 106 Taiwan
Tel: 886-2-27099669
Fax: 886-2-27038802
Email: mori@oreilly.com

CHINA
O'Reilly Beijing
SIGMA Building, Suite B809
No. 49 Zhichun Road
Haidian District
Beijing 100031, P.R. China
Tel: 86-10-8809-7475
Fax: 86-10-8809-7463
Email: beijing@oreilly.com

INDIA
Shroff Publishers & Distributors Pvt. Ltd.
12, "Roseland", 2nd Floor
180, Waterfield Road, Bandra (West)
Mumbai 400 050
Tel: 91-22-641-1800/643-9910
Fax: 91-22-643-2422
Email: spd@vsnl.com

JAPAN
O'Reilly Japan, Inc.
Yotsuya Y's Building
7 Banch 6, Honshio-cho
Shinjuku-ku
Tokyo 160-0003 Japan
Tel: 81-3-3356-5227
Fax: 81-3-3356-5261
Email: japan@oreilly.com

THAILAND
TransQuest Publishers (Thailand)
535/49 Kasemsuk Yaek 5
Soi Pracharat-Bampen 15
Huay Kwang, Bangkok
Thailand 10310
Tel: 662-6910421 or 6910638
Fax: 662-6902235
Email: puripat@.inet.co.th

ALL OTHER ASIAN COUNTRIES
O'Reilly & Associates, Inc.
101 Morris Street
Sebastopol, CA 95472 USA
Tel: 707-829-0515
Fax: 707-829-0104
Email: order@oreilly.com

AUSTRALIA
Woodslane Pty., Ltd.
7/5 Vuko Place
Warriewood NSW 2102
Australia
Tel: 61-2-9970-5111
Fax: 61-2-9970-5002
Email: info@woodslane.com.au

NEW ZEALAND
Woodslane New Zealand, Ltd.
21 Cooks Street (P.O. Box 575)
Waganui, New Zealand
Tel: 64-6-347-6543
Fax: 64-6-345-4840
Email: info@woodslane.com.au

ARGENTINA
Distribuidora Cuspide
Suipacha 764
1008 Buenos Aires
Argentina
Phone: 5411-4322-8868
Fax: 5411-4322-3456
Email: libros@cuspide.com

O'REILLY®

TO ORDER: **800-998-9938** • **order@oreilly.com** • **http://www.oreilly.com/**
OUR PRODUCTS ARE AVAILABLE AT A BOOKSTORE OR SOFTWARE STORE NEAR YOU.
FOR INFORMATION: **800-998-9938** • **707-829-0515** • **info@oreilly.com**